Collins

CSEC®

INTEGRATED SCIENCE

Anne Tindale and Peter DeFreitas
Reviewers: Naresh Birju and Shaun deSouza

Collins

William Collins' dream of knowledge for all began with the publication of his first book in 1819. A self-educated mill worker, he not only enriched millions of lives, but also founded a flourishing publishing house. Today, staying true to this spirit, Collins books are packed with inspiration, innovation and practical expertise. They place you at the centre of a world of possibility and give you exactly what you need to explore it.

Collins. Freedom to teach.

Published by Collins
An imprint of HarperCollins*Publishers*
The News Building
1 London Bridge Street
London
SE1 9GF
UK

HarperCollins*Publishers*
Macken House,
39/40 Mayor Street Upper,
Dublin 1,
D01 C9W8,
Ireland

> Browse the complete Collins Caribbean catalogue at
> *collins.co.uk/caribbeanschools*

© HarperCollins*Publishers* Limited 2025

10 9 8 7 6 5 4 3 2 1

ISBN 978-0-00-843201-0

Collins CSEC® Integrated Science is an independent publication and has not been authorised, sponsored or otherwise approved by **CXC®**.

CSEC® is a registered trademark of the *Caribbean Examinations Council (CXC®)*.

British Library Cataloguing in Publication Data

A catalogue record for this publication is available from the British Library.

The publishers gratefully acknowledge the permission granted to reproduce the copyright material in this book. Every effort has been made to trace copyright holders and to obtain their permission for the use of copyright material. The publishers will gladly receive any information enabling them to rectify any error or omission at the first opportunity.

Authors: Anne Tindale and Peter DeFreitas
Reviewers: Naresh Birju and Shaun deSouza
Publishers: Dr Elaine Higgleton and Catherine Martin
Product manager: Saaleh Patel
Project manager: Julianna Dunn
Copy editor: Aidan Gill
Proofreader: Mitch Fitton
Illustrator: Ann Paganuzzi
Production controller: Alhady Ali
Typesetter: Siliconchips Services Ltd
Cover designers: Kevin Robbins and Gordon MacGilp
Cover image: Gordon MacGilp

Printed and bound by Ashford Colour Ltd.

MIX
Paper | Supporting
responsible forestry
FSC™ C007454

This book contains FSC™ certified paper and other controlled sources to ensure responsible forest management.

For more information visit: www.harpercollins.co.uk/green

Contents

Section A – Organisms and Life Processes   1

Section B – Energy   139

Section C – Our Planet   287

Index   427

Getting the best from the book

Welcome to CSEC® Integrated Science

This textbook has been written as a comprehensive course designed to help you achieve **maximum success** in your CXC® CSEC® Integrated Science examination. Facts are presented in an easily understandable way, using **simple** and **clear language**. A variety of formats are used, including diagrams and tables, to make the facts easy to **understand** and **learn**. Colour **photographs** of real-life situations are also included to enliven and enrich your learning, and the relationship between **structure** and **function** is continually highlighted.

Key terms are highlighted in **bold** type and important **definitions**, which you must learn, are written in *italics* and highlighted in **colour**. These definitions are appropriately positioned within the text itself. No information is given in boxes to the side, which can be easily missed. All the information needed to fully cover the syllabus is given within the text, and only the required information is given.

Some **diagrams** are marked with a **star** (★). These are diagrams that are specifically identified in the syllabus as ones that you should know. These may have annotations alongside some of the labels; however, the important labels that you should know are highlighted in **bold** type.

Practical activities identified by the syllabus are fully covered within the **text** itself or in the **analysing data** questions at the end of the relevant units. In the case of the latter, the method used in each activity is outlined, possible results are given, and you are provided with a set of questions to help you **analyse** and **interpret** those results.

Useful techniques on tackling certain types of questions are outlined to provide you with the confidence required to always produce the correct answer. **Worked examples** are provided, where appropriate, that demonstrate how to answer a **spectrum of questions** on any topic which may confront you in the examination.

Just as the CSEC® Integrated Science syllabus is divided into three sections, the nineteen chapters of this book are divided into the same **three sections**. These are **colour coded** for clarity, and each chapter covers a particular topic in the syllabus.

- **Chapters 1 to 7** cover topics in Section A; **Organisms and Life Processes**
- **Chapters 8 to 12** cover topics in Section B; **Energy**
- **Chapters 13 to 19** cover topics in Section C; **Our Planet**

The chapters are broken down into clearly defined **units**, and the **learning objectives** of each unit are stated at the beginning of the unit so that you can see what you are expected to **learn** in the unit. These learning objectives relate fully to the **specific objectives** given in the syllabus. Using easy-to-see sub-titles, each unit is then divided into many sections that split information into manageable-sized chunks.

Each unit ends with a series of **differentiated practice exercises** which are designed to help you test your **knowledge** and **comprehension**, and to help you to improve your ability to **use your knowledge** by developing your **thinking**, **investigative** and **analytical skills**. The exercises are presented in three distinct levels of difficulty as outlined below, and these are **colour-coded** for clarity.

- **Recalling facts** – These exercises are designed to help you assess your **knowledge** and **understanding** of the facts, concepts and principles covered in the unit. You should be able to find the information necessary to answer the questions within the unit, and answering them should help you to **learn** this information.

- **Applying facts** – These exercises are designed to test how you **use** the facts, concepts and principles covered in the unit to answer questions, which are usually about unfamiliar or novel situations. They should help you to develop your ability to **apply** your knowledge, as well as developing your **critical thinking skills**.

- **Analysing data** – These exercises are designed to develop your **investigative** and **analytical skills**. They begin with some form of data or information for you to **analyse** and answer questions about. This information is usually in the form of one, or sometimes more, tables or graphs. You could be asked to read information directly from a table, graph or chart, use information in a table to draw a graph, perform accurate calculations using data given, identify relationships, patterns or trends, make predictions and draw conclusions. Some of these exercises give the results of **practical activities** for you to answer questions about.

If you **study** each unit in turn and **answer all the questions** that follow, you can then visit www.collins.co.uk/caribbeanschools to find the **correct answers**. This will enable you to assess your knowledge, help you to develop your thinking, investigative and analytical skills, and put you on the right path to achieve **maximum success** in your examination.

Key features of the book

Learning objectives inform you of what you are expected to **learn** ▷

Water and its uses

Learning objectives
- Discuss the **properties** of **water**.
- Distinguish between **hard water** and **soft water**.
- Explain the **uses** of **water**.
- Describe various **methods** used **locally** for **fishing**.

Key terms are in **bold** for emphasis ▷

Definitions are in *italics* and highlighted in **colour** for easy learning ▷

Energy, work and change

*Energy is the ability to do **work** (the ability to produce change).*

*Work is done when the point of application of a force moves and is measured as the product of the force and the distance moved in the **direction of the force**.*

The **joule** is the **SI unit** of work or energy.

1 joule is the work done (or energy used) when a force of 1 N moves an object through a distance of 1 m in the direction of the force.

Fully labelled diagrams highlight structural details ▷

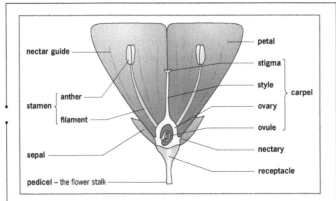

nectar guide
petal
stigma
style
carpel
stamen — anther
ovary
filament
ovule
sepal
nectary
receptacle
pedicel – the flower stalk

Blue stars mark important **diagrams** to be learnt ▷

★Figure 2.9 *A longitudinal section of a typical flower showing the main parts*

Tables highlight relationships between **structure** and **function** ▶

Table 2.2 *Structure and functions of the parts of a flower*

Flower part	Structure	Function(s)
Receptacle	Swollen top of the **pedicel** or flower stalk.	• Bears the flower parts.
Sepal	Leaf-like structure that is usually green in colour.	• Encloses and protects the developing flower when it is a bud.
Petal	Modified leaf which is usually brightly coloured and scented. Some have lines or markings called **nectar guides**.	• Attracts insects and other pollinators for pollination. • Nectar guides guide the pollinators to the nectar.
Nectary	Gland at the base of a petal or stamen.	• Produces **nectar**, a solution of sugars used to attract pollinators for pollination.
Anther	Oval-shaped structure composed of four pollen sacs containing pollen grains.	• Produces pollen grains which contain the male gametes.
Filament	Thin, stalk-like structure.	• Supports the anther and holds it in a position where it can best deliver pollen.
Ovary	Hollow, swollen base of the carpel containing one or more ovules.	• Produces ovules. • Houses and protects the ovules. • Develops into the fruit after fertilisation.
Ovule	Round- to oval-shaped structure inside the ovary. Contains the **embryo sac** which contains the female gamete.	• Produces and protects the female gamete. • Develops into the seed after fertilisation.
Style	Slender stalk that connects the ovary and the stigma.	• Holds the stigma in the best position to catch pollen grains.
Stigma	Sticky tip of the style.	• Catches the pollen grains during pollination.

Annotated diagrams show relationships between **form** and **function** ▶

Key terms are in **bold** for emphasis ▶

Common examples In **everyday life** ▶

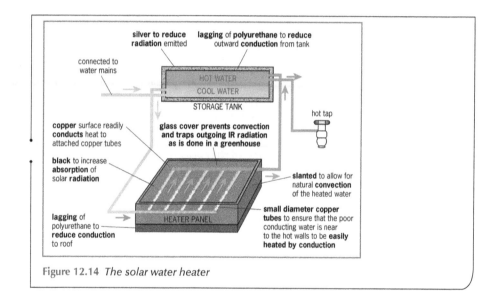

Figure 12.14 *The solar water heater*

Experiments important for **School-Based Assessment (SBA)** are fully described ▶

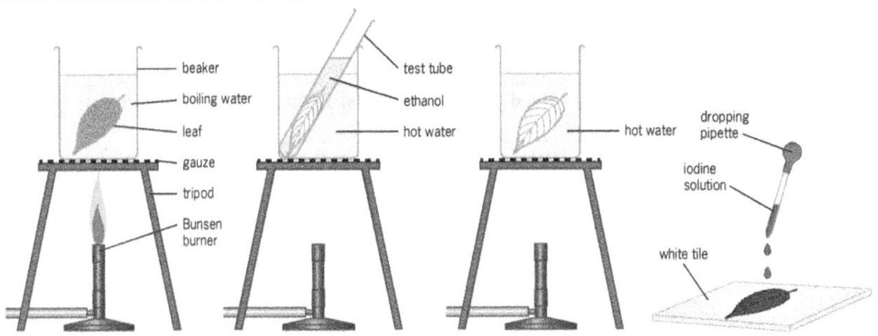

Full-colour diagrams enhance maximum interest ▶

beaker
boiling water
leaf
gauze
tripod
Bunsen burner

test tube
ethanol
hot water

hot water

dropping pipette
iodine solution
white tile

① The leaf is placed in **boiling water** for 1 minute to make the membranes of the cells permeable to chlorophyll and iodine solution.

② The leaf is placed in a test tube containing **ethanol** and the Bunsen burner is turned off. The tube is placed in the hot water and left until the chlorophyll has been removed from the leaf and the leaf is white. This enables any colour changes with iodine solution to be seen.

③ The leaf is dipped back into the **hot water** to soften it.

④ The leaf is placed flat on a white tile and covered with **iodine solution**. The leaf turns **blue-black** if it contains **starch**.

Figure 8.16 *Testing a leaf for starch*

Worked examples strengthen concepts taught ▶

Important notes give reasons for the approach to the question ▶

Detailed steps teach correct **equation solving** techniques ▶

Example 6

A toaster rated at 1300 W is to be used on a 110 V electrical mains supply.

a Calculate the amperage (current in A) that it takes.

b State, with reasons, which of the following fuses would be suitable to protect the device:

3 A, 5 A, 13 A, 20 A

c Calculate the energy consumed by the toaster when used for 3 minutes.

Solution

a $P = VI$ — Lay out the equation as you have learnt it.

$\therefore I = \dfrac{P}{V}$ — Make the subject of the equation the quantity you are solving for.

$I = \dfrac{1300\ \text{W}}{110\ \text{V}}$ — Substitute values using SI base units into the equation.

$I = 11.8\ \text{A}$ — Represent final answer with correct SI unit.

b The 13 A fuse is most suitable since its current rating is just above the normal operational current the toaster was designed to take.

- The 3 A and 5 A fuses will 'blow' as soon as the device is switched on.
- The 20 A fuse will allow a much larger current to flow than is necessary, which can result in overheating or damage to the components and may even cause an electrical fire.

c $P = \dfrac{E}{t}$

$\therefore E = P \times t$

$E = 1300\ \text{W} \times (3 \times 60\ \text{s})$

$E = 234\ 000\ \text{J}$

Full-colour photos of real-life situations enliven and enrich learning ▶

Figure 11.41 *Extinguishing a chemical fire using an atmosphere respirator*

Figure 11.42 *Extinguishing a bush fire using water bombs*

Recalling facts questions
help you to assess your
knowledge and
understanding of the
facts, concepts and
principles ▶

Applying facts questions
test your **use** of the facts,
concepts and principles ▶

Analysing data questions
develop your **investigative**
and **analytical skills** ▶

Recalling facts

 Identify the TWO factors that affect the absorption and transport of substances in living organisms.

 Explain why a mongoose has a well developed transport system in its body.

 Construct a table to show the different materials that are transported around the human body, where each substance enters the transport system and its destination, if applicable.

Applying facts

 The flatworm *Planaria* is a multicellular organism that is about 10 mm long, 4 mm in width and less than 1 mm thick. It is one of the largest organisms that lack transport systems. Explain how it manages without one.

Analysing data

 To investigate the effect of surface area to volume ratio on the rate of diffusion, some students were given blocks of agar, a permeable, jelly-like material. The blocks were different sizes and had been stained pink by using an alkali mixed with an indicator dye. The dye is pink in alkaline conditions and colourless in acidic conditions. The students submerged the blocks in hydrochloric acid, as shown in Figure 4.2, and recorded how long it took for the pink colour to disappear right through to the centre of each block. The times are given in Table 4.2.

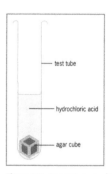

Figure 4.2 *Apparatus used to investigate the effect of surface area to volume ratio on the rate of diffusion*

Table 4.2 *The time taken for the pink colour to disappear in four cubes of different sizes*

Cube	Length of side (mm)	Surface area (mm²)	Volume (mm³)	Surface area to volume ratio	Time taken for pink colour to disappear (s)
W	1	6	1	6 : 1	10
X	2	24			25
Y	3		27		52
Z	6			1 : 1	240

a Complete the table by filling in the blanks.

b What effect did increasing the size of the cubes have on:

   i the surface area to volume ratio of the cubes

   ii the time taken for the pink colour to disappear

   iii the rate of disappearance of the pink colour?

c What conclusion can you draw from the results of the experiment?

d If each block represented a living organism, which organism would be the MOST likely to need a transport system? Explain how you arrived at your answer.

Analysing data questions
improve your **SBA**
performance and develop
your ability tackle the **data
analysis** question on your
examination paper ▶

Quantities and their SI units used in this course

Fundamental (base) quantities

Scientific quantities and their corresponding units can all be expressed in terms of **7 fundamental** (or **base**) quantities and units. For this course, the following **5** are used.

Note that the only base quantity whose SI unit carries a prefix is mass; it carries the prefix kilo.

Fundamental or base quantity	Name of SI unit	Symbol of SI unit
Mass	kilogram	kg
Length	metre	m
Time	second	s
Current	ampere	A
Temperature*	kelvin	K

*Temperature may be expressed in °C since an interval of 1 °C has the same size as an interval of 1 K.

Derived quantities

All other quantities and units are **derived** from, and expressed in terms of, the fundamental ones.

Sometimes we use '**special name**' units, particularly when the combinations of the fundamental units are complex.

Derived quantity	Name of SI unit	Symbol of SI unit using fundamental units	Special name SI unit
Area	square metre	m^2	
Volume	cubic metre	m^3	
Density	kilogram per cubic metre	kg/m^3	
Speed	metre per second	m/s	
Velocity	metre per second	m/s	
Acceleration	metre per second squared	m/s^2	
Momentum	kilogram metre per second	kg m/s	
Force	newton	$kg\ m/s^2$*	N
Work or energy	joule	$kg\ m^2/s^2$*	J
Power	watt	$kg\ m^2/s^3$*	W
Voltage	voltage	$kg\ m^2/s^3 A$*	V

*No need to learn these **complex** combinations since we can use the **simple** special name units. It would be ridiculous to hear someone speaking of a voltage of 6 $kg\ m^2/s^3 A^2$!

Important relations and formulae used in this course

Quantity	Worded equation	Symbolic equation
Work or energy	work or energy = force × distance (parallel to force)	$W = Fd_\parallel$ $E = Fd_\parallel$
Voltage	voltage = current × resistance	$V = IR$
Power	power = $\dfrac{energy}{time}$	$P = \dfrac{E}{t}$
Power	power = voltage × current	$P = VI$
Weight	weight = mass × acceleration due to gravity	$W = mg$
Weight	weight = mass × gravitational field strength	$W = mg$
Density	density = $\dfrac{mass}{volume}$	$\rho = \dfrac{m}{V}$
Speed	speed = $\dfrac{distance}{time}$	$s = \dfrac{d}{t}$
Resultant force	resultant force = mass × acceleration	$F_R = ma$
Moment	moment = force × perpendicular distance from force to pivot	$M = Fd_\perp$
Momentum	momentum = mass × velocity	$p = mv$
Momentum conservation	total momentum before event = total momentum after event	–
Useful work output	useful work output = load × distance moved by load	$W_{out} = Ld_L$
Work input	work input = effort × distance moved by effort	$W_{in} = Ed_E$
Efficiency	efficiency = $\dfrac{useful\ work\ or\ energy\ output}{work\ or\ energy\ input} \times 100\%$	$\eta = \dfrac{W_{out}}{W_{in}} \times 100\%$
Mechanical advantage	mechanical advantage = $\dfrac{load}{effort}$	$MA = \dfrac{L}{E}$

It is advisable when using equations comprised of special name units, to only use SI units.
Recall that the **only coherent SI unit with a prefix is the kg** (the unit of mass).

Examination tips

The following sections provide you with valuable information about the **format** of your CSEC®
Integrated Science examination, and how to **interpret** and **answer** examination questions.

The format of the CSEC® Integrated Science examination

The examination consists of **two papers** and your performance is evaluated using the following **three**
profiles.

* **Knowledge and comprehension**
* **Use of knowledge**
* **Experimental skills**

Paper 01 (1¼ hours)

Paper 01 is worth **60 marks**, which represents **30%** of your final examination mark. It consists of
60 multiple choice questions which test information drawn from **all** areas of the syllabus. Each question
is worth **1 mark**. Four **choices** of answer are provided for each question of which one is correct.

* Make sure you read each question **thoroughly**; some questions may ask which answer is **incorrect**.
* Some questions may give two or more correct answers and ask which answer is the **best**; you must
  consider each answer very carefully before making your choice.
* If you do not know the answer or are unsure of it, try to work it out by **eliminating** the incorrect
  answers. Never leave a question unanswered.

Paper 02 (2½ hours)

Paper 02 is worth **100 marks**, which represents **50%** of your final examination mark. It consists
of **six compulsory questions** which test information drawn from **all** areas of the syllabus and each
question may require knowledge of **several topics**. Each question is divided into several parts and
the answers are to be written in **spaces** provided on the paper. These spaces indicate the length of
answer required and answers should be restricted to them. Take time to **read the entire paper** before
beginning to answer any of the questions.

* **Question 1** is a **practical/investigative type question** which is worth **25 marks.** You will usually be
  provided with some form of **data**, such as the results obtained during a practical investigation,
  which you will be expected to answer questions about. The data might be in the form of a table or
  a graph. If you are given a table, you may be asked to draw a graph using the data and may then be
  asked questions about the graph.
* **Questions 2 to 6** are each worth **15 marks**. They often contain some kind of **stimulus material**, such
  as a diagram, table of data or a graph which you will be asked questions about. You may also have
  to perform calculations.

The **marks** allocated for the different parts of each question are clearly given. Since a total of
100 marks is available for Paper 02 and the time allowed is **150 minutes**, you should allow about
35 minutes for Question 1 and about **20 minutes** for each of the other five questions. This will allow
you time to read the paper fully before you begin and time to check over your answers when you
have finished.

Interpreting examination questions

It is essential that you **fully understand** what each question is **asking you to do** before you begin to answer. Always look at the **number of marks** allocated for each part of a question and make sure you include at least as many **points** in your answer as there are **marks**. The following **key instruction words** tell you the **type of detail** that you should give in your answers.

Account for: provide reasons for the information given.

Annotate: add brief notes to labels.

Apply: use knowledge and principles to solve problems.

Appraise: judge the quality or worth of the topic or issue in question.

Assess: give reasons for the importance of particular structures, relationships or processes.

Calculate: arrive at a solution to a numerical problem.

Classify: divide into groups based on observable characteristics.

Comment: state an opinion or view, giving supporting reasons.

Compare: give similarities and differences.

Construct: draw a line graph, bar graph, histogram, pie chart or table using data provided or obtained from practical investigations.

Contrast: give differences.

Deduce: make a logical connection between two or more pieces of information, or use data provided or obtained to arrive at a conclusion.

Define: state concisely the meaning of a word or term.

Demonstrate: show clearly by giving proof or evidence.

Derive: use data to logically determine a relationship, formula or result.

Describe: provide a detailed account, which includes all relevant information.

Determine: find the value of a physical quantity.

Design: plan and present ideas in a structured manner with relevant practical detail.

Develop: expand or elaborate on an idea or argument with supporting reasons.

Differentiate or **distinguish between** or **among:** give differences between or among items that place them into separate categories.

Discuss: provide a balanced argument, which considers points both for and against, or explain the relative merits of a case.

Draw: produce a line representation of a specimen or apparatus that accurately shows the relationship between the parts.

Estimate: arrive at an approximate quantitative result.

Evaluate: determine the significance or worth of the point in question.

Explain: give a clear, detailed account which makes the given information easy to understand and provides reasons for the information.

Formulate: develop and present ideas in a structured manner.

Identify: name or point out specific components or features.

Illustrate: make the answer clearer by including appropriate examples or diagrams.

Justify: provide adequate grounds for your reasoning.

Label: add names to identify structures or parts indicated by label lines or pointers.

List: itemise without detail.

Name: give only the name.

Outline: write an account which includes the main points only.

Predict: use information provided to arrive at a likely conclusion or suggest a possible outcome.

Relate: show connections between different sets of information or data.

State: give brief, precise facts without detail.

Suggest: put forward an idea.

Successful examination technique

- **Read the instructions** at the start of each paper very carefully and do **precisely** what they require.
- **Read through the entire paper** before you begin to answer any of the questions.
- **Read each question at least twice** before beginning your answer to ensure you **understand** what is being asked.
- **Study diagrams**, **graphs** and **tables** in detail and make sure that you **understand** the information they are giving before answering the questions that follow.
- **Underline the important words** in each question to help you answer precisely what the question is asking.
- **Reread** the question when you are **part way through** your answer to check that you are answering what it is asking.
- **Give precise** and **factual answers**. You will not get marks for information that is 'padded out' or irrelevant. The number of marks allocated for each answer indicates how long and detailed it should be.
- **Use correct scientific terminology** throughout your answers.
- Give any **numerical answer** the appropriate **unit** using the proper abbreviation/symbol e.g. cm^3, g, °C.
- If a question asks you to give a **specific number of points**, use **bullets** to make each separate point clear.
- If you are asked to give **similarities** and **differences**, you must make it clear which points you are proposing as similarities and which points as differences. The same applies if you are asked to give **advantages** and **disadvantages**.
- **Watch the time** as you work. Know the time available for each question and stick to it.
- **Check over your answers** when you have completed all the questions.
- **Remain in the examination room** until the **end** of the examination and recheck your answers again if you have time to ensure you have done your very best. Never leave the examination room early.

School-Based Assessment (SBA)

The **School-Based Assessment (SBA)** is an integral part of your CXC® CSEC® examination and is worth **20%** of your final examination mark. Your SBA assesses your achievements in the **experimental skills** and **analysis and interpretation skills** that are involved in laboratory and field work. It is intended to help build your **self confidence** and assist you in acquiring certain knowledge, attitudes and skills that are critical to the study of Integrated Science, in particular, your **critical thinking** and **problem solving skills**. The important points that you should note about the SBA are outlined below.

- The assessments are carried out at your school by **your teacher** during Terms 1 to 5 of your two-year period of study.
- The assessments are carried out during **normal practical classes** and not under examination conditions. You have every opportunity to gain a high score in each assessment if you make a **consistent effort** over the two-year period.
- Assessments are made of the following **five skills:**
  - Manipulation and Measurement
  - Observation, Recording and Reporting
  - Drawing
  - Planning and Designing
  - Analysis and Interpretation
- Each skill will be assessed at **least twice** over the two-year period with the exception of Drawing, which will only be assessed once. You will be awarded a mark between **0** and **10** for each assessment made.
- You will be **taught** the skills and be given enough opportunity to **develop** them before you are assessed. You will do a minimum of **eighteen** practical experiments over the two-year period.
- As an integral part of your SBA, you will also carry out an **Investigative Project** during the second year of your two-year study period (see page xx). This project assesses your **Planning and Designing**, and your **Analysis and Interpretation skills.**
- All your experimental reports are recorded in a **practical notebook**, which is subject to moderation by the CXC® Examination Board to assess the standard of marking in your school.

Manipulation and Measurement (MM)

Manipulation and Measurement is assessed whilst you are conducting experiments in the laboratory. In assessing this skill your teacher will be looking to see if you fulfil the following assessment criteria.

- Use **basic laboratory equipment** and **measuring devices** with care, competence and skill.
- Take **precise** and **accurate readings** when using laboratory equipment to make measurements.
- Use **appropriate units.**
- Show **mastery** of **laboratory techniques.**
- **Follow instructions.**

Observation, Recording and Reporting (ORR)

Your **laboratory reports** will be used to assess **Observation, Recording and Reporting**. In assessing this skill, your teacher will look to see that you fulfil the following.

- You use the **correct format** to present your report, with the appropriate headings in the correct order: Aim/Purpose, Apparatus and Materials, Method/Experimental Procedure, Results/Observations, Discussion, Conclusion.
- You use the **past tense** and **passive voice** when writing your report, and you use the correct **grammar** and **spelling** throughout.
- You use the **correct terminology** and **expressions** throughout.
- Your **method** contains all the important **steps** written concisely and in the correct sequence.
- You **draw** an appropriate **diagram** to accurately represent the **apparatus** as it was set up for use. Each diagram must be large enough to show all detail clearly. It must be drawn using a sharp pencil, must not be shaded and a ruler must be used to draw all straight lines. It must be two-dimensional, correctly proportioned, accurate and fully labelled following the guidelines for labelling on page xix. It must also bear an appropriate title below.
- You make appropriate use of **prose** to record written descriptions of your **observations**. It is important to include **all** the observations you made in your descriptions.
- You make the proper use of **tables** to record numerical data and observations, and the appropriate use of **graphs** to display numerical data, as explained in the following sections.

Drawing tables and graphs

Any **data** you collect whilst carrying out **experiments** or research projects, such as your **Investigative Project**, should be presented in the form of **tables** and **graphs**, therefore it is really important that you know how to construct these. You may also be asked to draw a table or graph when answering the **data analysis question** on your examination paper.

Variables

When carrying out an experiment or research project, **variables** are the factors that can be changed, controlled and/or measured by the investigator. Examples of variables include time, temperature, length, weight, voltage, current, concentration or blood groups. Usually the investigator wishes to find out how certain variables are related to each other, or how one variable affects another, in which case the variables are known as the **manipulated** or **independent variable**, and **responding variable** or **dependent variable**.

- The **manipulated** or **independent variable** is the factor that is **varied** or **adjusted** by the person carrying out the investigation. It **affects** the responding variable.
- The **responding** or **dependent variable** is the factor that **changes** as a result of the changes made to the manipulated variable. It is **affected by** the manipulated variable.

For example, if investigating how the **height** of a child changes with the child's **age**, the **manipulated variable** is **age** and the **responding variable** is **height**. This is because the age of a child affects the child's height, but not the other way round; the height of a child cannot affect the child's age.

Tables

Tables can be used to record numerical data or observations. When drawing a table:

- Use **lines** to **neatly enclose** the table, and draw vertical and horizontal **lines** to separate the columns and the rows.
- Show the **manipulated variable** in the **left-hand column** and the **responding variable(s)** in the **right-hand column(s)**.
- When drawing **numerical tables**, give the correct column headings which state the **physical quantities** measured and give the correct **units** using proper abbreviations/symbols, e.g. cm^3, g, °C.
- Give the appropriate number of **decimal places** when recording numerical data.

- When drawing **non-numerical tables**, give the correct column headings and **all observations**.
- Give the table an appropriate, underlined **title** at the top, which must include reference to the responding variable and the manipulated variable.

<u>Table showing the heart rate of a football player at 1 minute intervals before and during exercise</u>

Time (minutes)	Heart rate (beats per minute)
0	66
1	68
2	112
3	126
4	130
5	130

(**Time** is the **manipulated variable** and **heart beat** is the **responding variable**.)

Graphs

Graphs are used to display numerical data. They show the relationship between the responding variable and the manipulated variable. The main types of graphs are **line graphs** and **bar graphs**.

- **Line graphs** show how the responding variable **changes** with respect to the manipulated variable. They are very useful for illustrating **trends**.
- **Bar graphs** show data in **discrete categories** using **separated bars** of different heights.

Drawing a graph

- When drawing **all graphs**:
  - Use a **sharp HB pencil**, preferably a mechanical pencil with a 0.5 mm lead.
  - Plot the **manipulated variable** on the *x*-axis (horizontal axis) and the **responding variable** on the *y*-axis (vertical axis):
  - Choose appropriate **scales** which are easy to work with, and which use more than half of the graph grid in both the *x* and *y* directions. Avoid using scales having multiples of 3, 7 or 9 which make plotting difficult.
  - **Label** each axis with its correct **quantity** and **unit**, if any. To do this, use the **column headings** in the table of data.
  - Give a **key** if more than one set of data is being plotted on the same axes.
  - Give the graph an appropriate, underlined **title** at the top, which must include reference to the responding variable and the manipulated variable.
- When drawing a **line graph**:
  - Plot each **data point** accurately using a **small dot** surrounded by a circle or triangle, e.g. ⊙, to locate it. Alternatively, a small cross (x) may be used.
  - Draw a **smooth curve** or **straight line of best fit** passing between the data points such that the mean deviation from the points is minimum, as in Example 1 on page xviii.
- When drawing a **bar graph**, the height of each bar indicates the value of the responding variable:
  - Draw **vertical bars** of equal width and draw an accurately positioned **horizontal line** to show the top of each bar
  - Ensure that a **space** is left between the *y*-axis and the first bar, and **spaces** of equal width are left between each of the bars, as in Example 2 on page xviii.

Example 1

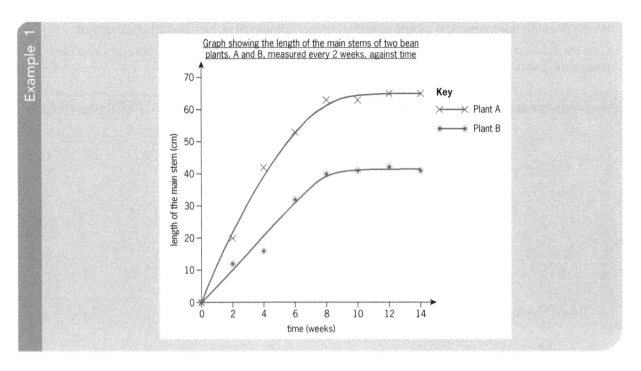

Example 2

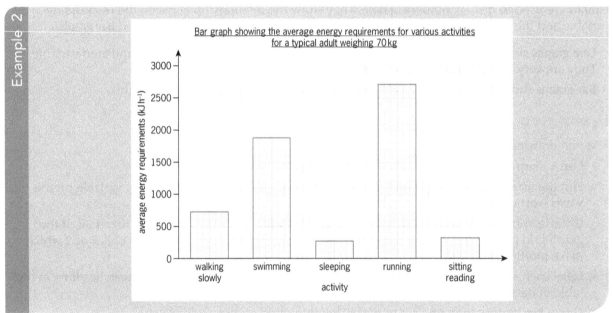

Planning and Designing (PD)

Your teacher will supply you with an **observation**, **scenario** or **problem statement**. You will be expected to suggest an appropriate hypothesis for the observation, scenario or problem, and then design a suitable experiment to test your hypothesis. A **hypothesis** is a testable proposal intended to explain certain facts or observations. You will be expected to include the following in your design.

- A clear, concise statement of your **hypothesis** in a form which is **testable** and which relates to the observation, scenario or problem statement.

- A clear statement of your **aim** which relates to your hypothesis.

- A list which contains all the essential **apparatus** and **materials** to be used in your design.

- A workable or feasible **method** which could be used to test your hypothesis. Your method must be clear, concise, written using **instructional language** and it must include the following.
  - All important **steps**, written in a **logical sequence**.
  - **Precautions** to be taken.
  - Method of **controlling variables**.
  - **Observations** to be made or **measurements** to be taken that will support or disprove your hypothesis.
  - Identification of **controlled**, **manipulated** and **responding variables**.
- An outline of the method you will use to display your **results** or **data**, such as tables, graphs, prose or drawings, and a clear statement of the results you expect to obtain that will support or disprove your hypothesis.
- An explanation of how the results you expect to obtain are to be **treated** or **interpreted** to support or disprove your hypothesis. This is the link that shows how the results you expect to obtain validate the hypothesis.
- A statement of any **assumptions** to be made, **precautions** to be taken and possible **sources of error** in your design.

Drawing (D)

Drawing is a very important **skill** in the study of Integrated Science and is considered a type of **data collection** because drawings help record information from biological specimens and materials in particular. When drawing any **biological drawing**, the drawing should be:

- Drawn on **plain** white, unlined paper.
- Placed in a **position** on the page that will allow for neat and clear labelling.
- **Large** enough to show all the structures clearly, leaving enough space at one or both sides for labels.
- Drawn using a **sharp HB pencil**, preferably a mechanical pencil with a 0.5 mm lead.
- Drawn with **single**, **clean**, **sharp**, **continuous lines** which are all of **even thickness**. The lines should not be sketchy and drawings should not be shaded or coloured.
- An **accurate representation** of the specimen. It must show structures typical of the specimen, but should not contain unnecessary detail. If a large number of small, repetitive structures are present, only a **few** should be drawn to show accurate detail.
- **Correctly proportioned** and all parts should be **accurately positioned**.
- **Fully labelled**. Label lines should be drawn using a **pencil** and **ruler**. As far as possible they should be **horizontal**, they should never cross and should begin **in** or **on** the structure being labelled. Labels **naming** structures should be neatly **printed** in **pencil** and appropriately **annotated** to indicate important features of structural and/or functional interest, where appropriate. If only a few structures are labelled (less than five), all labels should be on the **right** and lined up vertically below each other.
- **Appropriately titled**. The title must be neatly **printed** in **pencil** below the drawing and be **underlined**. The title should include: the **name** of the specimen or structure, the **view** from which the specimen was drawn or the **type of section**, and the **magnification** of the drawing. To calculate **magnification**:
  - Measure between **two appropriate points** of the drawing that are as far apart as possible.
  - Using the same units, measure between the **same two points** of the specimen.
  - Use the following formula to calculate magnification. Magnification has **no units** and is usually calculated to one decimal place.

$$\text{magnification} = \frac{\text{size of the drawing}}{\text{size of the specimen}}$$

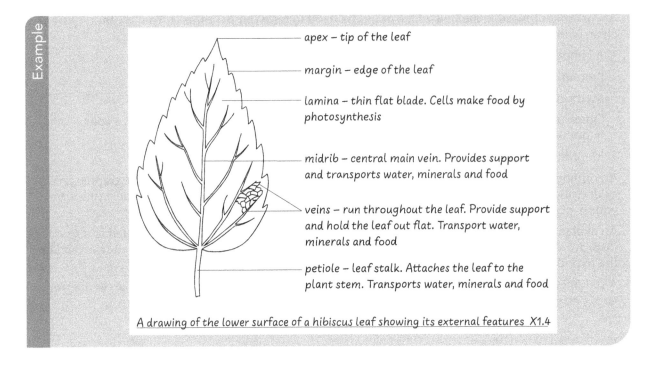

A drawing of the lower surface of a hibiscus leaf showing its external features X1.4

Analysis and Interpretation (AI)

Your teacher will use your laboratory reports to assess **Analysis and Interpretation**. As the name of the skill implies, your teacher will assess your ability to **analyse** and **interpret** your results and observations, and draw **conclusions**, by looking to see if you can fulfil the following criteria.

- Present relevant **background information.**
- Accurately identify and explain **relationships**, **patterns** and **trends** displayed by your results.
- Make **accurate calculations.**
- Discuss your **results** in relation to background/theoretical knowledge and the aim/hypothesis.
- Identify **precautions**, **sources of error** and **limitations.**
- Present the **relevance** between the experiment and real life, and/or the **impact** that the knowledge you gained had on yourself.
- Draw a **logical**, **accurate conclusion** that relates to the aim.

The Investigative Project

You will be expected to carry out an **Investigative Project** during your second year of study. To begin your project, your teacher may supply you with an **observation**, **scenario** or **problem statement**. Alternatively, you may be asked to come up with an observation, scenario or problem statement of your own. Your Investigative Project will then be divided into two parts: the **proposal** and the **implementation**.

The proposal

You will be expected to suggest an appropriate hypothesis for the observation, scenario or problem and then design a suitable experiment to test your hypothesis. This is your **proposal**, and your teacher will use it to assess your **Planning and Designing** skills. Your proposal is worth a maximum of 10 marks, and the criteria that will be used in its assessment are outlined below:

• Your **hypothesis** is clearly stated and testable.	*2 marks*
• Your **aim** clearly relates to your hypothesis.	*1 mark*
• The appropriate **materials** and **apparatus** are given.	*1 mark*
• Your **method** is logically sequenced and suitable, is written in instructional language and includes at least one manipulated or responding variable.	*3 marks*
• At least one **controlled variable** is stated.	*1 mark*
• Your **expected results** are reasonable and are linked to the method.	*1 mark*
• One **assumption, precaution** or **possible source of error** is stated.	*1 mark*
	10 marks

The Implementation

You will then be expected to carry out your experiment. This is your **implementation**, and your teacher will use it to assess your **Analysis and Interpretation** skills. Your implementation is worth a maximum of 20 marks, and the criteria that will be used in its assessment are outlined below.

• Your **method** is linked to the proposal and is written in the correct tense.	*1 mark*
• The method used for recording your **results (data)** is appropriate and accurate, and your results are accurate and acceptable.	*4 marks*
• Your **discussion** explains and interprets your results and states any trends.	*5 marks*
• At least one **precaution**, one **source of error** and one **limitation** are stated.	*3 marks*
• A written **reflection** on your work is given, which is written using the appropriate scientific language, grammar and clear expression, and which includes the relevance between your experiment and real life, the impact that the knowledge you gained from the experiment had on yourself and the justification for any adjustments you made during the experiment	*5 marks*
• A **conclusion** is stated which relates to the aim.	*2 marks*
	20 marks

Section A
Organisms and
Life Processes

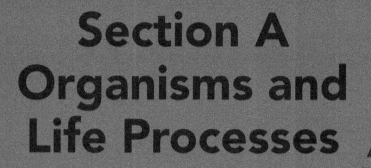

The topics covered in this section are:

- Cells
- Movement of substances into and out of cells
- Asexual and sexual reproduction compared
- Reproduction in plants
- Growth in plants and crop production
- Soil
- Reproduction in animals
- Growth in animals
- Transport systems in multicellular organisms
- The circulatory system in humans
- Transport systems in plants
- Excretion
- The sense organs
- The nervous and endocrine systems
- Microbes
- Disease, immunity and hygiene
- Drug use and abuse
- Pests and pest control
- Food contaminants and food preservation

1 Units of life

All living organisms are made of **cells.** Cells are so small that they can only be seen with a microscope and not with the naked eye. Substances move into and out of cells, and from one cell to another, by three processes: **diffusion, osmosis** and **active transport.**

Cells

Learning objectives

- Examine **animal** and **plant cells.**
- Describe the **functions** of the **cell structures** in **animal** and **plant cells.**
- Draw **annotated diagrams** to **describe** the **structures** of **animal** and **plant cells.**

An introduction to cells

A **cell** is the smallest unit of life. It is the basic structural and functional unit of all living organisms. Some organisms are composed of a single cell only and are known as **unicellular organisms,** whilst others are composed of many cells and are known as **multicellular organisms.** The latter includes **plants** and **animals.**

Animal and plant cells

Both **animal** and **plant cells** are surrounded by an extremely thin outer layer known as the **cell membrane,** which has jelly-like **cytoplasm** inside. The cytoplasm contains structures known as **organelles,** which are specialised to carry out one or more vital functions. Most organelles are surrounded by one or two **membranes.** Examples of organelles include the nucleus, mitochondria, ribosomes, chloroplasts and vacuoles. Whilst cells and most organelles can be seen under a **light microscope,** the detailed structure of the organelles can only be seen under an **electron microscope.**

Certain components are found in **both** animal and plant cells. These include the following:

- a **cell membrane** or **plasma membrane**
- **cytoplasm**
- a **nucleus**
- **mitochondria** (singular: **mitochondrion**)
- **ribosomes.**

In addition, **plant cells** possess the following:

- a **cell wall**
- **chloroplasts**
- a large **vacuole.**

Figure 1.1 on page 3 shows the structure of a generalised animal cell, Figure 1.2 on page 3 shows the structure of a generalised plant cell and Figure 1.3 on page 4 shows the appearance of animal and plant cells when viewed using a light microscope. The functions of the various components of these cells are summarised in Table 1.1 on page 4.

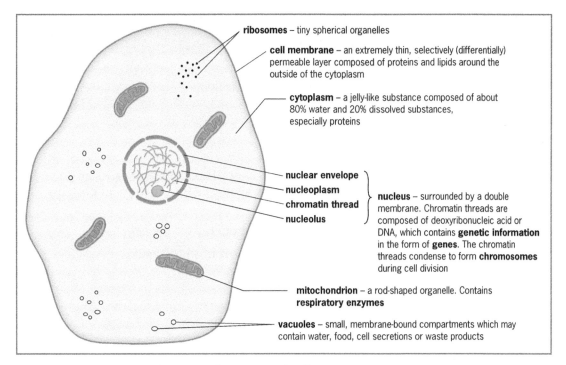

ribosomes – tiny spherical organelles

cell membrane – an extremely thin, selectively (differentially) permeable layer composed of proteins and lipids around the outside of the cytoplasm

cytoplasm – a jelly-like substance composed of about 80% water and 20% dissolved substances, especially proteins

nuclear envelope
nucleoplasm
chromatin thread
nucleolus

nucleus – surrounded by a double membrane. Chromatin threads are composed of deoxyribonucleic acid or DNA, which contains **genetic information** in the form of **genes**. The chromatin threads condense to form **chromosomes** during cell division

mitochondrion – a rod-shaped organelle. Contains **respiratory enzymes**

vacuoles – small, membrane-bound compartments which may contain water, food, cell secretions or waste products

★Figure 1.1 *Structure of a generalised animal cell*

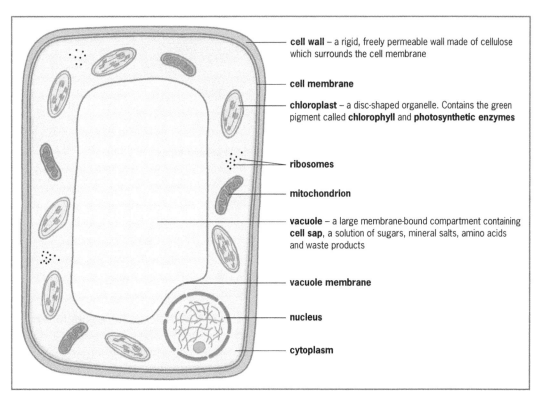

cell wall – a rigid, freely permeable wall made of cellulose which surrounds the cell membrane

cell membrane

chloroplast – a disc-shaped organelle. Contains the green pigment called **chlorophyll** and **photosynthetic enzymes**

ribosomes

mitochondrion

vacuole – a large membrane-bound compartment containing **cell sap**, a solution of sugars, mineral salts, amino acids and waste products

vacuole membrane

nucleus

cytoplasm

★Figure 1.2 *Structure of a generalised plant cell*

It is important to note that **plant cells** have **regular shapes**, usually round, square or rectangular, because they are surrounded by a rigid cell wall, whereas **animal cells** can have a **variety of shapes** because they are only surrounded by an extremely thin membrane; they have no cell wall.

Table 1.1 *A summary of the functions of the different components of cells*

Cell component	Function(s)
Cell membrane	• Keeps the cell contents inside the cell. • Controls what substances enter and leave the cell.
Cytoplasm	• Supports the organelles. • The site of many chemical reactions.
Nucleus	• Essential for cell division. • **Genetic information** in the form of **genes** controls the characteristics and functioning of the cell by controlling the synthesis (production) of proteins, especially enzymes, in the cell.
Mitochondrion	• Where **aerobic respiration** occurs to release energy for the cell.
Ribosome	• Where proteins are synthesised (produced) from amino acids.
Vacuole	• Stores food, cell secretions or cell waste. • Supports a **plant cell** when it is turgid (firm).
Cell wall	• Supports and protects a **plant cell** and gives it shape.
Chloroplast	• Where **photosynthesis** occurs in **plant cells** to produce food for the plant.

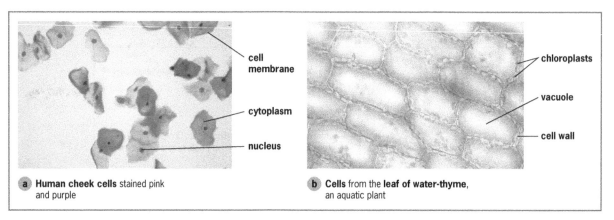

a **Human cheek cells** stained pink and purple

b **Cells** from the **leaf of water-thyme**, an aquatic plant

Figure 1.3 *Animal and plant cells seen under the light microscope*

Recalling facts

1 What are cells?

2 Draw a fully labelled <u>and</u> annotated diagram to describe the structure of a generalised animal cell.

3 Outline the function of EACH of the following cellular components:

a the cytoplasm   **b** the nucleus   **c** a vacuole   **d** a ribosome.

4 In what way is the function of a mitochondrion different from the function of a chloroplast?

Applying facts

5 Explain the relationship between cells and living organisms.

6 Distinguish between the cell membrane and the cell wall in terms of:

a their structure   **b** their properties.

7 Red blood cells lack nuclei. Explain the consequences to the cells of the absence of nuclei.

8 In which type of cell in the human body would you expect to find most mitochondria? Explain your answer fully.

9 Give THREE similarities and THREE differences between the structure of a typical plant cell and the structure of a typical animal cell.

Movement of substances into and out of cells

Learning objectives

- Analyse the **processes** of **diffusion, osmosis** and **active transport**.
- Explain the **roles** of **diffusion, osmosis** and **active transport** in **living organisms**.
- Cite **examples** of **diffusion** in **artificial** and **natural environments**.

Introduction

Cells must constantly take in useful substances and get rid of waste and harmful substances. To enter or leave cells, or pass from one cell to another, the substances must pass through the **membranes** of the cells, and they can do this by **passive transport** or **active transport**. **Passive transport** involves the movement of particles through cell membranes without using energy released in respiration, whereas **active transport** requires energy released in respiration. Passive transport includes **diffusion** and **osmosis**.

Diffusion

Diffusion is the net movement of particles down a concentration gradient from an area of higher concentration to an area of lower concentration until the particles are evenly distributed.

The particles, which can be **molecules** or **ions**, are said to move **down a concentration gradient** because they are moving from high concentration to low concentration, as shown in Figure 1.4. The greater the difference in concentration, the steeper the concentration gradient and the faster the particles diffuse. Particles in **gases**, **liquids** and **solutions** are capable of diffusing because they are in constant motion.

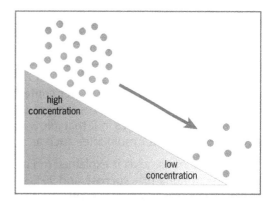

Figure 1.4 *Diffusion of molecules down a concentration gradient*

Diffusion can be **demonstrated** by placing a drop of blue food colouring into a glass of water. The molecules of blue food colouring slowly diffuse between the water molecules, forming a blue solution. This is shown in Figure 1.5.

drop of food colouring

molecules of the food colouring gradually **diffuse** into the water turning it blue

Figure 1.5 *Demonstrating diffusion*

The role of diffusion in living organisms

Diffusion plays an important **role** in living organisms because it is the way that cells obtain many of their requirements and get rid of their waste products which, if not removed, would poison them.

- **Oxygen**, for use in **aerobic respiration**, moves into organisms through respiratory surfaces and then into cells by diffusion, and **carbon dioxide**, produced in **aerobic respiration**, moves out of cells and out of organisms through respiratory surfaces by diffusion.
- Some of the **glucose** and **amino acids** produced in **digestion** are absorbed through the cells in the walls of the small intestine and into the blood by diffusion.
- **Carbon dioxide**, for use by plants in **photosynthesis**, moves into leaves and leaf cells by diffusion, and **oxygen**, produced by plants in **photosynthesis**, moves out of leaf cells and leaves by diffusion.

Osmosis

*Osmosis is the movement of **water molecules** through a selectively or differentially permeable membrane from a solution containing a lot of water molecules; for example, a dilute solution (or water), to a solution containing fewer water molecules; for example, a concentrated solution.*

Osmosis is a special form of diffusion. Only **water molecules** move by osmosis, and they always move from a solution with a **higher water content** (a more dilute solution) into a solution with a **lower water content** (a more concentrated solution) through a **selectively** or **differentially permeable membrane**. The membrane has tiny **pores** in it that allow tiny water molecules to move through, but they do not allow the passage of larger molecules such as sucrose (sugar) molecules.

The process of osmosis is **explained** in Figure 1.6 on page 7. In this explanation, the 10% sucrose solution contains 10% sucrose and 90% water, and the 50% sucrose solution contains 50% sucrose and 50% water. Therefore the **10% sucrose solution** is more dilute and has a **higher water content** than the 50% sucrose solution. Osmosis can be **demonstrated** using **Visking tubing** which is selectively permeable, as illustrated in Figure 1.7 on page 7.

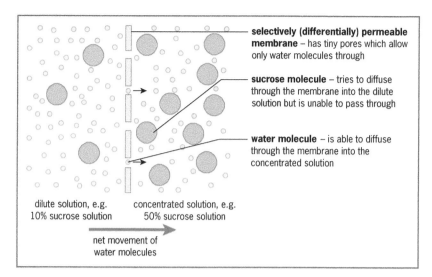

Figure 1.6 *Explanation of osmosis*

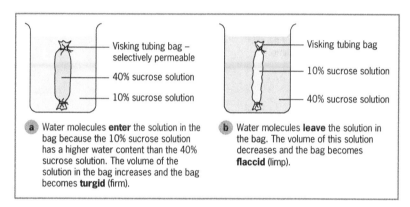

Figure 1.7 *Demonstrating osmosis using Visking tubing*

Osmosis in living cells

In any **living cell**, the **cell membrane** is selectively or differentially permeable. There is always **cytoplasm**, a solution of proteins and other substances in water, on the inside of the membrane and usually a solution, such as tissue fluid, on the outside. **Water molecules**, therefore, move into and out of living cells by **osmosis**. It is important to note that osmosis does **not** occur in **dead cells**.

If **animal cells** are placed in **water** or a solution that is **more dilute** than their cytoplasm, water enters the cytoplasm by osmosis causing the cells to **swell** and possibly **burst**. If animal cells are placed in a solution that is more **concentrated** than their cytoplasm, water leaves the cytoplasm causing the cells to **shrink**.

Plant cells are surrounded by a strong, freely permeable **cell wall**. Because of this they behave differently from animal cells when placed in solutions of different concentrations. If plant cells are placed in **water** or a solution that is **more dilute** than their cytoplasm and cell sap, water enters the cells by osmosis causing the cells to **swell** and become **turgid**, but the cell wall prevents them from bursting. If plant cells are placed in a solution that is more **concentrated** than their cytoplasm, water leaves the cytoplasm causing the cells to **shrink** and become **flaccid**. Osmosis occurring in plant tissue can be **demonstrated** by placing strips of potato in solutions of different concentrations as illustrated in Figure 1.8 on page 8.

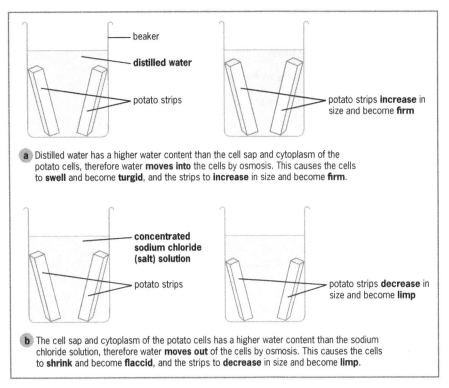

Figure 1.8 *Demonstrating osmosis in potato tissue*

The role of osmosis in living organisms

Osmosis plays an important **role** in living organisms because it is the way in which cells take in the **water** they need.

- **Water** moves into animal cells from blood plasma and body fluids by osmosis. This keeps the cells **hydrated**.
- **Water** is absorbed from the intestines into the blood by osmosis. This ensures the body obtains the water it needs from food and drink.
- **Water** is reabsorbed from the filtrate in the kidney tubules into the blood by osmosis. This prevents the body from losing too much water.
- **Water** is absorbed from the soil by the root hairs of plant roots, and then moves into and through the cells of roots and leaves by osmosis. This keeps water **moving** through plants and it ensures that the leaves get water for **photosynthesis**.
- **Water** that moves into plant cells by osmosis keeps the cells **turgid**. This causes non-woody stems to stand upright and keeps leaves firm.

Active transport

Active transport is the movement of particles through cell membranes against a concentration gradient using energy released in respiration.

Sometimes molecules and ions are in a **higher** concentration **inside** cells than they are outside, but the cells still require them, so they are absorbed into the cells by **active transport**. During active transport, protein molecules known as **carrier proteins**, which are present in cell membranes, pick up these molecules and ions and move them through the membranes into the cells. To do this, they use **energy** released in respiration.

1 Units of life

The role of active transport in living organisms

Active transport plays an important **role** in living organisms because it allows cells to accumulate high concentrations of important substances such as glucose, amino acids and various ions.

- Some of the **glucose** and **amino acids** produced in **digestion** are absorbed from the small intestine into the blood by active transport.
- **Useful substances** such as glucose, amino acids, hormones and vitamins are reabsorbed from the filtrate in the kidney tubules into the blood by active transport. This prevents the loss of these substances from the body.
- **Mineral ions** move from the soil into the cells of plant roots by active transport.

Diffusion, osmosis and active transport compared

Table 1.2 provides a comparison between diffusion, osmosis and active transport occurring in living organisms.

Table 1.2 *Diffusion, osmosis and active transport in living organisms compared*

	Diffusion	Osmosis	Active transport
Particles moving	Oxygen and carbon dioxide are the main molecules that move.	Only water molecules move.	Many different molecules and ions move
Direction of movement of particles	Molecules move down a concentration gradient.	Water molecules move from a solution with a higher water content to a solution with a lower water content.	Molecules and ions move against a concentration gradient.
Energy requirements	Energy is not required.	Energy is not required.	Energy is required.
Membrane requirements	Does not require a membrane, but can occur through cell membranes.	Requires a selectively (differentially) permeable membrane.	Requires carrier proteins in cell membranes.

Examples of diffusion in natural and artificial environments

Diffusion can be observed in a variety of natural and artificial environments. Some examples are outlined as follows.

- **Ash** is produced during **volcanic eruptions** and consists of rock and mineral particles of various sizes. During an eruption, the finest of these particles can remain suspended in the atmosphere forming ash clouds, and the particles in these clouds can **diffuse** long distances from the site of the eruption.

- **Smog** can be emitted from the **exhausts** of vehicles such as cars and lorries that burn gasoline (petrol) or diesel, and also from **industries** that burn fossil fuels. Smog is a mixture of nitrogen oxides, sulfur oxides, carbon oxides, ozone, volatile organic compounds and fine particulate matter. Smog **diffuses** from its source into the surrounding atmosphere, creating a hazy fog (see Figure 1.9).

Figure 1.9 *Smog emitted from the exhausts of vehicles*

- **Smoke** is produced when materials **burn**, which is a chemical reaction between the material and oxygen in the air. Wildfires, the combustion of fossil fuels in industry, intentional or accidental fires in landfills and cigarettes all produce smoke. Smoke contains a variety of gases and fine particulate matter, especially carbon particles, which **diffuse** from the fire into the surrounding atmosphere.
- **Perfume** contains molecules that produce a scent. When perfume is applied to the skin, these molecules gradually evaporate and **diffuse** into the surrounding air where they can be smelt.

Recalling facts

1 Provide definitions to distinguish between diffusion and osmosis.

2 What do the following terms mean:

 a concentration gradient **b** selectively permeable **c** active transport?

3 Give THREE ways diffusion is important to animals.

4 Explain what will happen to the following:

 a a human cheek cell that is placed in a solution that is more dilute than its cytoplasm.

 b a leaf cell that is placed in a solution that is more concentrated than its cell sap and cytoplasm.

5 Explain the role of EACH of the following in the life of a plant:

 a diffusion **b** osmosis **c** active transport.

6 Identify THREE examples of diffusion occurring in natural or artificial environments.

Applying facts

7 Human body cells are surrounded by body fluids. What would you expect the concentration of these fluids to be relative to the concentration of the cytoplasm of the cells? Explain your answer.

8 Salina noticed that certain types of lettuce leaves that had lost their crispness and become limp could be made crisp again by soaking them in water. Suggest an explanation for Salina's observations.

9 A scientist discovered that plants whose roots were treated with a poison that prevented them from respiring began to suffer from symptoms of mineral deficiency. Suggest an explanation for the scientist's discovery.

10 Give TWO similarities and TWO differences between the processes by which carbon dioxide enters the leaves of a hibiscus plant and water enters the roots of the same plant.

11 Use your knowledge of diffusion to explain why a glass of soda water that contains carbon dioxide bubbles goes flat when it is left on a table overnight.

12 Cylinders of potato were prepared, EACH 6.0 cm long and uniform in diameter. TEN cylinders were placed in Solution **X**, TEN were placed in Solution **Y** and TEN in Solution **Z**. They were removed after 1 hour, their lengths were re-measured and their textures were felt and compared with the original texture. The results are shown in Table 1.3.

Table 1.3 *The length and texture of potato cylinders after being left for 1 hour in different solutions*

	Average length of strips after 1 hour (cm)	Percentage change in length after 1 hour (%)	Texture after 1 hour
Solution X	5.4		Had become soft and limp.
Solution Y	6.3		Had become firm and crispy.
Solution Z	6.0		Texture had not changed.

a Explain why ten cylinders of potato tissue were placed in each solution and not just a single cylinder.

b Complete Table 1.3 by filling in the percentage change in length of the cylinders in each solution after 1 hour. Use a + or – sign, where appropriate, to indicate if the change was an increase or a decrease.

c What can you deduce about the concentration of EACH solution relative to the concentration of the cell sap and cytoplasm of the potato cells?

d Name the process that caused the changes in the potato cylinders.

e Account for:

  i the change in texture of the cylinders in Solution **X**.

  ii the change in length of the cylinders in Solution **Y**.

f The cylinders in Solution **X** were removed, placed in distilled water and left. What would you expect to have happened to the length and texture of the cylinders after 1 hour?

g State TWO ways in which the process occurring in this experiment is different from the one by which plant roots take up minerals from the soil.

13 To study osmosis, Xavier set up the apparatus shown in Figure 1.10 and measured the height of the sucrose solution in the capillary tube every 5 minutes for 30 minutes. His results are given in Table 1.4.

Table 1.4 *The height of the sucrose solution in the capillary tube every 5 minutes*

Time/min	Height of sucrose solution in the capillary tube/cm
0	0.0
5	3.8
10	7.9
15	12.5
20	16.7
25	20.3
30	24.0

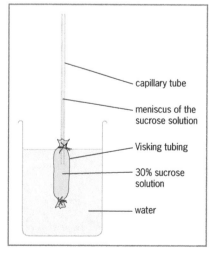

Figure 1.10 *Apparatus used to study osmosis*

a i Plot a line graph to show the height of the sucrose solution against time.

  ii What is the benefit of drawing graphs to display data such as the results of Xavier's investigation?

b What deduction can you make about Visking tubing?

c Explain why the sucrose solution gradually moved up the capillary tube.

d Xavier set up the apparatus again, but this time he placed water in the Visking tubing bag and 30% sucrose solution in the beaker. What would you expect to happen to the level of the water in the capillary tube? Explain your answer.

e The process occurring in Xavier's apparatus also occurs in the human body. Give ONE example of where it occurs.

14 Karen performed an experiment to investigate the movement of water through potato tissue. To do this, she peeled a potato, cut it in half and boiled one half to kill the cells. She then made a cavity in each half, placed the same volume of concentrated salt (sodium chloride) solution in each cavity and marked the levels of the solution using pins. She placed both halves in a trough of distilled water and left them. Figure 1.11 shows her observations after 3 hours.

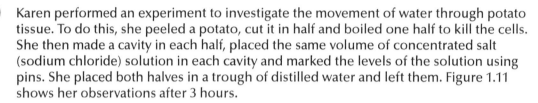
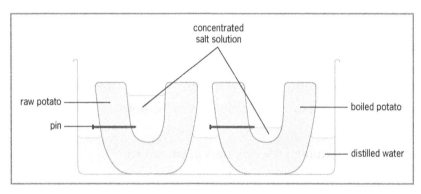

Figure 1.11 *Observations of the potato halves after 3 hours in distilled water*

a Name the process that Karen was studying.

b What had happened to the level of solution in EACH potato half after 3 hours?

c Explain the change in level of the solution in the raw potato.

d i Suggest a suitable control for the experiment.

  ii Explain the result that you would expect to obtain from the control suggested in **d i.**

e Suggest a reason for the results observed in the boiled potato.

f What conclusion might Karen have drawn from the results of her experiment?

2 Reproduction and growth in plants

All plants must **produce offspring** in order for their species to survive. They achieve this by reproduction of which there are two types: **asexual reproduction**, which requires only one parent, and **sexual reproduction**, which requires two parents. Plants also **grow**, and as they do so, they **develop**. Growth ensures that the plant is the correct size to survive in its environment.

Reproduction is the process by which living organisms generate new individuals of the same kind as themselves.

Growth is a permanent increase in the size of an organism.

Asexual and sexual reproduction compared

Learning objectives

- Distinguish between **asexual** and **sexual reproduction**.
- Explain the **role** of **mitosis** and **meiosis** in **asexual** and **sexual reproduction**.
- Discuss the **advantages** and **disadvantages** of **asexual reproduction**.

Asexual reproduction

Asexual reproduction involves only **one** parent and offspring are produced by a type of **cell division** known as **mitosis**. All offspring produced asexually from one parent are **genetically identical**, therefore they do not show variation, and they are collectively called a **clone**. Asexual reproduction occurs in unicellular organisms such as protozoans and bacteria. It also occurs in fungi, some plants and a few animals.

The role of mitosis in asexual reproduction

Mitosis ensures that each daughter (new) cell receives the **same number** and **type** of chromosomes as the parent cell. During mitosis, each **chromosome replicates** (makes a copy of itself) and forms a pair of **sister chromatids**. The cell then divides into **two daughter cells** such that each cell receives one chromatid from each pair. The chromatids then become known as chromosomes and the two daughter cells are **genetically identical** because they receive identical combinations of chromosomes, and therefore, of **genes**. They are also genetically identical to the original parent cell. Mitosis is summarised in Figure 2.1.

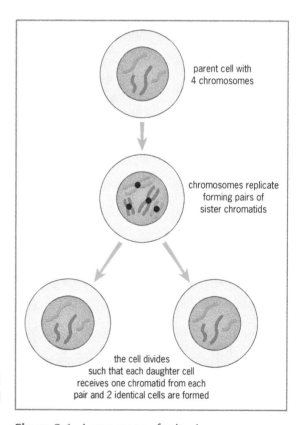

parent cell with 4 chromosomes

chromosomes replicate forming pairs of sister chromatids

the cell divides such that each daughter cell receives one chromatid from each pair and 2 identical cells are formed

Figure 2.1 *A summary of mitosis*

Sexual reproduction

Sexual reproduction involves **two** parents. **Gametes**, or **sex cells**, are produced in **reproductive organs** by a type of **cell division** known as **meiosis**. A male and a female gamete fuse during **fertilisation** to form a single cell called a **zygote**. The zygote then divides repeatedly by **mitosis** to form an **embryo** and ultimately an **adult**. Offspring produced sexually receive genes from both parents, therefore they possess characteristics of both parents and they show **variation**. Sexual reproduction occurs in most plants and animals.

The role of meiosis in sexual reproduction

Meiosis ensures that each gamete receives **half** the number of chromosomes as the parent cell, and that all gametes are **genetically non-identical**. During meiosis, each **chromosome replicates** as in mitosis and the chromatids **cross over** each other and exchange genetic material. The cell then divides twice, forming **four** daughter cells that all have **different** combinations of chromosomes, therefore different combinations of **genes**. By halving the number of chromosomes, meiosis ensures that when gametes fuse, the zygote has the **correct number** of chromosomes for the species, and because no two gametes have the same combination of genes, all offspring produced sexually show **variation**. The process of meiosis is summarised in Figure 2.2.

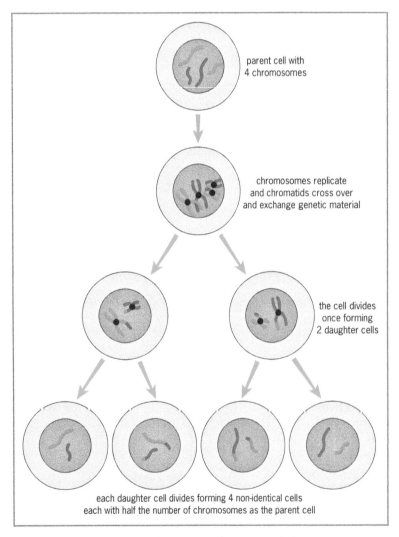

parent cell with
4 chromosomes

chromosomes replicate
and chromatids cross over
and exchange genetic material

the cell divides
once forming
2 daughter cells

each daughter cell divides forming 4 non-identical cells
each with half the number of chromosomes as the parent cell

Figure 2.2 *A summary of meiosis. The two red chromosomes are of maternal origin, having been passed on from the organism's mother, and the two blue are of paternal origin, having been passed on from the organism's father*

Table 2.1 *Asexual and sexual reproduction compared*

Asexual reproduction	Sexual reproduction
Involves only **one** parent.	Involves **two** parents, one male and one female.
Does not involve the production of gametes (sex cells).	Involves the production of male and female **gametes** by **meiosis** in male and female reproductive organs.
Offspring are produced by **mitosis** occurring in the parent.	Offspring are produced by the **fusion** of a **male** and a **female gamete** during **fertilisation** to form a single-celled **zygote**. The zygote then divides repeatedly to form an **embryo** and ultimately an **adult**.
All offspring produced asexually from one parent are **genetically identical** to each other and to their parent. In other words, they do **not** show variation.	Offspring receive genes from both parents, therefore they possess characteristics of both parents and are **genetically non-identical**. In other words, they show **variation**.
The process is **rapid** and **energy requirements** are **low** because it does not involve gamete production, finding a mate, mating, fertilisation and embryo development, so **large numbers** of offspring can be produced **quickly**.	The process is **slow** and **energy requirements** are **high** because it involves gamete production, finding a mate, mating, fertilisation and embryo development, so **small numbers** of offspring are produced **slowly**.

Advantages and disadvantages of asexual reproduction

Both asexual and sexual reproduction have advantages and disadvantages, several of which depend on the environmental conditions under which the organisms live. The advantages and disadvantages of **asexual reproduction** are discussed in the following sections.

Advantages of asexual reproduction

The **advantages** of asexual reproduction include the following.

- **All** offspring produced asexually from a single parent will be **well adapted** to their environment and have a **high** chance of survival if the parent is well adapted to the environment because they are all **identical**.
- **Beneficial** or **desirable characteristics** are retained within populations because all the offspring from a single parent are **identical**. This is of particular importance to commercial **crop growers** because if their crops are produced by asexual means, they can ensure that these crops possess the same **desirable traits** from generation to generation (see page 17).
- **Population sizes** can increase **rapidly** because the process is **rapid** and it does not require a lot of energy.
- Asexual reproduction allows organisms to reproduce when suitable mates are **scarce** or **absent**.

Disadvantages of asexual reproduction

The **disadvantages** of asexual reproduction include the following.

- **All** offspring produced asexually from a single parent will be **adversely affected** and have a reduced chance of survival if the environmental conditions change adversely because they are all **identical**. This is particularly detrimental to commercial **crop growers** because crops grown by asexual means will all be susceptible to the same adverse environmental conditions and diseases.
- Species reproducing asexually cannot change and adapt to changing environmental conditions. In other words, they **cannot improve** or **evolve**, because they are all **identical**.
- Asexual reproduction can lead to **overcrowding** and **competition** for resources because the offspring usually remain **close** to the parent.

Recalling facts

1. In your own words, provide a suitable definition for 'sexual reproduction'.

2. State THREE differences between asexual and sexual reproduction.

3. Outline the role of meiosis in sexual reproduction.

4. State TWO advantages of asexual reproduction.

Applying facts

5. Explain why all the offspring produced asexually from a single parent are genetically identical.

6. Under what conditions would asexual reproduction be of benefit to living organisms? Provide a suitable explanation for your answer.

7. Plant **X**, which reproduces asexually, and plant **Y**, which reproduces sexually, both live in the same woodland community. Which plant population is likely to be harmed to the greatest extent if a new disease enters the community? Explain your answer.

Reproduction in plants

Learning objectives

- Examine the different **methods** of **asexual reproduction** in **plants**.
- Examine the **process** of **sexual reproduction** in **plants**.
- Describe the **structure** and **function** of the **parts** of a **flower**.
- Explain **pollination** and **fertilisation**.
- Outline the **development** of **seeds** and **fruits**.

Asexual reproduction in plants

Many **plant** species are capable of reproducing **asexually** by **mitosis** occurring in certain structures of the parent plant. This process is known as **vegetative propagation**, and it results in new plants growing from these structures which are genetically identical to the parent plant. Humans can make use of vegetative propagation to **artificially propagate (produce)** plants. Vegetative propagation is a form of **cloning** because all individuals produced vegetatively from a single parent are identical.

Cloning is the process of making genetically identical individuals by non-sexual means.

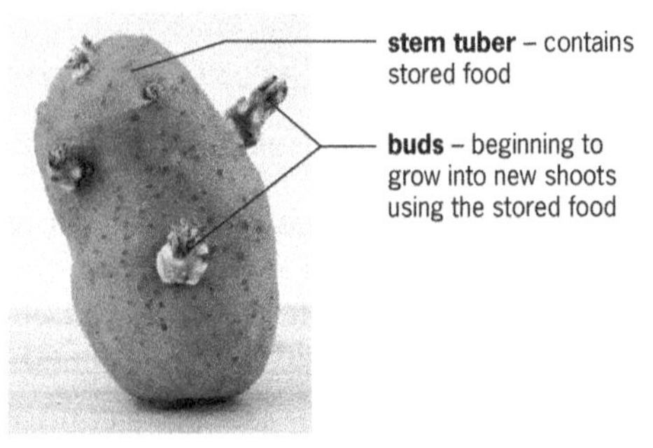

Natural vegetative propagation

Plants can propagate **naturally** by producing **perennating organs** such as **stem tubers**, **rhizomes**, **corms** and **bulbs**. These are usually **underground structures** that are swollen with **stored food** at the end of a growing season, such as the rainy season or summer months. The organs allow the

stem tuber – contains stored food

buds – beginning to grow into new shoots using the stored food

Figure 2.3 *A stem tuber with buds beginning to grow into new shoots*

plants to survive when conditions are unfavourable for photosynthesis, such as during the dry season or winter months. When conditions start to improve, several buds begin to grow from a single organ using the stored food. Each bud then continues to grow and develop into a new plant as shown in Figure 2.3 on page 16. Plants can also propagate by producing outgrowth called **runners** or **stolons**.

- **Stem tubers** are the swollen ends of underground stems; for example, yam and Irish potato.
- **Rhizomes** are swollen, horizontal underground stems that contain stored food (see Figure 2.4a). New shoots develop from buds and grow vertically; for example, turmeric and ginger.

a rhizomes   b corms   c bulbs

Figure 2.4 *Perennating organs produced by plants for asexual reproduction*

- **Corms** are short, swollen, vertical bases of stems that contain stored food (see Figure 2.4b). New shoots grow from buds that develop around the corm and grow vertically; for example, dasheen and eddo.

- **Bulbs** are composed of layers of fleshy, modified leaves arranged in a circular pattern (see Figure 2.4c). These leaves contain stored food. One or more buds develop inside a bulb, and these go on to develop into new plants; for example, lily and onion.

- **Runners** or **stolons** are **horizontal stems** that grow above ground from the base of the parent plant, as shown in Figure 2.5. Each runner has a bud at its tip which develops into a new plant. Once a new plant becomes established, more runners can develop from it; for example, savannah grass, spider plant and strawberry.

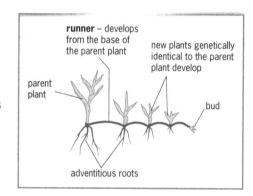

Figure 2.5 *Runners used for asexual reproduction*

Artificial vegetative propagation

Farmers and gardeners can **artificially** propagate plants by taking **cuttings** or by using techniques known as **grafting, budding** and **tissue culture**. Because all the plants produced from one parent by these methods are **genetically identical**, if the **cuttings, scions** used in grafting, **buds** used in budding or **explants** used in tissue culture are taken from plants with **desirable characteristics**, then all the plants produced will have the same desirable characteristics. These characteristics include a high yield, high quality, resistance to disease and fast growth rate.

- **Cuttings** are parts of stems, roots or leaves which, when removed and given suitable conditions, develop into new plants. **Sugar cane** and **hibiscus** are examples of plants that can be propagated using **stem cuttings**.

  - To propagate **sugar cane**, young sugar cane stems are cut up into pieces called **setts**, as shown in Figure 2.6. Each sett usually has two or three

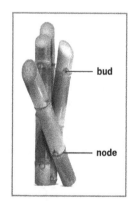

Figure 2.6 *Sugar cane setts, each with two nodes*

growth rings, known as **nodes**, and each node normally has a bud developing from it. The setts are planted horizontally and a new plant develops from the bud at each node.

♦ To propagate **hibiscus**, a stem bearing a few leaves at the top, is cut from a hibiscus plant. The cut end is often dipped into a rooting hormone to stimulate root growth and the stem is planted vertically into the soil. After a short period of time, roots grow from the cut end of the stem and a new plant develops.

- **Grafting** is often used to propagate fruit trees; for example, citrus and mango. It involves placing the cut stems of two plants in contact with each other so that their tissues join and they grow together. An actively growing shoot with several buds, called the **scion**, is taken from a plant with **desirable characteristics** that is to be propagated and its end is cut into a V-shape or obliquely. Another young plant, usually of the same or closely related species, which has an actively growing root system and is resistant to disease, is selected and its stem is cut to match the scion's cut surface (see Figure 2.7). This is known as the **rootstock** or **stock**, and it may have a few small branches. The two stems are then bound together and they grow into a new plant.

Figure 2.7 *Grafting two scions onto a rootstock*

- **Budding** is similar to grafting, and it can be used to propagate fruit trees and many ornamental plants. A **rootstock** is selected and a T-shaped cut is made into its bark. A **bud**, together with a small amount of bark, is cut from the plant to be propagated and inserted into the cut. The bud is secured in place with tape and it grows into a new plant using the root system of the rootstock.

- **Tissue culture** is used to artificially propagate plants such as orchids, potatoes and tomatoes (see Figure 2.8). Small pieces of tissue, called **explants**, are taken from a parent plant and grown in a nutrient-rich culture medium under sterile conditions. Each explant initially undergoes a period of cell division to form a cell mass known as a **callus**. Each callus is then treated with the appropriate plant hormones to stimulate it to develop into a **plantlet**, which can be transferred to the soil to grow and develop into a mature plant.

Figure 2.8 *Plants being grown by tissue culture under sterile conditions*

Sexual reproduction in flowering plants

Flowering plants produce **flowers** for **sexual reproduction**. Flowers show a wide variation in size, colour and structure to ensure that the end products of sexual reproduction, **seeds**, are produced. These seeds then **germinate** and produce **new plants**.

Flower structure

A **typical flower** is made up of an expanded stem tip, known as the **receptacle**, which bears **four** distinct whorls or rings of modified leaves.

- The **sepals** make up the outermost whorl.
- The **petals** lie inside the sepals.
- The **stamens** lie to the inside of the petals. These are the **male** reproductive organs. Each stamen is made up of an **anther** attached to a **filament**. The anthers produce **pollen grains**, which contain the **male gametes**.
- One or more **carpels** make up the innermost whorl. These are the **female** reproductive organs. Each carpel is made up of an **ovary**, which contains one or more **ovules**, a **style** and a **stigma**. The ovules contain the **female gametes**.

The **arrangement** of these parts varies considerably from species to species, and not all flowers have all four whorls. A longitudinal section through a typical flower is shown in Figure 2.9, and the structure and functions of the different parts are summarised in Table 2.2.

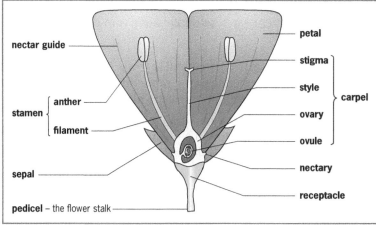

★**Figure 2.9** *A longitudinal section of a typical flower showing the main parts*

Table 2.2 *Structure and functions of the parts of a flower*

Flower part	Structure	Function(s)
Receptacle	Swollen top of the **pedicel** or flower stalk.	• Bears the flower parts.
Sepal	Leaf-like structure that is usually green in colour.	• Encloses and protects the developing flower when it is a bud.
Petal	Modified leaf which is usually brightly coloured and scented. Some have lines or markings called **nectar guides**.	• Attracts insects and other pollinators for pollination. • Nectar guides guide the pollinators to the nectar.
Nectary	Gland at the base of a petal or stamen.	• Produces **nectar**, a solution of sugars used to attract pollinators for pollination.
Anther	Oval-shaped structure composed of four pollen sacs containing pollen grains.	• Produces pollen grains which contain the male gametes.
Filament	Thin, stalk-like structure.	• Supports the anther and holds it in a position where it can best deliver pollen.
Ovary	Hollow, swollen base of the carpel containing one or more ovules.	• Produces ovules. • Houses and protects the ovules. • Develops into the fruit after fertilisation.
Ovule	Round- to oval-shaped structure inside the ovary. Contains the **embryo sac** which contains the female gamete.	• Produces and protects the female gamete. • Develops into the seed after fertilisation.
Style	Slender stalk that connects the ovary and the stigma.	• Holds the stigma in the best position to catch pollen grains.
Stigma	Sticky tip of the style.	• Catches the pollen grains during pollination.

Pollination

Pollination is the transfer of pollen grains from the anther of a flower to the stigma of a flower of the same species.

A male gamete in a pollen grain must be dispersed from the anther (see Figure 2.10) and then brought into contact with a female gamete in an ovule for **fertilisation** to take place in a flowering plant. **Pollination** is the first step towards bringing these gametes together, and it can take place in **two** different ways: **self-pollination** and **cross-pollination**.

- **Self-pollination** occurs when a pollen grain is transferred from an anther to a stigma of the **same flower** or to a stigma of another flower on the **same plant**.

- **Cross-pollination** occurs when a pollen grain is transferred from an anther of a flower on one plant to a stigma of a flower on a **different plant** of the **same species**.

Figure 2.10 *Yellow pollen grains being dispersed from the anther of a hibiscus flower*

Advantages of cross-pollination

Cross-pollination has certain **advantages** over self-pollination which increase the success of plant species.

- The **offspring** produced by cross-pollination show **greater variation** because gametes come from two different parent plants. This is advantageous because it increases the **chances of survival** of the offspring in changing environments and it helps species to adapt to changing environmental conditions, which enables them to **improve** or **evolve.**

- The **offspring** produced by cross-pollination can have **characteristics** that are **superior** to both parents, which increases their chances of survival; for example, they may show greater resistance to disease.

- The **seeds** produced by cross-pollination tend to be more **viable**, meaning that they are capable of surviving longer before they germinate and they are more likely to germinate.

Agents of pollination

Agents of pollination are responsible for transporting the pollen grains between flowers. These agents include the **wind** and small **animals**, including **insects** such as bees, wasps, flies, butterflies and moths, certain **bats** and some small **birds** such as hummingbirds. **Flowers** are usually **adapted** to be pollinated by either **wind** or **animals.**

- **Flowers** that rely on the **wind** to transport their pollen grains are usually small and inconspicuous, and have large anthers that hang outside the flower, as shown in Figure 2.11. These produce large quantities of lightweight pollen grains that can be easily carried by the wind, which increases their chances of pollinating other flowers as many are lost. The flowers also have large, feathery stigmas to trap

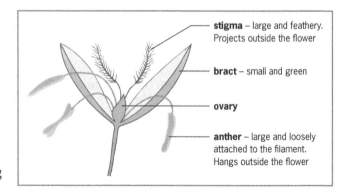

Figure 2.11 *A typical wind-pollinated flower*

the pollen grains. Examples include grasses, maize and sugar cane.

- **Flowers** that rely on **animals**, mainly **insects**, to transport their pollen gains are usually large, brightly coloured, conspicuous and often scented to attract the insects to feed on their nectar (see Figure 2.12). In doing this, the insects brush against the anthers and pick up pollen grains on their heads and bodies. They then move on to other flowers to feed and the pollen grains brush off onto their stigmas and few are lost. Examples include flamboyant, allamanda and pride of Barbados.

Figure 2.12 *A bee with pollen on its legs and body*

Fertilisation in flowering plants

After pollination has occurred, a male gamete has to reach a female gamete for **fertilisation** to take place. Each **pollen grain** contains a **male gamete** and each **ovule** is made up of an **embryo sac** surrounded by two protective layers that have a tiny hole in them called the **micropyle**. The embryo sac contains the **female gamete**. The mechanism of fertilisation in a flowering plant is explained in Figure 2.13.

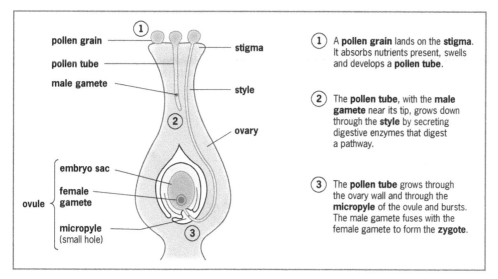

1. A **pollen grain** lands on the **stigma**. It absorbs nutrients present, swells and develops a **pollen tube**.

2. The **pollen tube**, with the **male gamete** near its tip, grows down through the **style** by secreting digestive enzymes that digest a pathway.

3. The **pollen tube** grows through the ovary wall and through the **micropyle** of the ovule and bursts. The male gamete fuses with the female gamete to form the **zygote**.

Figure 2.13 *Longitudinal section through a carpel showing the mechanism of fertilisation*

It is possible for **several** pollen grains to land on one stigma and to develop pollen tubes, however, the **first** male gamete to reach a female gamete is the one that fertilises it. If the ovary contains more than one ovule, each female gamete must be fertilised by a male gamete from a different pollen grain. Any pollen grains landing on the stigmas of flowers of a **different species** will **not** develop pollen tubes.

Development of seeds and fruits

After fertilisation, each **ovule** develops into a **seed** and the **ovary** develops into the **fruit**. The **stigma**, **style**, **stamens**, **petals** and **sepals** usually wither and drop off, though the **sepals** may remain; for example, in an eggplant or strawberry fruit.

Seed development

The **zygote** divides by **mitosis** forming the **embryo**, which is composed of three parts: the **plumule** or embryonic shoot, the **radicle** or embryonic root and one or two **cotyledons** that usually store food. The embryo is surrounded by the seed coat or **testa**. Water is withdrawn from the seed and it becomes **dormant**. Figure 2.14 shows the structure of a bean seed.

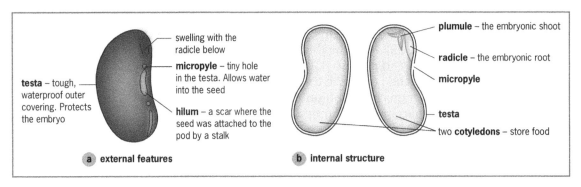

Figure 2.14 *Structure of a bean seed*

Fruit development

As the seeds are developing inside the ovary, the **ovary wall** develops into the **fruit**. A fruit, therefore, always contains one or more **seeds**. The ovary wall may become **succulent** (**fleshy and juicy**); for example, mango, guava, tomato and pumpkin, or it may become **dry** and **thin**; for example, the pods of pride of Barbados and pigeon pea. Fruits **protect** the seeds and they help to **disperse** or **spread** the seeds that they contain. Figure 2.15 shows the structure of a succulent fruit and of a dry fruit.

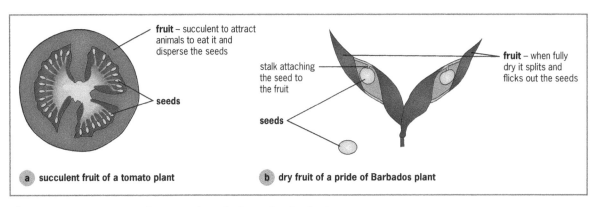

Figure 2.15 *Structure of a succulent fruit and a dry fruit*

Recalling facts

1. What is meant by the term 'vegetative propagation'?

2. Describe TWO different methods by which plants can propagate vegetatively in nature.

3. Explain how tissue culture is used to propagate tomato plants.

4. Why do plants produce flowers?

5. Outline the structure of a typical flower.

6   State the function of EACH of the following parts of a flower:

a the petals   b the style   c the pollen grains
d the sepals   e the filaments   f the stigma.

7   Clearly distinguish between the following:

a pollination and fertilisation   b self-pollination and cross-pollination.

8   What is an agent of pollination? Support your answer with examples.

9   Describe the events that follow pollination and lead to the development of a seed.

10   What is a fruit and why is it important for plants to produce fruits?

Applying facts

11   When a farmer plants Irish potato tubers, he usually removes all but two of the buds. Suggest TWO reasons for doing this.

12   You find a mango tree that produces extremely tasty, juicy mangoes. Explain how you could try to grow the same variety of mango tree in your garden.

13   A hibiscus plant with yellow flowers on all of its branches except two, which had red flowers, was found growing in the grounds of a large hotel. Explain how the plant could have been produced.

14   Despite the fact that some varieties of sugar cane produce seeds for reproduction, most sugar cane is grown from stem cuttings. Suggest TWO reasons why this method is usually employed.

15   Explain fully why some plants have developed mechanisms to prevent self-pollination.

16   Chemical insecticides designed to kill insect pests have been found to be harming bee populations worldwide. Discuss the long-term effects that this will have on farmers.

17   Suggest the advantages to flowers of having adaptations for attracting insects for pollination rather than relying on the wind.

Growth in plants and crop production

Learning objectives

- Identify the **conditions** necessary for **germination**.
- Analyse **growth patterns** in **annual plants**.
- Describe the **methods** used in the **production** of **crops**.

Germination and growth in annual plants

An **annual plant** is a plant that completes its life cycle, from germination of its seeds to the development of flowers, fruits and seeds, within a **single** growing season, usually the summer months or rainy season. This enables the plant to complete its life cycle before adverse conditions develop, usually during the winter months or dry season. Many **crops** are annual plants; for example, beans, maize (corn) and other grains, and their growth follows a similar pattern, which begins with **germination**.

Germination

Germination is the process by which the embryonic plant in a seed grows into a seedling.

Seeds require the following **three conditions** to germinate.

- **Water** to activate the enzymes so that chemical reactions can occur.
- **Oxygen** for aerobic respiration to occur and release the energy required for the process.
- A **suitable temperature**, usually between about 5 °C and 40 °C, to activate enzymes.

As **germination** begins, **water** is absorbed through the **micropyle** of the seed (see Figure 2.14, page 22). The water causes the seed to swell and it activates enzymes. The enzymes break down stored, insoluble food in the cotyledons into soluble food which the radicle and plumule use for **respiration** to release energy and for **growth**. As the **radicle** grows, it ruptures the testa, emerges, grows downwards into the soil and begins to form the **root system** which anchors the seedling, and absorbs water and minerals. The **plumule** then emerges, grows upwards out of the soil and forms the **first foliage leaves**. The process of germination is illustrated in Figure 2.16.

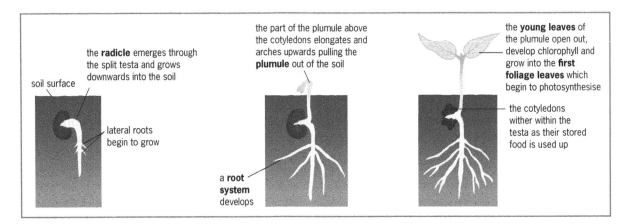

Figure 2.16 *Germination*

Growth patterns of annual plants after germination

As the first foliage leaves develop, the seedling starts to make food by **photosynthesis** and it uses this food to increase in size or to **grow** and to develop into a **plant**. The main stem grows upwards and usually begins to branch, the leaves increase in number and size, and the root system continues to develop within the soil. This period of **vegetative growth** continues until the plant approaches **maturity**, at which stage growth slows as it begins to develop **flowers** so that it can **reproduce** (see pages 18 to 22).

After pollination and fertilisation have occurred, each ovule develops into a **seed** and the ovary develops into the **fruit**, as described on pages 21 to 22. The plant itself **stops** growing during this **reproductive phase** as the food produced in photosynthesis is used in the growth and development of the flowers, seeds and fruits. When fully developed, the seeds are **dispersed**, the plant **dies** and the seeds remain **dormant** (inactive) until the next growing season when they **germinate**.

When the **height** of an annual plant is measured at regular intervals and plotted against time, a **growth curve** is obtained that is similar in shape for most annual plants. The curve is described as being **sigmoid shaped** or **S-shaped**, and is illustrated in Figure 2.17 on page 25.

2 Reproduction and growth in plants

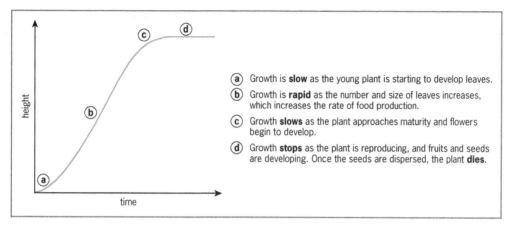

(a) Growth is **slow** as the young plant is starting to develop leaves.
(b) Growth is **rapid** as the number and size of leaves increases, which increases the rate of food production.
(c) Growth **slows** as the plant approaches maturity and flowers begin to develop.
(d) Growth **stops** as the plant is reproducing, and fruits and seeds are developing. Once the seeds are dispersed, the plant **dies**.

Figure 2.17 *A sigmoid growth curve for an annual plant*

Crop production

Farmers and gardeners use a variety of **methods** to produce **crops**, which are designed to maximise yields to meet the growing demand to provide humans with **food**. The methods used depend on factors such as climate, availability of land and other necessary resources, soil type and type of crop being grown, and include **strip planting**, **crop rotation**, **greenhouse farming**, **hydroponics**, **tissue culture**, **organic farming** and **container gardening**.

Strip planting

Strip planting involves growing crops in **strips** or **bands** across a field or following the contours of sloping land (see Figure 2.18). The strips are created by leaving unploughed strips between them or by creating raised beds. Crops are then planted and allowed to grow in the strips. Different crops or varieties can be planted in alternating strips to help reduce pests and diseases, and to optimise the use of resources. Strip planting reduces soil erosion, improves the use of mineral nutrients when different crops are planted in the strips, and can help to manage water runoff.

Figure 2.18 *Strip planting*

Crop rotation

Crop rotation involves growing different crops in a **specific order** over successive growing seasons on the same piece of land. The crops grown usually have different mineral nutrient requirements and different susceptibilities to pests and diseases. The rotation usually begins with a **legume** such as peas or beans to replenish **nitrates** in the soil. Crop rotation maintains or enhances soil fertility, helps to reduce soil erosion and helps to control pests and diseases, all of which lead to increased crop yields.

Greenhouse farming

Greenhouse farming involves growing crops in **greenhouses** that have walls and roofs made of a **transparent material** such as glass or plastic (see Figure 2.19). The climate in the greenhouse is carefully controlled, especially the temperature, humidity and,

Figure 2.19 *Greenhouse farming*

in some cases, the light. The greenhouse must also be well ventilated, and an irrigation system is often used to provide the plants with water and mineral nutrients. This method of crop production allows many different kinds of crops to be grown in places where the climate would not normally be suitable. It also allows for year-round crop production and protects the crops from adverse weather conditions, pests and diseases.

Hydroponics

Hydroponics involves growing crops in a **nutrient-rich solution** without soil. The plants are usually suspended with their roots in an inert growing medium such as perlite, vermiculite, clay pellets, rockwool or coconut coir, or in the nutrient-rich solution alone (see Figure 2.20). The solution contains a balanced mixture of the macronutrients and micronutrients required by the plants for healthy growth and development. The solution is usually pumped around the plant roots whilst ensuring that the roots are well oxygenated. Hydroponics eliminates damage due to soil-borne pests and diseases, enables high yields to be produced in limited space and allows crops to be grown in locations with poor soil quality.

Figure 2.20 *Growing lettuces using hydroponics*

Tissue culture

Tissue culture involves growing plants from small pieces of tissue, known as **explants**, which are taken from plants with certain desirable characteristics and grown initially in a nutrient-rich culture medium under sterile conditions, as described on page 18. The method allows large numbers of plants with desirable characteristics such as a high yield, resistance to disease or fast growth rates to be produced in a fairly short period of time.

Organic farming

Organic farming involves using **sustainable** and **ecologically friendly** methods to grow crops without the use of any synthetic inputs such as chemical pesticides, chemical fertilisers and antibiotics, or any genetically modified organisms (GMOs). Only **natural** pesticides and fertilisers are used, crops are rotated, organic matter (including animal manure) is recycled back into the soil, and soil conservation and preventative disease control are practised. Organic farming usually incurs higher labour costs and more careful management than conventional farming methods. However, it produces nutritious and healthy crops with very low levels of chemical residues and, at the same time, it enhances soil fertility and minimises the environmental impact associated with conventional crop growing practices.

Container gardening

Container gardening involves growing crops and herbs in appropriately sized **containers** that contain soil or a mixture of soil and potting mix, instead of growing them in the ground. These containers can include half-barrels, tubs and pots, and they must have drainage holes in the bottom. The plants should be watered regularly, inspected for any signs of pests or diseases and crops should be rotated in the containers to maximise productivity. Container gardening is especially useful in urban areas where outdoor space is limited as it can utilise unused spaces such as flat rooftops, patios and balconies (see Figure 2.21).

Figure 2.21 *Tomato plants growing in containers on a patio*

Recalling facts

1. What is meant by the following terms:

   a growth   **b** germination?

2. **a** Identify the conditions needed for germination and state the role of each.

   b Describe the process of germination of a seed until the first foliage leaves are formed.

3. Briefly describe EACH of the following methods that can be used to produce crops:

   a organic farming   **b** container gardening   **c** strip planting.

4. Explain THREE ways by which crop rotation leads to increased crop yields.

Applying facts

5. Suriyah, who had moved into her new home during the dry season, noticed that a few bean seedlings had begun to appear in one of her garden beds soon after the first rains began to fall. Provide a suitable explanation to account for Suriyah's observations.

6. To measure the growth of pigeon pea seeds as they germinate, Esme planted a large number of seeds. She then dug up ten seeds or seedlings every day, removed any soil, dried them completely by heating them in an oven at 100 °C, weighed them to determine their dry masses (masses without water) and took the average. Her results are shown in Figure 2.22.

   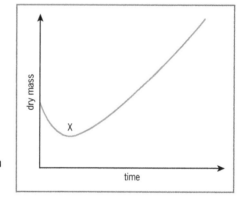

   Figure 2.22 *Graph showing the dry mass of germinating seeds against time*

   a Suggest why the dry mass of the seeds decreased at the beginning of the germination process.

   b Suggest what happened at point X on the graph to cause the dry mass of the seedlings to begin to increase and explain why the dry mass continued to increase.

   c What would you expect to happen to the dry mass of the plants after their fruits and seeds had developed and matured? Explain your answer.

7. Suggest FOUR reasons why Caleb, a specialised crop farmer, grows his lettuce plants hydroponically in greenhouses.

Soil

Learning objectives

- Describe the **characteristics** of **sandy**, **clay** and **loam soils**.
- Relate **soil fertility** to the **physical**, **chemical** and **biological properties** of **soil**.
- Describe the **causes** and **effects** of **soil erosion**.
- Explain **methods** to **prevent soil erosion**.
- Evaluate the **impact** of **soil erosion** on **food production**.

An introduction to soil

Soil is a complex and dynamic mixture of **six** components: **rock particles**, **organic matter**, **water**, **air**, **mineral salts** or **mineral nutrients** and **living organisms**.

- **Rock particles** form from rocks by weathering, and they provide support and anchorage for plant roots and shelter for burrowing animals.
- **Organic matter** or **humus** forms from dead and decaying plant and animal material and it helps to increase soil fertility and improve soil structure (see page 31).
- **Water** is held in a thin film around rock particles and is essential for photosynthesis in plants and to prevent soil organisms from drying out or desiccating.
- **Air** is present in the spaces between rock particles and it contains oxygen which is essential for aerobic respiration to take place in plant roots and other soil organisms.
- **Mineral nutrients** are dissolved in the water in the soil and are essential for healthy plant growth.
- **Living organisms** include microorganisms, earthworms and other burrowing animals which help to increase soil fertility (see page 31) and plant roots which help to prevent soil erosion (see page 32).

Soil forms continuously, but slowly, from the breakdown of rocks by physical and chemical weathering, and biological action. Soil is **important** for the survival of all terrestrial (land) organisms because it provides **support** for plant roots, and it contains the **water** and **mineral nutrients** that plants need to produce **food** for themselves and for all other terrestrial organisms that rely directly or indirectly on plants for their food (see pages 161 to 164).

Soil profiles

Soil is composed of layers known as **soil horizons**. A **soil profile** is a vertical section through the soil showing the horizons. The soils in the horizons differ in composition, structure, texture and colour. Most soils have **three** horizons: **A**, **B** and **C**. Some also have an **O** horizon, and the parent rock is known as the **R** horizon. A typical soil profile is shown in Figure 2.23.

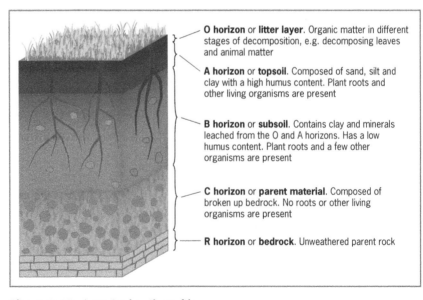

O horizon or **litter layer**. Organic matter in different stages of decomposition, e.g. decomposing leaves and animal matter

A horizon or **topsoil**. Composed of sand, silt and clay with a high humus content. Plant roots and other living organisms are present

B horizon or **subsoil**. Contains clay and minerals leached from the O and A horizons. Has a low humus content. Plant roots and a few other organisms are present

C horizon or **parent material**. Composed of broken up bedrock. No roots or other living organisms are present

R horizon or **bedrock**. Unweathered parent rock

Figure 2.23 *A typical soil profile*

Soil fertility

A **fertile soil** is one that is capable of supporting the growth of a large number of healthy plants. A fertile soil has a high **organic matter** content, is rich in **mineral nutrients**, has a **balanced pH**, usually between 6.0 and 7.5, and has a good **crumb structure** so that it is **well aerated**, it **drains well** whilst still retaining **water** and is **loosely packed**, making it easy for plant roots to penetrate and animals to burrow. The different **physical**, **chemical** and **biological properties** of soil all work together to determine the **fertility** of soil.

Types of soil and soil fertility

Soils can be classified into **sandy soil**, **clay soil** and **loam soil** based on the **size** of the rock particles that the soil contains. A **sandy soil** contains a high proportion of fairly large **sand** particles, a **clay soil** contains a high proportion of fairly small **clay** particles and a **loam soil** contains a mixture of different sized rock particles: **sand**, **silt** and **clay**. The sizes of these particles are given in Figure 2.24 on page 30.

The size of particles in the soil determines the **physical properties** of the soil. The properties of the three soil types are compared in Table 2.3.

Table 2.3 *Sandy, clay and loam soils compared*

Property	Sandy soil	Clay soil	Loam soil
Particle size	High proportion of **large** sand particles: 0.02 to 2.0 mm.	High proportion of **small** clay particles: less than 0.002 mm.	Mixture of **large** sand, **medium** silt and **small** clay particles.
Air content	**High:** the large particles have large air spaces between.	**Low:** the small particles have small air spaces between.	**Fairly high:** the different sized particles have fairly large air spaces between.
Water-holding capacity	**Poor:** the large particles have a small total surface area to retain water.	**Very good:** the small particles have a large total surface area to retain water.	**Good:** the different sized particles have a fairly large total surface area to retain water.
Drainage	**Good:** water passes through large air spaces quickly. The soil does not become waterlogged.	**Poor:** water passes through small air spaces slowly. The soil becomes waterlogged easily.	**Good:** water passes through the fairly large air spaces fairly quickly. The soil retains water, but does not become waterlogged.
Mineral nutrient content	**Low:** rapid drainage causes minerals to be leached (washed) through the soil.	**High:** slow drainage causes minerals to be leached through the soil very slowly.	**Relatively high:** the water retained around the particles retains dissolved minerals.
pH	Slightly acidic to very slightly alkaline. Typically ranges from **5.5** to **7.5**.	Moderately acidic to moderately alkaline. Typically ranges from **5.0** to **8.5**.	Very slightly acidic to very slightly alkaline. Typically ranges from **6.0** to **7.5**.
Ease of cultivation	**Very easy** to dig or plough and for plant roots to penetrate: the particles are loosely packed and have large spaces between.	**Hard** to dig or plough and for plant roots to penetrate: the particles stick together and have small spaces between.	**Easy** to dig or plough and for plant roots to penetrate: the particles are loosely packed and have fairly large spaces between.

A **loam soil** is described as being the **ideal soil** because it is the most **fertile** of the three types. It combines the **advantages** of both sandy and clay soils. It is **well aerated**, has good **drainage** whilst still retaining **water** and not becoming waterlogged, its **mineral nutrient** content is relatively high, its **pH** range is small and optimum for most plants, and it is easy to **cultivate**.

Investigating the composition of rock particles in soil

The **composition** of rock particles in a soil sample can be determined using the **sedimentation test**. A cylinder is half-filled with soil and water is added to almost fill the cylinder. The cylinder is covered, shaken for 5 minutes to break up the soil crumbs and then left undisturbed until the particles have settled into layers, as shown in Figure 2.24. The **depth** of each layer is then measured. Alternatively, a measuring cylinder can be used and the **volume** of each layer measured. In both methods, the percentage of each component can then be calculated.

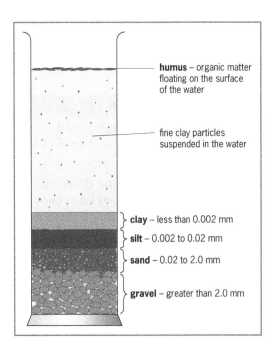

Figure 2.24 *The sedimentation test to determine the composition of rock particles in a soil sample*

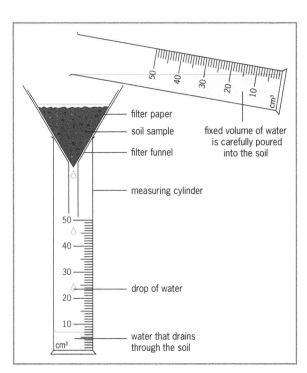

Figure 2.25 *To determine the water-holding capacity and rate of drainage of a soil sample*

Determining the water-holding capacity and rate of drainage of a soil sample

The **water-holding capacity** and **drainage rate** of a soil sample can be determined using the apparatus shown in Figure 2.25. A filter funnel is lined with filter paper, rested on a measuring cylinder and a sample of **dry soil** is placed inside the funnel. A **fixed volume** of **water** is carefully poured into the soil and a stopwatch is started as pouring begins. When obvious dripping stops, the stopwatch is stopped and the funnel is lifted off the measuring cylinder. The **volume** of water that drains through the soil and collects in the measuring cylinder, and the **time** taken for it to drain, are measured and recorded. These measurements are then used to calculate the following.

- volume of water retained (cm³) = volume of water added (cm³) – volume of water collected (cm³)

- rate of drainage (cm³ min⁻¹) = $\dfrac{\text{volume of water collected (cm}^3\text{)}}{\text{time taken for water to drain (min)}}$

The **smaller** the rock particles in a soil, the more water it retains and the slower it drains.

Determining the air content of a soil sample

To determine the **air content** of a soil sample, approximately 50 cm³ of soil is placed in a 100 cm³ measuring cylinder, the cylinder is tapped gently to help the soil to settle and its exact volume is measured. A second measuring cylinder is used to measure 50 cm³ of water and the water is slowly added to the soil. The soil and water are gently shaken until all the air is displaced from the soil, the new volume of soil and water is measured, and the volumes are used to calculate the percentage of air in the soil sample as follows.

- $$\text{volume of air (cm}^3) = \left[\text{volume of soil (cm}^3) + \text{volume of water added (cm}^3)\right] - \text{volume of soil and water (cm}^3)$$

- $$\text{percentage of air} = \frac{\text{volume of air (cm}^3)}{\text{volume of soil (cm}^3)} \times 100\ \%$$

Soil organisms and soil fertility

Soil organisms are important in increasing soil fertility.

- **Microorganisms**, mainly **bacteria** and **fungi**, feed on dead and waste plant and animal material (organic matter) causing it to **decompose**. During this process, they release mineral nutrients back into the soil, including nitrogen, phosphorous and potassium, which improves the soil's **fertility**. These organisms are known as **decomposers** and the nutrients that they release can be reabsorbed and re-used by plants.

- **Earthworms** improve the soil's **aeration** and **drainage** by burrowing through the soil (see Figure 2.26). They **fertilise** the soil by feeding on plant debris and soil particles and egesting **worm casts** which are rich in mineral nutrients. They also add **humus** to the soil by pulling plant debris into their burrows, which then decomposes.

- **Nematodes**, which are microscopic roundworms, consume bacteria and fungi in the soil and release **ammonium compounds** that can then be converted into **nitrates** for plant use (see page 32). They also **spread** useful bacteria and fungi through the soil on their bodies.

Figure 2.26 *Earthworms improve soil fertility*

Humus and soil fertility

Humus is formed by bacteria and fungi decomposing dead and waste **organic matter** in the soil. It is a dark brown, sticky material that coats soil particles and improves soil fertility in the following ways.

- Humus improves the **mineral nutrient content** of soil by adding minerals when the organic matter decomposes. It also absorbs and retains minerals, preventing them from being leached through the soil.

- Humus improves the **water content** of soil by absorbing and retaining water.

- Humus improves the **air content** and **drainage** of soil by binding finer soil particles together into larger **soil crumbs**. This also improves the structure of the soil, and makes it easier to cultivate and for plant roots to penetrate.

Cycling of nitrogen and soil fertility

Nitrogen is one of the most important elements that plants require for healthy growth, primarily to make proteins. However, plants are unable to use nitrogen (N_2) gas directly from the air; they must obtain it from the soil in the form of the **nitrate (NO_3^-) ion**. Certain **bacteria** in the soil are responsible for cycling nitrogen within the soil and this plays a crucial role in maintaining **soil fertility**.

- **Nitrifying bacteria** convert **ammonia (NH_3)** and **ammonium (NH_4^+) compounds** into **nitrites (NO_2^-)** and then into **nitrates**. The ammonia and ammonium compounds are formed initially when **decomposers** break down proteins in dead and waste organic matter in the soil.

- **Denitrifying bacteria** convert **nitrates** in the soil into **nitrogen gas**, which is returned to the air in the soil, and eventually to the atmosphere. They do this under anaerobic conditions, in other words, without oxygen. They are usually present in waterlogged or very compacted soil and lead to a **reduction** in soil fertility.

- **Nitrogen-fixing bacteria** are present in root nodules of legumes such as peas and beans, and they are also free-living in the soil. They convert **nitrogen gas**, which is present in the air in the soil, into **ammonium compounds**. The legumes can then use these compounds directly to make proteins, and those produced by free-living bacteria can be converted into **nitrates** by nitrifying bacteria in the soil.

Composting and soil fertility

Composting is a natural process by which microorganisms, mainly bacteria and fungi, convert organic material such as kitchen and garden waste into a nutrient-rich **soil conditioner**, known as **compost**, which can be used to improve **soil fertility** in a similar way to humus. Compost provides the soil with a balanced mixture of **mineral nutrients**, it improves the soil's ability to retain **nutrients** and **water**, it improves the **crumb structure**, which improves the soil's **aeration** and **drainage**, and it promotes the activity of **microorganisms** in the soil.

Soil erosion and its impact on food production

Soil erosion is the wearing away of the upper layer of soil due to the action of wind and water.

Soil is one of the world's most **important natural resources** and the upper layer, known as **topsoil**, is the most fertile because it contains the most decomposing organic matter. If the topsoil is removed, the remaining soil is less fertile, more compact and less able to retain water and nutrients, making it difficult for plants to grow.

Causes of soil erosion

Soil erosion occurs naturally and is speeded up if the soil has **no plants** growing in it to bind the particles together with their roots. A combination of **natural** and **human-induced** factors leads to soil erosion.

- **Rainfall** on the surface of the soil breaks down soil crumbs and separates the soil particles. These particles can then be washed away by the rainwater as it runs off the land, known as **surface runoff**.

- **Wind** picks up loose soil particles and carries them away as it blows. The stronger the force of the wind, the more particles it erodes away.

- **Deforestation**, where trees are cut down and not replanted, removes leaves that break the force of the rain and roots that bind the soil together. Deforestation leaves the soil barren and exposed to the rain and wind (see Figure 2.27).

Figure 2.27 *Deforestation exposes the soil to erosion*

- **Bad agricultural practices**; for example, leaving the soil barren after harvesting crops, overgrazing of animals, ploughing down hillsides instead of contour ploughing and using chemical fertilisers instead of organic fertilisers such as manure, can all lead to topsoil being washed away by the rain or blown away by the wind.

Effects of soil erosion

Soil erosion has many effects which go beyond those resulting directly from the loss of fertile soil, outlined as follows.

- Soil erosion leads to a reduction in the number of **trees** and **other plants** that can be grown which, in turn, leads to a decline in **biodiversity**.
- Soil erosion leads to reduced **agricultural productivity**. As fertile topsoil is lost, the yield of **agricultural crops** decreases, and this leads to a decrease in food production and an increase in global food insecurity (see page 34).
- Persistent soil erosion can lead to **desertification** in areas where the soil has become eroded to such an extent that plants can no longer grow.
- Soil erosion causes **sediment** to build up in bodies of water such as lakes, rivers and streams as surface runoff washes soil into them. The sediment reduces the quality of the water and light penetration, which causes a reduction in the growth of aquatic plants. It also clogs the gills of fish, smothers bottom-dwelling organisms and blocks waterways as it builds up.
- Soil erosion leads to an increase in **flooding** because eroded lands are less able to retain water during periods of heavy rainfall.

Prevention of soil erosion

A variety of measures can be implemented to **reduce soil erosion** and **conserve soil**.

- Practise **contour farming** when growing crops on **sloping land**, such as a hillside. This involves ploughing and planting crops along the **natural contours** of the land rather than up and down the slope. This method helps to retain water by reducing water runoff and it minimises soil loss.

- Cut **terraces** out of the sides of hills or mountains to create a series of flat steps or platforms that resemble a staircase (see Figure 2.28). Crops are then planted in the flat terraces. Like contour farming, this method, known as **terracing**, helps reduce rainwater runoff and minimises soil loss.

Figure 2.28 *Terracing helps to minimise soil erosion*

- Practise **crop rotation**, which involves growing different crops in a **specific order** over successive growing seasons on the same piece of land (see page 25) and often involves planting cover crops (see page 34). The varying root structures of the different crops help to improve soil structure and cover crops maintain soil cover, both of which help minimise soil erosion.
- Plant **windbreaks** around areas of land where the soil needs to be protected against erosion by the wind. These are rows of trees, shrubs or other vegetation that are planted around the edges of fields, or in well-planned positions within large areas of cropland. Windbreaks act as barriers to reduce the speed of the wind and they can also change its direction.

- Plant **cover crops**, which are plants that are grown to cover the soil and protect it against soil erosion, rather than to produce a crop for harvesting. They include legumes, such as clover, or grasses and are usually planted when the main crops are not being grown or immediately after their harvesting. Cover crops protect the surface of the soil against the wind and rain. They also help to reduce water runoff and their roots help to bind soil particles together.

The impact of soil erosion on food production

Food security exists when all people at all times have access to sufficient, safe and nutritious food to maintain a healthy and active life. Food security depends directly on **soil productivity**, and **soil erosion** is the principal cause of a decrease in soil productivity. According to the Food and Agricultural Organization of the United Nations (FAO), **soil degradation** is the single biggest threat to **global food security**. Estimates show that 33% of the Earth's soils are already degraded due to soil erosion and over 90% could become degraded by 2050.

It is estimated that soil erosion can cause up to 50% losses in **crop yields**. It can also lead to a decrease in the **quality** of crops and an increase in the **costs** associated with their production. All these factors can lead to economic losses for farmers, food shortages, higher food prices, hunger and starvation. **Food insecurity** already affects more than three quarters of a billion people worldwide, especially in tropical and sub-tropical regions, such as South Asia and Sub-Saharan Africa. Putting measures in place worldwide to prevent soil erosion is, therefore, crucial for ensuring global food security.

Recalling facts

1. What is soil and of what importance is it to living organisms?

2. What are the characteristics of a fertile soil?

3. Distinguish among a sandy soil, a clay soil and a loam soil in terms of
    a particle size   b pH   c drainage.

4. Explain how EACH of the following affects a soil's fertility:
    a the organisms living in the soil
    b its humus content
    c nitrifying bacteria.

5. a What do you understand by the term 'soil erosion'?
    b Explain FOUR ways in which soil can be eroded and FOUR measures that an agriculturalist can implement to reduce or prevent soil erosion.

Applying facts

6. Suggest why a clay soil is referred to as a 'heavy soil' and a sandy soil is referred to as a 'light soil'.

7. Explain how the size of soil particles affects the fertility of a soil.

8. To compare the air content of three soil samples: Soil A, Soil B and Soil C, to find out which would be best to use for growing pepper plants, Laila conducted the experiment described on page 31. Her results are given in Table 2.4 on page 35.

Table 2.4 *The percentage of air in three soil samples*

Soil sample	Volume of soil (cm³)	Volume of water added (cm³)	Volume of soil and water (cm³)	Percentage of air (%)
Soil A	47	50	85	
Soil B	49	50	91	
Soil C	51	50	82	

a Complete the table by calculating the percentage of air in EACH soil sample.

b Which soil would you advise Laila to put into the containers that she is going to use to grow her pepper plants? Provide suitable reasons to justify your choice.

9 On 26ᵗʰ February, 1937, President Franklin D. Roosevelt wrote the following in a letter to all State Governors: "The nation that destroys its soil destroys itself." Write an argument to support this very powerful statement.

Analysing data

10 A group of students analysed the composition of two soils, **X** and **Y**, and their results are given in Table 2.5.

Table 2.5 *The percentage of the different components of two soils*

Component	Percentage of component (%)	
	Soil X	Soil Y
Humus	4.2	11.8
Clay	18.6	53.0
Silt	15.7	12.1
Sand	52.1	13.5
Gravel	10.4	9.6

a i What would be another way to represent the data in Table 2.5?

 ii Use the method identified in **a i** to represent the data for Soil **X**.

b Suggest and explain which soil would be expected to have the higher air content.

c i Which soil is likely to contain the greater percentage of microorganisms?

 ii Give a reason for your answer to **c i**.

d To compare the water-holding capacity of the soils, the students then dried a sample of each in an oven at 100 °C, placed the same mass of each soil into two separate filter funnels lined with filter paper, rested the funnels on two measuring cylinders and carefully poured 50 cm³ of water into each soil sample. Figure 2.29 shows the volume of water that drained through each sample.

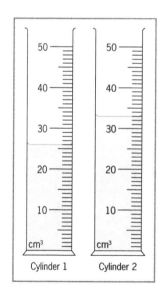

Figure 2.29 *Volume of water draining through two soil samples*

i Why did the students dry the soil samples?

ii What volume of water was retained by the soil sample in the funnel above
- Cylinder 1?
- Cylinder 2?

Show how you arrived at your answers.

iii Which measuring cylinder represents the water that drained through Soil **Y**?

iv Explain how you deduced your answer to **d iii**.

v Suggest a hypothesis for the students' investigation.

vi Identify ONE precaution that the students should take when carrying out their investigation.

3 Reproduction and growth in animals

Like plants, animals must also **produce offspring** in order for their species to survive, and they achieve this by reproducing. Some animals can reproduce **asexually**, however, most reproduce **sexually**. Animals also **grow** and **develop** which ensures that they are the correct size to survive in their environment.

Reproduction is the process by which living organisms generate new individuals of the same kind as themselves.

Growth is a permanent increase in the size of an organism.

Reproduction in animals

Learning objectives

- Outline **methods** of **asexual reproduction** in **animals**.
- Describe the **structure** and **function** of the **sexual reproductive organs** in **humans**.
- Analyse the **menstrual cycle** in **humans**.
- Explain **menopause**.
- Discuss the **stages** of **pregnancy**.
- Discuss the **methods** of **birth control**.
- Assess the **importance** of **prenatal** and **postnatal care** of **mothers** and **babies**.

Methods of asexual reproduction in animals

A few **animal** species are capable of reproducing **asexually**, in other words, they can produce offspring from a **single** parent by **mitosis** (see page 13). Several different methods are employed, including **budding**, **fragmentation** and **parthenogenesis**. Unicellular organisms such as protozoans and bacteria also reproduce asexually by a process known as **binary fission**.

Binary fission

Binary fission involves the division of a single parent cell into two identical cells by **mitosis**. Figure 3.1 shows how an amoeba (a protozoan) reproduces asexually.

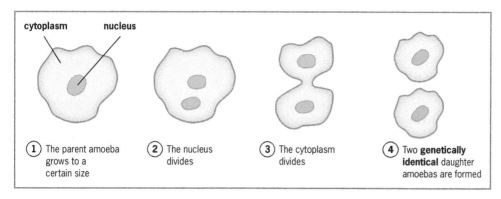

(1) The parent amoeba grows to a certain size

(2) The nucleus divides

(3) The cytoplasm divides

(4) Two **genetically identical** daughter amoebas are formed

Figure 3.1 *Binary fission in an amoeba*

Budding

Budding occurs in some simple animals; for example, coral polyps, jellyfish and hydra. In these animals, the new individuals develop from **buds** produced by cells dividing repeatedly by **mitosis** in specialised areas of the animal's body. Figure 3.2 illustrates the process of budding in hydra. Budding can also occur in some unicellular organisms; for example, yeast and bacteria, where the **bud** develops as a small protrusion on the surface of the cell. In yeast cells, the nucleus undergoes mitosis and one of the two nuclei moves into the bud as it grows. The bud then separates from the parent cell and forms a new yeast cell.

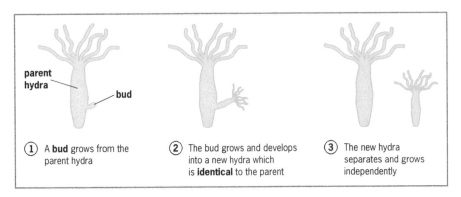

parent hydra

bud

① A **bud** grows from the parent hydra

② The bud grows and develops into a new hydra which is **identical** to the parent

③ The new hydra separates and grows independently

Figure 3.2 *Budding in hydra*

Note: Budding in animals and some unicellular organisms is a **natural** process and it must not be confused with the process of budding outlined on page 18, which is an **artificial** process used by humans to vegetatively propagate plants.

Fragmentation

Fragmentation occurs in some invertebrates; for example, certain species of flatworms and sponges. During fragmentation, the body of the parent splits into two or more pieces or **fragments**. Each fragment then grows and develops into a new individual. For example, if a flatworm, known as a planarian (see Figure 3.3), is cut into several pieces, each piece can develop into a new individual which is identical to the original planarian.

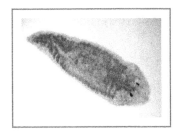

Figure 3.3 *A planarian under the microscope*

Parthenogenesis

Parthenogenesis is a form of asexual reproduction in which an **ovum** or **egg cell** is **activated** to divide by mitosis and form an embryo, without being fertilised. Activation can be caused by various factors; for example, certain environmental stresses, changes in day length, hormonal changes or a lack of mating opportunities. Parthenogenesis occurs in certain insects such as aphids, stick insects, and some ants, wasps and bees. It can also occur in certain reptiles, amphibians and fish.

Sexual reproduction in humans

Humans reproduce **sexually**, in other words, **two** parents are required to produce offspring (see page 14). Sexual reproduction involves the fusion of male and female **gametes** or **sex cells**. These gametes are produced in the male and female **reproductive systems**, which consist of both internal and external **reproductive organs**.

The female reproductive organs

The **female gametes** are called **ova** (singular: **ovum**) and they are produced in two **ovaries**, which form part of the female reproductive system. The ovaries are found at either side of the abdominal cavity and an **oviduct** or **fallopian tube** leads from each ovary to the **uterus**. The lower end of the uterus leads into the **vagina**. The vagina opens into the external part of the system, known as the **vulva**, directly behind the urethra, which leads from the bladder. The front and side views of the female reproductive system are shown in Figures 3.4 and 3.5, and the functions of the main parts are summarised in Table 3.1 on page 40.

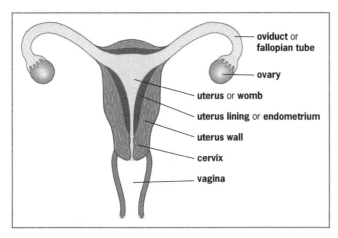

Figure 3.4 *Front view of the female reproductive system*

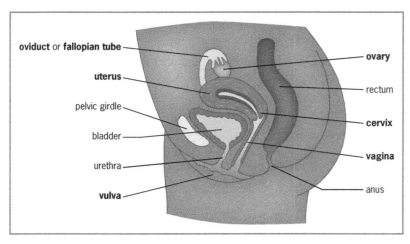

Figure 3.5 *Side view of the female reproductive system*

Table 3.1 *Structure and functions of the organs of the female reproductive system*

Part of the system	Structure	Function(s)
Ovary	Oval-shaped organ.	• Produces ova. • Secretes the female sex hormones: **oestrogen** and **progesterone**.
Oviduct or **fallopian tube**	Narrow tube with thin, muscular walls that are lined with cilia.	• Transports ova from the ovary to the uterus. • Where fertilisation occurs.
Uterus or **womb**	Pear-shaped organ.	• Where the foetus grows and develops during pregnancy.
Uterus lining or **endometrium**	Lining of the uterus wall composed of connective tissue with a rich supply of blood vessels. Its thickness changes during the menstrual cycle.	• Where the embryo is implanted and the placenta develops during pregnancy. • Supplies the developing foetus with food and oxygen, and removes carbon dioxide and other waste.
Uterus wall	Thick wall composed of three layers of muscle tissue.	• Stretches during pregnancy to accommodate the developing foetus. • Contracts during birth to push out the baby.
Cervix	Ring of muscle around the neck of the uterus.	• Allows blood and cells from the uterus lining to leave the uterus during menstruation and sperm to enter after intercourse. • Keeps the neck of the uterus closed during pregnancy.
Vagina	Thin-walled, muscular passage from the uterus to the outside of the body.	• Receives the male penis and where semen is deposited during intercourse. • Stretches to allow the baby to pass out during birth.

The male reproductive organs

The **male gametes** are called **sperm** or **spermatozoa** and they are produced in the **testes**, which form part of the male reproductive system. The testes are held outside the body in the **scrotal sac** or **scrotum**. The **epididymis** on the outside of each testis connects the testis to a **vas deferens** or **sperm duct** which leads upwards from the epididymis and joins into the urethra just after it has exited the bladder. A gland known as the **seminal vesicle** leads into each sperm duct before it joins the urethra. The urethra then passes through the **prostate gland** just below the bladder and exits the body by passing through the **penis**. Two **Cowper's glands**, one at each side, lead into the urethra just below the prostate gland. The front and side views of the male reproductive system are shown in Figures 3.6 and 3.7 on page 41, and the functions of the main parts are summarised in Table 3.2 on page 41.

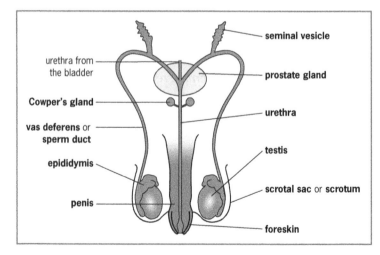

Figure 3.6 *Front view of the male reproductive system*

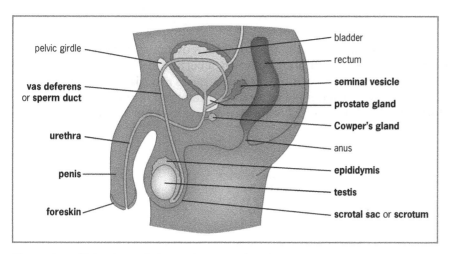

Figure 3.7 *Side view of the male reproductive system*

Table 3.2 *Structure and functions of the organs of the male reproductive system*

Part of the system	Structure	Function(s)
Testis	Oval-shaped organ composed of a mass of coiled tubules known as **seminiferous tubules.**	• Produces sperm. • Secretes the male sex hormone, **testosterone.**
Scrotal sac or **scrotum**	Loose, pouch-like sac of skin containing the testes.	• Holds the testes at a temperature slightly below 37 °C to enable sperm to develop normally and to survive.
Epididymis	Coiled tubule outside the testis, connected to the seminiferous tubules of the testis and the sperm duct.	• Where sperm mature. • Stores mature sperm.
Vas deferens or **sperm duct**	Thin-walled, muscular tube.	• Carries sperm from the epididymis to the urethra during intercourse.
Seminal vesicle	Sac-like gland.	• Secretes a sugar-rich fluid that mixes with sperm to form **semen** during ejaculation. The sugar supplies sperm with a source of energy to swim.
Prostate gland	Walnut-sized organ.	• Secretes a fluid rich in proteins and salts which is added to the semen to nourish the sperm.
Cowper's gland	Pea-sized organ.	• Secretes a viscous fluid just before ejaculation to neutralise any remnants of acidic urine in the urethra, and to cleanse and lubricate the urethra to help the semen pass through.
Urethra	Thin-walled, muscular tube.	• Carries semen out of the body during intercourse.
Penis	Organ composed of connective tissue with many blood spaces surrounding the urethra.	• Becomes erect during sexual intercourse to deposit semen containing sperm into the vagina.
Foreskin	Loose layer of retractable skin covering the head of the penis.	• Protects the head of the penis.

Ova and sperm

At birth, each female ovary contains many thousand **immature ova.** Each ovum is surrounded by a fluid-filled space that forms a **primary follicle.** Each month between **puberty** at about 11 to 13 years old, and **menopause** at about 45 to 55 years old, one immature ovum undergoes **meiosis** (see page 14) and one of the four cells produced develops into a **mature ovum**, which is released during **ovulation.** The events occurring in an ovary during the production and release of a mature ovum are summarised in Figure 3.8.

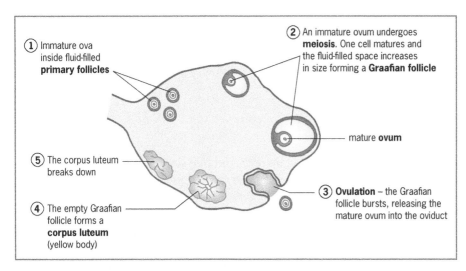

Figure 3.8 *Production of an ovum in an ovary*

Sperm cells are produced continuously from **puberty** in the **seminiferous tubules** of the **testes.** Cells in the tubule walls undergo **meiosis** and **all** the cells produced develop into sperm. These sperm mature in the **epididymis**, where they are stored until ejaculation.

The structures of a mature ovum and a mature sperm are shown in Figure 3.9.

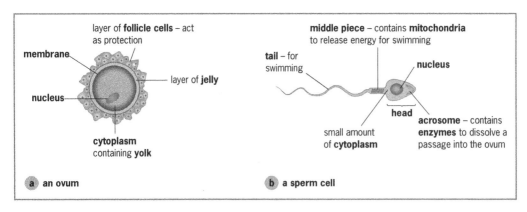

Figure 3.9 *Structure of an ovum and a sperm cell*

The menstrual cycle

The **menstrual cycle** is a cycle of about 28 days which prepares the uterus lining each month to receive the embryo if fertilisation occurs. The cycle comprises **two** main events: **ovulation** and **menstruation**.

Ovulation is the release of an ovum from an ovary.

Menstruation is the loss of the uterus lining from the body.

Menstruation starts to occur about 14 days after ovulation, if fertilisation has not occurred. The events occurring in an **ovary** and the **uterus** during one complete cycle are summarised in Table 3.3 and Figure 3.10 on page 44, where the **start** of each cycle is taken from the start of **menstruation**. However, not every person has this exact cycle; times vary between individuals and can vary from month to month in each individual.

Table 3.3 *A summary of the events occurring in an ovary and the uterus during the menstrual cycle*

Time	Events in an ovary	Events in the uterus
Day 1 to day 14	An immature ovum undergoes meiosis and one cell matures. The Graafian follicle develops around the ovum as it matures.	**Day 1 to day 5**: the uterus lining breaks down and is lost from the body (menstruation). **Day 6 to day 14**: the uterus lining thickens and its blood supply increases.
Day 14	The mature ovum is released (ovulation) and the Graafian follicle forms the corpus luteum.	
Day 14 to day 25	The corpus luteum remains.	The uterus lining continues to thicken slightly and remains thick.
Day 26 to day 28	The corpus luteum breaks down.	The uterus lining begins to break down.

Hormonal control of the menstrual cycle

The menstrual cycle is controlled by several **hormones** that synchronise the production of an ovum in an ovary with the lining of the uterus being ready to receive the embryo if the ovum is fertilised. Two of the main hormones are **oestrogen** and **progesterone**.

- **Oestrogen** is produced by the **Graafian follicle**, mainly during the **second week** of the cycle. It stimulates the lining of the uterus to thicken and its blood supply to increase after menstruation.

- **Progesterone** is produced by the **corpus luteum** during the **third week** of the cycle. It causes the uterus lining to increase slightly in thickness and remain thick. If fertilisation does not occur, the corpus luteum degenerates during the fourth week and reduces secretion of progesterone. The decrease in progesterone causes the uterus lining to begin to break down towards the end of the fourth week.

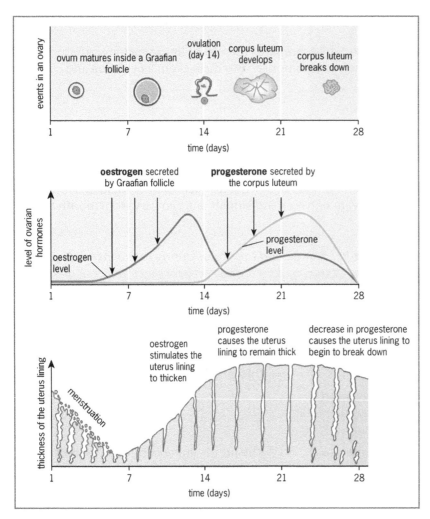

Figure 3.10 *A summary of the events occurring during the menstrual cycle*

Menopause

Menopause is the time in a female's life that marks the end of her menstrual cycles.

Menopause is considered to have occurred when a female has not had a menstrual period for 12 consecutive months. It typically happens between the ages of 45 and 55, and it marks the end of a female's fertility; the ovaries stop releasing ova and she can no longer become pregnant.

Menopause is preceded by **perimenopause**; this is the transitional stage that leads up to menopause and can last for several years. During perimenopause, the ovaries gradually reduce their secretion of **oestrogen** and **progesterone** which leads to irregular menstrual cycles and eventually menopause itself.

Perimenopause is often accompanied by a variety of symptoms including hot flushes, night sweats, anxiety, depression, mood swings, vaginal dryness and difficulty sleeping. These symptoms can also carry on for several years after menopause and can be alleviated by a variety of non-hormonal and hormonal treatments. The main treatment is **hormone replacement therapy (HRT)** which involves taking a combination of **oestrogen** and **progesterone**, or only **oestrogen**.

Fertilisation, implantation and pregnancy

Bringing sperm and ova together

When a male becomes sexually excited, blood spaces in the penis fill with blood. The penis becomes **erect** and is placed into the female vagina. **Semen**, composed of sperm and secretions from the seminal vesicles and prostate gland, is **ejaculated** into the top of the vagina by muscular contractions of the tubules of the epididymis and sperm ducts. The **sperm** swim through the cervix and uterus and into the fallopian tubes.

Fertilisation

If an **ovum** is present in one of the **fallopian tubes**, one **sperm** enters, leaving its tail outside. This is achieved by enzymes, which are contained in the acrosome at the anterior end of the sperm (see Figure 3.9, page 42), digesting a pathway into the ovum. A **fertilisation membrane** immediately develops around the ovum to prevent other sperm from entering, and the nuclei of the ovum and sperm fuse to form a **zygote**.

Implantation

The **zygote** divides repeatedly by **mitosis**, using **yolk** stored in the original ovum as a source of nourishment. This forms a ball of cells called the **embryo**, which moves down the fallopian tube and sinks into the uterus lining, a process called **implantation**. This is illustrated in Figure 3.11. Food and oxygen diffuse from the mother's blood in the uterus lining into the embryo, and carbon dioxide and other waste diffuse in the opposite direction, from the embryo into the mother's blood.

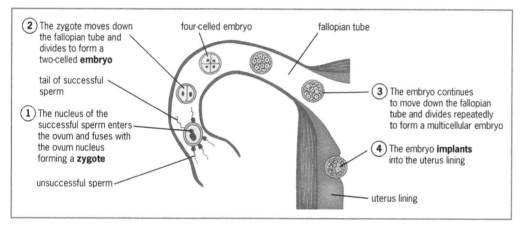

Figure 3.11 *Fertilisation and implantation*

Pregnancy and development

The cells of the **embryo** continue to divide and some of the cells develop into the **placenta**. The placenta is a disc of tissue with finger-like projections called **villi**, which project into the uterus lining and give the placenta a large surface area. Capillaries run throughout the placenta. The placenta allows exchange of materials between the mother's blood and the embryo's blood, but prevents mixing of the two bloods, and it also secretes **progesterone**. The embryo is joined to the placenta by the **umbilical cord**, which has an **umbilical artery** and **umbilical vein** running through. These connect the capillaries in the embryo with those in the placenta. The roles of the placenta, umbilical artery and umbilical vein are summarised in Figure 3.12 on page 46.

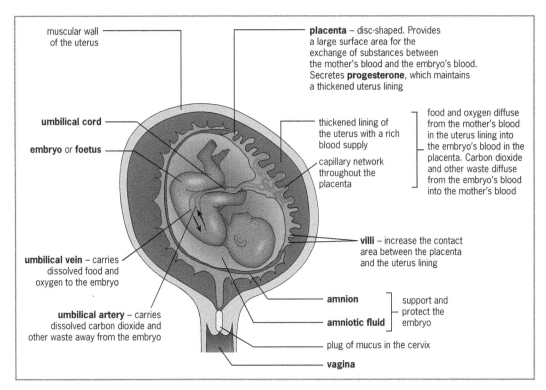

Figure 3.12 *The developing human embryo/foetus in the uterus*

The developing embryo is surrounded by a thin, tough membrane called the **amnion**, which forms a sac containing **amniotic fluid** to support the developing embryo and to protect it against mechanical damage by acting as a shock absorber. A summary of the development of the embryo/foetus is given in Table 3.4.

Table 3.4 *A summary of the development of a human embryo/foetus*

Time after fertilisation	Characteristics
7 to 10 days	A hollow ball of cells, which is implanted in the uterus lining.
4 weeks	The brain, eyes and ears are developing along with the nervous, digestive and respiratory systems. Limb buds are forming and the heart is beginning to beat.
8 weeks	The embryo has a distinctly human appearance. All the vital organs have been formed and limbs with fingers and toes are developed.
10 weeks	The embryo is now known as a **foetus**. External genitals are beginning to appear, fingernails and toenails form and the kidneys start to function.
11 to 38 weeks	The foetus continues to grow and the organs continue to develop and mature.
38 weeks	Birth occurs.

Note: The **gestation period (pregnancy)** is considered to last for 40 weeks or 280 days, since it is calculated from the first day of the last menstrual cycle and not from the time of fertilisation.

Birth

Towards the end of the pregnancy, the baby turns so it lies head down and as it continues to grow, it stretches the uterus wall to a point where **stretch receptors** are stimulated. This inhibits secretion of progesterone by the placenta and stimulates the **pituitary gland** to secrete the hormone **oxytocin** into the blood. Oxytocin then begins the **birthing process**, which is divided into **three** stages: **dilation** of the **cervix**, **birth** and **expulsion** of the **placenta**. These stages are shown in Figure 3.13.

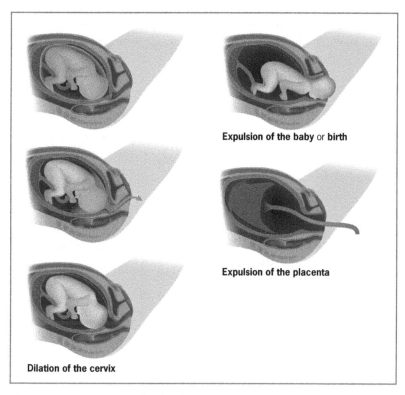

Figure 3.13 *Stages in the birthing process*

Dilation of the cervix

Oxytocin stimulates the muscles in the wall of the uterus to start **contracting**, which causes **labour** to begin. At some point during these contractions, the amnion bursts and the amniotic fluid is released; this is referred to as **water breaking** or **waters breaking**. The contractions gradually strengthen and cause the **cervix** to gradually **dilate (widen)**, and they push the baby towards the cervix. This stage comes to an end when the cervix has dilated to **10 cm**.

Expulsion of the baby or birth

Pressure of the baby's head on the **cervix** when it is fully dilated gives the mother the urge to **push**. Strong **contractions** of the uterus wall continue and the mother aims to push with each contraction by contracting her abdominal muscles. This pushes the baby, head-first, through the cervix into the vagina. **Crowning** occurs as the top of the baby's head emerges through the opening of the vagina and is visible. The rest of the baby's head then emerges through the vaginal opening, followed by the baby's body. Once outside the mother's body, the baby starts to **breathe** and the **umbilical cord** is clamped and cut.

Expulsion of the placenta

After the baby is born, the **placenta** detaches from the uterus lining and is expelled from the mother's body as the **afterbirth** by further **contractions** of the uterus wall.

Methods of birth control (contraception)

Birth control is used to **prevent unintended pregnancies**. A variety of methods are available that are designed to **prevent fertilisation** or to **prevent implantation**. These methods can be **natural, barrier, hormonal** or **surgical**. Two methods, **abstinence** and the **condom**, also protect against the spread of sexually transmitted infections (STIs) such as HIV/AIDS. When choosing a method, its reliability, availability, side effects and if both partners are comfortable using it must be considered. The different methods of birth control, with their advantages and disadvantages are summarised in Table 3.5, and examples are shown in Figure 3.14 on page 51.

Table 3.5 *Methods of birth control*

Method	How the method works	Advantages	Disadvantages
Abstinence	• Refraining from sexual intercourse.	• Completely effective.	• Relies on self-control from both partners.
Withdrawal	• Penis is withdrawn before ejaculation.	• No artificial device needs to be used or pills taken – it is **natural**, therefore is acceptable to all religious groups.	• Very unreliable since some semen is released before ejaculation. • Relies on self-control.
Rhythm method	• Intercourse is restricted to times when ova should be absent from the oviducts.	• No artificial device needs to be used or pills taken – it is **natural**, therefore is acceptable to all religious groups.	• Unreliable since the time of ovulation can vary. • Restricts the time when intercourse can occur. • Unsuitable for women with irregular menstrual cycles.
Billings method	• Refraining from sexual intercourse when the cervical mucus is slippery and elastic, and for three days afterwards. Mucus is slippery from a few days before ovulation until ovulation.	• No artificial device needs to be used or pills taken – it is **natural**, therefore is acceptable to all religious groups.	• Restricts the time when intercourse can occur. • Requires commitment, accurate observations of the cervical mucus and a proper understanding of the method. • Reliability varies.
Condom	• A latex rubber or polyurethane sheath placed over the erect penis or into the female vagina before intercourse. • Acts as a physical **barrier** to prevent sperm entering the female body.	• Very reliable if used correctly. • Easy to use. • Readily available. • Protects against sexually transmitted infections.	• May reduce sensitivity, so interferes with enjoyment. • Condoms can tear, allowing sperm to enter the vagina. • Latex may cause an allergic reaction.

Method	How the method works	Advantages	Disadvantages
Diaphragm and cervical cap	• A **diaphragm** is a dome-shaped latex or silicone cup inserted over the cervix and surrounding area before intercourse. • A **cervical cap** is a silicone cap that fits snugly over the cervix only, inserted before intercourse. • Both are used with a spermicide to kill sperm. • Both act as physical **barriers** to prevent sperm entering the uterus.	• Both are fairly reliable if used correctly. • They are not felt, therefore do not interfere with enjoyment. • Both are easy to use once the female is taught.	• Must be left in place for 6 hours after intercourse, but no longer than 24 hours in the case of the diaphragm and 48 hours in the case of the cervical cap. • Latex in latex diaphragms may cause an allergic reaction. • Both may slip out of place if not fitted properly.
Intra-uterine device (IUD or coil)	• A T-shaped plastic device, usually containing copper or **progestin** (synthetic form of **progesterone**), inserted into the uterus by a doctor. • Prevents sperm reaching the ova or prevents implantation.	• Very reliable. • Once fitted, no further action is required except an annual check-up. • Long-acting; can work for 3 to 10 years. • No need to think further about contraception. • Few, if any, side effects.	• Must be inserted by a medical practitioner. • May cause menstruation to be heavier, longer or more painful.
Contraceptive pill	• A **hormone** pill, taken daily, which contains **oestrogen** and **progestin** or **progestin** only. • Prevents ovulation. • Makes cervical mucus thicker and more difficult for sperm to swim through. • Thins the uterus lining, making it less suitable for implantation if fertilisation occurs.	• Almost totally reliable if taken daily. • Menstruation is lighter, shorter and less painful.	• Ceases to be effective if one pill is missed. • May cause side effects in some women, especially those who smoke.
Contraceptive patch	• A small, sticky patch attached to the skin and replaced weekly. • Releases **oestrogen** and **progestin** into the bloodstream. • Works in the same way as the contraceptive pill.	• Almost totally reliable if replaced every 7 days. • Menstruation is lighter, shorter and less painful.	• Ceases to be effective if not changed for 9 days or longer. • May cause side effects in some women, especially those who smoke.

Method	How the method works	Advantages	Disadvantages
Contraceptive injection	• An injection containing **progestin** given by a doctor every 3 months. • Prevents ovulation. • Thickens cervical mucus and thins the uterus lining.	• Almost totally reliable. • Once injected, no further action is required for 3 months. • Can reduce heavy, painful menstruation.	• May cause side effects in some women. • Can take up to 1 year for fertility to return to normal after injections are discontinued.
Contraceptive implant	• A small, flexible plastic rod placed under the skin of the upper arm by a doctor every 3 years. • Releases **progestin** into the bloodstream which prevents ovulation. • Thickens cervical mucus and thins the uterus lining.	• Almost totally reliable. • Once fitted, no further action is required for 3 years. • Can be removed at any time and fertility returns immediately. • Can reduce heavy, painful menstruation.	• May cause side effects in some women.
Surgical sterilisation (**vasectomy** in males, **tubal ligation** in females)	• The sperm ducts or oviducts are **surgically** cut and tied off. • Prevents sperm leaving the male body or ova passing down the oviducts in females.	• Totally reliable. • No artificial device needs to be used or pills taken. • No need to think further about contraception.	• Usually irreversible.
Hysterectomy	• The uterus, and usually the cervix, are **surgically** removed. • Usually only recommended when the individual is experiencing a serious medical condition, such as fibroids or cancer.	• Totally reliable. • No artificial device needs to be used or pills taken. • No need to think further about contraception. • No more menstrual periods.	• A major surgical procedure that has risks associated with it. • Irreversible.

Note: One **disadvantage** of all methods, except abstinence and condoms, is that they do not protect against sexually transmitted infections.

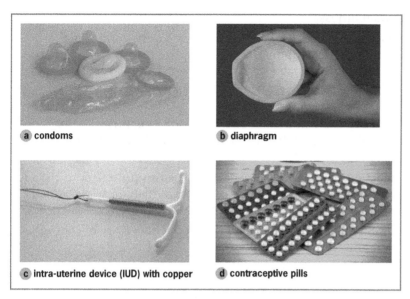

a condoms   b diaphragm

c intra-uterine device (IUD) with copper   d contraceptive pills

Figure 3.14 *Methods of birth control*

The importance of prenatal (antenatal) care

Prenatal care, or care before birth, is essential to ensure the foetus **grows** and **develops normally** and **healthily**, and that the mother **remains healthy** throughout her pregnancy. During pregnancy, it is important that the mother follows the procedures outlined below.

- She should attend regular **prenatal check-ups** with her doctor or clinic to monitor her health and the development of her baby.

- She should have two **ultrasound scans** if possible, one at about 6 to 8 weeks and the other at about 18 to 20 weeks. These scans use high-frequency sound waves to create an **image** of the baby to monitor its growth and development to ensure it is progressing normally, and to detect any abnormalities or birth defects, as shown in Figure 3.15.

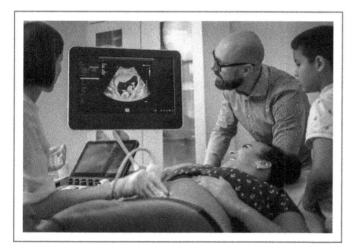

Figure 3.15 *A pregnant woman having an ultrasound scan*

- She should eat a **balanced diet** which contains adequate quantities of proteins, carbohydrates, vitamins and minerals, especially folic acid or vitamin B_9, vitamin D, calcium and iron, in the correct proportions to ensure the foetus obtains all the nutrients it needs to grow and develop. Her diet must also contain sufficient fibre to help prevent constipation, and she should stay well-hydrated and avoid certain foods such as raw fish, cured meats and too much caffeine.

- She should **exercise** regularly to maintain fitness.
- She should not use unprescribed **drugs** of any kind, especially alcohol, cigarettes and illegal drugs, which can interfere with normal foetal development and damage foetal organs. They can increase the chances of a miscarriage and result in babies being born with low birth weights and birth defects, and children with deficiencies in physical growth, and impaired intellectual and behavioural development.
- She should protect herself against harmful **X-rays** due to the risks that radiation poses to her developing foetus, including the risk of slowed growth, birth defects and children with impaired learning abilities.
- She should protect herself against **infectious diseases** because certain diseases pose serious risks to both the mother and her foetus; examples of the latter include rubella (German measles), which can cause birth defects and Zika fever, which can cause microcephaly (an abnormally small head).
- She should be tested for **sexually transmitted infections (STIs)** and treated if necessary because they can pose significant health risks to her baby.

Postnatal care

Postnatal care, or care after birth, is essential to ensure the baby **grows** and **develops healthily**, and that the mother remains both physically and emotionally **healthy**.

- The **newborn baby** should be **breastfed**, if possible, for a minimum of 6 months for several important reasons.
  - Breast milk contains all the **nutrients** the baby needs in the correct proportions.
  - Breast milk contains **antibodies** which protect the baby against bacterial and viral diseases.
  - Breast milk is **sterile**, so it reduces the risk of infection, it is at the correct **temperature**, and it is **available** whenever needed.
  - Breastfeeding lowers the baby's risk of developing **asthma**, **allergies** and other **non-communicable diseases** as it grows older.
  - Breastfeeding creates a strong **emotional bond** between mother and baby.
- The **newborn baby** must be kept **warm** and **clean**, have plenty of **interaction** with both parents and its surroundings, and be taken for regular **check-ups** with the doctor. As the baby grows, it must be **weaned** onto semi-solid and solid food, **cared for** physically and emotionally, and given continual **teaching**.
- The **baby** must be **vaccinated** to **immunise** it against a variety of different infectious diseases, following a vaccination or immunisation programme. This helps protect the health of the child as he or she grows up and also the health of the wider community.

Recalling facts

1. Identify THREE different methods by which animals can reproduce asexually.

2. Describe the structure and function(s) of EACH of the following parts of the female reproductive system:

   a uterus wall   b cervix   c vagina.

3. Construct a table to give the functions(s) of EACH of the following parts of the male reproductive system: the seminal vesicles, the urethra, the epididymis, the penis and the testes.

4 Describe the events that take place in EACH of the following during one menstrual cycle:

    a an ovary   **b** the uterus.

5 Explain the roles of oestrogen and progesterone in the menstrual cycle.

6 Describe the events that must occur for an ovum to be fertilised.

7 Explain the role of EACH of the following in the development of Joyann's baby:

    a the placenta   **b** the umbilical cord   **c** the amniotic fluid.

8 Outline the events that take place as Joyann gives birth to her baby.

9 Using the FOUR headings: natural, barrier, hormonal and surgical, classify EACH of the following methods of birth control: condom, contraceptive pill, vasectomy, rhythm method, abstinence, spermicides, tubal ligation, withdrawal, diaphragm and contraceptive implant.

10 Explain how EACH of the following methods of birth control works to prevent pregnancy, state how effective it is and give ONE advantage and ONE disadvantage of its use other than its effectiveness:

    a the rhythm method   **b** a diaphragm   **c** a vasectomy.

11 As well as serving as a contraceptive device, what is the other major advantage of using a condom during sexual intercourse?

12 Outline FIVE steps that a pregnant woman should take to ensure that her developing baby remains healthy throughout her pregnancy.

13 After the birth of her baby, Ryan, what steps should June take to ensure that he grows and develops in a healthy way?

Applying facts

14 For EACH of the following structures found in females, identify the equivalent structures in males and say why the structure is equivalent:

    a ova   **b** the ovaries   **c** the oviducts.

15 Certain diseases can cause sterility in both males and females. Using your knowledge of the structure of the male and female reproductive systems, suggest TWO ways this could happen in males and TWO ways it could happen in females.

16 Suggest a reason for EACH of the following.

    a Semen contains a very large number of sperm.

    b Sperm cells are extremely small.

    c An ovum is larger than a sperm cell.

17 A certain study found that men who wore tight-fitting underwear every day were 25% less fertile than those who wore boxer shorts daily. Explain the possible reason for these findings.

18 Felicia, who just celebrated her 47th birthday, begins to notice that her menstrual periods are becoming irregular and she is starting to have hot flushes. Write a suitable explanation that you could give to Felicia to help her to understand her symptoms, how they can be alleviated and their eventual outcome.

19 By means of a flow chart, show the journey that a sperm cell would take from the testis until it has fertilised an ovum in an oviduct.

20 It is possible for the ovum to become implanted in a fallopian tube, causing what is known as an ectopic pregnancy. Suggest and explain what the possible consequences might be if the pregnancy continues.

21 After reading an article suggesting that an enzyme in unripe paw paw can inactivate progesterone if eaten in large quantities, Naomi immediately advised her pregnant friend, Tianna, not to eat any green paw paw during her pregnancy. Explain the reason for Naomi's advice.

22 Shaunette and Kenley are a happily married, career-driven couple and they wish to pursue their careers for a few years before they have a family.

   a Which method of birth control do you think would be MOST suitable for them to use? Support your answer with TWO reasons.

   b State, with a reason in EACH case, which TWO methods of birth control you think would be the least suitable.

23 Khadija is advised by her mother to breast feed her baby for at least 6 months after she is born. However, her friend, Onica, says she should bottle-feed her because it is much easier. Whose advice should Khadija follow? Give FOUR reasons to support your answer.

24 Explain TWO important ways that parents of newborn babies can help to reduce infant mortality rates.

Growth in animals

Learning objectives

- Compare **growth patterns** of **males** and **females**.
- Discuss the **need** for **human population control**.

Growth patterns

When the height or weight of a typical boy or girl is plotted against age, a **height** or **weight curve** is obtained, which shows the boy's or girl's **pattern** of **growth**. Both boys and girls have a similar growth pattern, however there are some differences.

- **Boys** and **girls** both grow **rapidly** during **infancy** and **very early childhood**, from birth to about 3 years old. Their growth rates then slow slightly during **childhood**, with **boys** in general being slightly **taller** and **heavier** than girls at all ages.

- As a child approaches **puberty**, which is the time when the child's physical and sexual characteristics begin to mature, his or her **growth rate** begins to **increase**. The average age for **girls** to start puberty is **earlier** than boys, with girls starting anywhere between 8 and 13 year old and boys anywhere between 9 and 14 years old. Since **girls** typically enter puberty **earlier** than boys, their growth rate begins to increase at a **younger age**, such that they become **taller** and **heavier** than boys of their age during this period.

- Towards the **end** of **puberty**, the growth rate of both girls and boys **decreases**. This happens at a younger age in girls than boys and, once again, **boys** become **taller** and **heavier** than girls of their age when this happens.
- **Girls** typically **stop growing** earlier than boys; most girls reach their maximum size and stop growing by about 14 to 16 years old, while boys usually continue to grow for another 2 years, reaching their maximum size at about 16 to 18 years old. At this age, boys are, in general, significantly taller and heavier than girls.

Figure 3.16 shows a **height curve** and Figure 3.17 shows a **weight curve** for girls and boys up to the age of 18.

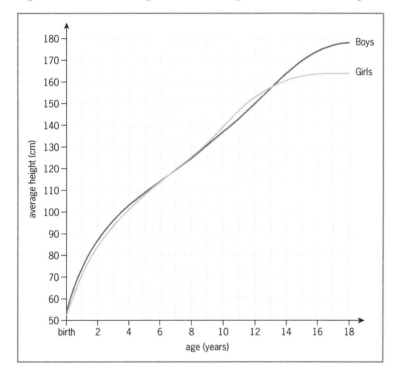

Figure 3.16 *Average height against age of boys and girls up to age 18*

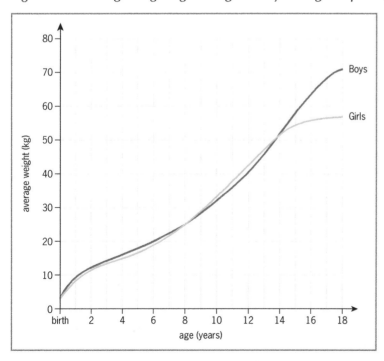

Figure 3.17 *Average weight against age of boys and girls up to age 18*

Human population growth and control

Populations grow when the **birth rate** is **higher** than the **death rate**. The **human population** is currently growing **rapidly** or **exponentially**, as shown in Figure 3.18. Estimates show that the world population was approximately 5 million in the year 8000 BC. It then took up until 1804 AD, a total of 9804 years, to reach 1 billion and 218 years later in 2022, it reached 8 billion.

It is currently estimated that the human population will continue to increase, but at a **slower rate** compared to the recent past, reaching 9 billion by 2037 and 10 billion by 2058.

Problems arising from human population growth

Human population growth, leading to the possibility of countries becoming **overpopulated**, can cause a variety of interconnected issues that impact the environment, society and economy of countries.

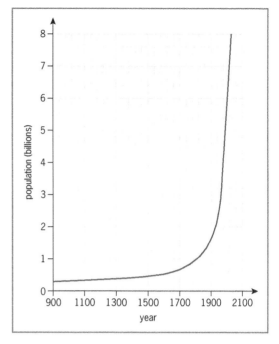

Figure 3.18 *The growth of the human population since 900 AD*

- It can cause the **depletion** of both **natural** and **material** resources. **Natural resources** are substances that occur **naturally** in the environment. They can be classified as either non-renewable or renewable. **Non-renewable resources** include fossil fuels such as coal, crude oil and natural gas, and mineral resources such as iron ore, bauxite (aluminium ore), zinc ore, copper, tin and gold. **Renewable resources** include land, wildlife, forests, soil and water. **Material resources** are produced from natural resources; for example, glass, plastics, textiles, processed foods, fertilisers and construction materials such as cement, concrete blocks, steel and lumber.

  As the human population increases, the **demand** for these resources **increases. Non-renewable** resources cannot be replaced and some are **running out** rapidly. Based on known reserves and annual production levels in 2019, it has been estimated that oil will last until 2052, natural gas until 2060 and coal until 2090. Many **renewable resources** are also being **depleted** at a faster rate than they can be replenished. This depletion of natural resources will lead to worldwide **shortages** of both **natural resources**; for example, shortages of fuel, food, land and water, and the **material resources** produced from them; for example, shortages of construction materials.

- It can lead to **food insecurity** as a rapidly growing human population has the potential to outpace agricultural production leading to food shortages, increased food prices, hunger and starvation, especially in developing countries with limited resources.

- It can lead to a variety of other issues including increased **pollution** and the build-up of **waste**, degradation of the **environment**, **overcrowding**, increased **unemployment** and **poverty**, and an increase in the **spread of disease**, all leading to decreased **living standards**.

Controlling and **reducing** human population growth should help to **reduce** the depletion of natural resources, pollution, the degradation of the environment, overcrowding, unemployment, poverty and the spread of disease, and **increase** worldwide food security, standards of living and the overall quality of people's lives.

Effects of teenage pregnancy on human population growth

Teenage pregnancy contributes significantly to **human population growth**, especially in developing countries. It is estimated that about 16 million girls between the ages of 10 and 19 give birth every year. This affects population growth in a variety of ways.

- Girls who become **pregnant** during their **teenage years** are starting to have children very early in their reproductive life. This means that they have many **more years** to continue to give birth than women who become pregnant for the first time later in life and, as a result, they can have **more children** during their reproductive lifespan, which increases birth rates within populations.

- The **cycle** of girls born to teenage mothers becoming pregnant themselves during their teenage years can continue through generations if proper interventions are not put in place to break the cycle, and this contributes to higher birth rates within populations.

- High rates of teenage pregnancy in populations affect the **age distribution** within these populations and create the 'youth bulge' phenomenon in which populations have a higher proportion of **young individuals** compared to older individuals. This can then affect education systems, labour markets, healthcare services and social welfare programmes, as they all need to accommodate a younger population.

Effects of birth control on human population growth

Using **birth control** can play a significant role in **reducing** human population growth.

- Most birth control methods are highly effective in preventing **unintended pregnancies**, if used correctly. This allows individuals to control their own **fertility**, which in turn helps to reduce birth rates in populations.

- Birth control allows parents to control **when** they have children, and this enables them to **delay** having children until later in life after they have pursued their careers and become more emotionally, financially and socially ready to become parents, and this can lower a population's birth rate.

- Using birth control allows parents to control the **number** of children they have, which enables them to **restrict the size** of their family, thus reducing birth rates within populations.

Recalling facts

 Describe the growth pattern of the human population from 8000 BC until today.

 Discuss THREE effects of EACH of the following on the growth of the human population:

   a birth control   b teenage pregnancy.

Applying facts

 Describe the similarities and differences in the patterns of growth of boys and girls from birth until 18 years of age.

 There is a continuing debate on the need to control human population growth. Explain the reasons why many people take the view that this growth should be controlled.

4 Transport systems

Living organisms need to constantly exchange substances with their environment. They need to take in useful substances and get rid of waste. **Transport systems** provide a means by which these substances are moved between the surfaces where they are exchanged and body cells.

Transport systems in multicellular organisms

Learning objectives

- Justify the **need** for **transport systems** in **living organisms**.
- Identify the **materials** that need to be **transported** in **animals** and **plants**.

The need for a transport system in multicellular organisms

The absorption and transport of substances in living organisms are affected by **two** factors.

- The **limitations of diffusion**. Diffusion is a relatively slow process, therefore it is only effective over short distances.
- The **surface area to volume ratio** of an organism. This determines the effectiveness of diffusion occurring through the surface of the organism.

As organisms increase in size, their **surface area** increases at a slower rate than their **volume**. In other words, the **ratio** of the surface area to the volume of their body **decreases**. This is seen when comparing the surface area to volume ratio of three cubes of different sizes as shown in Table 4.1. The **smallest** cube, **A**, has the **biggest** surface area to volume ratio and the **biggest** cube, **C**, has the **smallest** ratio.

Table 4.1 *The concept of surface area to volume ratio*

	Cube A	Cube B	Cube C
	0.1 cm 0.1 cm 0.1 cm	1.0 cm 1.0 cm 1.0 cm	10.0 cm 10.0 cm 10.0 cm
Surface area	$6 \times (0.1 \times 0.1)$ cm^2 = **0.06 cm^2**	$6 \times (1.0 \times 1.0)$ cm^2 = **6.0 cm^2**	$6 \times (10.0 \times 10.0)$ cm^2 = **600.0 cm^2**
Volume	$0.1 \times 0.1 \times 0.1$ cm^3 = **0.001 cm^3**	$1.0 \times 1.0 \times 1.0$ cm^3 = **1.0 cm^3**	$10.0 \times 10.0 \times 10.0$ cm^3 = **1000.0 cm^3**
Surface area : volume ratio	0.06 : 0.001 = **60 : 1**	6.0 : 1.0 = **6 : 1**	600.0 : 1000.0 = **0.6 : 1**

Diffusion would be **adequate** for substances to be absorbed through the surface of **Cube A** and reach the centre of the cube because of its **large** surface area to volume ratio and small size. **Diffusion** would be **inadequate** for the same substances to be absorbed through the surface of **Cube C** and reach the centre of the cube because of its **small** surface area to volume ratio and large size. This concept can be applied to living organisms.

Unicellular organisms; for example, an amoeba, are very small and have a **large** surface area to volume ratio. Diffusion through their body surface is adequate to take in their requirements, such as oxygen, and remove their waste, such as carbon dioxide, as shown in Figure 4.1. In addition, no part of their body is far from its surface and substances can move these short distances by **diffusion**. They do not need a transport system to carry substances around their bodies.

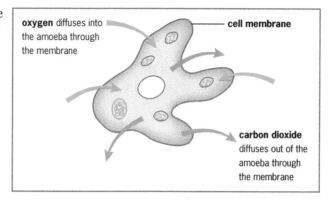

Figure 4.1 *Diffusion occurring across the surface of an amoeba*

Large, **multicellular organisms** have a **small** surface area to volume ratio. Because of this, diffusion through their limited body surface is not adequate to supply all their body cells with their requirements and remove their waste. In addition, most of their body cells are too far from the body surface for substances to move through them quickly and efficiently enough by diffusion. These organisms have, therefore, developed **transport systems** to carry **useful substances** from specialised organs which absorb them, such as the lungs and small intestine, to body cells, and to carry **waste substances** from body cells to specialised organs which excrete them, such as the lungs and kidneys.

Materials transported in animals and plants

Nutrients, **gases**, **excretory products** and **metabolic products** are transported around the bodies of **animals**. These include the following.

- **Products of digestion**, mainly **glucose**, **amino acids**, **vitamins** and **minerals**, are carried from the intestines, where they are absorbed, to the body cells.
- **Oxygen** is carried from the lungs, where it is absorbed, to the body cells which use it in respiration.
- **Carbon dioxide** is carried from the body cells, where it is produced in respiration, to the lungs which excrete it.
- **Nitrogenous waste**, mainly **urea**, is carried from the liver, where it is produced, to the kidneys which excrete it.
- **Hormones** are carried from the glands that produce them, to their target organs.
- **Heat energy** is carried mainly from the liver and muscles, where it is produced predominantly by respiration, to the rest of the body.
- Other substances that are transported include **antibodies**, **blood** or **plasma proteins** and **water**.

The following substances are transported around **plants**.

- **Water** and **mineral salts** are carried from the roots, where they are absorbed, to the leaves.
- **Sucrose** and **amino acids** are carried from the leaves, where they are made, to all other plant organs.

Recalling facts

 Identify the TWO factors that affect the absorption and transport of substances in living organisms.

 Explain why a mongoose has a well developed transport system in its body.

 Construct a table to show the different materials that are transported around the human body, where each substance enters the transport system and its destination, if applicable.

Applying facts

4 The flatworm *Planaria* is a multicellular organism that is about 10 mm long, 4 mm in width and less than 1 mm thick. It is one of the largest organisms that lack transport systems. Explain how it manages without one.

Analysing data

5 To investigate the effect of surface area to volume ratio on the rate of diffusion, some students were given blocks of agar, a permeable, jelly-like material. The blocks were different sizes and had been stained pink by using an alkali mixed with an indicator dye. The dye is pink in alkaline conditions and colourless in acidic conditions. The students submerged the blocks in hydrochloric acid, as shown in Figure 4.2, and recorded how long it took for the pink colour to disappear right through to the centre of each block. The times are given in Table 4.2.

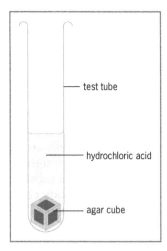

Figure 4.2 *Apparatus used to investigate the effect of surface area to volume ratio on the rate of diffusion*

Table 4.2 *The time taken for the pink colour to disappear in four cubes of different sizes*

Cube	Length of side (mm)	Surface area (mm²)	Volume (mm³)	Surface area to volume ratio	Time taken for pink colour to disappear (s)
W	1	6	1	6 : 1	10
X	2	24			25
Y	3		27		52
Z	6			1 : 1	240

a Complete the table by filling in the blanks.

b What effect did increasing the size of the cubes have on:

  i the surface area to volume ratio of the cubes

  ii the time taken for the pink colour to disappear

  iii the rate of disappearance of the pink colour?

c What conclusion can you draw from the results of the experiment?

d If each block represented a living organism, which organism would be the MOST likely to need a transport system? Explain how you arrived at your answer.

The circulatory system in humans

Learning objectives

- Relate the **structures** in **transport systems** to their **functions**.
- Describe the **composition** of **blood**.
- Relate the **structures** of **red** and **white blood cells** and **platelets** to their **functions**.
- Name the **major blood vessels** connected to the **heart**.
- Relate the **internal structures** of the **heart** to their **functions**.
- Explain the **events** occurring in one **heartbeat**.
- Distinguish among the **different blood groups**.

An introduction to the circulatory system

The **circulatory system**, also known as the **cardiovascular system**, consists of **three** basic components:

- **Blood**, which serves as the **medium** to **transport** substances around the body.
- **Blood vessels**, which are **tubes** through which the blood flows to and from all parts of the body.
- The **heart**, which **pumps** the blood through the blood vessels.

The composition of blood

An average adult has about 4.5 to 5 litres of blood circulating around his or her body. **Blood** is a **tissue** composed of **three** types of cells: **red blood cells**, **white blood cells** and **platelets**, which are cell fragments. These cells are suspended in a fluid called **plasma**. The cells make up about 45% by volume of the blood and the plasma makes up about 55%.

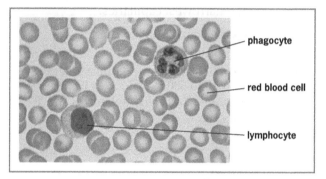

Figure 4.3 *Red and white blood cells (a phagocyte and a lymphocyte) under the microscope*

Plasma

Plasma is a yellowish fluid composed of about 90% **water** and 10% **dissolved substances**. The dissolved substances include the following.

- **Products of digestion**, mainly glucose, amino acids, vitamins and minerals.
- **Waste products**, mainly dissolved carbon dioxide and urea.
- **Hormones** such as insulin and thyroxine.
- **Blood** or **plasma proteins** such as fibrinogen, prothrombin, albumin and antibodies.

The main function of plasma is to **transport** dissolved substances around the body.

Blood cells

On average, an adult human has approximately 4.5 to 6.5 million cells per cubic millimetre of blood. The structure and functions of these cells are summarised in Table 4.3 on page 62.

Table 4.3 *Structure and functions of blood cells*

Cell type and structure	Formation of cells	Functions
Red blood cells (erythrocytes) cell membrane cytoplasm rich in **haemoglobin**, an iron-containing protein • **Biconcave discs** with a thin centre and relatively large surface area to volume ratio so gases can diffuse in and out easily. • Have **no nucleus**, therefore they cannot divide and can only live for about 3 to 4 months. • Contain the red pigment **haemoglobin**, a protein containing iron. • Slightly **elastic**, which allows them to squeeze through the narrowest capillaries.	• Formed in the red bone marrow found in flat bones, e.g. the pelvis, scapula, ribs, sternum, cranium and vertebrae, and in the ends of long bones, e.g. the humerus and femur. • Broken down mainly in the liver and spleen.	• Transport **oxygen** as **oxyhaemoglobin** from the lungs to the body cells. • Transport small amounts of **carbon dioxide** from the body cells to the lungs.
White blood cells (leucocytes) These are slightly larger than red blood cells and less numerous. Blood contains approximately 1 white blood cell to 600 red blood cells. There are two main types: 25% are **lymphocytes** and 75% are **phagocytes**.		
Lymphocytes cell membrane large, round **nucleus** non-granular **cytoplasm** • Have a **rounded** shape. • Have a large, **round nucleus** which controls the production of antibodies. • Have only a small amount of cytoplasm.	• Develop from cells in the red bone marrow and mature in other organs, e.g. lymph nodes, spleen and thymus gland.	• Produce **antibodies** to destroy disease-causing bacteria and viruses, also known as pathogens. • Produce **antitoxins** to neutralise toxins produced by pathogens.
Phagocytes cell membrane lobed **nucleus** granular **cytoplasm** • Have a **variable** shape. • Move by **pseudopodia** or **false feet**. They can move out of capillaries by passing between the cells in their walls and engulf pathogens using their pseudopodia by a process known as **phagocytosis**. • Have a **lobed nucleus**.	• Formed in the red bone marrow.	• Engulf and destroy pathogens. • Engulf pathogens destroyed by antibodies.

Cell type and structure	Formation of cells	Functions
Platelets (thrombocytes) — cell membrane — cytoplasm • Cell **fragments**. • Have **no nucleus** and only live for about 10 days.	• Formed from cells in the red bone marrow.	• Help the blood to **clot** at a cut or wound.

Blood doping

Blood doping is an unethical and illegal method used by athletes to **artificially** boost their blood's ability to carry oxygen to their muscle cells, usually by increasing the number of **red blood cells** in their blood. It is carried out to improve an athlete's endurance and stamina, thereby improving his or her **athletic performance**. It can be done by **transfusing blood** into the athlete before a competition or by injecting the hormone **erythropoietin (EPO)** into the athlete to stimulate his or her body to produce higher than normal numbers of red blood cells. **Synthetic oxygen-carrying chemicals** can also be injected into the athlete's blood.

Blood vessels

There are **three** main types of blood vessels in the circulatory system: **arteries**, **capillaries** and **veins**.

Arteries carry blood **away** from the heart. On entering an organ, an artery branches into smaller arteries called **arterioles**, which then branch into a network of **capillaries** that run throughout the organ. Capillaries then join into small veins called **venules**, which join to form a **vein** that leads back from the organ **towards** the heart. The **exchange** of substances between the blood and body cells occurs in the **capillaries**. The relationship between different blood vessels and the heart is illustrated in Figure 4.4.

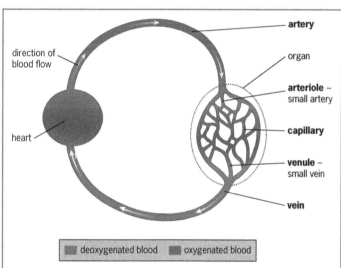

Figure 4.4 *The relationship between the different blood vessels*

Arteries carry blood which is under **high pressure**, therefore they have thick muscular walls to withstand the pressure. **Veins** carry blood which is under **low pressure**, therefore they have **thinner** muscular walls and **valves** to prevent the blood from flowing backwards. **Capillaries** have walls which are **one cell thick** so that nutrients and oxygen can easily pass from the blood into body cells, and carbon dioxide and other waste can pass back into the blood.

The **major arteries** in the human body are the **aorta** and the **pulmonary artery**, which carry blood directly out of the heart. The **major veins** are the **anterior vena cava**, **posterior vena cava** and the **pulmonary veins**, which carry blood directly into the heart, as shown in Figure 4.5 on page 64.

The heart

The **heart** acts as a **pump** to maintain a constant circulation of blood around the body. The walls of the heart are composed of **cardiac muscle**, which contracts without nerve impulses and does not get tired.

The heart is divided into **four** chambers. The two on the right contain **deoxygenated blood** and are completely separated from the two on the left, which contain **oxygenated blood**, by a dividing wall known as the **septum**.

- The top two chambers are called **atria**. They have thin walls and they collect blood entering the heart via **veins** known as the **anterior vena cava**, **posterior vena cava** and the **pulmonary veins**. Their walls are **thin** because they only have to pump blood a short distance into the ventricles below.
- The bottom two chambers are called **ventricles**. They have thick walls and they pump blood out of the heart via **arteries** known as the **pulmonary artery** and **aorta**. Their walls are **thick** because they have to pump blood longer distances to the lungs and around the rest of the body, therefore they have to pump with more force than the atria.

  The **left ventricle** has a **thicker** muscular wall than the right ventricle because it has to pump blood **longer distances**; the left ventricle pumps blood to all the body cells, so it has to pump with more force. The right ventricle only pumps blood to the lungs, which are next to the heart.

Valves are present between each atrium and ventricle, and in the pulmonary artery and aorta as they leave the ventricles. These valves ensure that blood flows through the heart in **one direction** by opening to allow the blood to flow through and closing to prevent it from flowing backwards. The **coronary arteries** branch from the aorta as it leaves the heart and supply the muscle of the heart with oxygen. The internal structure of the human heart and the functions of the different parts are shown in Figure 4.5.

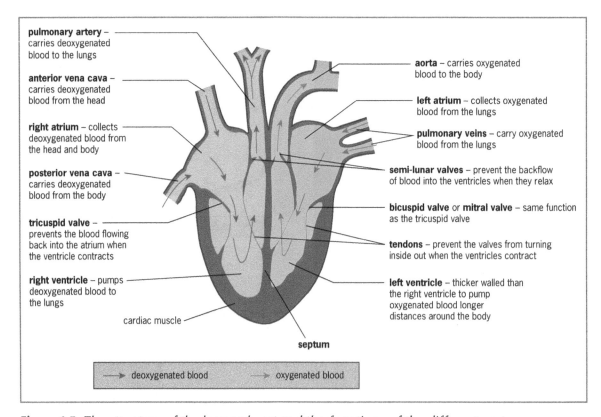

Figure 4.5 *The structure of the human heart and the functions of the different parts*

Note: In diagrams of the heart, the right side of the heart is shown on the left side of the diagram, and the left side of the heart is shown on the right side of the diagram. This is because the diagram shows the heart from **front view**, or as it would appear in a person's body that is facing the observer.

Heartbeat

As the **heart beats**, the atria and ventricles at both sides contract and relax together. The **contraction** of a chamber is called **systole** and its **relaxation** is called **diastole**. One **cardiac cycle** or **heartbeat** involves the events outlined as follows and these are illustrated in Figure 4.6.

- **Diastole** – the **atria** and **ventricles relax** together, the semi-lunar valves close, the atria fill up with blood from the anterior vena cava, posterior vena cava and pulmonary veins, and the blood flows into the ventricles. This takes 0.4 seconds.
- **Atrial systole** – the **atria contract** together forcing any remaining blood through the tricuspid and bicuspid valves into the ventricles. This takes 0.1 second.
- **Ventricular systole** – the **ventricles contract** together, the tricuspid and bicuspid valves close and blood is forced through the semi-lunar valves into the pulmonary artery and aorta. This takes 0.3 seconds.

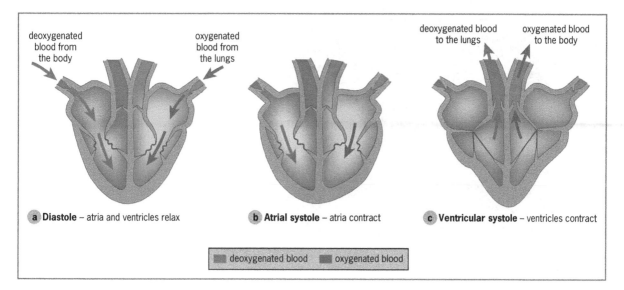

Figure 4.6 *One heartbeat*

A group of **specialised cells** in the wall of the **right atrium**, called the **pacemaker**, controls the rhythm of a normal heartbeat. The cells spontaneously produce electrical impulses which travel through the heart muscle, causing it to contract about 75 times per minute. This rate can be **modified** by nerve impulses or the hormone adrenaline; for example, the rate increases during exercise or when nervous.

Blood groups

Blood can be classified into different **blood groups** or **types** based on chemicals known as **antigens** which are present on the surface of red blood cells. A person's blood type is **inherited** from his or her parents and there are **two** grouping systems: the **ABO blood group system** and the **rhesus blood group system**.

The ABO blood group system

The **ABO system** divides blood into **four** groups: group A, group B, group AB and group O. These are determined by the presence or absence of two **antigens**, known as **A** and **B**, on the surface of the red blood cells and also two **antibodies**, known as **anti-A** and **anti-B**, in the plasma. These are summarised in Table 4.4 on page 66.

Table 4.4 *Antigens and antibodies of the ABO blood grouping system*

Blood group	Antigen on the surface of red blood cells	Antibody in the plasma
Group A	A	Anti-B
Group B	B	Anti-A
Group AB	Both A and B	No antibodies
Group O	No antigens	Both anti-A and anti-B

The antibodies in the plasma must be different from the antigens on the red blood cells. If they are the same, the antibodies bind to the antigens causing **agglutination** or **clumping** of the red blood cells, as seen in Figure 4.7.

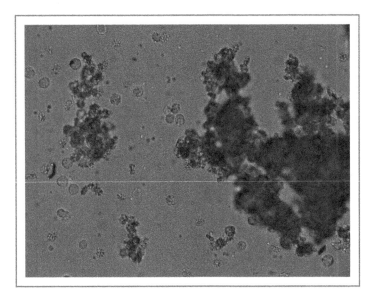

Figure 4.7 *Agglutination of red blood cells*

The Rhesus (Rh) blood group system and risks in pregnancy

The **Rhesus** or **Rh system** divides blood into **two** groups: Rh-positive and Rh-negative. These are determined by the presence or absence of an **antigen**, known as the **Rh antigen** or **Rh factor** on the surface of the red blood cells. If the antigen is present, the person has **Rh-positive** blood. If the antigen is absent, the person has **Rh-negative** blood.

The **Rh antigen** poses a risk to a woman with **Rh-negative** blood who wishes to have children. If she carries a baby with **Rh-positive** blood, a small amount of the baby's blood may enter her bloodstream, mainly during the last three months of her pregnancy and, more especially, during labour. This causes her immune system to react and produce **anti-Rh antibodies**. During any **subsequent pregnancies** with Rh-positive babies, these antibodies can pass across the placenta and attack the baby's red blood cells causing **Rhesus disease**, characterised by anaemia, jaundice, an enlarged liver and spleen, fluid retention and swelling. To prevent this, the mother is usually given an **injection** of a substance called **anti-D** at about 28 weeks into her pregnancy and then again immediately after delivery if her baby is Rh-positive to stop her from making any anti-Rh antibodies.

Precautions for blood transfusions

During a **blood transfusion**, blood from a healthy person is given to a person who has lost blood. Certain **precautions** have to be followed when handling and transfusing blood.

- Persons handling blood for transfusion must **avoid direct contact** with the blood; for example, by wearing medical gloves.

- Blood should **not** be taken from a person who is pregnant or has anaemia.
- Donated blood must be **screened** for pathogens such as HIV, hepatitis B and C.
- Blood from the donor must be **cross-matched** with the recipient's blood to ensure that their blood groups are **compatible** (see Figure 4.8). This prevents **agglutination** of red blood cells in the **donated** blood. If agglutination occurs, blood vessels may become blocked and the agglutinated cells **disintegrate**, which can be fatal. To ensure compatibility, the recipient's blood must not contain antibodies against the antigens present in the donor's blood.

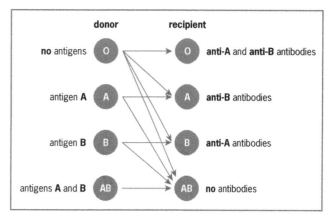

Figure 4.8 *ABO blood group system donors and recipients*

Type **O Rh-negative blood** or **O–** is known as the **universal donor** type because it has no A, B or Rh antigens, so it can be given to anybody. Type **AB Rh-positive blood** or **AB+** is known as the **universal recipient** type because it has no A, B or Rh antibodies, so a person with it can receive blood of any type.

Recalling facts

1. a What is plasma?
    b Identify FOUR components of plasma other than water.

2. a Construct a table to give THREE differences between the structure of a red blood cell and a phagocyte.
    b Outline THREE ways that the structure of a red blood cell helps it to function.

3. State the functions of red blood cells, phagocytes and lymphocytes.

4. Describe the relationship between arteries, capillaries and veins.

5. Name the type of muscle that makes up the walls of the heart and explain what is special about it.

6. Construct a table that names the FOUR chambers of the heart, gives the function of EACH chamber and names the blood vessel(s) connected to EACH.

7. Name THREE different valves found in the heart and state the function of EACH.

8. Explain why the wall of the left ventricle of the heart is thicker than the wall of the right ventricle.

9. Identify the events that occur in a person's heart during one heartbeat.

10. Name TWO different blood grouping systems and explain why these different blood groups exist.

11. Outline THREE precautions that should be taken when handling and transfusing blood.

12   Suggest and explain THREE reasons why it is dangerous to lose more than 2 litres of blood.

13   If a person who lives at sea level travels to a place at high altitude, where the air is 'thinner' or less dense, the number of red blood cells per mm^3 of blood increases by as much as 30% in the first 2 to 3 weeks.

     a   Suggest an explanation for this increase in the number of red blood cells per mm^3 of blood.

     b   Wallace, an elite athlete, decides to train at high altitude for a few weeks just before an important race, even though the race is being held at sea level. Suggest the advantage that this high-altitude training should give Wallace.

14   Suggest and explain why blood doping is illegal.

15   Jasmine finds that she lacks energy and gets tired easily. On visiting her doctor, she is told that she is anaemic because her red blood cell count is low. Explain why Jasmine has these symptoms.

16   'Vascular trauma' refers to an injury to a blood vessel that can be caused by the vessel being punctured. Suggest why this would be much more dangerous if it happened to an artery than to a vein.

17   Rosa suffers from mitral valve prolapse in which the two flaps of the mitral (bicuspid) valve do not close properly, and she finds that she gets tired more easily than the rest of the players on her netball team. Explain the possible cause of Rosa's tiredness.

18   Samara, who has Rh-negative blood, finds that she is pregnant and her husband, Kevon, has Rh-positive blood.

     a   What precaution should be taken by Samara's doctor during her pregnancy and immediately after she gives birth?

     b   Explain your answer to **a**.

19   Complete Table 4.5 by placing a ✓ to indicate if the transfusion would be successful and a ✗ if the transfusion would be unsuccessful.

Table 4.5 *Compatibility of ABO blood groups for transfusion*

Blood type of donor	Blood type of recipient			
	A	B	AB	O
A	✓	✗		
B				
AB				
O				

Transport systems in plants

Learning objectives

- Relate the **structures** of **xylem** and **phloem** to their **functions**.
- Explain the **role** of **transpiration** in **plants**.
- Investigate **environmental factors** that **affect** the **rate** of **transpiration**.

Structure and functions of xylem and phloem

Substances are transported around plants by **vascular tissue** which is composed of **two** different tube-like tissues: **xylem tissue** and **phloem tissue**. Vascular tissue runs throughout roots and stems of plants and it makes up the midrib and veins of leaves, as shown in Figure 4.9.

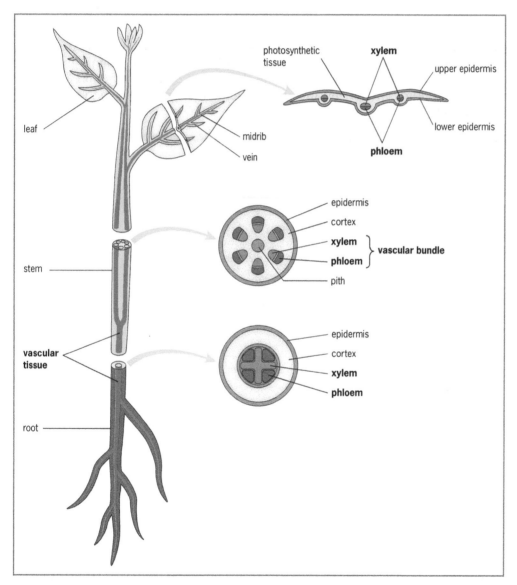

Figure 4.9 *The arrangement of vascular tissue in a plant*

Xylem tissue

Xylem tissue is made up of **xylem vessels**, grouped closely together. **Xylem vessels** are long, extremely narrow, hollow tubes that are non-living and they have walls that are thickened with **lignin**, a tough material, which is arranged in rings, spirals or a net-like pattern, as shown in Figure 4.10a. **Wood** is composed almost entirely of lignified xylem vessels.

Xylem vessels transport **water** and dissolved **mineral salts** from the roots, where they are absorbed from the soil, up the plant stem and into the leaves for use in photosynthesis. The main process responsible for moving water upwards through the xylem vessels is **transpiration**, which is explained below.

Phloem tissue

Phloem tissue is made up of **phloem sieve tubes** and **companion cells**, grouped closely together. **Phloem sieve tubes** are long, narrow tubes that contain living cytoplasm but no nuclei and they have perforated cross walls along their length as shown in Figure 4.10b.

The **phloem sieve tubes** transport **soluble organic food**, mainly **sucrose** and some **amino acids**, from the leaves where it is made in photosynthesis to all other parts of the plant that need it, mainly growing parts and storage organs. The food moves into and out of the sieve tubes by **active transport** (see page 8) and it can move both upwards and downwards. The movement of food through the sieve tubes is known as **translocation**.

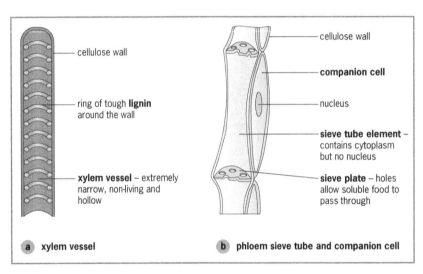

Figure 4.10 *Longitudinal section through a xylem vessel and a phloem sieve tube and companion cell*

Transpiration and its role in plants

Transpiration is the loss of water vapour from the surface of leaves.

Water moves in a **continuous stream** through the xylem vessels of a plant from the roots, where it is absorbed, up the stem, and into the leaves, where most of it is lost to the atmosphere as water vapour which diffuses out of the leaves, mainly through the stomata. **Transpiration** provides the suction, known as the **transpiration pull**, which is necessary to draw the water up into the leaves, as explained in Figure 4.11 on page 71.

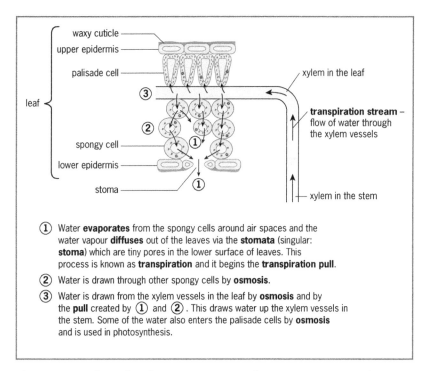

Figure 4.11 *The role of transpiration in drawing water up xylem vessels*

The numbered descriptions in the figure:

① Water **evaporates** from the spongy cells around air spaces and the water vapour **diffuses** out of the leaves via the **stomata** (singular: **stoma**) which are tiny pores in the lower surface of leaves. This process is known as **transpiration** and it begins the **transpiration pull**.

② Water is drawn through other spongy cells by **osmosis**.

③ Water is drawn from the xylem vessels in the leaf by **osmosis** and by the **pull** created by ① and ②. This draws water up the xylem vessels in the stem. Some of the water also enters the palisade cells by **osmosis** and is used in photosynthesis.

Transpiration is important to plants for the following reasons.

- It draws water from the soil up to leaves for use in **photosynthesis**.
- Moving water carries dissolved **mineral salts** up to the leaves for use in processes such as photosynthesis, healthy growth and development.
- It supplies plant cells with water to keep them **turgid**. This **supports** non-woody stems and leaves.
- Evaporation of water from the surface of leaves **cools** the leaves as it removes heat energy from them.

Environmental factors affecting the rate of transpiration

If the water supply in the soil is **plentiful**, the **rate of transpiration** is controlled by the interaction of different **environmental factors** that affect the rate at which water **evaporates** from the spongy cells inside leaves and water vapour **diffuses** out of the stomata. These factors include the environmental **temperature**, the **humidity** of the air, the **wind speed** and the **light intensity**.

- As **temperature increases** the rate of transpiration **increases**. This is because the rate at which water evaporates from the spongy cells and water vapour diffuses out through the stomata increases as temperature increases, and the amount of water vapour the air can hold also increases.
- As **humidity decreases** the rate of transpiration **increases**. This is because the amount of water vapour in the air decreases as humidity decreases. This increases the concentration gradient between the water vapour in the air spaces of leaves and in the air around the leaves, and enables water vapour to diffuse out of the leaves faster.
- As **wind speed increases** the rate of transpiration **increases**. This is because the increase in wind speed increases the speed at which water vapour is carried away from the leaves.
- As **light intensity increases** the rate of transpiration **increases**. This is because the stomata open more fully as light intensity increases, allowing more water vapour to diffuse out.

Comparing the rate of water uptake in different environments

The effect that the different environmental conditions have on the **rate** of **water uptake** by a leafy stem can be studied using a piece of apparatus known as a **potometer**, which is illustrated in Figure 4.12. This gives an **indirect** measurement of the **rate of transpiration** because most of the water taken up by the plant will leave by transpiration. However, a small amount of the water taken up is used by the plant in photosynthesis and does not leave by transpiration.

A **leafy stem** is cut and sealed into the potometer, ensuring the cut end is kept in water at all times so that no air is sucked into the xylem vessels. An air bubble is allowed to enter the apparatus and its position is controlled by using the tap on the water reservoir. As the leaves transpire, water is drawn into the xylem vessels in the stem causing the air bubble to move. The **time taken** for the bubble to move a **fixed distance** is measured under different environmental conditions.

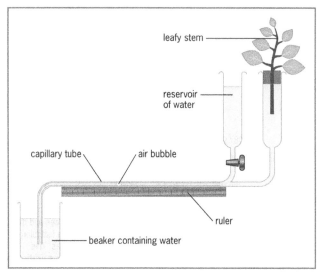

Figure 4.12 *A potometer used to compare the rate of water uptake in different environmental conditions*

Recalling facts

1. Construct a table that names the TWO types of tissue responsible for transporting substances around plants, identifies the substance(s) carried by EACH tissue, and gives the starting point of EACH substance and its final destination.

2. **a** Define transpiration.

   b Give FOUR reasons why transpiration is important in the life of a flowering plant.

3. Explain why water moves up the stem of a hibiscus plant faster on a hot, windy, dry day than on a cool, still, humid day.

Applying facts

4. Suggest ONE similarity and TWO major differences between transport systems in plants and those in humans.

5. Construct a table to give THREE structural differences between xylem vessels and phloem sieve tubes.

6. Franz cut a leafy stem of a plant with green and white leaves and immediately placed the cut end into a very dilute solution of eosin, which is a pink dye. After 2 hours, he discovered that the veins of the leaves were pink.

   a Provide a suitable explanation for Franz's observation.

   b Why did Franz place the cut end of the stem into the eosin solution immediately after it was cut?

7. Suggest why aphids stick their tube-like, sucking mouthparts, known as stylets, into the phloem in the leaves of a mango tree.

Analysing data

8 To compare the rate of transpiration occurring in three different species of plants, small pieces of dry cobalt chloride paper were attached onto the lower surfaces of the leaves of each plant using transparent tape, as illustrated in Figure 4.13. Cobalt chloride paper is blue when dry and turns pink when it is wet. The rate of transpiration was compared by recording the time taken for each piece of paper to change completely from blue to pink. The data collected by the three students is given in Figure 4.14.

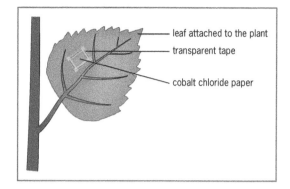

Figure 4.13 *Cobalt chloride paper attached to the leaf of a plant*

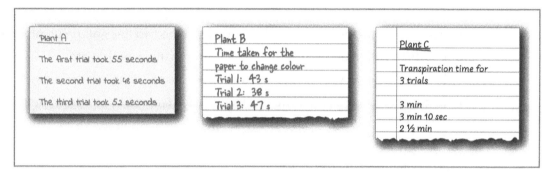

Figure 4.14 *Data collected by three students*

a Construct a suitable table and record the results obtained by the three students. Give your table a title.

b Which of the three plants was transpiring at the fastest rate? Explain how you arrived at your answer.

c Suggest ONE way in which the students could improve the accuracy of their results.

d State ONE precaution that the students should take when setting up and conducting the experiment.

e Three other students in the same class wished to check the accuracy of their classmates' results. Identify THREE additional details they would need to know about the method and/or conditions under which the investigation was carried out.

9 Renee set up a potometer, similar to the one illustrated in Figure 4.12 on page 72, to investigate the rate of transpiration in a leafy stem of a plant known as geranium aralia. She placed the potometer on a table in the laboratory, opened the tap on the reservoir to return the air bubble to zero, closed the tap and recorded the distance travelled by the bubble every 2 minutes for 14 minutes. She then repeated the experiment, but this time she very gently blew air from a fan onto the leaves. Her results are given in Table 4.6 on page 74.

Table 4.6 *Distance moved by the air bubble in the potometer every 2 minutes*

Time (min)	Distance moved by air bubble (cm)	
	In the laboratory	In front of a fan
2	0.9	1.3
4	1.7	3.0
6	2.6	4.8
8	3.7	6.1
10	4.6	7.9
12	5.4	9.3
14	6.3	10.4

a Draw a graph to represent the data given in Table 4.6.

b Write a suitable aim for Renee's experiment.

c Account for the difference in the gradient of the two lines of the graph drawn in **a**.

d i Which condition represented the control in the experiment?

ii Identify the MAIN assumption that Renee was making in her method.

e Renee then covered the lower surface of each leaf with waterproof petroleum jelly and repeated the experiment without using the fan.

i What results would you expect Renee to obtain?

ii Explain your answer to **e i**.

5 Excretion

Chemical reactions occurring in living organisms constantly produce **waste** and **harmful** substances which the organisms must get rid of from their bodies. **Excretion** is responsible for getting rid of these substances. It is also essential that the body's internal environment is kept constant, and excretion plays a part in this by helping to keep certain conditions surrounding cells constant.

Learning objectives

- Distinguish between **excretion** and **egestion**.
- Identify **metabolic waste products** and **excretory organs** in **humans**.
- Explain the **mechanism** of **excretion** by the **kidneys**.
- Explain the **osmoregulatory function** of the **kidneys**.
- Discuss the **use** of **dialysis** for **malfunctioning kidneys**.
- Relate the **structure** of the **skin** to **excretion** and **temperature control**.
- Identify the **methods** of **excretion** in **flowering plants**.

Excretion and egestion in living organisms

Excretion is the process by which waste and harmful substances, produced by the body's metabolism, are removed from the body.

The **body's metabolism** refers to all the **chemical reactions** occurring within the cells of living organisms, many of which produce waste and harmful substances that organisms must get rid of from their bodies. Excretion is **important** in living organisms for the following reasons.

- It prevents **toxic** metabolic waste substances from building up in the body and damaging **or** killing cells.
- It plays an important role in **homeostasis**, that is, keeping the conditions surrounding cells within the body **constant** so that the conditions are at their **optimum** for enzyme action (see page 180) and for cells to function properly.

Egestion is the process by which undigested dietary fibre and other undigested materials are removed from the body as faeces.

Excretion and **egestion** must **not** be confused. The undigested dietary fibre and other indigestible materials that are removed during egestion are **not** produced by the body's metabolism, so their removal cannot be classed as excretion. However, faeces do contain bile pigments which are excretory products that are made in the liver by the breakdown of haemoglobin. These pigments give faeces their brown colour.

Excretory products and organs in humans

Humans produce the following waste substances during metabolism.

- **Carbon dioxide** is produced by **respiration**, which occurs in all body cells.
- **Water** is produced by **respiration**, which occurs in all body cells.
- **Nitrogenous waste** is produced by the liver from excess **amino acids** in the diet (see page 183). **Urea** is the main nitrogenous waste produced.
- **Bile pigments** are produced by the **breakdown of haemoglobin** from red blood cells in the liver.
- **Heat** is produced in general metabolism, especially by **respiration**.

Table 5.1 summarises the excretory organs in humans and the metabolic waste substances that each excretes.

Table 5.1 *Excretory organs in humans*

Excretory organ	Substances excreted
Kidneys	• Water, urea and salts are excreted in **urine** (see Figure 5.3 on page 78).
Lungs	• Carbon dioxide and water vapour are excreted in **exhaled air** during **exhalation** (see page 193).
Skin	• Water, urea and salts are excreted in **sweat** (see Figure 5.6 on page 81). • Heat is also excreted.
Liver	• Bile pigments are excreted in **bile**, which passes into the intestines and is excreted in faeces. • Urea is made in the liver and is carried by the blood to the kidneys to be excreted.

The kidneys and excretion in humans

Humans have two **kidneys**, which form part of the **urinary system**. The kidneys have **two** main **functions**.

• They **excrete** metabolic waste, mainly urea, from the body as **urine**.
• They **regulate** the volume and concentration of blood plasma and body fluids by regulating the amount of water they contain, a process known as **osmoregulation** (see pages 78 to 79).

The **kidneys** are bean-shaped organs which are situated at the back of the abdominal cavity. Each kidney has a long, thin tube with muscular walls called the **ureter** leading from it to the bladder. The **bladder** is a bag-like structure with muscular walls and a ring of muscle, known as the **sphincter muscle**, around its exit. A thin tube called the **urethra** leads from the bladder to the outside of the body. A **renal artery** carries oxygenated blood containing **urea** from the aorta to each kidney, and a **renal vein** carries deoxygenated blood lacking urea from each kidney to the posterior vena cava. The structure of the urinary system and functions of the different parts are shown in Figure 5.1.

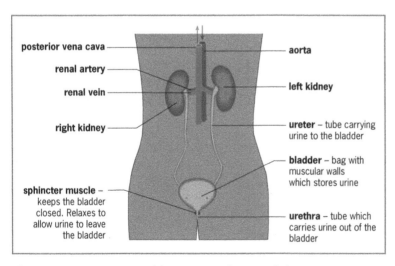

Figure 5.1 *Structure and functions of parts of the urinary system in a human*

Kidney structure

Each **kidney** is divided into **three** regions: an outer region called the **cortex**, an inner region called the **medulla**, and a central hollow region called the **pelvis**, which leads into the top of the ureter. Each kidney is composed of about 1 million thin-walled, microscopic **kidney tubules** or **nephrons**. Urine is produced in the nephrons. Each nephron begins with a cup-shaped **Bowman's capsule** in the cortex, which surrounds an intertwined cluster of capillaries, called a **glomerulus** (plural: **glomeruli**). After the Bowman's capsule, each nephron is divided into the following **three** sections.

- The **first convoluted (coiled) tubule** or **proximal convoluted tubule** in the cortex.
- The **loop of Henle** in the medulla.
- The **second convoluted (coiled) tubule** or **distal convoluted tubule** in the cortex.

An **afferent arteriole**, which branches from the renal artery, leads into each glomerulus. An **efferent arteriole** leads out of each glomerulus and branches to form a **network of capillaries** that wrap around each nephron and then join into a venule, which leads into the renal vein. Nephrons join into **collecting ducts** in the cortex and these ducts lead through the medulla and out into the pelvis. The structure of a kidney showing the glomeruli and position of a nephron is shown in Figure 5.2.

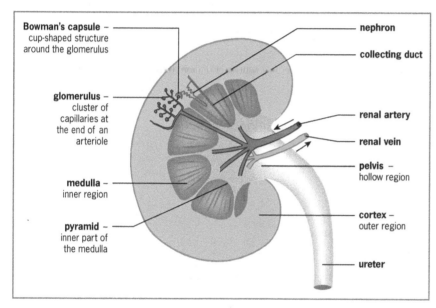

Figure 5.2 *A longitudinal section through a kidney showing the position of a nephron*

Formation of urine

Urine is produced in the nephrons by **two** processes.

- **Ultra-filtration** or **pressure filtration**.
- **Selective reabsorption**.

The detailed structure of a nephron and an explanation of the mechanism by which urine is formed are given in Figure 5.3 on page 78.

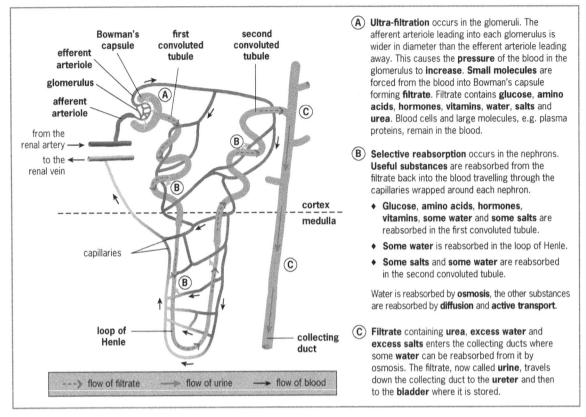

The figure contains the following labels and annotations:

Bowman's capsule, first convoluted tubule, second convoluted tubule, efferent arteriole, glomerulus, afferent arteriole, from the renal artery, to the renal vein, cortex, medulla, capillaries, loop of Henle, collecting duct

- - -> flow of filtrate   ⟶ flow of urine   ⟶ flow of blood

(A) **Ultra-filtration** occurs in the glomeruli. The afferent arteriole leading into each glomerulus is wider in diameter than the efferent arteriole leading away. This causes the **pressure** of the blood in the glomerulus to **increase**. **Small molecules** are forced from the blood into Bowman's capsule forming **filtrate**. Filtrate contains **glucose, amino acids, hormones, vitamins, water, salts** and **urea**. Blood cells and large molecules, e.g. plasma proteins, remain in the blood.

(B) **Selective reabsorption** occurs in the nephrons. **Useful substances** are reabsorbed from the filtrate back into the blood travelling through the capillaries wrapped around each nephron.

♦ **Glucose, amino acids, hormones, vitamins, some water** and **some salts** are reabsorbed in the first convoluted tubule.

♦ **Some water** is reabsorbed in the loop of Henle.

♦ **Some salts** and **some water** are reabsorbed in the second convoluted tubule.

Water is reabsorbed by **osmosis**, the other substances are reabsorbed by **diffusion** and **active transport**.

(C) **Filtrate** containing **urea, excess water** and **excess salts** enters the collecting ducts where some **water** can be reabsorbed from it by osmosis. The filtrate, now called **urine**, travels down the collecting duct to the **ureter** and then to the **bladder** where it is stored.

Figure 5.3 *Detailed structure of a nephron explaining how urine is formed*

The kidneys and osmoregulation

Osmoregulation is the regulation of the concentration of blood plasma and body fluids.

Osmoregulation helps to keep the conditions surrounding cells within the body **constant**. The concentration of blood plasma and body fluids must be kept constant to prevent water moving into and out of body cells unnecessarily.

- If the body fluids become **too concentrated**, water will **leave** body cells by osmosis. The cells will shrink and the body will become **dehydrated**. If too much water leaves cells, metabolic reactions cannot take place and cells die. Not drinking enough, excessive sweating or eating a lot of salty foods can cause body fluids to become too concentrated.

- If the body fluids become **too dilute**, water will **enter** body cells by osmosis. The cells will swell and may burst. Drinking a lot of liquid or sweating very little because of being in cold weather can cause body fluids to become too dilute.

Table 5.2 summarises the main ways that the human body gains and loses water, and the process of osmoregulation is explained in the following sections and summarised in Figure 5.4 on page 79.

Table 5.2 *Water gain and loss by the human body*

Water gain	Water loss
• In **drink**.	• From the kidneys in **urine**.
• In **food**.	• From the skin in **sweat**.
• **Metabolic water** is produced by cells during **respiration**.	• From the respiratory system during **exhalation**.

The **kidneys** regulate the concentration of the blood plasma and body fluids by controlling how much **water** is reabsorbed into the blood plasma during **selective reabsorption**. This determines how much water is lost in urine. Control involves the following.

- The **hypothalamus** of the **brain** (see page 102), which detects changes in the concentration of blood plasma.
- The **antidiuretic hormone (ADH)**, which is produced by the **pituitary gland** at the base of brain in response to messages from the hypothalamus. ADH is carried by the blood to the kidneys where it controls the **permeability** of the walls of the second convoluted tubules and collecting ducts to water.

If the body fluids become too concentrated

If the body fluids become **too concentrated**, the hypothalamus detects that the blood plasma is too concentrated and stimulates the pituitary gland to secrete antidiuretic hormone (ADH). The blood carries the ADH to the kidneys where it makes the walls of the second convoluted tubules and collecting ducts **more permeable** to water. Most of the water is reabsorbed from the filtrate into the blood and very **small quantities** of **concentrated** urine are produced. The hypothalamus also triggers the feeling of **thirst**, which causes a person to drink.

If the body fluids become too dilute

If the body fluids become **too dilute**, the pituitary gland secretes very little or no ADH. Without ADH, the walls of the second convoluted tubules and collecting ducts remain almost **impermeable** to water and so very little water is reabsorbed from the filtrate into the blood. **Large quantities** of **dilute** urine are produced.

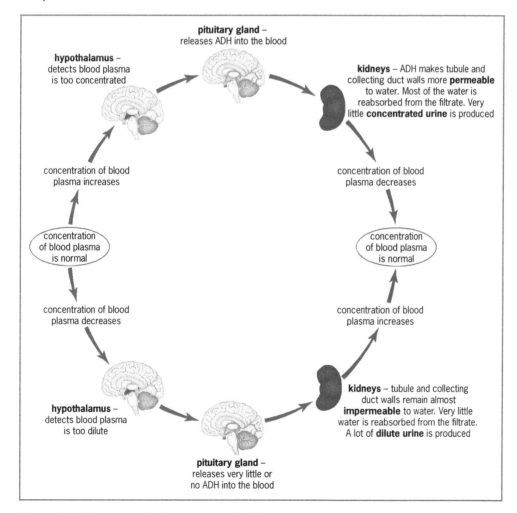

Figure 5.4 *Osmoregulation summarised*

Dialysis for malfunctioning kidneys

When nephrons stop functioning properly, the kidneys are unable to **remove waste** from the blood and regulate the **volume** and **composition** of blood plasma and body fluids. Harmful waste, especially urea, builds up in the blood and can reach toxic levels, resulting in death. Malfunctioning kidneys can be treated by a **kidney transplant** or **renal dialysis**.

During **renal dialysis**, blood from a blood vessel, usually in the arm, flows through a **dialysis machine** or **dialyser** and is then returned to the body, as shown in Figure 5.5. In the machine, the blood is separated from **dialysis fluid** by a series of partially permeable membranes. **Waste products**, mainly **urea**, together with **excess water** and **excess salts**, pass from the blood into the dialysis fluid. In this way, waste is removed from the blood and the volume and composition of the blood plasma and body fluids are regulated. Dialysis must occur at regular intervals; most people require three sessions per week, each lasting 4 hours.

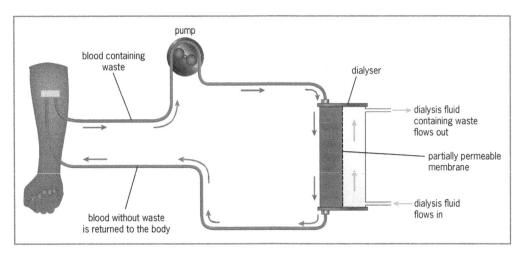

Figure 5.5 *Dialysis*

The skin and excretion

The **skin** is the largest organ in the human body. It is made up of **three** layers: the **epidermis**, the **dermis** and the **subcutaneous layer**.

- The **epidermis** is the outermost layer. It is waterproof and is, itself, made of three different layers: the outer **cornified layer**, the middle **living layer** and the **Malpighian layer** at the bottom.
- The **dermis** is found below the epidermis. It is made of **connective tissue** and has **nerve endings** which are responsible for detecting touch, pressure, pain, temperature and hair movement, **hair follicles**, **sweat glands** and **blood vessels** throughout.
- The **subcutaneous layer** is the innermost layer. It is composed of **adipose tissue**, a connective tissue consisting mainly of **fat cells** that contain large droplets of fat. The layer varies in thickness depending on where it is found in the body.

The skin has a variety of important functions. These include **excreting waste** in the form of **sweat** when the body temperature rises above 37 °C. The structure of the human skin is shown in Figure 5.6 on page 81, together with an explanation of the mechanism by which sweat is formed.

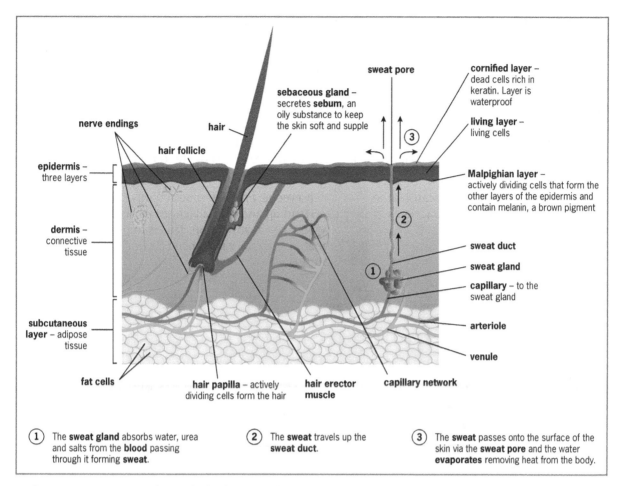

The sweat gland absorbs water, urea and salts from the **blood** passing through it forming **sweat**.

The **sweat** travels up the **sweat duct**.

The **sweat** passes onto the surface of the skin via the **sweat pore** and the water **evaporates** removing heat from the body.

★Figure 5.6 *A section through the human skin showing its structure and the mechanism of sweat formation*

The skin and temperature control

Humans must maintain a **constant** internal body temperature of about **37 °C** for **enzymes** to function properly (see page 180). They **gain** most of their body heat from internal **metabolic processes**, mainly respiration, and the blood carries this heat around the body. Heat is **lost** from the body mainly by conduction, convection and radiation through the skin, and evaporation of water during exhaling and sweating.

The **human skin** plays a major role in regulating body temperature. The **hypothalamus** of the brain detects if the body temperature rises above 37 °C or drops below 37 °C by detecting the temperature of the blood flowing through the brain. It then sends messages along nerves to appropriate structures in the skin causing the responses summarised in Table 5.3 on page 82.

Table 5.3 *How the skin helps to maintain a constant body temperature*

Body temperature rises above 37 °C	Body temperature drops below 37 °C
Sweating occurs: water in the sweat **evaporates** and removes heat from the body (see page 279).	**Sweating stops:** there is no water to evaporate and remove heat from the body.
Vasodilation occurs: the blood vessels in the dermis of the skin **dilate** so more blood flows through them and more heat is lost to the environment from the blood (see Figure 5.7).	**Vasoconstriction occurs:** the blood vessels in the dermis of the skin **constrict** so very little blood flows through them and very little heat is lost. The heat is retained by the blood flowing through vessels deeper inside the body.
Hair erector muscles relax: this causes the hairs to **lie flat** so no insulating layer of air is created.	**Hair erector muscles contract:** this causes the hairs to **stand up** and trap a layer of air next to the skin, which acts as **insulation.** This is important to prevent heat loss in hairy mammals and creates 'goose bumps' in humans.

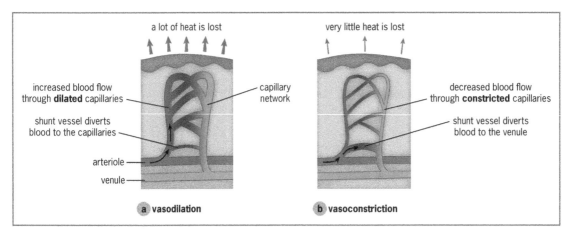

Figure 5.7 *Vasodilation and vasoconstriction*

Excretion in flowering plants

Plants produce several **waste substances** during metabolism.

- **Oxygen** is produced in **photosynthesis**, which occurs during daylight hours. It is excreted during the **day** when the rate of photosynthesis is higher than the rate of respiration and more oxygen is being produced in photosynthesis than is being used in respiration.
- **Carbon dioxide** is produced in **respiration**, which occurs at all times. It is excreted during the **night** when no photosynthesis is occurring to use the carbon dioxide produced.
- **Water** is produced in **respiration**. It is excreted as water vapour during the **night** when no photosynthesis is occurring to use the water produced.

Plants, unlike animals, do not have any specialised excretory organs to get rid of their waste products. **Oxygen**, **carbon dioxide** and **water vapour** are all excreted by **diffusion**. All three gases diffuse out of leaves through **stomata**, which are tiny pores in the undersurface of the leaves, and they diffuse out of bark-covered stems and roots through **lenticels**, which are small areas of loosely packed cells in the bark. Stomata and lenticels are shown in Figures 5.8 and 5.9 on page 83.

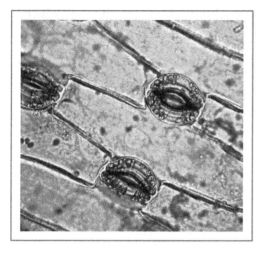

Figure 5.8 *Stomata in the lower surface of a leaf seen under the microscope*

Figure 5.9 *Lenticels in the bark of a tree trunk*

Recalling facts

1 **a** Provide a definition of excretion.

   b Is the removal of faeces from the body considered to be excretion? Explain your answer.

2 State the role of EACH of the following organs in excretion in humans:

   a the lungs   **b** the skin   **c** the kidneys.

3 Outline the TWO main functions of the human kidneys.

4 Describe the structure of a kidney tubule.

5 Explain the significance of the difference in diameter between the afferent arteriole leading into a glomerulus and the efferent arteriole leading away from the glomerulus.

6 Construct a table to give the function of EACH of the following in the formation of urine: glomerulus, Bowman's capsule, first convoluted tubule, loop of Henle, second convoluted tubule, collecting duct.

7 Distinguish between ultra-filtration and selective reabsorption.

8 **a** What is osmoregulation?

   b Name the hormone involved in osmoregulation and the gland responsible for producing it.

9 Explain why it is important to regulate the concentration of blood plasma and body fluids.

10 What effect would drinking three large glasses of soda have on the quantity and composition of a person's urine?

11 Why is it important for humans to maintain a constant internal body temperature?

12 Identify the MAIN processes that produce heat in the human body and those by which heat is lost from the body.

13 List THREE responses made by the skin of a human if the body temperature drops below normal.

14 Identify the MAIN excretory products in plants and outline how they are excreted.

Applying facts

15 Explain what would happen to Simeon if he was unable to excrete waste from his body.

16 How would you expect the loops of Henle in the kidneys of desert mammals such as the kangaroo rat to differ from those found in a human kidney? Give a reason for your answer.

17 It has been suggested that people pass less urine when the days are hotter than normal. Plan and design an experiment to see if this suggestion could be correct. Your design must contain the hypothesis you are testing, your aim and the results you expect to obtain if the suggestion is correct.

18 Members of a hiking group were advised by their leader to take water with them on their 5-hour hike into the mountains on a hot day. Gavin decided to drink a large quantity of water before leaving on the hike to save having to take any with him.

   a Explain how Gavin's body functioned to deal with the excess water.

   b Do you think Gavin's decision was wise? Support your answer with reasons.

19 Whilst running a 10 kilometre race, Lucinda failed to pick up any water from any of the water stops along the way, even though the weather was very hot.

   a What effect will Lucinda's behaviour have on the volume and composition of her urine?

   b Give a full explanation for your answer to **a**.

20 Otis was told by his doctor that his kidneys were beginning to malfunction. Explain the effect of this malfunction on his body and suggest what treatment his doctor will prescribe to deal with the situation.

21 The day is very hot and humid and Kadene notices that her skin looks redder than normal and appears wet. Provide a suitable explanation for Kadene's observations.

22 Suggest why it is an advantage for the ears of African elephants that live in hot climates to be particularly big.

23 Explain fully why plants excrete both oxygen and carbon dioxide during a 24-hour period, but animals only excrete carbon dioxide during the same period.

Analysing data

24 An average adult produces between about 1.0 dm³ and 1.5 dm³ of urine per day, after producing between 150 dm³ and 180 dm³ of glomerular filtrate per day. Table 5.4 shows the concentration of dissolved substances (solutes) in the blood plasma, glomerular filtrate and urine of an average healthy adult.

Table 5.4 *The concentration of dissolved substances (solutes) in the blood plasma, glomerular filtrate and urine of an average healthy adult*

Solute	Concentration of solute (g per dm³)		
	Blood plasma	**Glomerular filtrate**	**Urine**
Glucose	1.0	1.0	0.0
Amino acids	1.5	1.5	0.0
Proteins	80.0	0.0	0.0
Urea	0.3	0.3	20.0
Salts	3.2	3.2	1.6

a State the overall conclusion that can be drawn from the data given in the table.

b Explain why less than 1% of the filtrate becomes urine each day.

c Suggest why it is important that most of the filtrate never becomes urine.

d Suggest an explanation for EACH of the following.

   i Glucose and amino acids are present in glomerular filtrate but not in urine.

   ii There are no proteins in the glomerular filtrate.

   iii The concentration of urea in urine is much higher than it is in glomerular filtrate.

   iv There are some salts in urine, but their concentration is lower than in the blood plasma and glomerular filtrate.

e Why does the volume of urine produced by a person each day vary?

25 The concentration of a substance present in the filtrate in a nephron can be compared with its concentration in the blood plasma using the filtrate to plasma ratio as follows:

$$\text{filtrate to plasma ratio} = \frac{\text{concentration of substance in the filtrate}}{\text{concentration of substance in the plasma}}$$

Samples of filtrate were taken from Bowman's capsule and different distances along the first convoluted tubule. The concentrations of glucose and urea were measured and used to calculate the filtrate to plasma ratio of each sample. The kidney was then treated with chemical X and the process was repeated. The filtrate to plasma ratio of both glucose and urea in Bowman's capsule was found to be 1.0 in both the untreated and treated kidney. The results for the samples from the tubule are shown in Figure 5.10 on page 86.

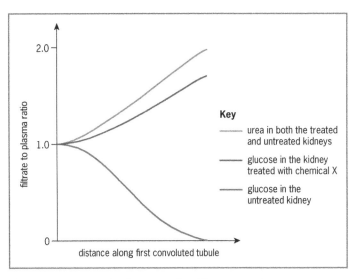

Figure 5.10 *Graph showing the filtrate to plasma ratio of urea and glucose at different distances along the first convoluted tubule of an untreated kidney and a kidney treated with chemical X*

a Explain why the filtrate to plasma ratio of both urea and glucose in Bowman's capsule is 1.0.

b Explain the trend shown in the filtrate to plasma ratio of urea along the length of the tubule.

c Describe and explain how the filtrate to plasma ratio of glucose changes along the length of the tubule in:

i the untreated kidney.

ii the kidney treated with chemical X.

d Suggest how chemical X could have caused the effect described in c ii.

26 To investigate the effectiveness of sweating in cooling the body, two identical 1000 cm³ flasks, labelled **A** and **B**, were set up. Flask **A** was wrapped with wet paper towel and flask **B** with the same thickness of dry paper towel. Each flask was filled with 1000 cm³ of water at 56 °C and sealed with corks which held thermometers, as shown in Figure 5.11. The temperature of each flask was recorded every 2 minutes for 16 minutes. The results are given in Table 5.5 on page 87.

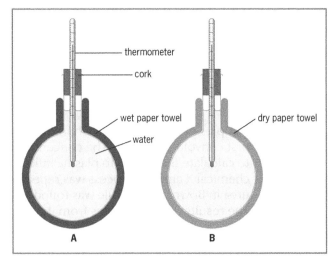

Figure 5.11 *Apparatus used to investigate the effectiveness of sweating as a cooling mechanism*

Table 5.5 *The temperature of the contents of two flasks at 2-minute intervals*

Time (min)		0	2	4	6	8	10	12	14	16
Temperature of water (°C)	Wet towels	56	50	46	42	39	36	34	32	31
	Dry towels	56	52	49	46	44	42	41	40	39

a Draw a graph to display the data in Table 5.5.

b Determine the overall temperature change:

   i   in flask **A**.

   ii in flask **B**.

c Describe the pattern of temperature change in the two flasks shown in your graph.

d What conclusion can you draw from the results?

e Explain the difference in heat loss by the two flasks.

f The investigation was repeated, but this time a 500 cm³ flask, labelled **C**, was set up with a cork and thermometer. The flask had the same shape as **A** and **B**, and it was wrapped with wet paper towel and filled with 500 cm³ of water at 56 °C. Would the rate of heat loss from flask **C** be the same, higher or lower than that from flask **A** in the first experiment? Explain your answer.

6 Sense organs and coordination

Humans must constantly monitor their environment and **respond** appropriately to any changes that they detect in this environment to help them survive. To do this, two systems are involved: the **nervous system** and the **endocrine** or **hormonal system**, and the **sense organs** play a critical role in detecting environmental changes.

The sense organs

Learning objectives

- Describe the **sense organs** and their **functions**.
- Relate the **structures** of the **mammalian eye** to their **functions**.
- Explain how an **image** is formed in the **eye**.
- Explain **accommodation** in the **eye**.
- Analyse the **causes** of, and **corrective measures** for, **sight defects**.
- Relate the **structures** of the **mammalian ear** to their **functions**.

Human sense organs

Humans have **five sense organs**: the **eyes**, the **ears**, the **nose**, the **tongue** and the **skin**. These organs contain specialised cells known as **receptor cells** that detect changes in the environment, also known as **stimuli**. The cells turn these stimuli into **electrical impulses**, which travel along nerves to the brain. The brain then interprets the impulses as **sensations** of **seeing**, **hearing**, **smelling**, **tasting** and **touching**, respectively. Table 6.1 gives the sense organs of the human body and stimuli that they detect.

Table 6.1 *Sense organs in the human body*

Sense organ	Specialised receptor cells	Stimuli detected
Eyes	Rods and cones (photoreceptors) in the retina.	Light. Light intensity and colour are detected.
Ears	Hair cells (mechanoreceptors) in the inner ear.	Sound waves and the position of the head.
Nose	Olfactory cells (chemoreceptors) in the top of the nasal cavities.	Chemicals in the air.
Tongue	Taste receptor cells (chemoreceptors) in the taste buds on its upper surface.	Chemicals in food. Five tastes are detected: sweet, sour, salty, bitter and umami (savoury).
Skin	Touch receptor cells.	Touch and texture.
	Pressure receptor cells.	Pressure.
	Pain receptor cells.	Pain and itching.
	Temperature receptor cells.	Hot and cold.

Structure of the eye

The **eyes** detect **light** that has been reflected from objects. This light causes changes in the specialised receptor cells found in the **retina** at the back of each eye. These changes set up **electrical impulses** which are transmitted along the **optic nerve** to the brain. The brain then translates the impulses into a precise picture of the object.

The eyes are situated in bony sockets of the skull called **orbits** and have muscles attached to move them. The orbits protect the back of each eye from damage, and the **eyelids** and **eyelashes** protect the front from foreign particles. **Tears**, produced by tear glands above each eye, keep the eyes moist, wash away foreign particles and contain an enzyme that destroys microorganisms.

Figure 6.1 shows a longitudinal section through the human eye, and the structure and functions of the main parts as they relate to **sight** are summarised in Table 6.2.

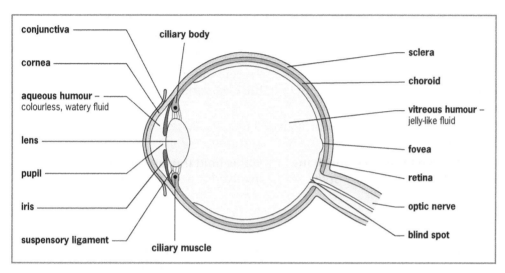

★**Figure 6.1** *A longitudinal section through the human eye*

Table 6.2 *Structure and functions of the main parts of the human eye*

Part of the eye	Structure	Function(s)
Sclera or **sclerotic coat**	Tough, white, fibrous coat around the outside of the eyeball.	Protects the eyeball.
Choroid	Layer lining the sclera. Contains blood vessels and the dark brown pigment known as **melanin.**	Blood vessels supply the retina with food and oxygen and remove waste. Melanin prevents reflection of light inside the eye.
Retina	Layer of light-sensitive cells known as **rods** and **cones** that lines the back of the eye.	Rods and cones convert light rays that focus on the retina into electrical impulses that are sent to the brain.
Fovea	Small depression in the retina directly in line with the centre of the lens. Contains cones only.	The most sensitive part of the retina where most light rays are focused.
Optic nerve	Nerve running from the retina to the brain.	Carries electrical impulses from the retina to the brain.
Blind spot	Point where the optic nerve leaves the eye. No light-sensitive cells are present.	Light rays falling on the blind spot are not detected.

Part of the eye	Structure	Function(s)
Conjunctiva	Thin, transparent layer over the front of the eye, continuous with the lining of the eyelids.	Protects the cornea beneath.
Cornea	Transparent layer connected to the sclera which covers the front part of the eye.	Refracts (bends) light rays onto the retina (see Figure 6.2).
Iris	A coloured disc in front of the lens composed of circular and radial muscles.	Controls the amount of light entering the eye by controlling the size of the pupil (see Figure 6.3 on page 91).
Pupil	A hole in the centre of the iris.	Allows light to enter the eyeball.
Lens	A transparent, elastic, biconvex structure.	Refracts light rays, making fine adjustments to focus them onto the retina during accommodation (see Figure 6.4 on page 92).
Ciliary body	Circular, forward continuation of the choroid that runs around the edge of the lens beneath the iris.	Secretes aqueous humour and contains the ciliary muscle.
Ciliary muscle	Circular ring of muscle running through the ciliary body.	Alters the shape of the lens during accommodation.
Suspensory ligament	A series of tough fibres that attach the edge of the lens to the ciliary body.	Fibres hold the lens in place and are involved in accommodation.

Image formation

In order to see, light rays reflected from an object must be **refracted** (bent) as they enter the eye so that they form a clear **image** of the object on the receptor cells of the retina. Being **convex** in shape, both the **cornea** and the **lens** refract the light rays; the cornea refracts them to the greatest extent and the lens then makes fine adjustments to focus them onto the retina. Figure 6.2 explains how an image is formed in the eye.

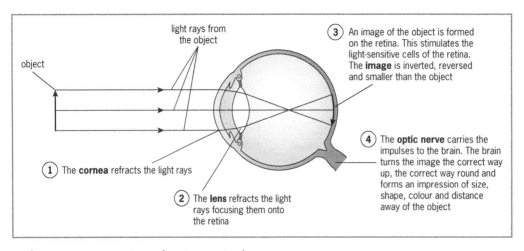

★Figure 6.2 *Formation of an image in the eye*

Detection of light intensity and colour by the eye

The **retina** is composed of **two** types of specialised **light-sensitive cells** or **photoreceptors**. These are known as **rods** and **cones**.

- **Rods** function in **low light intensities**. They are responsible for detecting the **brightness** of light and are located around the sides of the retina. Images falling on the rods are seen in **shades** of black and white only.

- **Cones** function in **high light intensities**. They are responsible for detecting **colour** and **fine detail**, and are mainly located around the back of the retina. The **fovea** is composed entirely of cones which are packed closely together. Light rays focusing onto the fovea produce the **sharpest** image. There are **three** different types of cones, which detect either the **red**, **green** or **blue** wavelengths of light, and they work together allowing the whole spectrum of colours to be seen.

Control of light entering the eye

The **iris** is composed of **two** sets of muscles: **circular muscles** and **radial muscles**. These muscles control the size of the **pupil**, and the size of the pupil controls the amount of light that enters the eye. The wider the pupil, the more light can enter. The mechanism by which the muscles of the iris control the size of the pupil is explained in Figure 6.3.

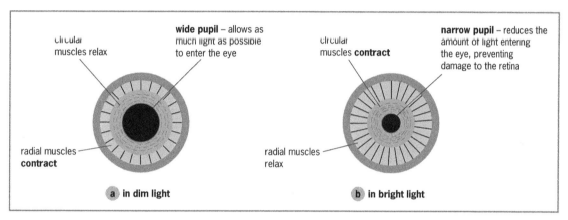

★ Figure 6.3 *Controlling the amount of light entering the eye*

Focusing light onto the retina – accommodation

Accommodation is the process by which the shape of the lens is changed to focus light coming from different distances onto the retina.

By its **shape** changing, the **lens** makes fine adjustments to focus light rays coming from objects different distances away onto the retina. This change in shape is brought about by the **ciliary muscle** in the ciliary body and the elasticity of the **lens**, as illustrated in Figure 6.4 on page 92.

- To focus on a **distant object**, the light rays need to be bent only slightly. To do this, the lens must be in a **flattened** shape. This is achieved by the ciliary muscle in each eye **relaxing**, which increases its circumference and causes the fibres making up the suspensory ligament to be **pulled tight**. The ligament then pulls the lens into a flattened shape.

- To focus on a **near object**, the light rays need to be bent a lot. To do this, the lens must be in a **bulged** shape. This is achieved by the ciliary muscle in each eye **contracting**, which decreases its circumference and causes the fibres of the suspensory ligament to become **slack**. Without the tension in the ligament, the elasticity of the lens allows it to spring into a bulged shape.

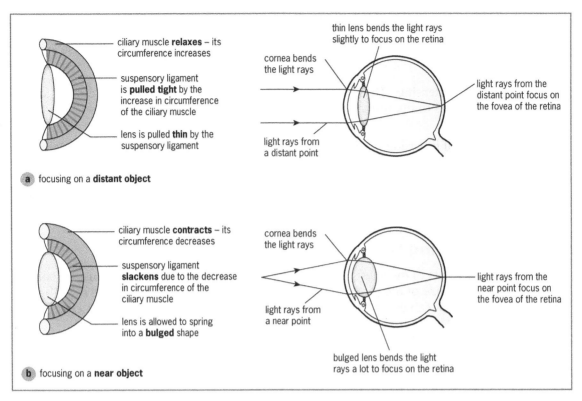

ciliary muscle **relaxes** – its circumference increases

suspensory ligament is **pulled tight** by the increase in circumference of the ciliary muscle

lens is pulled **thin** by the suspensory ligament

thin lens bends the light rays slightly to focus on the retina

cornea bends the light rays

light rays from the distant point focus on the fovea of the retina

light rays from a distant point

a focusing on a **distant object**

ciliary muscle **contracts** – its circumference decreases

suspensory ligament **slackens** due to the decrease in circumference of the ciliary muscle

lens is allowed to spring into a **bulged** shape

cornea bends the light rays

light rays from the near point focus on the fovea of the retina

light rays from a near point

bulged lens bends the light rays a lot to focus on the retina

b focusing on a **near object**

★Figure 6.4 *Accommodation*

Sight defects and their corrections

Any condition that prevents light rays from focusing properly on the retina causes a person's sight to be **defective**. The most common sight defects are **short-sightedness** and **long-sightedness**. Others include **astigmatism**, **glaucoma** and **cataract**. Most of these can be corrected by wearing **corrective lenses** as spectacles or contact lenses.

Short-sightedness (myopia)

A person with **short sight** can see **near** objects clearly, but distant objects are out of focus. This is because light rays from near objects focus on the retina, whereas light rays from **distant** objects focus **in front** of the retina. It is caused by the eyeball being too **long** from front to back, or by either the cornea or the lens being too **curved**. It is corrected by wearing **diverging (concave) lenses** as spectacles or contact lenses to bend the light rays from a distant object **outwards**, or **diverge** the rays, before they hit the cornea, as shown in Figure 6.5.

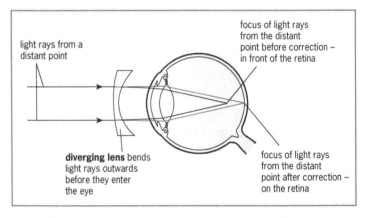

light rays from a distant point

focus of light rays from the distant point before correction – in front of the retina

diverging lens bends light rays outwards before they enter the eye

focus of light rays from the distant point after correction – on the retina

Figure 6.5 *The cause and correction of short sight*

Long-sightedness (hyperopia or hypermetropia)

A person with **long sight** can see **distant** objects clearly, but near objects are out of focus. This is because light rays from distant objects focus on the retina, whereas light rays from **near** objects focus **behind** the retina. It is caused by the eyeball being too **short** from front to back, or by either the cornea or the lens being too **flat**. It is corrected by wearing **converging (convex) lenses** as spectacles or contact lenses to bend the light rays from a near object **inwards**, or **converge** the rays, before they hit the cornea, as shown in Figure 6.6.

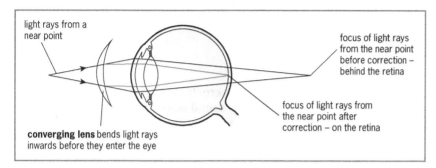

light rays from a
near point

converging lens bends light rays
inwards before they enter the eye

focus of light rays
from the near point
before correction –
behind the retina

focus of light rays from
the near point after
correction – on the retina

Figure 6.6 *The cause and correction of long sight*

Astigmatism

A person who has **astigmatism** finds that both near and distant objects appear **blurry** or **distorted**. It occurs if either the cornea or the lens is **unevenly curved**, so not all light rays from an object are equally refracted and not all focus on the retina. It is corrected by wearing **unevenly curved lenses** that counteract the uneven curvature of the cornea or lens.

Glaucoma

Glaucoma is a condition in which the **pressure** of the fluid within the eye **increases** because the drainage channels that allow aqueous humour to flow from the eye become blocked. If left untreated, the optic nerve becomes damaged and it can lead to permanent **blindness**. The most common type develops slowly and causes a gradual loss of peripheral (side) vision. Glaucoma is treated with **eye drops** to reduce fluid production or to improve the flow of fluid from the eye, or by **laser treatment** or **surgery** to open the drainage channels. Glaucoma tends to run in families.

Cataract

A **cataract** is a **cloudy** area that forms in the lens (see Figure 6.7). It develops slowly and, as it increases in size, it leads to cloudy or blurred vision, halos forming around lights, colours appearing faded, and difficulty seeing in bright light and at night. It is usually caused by **ageing** and is usually corrected by **surgery** to remove the clouded lens and to replace it with an **artificial lens**.

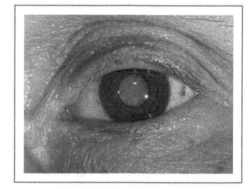

Figure 6.7 *An eye with a cataract*

Colour blindness

Colour blindness occurs if one or more of the **cone types** in the retina do not function properly and the sufferer is unable to distinguish differences between certain colours. The commonest form is red-green colour blindness where the sufferer is unable to distinguish differences between red and green. Another less common form makes it difficult to distinguish blue and yellow. Most forms of colour blindness are **inherited**.

Damage to the eyes

The eyes can be **damaged** in various ways. Staring directly at the **Sun** or very **bright lights** can damage the **retina** at the back of the eye and cause blind spots to develop. Extended exposure to **ultraviolet**

light from the Sun can lead to **cataracts** developing and can also damage the **cornea** or the **retina**. Damage to the retina may lead to **blindness**.

Eyes can also be **physically injured** by being poked; for example, with a stick or finger, by flying objects getting into the eye, such as small pieces of metal or sand, by being hit by a sports ball, such as a cricket, tennis or squash ball, or by being hit with a fist during a fistfight.

Structure of the ear

Sounds are produced when objects **vibrate**. These vibrating objects create pressure waves, known as **sound waves**, which travel through the air. The **ear** detects these **sound waves** and converts them into **electrical impulses**, which are transmitted along the **auditory nerve** to the brain. The brain then interprets the impulses as **sound**. The ear also detects the **position** and **movement** of the head, and this helps to control **balance** and **posture**.

The ear is divided into **three** regions: the **outer ear** consisting of the visible **pinna** and the **ear canal**, the **middle ear** which is a small, air-filled cavity in the skull containing three tiny bones known as **ear bones** or **ear ossicles**, and the **inner ear** which is filled with fluid and composed of three **semicircular canals** and the **cochlea**. Figure 6.8 shows the structure of the human ear and the structure and functions of the main parts are summarised in Table 6.3.

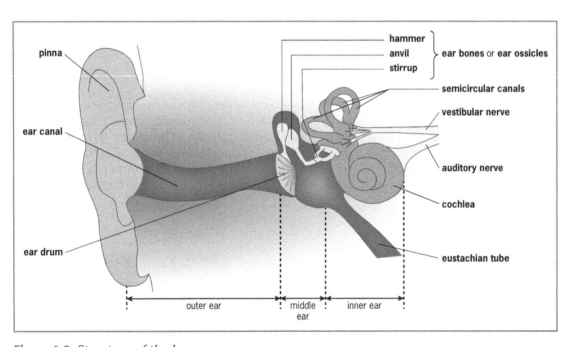

Figure 6.8 *Structure of the human ear*

Table 6.3 *Structure and functions of the main parts of the human ear*

Part of the ear	Structure	Function(s)
Pinna	Funnel-shaped, external part of the ear composed of cartilage covered with skin.	Collects and directs sound waves into the ear canal.
Ear canal	Tube-like structure leading from the pinna to the ear drum.	Transmits sound waves from the pinna to the ear drum.
Ear drum	Skin-like membrane stretching across the end of the ear canal separating the canal and the middle ear.	Vibrates when hit by sound waves and transmits these vibrations to the ear ossicles. Helps protect the delicate ear ossicles.

Part of the ear	Structure	Function(s)
Ear bones or **ossicles**	Three tiny bones: the **hammer**, **anvil** and **stirrup**, which have joints between. Form a chain connecting the ear drum to the inner ear.	Transmit vibrations from the ear drum to the cochlea. Amplify or strengthen the vibrations transmitted.
Semicircular canals	Three fluid-filled canals at 90° to each other containing movement-sensitive cells known as **hair cells**.	Rotational movements of the head cause the fluid to move and set up electrical impulses in the hair cells. Essential for maintaining **balance**, **posture** and **spatial orientation**.
Cochlea	Fluid-filled, spiral-shaped tube containing **hair cells**.	Vibrations of the stirrup cause the fluid to vibrate and set up electrical impulses in the hair cells. Essential for **hearing** (see Figure 6.9).
Vestibular nerve	Nerve running from the semicircular canals to the brain.	Carries electrical impulses from the semicircular canals to the brain.
Auditory nerve	Nerve running from the cochlea to the brain.	Carries electrical impulses from the cochlea to the brain.
Eustachian tube	Narrow tube that connects the inner ear to the upper part of the throat behind the nose.	Keeps the pressure on each side of the ear drum equal.

The mechanism of hearing

Figure 6.9 illustrates the mechanism of hearing.

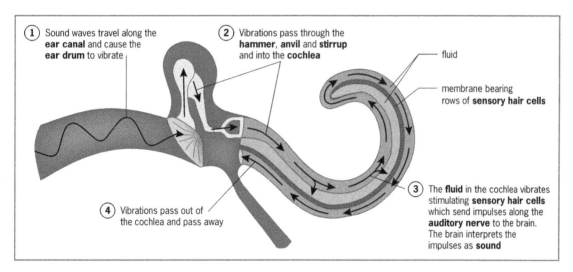

(1) Sound waves travel along the **ear canal** and cause the **ear drum** to vibrate

(2) Vibrations pass through the **hammer**, **anvil** and **stirrup** and into the **cochlea**

fluid

membrane bearing rows of **sensory hair cells**

(3) The **fluid** in the cochlea vibrates stimulating **sensory hair cells** which send impulses along the **auditory nerve** to the brain. The brain interprets the impulses as **sound**

(4) Vibrations pass out of the cochlea and pass away

★**Figure 6.9** *The mechanism of hearing*

Controlling balance and posture

The **semicircular canals** are important in controlling **balance** and **posture**. When the head moves, the fluid inside the canals moves and stimulates the **hair cells**. Impulses travel along the **vestibular nerve** to the brain. The brain processes these impulses and integrates the information received with information that it receives from the eyes and other parts of the body, such as muscles and joints. It then sends impulses back to muscles to help maintain balance and posture, help coordinate movement and provide an awareness of spatial orientation.

Sound

Sound waves travelling through the air are made of areas of high pressure alternated with areas of low pressure. A sound can be described in terms of its **loudness** and its **pitch**.

Loudness

The **loudness** of a sound depends on the **amplitude** or **height** of the sound wave. The greater the amplitude, the louder the sound (see Figure 6.10). Loudness is measured in **decibels** or **dB**. A ticking watch is about 20 dB, normal conversation is approximately 60 dB, traffic noise is about 80 dB, very loud music is 120 dB, a jet engine is 140 dB and a gunshot is about 150 dB.

Humans can **safely** listen to sounds up to **70 dB** for as long as they wish. However, prolonged or repeated exposure to very loud sounds of **85 dB** and higher can lead to permanent damage to the hair cells of the cochlea and this leads to permanent **hearing loss**. Exposure to sounds exceeding **120 dB** can cause **immediate** damage to the hair cells and immediate hearing loss, and the pressure created by sounds above 150 dB can cause the ear drums to rupture and can damage the ear ossicles.

Pitch

The **pitch** of a sound is how low or high the sound is, and this depends on the **frequency** of the sound waves. Frequency is the **number** of waves per second. The higher the frequency, the higher the pitch (see Figure 6.10). Frequency is measured in **hertz** or **Hz**.

The approximate **audio frequency range** of human hearing is **20 Hz** to **20 000 Hz**. Frequencies below 20 Hz are called **infrasound** and are more typically felt as vibrations rather than being heard. Frequencies higher than 20 000 Hz are called **ultrasound** and are beyond the range of human hearing. The ear is most sensitive to sounds between **2000 Hz** and **5000 Hz**, which roughly corresponds to the frequencies of human speech. As a person **ages**, the audio frequency range **decreases** and a person often finds that it becomes increasingly difficult to hear high pitch sounds.

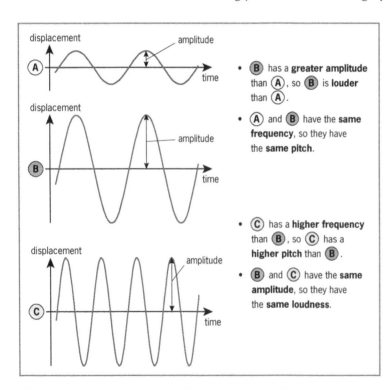

Figure 6.10 *Sound waves with different amplitudes and frequencies*

Recalling facts

1. Name the FIVE sense organs in the human body and state the stimulus or stimuli detected by EACH.

2. State the function of EACH of the following parts of the eye:
   a the sclera   b the choroid
   c the pupil   d the optic nerve.

3. Name the TWO types of cells found in the retina and distinguish between them.

4. a Identify the structures that control the amount of light entering the eye.
   b How do the structures named in **a** function in bright light?

5. a What is meant by accommodation in the eye?
   b Name the THREE parts of the eye that are involved in accommodation and state the function of EACH.

6. Explain the cause of short-sightedness and how it is corrected.

7. What is glaucoma and how can it be treated?

8. Identify the THREE bones that make up the ear bones or ossicles.

9. Explain how the parts of the ear function:
   a to detect sound
   b to help control balance and posture.

10. What is the approximate audio frequency range of the human ear?

Applying facts

11. Your friend Everton cannot understand that the image formed on the retina of each eye is upside down. Provide a suitable explanation to convince him that this is true and to help him understand why he does not see objects upside down.

12. Explain the reason for EACH of the following.
    a It is important to look directly at the pages of your notes when you are studying.
    b In the evening, when it is getting dark, it is not possible to see the colours of the cars on the road.

13. Abby walks from a brightly lit room into a dimly lit corridor. What changes would take place in her eyes to enable her to see as much as possible in the corridor?

14. Explain the changes occurring in Keisha's eyes as she looks down to read her book after watching her dog chase a cat at the bottom of her garden.

15 As people age, the lenses of their eyes often begin to lose their elasticity and their ciliary muscles weaken. Suggest and explain how this affects their eyesight and what action they must take to correct the defect.

16 Explain why Lawson, who works at his local airport directing the movement of aircraft on the ground, is told by his employer that he must wear ear protectors at all times when working.

17 Lucinda, who has perfect hearing, does not think that the dog whistle she uses to call her dog, Fritz, makes any sound when blown. However, Fritz always comes running to her when she blows it. Suggest and explain the reasons for Lucinda's observations.

Analysing data

18 Table 6.4 gives the cataract surgical rates (CSR) for the year 2000 for eleven Caribbean countries, measured as the number of cataract operations performed during the year per million population.

Table 6.4 *The cataract surgical rate for the year 2000 for eleven Caribbean countries*

Country	Population (thousands)	Cataract surgical rate (operations per million population)
Antigua	67	1343
Barbados	269	4000
Belize	235	600
Dominica	71	1746
Grenada	93	1700
Guyana	885	600
Haiti	8087	247
Jamaica	2560	500
St. Lucia	152	1000
St. Vincent	113	1300
Trinidad	1289	2600

a Suggest why the data is expressed as operations performed per million population instead of total number of operations per country.

b i Which country had the highest surgical rate?

   ii Suggest TWO reasons why the rate might be the highest in this country.

c i Which country had the lowest surgical rate?

   ii Suggest TWO reasons, which are different from those suggested in **b ii**, why the rate might be so low in this country.

d Explain why blindness caused by glaucoma is more serious than blindness caused by cataracts.

e The data given in the Table 6.4 was obtained from the Strategic Plan for Vision 2020 in the Caribbean prepared by the Pan American Health Organization and the World Health Organization in 2002. Suggest THREE proposals that could possibly have been put forward within the Plan to reduce the prevalence of preventable or curable blindness in the Caribbean.

19 Figure 6.11 shows an audiogram displaying the results of Clarissa's hearing test for each ear. The test was performed by an audiologist who began by playing a series of beeps into Clarissa's left ear at a volume she could hear. He then gradually reduced the volume of the beeps until Clarissa indicated that she could no longer hear the sound. The audiologist recorded this volume and repeated the test at different frequencies for Clarissa's left ear and then again for her right ear.

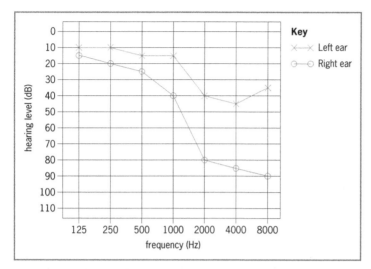

Figure 6.11 *An audiogram displaying the results of Clarissa's hearing test*

a Construct a suitable table and record the data used by the audiologist to plot the audiogram shown in Figure 6.11.

b Describe the trends shown by the audiogram for:

   i Clarissa's left ear

   ii Clarissa's right ear.

c i In which ear is Clarissa most likely to need to use a hearing aid?

   ii Explain how you arrived at your answer to c i.

   iii Suggest what could have caused Clarissa's hearing loss in the ear identified in c i.

d If the test is repeated using beeps with a frequency of 16 000 Hz, what results would you expect the audiologist to obtain for Clarissa's right ear? Give a reason to justify your answer.

The nervous and endocrine systems

Learning objectives

- Relate the **structures** of the **human nervous system** to their **functions**.
- Describe the **functions** of **sensory**, **motor** and **relay neurones**.
- Describe the **functions** of the **main regions** of the **brain**.
- Describe the **function** of the **spinal cord**.
- Cite **examples** of **voluntary** and **involuntary actions**.
- Relate the **structures** of the **endocrine system** to their **functions**.

Some important definitions

The following **terms** are important when discussing the nervous system.

A *stimulus is a change in the internal or external environment of an organism that initiates a response.*

A *response is a change in an organism or part of an organism that is brought about by a stimulus.*

A *receptor is the part of the organism that **detects** the stimulus.*

An *effector is the part of an organism that **responds** to the stimulus.*

The structure of the nervous system

The **nervous system** is responsible for coordinating and controlling all the activities of the body. It is made up of **neurones** or **nerve cells** which transmit messages as **electrical impulses** throughout the system. Neurones link **receptors**, which are present in the sense organs, to **effectors**, which are muscles and glands. The system is divided into **two** parts: the **central nervous system** and the **peripheral nervous system**, as shown in Figure 6.12.

- The **central nervous system (CNS)** consists of the **brain** and the **spinal cord**.
- The **peripheral nervous system (PNS)** consists of **cranial** and **spinal nerves** that connect the central nervous system to all parts of the body. The cranial nerves emerge from the brain and the spinal nerves emerge from the spinal cord.

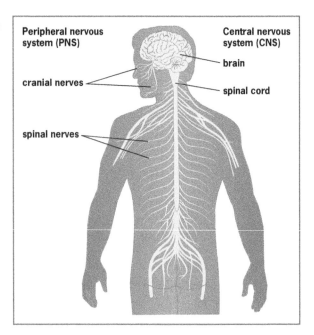

Figure 6.12 *The human nervous system*

Neurones

Neurones are specialised cells that conduct nerve impulses throughout the nervous system.

Neurones make up both the CNS and PNS. All neurones have a **cell body** with thin fibres of cytoplasm extending from it called **nerve fibres**. Nerve fibres that carry impulses **towards** the cell body are called **dendrites**. Nerve fibres that carry impulses **away from** the cell body are called **axons**; each neurone has only **one** axon, but most have many dendrites. The nerve fibres in certain types of neurones are covered with a fatty sheath known as a **myelin sheath**. There are **three** types of neurones: **sensory neurones**, **motor neurones** and **relay** or **intermediate neurones**.

- **Sensory neurones** transmit impulses from **receptors** to the **CNS**. The cell bodies of sensory neurones lie just outside the CNS. Each sensory neurone has a short axon, as shown in Figure 6.13 on page 101.
- **Motor neurones** transmit impulses from the **CNS** to **effectors**. The cell bodies of motor neurones lie inside the CNS. Each motor neurone has a long axon, as shown in Figure 6.14 on page 101.
- **Relay** or **intermediate neurones** transmit impulses throughout the **CNS**. They link sensory and motor neurones and their nerve fibres lack myelin sheaths.

Nerves are made up of bundles of nerve fibres of sensory and/or motor neurones surrounded by connective tissue. The **brain** and **spinal cord** are made up mainly of relay neurones and the cell bodies of motor neurones.

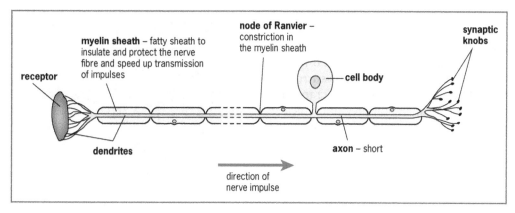

Figure 6.13 *Structure of a sensory neurone*

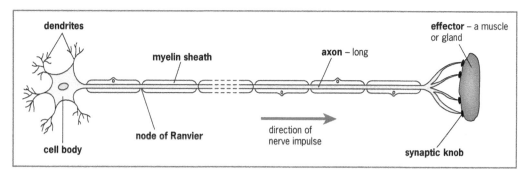

Figure 6.14 *Structure of a motor neurone*

When a **receptor** is stimulated, impulses pass from the receptor along **sensory neurones** into the CNS, where they pass into **relay neurones**. The impulses then pass into **motor neurones** which carry them out of the CNS to **effectors**. The connection between the three types of neurones is summarised in Figure 6.15.

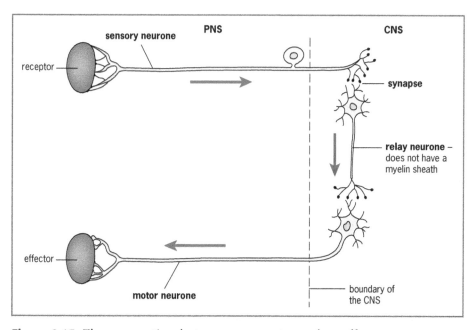

Figure 6.15 *The connection between a receptor and an effector*

The brain

The **human brain** is an extremely complex organ composed of billions of interconnected **neurones** (see Figure 6.16). The brain is housed in the **cranium** of the skull and is surrounded by three layers of tissue known as **meninges**. The cranium and meninges protect the brain against injury, and it is also cushioned and protected by being surrounded by a layer of **cerebrospinal fluid** between the two inner meninges.

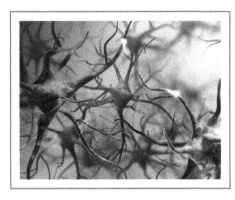

Figure 6.16 *A network of inter-connected neurones in the brain*

The brain has **five** main regions:

- The **cerebrum**, which is composed of two **cerebral hemispheres**.
- The **cerebellum**.
- The **medulla oblongata**, which is often referred to as the **medulla**.
- The **hypothalamus**.
- The **pituitary gland**.

Each region is concerned with different functions. The positions of these regions are shown in Figure 6.17 and their functions are summarised in Table 6.5.

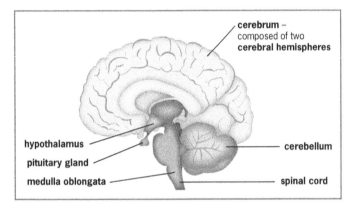

Figure 6.17 *The main parts of the human brain*

Table 6.5 *Functions of the main parts of the brain*

Part of the brain	Function(s)
Cerebrum	• Controls conscious thought, problem solving, decision making, planning and emotions. • Responsible for intelligence, memory, personality, learning, speech and language. • Processes visual, auditory and other external information. • Coordinates voluntary actions.
Cerebellum	• Controls balance and posture. • Coordinates muscular activity and movement.
Medulla oblongata	• Controls automatic, involuntary actions, e.g. heart rate, breathing rate, blood pressure and peristalsis.
Hypothalamus	• Plays a vital role in regulating the body's internal environment, e.g. it regulates body temperature (see page 81) and the concentration of body fluids by controlling the release of antidiuretic hormone (ADH) by the pituitary gland (see page 79).
Pituitary gland	• Secretes a variety of hormones, e.g. ADH and growth hormone (see Table 6.6 on page 104).

The spinal cord

The **spinal cord** is a long, thin structure that runs through the vertebral column (see page 100) from the medulla oblongata of the brain almost to the bottom of the column. It is protected by the **vertebrae** of the column (see Figure 6.18) and is made up of interconnected **neurones**. The spinal cord is responsible for transmitting messages backwards and forwards between the **brain** and the **rest of the body**.

Sensory neurones in **spinal nerves** carry messages from receptors in the body into the spinal cord. Messages then travel to and from the brain through **relay neurones**. **Motor neurones** in **spinal nerves** then carry messages back out to effectors in the body. In this way, the spinal cord helps coordinate and control body movements and other body processes. It also coordinates certain reflex actions without involving the brain.

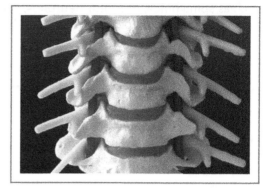

Figure 6.18 *Model showing pairs of spinal nerves exiting the spinal cord between the vertebrae*

Voluntary and involuntary actions

*A **voluntary action** is an action that is consciously controlled by the **brain**.*

The **cerebrum** of the brain is responsible for initiating voluntary actions. It does this in one of two ways, both of which involve **conscious thought**.

- The cerebrum can receive **incoming information** from sensory neurones, **process** this information and then initiate an action. For example, your friend asks you if you would like one of his oranges. You can **decide** whether to accept the orange or not.
- The cerebrum can **spontaneously** initiate an action without receiving any incoming information. For example, you **decide** to go for a ride on your bicycle.

Voluntary actions have the following **characteristics**: they are **learned**, they are relatively **slow** and they are **complex** because a variety of **different responses** can result from **one stimulus**.

Other **examples** of voluntary actions include talking, writing, running, eating, reading, watching TV and playing a game of football.

*An **involuntary action** is an action that occurs without conscious thought.*

Involuntary actions have the following **characteristics**: they are **not learned**, they are **rapid** and they are **simple** because the **same response** always results from the **same stimulus**.

Examples of involuntary actions include breathing, digestion, peristalsis, control of blood pressure and **reflex actions** such as the withdrawal reflex in response to pain, the knee jerk reflex, the pupil reflex, blinking, sneezing, coughing and saliva production.

Malfunctioning of the nervous system

Malfunctioning of the nervous system can lead to a variety of different conditions, including **paralysis** and other **physical disabilities. Paralysis** occurs when a person loses control of one or more muscles. The muscles stop being able to contract and bring about movement due to messages not passing from the central nervous system to them. It is mainly caused by **injury** to the spinal cord or by a **stroke**.

Physical disabilities affect a person's physical abilities and/or mobility. They can be caused by **injuries** to the brain or to the spinal cord; for example, visual impairment can be caused by an injury to the brain and bladder or bowel dysfunction can be caused by an injury to the spinal cord. They can also be caused by **conditions** or **diseases** that affect the brain, such as cerebral palsy, or the spinal cord, such as spina bifida, or motor neurones, such as motor neurone disease. Damage to the **cerebrum** of the brain can also affect a person's mental ability, memory and personality.

The structure of the endocrine (hormonal) system

The **endocrine system** is composed of **endocrine glands** which secrete chemicals known as **hormones**. Endocrine glands are also known as **ductless glands** because they do not posses any ducts; as a result, they secrete the hormones directly into the blood. Hormones are also known as **chemical messengers** and they help coordinate and control the body's activities. Figure 6.19 shows the positions of the main endocrine glands in the human body.

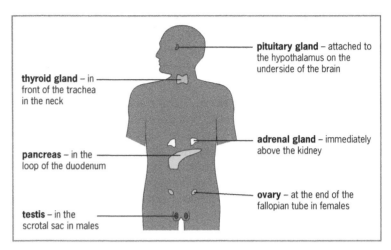

★**Figure 6.19** *The position of the main endocrine glands*

The role of the main hormones in the human body

Hormones are carried around the body by the **blood.** Some of these hormones have an effect on specific organs, known as **target organs**; for example, antidiuretic hormone (ADH) only has an effect on the kidneys. Other hormones have an effect on cells and tissues throughout the body; for example, thyroxine controls the rate of metabolism in all the cells of the body. Table 6.6 outlines the functions of some of the main hormones in the body.

Table 6.6 *Hormones produced by the main endocrine glands and their functions*

Endocrine gland	Hormone(s)	Function(s)
Pituitary gland	**Antidiuretic hormone (ADH)**	ADH controls the **water content** of blood plasma and body fluids by controlling water reabsorption in the **kidneys.** It is secreted when the blood plasma and body fluids become too concentrated (see page 79).
Thyroid gland	**Thyroxine**	Thyroxine controls the **rate of metabolism** and energy production in cells. It also controls physical **growth** and **mental development**, especially in children.
Adrenal glands	**Adrenaline** (flight, fright or fight hormone)	Adrenaline is released in large quantities when a person is frightened, excited or anxious. It speeds up **metabolism**, mainly respiration, and stimulates the liver to convert glycogen to glucose, which increases blood sugar levels. It also increases the heart rate, breathing rate and blood supply to muscles. In other words, it triggers the **fight-or-flight response** and gives the feeling of **fear**.
Pancreas	**Insulin**	Insulin regulates **blood glucose** levels. It is secreted when blood glucose levels rise, and it stimulates body cells to absorb glucose for respiration and liver cells to convert excess glucose to glycogen (animal starch). This causes blood glucose levels to drop.

Endocrine gland	Hormone(s)	Function(s)
Ovaries	**Oestrogen** (produced by the Graafian follicle)	Oestrogen controls the development of female **secondary sexual characteristics** at puberty; these include the development of breasts, pubic and underarm hair, and widening of the pelvis. It also helps regulate the **menstrual cycle** by stimulating the **uterus lining** or **endometrium** to thicken each month after menstruation (see page 43).
	Progesterone (produced by the corpus luteum)	Progesterone helps regulate the **menstrual cycle** by maintaining a thickened **uterus lining** after ovulation each month (see page 23).
Testes	**Testosterone**	Testosterone controls the development of the male **reproductive organs** and **secondary sexual characteristics** at puberty; these include the development of a deep voice, facial and body hair, muscles and broad shoulders. It also controls **sperm** production in the testes.

Recalling facts

1. a What is the role of the nervous system?
    b Identify the MAIN divisions of the nervous system.

2. a Name the THREE types of neurones that make up the nervous system and state the function of EACH.
    b Explain the relationship between the neurones identified in **a**.

3. Outline the functions of the following regions of the brain:
    a the medulla oblongata   b the cerebellum   c the hypothalamus.

4. What is the MAIN function of the spinal cord?

5. Distinguish between a voluntary action and an involuntary action and give THREE examples of EACH.

6. a What are hormones also known as?
    b Explain the meaning of the terms 'endocrine gland' and 'target organ'.

7. For EACH of the following hormones, name the gland that secretes it, state where the gland is located in the body and give the function(s) of the hormone in the body:
    a oestrogen   b thyroxine   c testosterone.

8. After a meal rich in carbohydrates, Bertha's blood glucose level rises. Explain how her body functions to return her blood glucose level to normal.

Applying facts

9 Suggest ONE reason why a central nervous system is necessary in humans, even though it would be much quicker for messages to go directly from receptors to effectors.

10 Delano survived a fall from a four-storey building but his personality changed after the fall, and he finds it difficult to remember information given to him and to keep his balance when walking. Suggest, with reasons, which parts of his brain were possibly damaged by his fall.

11 Sally suffered from a stroke which caused cells in the medulla oblongata of her brain to die due to a lack of oxygen. Outline the possible consequences of Sally's stroke.

12 Harry falls off his horse and damages the lower part of his spinal cord, which results in his legs becoming paralysed. Suggest an explanation for Harry's paralysis.

13 Endocrine glands have a large number of small capillaries passing between all their cells. Suggest the reason for this.

14 Which hormone is similar to the nervous system in its actions? Explain your answer.

15 Consuming excessive quantities of alcohol reduces the secretion of the antidiuretic hormone by the pituitary gland. Explain the possible consequences of this.

Analysing data

16 A group of students used a computer programme called 'Reaction Time Test' to carry out a study on the effect of age on reaction time. The programme measures the time taken for a person to react, in milliseconds (ms), by getting the person to click on the computer screen as soon as it changes colour from red to green. They used a large number of individuals of each chosen age, asked each of them to repeat the test 5 times and averaged all times for each age. The results are given in Table 6.7.

Table 6.7 *The average reaction time of individuals of different ages*

Age (years)	10	20	30	40	50	60	70	80
Average reaction time (ms)	257	224	212	221	237	268	325	446

a i How could you display the results in a more visual way?

ii Use the method suggested in **a i** to display the results.

b Why did the students use a large number of individuals of each age and ask each of them to repeat the test 5 times?

c i What is the age of the persons who had the fastest reaction?

ii Explain how you arrived at your answer to **c i**.

d What can you deduce about the effect of age on the speed of reaction of persons between 10 and 30 years of age?

e i Describe the trends seen in the reaction time of persons between 30 and 80 years of age.

ii Suggest a reason for your observations in **e i**.

f Outline the events occurring in a person's nervous system during each test.

7 Health

The World Health Organization (WHO) is a specialised agency of the United Nations (UN) responsible for **international public health.** The Constitution of the WHO states that its main objective is 'the attainment by all people of the highest possible level of health'. According to the WHO, **healthy people** are able to function well physically, mentally and socially.

Health is a state of complete physical, mental and social wellbeing and not merely an absence of disease and infirmity.

Microbes

Learning objectives

- Discuss **viruses**, **bacteria** and **fungi**.
- Discuss the **positive** and **negative** effects of **microbes**.

An introduction to microbes

Microbes or **microorganisms** are extremely small organisms which include **viruses, bacteria, protozoans** and some **fungi**. They play an **important role** in maintaining life on Earth; however, they can also be extremely **harmful.**

Viruses

Viruses are considered to be **particles** and not cells because they do not have a cell membrane, cytoplasm or organelles found in plant and animal cells. Each **virus particle** is composed of **nucleic acid** (**DNA** or **RNA**) surrounded by a coat of protein (see Figure 7.1). All viruses live **parasitically** inside living cells, and they can only reproduce inside these cells. This is because they must use the components of host cells in order to replicate or make copies of themselves. This process usually damages the host cells and can lead to their death, and it often causes **disease** in plants and animals.

Bacteria

Bacteria are unicellular organisms; however, their cells lack true nuclei and other membrane-bound organelles. The **DNA** of bacterial cells is found in a region called the **nucleoid**, which lacks a nuclear membrane. Bacterial cells can have a variety of different shapes such as spherical, rod-shaped, spiral-shaped or comma-shaped (see Figure 7.1). They can be found in almost every environment found on Earth, including extreme environments such as hot springs and deep-sea hydrothermal vents. Many are **beneficial** to the environment and other living organisms, while others cause **disease.**

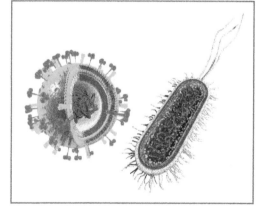

Figure 7.1 *The influenza virus (left) and the E. coli bacterium (right)*

Fungi

Fungi that are considered to be microbes include **yeasts**, which are unicellular, and **moulds**, which are multicellular. In multicellular fungi, the cells form thread-like, branching filaments called **hyphae**. A network of hyphae, known as a **mycelium**, then makes up the body of the fungus. Many fungi produce microscopic **spores** in order to reproduce. Fungi obtain their food by producing digestive enzymes (see page 181) to break down complex organic compounds in their environment and they then absorb the simpler breakdown products. Fungi can be found living in a variety of different environments and many are **beneficial** to their environment and other living organisms, while a few cause **disease**.

Positive effects of microbes

- Some **bacteria** and **fungi** contribute to **soil fertility** by feeding on dead and waste plant and animal material (organic matter), causing it to **decompose**. During this process **mineral nutrients** are released into the soil, which increase its fertility. Bacteria are particularly important in the cycling of **nitrogen** in the soil (see pages 31 to 32).

- Certain **bacteria** and **fungi** are used in **food production** and **processing**. The unicellular fungus, **yeast**, is used in making bread and alcoholic beverages. The yeast converts sugars present in the raw ingredients into **carbon dioxide** and **ethanol** (alcohol). The carbon dioxide causes the bread dough to rise and the ethanol is a component of alcoholic beverages (see page 187). **Lactic acid bacteria** are used to make **fermented products** such as yoghurt, sour cream, buttermilk, kimchi and sauerkraut. The bacteria convert sugars present in the raw ingredients into **lactic acid** which gives the foods a tangy, sour flavour. **Acetic acid bacteria** are used to produce **vinegar** by converting ethanol in various fermented beverages, such as wine or cider, into **acetic acid**, also known as vinegar.

- Certain **bacteria** are used to break down domestic and industrial organic waste during the **treatment** of **sewage** in sewage treatment plants. This forms **fertiliser** from harmful waste.

- Certain **bacteria** and **fungi** enable herbivores such as cows and rabbits to **digest** their food. These microbes are found in the digestive systems of the herbivores where they break down the cellulose and other plant fibre present in the food that the animals eat, making nutrients available to the animals.

Negative effects of microbes

- Some **bacteria** and **fungi** cause **food** to **spoil** (see Figure 7.2). They produce enzymes which break down food and cause its appearance, texture, flavour and odour to change. Some also produce acids or gases such as carbon dioxide and hydrogen sulfide, which can also change the appearance, texture, flavour and odour of food. Others produce **toxic chemicals**, which can cause food poisoning (see page 134).

- **Viruses**, certain **bacteria** and some **fungi** cause **disease** in both plants and animals. Microbes that cause disease are known as **pathogens** and the diseases they cause can range from mild to severe. Some can even lead to the death of the infected plant or animal.

- Certain **viruses**, **bacteria** and **fungi** cause **damage** to **food crops** by growing parasitically on various parts of the plants and causing **disease**. This can considerably reduce **yields** and affect the **quality** of the crop, and ultimately lead to food insecurity in a similar way to soil erosion (see page 34).

Figure 7.2 *Mould causes bread to spoil*

Recalling facts

1 Why are viruses referred to as particles and not cells?

2 Name TWO types of microbes other than viruses and briefly describe EACH.

3 Explain how microbes are used:

   a in food production and processing   b to improve soil fertility.

4 Identify THREE negative effects of microbes.

Applying facts

5 Suggest the MAIN reason why viruses are not considered to be living by many scientists.

6 Which type of microbe is MOST likely to be found living in a glacier? Explain how you arrived at your answer.

7 Sariyah discovered that the lid on a can of tomatoes in her cupboard had begun to look bulged, and when she opened the can, the tomatoes inside were mushy and smelt 'sour'.

   a Suggest and explain the possible cause of Sariyah's observations.

   b What would you advise Sariyah to do with the contents of the can? Give a reason to support your advice.

Disease, immunity and hygiene

Learning objectives

- Discuss **communicable** or **infectious diseases**.
- Discuss **sexually transmitted infections (STIs)**.
- Outline how the **principles** of **immunisation** are used to **control communicable diseases**.
- Discuss **non-communicable** or **non-infectious diseases**.
- Examine the **physiological effects** of **exercise**.
- Discuss the **importance** of **practising good hygiene**.

Communicable or infectious diseases

A **disease** is a condition that impairs the normal functioning of part or all of an organism and leads to a loss of good health.

A **communicable disease** is a disease that can be passed from one person to another and is caused by a **pathogen**.

Pathogens are **microscopic parasites** that cause disease in their hosts and include **viruses**, **bacteria**, **fungi** and **protozoans**. For this reason, communicable diseases are also known as **pathogenic diseases**, and because the pathogen **infects** its host, they are also known as **infectious diseases**. The pathogens can also be referred to as **causative agents** of the disease.

Some communicable diseases are described as being **contagious** because they are spread by **direct bodily contact** with an infected person, contact with their **discharges** such as saliva, blood, urine, semen and airborne respiratory droplets (see Figure 7.3), or contact with an **object** or **surface** that they have contaminated. Not all infectious diseases are contagious; for example, dengue is spread by mosquitoes, not by contact with an infected person.

Sexually transmitted infections (STIs)

Sexually transmitted infections or **STIs** are infectious diseases that are passed on from one person to another during **unprotected sexual contact**, including vaginal, anal and oral sexual contact. The **causative agents** include viruses, bacteria and fungi, and they pass from person to person in vaginal fluids, semen, blood and other body fluids. Some can also be transmitted from mother to child during pregnancy, childbirth and breastfeeding, and through infected blood and blood products during transfusions.

The causes, signs/symptoms and methods of treatment of some common STIs are summarised in Table 7.1. When **treating** a disease, the aim is to **relieve the symptoms** experienced by the person suffering from the disease and to **cure** the disease, if possible. When **controlling** a disease, the aim is to **prevent further development** and **spread** of the disease so that the incidence of the disease in the population is gradually reduced. Treating a disease is always one method to control it. There are several other methods that can be used to **prevent** and **control all** STIs, which are summarised after Table 7.1.

Figure 7.3 Airborne respiratory droplets can spread diseases

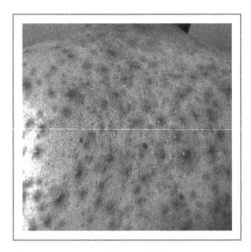

Figure 7.4 A syphilitic rash experienced during secondary syphilis

Table 7.1 *Causes, signs/symptoms and treatment of some common STIs*

Infection	Cause	Signs/symptoms	Treatment
AIDS – acquired immune deficiency syndrome	**Virus** known as the human immuno-deficiency virus or HIV	• **Primary infection:** Flu-like symptoms lasting 1 to 2 weeks may develop 2 to 6 weeks after infection. Some people have no symptoms. • **Asymptomatic stage:** Usually no symptoms are experienced for 10 years or more, but the virus is damaging the immune system and the person can pass on the virus without knowing. • **Symptomatic stage:** Symptoms of **AIDS** begin to develop, including weight loss, prolonged fever, severe tiredness, night sweats, chronic diarrhoea, swollen glands and skin rashes. Severe damage to the body's immune system also leaves the person vulnerable to **opportunistic infections**, e.g. pneumonia, tuberculosis and some types of cancer such as lymphoma and Kaposi's sarcoma.	• **Antiretroviral drugs** to prevent the virus from replicating and reduce the level of the virus in the body. • **Drugs** to treat opportunistic infections. • No cure exists.

Infection	Cause	Signs/symptoms	Treatment
Genital herpes	**Virus** known as the herpes simplex virus or HSV	• Recurrent painful blisters on the genitals and surrounding areas. • Flu-like symptoms such as fever, muscle and body aches, and swollen glands may accompany the initial appearance of the blisters and become reduced in severity during subsequent outbreaks.	• **Antiviral drugs** to slow replication of the virus and reduce symptoms. • No cure exists.
Hepatitis B	**Virus** known as the hepatitis B virus or HBV	• Fatigue, jaundice (yellowing of the skin and whites of the eyes), dark coloured urine, joint pain, abdominal pain, loss of appetite, nausea, vomiting and fever. Symptoms usually appear within 2 to 3 months after infection and last up to 6 months. Some people have no symptoms. • Can lead to serious liver damage if left untreated, e.g. cirrhosis and liver cancer.	• **Antiviral drugs** to slow replication of the virus and reduce symptoms. • No cure exists.
Gonorrhoea	**Bacterium** known as *Neisseria gonorrhoeae*	• **In females:** abnormal vaginal discharge, pain or burning sensation when urinating, pain or tenderness in the lower abdomen and bleeding between periods. • **In males:** abnormal discharge from the tip of the penis, pain or burning sensation when urinating and pain or swelling in the testes. If left untreated, it can lead to infertility.	• **Antibiotics** to kill the bacterium.
Chlamydia	**Bacterium** known as *Chlamydia trachomatis*	• **In females:** abnormal vaginal discharge, burning sensation when urinating, pain during sexual intercourse, itching or soreness in or around the vagina and bleeding between periods. • **In males:** abnormal discharge from the tip of the penis, burning sensation when urinating, itching or burning around the opening of the penis and pain or swelling in the testes. People are often without symptoms in the early stages. If left untreated, it can cause serious health problems, including damage to the reproductive organs and infertility, especially in females.	• **Antibiotics** to kill the bacterium.
Syphilis	**Bacterium** known as *Treponema pallidum*	Syphilis develops in stages: • **Primary syphilis:** painless, round sores called **chancres** develop on the genitals at the point of infection and last for 3 to 6 weeks. • **Secondary syphilis:** a red, non-itchy rash spreads over the body (see Figure 7.4 on page 110) and may be accompanied by patchy hair loss, fever, sore throat and swollen lymph glands. These symptoms eventually go away. • **Latent syphilis:** no symptoms occur for years. • **Tertiary syphilis:** damage to the brain, nerves, heart, blood vessels and other organs can occur many years after the original infection, if left untreated.	• **Antibiotics** to kill the bacterium.

Infection	Cause	Signs/symptoms	Treatment
Candidiasis, yeast infection or thrush	A yeast-like **fungus** – *Candida albicans*	• **In females:** white vaginal discharge, itching or soreness of the vagina and surrounding area, and vaginal burning during intercourse or urination. • **In males:** irritation or burning at the head of the penis, soreness during intercourse, white discharge from the penis and redness of the penis. Much more common in females than males and can develop without any sexual activity.	• **Antifungal medications** such as tablets and creams to kill the fungus.

Note: Hepatitis A and **hepatitis C** have similar symptoms to hepatitis B and they can also be transmitted by sexual contact, however, this means of transmission of both is rare.

Prevention and control of STIs

The following methods can be employed to **prevent** or **control** the spread of **all STIs.**

- **Abstain** from sexual intercourse or keep to **one**, uninfected sexual partner.
- Use **condoms** during sexual intercourse.
- Visit a doctor or healthcare facility to be **tested** if an infection is suspected and, if an STI is diagnosed, undergo the correct **treatment.**
- **Trace** and **treat** all sexual contacts of infected persons.
- Set up **education programmes** to educate populations about STIs and how to prevent their spread.

Currently, the only STI referred to in Table 7.1 that can be controlled by **vaccination** is hepatitis B. **No vaccine** currently exists for syphilis, gonorrhea, chlamydia, genital herpes, HIV/AIDS or candidiasis.

Prevention and control of HIV/AIDS and hepatitis B

The measures outlined above can be used to prevent or control the spread of HIV/AIDS and hepatitis B. In addition, the following **specific measures** can be taken.

- Do not use intravenous drugs or share cutting instruments.
- Use sterile needles for all injections and dispose of all used needles following strict guidelines.
- Test all human products to be given intravenously for HIV and hepatitis B.
- Prevent mother to baby transmission by ensuring pregnant women who are HIV or hepatitis B positive receive antiretroviral drugs and their babies receive the appropriate medication after birth.
- Give **pre-exposure prophylaxis** or **PrEP**, a daily **HIV** drug, to all persons who are at a high risk of HIV infection, such as those with an HIV positive partner. This reduces their risk of being infected with HIV.
- **Vaccinate** all babies against **hepatitis B**, and also children and adults who have not been vaccinated, especially those in high risk groups.

The immune system and immunity

The **immune system** is a complex network of cells, tissues, organs and proteins that work together to defend the body against **pathogens**. It also helps to protect the body against **abnormal cells**, such as cancer cells, and other **harmful substances**, such as toxins and allergens. The immune system provides the body with **immunity**.

Immunity is the body's temporary or permanent resistance to a disease.

Immunity can be **innate** or **acquired**.

- **Innate immunity** refers to the inborn ability of the body to resist disease. It is provided by physical barriers, such as the **skin** and **mucous membranes**, and white blood cells known as **phagocytes** (see Table 4.3 on page 62). Innate immunity is present at **birth**.

- **Acquired immunity**, also known **as adaptive immunity**, is **highly specific** and it develops in response to a specific pathogen or toxin in the body. Acquired immunity involves white blood cells known as **lymphocytes** and it takes time to develop, but it can last a lifetime (see below).

Impact of diseases on the immune system

A variety of **diseases** can affect the way the immune system functions.

- **Immunodeficiency diseases** occur when the immune system is **suppressed** or **weakened**, making those affected more vulnerable to infections. These diseases can be **inherited**; for example, severe combined immunodeficiency (SCID). They can also be caused by another **disease**; for example, measles, mononucleosis, certain cancers and HIV/AIDS, or by taking certain **medications**; for example, chemotherapy and other drugs to treat cancer, and drugs taken to prevent organ rejection after an organ transplant.

- **Allergic diseases** occur when certain substances in the environment, known as **allergens**, cause the immune system to respond in an **overactive** way. This can lead to a variety of conditions such as **asthma, eczema, allergic rhinitis (hay fever)** and **food allergies** (see pages 115 to 116).

- **Autoimmune diseases** occur when the immune system attacks the body's own normal, healthy cells and tissues; for example **type 1 diabetes, rheumatoid arthritis** and **lupus** (see page 116).

Acquired immunity

The body **acquires** much of its immunity over time, usually due to its response to the presence of specific **antigens** that enter, and the body's **lymphocytes** are essential for the development of this immunity. However, immunity can also be acquired by specific **antibodies** or **antitoxins** entering the body.

*An **antigen** is a substance that is recognised as being foreign to the body and it stimulates the lymphocytes to produce antibodies.*

*An **antibody** is a specific protein that is produced by lymphocytes in response to the presence of a specific antigen.*

*An **antitoxin** is an **antibody** that is produced in response to a specific toxin, and it is able to neutralise this toxin.*

Antigens are usually **proteins** on the surface of **pathogens** such as **bacteria, viruses** and **fungi**. They may also be **toxins** produced by the pathogens. Antigens are specific to a particular pathogen, and when **antigens** are detected in the body, **lymphocytes** produce specific **antibodies**, including **antitoxins**, against them.

The **antibodies** bind to the **antigens** on the surface of the pathogens and cause the pathogens to clump together so that the phagocytes can engulf them, or they cause the pathogens to disintegrate. This is shown in Figure 7.5. The **antitoxins** neutralise any toxins produced by the pathogens. Antibody production is an essential part of the body's **immune response**.

There are **two** main types of acquired immunity: **natural immunity** and **artificial immunity**.

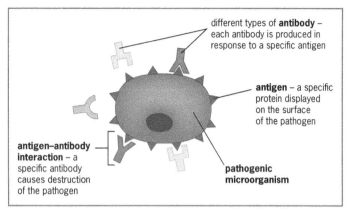

Figure 7.5 *The antibody–antigen interaction*

Natural immunity

Natural immunity is acquired by a person being exposed to a pathogenic disease. When a pathogen enters the body, lymphocytes make specific antibodies in response to the specific antigens of the pathogen. These **antibodies** destroy the pathogens or neutralise their toxins.

Production of antibodies takes time and whilst it is happening, the person experiences **symptoms** of the disease. When enough antibodies have been produced to destroy the pathogens or neutralise their toxins, the person recovers. The antibodies then gradually disappear from the blood and some lymphocytes develop into **lymphocyte memory cells** which remember the specific antigens.

When the same pathogen re-enters the body, the memory lymphocytes recognise the antigens, multiply and produce **large quantities** of the specific antibodies **rapidly**, as shown in Figure 7.6. The antibodies destroy the pathogen, or neutralise its toxins so quickly that the person does not develop any symptoms. The person has become **immune** to the disease. Depending on the type of pathogen, immunity may last for a **short time**; for example, against the common cold, or a **long time**; for example, chicken pox is rarely caught twice.

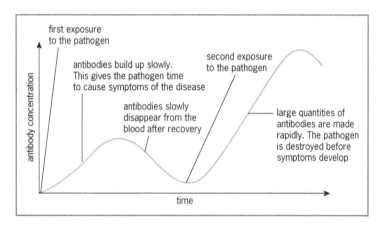

Figure 7.6 *Antibody production during the acquisition of natural active immunity*

Natural immunity can also acquired by a **baby** receiving antibodies from his or her mother. These can pass across the **placenta** before birth or be obtained from **breast milk** during breastfeeding. The immunity only lasts a **short time** because no lymphocyte memory cells are produced in the baby's body, and the antibodies gradually disappear from the baby's blood.

Artificial immunity

Artificial immunity is acquired by the deliberate introduction of the specific **antigens** into a person's body. This process is known as **vaccination** and the biological preparation that contains the antigens is known as a **vaccine**. A vaccine may contain any of the following.

- **Live** pathogens that have been **weakened** or **attenuated**; for example, the oral polio vaccine.
- **Killed** or **inactivated** pathogens; for example, the inactivated polio vaccine.
- **Antigens** from the coats of pathogens that have been produced by genetic engineering; for example, the hepatitis B vaccine.

- **Toxins** from the pathogens that have been made harmless; for example, the tetanus vaccine.
- **Viral vectors**, which are harmless viruses that contain genetic material from the pathogen. This material initiates an immune response; for example, the AstraZeneca and Johnson & Johnson COVID-19 vaccines.
- **Messenger RNA (mRNA)** from the pathogen enclosed in microscopic lipid (fat) particles. The mRNA provides instructions for production of the antigen of the pathogen, and the antigen then initiates an immune response; for example, the Pfizer-BioNTech and Moderna COVID-19 vaccines.

Vaccines do not cause the disease, but lymphocytes still make **antibodies** in response to the specific **antigens** or **toxins** in the vaccine. **Lymphocyte memory cells** are also produced so that an **immune response** is set up whenever the pathogen enters the body. Vaccines may provide **short-term** protection; for example, against cholera, or **long-term** protection; for example, against tuberculosis.

Artificial immunity can also be acquired when **antiserum** containing **specific antibodies** or **antitoxins** is injected into a person's body for **immediate** immunity and relief of symptoms of a specific disease. The immunity only lasts a **short time** because no lymphocyte memory cells are produced, and the antibodies gradually disappear from the body.

Non-communicable or non-infectious diseases

A **non-communicable disease** is a disease that cannot be passed from one person to another and is not caused by pathogens.

Many **non-communicable diseases** or **NCDs** are long-term medical conditions that can worsen over time. They are often influenced by genetic, environmental and lifestyle factors, they often require ongoing medical attention and may limit a person's daily activities. There are several different **types** of NCDs.

- **Nutritional deficiency diseases** are caused by the shortage or lack of a particular **nutrient** in the diet. These diseases include vitamin and mineral deficiency diseases, such as rickets and anaemia, and protein-energy malnutrition (see page 175).
- **Degenerative diseases** are caused by a gradual **deterioration** of body tissues or organs over time which prevents them from functioning normally. These diseases include Alzheimer's disease, Parkinson's disease and osteoporosis.
- **Inherited disorders** are passed on from one generation to the next via genes and are caused by an **abnormal gene**; for example, sickle cell anaemia, cystic fibrosis and Huntington's disease.
- **Mental health problems** affect how a person feels, thinks, behaves and interacts with other people. These include depression, anxiety disorders, neurosis, stress, schizophrenia and eating disorders.
- **Immune system diseases** disrupt the normal functioning of the immune system in a variety of ways. They can weaken the body's ability to protect itself against pathogens, and can result in allergic reactions and autoimmune diseases (see below and page 116).
- **Lifestyle diseases** are linked to the way people **live** their lives; for example, obesity, type 2 diabetes and hypertension (see pages 116 to 118 and page 175).

Allergies

Allergies result from an **overactive response** of the immune system to various substances in the environment, known as **allergens**, which are harmless to most people. Allergens stimulate the immune system to release **histamines**, **cytokines** and other **inflammatory substances** which cause responses associated with allergic reactions in the affected parts of the body. Allergens include pollen, dust mites, fungal spores, dust, animal dander (skin flakes), smoke and other air pollutants (see page 415), certain components of food, certain drugs and the venom in insect stings. The following are some common allergic reactions.

- **Asthma** is a chronic inflammation of the walls of the bronchi and bronchioles of the lungs. This makes the airways narrower, which causes breathing to become extremely difficult.

- **Allergic rhinitis** or **hay fever** mainly affects the nasal passages and eyes, causing sneezing, a runny or blocked nose, itchy or watery eyes and pain around the temples.

- **Eczema** affects the skin causing it to become dry, itchy, cracked, scaly, red and inflamed (see Figure 7.7).

- **Food allergies** occur when the immune system reacts to certain components in food, mainly proteins. Foods that cause most allergic reactions include milk, eggs, tree nuts, peanuts, shellfish, wheat, soybeans, fish and sesame seeds. When eaten, these foods affect various parts of the

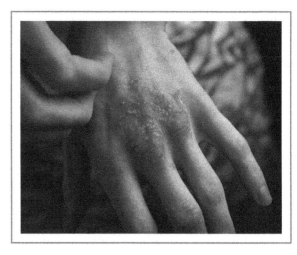

Figure 7.7 A person scratching an eczema rash on his hand

body and their effects can vary from mild itching or swelling to severe **anaphylaxis**, which is a life-threatening allergic reaction characterised by extreme difficulty breathing, a dip in blood pressure and loss of consciousness.

Autoimmune diseases

Autoimmune diseases are caused by the immune system mistakenly developing an immune response to the antigens of its own, healthy cells, tissues and organs as if they were foreign. In addition to the autoimmune diseases discussed below, others include **multiple sclerosis (MS)**, **Graves' disease**, **celiac disease**, **psoriasis**, **inflammatory bowel disease** and **type 1 diabetes**.

- **Rheumatoid arthritis** is an inflammatory disorder that mainly affects the joints causing pain, swelling, stiffness and loss of function, leading to decreased mobility.

- **Lupus** is an autoimmune disease that can affect various tissues and organs including the skin, joints, kidneys, heart, lungs and brain. Symptoms vary widely among individuals, and they often appear and disappear in cycles. These symptoms include fatigue, joint pain, skin rashes, fever, hair thinning, chest pain and organ dysfunction.

Diabetes

Diabetes is a condition in which the **blood sugar level** is consistently **high** over a prolonged period. The level is so high that the kidneys are unable to reabsorb all of the glucose from the filtrate (see Figure 5.3 on page 78) and some is passed out in the urine.

Causes of diabetes

There are **two** types of diabetes which have different **causes**.

- **Type 1** or **insulin-dependent diabetes** is the most common type in people under the age of 30 years. It is **caused** by the pancreas not producing any insulin because the insulin-producing cells have been damaged, usually by the body's own immune system.

- **Type 2** or **non-insulin dependent diabetes** is the type that occurs most often in people that are over 40 years old. It is **caused** by the pancreas not producing enough insulin and/or by the body cells developing resistance to the insulin so that they do not respond to it. Being overweight or obese, or having family history of type 2 diabetes, increases a person's chances of developing the condition.

Effects of diabetes

Symptoms of diabetes include glucose in the urine, frequent urination, excessive thirst, fatigue, blurred vision, excessive hunger, unexplained weight loss, tingling or numbness of the hands and feet, and slow healing of wounds. There is **no cure** for diabetes, however symptoms can be controlled with the correct **treatment** and **management**, and people with it can live long, healthy and active lives.

Management of diabetes can be demanding since blood sugar levels require constant monitoring and medication schedules must be carefully adhered to, which can involve regular injections of insulin (see Figure 7.8). It also requires following a carefully planned diet and making lifestyle modifications. All of these can have economic and social implications.

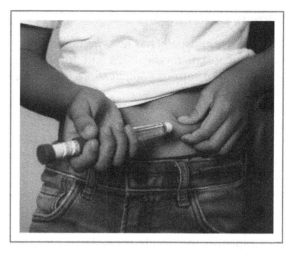

Figure 7.8 *A diabetic child injecting insulin with an insulin pen*

If diabetes is not managed properly, it can lead to a variety of **complications** over time such as **heart disease**, **nerve damage**, **vision loss**, **kidney disease**, **foot complications** and an increased risk of **skin infections**, all of which can affect the individual's **health** and **wellbeing**.

Hypertension

Hypertension or **high blood pressure** is a condition in which the pressure of blood in the **arteries** is consistently higher than normal; in other words, **140/90 mm Hg** or **higher**, as shown in Figure 7.9. It can be detected by measuring the blood pressure in the upper arm using a **blood pressure monitor**.

Causes of hypertension

A number of **factors** can put a person at risk of developing hypertension. Many of these are known as **modifiable risk factors** because a person can **adjust** or **change** them in order to prevent or manage hypertension. These factors include the following.

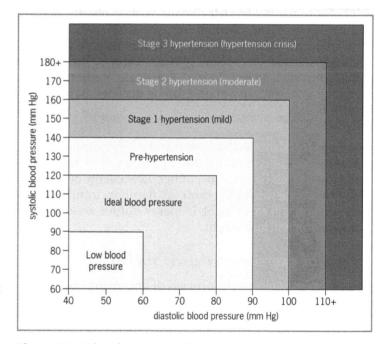

Figure 7.9 *Blood pressure chart*

- Being **overweight** or **obese**.
- Being **physically inactive**.
- Consuming too much **saturated fat** and **salt** in the diet.
- **Smoking**.
- Drinking too much **alcohol**.
- Being under **stress**.

Effects of hypertension

Hypertension usually has **no symptoms**; it is known as the 'silent killer'. However, if it is not treated with appropriate medications and properly managed by making lifestyle modifications, it can lead to a variety of serious **complications** including **heart disease**, **stroke**, **kidney failure**, **impaired vision** and **dementia**.

Physiological effects of exercise

During exercise, **respiration** speeds up in muscles cells in order to meet their increased demands for **energy** so that they can work harder. As a result, heart rate and breathing rate increase to supply the muscles with the extra oxygen and glucose they need, and to remove the extra carbon dioxide produced (see page 186). **Exercise** has many **benefits**, including the following.

- It improves the **circulatory system**. This is because it strengthens the heart muscles and increases cardiac output, which is the amount of blood pumped by the heart per minute. It also lowers the resting heart rate, lowers blood pressure, improves circulation and it reduces the risk of hypertension, heart disease and stroke.

- It improves the **respiratory system**. This is because it strengthens the diaphragm and intercostal muscles (see page 192) and increases lung capacity, which is the volume of air that the lungs can hold. It also increases the efficiency of gaseous exchange and it improves the body's ability to use oxygen.

- It helps to control **lifestyle diseases** such as **obesity**, **diabetes**, **hypertension** and **heart disease**. Engaging in regular, **aerobic exercise** such as swimming, walking and aerobics increases a person's metabolism, which helps to limit weight gain, and this helps to reduce a person's risk of developing **obesity**. It also lowers blood glucose levels by increasing respiration in muscle cells and increasing their sensitivity to insulin so that the cells are better able to use any available insulin, and this helps reduce a person's risk of developing **diabetes**. Since it improves the functioning of the circulatory system, exercise also reduces a person's risk of developing **hypertension** and **heart disease**.

- It helps to **balance** energy input and energy output. To maintain a **healthy body**, it is essential that a person's daily **energy input** from the food eaten balances his or her daily **energy output** as a result of daily activities, including exercise. If energy input exceeds output, the person will **gain weight**. If energy output exceeds energy input, the person will **lose weight**.

Effects of exercise on muscle toning

Muscle toning refers to the process of improving muscle shape, strength and firmness, and reducing body fat to give the body a lean and defined physique, and to improve overall physical health and appearance. **Exercise** plays a crucial role in muscle toning by stimulating muscle growth and improving muscle definition, overall strength and endurance whilst, at the same time, reducing excess body fat (see Figure 7.10).

Figure 7.10 *Exercise improves muscle toning*

Personal hygiene practices

Personal hygiene refers to the practices carried out by individuals in order to maintain **cleanliness** of their bodies and clothing to preserve overall **good health** and **wellbeing**. Eliminating **body odours** and taking care of **genitalia** are two very important **practices** in maintaining good personal hygiene.

Elimination of body odours

Body odours or **BO** can affect anyone, however certain factors increase a person's likelihood of developing BO, especially excessive **sweating**. When water evaporates from the sweat it leaves salts, urea and dead skin cells on the surface of the skin. **Bacteria** then break down these substances and produce unpleasant smelling chemicals that cause BO. This happens especially under the arms, and in the groin and genital areas. Other factors that can lead to BO include certain foods, such as garlic, certain medical conditions, such as hormonal imbalances and practising poor personal hygiene.

Eliminating body odour involves practising good personal hygiene and, in some cases, making lifestyle changes or obtaining medical treatment. **Good personal hygiene practices** include **washing** the **body** daily using soap and water, paying particular attention to the armpits, groin, genitals and feet. **Hair** should also be **washed** with shampoo at least once a week. **Skin** and **hair** should be **dried** thoroughly after washing. **Antiperspirant** or **deodorant** should be applied to the clean, dry skin of the armpits and **foot powder** applied to the feet, if necessary. **Clothes** should also be changed and washed regularly, especially undergarments and socks, which should be changed daily.

Care of the genitalia

Keeping the **genitals** and surrounding areas clean is particularly important to prevent **odours** and **infection**. To do this, they should be **washed** thoroughly each day using mild, unscented soap and water, especially during **menstruation** in females. **Females** should be particularly careful to prevent any bacteria from building up in vaginal secretions and entering the **vagina**. Female genitalia should be cleaned from front to back to prevent any faeces from reaching the vaginal area, and sanitary products should be changed regularly.

Males should be particularly careful to keep the area beneath the **foreskin** clean to prevent a build-up of secretions from the foreskin and dead cells, known as **smegma**. If whitish, pasty smegma builds up, bacteria start to accumulate in it and cause an unpleasant odour. Uncircumcised males must ensure that the foreskin is pulled back once a day to clean beneath it and remove any smegma.

Benefits of good personal hygiene

Maintaining good personal hygiene has several **benefits**, two of the most important are as follows.

- It promotes **social acceptance** by reducing or eliminating body odours, preventing bad breath, enhancing a person's appearance, and promoting greater self confidence and self-esteem. All of these enhance social interactions and interpersonal relationships, and lead to greater success in a person's professional endeavours.

- It significantly reduces the risk of **catching** and **spreading infections** such as skin, respiratory, gastrointestinal and sexually transmitted infections, by reducing the growth of microorganisms on the body. As a result, it leads to better overall health.

Recalling facts

1 Provide a suitable definition for EACH of the following:

    a a disease   **b** a communicable disease   **c** a pathogen.

2 Distinguish between the treatment and the control of a disease.

3 **a** What is an STI?

    b Chlamydia, genital herpes and candidiasis are three STIs. For EACH infection, identify the cause, describe the effects it has on the body and how it can be treated.

    c Outline FOUR measures that can be taken to control the spread of the STIs discussed in **b**.

    d Give FOUR measures NOT outlined in **c** that can be taken to control the spread of HIV/AIDS.

4 **a** What is the immune system?

    b What is meant by the term 'immunity'?

5 Distinguish between the following types of immunity:

    a innate and acquired   **b** natural and artificial.

6 Identify THREE types of disease that affect the immune system.

7 Explain how antibodies function to protect the body against pathogens.

8 **a** What is a vaccine?

    b Explain how the rubella (German measles) vaccine provides Anika with immunity to rubella.

9 **a** What is a non-communicable disease?

    b Identify THREE different types of non-communicable diseases.

10 **a** Distinguish between allergies and autoimmune diseases.

    b Give THREE named examples of EACH disorder in **a**.

11 Discuss the causes of diabetes and the effects that the disease has on a person's body.

12 Outline the effects of exercise on EACH of the following:

    a the respiratory system   **b** lifestyle diseases   **c** muscle toning.

13 Why is it important that Nina balances her daily energy input and her daily energy output?

14 **a** What causes body odour and how can it be reduced or prevented?

    b Suggest TWO important benefits of practising good personal hygiene.

Applying facts

15 Explain why Zika fever, caused by a virus, is described as being infectious, but not contagious.

16 Darius notices that he has a sore on his penis, however he ignores it because it does not hurt. After a few weeks the sore disappears, but he then develops a non-itchy rash on his back and a sore throat, both of which he ignores until they finally go away.

    a Suggest the possible cause of Darius's symptoms.

    b Outline the consequences of Darius's failure to seek medical intervention for his symptoms.

17 Although HIV/AIDS is a sexually transmitted infection, it does not affect the reproductive system. Explain fully the reason for this.

18 It is easier to control the spread of gonorrhoea than HIV/AIDS. Suggest why the spread of gonorrhoea is relatively easy to control and FOUR factors that make the spread of HIV/AIDS difficult to control.

19 Identify the type of immunity gained in EACH of the following situations.

    a Jovan being given a yellow fever vaccine before travelling to another country.

    b Ramon contracting chikungunya during the rainy season.

    c Baby Lisa being breastfed by her mother.

20 Kaia contracted chicken pox, caused by a virus, when she was a child and her son, Ashton, recently caught the disease from one of his classmates. Explain fully how Kaia remained healthy despite her close contact with Ashton throughout his illness.

21 Within a few minutes of being stung by a bee, Kamaya's tongue and throat begin to swell and she begins to have difficulty breathing. Explain the possible cause of Kamaya's symptoms.

22 Until the 1800s, 'water tasters' diagnosed diabetes by tasting a person's urine. Explain the reason for this.

23 Research has shown that in some countries hypertension is most common among rich, successful executives. Explain how their lifestyles could account for this.

24 What advice would you give to Zuri, who recently started menstruating, on how to take care of her genitalia?

25 The bar graph in Figure 7.11 shows the number of deaths caused by six vaccine-preventable diseases worldwide in 1990 and 2017, rounded to the nearest 1000.

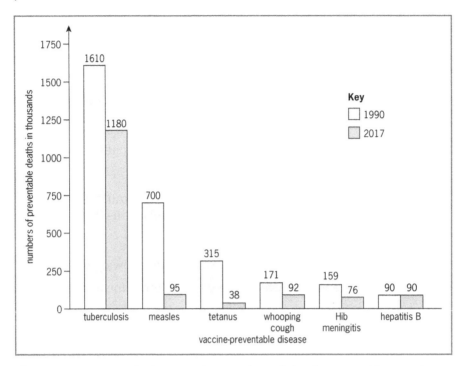

Figure 7.11 *Bar graph showing the number of deaths caused by vaccine-preventable diseases worldwide in 1990 and 2017*

a Draw a suitable table and record the data shown in the graph.

b i   Describe the overall trend in number of deaths between 1990 and 2017.

   ii Which disease does not fit into the trend described in **b i**?

   iii Explain your answer to **b ii**.

c Suggest the MAIN reason for the trend described in **b i**.

d Which disease do you think is of most concern to the World Health Organization and why?

e Many authorities prevent children who have not been immunised from entering public school. Suggest TWO reasons why some parents might have valid concerns about immunising their children and TWO reasons why authorities maintain their position.

26 The global burden of communicable and non-communicable diseases between 1990 and 2015, measured as the total number of healthy years of life lost per year worldwide due to premature death or years lived with a disability, is given in Table 7.2 on page 123, rounded to the nearest ten million.

Table 7.2 *The global burden of communicable and non-communicable diseases between 1990 and 2015*

Year	Total number of healthy years of life lost in millions due to:	
	communicable diseases	non-communicable diseases
1990	770	1070
1995	730	1150
2000	700	1200
2005	640	1260
2010	550	1330
2015	440	1430

a Plot a graph to show the information given in Table 7.2. Give your graph a suitable title.

b Name TWO communicable diseases and TWO non-communicable diseases that would be included in the numbers given in Table 7.2.

c Describe the trends shown in the number of healthy years of life lost from 1990 to 2015 due to:

  i communicable diseases   **ii** non-communicable diseases.

d Suggest TWO possible reasons for the trends shown in the number of healthy years of life lost from 1990 to 2015 due to:

  i communicable diseases   **ii** non-communicable diseases.

27 To investigate the effect of exercise and fitness on heart rate, Lisa enlisted the help of two classmates, Deane and Malik. In his spare time, Deane is always playing football and is a member of the school football team, whilst Malik spends all of his spare time playing computer games and does not like sports. Using digital fitness trackers worn by Deane and Malik, Lisa measured their pulse rates at rest and then asked them to run around the track for 5 minutes and recorded their pulse rates every minute during exercise and after exercise. Lisa's results are given in Table 7.3.

Table 7.3 *The heart rate of two students before, during and after exercise*

Time (minutes)	Heart rate (beats per minute)	
	Deane	Malik
0	64	80
1	66	80
2	110	128
3	122	142
4	128	148
5	130	152
6	130	154
7	98	128
8	80	112
9	68	96
10	64	88

a Plot a line graph to show heart rate against time for both Deane and Malik on the same axes. Clearly distinguish each curve.

b With a reason, state which student's heart rate had returned to normal after 10 minutes.

c What deduction can you make about the effect of fitness on the time taken for the heart rate to return to normal after exercise?

d Excluding the deduction you made in **c**, give TWO other conclusions that can be drawn about the effect of fitness on heart rate.

e i Describe the effect of exercise on Deane's heart rate.

   ii Explain why exercise had the effect described in **e i**.

Drug use and abuse

Learning objectives

- Evaluate the effects of **drug** use.
- Distinguish between **prescription drugs** and **non-prescription drugs**.
- Describe the **effects** of **drugs** on the **nervous system**.
- Describe the **social** and **economic effects** of **drug use** and **abuse**.

Prescription drugs and non-prescription drugs

*A **drug** is any chemical substance that alters the functioning of the body physically and/or psychologically.*

People take **drugs** for different reasons and in different ways. Many drugs are used to **treat** or **prevent** medical conditions with the aim of **improving health**, whilst others are taken for **recreational** purposes. Some drugs are **illegal** and all drugs, whether legal or illegal, can be harmful to the body if they are used incorrectly, in other words, **misused** or **abused**.

Drugs affect the body in different ways. They can have **physiological effects** because they affect the way organs and systems of the body function, which affects the person's **physical health**. They can also have **psychological effects** because they affect the way a person's brain functions, which affects the person's **mental health**.

Drugs can be **classified** in various different ways; one way is based on how the drugs are obtained, and it classifies them into **prescription drugs** and **non-prescription drugs**.

Prescription drugs

A **prescription drug** is a **legal** drug that requires a **prescription** from a medical practitioner to be dispensed. Prescription drugs can be **misused** by persons taking the drugs in doses other than prescribed, taking someone else's prescription drugs or taking drugs for a purpose other than the one intended; for example, taking opioid pain relievers for anxiety or stimulants to enhance academic performance. Prescription drugs can also be **abused** by persons using the drugs in ways that are **harmful** or **dangerous** to the body; for example, taking the drugs to feel euphoria (get a high) or to escape from reality. Prescription drugs include opioid pain relievers, sedatives, tranquillisers, antibiotics, steroids, diet pills, amphetamines and hormonal injections.

Non-prescription drugs

A **non-prescription drug** is any drug that can be obtained without a prescription. Some non-prescription drugs are **legal** and include **alcohol**, **tobacco** and **over-the-counter drugs**. Alcohol and tobacco, however, can only be used legally by persons over a certain age, which differs from country to country. Over-the-counter drugs are medicinal drugs that can be obtained from a pharmacy without a prescription; for example, cough medicines, decongestants, painkillers, nonsteroidal anti-inflammatory drugs (NSAIDs) and laxatives. Other non-prescription drugs are **illegal** and include **cocaine**, **methamphetamine**, **ecstasy** and **marijuana** (in most countries). Alcohol, tobacco and illegal drugs are also known as **recreational drugs** because they are usually used for **non-medical** purposes such as pleasure-seeking. All non-prescription drugs can be **misused** and **abused**.

Effects of drugs on the nervous system

Drugs can also be **classified** into **four** categories based on the effects they have on the **nervous system: stimulants**, **depressants**, **hallucinogens** and **narcotics**. Some drugs can fall into more than one category; for example, marijuana (cannabis) can be classified as a stimulant, depressant or hallucinogen (see Figure 7.12), ecstasy is both a stimulant and a hallucinogen, and opioids are both depressants and narcotics.

Figure 7.12 *Marijuana flowers are dried, rolled into joints and smoked*

- **Stimulants** are also known as **'uppers'**. They **speed up** the body's functions and the functioning of the central nervous system. They increase the activity of two chemicals in the brain, known as **dopamine** and **norepinephrine**, and these make a person feel more awake, alert, attentive and anxious, and they produce feelings of pleasure and euphoria. They also stimulate the peripheral nervous system, leading to an increase in heart rate and blood pressure, and they increase energy levels and physical stamina. Examples include nicotine, caffeine, amphetamines, marijuana, methamphetamine, cocaine (see Figure 7.13) and ecstasy.

Figure 7.13 *Cocaine powder on dried coca leaves from which it is extracted*

- **Depressants** are also known as 'downers'. They **slow down** the body's functions and the functioning of the central nervous system. They enhance the activity of a chemical called **gamma-aminobutyric acid (GABA)** in the brain, which inhibits the activity of neurones (nerve cells). This leads to a person feeling calm, relaxed and drowsy or fatigued, and helps reduce anxiety, tension and stress. They also inhibit the activity of neurones in the peripheral nervous system, which can cause skeletal muscles to relax, impair coordination and lower heart rate, blood pressure and breathing rate. Examples include alcohol, sedatives, tranquillisers, marijuana and opioids, such as heroin.

- **Hallucinogens** are drugs that alter a person's **perception of reality** by altering how impulses are transmitted in the brain. They can make a person see, hear, feel or experience things that are not there or are distorted from reality. They can alter thought patterns leading to changes in a person's perception of time, space and self-awareness, and they lead to irrational or bizarre behaviour, aggression and/or paranoia, anxiety, mood changes and loss of contact with reality. Examples include ecstasy, LSD (acid), marijuana, mescaline and magic mushrooms.
- **Narcotics**, also known as **opioids**, are drugs that give **relief** from moderate to severe **pain** by binding to tiny parts of nerve cells, known as opioid receptors, in the brain and blocking the feeling of pain. They can also cause relaxation, drowsiness, impaired judgment, confusion, nausea, slowed breathing and a feeling of euphoria. Examples include codeine, oxycodone, fentanyl, morphine and heroin.

Social and economic effects of drug use and abuse

Drug abuse refers to the use of legal or illegal drugs for unintended purposes or in excessive amounts.

Drug use and **abuse** can have a devastating impact on **individuals**, **families** and **communities**. It harms the user physically and psychologically, and often shortens lives. It can lead to loss of self-worth and emotional stability, personal neglect, loss of earnings or job loss, health issues and financial problems. Higher suicide rates and anti-social behaviour are also associated with drug use and abuse.

Financial and other problems experienced by the **user** can begin a cycle of lying and deceit, and can cause the user to turn to crime or prostitution to get money to pay for the drugs. Crime can lead to arrest and imprisonment, and prostitution exposes the user to infection with STIs. Use of intravenous drugs exposes the user to HIV/AIDS and hepatitis B and C if unsterilised needles are used, and babies born to addicts may have developmental problems or be addicted to the drug themselves.

Drug abuse also upsets relationships with **family** and **friends**, and can lead to neglect or abuse of family members, especially children and the elderly, resulting in unstable and disturbing family environments. It may also cause children to lose one or both parents, and ultimately leads to dysfunctional families.

The cost to **society** of drug abuse is high. Job losses can lead to reduced productivity and weakened economies. Increases in automobile accidents that occur when users drive under the influence of drugs can lead to serious injury and loss of life, and violent crimes associated with drug use cause injury, loss of life and communities to live in fear. More and more resources have to be used to treat and rehabilitate drug users and addicts, to fight drug related crimes, and to apprehend, convict and imprison traffickers and pushers of illegal drugs. Ultimately, economies suffer, standards of living are reduced, and human resources are lost through drug use and abuse.

Recalling facts

1.
   a Define the term 'drug'.
   b Distinguish between prescription drugs and non-prescription drugs.
   c Give THREE examples of prescription drugs and THREE examples of non-prescription drugs.

2. Drugs can be classified into FOUR categories based on their effects on the nervous system. Name these categories, outline the effects that drugs in EACH category have on the body and give <u>named</u> examples of TWO drugs in EACH category.

3. Describe the effects of drug use and abuse on society.

Applying facts

4 Explain why cough syrup that can be bought off the shelf at any pharmacy is considered to be a drug.

5 Suggest why it is illegal to drive with a blood alcohol content (BAC) over a certain, fixed limit in most countries of the world.

6 Daniel recently finished school, and soon after starting a new job one of his colleagues introduced him to cocaine. Explain the possible consequences if Daniel's cocaine use continues.

Analysing data

7 The bar graph in Figure 7.14 shows the total number of healthy years of life lost due to premature death or years of life lived with a disability that can be attributable to drug use globally in 2015, rounded to the nearest 100 000, and the percentage change in years lost from 2005.

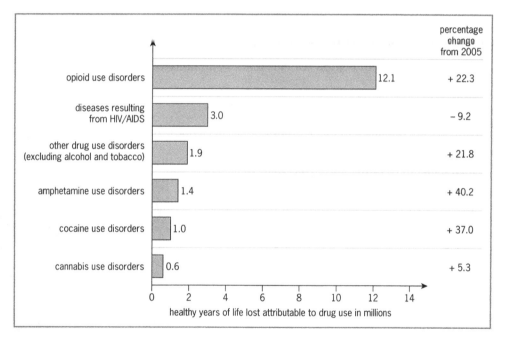

Figure 7.14 *Bar graph showing the number of healthy years of life lost attributable to drug use in 2015 and the percentage change in years lost from 2005*

a i Which drug caused the lowest number of healthy years of life to be lost in 2015?

ii Which drug showed the greatest percentage change in healthy years of life lost between 2005 and 2015? Did this change show an increase or decrease in years lost?

iii Which drug appears to have the MOST severe effects on the body? Explain how you deduced your answer.

b i Describe the overall trend in healthy years of life lost due to drug use disorders from 2005 to 2015.

ii What deduction can be made about the trends in global drug use from your answer to **b i**? Explain your answer.

iii Identify THREE possible consequences of the trend described in **b i** on societies worldwide.

c i Explain why diseases resulting from HIV/AIDS are included in this bar graph.

ii Suggest ONE possible reason why the number of healthy years of life lost due to diseases resulting from HIV/AIDS, that were attributable to drug use, decreased from 2005 to 2015.

d Name TWO drugs that could be contributing to the number of 'other drug use disorders'.

Pests and pest control

Learning objectives

- Define **pest**, **parasite**, **pathogen** and **vector**.
- Discuss **conditions** that **encourage** the **breeding** of **household pests**.
- Recommend **appropriate methods** of **pest control**.
- Describe **relevant methods** of **control** for **mosquitoes** and **houseflies**.

Pests, parasites, pathogens and vectors

*A **pest** is any organism, usually a plant or animal, that has a harmful effect on humans, their food or their living conditions.*

Pests can cause damage to crops and other resources, such as forests, and they can compete with humans for natural resources. **Household pests** invade homes and can damage structures, deposit faecal pellets, eat human food, damage clothing and bite or sting humans. Many of these pests are also **vectors of disease** because they carry **pathogens** in or on their bodies. Household pests include **cockroaches** (see Figure 7.15), **flies, ants, rats, mice, termites, bed bugs, clothes moths** and **mosquitoes**.

*A **parasite** is an organism that lives in or on another living organism known as its **host** and gains benefit at the expense of the host.*

Parasites obtain their **food** from their host and they usually harm their host to varying extents, from mild irritation to severe disease or death. Parasites include tapeworms, hookworms, ticks, fleas, bed bugs and lice.

Figure 7.15 *Cockroaches are household pests*

*A **pathogen** is a parasitic microorganism that causes **disease** in its host.*

Pathogens damage the health of their host. Pathogens include **viruses** such as those causing dengue fever, HIV/AIDS, COVID-19, the common cold and influenza, **bacteria** such as those causing gonorrhoea, syphilis, tuberculosis and cholera, **fungi** such as those that causing athlete's foot, canididiasis (thrush) and ringworm, and **protozoans** such as those causing malaria, amoebic dysentery and sleeping sickness.

*A **vector** is an organism that carries **pathogens** in or on its body and transmits the pathogens from one host to another.*

Vectors can transmit pathogens by carrying them **inside** their bodies, where the pathogens **multiply** and are then usually delivered to the new host by the vector biting the host. They can also transmit pathogens by picking them up on the **outside** of their bodies, and then delivering them to the new host by physical contact. Vectors are **not** usually harmed by the pathogens they carry and include **mosquitoes** which can transmit malaria, yellow fever, dengue fever, chikungunya and Zika fever, **rats** which can transmit leptospirosis, **houseflies** which can transmit gastroenteritis, cholera and typhoid, **ticks** which can transmit Lyme disease and **fleas** which can transmit bubonic plague.

Conditions that encourage breeding of household pests

The **improper disposal of waste** and **improper household hygiene** provide a variety of **conditions** that can encourage **household pests** to breed by providing them with favourable environments in which to live and reproduce. Many of these pests are also **vectors** of disease, including cockroaches, flies, rats and mosquitoes.

Improper disposal of waste

Many human activities, both **domestic** and **industrial**, produce **waste** which must be properly treated and disposed of so that it does not provide a breeding ground for household pests. This waste can be divided into **sewage** and **solid waste**.

- **Sewage** is **wastewater** that comes from homes, schools, hospitals, industry and rainwater runoff from the streets that enters drains. It can contain a variety of components, including faeces, urine, detergents, organic matter and food particles, and it must be properly treated before being released into the environment. If **untreated sewage**, known as **raw sewage**, is deliberately disposed of in the environment, or enters from poorly maintained sewage and drainage systems, it promotes the breeding of household pests and pathogens.

- **Solid waste** such as **domestic refuse** includes paper and packaging, cans, glass and plastic items, textiles, food waste and garden waste. This should be stored in sealed containers, collected at least once a week and transported in enclosed trucks to a disposal facility. If it is not stored correctly before collection and not collected regularly, it provides a breeding ground for household pests (see Figure 7.16).

Figure 7.16 *Improper disposal of refuse provides ideal conditions for pests to breed*

Organic matter, food particles or **food waste** in raw sewage or unsealed refuse attracts pests such as cockroaches, flies, ants, rats and mice to feed and breed, and **standing water** in raw sewage or collecting in open containers provides a place for mosquitoes to lay their eggs. Unsealed garbage also provides pests with a place to **hide** from predators and a safe place to reproduce, and **unpleasant odours** given off by waste attract flies, cockroaches and rats to the waste, where they can then breed.

Improper household hygiene

Household environments that are not kept properly **clean** and **tidy** can create a variety of conditions that promote the breeding of household pests.

- **Uncovered** or **incorrectly stored food**, **food spills** and **crumbs of food** left lying around provide readily available **food sources** for pests such as flies, cockroaches, ants, rats and mice. These pests are then more likely to remain and breed in these places with food present.

- Pools of **standing water** in sinks, uncovered drains or in any water-holding containers left lying about, or caused by leaking taps, attract mosquitoes to lay their eggs.

- **Organic waste** such as scraps of food, kitchen waste and pet faeces left lying around provide flies with the ideal conditions to lay their eggs, and it releases unpleasant odours which attract cockroaches and rats, as well as flies.

- **Unclean toilets**, **work surfaces**, **cupboards**, **tables** and **floors**, **unwashed dishes** (see Figure 7.17) and **uncovered drains** attract pests such as cockroaches, ants, flies and rats.

- **Clutter**, **debris** and any **unused items** left lying about create hiding places for pests such as cockroaches, rats, mice and mosquitoes, and safe places in which to reproduce.

Methods of pest control

Pests can be controlled by **four** main methods: **biological control**, **chemical control**, **sanitary control** and **mechanical control**.

- **Biological control** involves using **natural enemies** of the pests to kill them, such as predators or parasites. For example, ladybird beetles are natural predators of small, sap-sucking insects known as aphids that can damage crops. When released into the environment, these beetles can consume large numbers of aphids (see Figure 7.18). A parasitic wasp is also used to control the pink hibiscus mealybug in the Caribbean and a fish known as tilapia is used to control mosquitoes (see Table 7.4 on page 132). Care must be taken to ensure that the natural enemy does not become a pest itself.

- **Chemical control** involves using **chemicals**, known as **pesticides**, to kill pests. These include insecticides, used to kill insects and rodenticides, used to kill rodents such as rats and mice. These can be applied by spraying (see Figure 7.19), dusting, fogging or as baits.

Figure 7.17 *Unwashed dishes and food scraps attract rats*

Figure 7.18 *Biological control of aphids by a ladybird beetle*

Figure 7.19 *Spraying a chemical to control pests*

Pesticides, however, can be harmful to harmless and beneficial organisms such as bees which are essential for pollination, and they can disrupt ecosystems and pollute land, water and the air.

- **Sanitary control** involves **removing conditions** that attract pests. For example, treating all sewage, sealing all refuse, collecting refuse regularly and disposing of it in the correct manner, and keeping household environments clean, tidy and free of improperly stored food, standing water and organic waste.

- **Mechanical control** involves **physically removing** or **excluding** pests from an area. For example, using traps, sealing entry points and using fencing or other barriers such as nets and screens.

Control of mosquitoes and houseflies

Mosquitoes and **houseflies** are **vectors** of several diseases, some of which can be fatal (see page 129). Some of these have no effective cures or medical measures available to prevent them such as vaccines and drugs, therefore, to reduce the incidence of these diseases within populations it is crucial that measures are put in place to **control** their **vectors**. Understanding the **life cycles** of these vectors is essential to develop the most effective methods to control them.

Life cycle of a mosquito

The life cycle of a mosquito has **four distinct stages**. These are illustrated in Figure 7.20.

- **Egg** – The adult female lays eggs in standing water and the eggs float on the surface of the water.
- **Larva** – The larva hatches from the egg. Larvae live in the water. They hang from the surface and breathe air through breathing tubes, **feed** on microscopic organisms in the water and **grow**.
- **Pupa** – The pupa develops from the larva. Pupae live in the water, where they hang from the surface and breathe air through breathing tubes. **Larval tissue re-organises** into adult tissue in the pupa.
- **Adult** or **imago** – The adult emerges from the pupa. Adults rest in cool, dark places around human residences during the day, and fly and feed on nectar and sugars from plants in the evenings. After mating, the female requires a **blood meal** to mature her eggs before she lays them. She usually obtains the blood from a human and can transmit any pathogens she is carrying whilst feeding.

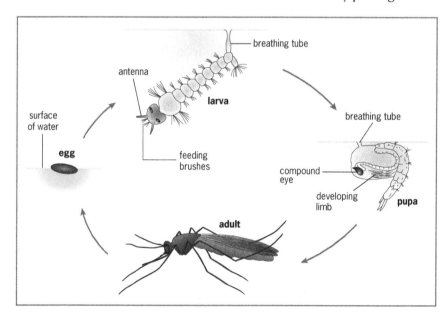

Figure 7.20 *The life cycle of a mosquito*

Life cycle of a housefly

The life cycle of a housefly has the **same four stages** as the mosquito. These are illustrated in Figure 7.21. The adult female lays her **eggs** in decaying organic matter such as compost, faeces, manure and the bodies of dead animals. The **larvae** hatch from the eggs and they feed on the organic matter, grow and pupate, forming **pupae**. An **adult** then emerges from each pupa and starts to fly, feeding on decaying organic matter and human food.

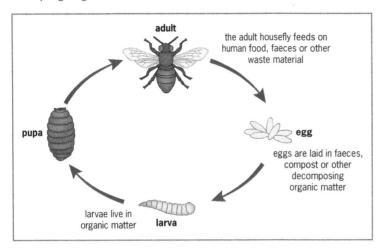

Figure 7.21 *The life cycle of a housefly*

Methods used to control mosquitoes and houseflies

Specific measures that can be used to **control** mosquitoes and houseflies are summarised in Table 7.4.

Table 7.4 *Methods used to control mosquitoes and houseflies*

Pest	Methods of control
Mosquitoes	To control mosquito **eggs**, **larvae** and **pupae** • **Drain** all areas of standing water and remove all containers that collect water so that females have nowhere to lay their eggs. • Add **insecticides** to breeding areas to kill larvae and pupae. • Introduce **fish**, such as tilapia or mosquito fish, into breeding areas to feed on larvae and pupae. • Add mosquito dunks, containing a soil **bacterium** that produces toxins harmful to mosquito larvae, to areas of standing water. • Spray **oil**, **kerosene** or non-toxic **lecithins** onto still-water breeding areas to prevent females from laying eggs, and larvae and pupae from breathing. To control **adult** mosquitoes • Spray with **insecticides** to kill adults. • Remove **dense vegetation** to reduce protection for adults during daylight hours. • Place **mosquito screens** over windows and doors to prevent adults entering buildings, and place **mosquito nets** impregnated with insecticide over beds at night.
Houseflies	• Spray adults with **insecticides** to kill them. • Use **fly traps** to kill adults. • **Dispose** of all human and animal waste properly so that females have nowhere to lay their eggs. • **Treat** all sewage. • **Cover** food so that adults are not attracted to it and cannot land on it.

Recalling facts

1 Distinguish among a pest, a parasite and a pathogen.

2 Outline FOUR ways that improper household hygiene can encourage household pests to breed.

3 Differentiate between the following:

  a biological and chemical pest control

  b mechanical and sanitary pest control.

4 **a** What is a vector?

  b Why is it important to understand the life cycle of a vector?

5 Identify the FOUR stages in the life cycle of a mosquito and state where EACH is found.

6 Suggest FOUR ways you could control houseflies in your home.

Applying facts

7 Many households in the islands of the Caribbean lack connections to sewage systems and also regular refuse collections. Discuss the possible consequences of this.

8 The Sterile Insect Technique (SIT), which involves rearing large numbers of male mosquitoes, sterilising them using radiation and then releasing them into the environment, is being used in various parts of the world to control mosquito populations.

  a Identify the type of pest control described.

  b Explain how SIT controls mosquito populations.

  c Suggest, with a reason, whether you consider SIT or spraying with insecticides to be the BEST method to control mosquitoes.

9 You read in your local newspaper that there is an outbreak of dengue in your country. Outline measures that individuals in your community can take to protect themselves against the disease.

Food contaminants and food preservation

Learning objectives

- Describe the **types** of **food contaminants**.
- Determine **conditions** which **promote** the **growth** of **microorganisms**.
- Describe the **effects** of **microorganisms** in **food spoilage**, **production** and **processing**.
- Describe **procedures** to **prevent** the **growth** of **bread mould**.
- Apply the **principles** used in **food preservation**.

Types of food contaminants

Food contaminants are substances that enter food supplies unintentionally and have the potential to cause harm to the consumer. Food contaminants include **pathogens**, **chemical contaminants** and **physical contaminants.**

- **Pathogens** that contaminate food include **viruses**, **bacteria**, **fungi** and **parasitic protozoans**. If food containing pathogens is consumed, it can cause a variety of **food-borne illnesses** including **gastrointestinal infections** caused by the pathogens themselves and **food poisoning** caused by toxins produced by the pathogens. These pathogens can be found in a variety of food, especially uncooked or undercooked meat, poultry, eggs and seafood, unpasteurised dairy products, processed and ready-to-eat foods such as processed meats, and fresh fruits and vegetables that become contaminated during growing, harvesting or processing.

- **Chemical contaminants** include insecticides, herbicides and other pesticides, heavy metal ions such as lead, mercury, cadmium and arsenic ions, industrial chemicals such as polychlorinated biphenyls or PCBs and dioxins, and chemicals from certain food packaging materials such as plasticisers. These chemicals can be **directly toxic** if consumed or they can cause **chronic** (long-lasting) health problems, including cancer. **Food additives** such as artificial colourings, flavour enhancers and preservatives can also be considered chemical contaminants because they can pose health risks if consumed in excessive amounts and can cause allergic reactions in sensitive individuals (see pages 115 to 116).

- **Physical contaminants** include foreign objects that accidently get into food products during processing or packaging; for example, pieces of broken glass, metal and plastic, including microplastics, splinters of wood, soil, fingernails, hair and dead insects. These can cause damage to teeth, choking, injury to the digestive system and other digestive issues.

Conditions that promote the growth of microorganisms

Microorganisms, including bacteria and fungi, need certain **conditions** in order to grow. **All** microorganisms require **moisture**, an **optimal temperature** and **nutrients**.

- Microorganisms require a certain amount of **moisture** to grow because water is essential for enzyme activity and for chemical reactions to occur in their cells.

- Microorganisms require a certain **optimal (ideal) temperature** so that their **enzymes** can function as efficiently as possible (see page 180). This is between about 20 °C and 40 °C for most microorganisms.

- Microorganisms require a source of **food** to provide them with the **nutrients** they need to grow and reproduce.

- Many microorganisms require **oxygen** so that they can carry out aerobic respiration, which provides them with the **energy** they need to grow and reproduce. Some, however, obtain this energy from anaerobic respiration, which does not require oxygen.

- Most microorganisms require a **pH** range of 6.5 to 7.5 so that their enzymes can function efficiently.

Effects of microorganisms in food spoilage, production and processing

When provided with **moisture**, a suitable **temperature** and a source of **nutrients**, certain microorganisms cause **food** to **spoil**, while others are used in the **production** and **processing** of certain foods. These were discussed in detail on page 108.

Procedures to retard and prevent the growth of bread mould

Various species of **moulds** (multicellular fungi) can grow on bread, where they often form fuzzy-looking patches of different colours including green, blue, black, yellow and white (see Figure 7.2 on page 108). If **spores** from any of these species land on bread, they can germinate and form thread-like **hyphae** which grow over the surface of the bread by absorbing moisture and nutrients from the bread (see page 108). The growth of bread mould can be slowed or prevented in various ways.

- Store the bread in a clean, dry, **air-tight container** to exclude oxygen and prevent any spores in the air from landing on the bread and germinating.
- Store the bread in a **cool temperature** such as a refrigerator to slow down the growth of the mould by slowing down enzyme activity (see page 180).
- **Freeze** the bread in moisture-proof packaging to inhibit enzyme activity and remove any available moisture by converting it into ice crystals.
- Include a **preservative** in the dough when making bread to inhibit the growth of bread mould. Natural preservatives are preferable; for example, ascorbic acid.

Principles used in food preservation

Food preservation refers to the process of treating and handling food in such a way as to stop or greatly slow down spoilage and prevent food-borne illness while maintaining nutritional value.

Food preservation aims to create conditions that are **unfavourable** for the growth of microorganisms that cause food to spoil or to become contaminated with toxins that cause food poisoning, whilst maintaining the **quality** of the food, mainly its nutritional value, flavour, colour and texture. This can be achieved in several ways.

- Removing **moisture** from the food to prevent the growth of microorganisms by inhibiting enzyme activity and cellular reactions.
- Storing the food at **low temperatures** to slow down or stop the growth of microorganisms by slowing down or stopping enzyme activity.
- **Heating** the food to kill any microorganisms present and then sealing it in an **airtight** container to prevent microorganisms from re-entering and to exclude oxygen.
- Lowering the **pH** of the food to make conditions too **acidic** for microorganisms to grow due to their enzymes becoming denatured (see page 180).
- Adding chemicals known as **preservatives** to the food to inhibit the growth of microorganisms, mainly due to the antimicrobial properties of the preservatives.

Methods used to preserve food

A variety of different **methods** can be used to **preserve food**. Each method uses one or more of the principles outlined above. These methods are summarised in Table 7.5 and examples are shown in Figure 7.22 on page 137.

Table 7.5 *Methods of preserving food*

Method	Principles of the method
Salting	**Salt (sodium chloride)** is rubbed into the food and left for a certain period so it can penetrate into the food. Alternatively, the food is placed into a concentrated salt solution known as **brine**. The salt **withdraws water** from the food by **osmosis** so microorganisms cannot survive and grow. It also enhances the flavour of the food. Examples include salt fish, salt pork and olives.
Adding sugar	The food is boiled in a concentrated **sugar** solution, sometimes to the point of crystallisation. The sugar **withdraws water** from the food by **osmosis** so microorganisms cannot survive and grow. It also adds sweetness to the food. For example, jams and crystallised or candied fruits.
Curing	A mixture of **salt**, **sodium nitrate** or **nitrite**, and sometimes **sugar**, is rubbed into the food, usually meat, and left for a certain period to penetrate. The nitrates and nitrites have **antimicrobial properties** which inhibit the growth of microorganisms, especially the bacterium *Clostridium botulinum* that causes botulism, a potentially fatal illness. The mixture also **withdraws water** from the food, enhances flavour and helps develop the pink colour of cured meats. For example, ham, bacon, corned beef and salami.
Drying	The food is **dried** to **remove all water** present so microorganisms are unable to survive and grow. This can be done naturally or artificially. • When dried **naturally**, the food is placed on racks or trays in direct **sunlight**. Alternatively, it can be placed on racks or trays in a **solar dryer**, which consists of a well-ventilated chamber with transparent walls that trap **heat** from the Sun (see Figure 7.23 on page 137). • When dried **artificially**, the food is placed in an **oven** at about 60 °C to 70 °C or in a **dehydrator** specifically designed to dry food at between 35 °C and 60 °C. Examples include sun-dried tomatoes, dried fruits and vegetables, grains, herbs and spices, and dried milk powders.
Pickling	The food is placed in **vinegar**, which is a dilute solution of **ethanoic (acetic) acid**. The vinegar **lowers** the **pH** of the food so that it is too low or too acidic for microorganisms to grow. Salt and spices are often added to the vinegar. Pickling adds a tangy flavour and crisp texture to the food. For example, pickled onions and cucumbers.
Heating	The food is **heated** to **kill** any microorganisms present and then **sealed** in airtight containers to prevent microorganisms from re-entering. Various techniques can be used which heat the food to different temperatures. • **Canning** involves heating food in sealed jars or cans in a boiling water bath at **100 °C**, a steam bath or a pressure canner for a specified time. Examples include canned fruits, vegetables, fish and meat. • **Pasteurisation** involves heating the food to **72 °C** for 15 to 25 seconds and cooling it rapidly. For example, milk. • **Ultra-high temperature treatment (UHT)** involves heating food to temperatures higher than **135 °C** for 1 to 2 seconds and cooling it rapidly. For example, UHT milk, soups and baby foods.

Method	Principles of the method
Refrigeration	The food is stored at **low temperatures** to **slow down** or **stop** the growth of microorganisms. This can be done in two ways.
	• Placing the food in a **refrigerator** which keeps it at about **4 °C**. This **slows** the growth of microorganisms; it does not completely stop their growth. Energy efficient, **inverter type refrigerators** are preferable because they use variable speed compressors that adjust their power output to match the cooling demands, which saves energy.
	• **Freezing** the food at temperatures of **−18 °C** and below stops the growth of microorganisms. Examples include frozen meat, fish and vegetables.
Treating with other preservatives	A variety of other **chemical preservatives** can be added to food to **inhibit** the growth of microorganisms.
	• **Sulfur dioxide** and **sulfites** are used to preserve foods and beverages such as dried fruits, fruit juices, soft drinks, fish, wine and beer.
	• **Benzoates** are often used to preserve acidic foods and beverages such as fruit purees, jams, fruit juices and soft drinks.
	• **Sorbates** are used to preserve foods and beverages such as cheese, baked goods and wine.

a salt fish   b candied fruits   c cured meats and brined olives

Figure 7.22 *Preserved foods*

a a simple solar dryer   b herbs being dried in a solar dryer greenhouse

Figure 7.23 *Solar dryers*

Recalling facts

1. a What are food contaminants?
   b Identify THREE different types of food contaminants and distinguish among them.

2. Name THREE conditions that all microorganisms require to grow.

3. Explain how microorganisms cause food to spoil.

4. Explain how Sara can slow down the growth of mould on her bread.

5. a What do you understand by the term 'food preservation'?
   b Outline the principles involved in food preservation.

6. Explain how EACH of the following methods preserves food:
   a curing   b adding sugar   c refrigeration.

7. Explain how a solar dryer functions to preserve food.

Applying facts

8. Suggest why 'use by' dates are placed on certain food items, such as raw meat and poultry.

9. What type of food contaminant is EACH of the following:
   a a human hair   b tartrazine, a yellow dye   c norovirus?

10. Kamal notices that mould grows much faster on bread stored in a transparent plastic bag on his kitchen counter than if it is stored in the same type of bag in his refrigerator.
    a Suggest a hypothesis for Kamal's observation.
    b Design an experiment that you could perform to test your hypothesis. Your design must include the aim of your experiment, your method and the results you would expect to get if your hypothesis is correct.
    c Identify the controlled variables, manipulate variable and responding variable.

11. Construct a table using the following column headings: heating, lowering pH and removing moisture. Place EACH of the following methods of preserving food into one or more of the columns: curing, pickling, drying, canning, salting, adding sugar and pasteurisation.

12. Distinguish between using vinegar and sodium chloride as methods of preserving food.

Section B
Energy

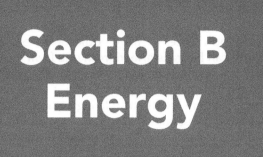

The topics covered in this section are:

- Energy and its interconversions
- Photosynthesis and energy transfer in the environment
- The human diet
- Digestion in humans
- Respiration
- Breathing, gaseous exchange and smoking
- Fossil fuels and alternative sources of energy
- Current electricity and its applications
- Reducing the impact of electrical and fire hazards
- Temperature control and ventilation

8 Conservation of energy

Energy is important in our everyday lives. When we apply **forces** to move bodies, we are using **energy** and doing **work**. Energy can exist in many forms and can be **transformed** from one **form** to another. The **Sun** supplies the energy needed to carry out most of the large number of processes which occur on Earth: the **motion** of our rivers, oceans and winds; the changes in our **weather**; the making of their own **food** during **photosynthesis** by **plants**, which pass on **energy** to other **living organisms** through **food chains**; the **sports** that we play; the **light** that we see and the **sounds** that we hear, are all phenomena linked with energy being transferred from one place to another and transformed from one form to another.

Energy and its interconversions

Learning objectives

- Explain that **energy** can produce **change** as it does **work**.
- Explain that energy can exist in different **forms**.
- Discuss the **transfer** of **energy** from one **place** to another.
- Discuss the **transformation** of **energy** from one **form** to another.
- Discuss the **interconversion** between **mass** and **energy**.
- Describe the methods used to **save energy** supplied to vehicles.
- Describe the effects of the **internal combustion engine** on the **environment** and how they can be **reduced**.

Energy, work and change

*Energy is the ability to do **work** (the ability to produce change).*

*Work is done when the point of application of a **force** moves and is measured as the **product** of the force and the **distance moved in the direction of the force**.*

The **joule** is the **SI unit** of work or energy.

*1 **joule** is the work done (or energy used) when a force of 1 N moves an object through a distance of 1 m in the direction of the force.*

Figure 8.1 on page 141 shows FOUR forces (F, f, mg, R) acting on a block being pushed through a distance, d. Forces are discussed in more detail in Chapter 16.

Work is done by the pushing force, F: $W_F = F \times d$
(**positive work** since the force and distance are similarly directed)

Work is done by the frictional force, f: $W_f = - f \times d$
(**negative work** since the force and distance are oppositely directed)

No work is done by the weight, mg: $W_{mg} = 0$
(**no work** is done since the force and distance are perpendicular to each other)

No work is done by the normal reaction, R: $W_R = 0$
(**no work** is done since the force and distance are perpendicular to each other)

Forces can do work on an object, but only when the force acts along the **same line** as the **distance** through which the object moves.

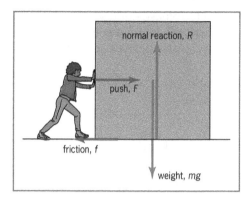

Figure 8.1 *Forces can do work*

Energy can cause different types of change

* Energy **stored** in a compressed spring produces a **change of position** or **motion** when **released**.
* Energy **added** to water in the form of heat causes a **change of temperature**.
* Energy **absorbed** by ice as it melts causes a **change of physical state**.
* Energy from a spark plug of a car engine causes a **change of chemical state** of the gasoline as it produces water vapour and oxides of carbon on **combustion**.

Forms of energy

Many of the different forms of energy are shown in Table 8.1.

Table 8.1 *Some forms of energy*

Energy	Description
Gravitational potential energy	**Energy stored by a body** due to its **position** in a **gravitational force field.**
	It increases as the body **rises** above the Earth's surface.
	A coconut in a tree has gravitational potential energy. If it disconnects from the tree, it has the potential to fall to the ground.
Elastic potential energy	**Energy stored by a body** due to its **stretched or compressed state.**
	A **stretched** elastic band has the potential to propel an object from a slingshot.
	A **compressed** spring has the potential to shoot a toy rocket into the air.
	An inflated balloon containing **compressed air** can dart around the room if its neck is opened.
Nuclear potential energy	**Energy stored in an atomic nucleus** due to the **physical state of the nucleus.**
	Unstable atomic nuclei have the potential to shoot out **particles** and gamma **radiation.** This is how nuclear power plants obtain energy to generate electricity.

Energy	Description
Chemical potential energy	**Energy stored by a body** due to its **chemical state**.
	Food has the potential to release energy as **chemical bonds are broken** during **respiration**. This is how we obtain energy to perform all our body functions.
	Fuels such as gasoline and diesel have the potential to release energy as chemical bonds are broken during their **combustion**. This is how the **internal combustion engine** (see page 153) provides energy to vehicles and other devices so that they can do **work** as they **move things** around.
	Batteries contain **chemicals** which have the potential to release electrical energy when **bonds are broken** during their chemical reactions.
Electrical energy	**Energy carried by** moving **positive** or **negative charges**.
	Negatively charged particles known as **electrons** transfer electrical energy through **metal** wires in electrical circuits.
	Positive and **negative ions** can transfer electrical energy through **ionic solutions** or **molten ionic substances**. An example of a molten ionic substance is table salt that has been heated past its melting point.
Kinetic energy	**Energy stored by a body** due to its **motion**.
	The kinetic energy of a body depends on two factors, **mass** and **speed**. A fast-moving cricket ball has a high kinetic energy due to its **high speed**. A heavy truck has a high kinetic energy due to its **large mass**.
Thermal energy	**Energy possessed by a body** due to the **motion of its particles** (atoms, molecules, ions).
	As a body is heated, its particles gain **kinetic energy** and this is expressed as an increase in **temperature**.
Heat energy	**Thermal energy** transferred from **hotter** to **cooler bodies** due to their **temperature difference**.
	NOTE: Thermal energy and heat energy are usually used interchangeably at the level of this course. To be more scientific, however, thermal energy becomes heat energy when it **transfers** from a body of **higher temperature** to one of **lower temperature**.
Sound energy	**Energy transferred** as **particle vibrations** through a material (solid, liquid or gas) in the form of a **longitudinal** wave (see Figure 8.6 and 8.7, page 147).
	The **speed of sound** in solids is greater than in liquids, and in liquids it is greater than in gases. This is because faster transmission occurs when the particles are closer together.
	Loudness: The **greater** the **amplitude** (maximum displacement) of the vibration, the **louder** is the sound as it pushes and pulls our eardrum to a greater extent.
	Pitch: The **higher** the **frequency** (number of vibrations per second), the **higher** the **pitch**. '*Do-re-mi-fa-so-la-ti-do*' are notes of increasing pitch.
	A soft but high-pitched **squeak** of a **mouse** has a **small amplitude** and **high frequency**. A loud, high-pitched screech of the **brakes** of a **train** has a **large amplitude** and a **high frequency**.
	Astronauts in space communicate by radio waves since **sound cannot pass through a vacuum**.

Energy	Description
	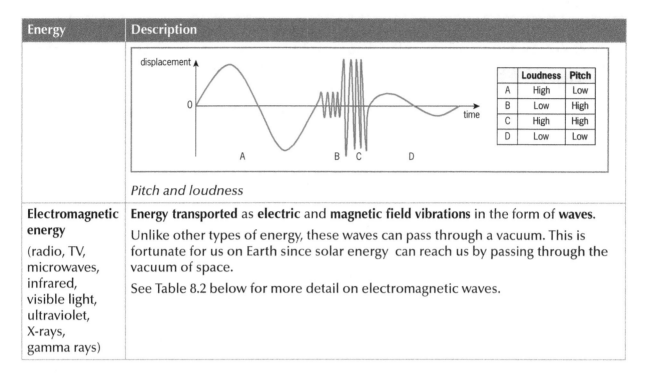 *Pitch and loudness*
Electromagnetic energy (radio, TV, microwaves, infrared, visible light, ultraviolet, X-rays, gamma rays)	**Energy transported** as **electric** and **magnetic field vibrations** in the form of **waves**. Unlike other types of energy, these waves can pass through a vacuum. This is fortunate for us on Earth since solar energy can reach us by passing through the vacuum of space. See Table 8.2 below for more detail on electromagnetic waves.

Potential energy

Table 8.1 includes several types of potential energy. A **general definition** is given below:

*The **potential energy** of a body is the energy which it stores due to:*

- *its **position in a force** field; for example, gravitational force field, elastic force field or electric force field*
- *its **state** (stretched, compressed, chemical or physical).*

A closer look at electromagnetic waves

Table 8.2 *Wavelengths, production and properties of electromagnetic wave energy*

Type	Relative wavelength	Production and properties
Radio (includes microwaves)		**Production: Aerials** of **radio transmitters** emit radio waves due to electrical circuits oscillating within them. • Detected by **aerials** of **radio receivers**. • Can **diffract (deviate around obstacles) more** than the other electromagnetic waves since they are of relatively long wavelength. They are therefore used for **radio communication** so they can carry information around mountains, buildings, etc. • Microwaves have the smallest wavelength of the radio wave band. They have a **heating effect** on water and fat molecules and so are used to heat our food. • Microwaves are also used for **cell phone communication**.
Infrared (IR)		**Production:** All bodies above 0 K (−273 °C) emit IR. • Detected as **warmth** when incident on our skin. • Detected by certain **photographic** (film).

Type	Relative wavelength	Production and properties
Light (RO GBIV)	∧∧∧	**Production:** Bodies above **1100 °C** emit light. • Detected by the eye. • Is comprised of seven colours (red, orange, yellow, green, blue, indigo, violet) which when **combined** form **white light**. • Detected by certain types of **photographic film**.
Ultraviolet (UV)	∧∧∧∧	**Production:** Very hot bodies such as the Sun, welding torches, lightning, filaments of lamps, etc. • Produces **fluorescence** of certain materials (see page 244). • **Destroys living tissue** and causes sunburn. • Detected by certain types of **photographic film**.
X-rays and gamma rays	∧∧∧∧∧	**Production: X-rays** can be produced by **high voltage machines**. **Gamma rays** are produced **naturally** and **spontaneously** in the **atomic nuclei** of **unstable atoms**. • Both are used to **transfer energy through flesh and metals to form images** on **photographic film**. • Detected by certain types of **photographic film**. • Gamma rays, emitted during nuclear reactions, can carry energy through our flesh just like X-rays. • Both are high frequency electromagnetic waves and can be **hazardous to our health** since they can **ionise atoms** in our body cells to produce **cancer**. • Both cause **fluorescence**. • Both can be used for **cancer therapy** as they can both destroy cancerous tumours.

Transformation, transfer and transport of energy

Energy can be **transformed**, **transferred** and **transported**.

*Energy is **transformed** when it changes from **one type to another**.*

*Energy is **transferred** when it passes from one **body** (solid, liquid, gas) **to another**.*

*Energy must be **transported** between two bodies if an **energy transfer** is being made between bodies which are **in different locations**.*

The following situations show how energy can be transformed, transferred and transported.

Conduction

If we touch a hot pot on a stove, heat energy is **transferred** from the pot to our hand by **conduction**. In this case, the hand and pot are in the same location and so there is no need for transport.

As one end of a bar is **heated**, atoms or molecules there absorb the energy and begin to **vibrate faster** than before. They **transfer** the **increased kinetic energy** among themselves on **collision** as each collision occurs at a particular location.

Radiation

If, however, we stand away from the stove and feel the radiation, the radiant energy is only **transferred** to us after it has been **transported** by an **electromagnetic wave** and is **received by our body**.

Collisions

During a **collision**, energy is **transferred** between two bodies at the point of contact (same location) and so there is no transport involved.

Convection

During convection, energy is **transported** upwards by particles moving from a **warmer region** to a **cooler region**.

Electrical

Chemical energy in a battery can be **transformed** to electrical energy as the chemicals react.

This energy is **transferred** as electrons leave the battery and enter the wires.

The conducting wires then can **transport** the energy to a filament lamp.

At the lamp the energy is **transformed** to electromagnetic energy, some in the form of infrared (which we detect as warmth) and some to visible light.

Waves

Energy is **transported** across the surface of water by a **water** wave. Kinetic energy of vibrating water particles is **transferred** between adjacent particles as the **transverse** wave progresses.

Similarly, energy is **transported** through a material by a **sound** wave. Kinetic energy of vibrating particles of the material is **transferred** between adjacent particles as the **longitudinal** wave progresses.

Electromagnetic waves, due to the **vibration** of **electric** and **magnetic fields**, can **transport** energy such as light or X-rays, through glass, water, air and even through a vacuum!

Rolling

Kinetic energy can be **transferred** from a moving hand to a bowling ball as it is tossed.

The kinetic energy is then **transported** by the rolling **ball** to the **bowling pins**.

On striking the pins, kinetic energy is **transferred** from the **ball** to the **pins**.

Example 1

Figure 8.2 shows the energy transfers that occur when a cricket ball is struck and caught.

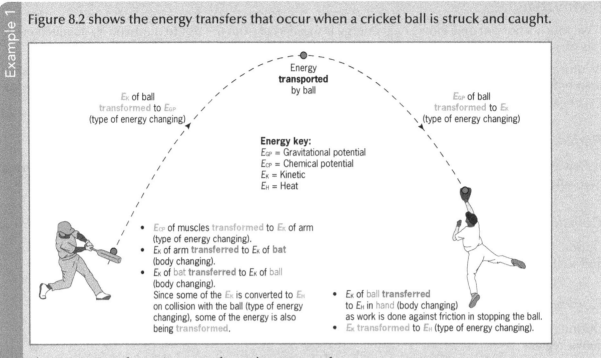

Figure 8.2 *Transformation, transfer and transport of energy*

Example 2

Thermal energy from the Sun can be transported by electromagnetic waves through the vacuum of space (see Figure 8.3). The **energy transfer** is **complete** only when the **Earth absorbs the radiation**.

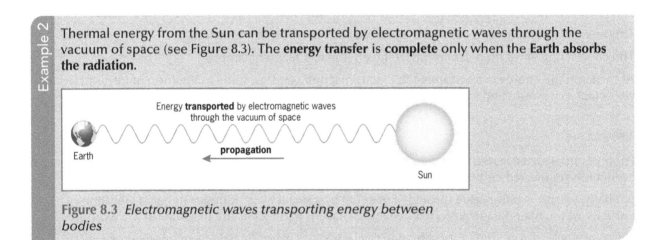

Figure 8.3 *Electromagnetic waves transporting energy between bodies*

Transfer of energy by different types of waves

Waves are produced by vibrations and may be transverse or longitudinal.

Transverse waves

Transverse waves are those whose vibrations are perpendicular to the direction of propagation of the wave.

There is a series of **crests** and **troughs** along the profile of a transverse wave.

Examples include **water** waves, **electromagnetic** waves and the **waves along a rope** or **slinky spring** vibrated **perpendicular** to its **length** from one end (see Figures 8.4 and 8.5 on page 147).

Electromagnetic waves (see Table 8.1) are **transverse** waves that, **unlike other types of waves,** can also travel through a **vacuum.**

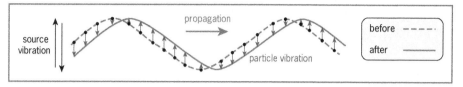

Figure 8.4 *Transverse waves along a rope*

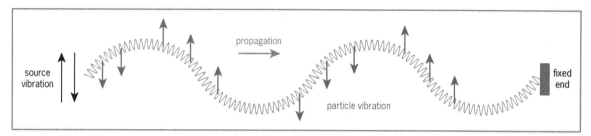

Figures 8.5 *Transverse waves along a slinky spring*

Longitudinal waves

*Longitudinal waves are those whose **vibrations** are **parallel** to the direction of **propagation** of the wave.*

There is a series of regions of **high pressure** and **low pressure** known as **compressions** (C) and **rarefactions** (R) respectively along their profile.

Examples are the wave on a **slinky spring,** vibrated **parallel** to its **length** from one end (Figure 8.6) and sound waves (Figure 8.7).

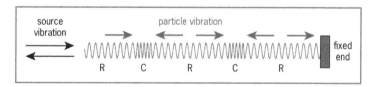

Figure 8.6 *Longitudinal wave along a slinky spring*

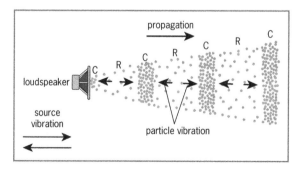

Figure 8.7 *Sound waves in air*

Reflection and focusing of wave energy

Reflectors with parabolic curvature can be used to focus radio and TV waves onto a receiver aerial or to focus a beam of solar radiation in a solar cooker as in Table 10.5, page 210. They can also produce a concentrated beam from the headlamps of vehicles and provide a wide-angled view from rear-view mirrors. These uses are shown in Figure 8.8.

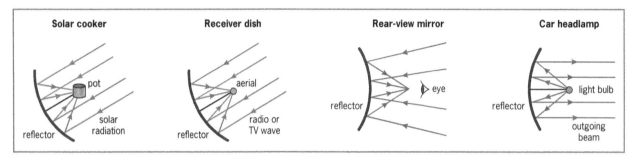

Figure 8.8 *Curved reflectors*

Law of conservation of energy

The law of conservation of energy states that energy cannot be created or destroyed but can be transformed from one type to another.

For example, **chemical energy** stored in batteries, and **gravitational potential energy** stored in water behind a river dam, can be transformed into **electrical energy** as needed.

Whenever **energy is transformed**, an equal amount of **work is done**. This can:

* put objects into motion if the transformation is to **kinetic energy**
* raise objects if the transformation is to **gravitational potential energy**
* produce **heat** and **sound energy** as work is done against frictional forces when the surfaces of objects slide over each other
* produce **heat energy** as electrons are forced through resistors in electrical circuits.

When **heat energy** is produced, it is **lost** to the surroundings (absorbed by the surroundings).

Several examples of energy transformations are outlined below.

Examples of energy transformations

Coconut falling to the ground

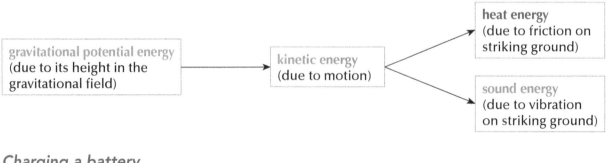

Charging a battery

Filament lamp in use

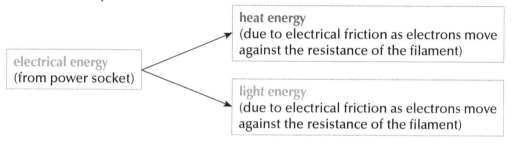

electrical energy
(from power socket)

→ heat energy
(due to electrical friction as electrons move
against the resistance of the filament)

→ light energy
(due to electrical friction as electrons move
against the resistance of the filament)

Photovoltaic (PV) electrical generation (solar panels)

light energy
(from Sun – 'solar energy') → electrical energy
(generated by PV panel)

Photosynthesis

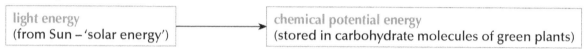

light energy
(from Sun – 'solar energy') → chemical potential energy
(stored in carbohydrate molecules of green plants)

Solar powered calculator

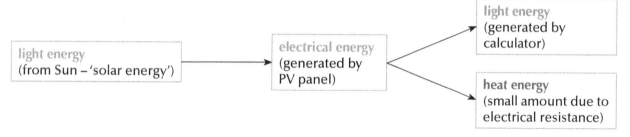

light energy
(from Sun – 'solar energy') → electrical energy
(generated by
PV panel) → light energy
(generated by
calculator)

→ heat energy
(small amount due to
electrical resistance)

Electrical motor lifting a load

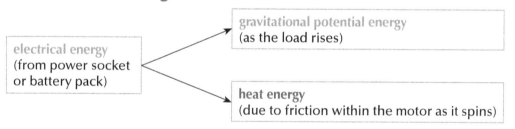

electrical energy
(from power socket
or battery pack)

→ gravitational potential energy
(as the load rises)

→ heat energy
(due to friction within the motor as it spins)

Hydro-electric power station (using an elevated reservoir or river dam)

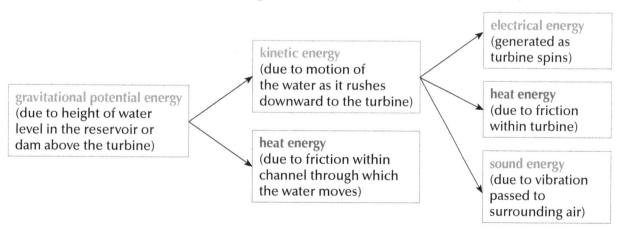

gravitational potential energy
(due to height of water
level in the reservoir or
dam above the turbine)

→ kinetic energy
(due to motion of
the water as it rushes
downward to the turbine)

→ heat energy
(due to friction within
channel through which
the water moves)

→ electrical energy
(generated as
turbine spins)

→ heat energy
(due to friction
within turbine)

→ sound energy
(due to vibration
passed to
surrounding air)

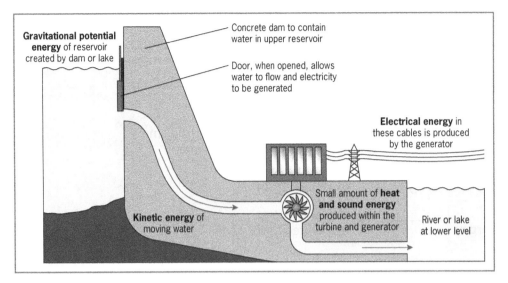

Figure 8.9 *Hydro-electric power*

Nuclear-electric power station

nuclear potential energy (stored in atomic nuclei of uranium) → heat energy (due to nuclear emissions; this produces steam from boiling water) → kinetic energy (due to pressure of steam; spins the turbine) → electrical energy (generated as turbine spins) / heat energy (due to friction within turbine) / sound energy (due to vibration passed to surrounding air)

Microphone

sound energy (due to vibration of air as it passes through larynx/voice-box) → kinetic energy (vibration of microphone's diaphragm) → electrical energy (generated as diaphragm vibrates)

Loudspeaker

electrical energy (AC fed to speaker) → kinetic energy (vibration of speaker cone) → sound energy (vibration of air caused by vibration of speaker cone)

Note: The energy changes in the microphone and speaker are the reverse of each other.

Microwave oven warming food

electromagnetic energy (microwaves) → heat energy (produced as water and fat molecules in the food resonate with approximately the same frequency as the microwaves)

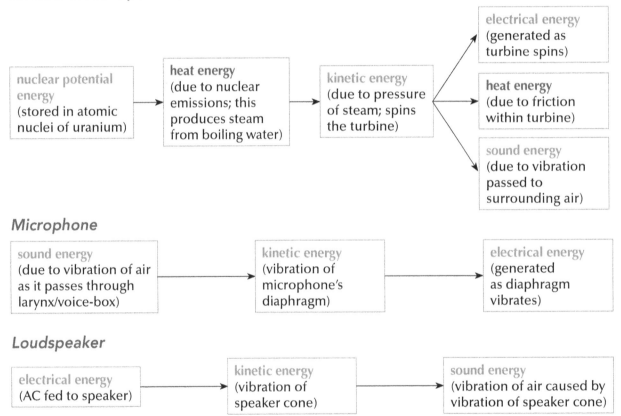

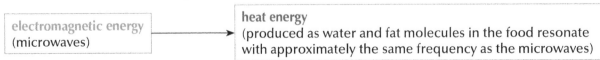

Vehicle braking and coming to rest

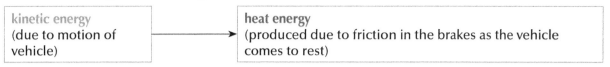

Block sliding down rough incline

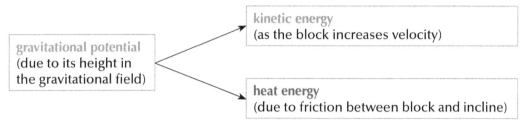

Swinging simple pendulum

Figure 8.10 shows a pendulum at different points of its swing.

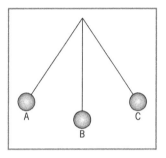

Figure 8.10 *Swinging pendulum*

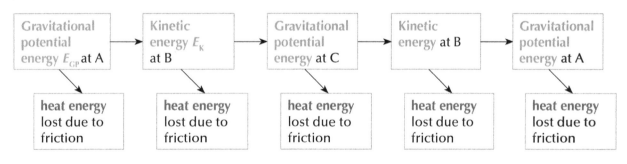

At A and C: $E_K = 0$ since the ball is momentarily at rest.

E_{GP} is then maximum since the ball is now at its maximum height for that swing.

At B: E_K is maximum since the ball moves fastest.

E_{GP} is then minimum since the ball is at its lowest point.

As the ball swings, a **small amount** of **heat** is **continuously lost** to the environment due to **friction**. Usually this can be ignored since **friction associated with simple pendulums is negligible**.

Interconversion of mass and energy

Nuclear fission

*Nuclear fission is the **splitting** of a **large atomic nucleus** into smaller atomic nuclei, resulting in a **large output of energy** and a **small loss in mass**.*

Not only can energy change from one form to another; it can also convert to mass, and mass can convert to energy.

Note: A **single uranium pellet**, just **1 inch tall**, generates the same energy as **120 gallons of crude oil**. Less than 10 of these pellets can supply a household with energy for an entire year!

- **Nuclear reactors of power plants** produce electricity by the **nuclear fission** of **uranium**. Large **uranium** nuclei **split** into smaller atomic nuclei of **barium** and **krypton**. The total mass of the products is **less** than the mass of the uranium from which they were formed since the **loss in mass converts to energy**. The energy is used to boil water to produce steam pressure that turns a turbine to generate electricity.

- **The atomic bomb**, known as the **A-bomb**, is a weapon that utilises a violent **nuclear fission** reaction.

Nuclear fusion

*Nuclear fusion is the **joining** of two very **small atomic nuclei** to form a larger atomic nucleus, resulting in a **large output of energy** and a **small loss in mass**.*

- In the **very hot core** of the **Sun**, electromagnetic energy in the form of gamma radiation is produced when **hydrogen** nuclei undergo **nuclear fusion** to form **helium** nuclei. The mass of the helium produced is less than the total mass of the hydrogen producing it since some of the mass converts to energy. Much of this radiant electromagnetic energy comes to us in the form of solar radiation: infrared, light and ultraviolet radiation.

- The **hydrogen bomb** is commonly called the **H-bomb** because it uses **hydrogen** nuclei in the **nuclear fusion** process as it converts to **helium**. It is much more powerful than the atomic bomb, which depends on nuclear fission.

Nuclear fission and nuclear fusion are illustrated in Figure 8.11.

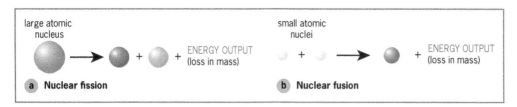

Figure 8.11 *Nuclear fission and nuclear fusion*

Simple nuclear equations

Fission: uranium → barium + krypton + energy   … compare with Figure 8.11a

Fusion: hydrogen + hydrogen → helium + energy   … compare with Figure 8.11b

Energy supplies for use in space

Energy sources are needed by all satellites and spacecraft. For example:

- To **operate devices** on **satellites** that orbit planets.
- To provide the **propulsion** of **spacecraft**.

Suitable sources include nuclear fission devices and solar cells.

- **Nuclear fission** devices can be **small**, **portable** and **reliable** for long periods. They are also **extremely energy efficient**, so a small sample of nuclear material can provide an enormous output of energy.

- **Solar** cells are **lightweight**, **compact** and **do not produce dangerous emissions**. The **energy input** comes from the **Sun**, so a satellite or spacecraft using a solar cell does not need to carry any **fuel** to power its systems. Also, solar cells operate with a **higher efficiency** in the **vacuum of space** than they do in the **atmosphere of the Earth**.

The internal combustion engine (ICE)

The internal combustion engine is a **heat engine** that burns a mixture of **fossil fuel** and **air**. Most motor vehicles are powered by an internal combustion engine. The combustion is done **internally** within cylinders of the engine, producing **hot gases** which **expand** and **set pistons in motion**. This motion is relayed through a mechanical system to cause the entire vehicle to move.

Negative effects of the internal combustion engine

The fuels used are fossil fuels, typically **gasoline** and **diesel**. When burnt, they produce the following **harmful exhaust contaminants** (see Figure 8.12):

- carbon monoxide
- oxides of nitrogen and sulfur
- volatile hydrocarbons
- particulate matter
- heavy metal ions.

Please refer now to **Table 10.3**, page 209 to learn about the negative effects of these harmful emissions.

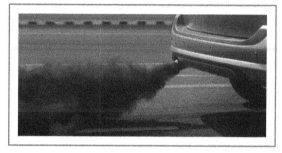

Figure 8.12 *Pollution from exhaust contaminants*

Industrial methods taken to increase efficiency and reduce pollution caused by the ICE

- **Government regulations** ensure that **air quality** resulting from vehicular emissions is monitored to meet specific standards.

- **Better-quality engines** and **fuels** have been developed to produce **higher fuel efficiency** and **less pollution**.

- **Streamlined aerodynamic shapes** (see Chapter 16, page 354) of vehicles increase efficiency by **reducing air friction**.

- **'Idle off' systems** save fuel by automatically **switching off** the engine when the car stops.

- **Solar cells**, **LED lighting** and **energy-efficient air conditioners** save on energy consumption in vehicles and make us less dependent on fossil fuels.

- **Catalytic converters** in the exhaust pipes of vehicles convert **dangerous** gaseous pollutants into **harmless** gases (see Figure 8.13).

- Modern **cooling systems reuse** the **heat energy** produced by the engine.

Figure 8.13 *Catalytic converter*

- Modern **suspension systems generate electricity** by absorbing energy whenever an object accelerates, decelerates or encounters a bump in the road.
- **Planting trees** helps remove **carbon dioxide** (a greenhouse gas; see Chapter 10, page 206) produced by ICE-powered vehicles.
- **Replacing ICE-powered vehicles** with **electric vehicles (EVs)** reduces pollution. EVs are also more efficient than ICEs in transforming stored energy to kinetic energy.
- **Regenerative braking systems recharge** the batteries of electric vehicles.

Methods taken by individuals to increase efficiency and reduce pollution of the ICE

- Maintain the recommended **tyre pressure** to increase **fuel efficiency**.
- Ensure that the engine is **well tuned** to reduce the emission of **toxins** and to utilise **less fuel**.
- Ensure that the **engine oil** is **changed** regularly to maintain **engine efficiency**.
- Ensure that **air filters** are **changed** as needed to maintain **good combustion**.
- **Avoid unnecessary idling** to **save fuel**.
- **Avoid unnecessary braking** by driving slowly and increasing the distance to the vehicle ahead.
- **Comply with speed limits** since increased speed requires **increased energy consumption**.
- **Combine** several **chores** in a single trip to **save fuel**.
- **Carpool** with others, or use **public transportation** or **bicycles**, when possible, to **save fuel**.
- **Keep windows up** when travelling at high speeds on highways to reduce air friction and so increase **fuel efficiency**.

Recalling facts

a Define:

   i work.   **ii** energy.   **iii** the joule.

b Define:

   i gravitational potential energy.

   ii elastic potential energy.

   iii chemical potential energy.

   iv electromagnetic energy.

   v kinetic energy.

c State TWO types of change that can be brought on by an input of energy, giving an example in each case.

What type of energy can cause the following?

a A change from liquid to gas.

b An increase in temperature.

c Photosynthesis.

3 **a** Define:

  i transverse waves.   **ii** longitudinal waves.

 b Categorise the following into transverse and longitudinal waves:

  i sound waves.

  ii electromagnetic waves.

  iii water waves.

  iv waves produced by rope vibrated perpendicular to its length from one end.

  v waves produced by slinky spring vibrated parallel to its length from one end.

4 **a** Electromagnetic energy exists as groups of waves of different frequencies. Rewrite and complete the list below in order of increasing frequency:

  ………………….., …………………………, light, …………………………, X-ray and gamma.

 b State the type of electromagnetic energy associated with each of the following.

  i Gives our nerve endings a feeling of warmth.

  ii Brings our television programmes and the news.

  iii Produces photographs of our bones.

5 **a** List TWO energy sources which suitably provide spacecraft with their energy needs.

 b Give TWO reasons why EACH source you have chosen is a good choice.

6 **a** Define the following:

  i nuclear fission.   **ii** nuclear fusion.

 b Rewrite and complete the following sentences.

  i Nuclear ……………………… is a process occurring in the hot core of the Sun.

  ii Uranium undergoes nuclear …………………… in our nuclear generating plants.

  iii Nuclear ……………… releases more energy per gram than does nuclear ……………………… .

  iv During nuclear **fission**, energy is released, and mass is lost. During nuclear **fusion**, energy is ………………………….. and mass is ………………………….. .

7 **a** Define an internal combustion engine.

 b List FOUR harmful exhaust contaminants from an internal combustion engine.

8 A boy of weight 400 N pushes a box of weight 50 N across the floor of a room using a force of 25 N through 3 m.

  a **i** Which force should be used to calculate the work done by the boy?

    ii Give a reason for your answer.

  b Give a worded equation which can be used to calculate work or energy.

  c What work is done by each of the following forces?

    i The weight of the box, 50 N.

    ii The push, 25 N.

    iii The weight of the boy, 400 N.

9 **a** State the law of conservation of energy.

  b Using arrow diagrams, describe the MAIN energy transformations occurring in each of the following.

    i A truck applying brakes.

    ii A microwave oven warming food.

    iii A filament lamp powered by a battery.

    iv An active hydroelectric power station.

    v Photosynthesis.

10 Rewrite and complete the following sentences using the verbs **transport**, **transfer** or **transform**.

  a As a ball rolls across a room, it .... kinetic energy. It then strikes another ball and .... its kinetic energy to it. Some of its kinetic energy is also .... to heat and sound during the collision.

  b Electrical energy is .... through electrical wires. On passing through a filament lamp, it gets very hot as the electrical energy is .... to thermal energy which then emits infrared, visible light and ultraviolet radiations. This radiant electromagnetic wave energy is .... across the room where some of it .... to the walls, producing heat as it .... to thermal energy.

11 **a** A ball has 400 J of potential energy at the top of an incline. Assuming friction is negligible, determine the maximum kinetic energy it can acquire as it **rolls** down the slope.

  b A block, having 400 J of potential energy at the top of the incline, **slides** down the slope, dissipating 100 J of heat energy in the process. What is its kinetic energy at the lowest point?

12 Explain why a loaded concrete truck possesses more kinetic energy than a small car travelling at the same speed.

13 Rewrite and complete the following sentences.

   a An atomic bomb is dangerous due to its .... potential energy.

   b Raising a book to a shelf increases its .... energy.

   c Gasoline provides a car with .... energy.

   d Increasing the speed of a car, increases its .... energy.

   e Stretching a bungee cord, increases its .... energy.

   f The energy stored in a battery is .... energy.

   g A bowl of cereal gives us .... energy.

   h Infrared, visible light and ultraviolet radiations are forms of .... energy.

14 Describe FOUR industrial means by which the negative effects of the internal combustion engine are being reduced.

Analysing data

15 Matt performed an experiment to investigate how temperature is affected when a small sample of beeswax was heated in a heat-resistant test tube. Readings of temperature were taken every 2 minutes and heating continued for a few minutes after the wax had all melted. His results are shown in graphical form in Figure 8.14.

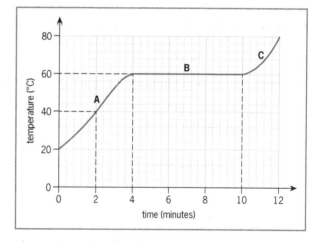

   a What type of change did the heat energy produce during each of the following stages?

     i Stage A.

     ii Stage B.

Figure 8.14 *Graph of temperature against time for Question 15*

     iii Stage C.

   b From the graph, what is the melting point of the beeswax?

   c For how long did melting continue?

   d Which stage corresponds to the liquid state?

   e Construct a table showing temperature and time by taking SIX pairs of readings from the graph.

   f Determine the slope (gradient) of the graph in stage A.

   g What was the rate of increase in temperature during stage A?

16 Zoe has TWO blocks, A and B, of the same weight but of differently textured surfaces. She pushes the blocks across a room at constant velocity and plots graphs of the forces used against the distances through which the blocks are pushed. Her results are shown in Figure 8.15.

Use the graphs to determine the following.

a The distance across the room.

b The block which presented the most friction.

c The work done on pushing:

   i block A.

   ii block B.

d What type of energy:

   i is Zoe using?

   ii is the friction producing?

e Explain why the weights of the blocks are not used in this calculation.

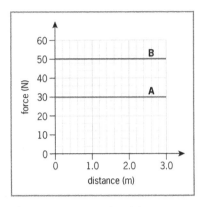

Figure 8.15 *Graph of forces against distance for Question 16*

Photosynthesis and energy transfer in the environment

Learning objectives

- Examine the **role** of **photosynthesis** in the **conversion** of **energy**.
- Identify the **substrates**, **conditions** and **products** of **photosynthesis**.
- Analyse the **transfer** of **energy** in the **environment**.

Photosynthesis and energy conversion

Photosynthesis is the process by which green plants convert carbon dioxide and water into glucose by using energy from sunlight, which is absorbed by chlorophyll in chloroplasts. Oxygen is produced as a by-product.

Photosynthesis occurs in the **chloroplasts** of plant cells, mainly in cells that are found in the **leaves** of plants, though any plant structure that contains **chlorophyll** (in other words, is green) can carry out photosynthesis. During photosynthesis, the **chlorophyll** molecules in the chloroplasts absorb **energy** from sunlight and use it to bring about the reaction between **carbon dioxide** and **water**. The **products** of the reaction are **glucose** and **oxygen**.

Photosynthesis can be summarised by the following **equations**.

Word equation

$$\text{carbon dioxide + water} \xrightarrow{\text{energy from sunlight absorbed by chlorophyll}} \text{glucose + oxygen}$$

Chemical equation

$$6CO_2 + 6H_2O \xrightarrow{\text{energy from sunlight absorbed by chlorophyll}} C_6H_{12}O_6 + 6O_2$$

Photosynthesis is known as a **photochemical reaction** because it is initiated by the absorption of **light energy**. This light energy is **converted** into **chemical energy**, which is stored within the glucose molecules.

Substrates and conditions for photosynthesis

Photosynthesis requires the following **two** raw materials, which are also known as **substrates.**

- **Carbon dioxide**, which diffuses into the leaves from the air through small pores in the undersurface of the leaves known as **stomata.**
- **Water**, which is absorbed from the soil by the roots.

In addition to the above substrates, photosynthesis requires several **conditions.**

- **Energy from sunlight**, which is absorbed by the chlorophyll in chloroplasts of leaf cells.
- **Chlorophyll**, the green pigment which is present in chloroplasts.
- **Enzymes**, which are present in chloroplasts.
- A **suitable temperature** of between about 5 °C and 40 °C, so that the enzymes can function.

Certain **mineral ions** are also indirectly required. Magnesium (Mg^{2+}), iron (Fe^{3+}) and nitrate (NO_3^-) ions are needed by plants to manufacture **chlorophyll**, and magnesium (Mg^{2+}) and potassium (K^+) ions are needed to assist or activate the enzymes that control photosynthesis.

The products of photosynthesis and their importance

Photosynthesis produces **two** products: **glucose** and **oxygen.**

- Some of the **glucose** produced during photosynthesis is used by plant cells in **respiration,** during which the stored **energy** is released and used by the plants in life processes. The rest can be converted to a variety of other useful **organic compounds** (carbon-containing compounds). These compounds include the following.
  - **Sucrose** and **starch**, which are stored by the plants for later use.
  - **Cellulose**, which is used to make cell walls in growing plant parts.
  - **Amino acids** and **proteins**, which the plants use for growth.
  - **Lipids**, which the plants store, mainly in seeds.
- The **oxygen** produced during photosynthesis is used by the leaf cells in **aerobic respiration.** Any oxygen not used in this way diffuses out of the leaves into the air and is used by other living organisms.

Testing for the presence of starch produced in photosynthesis

Leaf cells usually convert some of the glucose produced in photosynthesis into **starch** and then **store** the starch. This starch can then be converted back into glucose for use when needed; for example, during the night when the plant is not photosynthesising. One way to find out if a plant has been photosynthesising is to test its leaves for the presence of starch. Figure 8.16 on page 160 illustrates the method that is used to test a leaf for starch.

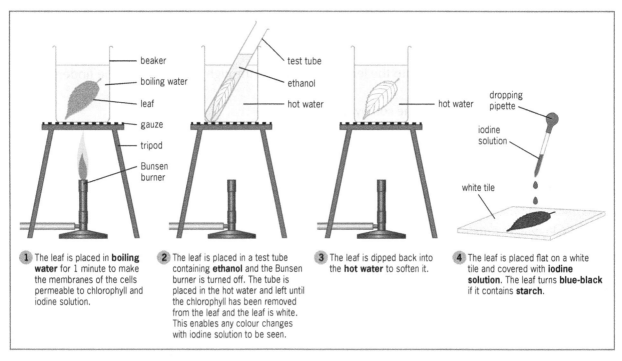

1 The leaf is placed in **boiling water** for 1 minute to make the membranes of the cells permeable to chlorophyll and iodine solution.

2 The leaf is placed in a test tube containing **ethanol** and the Bunsen burner is turned off. The tube is placed in the hot water and left until the chlorophyll has been removed from the leaf and the leaf is white. This enables any colour changes with iodine solution to be seen.

3 The leaf is dipped back into the **hot water** to soften it.

4 The leaf is placed flat on a white tile and covered with **iodine solution**. The leaf turns **blue-black** if it contains **starch**.

Figure 8.16 *Testing a leaf for starch*

Investigating the conditions necessary for photosynthesis

The presence of **starch** in a leaf is considered to be **proof** that the leaf has been photosynthesising. Therefore, the method used to test a leaf to see if it contains starch, described in Figure 8.16, can be used to investigate if **light** and **chlorophyll** are necessary for photosynthesis, as described in Figures 8.17 and 8.18 on page 161. All of these investigations must begin with a plant that contains **no starch**, known as a **destarched plant**. To destarch a plant, it is placed in the dark for about 7 days. During this time, any starch present in the leaves is converted back to glucose and used in respiration.

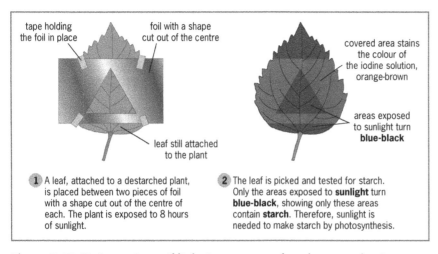

1 A leaf, attached to a destarched plant, is placed between two pieces of foil with a shape cut out of the centre of each. The plant is exposed to 8 hours of sunlight.

2 The leaf is picked and tested for starch. Only the areas exposed to **sunlight** turn **blue-black**, showing only these areas contain **starch**. Therefore, sunlight is needed to make starch by photosynthesis.

Figure 8.17 *To investigate if light is necessary for photosynthesis*

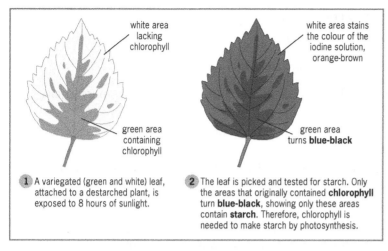

Figure 8.18 *To investigate if chlorophyll is necessary for photosynthesis; Figure 8.19 shows a suitable plant*

Figure 8.19 *A variegated hibiscus plant*

An introduction to the environment

Living organisms are constantly interacting with each other and the environment in which they live. It is important to understand certain **terms** that are used when talking about these interactions.

- **Environment** refers to the combination of factors that surround and act on an organism.
- **Habitat** is the place where a particular organism lives.
- A **species** is a group of organisms of common ancestry that closely resemble each other and are normally capable of interbreeding to produce fertile offspring.
- A **population** is composed of all the members of a particular species living together in a particular habitat.
- A **community** is composed of all the populations of different species living together in a particular area.
- An **ecosystem** is a community of living organisms interacting with each other and with their physical (non-living) environment. Examples of ecosystems include a pond, a coral reef, a mangrove swamp and a forest.

Transfer of energy in the environment

During **photosynthesis**, **energy** from sunlight is incorporated as **chemical energy** into the **organic food molecules** made by plants. Glucose is produced initially, and this can then be converted into other carbohydrates, proteins or lipids by the plants (see page 159). Because **green plants** make their own food, they are known as **producers**. The food molecules made by the plants, and the **energy** they contain, are then passed on to other organisms, known as **consumers**, through **food chains** and **food webs**.

Food chains

*A **food chain** is a linear diagram showing the flow of food and energy from one organism to the next in an ecosystem.*

Any **food chain** always begins with a producer and includes the following.

- A **producer**, in other words, a green plant.
- A **primary consumer** that eats the producer.

- A **secondary consumer** that eats the primary consumer.
- A **tertiary consumer** that eats the secondary consumer.

Consumers can also be classified according to what they **consume**.

- **Herbivores** consume plants or plant material only. Examples include cows, grasshoppers, snails, slugs, parrot fish and sea urchins.
- **Carnivores** consume animals or animal material only. Examples include lizards, toads, spiders, centipedes, eagles, octopuses and sharks.
- **Omnivores** consume both plants and animals, or plant and animal material. Examples include hummingbirds, crickets, mice, humans and crayfish.

Organisms that are not consumed eventually **die**. **Decomposers**, which are mainly bacteria and fungi, obtain their food containing energy from the bodies of these dead organisms and, at the same time, they cause the dead organisms to **decompose**, which releases **mineral nutrients** back into the environment.

The organisms in a food chain are linked by **arrows** that show the direction in which the **food** and **energy** flow. The **position** that an organism occupies in a food chain is known as its **trophic level** and each trophic level is given a number, starting at one for the trophic level of the producer. A terrestrial (land) food chain and a marine (seawater) food chain are shown in Figure 8.20.

Trophic level refers to the position or level that an organism occupies in a food chain.

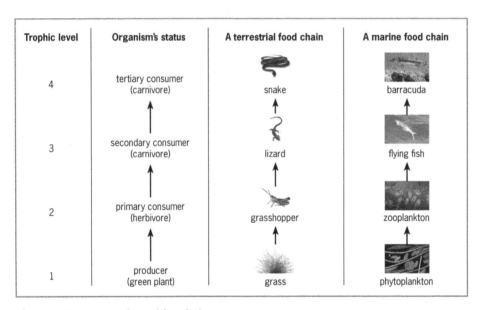

Figure 8.20 *Examples of food chains*

Food chains can also be written horizontally, as shown in the following example from a **mangrove swamp**:

green algae ⟶ insect larvae ⟶ tilapia ⟶ egret

Food webs

Food chains show how one organism feeds on another; however, feeding relationships are usually more **complex** than this. Any ecosystem usually has more than one producer and most consumers have more than one source of food. Consequently, food chains are interconnected to form **food webs**. A terrestrial food web and a freshwater food web are shown in Figures 8.21 and 8.22, respectively, on page 163.

A **food web** is a diagram that links food chains together to show all the pathways along which food and energy flow between organisms in an ecosystem.

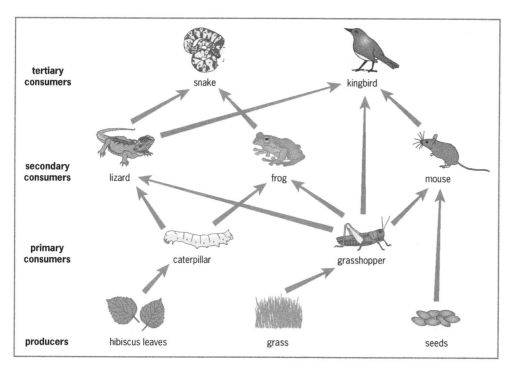

Figure 8.21 *An example of a terrestrial food web*

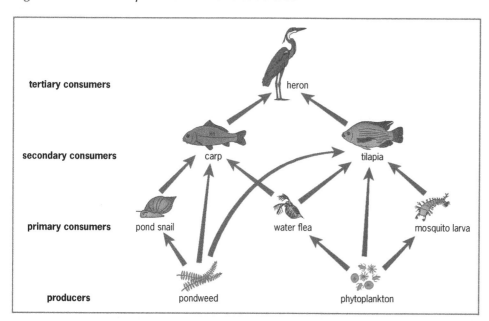

Figure 8.22 *An example of a food web from a freshwater lake*

Energy transfer in food chains

Not all the energy incorporated into the organic food molecules made by green **plants** during photosynthesis is passed along a food chain; some is **used** and some is **lost** at each trophic level. The plants use some of the food in **respiration**. This releases energy which the plants **use** in life processes (see page 186) or **lose** as heat energy, so this energy is not passed on to consumers. The rest of the food is used by the plants for **growth** or is **stored**.

When plants are eaten by **herbivores**, some of the organic matter containing energy is **lost** in **faeces** or **excretory products**, such as urea, and some is used in **respiration**, during which the stored energy is released and **used** by the herbivores or is **lost** as heat energy. The remaining food containing energy is used to **build body tissues** or is **stored**, and is then passed on to the next trophic level when herbivores are consumed. This then continues at each trophic level in a food chain.

Organisms that are not consumed eventually **die**. These dead organisms, together with faeces and excretory products, are **decomposed** by **decomposers** and the stored energy is released in respiration and **used** or **lost**. In general, only about **1** to **2%** of the energy from sunlight is absorbed by plants and used in photosynthesis, and only about **10%** of the energy from one trophic level is transferred to the next level. This is summarised in Figure 8.23.

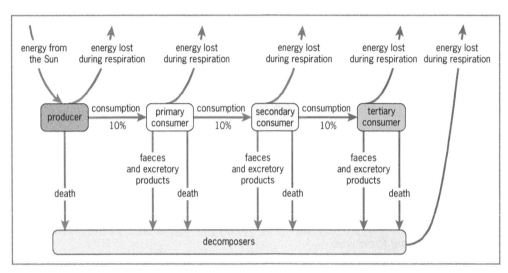

Figure 8.23 *Energy flow through a food chain*

Ecological pyramids

An **ecological pyramid** is a graphical representation in the form of a pyramid that shows the relationship between organisms at different trophic levels in a **food chain**. Each **bar** in the pyramid represents a different trophic level, starting from producers at the bottom, and the **width** of each bar is proportional to the quantity of the factor being measured.

There are **three** types of ecological pyramids.

- A **pyramid of numbers** shows the total **number** of organisms at each trophic level, without considering their size.
- A **pyramid of energy** represents the total amount of **energy** stored in organisms at each trophic level.
- A **pyramid of biomass** represents the total **dry mass** (mass without water) of organisms, known as **biomass**, at each trophic level.

Ecological pyramids are usually **upright** pyramids because the total amount of energy **decreases** at successive trophic levels, and there are usually **fewer** primary consumers with a **lower** total biomass than producers, and fewer secondary consumers with a lower total biomass than primary consumers, and so on, as shown in Figure 8.24a on page 165. However, when the producer is a **tree**, the **pyramid of numbers** is shaped as shown in Figure 8.24b on page 165 because a single tree, especially a large one, can support a large number of other organisms.

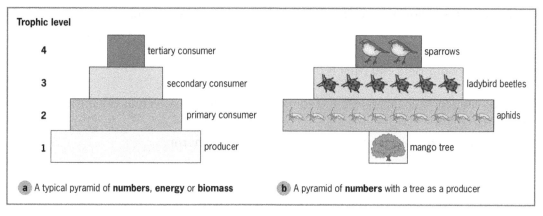

Figure 8.24 *Ecological pyramids showing four trophic levels*

Ecological balance and environmental sustainability

Ecosystems are influenced by complex and often unpredictable interactions among the species present and their environment, and these systems have evolved mechanisms to maintain **stability**. A **stable** ecosystem is one that is **ecologically balanced**, and where species coexist with each other and with their environment in a **sustainable** way.

Maintaining ecological balance is essential because it ensures the **stability** and **sustainability** of ecosystems for all forms of life. It helps **preserve biodiversity**, which ensures the continuous existence of species and availability of natural resources, and it maintains the **health** of ecosystems. If ecological balance is **disrupted** by natural or human-induced factors it can lead to habitat loss, the loss of biodiversity and the extinction of species, and it has a negative impact on human life such as creating shortages of food and other natural resources, and sometimes leading to the outbreak of disease.

Recalling facts

1
a Name the substrates needed and identify FOUR other requirements for photosynthesis.

b Provide a definition for photosynthesis and explain the energy interconversion that occurs during the process.

c Write a word equation and a chemical equation to summarise photosynthesis.

2
a For what process do leaves <u>immediately</u> use the products of photosynthesis?

b Suggest THREE other ways that a plant can use the glucose produced in photosynthesis.

3 Describe, giving <u>full</u> experimental details, the method you would use to prove that a leaf, which has been exposed to 8 hours of sunlight, contains starch.

4 Explain how you could prove to your friend that chlorophyll is necessary for photosynthesis.

5 Define the following terms:

a habitat   b population   c ecosystem.

6
a Distinguish between a food chain and a food web.

b What type of organism always begins a food chain?

7 For EACH of the following, explain the term and give a <u>named</u> example:

    a herbivore   **b** secondary consumer   **c** omnivore.

8 What are decomposers and what is their role in ecosystems?

9 The following food chain gives the feeding relationship between four organisms in a mangrove swamp:

    water weed ⟶ insect larvae ⟶ tilapia ⟶ heron

    From the organisms in the swamp, name:

    a a carnivore   **b** a primary consumer   **c** a producer.

10 What are ecological pyramids and what do they show?

Applying facts

11 When investigating the effect of different environmental factors on the production of starch in a potted plant, Ethan first puts the plant in darkness for 7 days. Explain clearly why Ethan did this.

12 Some leafhoppers were seen feeding on the leaves of sweet potato plants in a farmer's field, and a few of these leafhoppers were seen trapped in a spider's web. A falcon was also observed attacking and killing a sparrow for food, and sparrows are known to eat spiders. Use this information to draw:

    a a food chain for the organisms in the field.

    b a pyramid of energy for the organisms in the field.

13 Shantelle noticed that many of the leaves on her lime tree were beginning to look unhealthy and their edges were starting to curl. When she turned some over, she saw that their lower surfaces were covered in parasitic whiteflies and a few ladybird beetles were feeding on the whiteflies. She also saw a tree frog catch and consume a ladybird beetle. Describe how energy flows through the organisms on Shantelle's lime tree.

14 **a** In a marine ecosystem, zooplankton and shrimp feed on phytoplankton, and crabs feed on the shrimp. Jellyfish eat both shrimp and zooplankton, and sea turtles eat the crabs and jellyfish. Use this information to construct a food web for the named organisms.

    b Suggest why it is important for consumers to have more than one source of food.

    c Suggest TWO similarities between an aquatic food web and a terrestrial food web.

Analysing data

15 Marcus sets up the apparatus shown in Figure 8.25 and uses it to determine the effect of light intensity on the rate of photosynthesis in pondweed, an aquatic plant. He does this by changing the distance between the lamp and the apparatus and counting the number of bubbles produced in a 2-minute period. His results are given in Table 8.3.

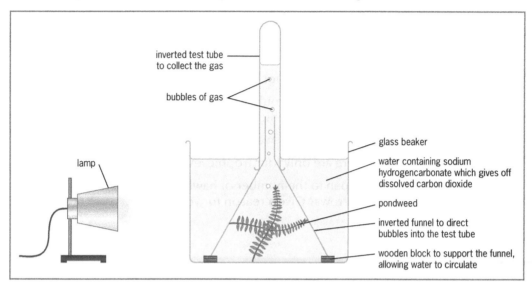

Figure 8.25 *Apparatus to determine the effect of light intensity on the rate of photosynthesis in pondweed*

Table 8.3 *The average number of bubbles produced in 2 minutes by pondweed when exposed to different light intensities*

Distance between the lamp and the apparatus/cm	Number of bubbles produced in 2 min					Average number of bubbles produced in 2 min
	Trial 1	Trial 2	Trial 3	Trial 4	Trial 5	
10	16	15	14	14	16	
20	11	12	10	11	11	
30	7	8	8	9	8	
40	4	6	4	5	6	
50	2	3	4	3	3	

a What gas would Marcus expect to find in the bubbles?

b Complete Table 8.3 by calculating the average number of bubbles produced in 2 minutes for each distance.

c i Plot a line graph to show the average number of bubbles against distance between the lamp and the apparatus.

ii Describe what the graph shows.

d What conclusion did Marcus draw about the effect of light intensity on the rate of photosynthesis in pondweed?

e i Suggest ONE limitation of the method used by Marcus.

ii Explain ONE way in which Marcus could adapt his apparatus or method to improve the accuracy of his results.

f How could Marcus adapt the apparatus to investigate the effect of temperature on the rate of photosynthesis in pondweed?

16 Table 8.4 gives the total biomass of each of four organisms in an ecosystem.

Table 8.4 *The biomass of four organisms in an ecosystem*

Organism	Total biomass/kg
Sparrows	50
Oak tree	1250
Hawks	10
Caterpillars	250

a Draw a pyramid of biomass for the ecosystem.

b i What difference, if any, would you expect in your pyramid if it showed the number of organisms at each trophic level instead of biomass?

  ii Give a reason for your answer to **b i**.

c Suggest why there are only four trophic levels in the ecosystem.

d What might happen to the number of hawks in the ecosystem if a disease suddenly killed all the sparrows? Give a reason for your answer.

9 Energy in life processes

Living organisms need a variety of **nutrients** to provide them with the **energy** and important chemicals they need to carry out the different life processes. These nutrients are contained in the **food** that they make or obtain. After humans consume their food, it must be broken down by **digestion** into a form that is useful for the body's activities. To obtain **energy** from the digested food, it must then be **respired** by body cells. Most living organisms respire **aerobically**, and the process of **breathing** is responsible for taking in the oxygen they need for aerobic respiration and getting rid of the carbon dioxide produced.

The human diet

Learning objectives

- Examine the **importance** of **food** as a **source** of **energy**.
- State the **sources** and **functions** of the **main nutrients** in a **balanced diet**.
- Explain the **effects** of **age**, **sex** and **occupation** on **dietary needs**.
- Discuss the **effects** of **food additives** and an **unbalanced diet** on **health**.

A balanced diet

The **food** an animal eats is called its **diet**. The human diet must contain the following **seven** components.

- **Carbohydrates**, **proteins** and **lipids (fats and oils)**, which are also known as **macronutrients**.
- **Vitamins** and **minerals**, which are also known as **micronutrients**.
- **Dietary fibre** or **roughage** and **water**.

*A **balanced diet** is a diet that contains carbohydrates, proteins, lipids, vitamins, minerals, dietary fibre and water in the **correct proportions** to maintain **growth** and **good health**.*

Humans must consume a **balanced diet** each day to supply the body with enough **energy** for daily activities, to supply the body with the correct materials for **growth**, **repair**, **development** and to **manufacture** biologically important molecules, and to keep the body in a **healthy state**.

A balanced diet should contain a **variety** of foods selected from each of the **six** different **Caribbean food groups** shown in Figure 9.1. Each group contains foods which supply similar nutrients in similar proportions. The **size** of each sector indicates the **relative amount** of each group that should be eaten daily, as recommended by the Caribbean Food and Nutrition Institute.

Figure 9.1 *The six Caribbean food groups*

Table 9.1 *Foods in the six Caribbean food groups*

Food group	Examples of foods in the group	Nutrients supplied
Staple foods	Cereals, bread, spaghetti, rice, yam, cassava, eddo, potato, breadfruit, plantain.	Carbohydrates (mainly starch), vitamins, minerals, fibre.
Legumes and nuts	Peas, beans, lentils, peanuts, cashew nuts.	Proteins, carbohydrates (mainly starch), vitamins, minerals, fibre.
Foods from animals	Meat, poultry, fish, eggs, cheese, milk.	Proteins, lipids, vitamins, minerals.
Fruits	Mangoes, paw paws, guavas, West Indian cherries, citrus fruits, bananas.	Carbohydrates (mainly sugars), vitamins, minerals, fibre.
Non-starchy vegetables	Spinach, callaloo, string beans, broccoli, pumpkin, carrots, tomatoes.	Vitamins, minerals, fibre.
Fats and oils	Butter, margarine, vegetable oil, ghee, fat on meat.	Lipids, vitamins.

Carbohydrates, proteins and lipids

Carbohydrates, **proteins** and **lipids** are required in relatively large quantities. They are **organic compounds** because their molecules contain carbon, hydrogen and oxygen atoms. They supply the body with the **energy** it needs, and the materials it needs for **growth**, **repair** and to **manufacture** biologically important molecules.

- **Carbohydrates** include **sugars** and **starch** and can be classified into **three** groups based on the chemical structure of their molecules: **monosaccharides**, **disaccharides** and **polysaccharides.** These are shown in Figure 9.2.
  - **Monosaccharides** are the simplest carbohydrate molecules. Many have the formula $C_6H_{12}O_6$. They include glucose, fructose and galactose.
  - **Disaccharides** are formed by chemically joining two monosaccharide molecules together, they have the formula $C_{12}H_{22}O_{11}$. They include maltose, sucrose and lactose.
  - **Polysaccharides** are formed by joining many monosaccharide molecules into straight or branched chains. They include starch, cellulose and glycogen (animal starch).

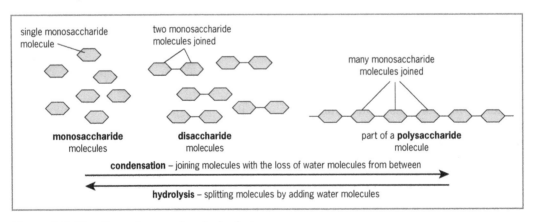

Figure 9.2 *The three types of carbohydrates*

- **Proteins** are large molecules composed of hundreds or thousands of small molecules known as **amino acids** which are joined together in long chains by **peptide links**, as shown in Figure 9.3.

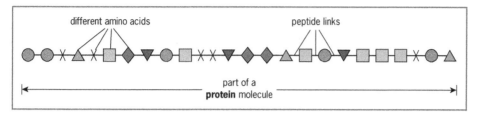

Figure 9.3 *Part of a protein molecule*

- **Lipids** are **fats** and **oils**. Their molecules are composed of **four** smaller molecules joined together; three **fatty acid** molecules and one **glycerol** molecule, as shown in Figure 9.4.

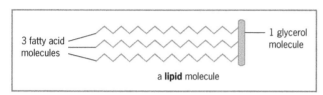

Figure 9.4 *A lipid molecule*

Sources and functions of carbohydrates, proteins and lipids

The **sources** and **functions** of carbohydrates, proteins and lipids are summarised in Table 9.2.

Table 9.2 *Sources and functions of carbohydrates, proteins and lipids in the human body*

Macronutrient	Sources	Functions
Carbohydrates	**Sugars**: fruits, cakes, sweets, jams, sugar-sweetened beverages. **Starch**: yams, potatoes, rice, pasta, bread.	• To provide **energy**: 1 g of carbohydrate releases 16 kJ of energy. This energy is easily released when carbohydrates are respired. • For **storage**: glycogen (animal starch) granules are stored in the cytoplasm of many cells.
Proteins	Fish, lean meat, milk, cheese, eggs, peas, beans, nuts.	• To make **new cells** for growth and to repair damaged tissues. • To make **enzymes** to catalyse (speed up) chemical reactions in the body. • To make **hormones** to control various processes in the body. • To make **antibodies** to fight disease. • To provide **energy**: 1 g of protein releases 17 kJ of energy. Proteins are used to provide energy only when stored carbohydrates and lipids have been used up.
Lipids	Butter, vegetable oils, margarine, nuts, fatty meats.	• To make **cell membranes** of newly formed cells. • To provide **energy**: 1 g of lipid releases 38 kJ of energy. Lipids are used to provide energy after carbohydrates because their metabolism is more complex and takes longer. • For **storage**: fat is stored under the skin and around organs. • For **insulation**: fat under the skin acts as an insulator.

Recognising carbohydrates, proteins and lipids

Tests can be performed in the laboratory to identify carbohydrates, proteins and lipids. Apart from the tests for lipids, the tests are usually carried out on about 2 cm³ of a **solution** of the test substance in a test tube. When testing a solid food item, a small piece of the food item is usually **crushed** with a small volume of water to create the necessary solution. The tests are summarised in Table 9.3 and are illustrated in Figure 9.5.

Table 9.3 *Laboratory tests to identify carbohydrates, proteins and lipids*

Macronutrient	Test	Positive result
Reducing sugars, e.g. glucose and maltose	Add an equal volume of **Benedict's solution** and shake. Heat the mixture.	An **orange-red** precipitate forms.
Non-reducing sugars, e.g. sucrose	Add a few drops of dilute **hydrochloric acid** and heat for 1 minute. Cool the solution and add small quantities of **sodium hydrogencarbonate** until effervescence stops. Add an equal volume of Benedict's solution and shake. Heat the mixture.	An **orange-red** precipitate forms. *Explanation:* The **acid** splits the disaccharide molecules into monosaccharide molecules which then react with the Benedict's solution. The sodium hydrogencarbonate neutralises the acid.
Starch	Add a few drops of **iodine solution** and shake.	Solution turns **blue-black**.
Proteins – the biuret test.	Add an equal volume of **sodium hydroxide solution** and shake. Add a few drops of dilute **copper sulfate solution** and shake. Or add an equal volume of **biuret reagent** and shake.	Solution turns **purple**.
Lipids – the emulsion test.	Place 4 cm³ of **ethanol** in a dry test tube. Add 1 drop of test substance and shake. Add an equal volume of **water** and shake.	A **milky-white** emulsion forms.
Lipids – the grease spot test.	Rub a drop of test substance onto **absorbent paper**. Leave for 10 minutes.	A **translucent mark** or grease spot remains.

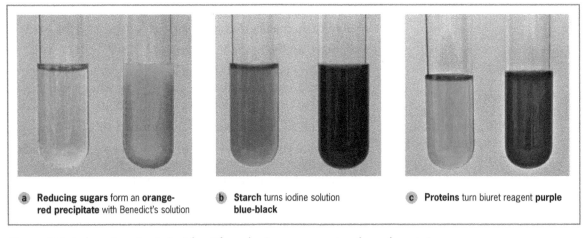

a **Reducing sugars** form an **orange-red precipitate** with Benedict's solution

b **Starch** turns iodine solution **blue-black**

c **Proteins** turn biuret reagent **purple**

Figure 9.5 *Laboratory tests to identify reducing sugars, starch and proteins*

Vitamins and minerals

Vitamins and **minerals** are required in small amounts for healthy growth and development. Some important vitamins and minerals required by the body, together with their **sources** and **functions**, are summarised in Tables 9.4 and 9.5.

Table 9.4 *Some important vitamins required by the human body*

Vitamin	Sources	Functions
A	Liver, cod liver oil, yellow and orange vegetables and fruits, e.g. carrots and pumpkin, green leafy vegetables, e.g. spinach.	• To help keep the skin, cornea and mucous membranes healthy. • To help vision in dim light (night vision). • To strengthen the immune system.
B_{12}	Animal products, e.g. meat, liver, poultry, fish, dairy products and eggs.	• To help regulate the formation of red blood cells in red bone marrow. • To aid in respiration to produce energy. • Important for the proper functioning of the nervous system.
C	West Indian cherries, citrus fruits, raw green vegetables.	• To keep tissues healthy, especially the skin and connective tissue. • To strengthen the immune system. • To help the body absorb iron in the ileum.
D	Oily fish, eggs, cod liver oil. Made in the body by the action of sunlight on the skin.	• To promote the absorption of calcium and phosphorus in the ileum. • To help build and maintain strong bones and teeth. • To strengthen the immune system.

Table 9.5 *Some important minerals required by the human body*

Mineral	Sources	Functions
Calcium (Ca)	Dairy products, e.g. milk, cheese and yoghurt, green vegetables, e.g. broccoli.	• To build and maintain healthy bones and teeth. • To help blood to clot at cuts.
Iron (Fe)	Red meat, liver, eggs, beans, nuts, dark green leafy vegetables.	• To make haemoglobin, the red pigment in red blood cells. Haemoglobin transports oxygen around the body for use in respiration.
Iodine (I)	Sea foods, e.g. fish, shellfish and seaweed, iodised table salt, milk, eggs.	• Used by the thyroid gland to make the hormone thyroxine (see Table 6.6 on page 104).

The importance of dietary fibre and water to health

Dietary fibre (roughage)

Dietary fibre is food that **cannot be digested**. It consists mainly of the cellulose of plant cell walls, lignin of plant xylem vessels (see page 70), husks of brown rice and bran of whole-grain cereals. Fruits, vegetables, legumes, nuts and whole grains are excellent sources of dietary fibre (see Figure 9.6 on page 174).

Dietary fibre has several health benefits. It adds bulk to the food so that food is kept moving through the digestive system, which helps prevent constipation and reduces the risk of colorectal (bowel) cancer. It makes a person feel full more easily, which reduces overall food intake and this, in turn, helps to reduce obesity. It also lowers cholesterol, which can reduce the risk of cardiovascular disease and it reduces the risk of a person developing type 2 diabetes.

Water

The human body is about 65% water. Water is present in blood plasma, tissue fluid and the cytoplasm of cells. Consumption of water in the diet is essential for maintaining good overall health. It keeps body cells hydrated so that chemical reactions can occur, and the water in blood plasma dissolves and transports nutrients and other useful substances to body cells and removes their waste products (see page 61). It aids in digestion of food in the digestive system and it cools the body when it evaporates from sweat. It also helps lubricate joints, keeps skin hydrated and healthy and it plays a crucial role in the functioning of the kidneys so that waste substances are excreted from the body.

Figure 9.6 *High-fibre foods*

Factors affecting dietary needs

To help maintain a healthy body, it is essential that a person's daily energy input from the food eaten balances his or her daily energy output, which is the amount of energy the person uses daily. If energy input exceeds energy output, the person will gain weight. If energy output exceeds energy input, the person will lose weight.

A person's energy output depends on many factors, including the person's basal metabolic rate (BMR), which is the energy the person uses when resting, the person's body mass, the person's age, the person's occupation or level of physical activity, and the person's sex.

- Effect of age – As age increases up to about 18 years, daily energy requirements increase, mainly because as children grow, they need increasing amounts of energy to sustain this growth. Energy requirements then remain fairly constant throughout adulthood up to old age, when less energy is required daily because older people tend to be less active, have less muscle mass and slower metabolic rates. Because children and adolescents are growing, they also need a higher proportion of protein in their diets than adults.
- Effect of occupation or level of physical activity – As activity increases, daily energy requirements increase because a person's metabolic rate increases as he or she becomes more active. For example, a manual labourer requires more energy than a person working in an office, and a sportsperson requires more energy than someone who never plays any sport.
- Effect of sex – Daily energy requirements are generally higher in males than in females of the same age and occupation. This is mainly because males generally have larger bodies and greater muscle mass than females. Women require more iron than men up to menopause to replace that lost each month during menstruation, and after menopause they require more vitamin D and calcium than men because their risk of developing osteoporosis is higher.

Food additives and their effects on health

Food additives are chemicals added to food during processing to prevent it from spoiling, or to improve its colour, flavour or texture. Food additives include artificial colourings such as yellow tartrazine, orange beta-carotene and red cochineal, artificial sweeteners such as aspartame, sucralose and saccharin, **salt** (sodium chloride), **monosodium glutamate** or **MSG**, a flavour enhancer, and **preservatives** such as nitrates, nitrites, sulfites, benzoates and sorbates (see Table 7.5 on pages 136 to 137).

Whilst many additives are generally recognised as being safe, some people are **sensitive** to certain additives and they can cause **allergic reactions** in these individuals such as hives, skin rashes, itching, swelling, rhinitis, sinusitis and difficulty breathing. They can also cause **asthma**, **digestive problems** such as diarrhoea and abdominal pain, and **hyperactivity** in children. Some of these additives may also increase a person's risk of developing **cancer**.

An unbalanced diet

When a person's diet does not contain the right amount of nutrients, it is said to be **unbalanced**. An unbalanced diet may be **lacking** in certain nutrients or certain nutrients may be in **excess**. Both can lead to certain serious health conditions, including **protein-energy malnutrition** or **PEM**, **deficiency diseases**, **obesity** and **type 2 diabetes**.

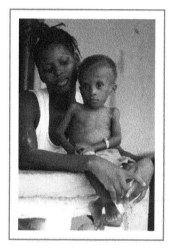

- **Protein-energy malnutrition (PEM)** refers to a group of related disorders which include **kwashiorkor** and **marasmus**. **Kwashiorkor** is caused by a severe shortage of **protein** in the diet. Its symptoms include loss of muscle mass and oedema (swelling) of the abdomen and legs. **Marasmus** is caused by a severe shortage of **protein** and **energy-rich foods** such as carbohydrates. Its symptoms include low body weight, thin face, and thin arms and legs with very little muscle and fat. These disorders mainly affect young children in developing countries (see Figure 9.7).

Figure 9.7 A child with marasmus

- **Deficiency diseases** are caused by a shortage or lack of a particular vitamin or mineral in the diet. These include **night blindness**, caused by a deficiency of vitamin A, **scurvy**, caused by a deficiency of vitamin C, **rickets**, caused by a deficiency of vitamin D or calcium, **anaemia**, caused by a deficiency of iron and **goitre**, caused by a deficiency of iodine.

- **Obesity** is generally caused by the excessive consumption of energy-rich foods high in **carbohydrates**, especially sugar, and/or **fat**, especially animal fat, and a **lack of physical activity**. It is characterised by an excessive accumulation and storage of **fat** in the body.

- **Type 2 diabetes** (see page 116) can be caused by consuming a diet high in **refined carbohydrates** such as white bread, flour and rice, **sugars** and **unhealthy fats** such as animal fats. It can also be caused by being overweight or obese.

Recalling facts

1. **a** What is a balanced diet?
   b Explain why it is important that Darian consumes a balanced diet daily.

2. Construct a table to give TWO sources and TWO uses of EACH of the following macronutrients in the human diet: starch, proteins and lipids.

3. Name TWO foods that are rich in EACH of the following, explain the importance of EACH in the human diet and name ONE deficiency disease caused by a shortage or lack of EACH:

   a vitamin A   **b** vitamin C   **c** iodine   **d** iron.

4. What is dietary fibre?

5 Identify THREE factors that can affect a person's dietary needs and outline the effect of EACH.

6 What dietary advice would you give to a person who suffers from type 2 diabetes?

Applying facts

7 Explain why Jared, a competitive swimmer, is advised to eat foods rich in carbohydrates before he races rather than foods rich in lipids, even though lipids release a lot more energy when they are respired.

8 Explain why prisoners who go on hunger strikes can survive for several weeks without food, but they must drink adequate quantities of water daily.

9 Calvin rarely includes any fruit, vegetables or cereals in his diet. Provide a full explanation of the likely consequences of his behaviour.

10 Soon after eating a packet of orange corn curls and drinking a Diet Coke, Wanda's skin begins to itch and her lips, tongue and throat start to swell. Suggest and explain TWO possible causes of Wanda's symptoms.

11 Two young boys, Kemar and Nathan, suffer from marasmus and kwashiorkor respectively. What foods would you recommend for EACH child and why?

Analysing data

12 Table 9.6 shows the results of a survey carried out on three groups of secondary school students about the average number of servings of each of the six Caribbean food groups that they ate over a 10-day period.

Table 9.6 *The average number of servings eaten by three groups of students over a 10-day period*

Student group	Average number of servings eaten					
	Staples	Legumes and nuts	Fats and oils	Food from animals	Fruits	Non-starchy vegetables
X	44	23	71	42	8	12
Y	38	33	28	30	35	36
Z	78	43	10	21	22	26

a i Name THREE examples of foods which are classified as 'staples'.

  ii Name THREE examples of foods from animals.

b Which group of students had the MOST balanced diet? Give a reason for your answer.

c Which students are MOST likely to become obese if they continue with their current diet? Support your answer with a reason.

d Suggest ONE factor, other than diet, that could contribute to the students identified in part **c** developing obesity.

e With a reason, state which students are MOST likely to suffer from constipation.

13 To determine which nutrients are present in three different food items, **A**, **B** and **C**, a piece of each food item was crushed thoroughly with some distilled water to create a solution and 2 cm³ portions of the solution were tested with the reagents indicated in Table 9.7. The results of the tests are given in the table.

Table 9.7 *The results of food tests carried out on three different food items*

Test reagent	Resultant colour		
	Food item A	Food item B	Food item C
Benedict's solution	Blue	Orange-red	Orange-red
Biuret solution	Purple	Blue	Purple
Iodine solution	Orange-brown	Blue-black	Orange-brown

a Suggest what macronutrient(s) is/are present in EACH food item.

b Is food item **B** MOST likely to be mango, kingfish, sweet potato or ham? Give a reason for your answer.

c Which TWO food items would be best for bodybuilding and why?

d i A suggestion was made that food item **A** might contain a non-reducing sugar. Outline the test that could be performed on **A** to see if the suggestion could be correct.

   ii Explain why it would be of no value to carry out the test outlined in **d i** on food item **B**.

e How would you test food item **C** to see if it contains lipids?

Digestion in humans

Learning objectives

- Examine the **process** of **digestion** in **humans**.
- Relate the **structure** of **teeth** to their **functions** in **mechanical digestion**.
- Describe the **effects** of **temperature** and **pH** on **enzyme activity**.
- Explain the **role** of **enzymes** in **chemical digestion**.
- Discuss **absorption**, **egestion** and **assimilation**.

Digestion and its importance

*Digestion is the process by which food is **broken down** into a form that is useful for body activities.*

To be **useful** for body activities, large food molecules such as polysaccharides, disaccharides, proteins and lipids must be broken down into **simple**, **soluble food molecules**, namely monosaccharides, amino acids, fatty acids and glycerol. These large food molecules are broken down during **digestion**.

Digestion occurs in the **alimentary canal**. The canal is a tube 8 to 9 metres long with muscular walls which runs from the **mouth** to the **anus**. Between the mouth and the anus, the canal is divided into the **pharynx**, **oesophagus**, bag-like **stomach**, **small intestine** composed of the **duodenum** and **ileum**, and the **large intestine** composed of the **caecum**, **colon** and **rectum**.

Three pairs of **salivary glands** lead into the mouth, and the **gall bladder** and **pancreas** lead into the duodenum via the **bile duct** and **pancreatic duct**, respectively. The exit from the stomach is closed by a ring of muscle called the **pyloric sphincter** and the anus is closed by the **anal sphincter**. The alimentary canal and its associated organs, including the liver, gall bladder and pancreas, make up the **digestive system** shown in Figure 9.8 on page 178.

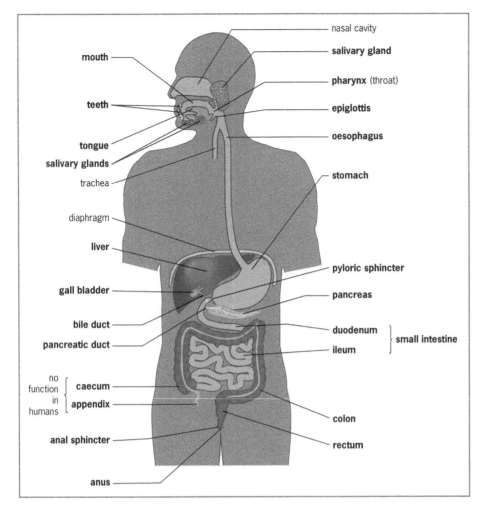

Figure 9.8 *The human digestive system*

Digestion involves **two** processes: **mechanical digestion** and **chemical digestion**.

- During **mechanical digestion**, large **pieces** of food are broken down into smaller pieces. Mechanical digestion begins in the **mouth**, where food is broken into smaller pieces by the **teeth** chewing it and the **tongue** moving it around. It then continues in the **stomach**, where contractions of the muscles in the stomach wall churn the food, which helps to break it down.

- During **chemical digestion**, large, usually insoluble **food molecules** are broken down into small, soluble food molecules by digestive **enzymes** (see page 181). Chemical digestion begins in the **mouth** and is completed in the **small intestine**.

The teeth and mechanical digestion

When food is **chewed** in the mouth, the teeth help to break up **large pieces** of food into **smaller pieces**. This is important in digestion for **two** reasons.

- It gives the pieces of food a **larger surface area** for digestive enzymes to act on, making chemical digestion quicker and easier.
- It makes food easier to **swallow**.

Types of teeth

Humans have **four** different types of teeth: **incisors**, **canines**, **premolars** and **molars**. The arrangement of these in the upper jaw of an adult is shown in Figure 9.9 and the structure and function of each type is given in Table 9.8. An adult has **8** incisors (i), **4** canines (c), **8** premolars (pm) and **12** molars (m). The **dental formula** of an adult gives the number of teeth of each kind in one half of the upper and lower jaw as follows:

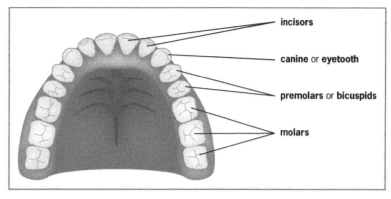

Figure 9.9 *Teeth of the upper jaw of an adult human*

$$i\frac{2}{2} \quad c\frac{1}{1} \quad pm\frac{2}{2} \quad m\frac{3}{3}$$

Table 9.8 *The different types of teeth in humans*

Type	Position	Shape		Functions
Incisor	At the front of the jaw.	Chisel-shaped with sharp, thin edges.	— crown — root	To cut food. To bite off pieces of food.
Canine (eye tooth)	Next to the incisors.	Cone-shaped and pointed.		To grip food. To tear off pieces of food.
Premolar	At the side of the jaw next to the canines.	Have a fairly broad surface with two pointed cusps.	— cusp — root	To crush and grind food.
Molar	At the back of the jaw next to the premolars.	Have a broad surface with 4 or 5 pointed cusps.		To crush and grind food.

Importance of tooth care

Caring for teeth and gums by following the guidelines outlined below is extremely **important** in helping prevent tooth decay and gum disease.

- **Brush** teeth and gums in the proper way for about 2 minutes, at least twice a day, to remove **food particles** and **plaque** that can cause tooth decay and gum disease.
- Use a **fluoride tooth paste** to help strengthen tooth enamel and a good quality **tooth brush** when brushing. Replace the brush every 3 to 4 months.

- Use **dental floss** and an **interdental brush** once a day to clean between the teeth.
- Use an **antibacterial mouthwash** after brushing and flossing to kill any remaining bacteria.
- Eat plenty of **tooth-healthy foods** such as fresh fruits and raw vegetables, and drink water or unsweetened and non-carbonated beverages. **Avoid** eating sugary and starchy foods and drinking sugar-sweetened and carbonated beverages, especially between meals and before going to bed.
- Visit a **dentist** regularly for a check-up and have teeth **professionally cleaned** twice a year.

An introduction to enzymes

Enzymes are biological catalysts that are produced by all living cells. They speed up chemical reactions occurring in living organisms without being changed themselves.

Enzymes are **protein molecules** which animal cells produce from **amino acids** that they obtain from their diet, and plant cells produce from the glucose they make during photosynthesis. Without enzymes, chemical reactions would occur too slowly to maintain life. Enzymes function by **lowering** the energy required to initiate a chemical reaction, known as the **activation energy**. This makes the reaction proceed at a much **faster rate** than it would without the enzymes.

Effects of temperature and pH on enzymes

Enzymes are **specific**, meaning that each type of enzyme catalyses only one type of reaction, and they are affected by **temperature** and **pH**. Questions 15 and 16 on pages 184 to 185 give details of experiments that can be performed to investigate the effect of temperature and pH on enzyme action.

- Enzymes work best at a particular **temperature**, known as the **optimum temperature**. This is about **37 °C** for human enzymes. Enzyme activity is reduced below or above this temperature, as shown in Figure 9.10. At temperatures below 0 °C, enzymes are not active. At temperatures above 40 °C to 45 °C, most enzymes start to be **denatured**; this means that they are **inactivated** and can no longer function.

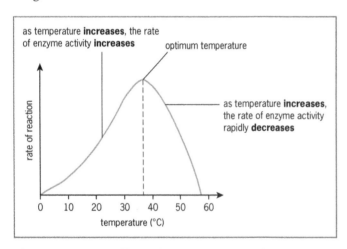

Figure 9.10 *The effect of temperature on the rate of a reaction catalysed by enzymes*

- Enzymes work best at a particular **pH** known as the **optimum pH**. This is about **pH 7** for most enzymes. Enzyme activity is reduced below or above the optimum pH, as shown in Figure 9.11 on page 181. This is because an increase in acidity or alkalinity begins to **denature** enzymes. Extremes of acidity or alkalinity denature most enzymes.

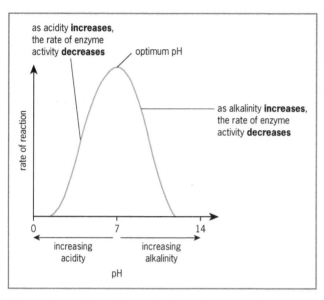

Figure 9.11 *The effect of pH on the rate of a reaction catalysed by enzymes*

Chemical digestion

Digestive enzymes are responsible for breaking down the large, usually insoluble molecules present in food into small, soluble molecules during **chemical digestion**.

The digestive system produces **three** categories of **digestive enzymes**. These are named after the food molecules they break down, also known as their **substrates**. These categories are given in Table 9.9. Several different enzymes may belong to each category and they are found in the **digestive juices** such as saliva, gastric juice and intestinal juice, which are produced in different regions of the alimentary canal. These are summarised in Table 9.10 on page 182.

Table 9.9 *The three categories of digestive enzymes*

Category of digestive enzyme	Food molecules digested (substrate)	Products of digestion
Carbohydrases	polysaccharides disaccharides	monosaccharides
Proteases	proteins	amino acids
Lipases	lipids	3 fatty acids glycerol

Table 9.10 *A summary of the enzymes involved in chemical digestion*

Organ (digestive juice)	Enzyme(s) present	Function of the enzyme
Mouth (saliva)	• **Salivary amylase**	• Begins to digest **starch** into **maltose** (a disaccharide).
Stomach (gastric juice)	• **Rennin** • **Pepsin**	• Produced in infants to clot the insoluble **protein** in milk so the protein is retained in the stomach for pepsin to act on. • Begins to digest **proteins** into **peptides** (shorter chains of amino acids).
Small intestine (duodenum and ileum) (pancreatic juice and intestinal juice)	• **Pancreatic amylase** • **Trypsin** • **Pancreatic lipase** • **Maltase** • **Sucrase** • **Lactase** • **Peptidase** or **erepsin**	• Continues to digest **starch** into **maltose**. • Continues to digest **proteins** into **peptides**. • Digests **lipids** into **fatty acids** and **glycerol**. • Digests **maltose** into **glucose** (a monosaccharide). • Digests **sucrose** (a disaccharide) into **glucose** and **fructose** (monosaccharides). • Digests **lactose** (a disaccharide found in milk) into **glucose** and **galactose** (monosaccharides). • Digests **peptides** into **amino acids**.

The role of bile

Bile is produced in the **liver**, stored in the **gall bladder** and enters the small intestine via the **bile duct**. It contains bile pigments, which are excretory products from the breakdown of haemoglobin in the liver, and **organic bile salts**, which play an essential role in the digestion of **lipids**. These bile salts break down large lipid droplets into smaller droplets. This increases the **surface area** of the droplets for the pancreatic lipase to work on, which makes the digestion of any lipids in the diet much quicker and easier. This process is known as **emulsification**.

Absorption

Absorption is the process by which soluble food molecules, produced in digestion, move into the body fluids.

The **soluble food molecules** which are produced in digestion must move from inside the intestines into the body fluids, namely the blood and lymph, to be transported around the body for body cells to use. The process of **absorption** occurs in the **small intestine** and **colon**.

Absorption in the small intestine

The products of digestion are **absorbed** through the lining of the small intestine, mainly the ileum, and into the **blood** flowing through the **blood capillaries** and **lymph** flowing through the **lacteals** (**lymph capillaries**) in its walls. Substances absorbed include monosaccharides, amino acids, fatty acids, glycerol, vitamins, minerals and water. Water is absorbed by **osmosis** and the other substances are absorbed by a combination of **diffusion** and **active transport**.

Absorption in the colon

Any food that has not been digested and absorbed in the small intestine passes into the **colon**, where **water** and **mineral salts** are absorbed from it. As this undigested waste moves along the colon to the rectum, it becomes progressively more solid as the water is absorbed from it.

Egestion

Egestion is the process by which undigested food material is removed from the body.

The almost solid material entering the rectum is called **faeces** and consists of undigested dietary fibre, dead bacteria and intestinal cells, mucus and bile pigments. Faeces are stored in the rectum and **egested** at intervals through the **anus** when the **anal sphincter** relaxes.

Egestion must not be confused with **excretion** which is the removal, from the body, of waste and harmful substances produced by the body's metabolism. Other than the bile pigments, the components of faeces are not produced by the body's metabolism, so their removal cannot be classed as excretion.

Assimilation

Assimilation is the process by which the body uses the soluble food molecules absorbed after digestion.

* **Monosaccharides**, namely glucose, fructose and galactose, are taken by the **blood** to the liver and the liver converts any non-glucose monosaccharides to **glucose**. The glucose then enters the general circulation and is used by body cells in **respiration** to release **energy**. Any excess glucose can be converted to **glycogen** (animal starch) by cells in the **liver** and **muscles**, and stored. The glycogen can then be converted back to glucose when needed. Alternatively, excess glucose can be converted to **fat** by cells in **adipose (fat) tissue** under the skin and around organs, and stored.

* **Amino acids** are taken by the **blood** to the liver and they then enter the general circulation and are used by body cells to make **proteins** for cell growth and repair. They can also be used to make **enzymes**, **hormones** and **antibodies**. Any excess amino acids are taken to the liver, where the nitrogen-containing part of each molecule is removed and converted into **urea**. The urea is then taken by the blood to the kidneys and excreted. The remaining part of each molecule is converted to glucose, glycogen or fat.

* **Fatty acids** and **glycerol** are carried by the **lymph** to the general circulation and used to make **cell membranes** of newly forming cells. They can also be used by body cells in **respiration** and any excess are converted to **fat** and **stored** in adipose tissue under the skin and around organs.

Recalling facts

1. What is digestion and why is it important?

2. Distinguish between mechanical and chemical digestion.

3. **a** Identify the types of teeth present in the mouth of an adult.
   b Describe the shape and state the function of EACH type of tooth named in **a**.

4. **a** What are enzymes?
   b Name the THREE categories of digestive enzymes produced in the alimentary canal. For EACH category named, identify the macronutrient digested and the products of digestion.

5. Starting with the mouth, list the organs that make up the alimentary canal in the correct order.

6. Distinguish between the following:
   a absorption and assimilation.   **b** egestion and excretion.

7. Describe how the body uses any monosaccharides that are absorbed into the bloodstream.

Applying facts

8 As people age, they often lose some of their teeth. Explain how this can affect their ability to digest their food.

9 Ramon develops a toothache which he tries to ignore, however it gradually worsens until he is forced to visit his dentist who tells him that his tooth is decaying. Outline the procedures Ramon should follow to prevent the same thing happening to any of his other teeth.

10 Hailey decided to use a 'biological' washing powder containing enzymes to remove food stains from her clothes, but she was advised to keep the temperature of the water between 35 °C and 40 °C, and definitely not let it get above 60 °C. Suggest an explanation for these TWO pieces of advice.

11 The enzyme pepsin has an optimum pH of 2.0 and it is inactive below pH 0.5 and above pH 3.5. By means of a sketch graph, show the effect of increasing the pH from pH 0 to pH 5.0 on the activity of pepsin.

12 For lunch, Xavier consumes a lean steak accompanied by a baked potato with butter. Construct a table to show how Xavier's lunch is digested using the following column headings: food item, main macronutrient present, region of the alimentary canal, digestive enzymes, products of digestion.

13 Eduardo has his gall bladder removed. Suggest and explain the change he should make to his diet after the operation.

14 Explain why it is essential that Gavin eats a balanced diet containing sufficient protein, but it may be unwise for him to consume excessive amounts of protein daily.

Analysing data

15 To determine the effect of pH on the activity of amylase, Marcia placed 2 cm³ of amylase solution and 5 drops of iodine solution into each of 5 test tubes. She added 1 cm³ of buffer solution with a different pH to each tube, as shown in Table 9.11, and shook the tubes. She then added 2 cm³ of starch solution to the first tube, shook the tube thoroughly and recorded the time taken for the blue-black colour to disappear completely. She repeated this for the other 4 tubes. Her results are given in Table 9.11.

Table 9.11 *The time taken for the blue-black colour to disappear under different pH conditions*

pH of test tube contents	Time taken for blue-black colour to disappear (s)
5	120
6	60
7	30
8	70
9	150

a What condition, not mentioned in the method, must be kept constant for all tubes to ensure that the results are accurate?

b Explain why the blue-black colour disappeared in each tube.

c Plot a graph to show the time taken for the blue-black colour to disappear against pH.

d Account for the shape of the graph between:

   i pH 5 and 7.   **ii** pH 7 and 9.

e Suggest the MAIN limitation of Marcia's method.

f The experiment was repeated using a buffer solution of pH 10 and the blue-black colour did not disappear. Explain fully the reason for this.

g Describe how the experiment could be adapted to investigate the effect of pH on the activity of an enzyme that breaks down gelatin, a protein.

16 A group of students used the apparatus illustrated in Figure 9.12 to investigate the effect of temperature on the activity of the enzyme catalase, which is found in potato tissue and breaks down hydrogen peroxide into oxygen and water. To do this, they cut a cube of potato measuring 1 cm × 1 cm × 1 cm into 8 pieces of equal size. They added the pieces to 10 cm³ of hydrogen peroxide in a measuring cylinder standing in a water bath at 5 °C. The bubbles formed by the reaction created foam and the students measured the volume of foam after 2 minutes. They then repeated the experiment at different temperatures and their results are shown in the graph in Figure 9.13.

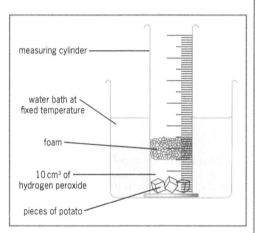

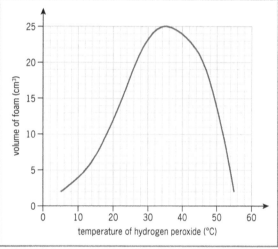

Figure 9.12 Apparatus used to determine the volume of foam produced when potato tissue is added to hydrogen peroxide

Figure 9.13 Graph showing the volume of foam produced against temperature of the hydrogen peroxide

a Construct a suitable table that gives six data points that the students would have used to plot the graph.

b Explain the relationship between the volume of foam produced and the rate of the reaction occurring in the measuring cylinder.

c i Of the temperatures studied, what was the optimum temperature for the enzyme catalase?

   ii How did you arrive at your answer to part **c i**?

d Using the results illustrated in the graph, explain the effect that temperature had on the activity of catalase.

e Suggest TWO precautions that the students should take when doing this experiment.

Respiration

Learning objectives

- Evaluate the **importance** of **respiration** in **providing energy** to **living organisms**.
- Distinguish between **aerobic** and **anaerobic respiration**.
- Discuss the **relevance** of **anaerobic respiration** to **sports** and **industries**.

Respiration and its importance

Respiration is the process by which energy is released from food by all living cells.

Respiration takes place in all living cells all of the time. It provides cells with a constant supply of **energy** to carry out their essential functions and remain alive. Respiration is catalysed by **enzymes** and it occurs **slowly** in a large number of **stages** to prevent a sudden release of heat energy that would harm or kill cells.

During respiration, about 60% of the energy is released as **heat energy** and this helps many organisms to maintain their body temperatures; for example, it helps humans to maintain a body temperature of **37 °C**. The rest of the energy released at each stage is used by cells in the following ways.

- To **manufacture** complex, biologically important molecules such as proteins and DNA.
- For **cell growth** and **repair**.
- For **cell division**.
- In **active transport** to move molecules and ions into and out of the cells through their membranes.
- For **special functions** in specialised cells; for example, for the contraction of muscle cells and the transmission of impulses in nerve cells.

There are **two** types of respiration: **aerobic respiration** and **anaerobic respiration**.

Aerobic and anaerobic respiration compared

Aerobic respiration

Aerobic respiration is the process by which energy is released from food by living cells using oxygen.

Aerobic respiration occurs in most cells. It **uses oxygen** and takes place in the **mitochondria** of the cells. The amount of energy produced depends on the type of molecules respired, known as **respiratory substrates**, as given in Table 9.12.

Table 9.12 *Amount of energy produced by different respiratory substrates*

Respiratory substrate	Energy produced (kJ g^{-1})
Carbohydrates	16
Lipids	38
Proteins	17

The main respiratory substrate is **glucose**, and the glucose molecules are **completely** broken down so that **all** their stored energy is released. Aerobic respiration always produces **carbon dioxide**, **water** and **energy** and can be summarised by the following **word** and **chemical equations**.

$$\text{glucose} + \text{oxygen} \xrightarrow[\text{mitochondria}]{\text{enzymes in}} \text{carbon dioxide} + \text{water} + \text{energy}$$

$$C_6H_{12}O_6 + 6O_2 \xrightarrow[\text{mitochondria}]{\text{enzymes in}} 6CO_2 + 6H_2O + \text{energy}$$

Anaerobic respiration

Anaerobic respiration is the process by which energy is released from food by living cells without the use of oxygen.

Anaerobic respiration occurs in some cells. It takes place **without oxygen** in the **cytoplasm** of the cells. The main respiratory substrate is **glucose** and the products of anaerobic respiration vary. It produces considerably **less energy** per molecule of glucose than aerobic respiration because the glucose molecules are only **partially** broken down and at least one of the products still contains energy. Yeast cells, certain bacteria and muscle cells are capable of carrying out anaerobic respiration.

Table 9.13 **compares** aerobic and anaerobic respiration.

Table 9.13 *Aerobic and anaerobic respiration compared*

Aerobic respiration	Anaerobic respiration
Uses oxygen.	Does **not** use oxygen.
Occurs in the **mitochondria** of cells.	Occurs in the **cytoplasm** of cells.
Releases **large amounts** of energy per glucose molecule.	Releases **small amounts** of energy per glucose molecule.
The products are always **inorganic**, i.e. carbon dioxide and water.	The products are variable, at least one is always **organic**, e.g. ethanol, lactic acid or methane.
Glucose is **completely** broken down and the products contain no energy.	Glucose is only **partially** broken down. The organic products still contain energy.

Relevance of anaerobic respiration

Making bread and alcoholic beverages

Yeast cells carry out a type of anaerobic respiration known as **fermentation** which produces **ethanol, carbon dioxide** and **energy**. Fermentation can be summarised by the following **word** and **chemical equations**.

$$\text{glucose} \xrightarrow[\text{cytoplasm}]{\text{enzymes in}} \text{ethanol} + \text{carbon dioxide} + \text{energy}$$

$$C_6H_{12}O_6 \xrightarrow[\text{cytoplasm}]{\text{enzymes in}} 2C_2H_5OH + 2CO_2 + \text{energy}$$

When **making bread**, the yeast is mixed with flour, water and a small amount of sugar to produce dough. The yeast ferments sugars present in the dough and the **carbon dioxide** produced forms **bubbles** which cause the dough to rise. When baked, heat from the oven causes the bubbles to expand, kills the yeast and evaporates the ethanol.

When making **alcoholic beverages** such as beer, wine, rum and other spirits, the yeast is mixed with grains, fruits or molasses which provide a source of sugar. The yeast ferments the sugars present and the **ethanol** builds up in the fermentation mixture. Fermentation stops when the ethanol concentration reaches about 14–16% because it kills the yeast cells, therefore the ethanol content of beer and wine is always below about 16%. Spirits are made by **distillation** of the fermentation mixture, which increases the concentration of ethanol present.

Anaerobic respiration in sports

Anaerobic respiration plays an important role in **sports**, especially activities requiring short bursts of high-intensity effort such as sprinting, football, rugby, tennis, hockey, gymnastics and weightlifting. During intense physical activity, the body's demands for energy can exceed the amount that can be supplied by aerobic respiration alone. As a result, muscle cells begin to respire **anaerobically**. This produces **lactic acid** and provides the muscle cells with a rapid source of **energy** for short-term, high-intensity activities. This is summarised by the following **word** and **chemical equations**.

$$\text{glucose} \xrightarrow[\text{cytoplasm}]{\text{enzymes in}} \text{lactic acid} + \text{energy}$$

$$C_6H_{12}O_6 \xrightarrow[\text{cytoplasm}]{\text{enzymes in}} 2C_3H_6O_3 + \text{energy}$$

Anaerobic respiration can only go on for a short period of time because the lactic acid builds up in the muscle cells and begins to harm them, causing **fatigue** and even collapse as they stop contracting. The muscle cells are said to have built up an **oxygen debt**. This debt must be **repaid** directly after exercise by resting and breathing deeply so that the lactic acid can be removed by respiring it **aerobically**.

Regular **anaerobic training** involving short bursts of high-intensity exercises improves the **efficiency** of anaerobic respiration in muscles cells allowing athletes to perform at higher intensities for longer periods before becoming fatigued. This improves their overall performance in sports.

Showing that carbon dioxide is produced in anaerobic respiration

The apparatus illustrated in Figure 9.14 is used to show that **carbon dioxide** is produced during anaerobic respiration. A 10% glucose solution is made using water that has been boiled to remove the dissolved oxygen. 20 cm³ of the solution is placed into a boiling tube, some live yeast is added and the mixture is covered with a layer of cooking oil to prevent oxygen from re-entering. The boiling tube is corked with a delivery tube passing through the cork into a test tube containing **bicarbonate indicator solution**, which changes colour from red-purple to yellow in the presence of carbon dioxide. A **control** is also set up in the same way, using yeast that has been killed, and both sets of apparatus are observed.

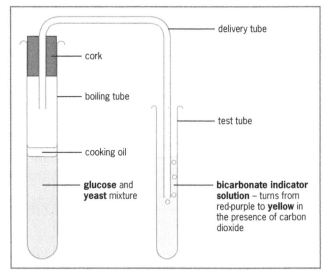

Figure 9.14 *Showing that carbon dioxide is produced during anaerobic respiration in yeast*

Effervescence (bubbling) occurs in the **experiment** and the bicarbonate indicator solution changes colour from red-purple to **yellow**, whereas no bubbling occurs in the control and the indicator solution remains red-purple. This shows that carbon dioxide is produced during anaerobic respiration in yeast.

Note: Question 10 on page 189 gives details of an experiment that can be performed to show that **heat energy** is produced in aerobic respiration.

Recalling facts

1 Define respiration and state its importance to living cells.

2 Give FOUR ways that body cells can use the energy released in respiration.

3 Place the following in descending order of energy released when 1 g of each is respired: carbohydrates, proteins and lipids.

4 State FOUR differences between aerobic and anaerobic respiration.

5 Write a word equation and a chemical equation to summarise aerobic respiration.

6 Outline how anaerobic respiration is used in the brewing industry. Include a relevant word equation in your answer.

Applying facts

7 Suggest why most living organisms use aerobic respiration rather than anaerobic respiration.

8 Darik the baker always uses yeast when making his dough, and he finds that it rises faster on days that are more humid than normal. Suggest a hypothesis for Darik's observation. Design an experiment that you could perform to test if your hypothesis could be correct. Include your expected results if your hypothesis is correct.

9 Karli did very little training before her school Sports Day; however, she decided to run the 400 m as a sprint on the day and collapsed before she reached the finish line.

  a Explain the cause of Karli's collapse. Support your answer with relevant word and chemical equations.

  b What should Karli have been doing in the months before her Sports Day to try to ensure that she did not collapse during the race? Explain your answer.

Analysing data

10 To investigate if heat is produced in aerobic respiration, a Thermos flask was set up as illustrated in Figure 9.15. The flask contained bean seeds that had been soaked in water to start the germination process and then rinsed in dilute disinfectant to prevent the growth of bacteria and fungi. A control was set up in the same way, but this contained bean seeds that had been soaked and then boiled to kill them before rinsing with disinfectant. The temperature of each flask was recorded at 8:00 am and 4:00 pm every day for 3 days. The results are recorded in Table 9.14 on page 190.

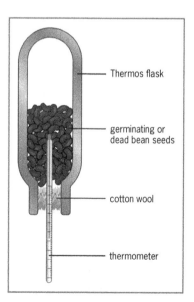

Figure 9.15 *Apparatus used to investigate if heat is produced in aerobic respiration*

a Construct a line graph to show the temperature of the two sets of seeds against time of day. Give your graph a title and clearly distinguish the two curves.

b **i** Account for the shape of the graph for the living seeds between 8:00 am on Day 1 and 8:00 am on Day 3.

Table 9.14 *The temperature of living and dead bean seeds recorded over a three-day period*

Day	Time of day	Temperature (°C)	
		Living bean seeds	Dead bean seeds
1	8:00 am	28.5	28.7
	4:00 pm	31.2	29.8
2	8:00 am	36.8	28.4
	4:00 pm	42.0	29.6
3	8:00 am	45.9	28.6
	4:00 pm	41.8	30.0

ii Suggest TWO reasons why the temperature of the living seeds decreased between 8:00 am and 4:00 pm on Day 3.

iii Account for the trends shown by the temperature of the dead seeds over the three days.

c Suggest TWO reasons why the Thermos flasks were inverted.

d Identify TWO precautions that the investigator should take when setting up and conducting the experiment, and ONE limitation of the method.

e Write a conclusion for the experiment.

11 An experiment was set up, using the apparatus shown in Figure 9.14 on page 188, to determine the effect of temperature on the rate of anaerobic respiration in yeast cells. The time taken for the indicator to turn fully yellow was measured by repeating the experiment at different temperatures. The results are given in Figure 9.16.

a Using any FIVE temperature values, construct a table and record in it the data used to plot the graph. Give your table a suitable title.

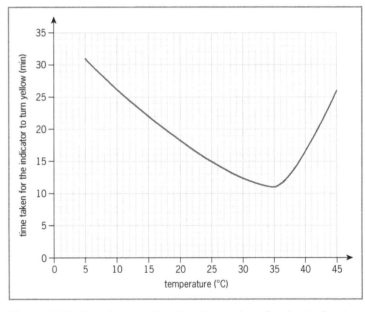

Figure 9.16 *Graph showing the time taken for the indicator to turn yellow against temperature*

b Explain why the indicator turned yellow and provide a balanced chemical equation to support your answer.

c **i** At what temperature was the rate of respiration at its fastest?

ii Explain how you deduced your answer to **c i**.

d Suggest an explanation for the results:

i as the temperature increased from 5 °C to 35 °C.

ii as the temperature increased from 35 °C to 45 °C.

e It was found that the indicator did not change colour at 55 °C. Suggest a reason why.

Breathing, gaseous exchange and smoking

Learning objectives

- Examine the **mechanism** of **breathing**.
- Outline the **stages** of **CPR**.
- Explain the **importance** of **gaseous exchange** in **organisms**.
- Explain the **effects** of **smoking** on **gaseous exchange**.

An introduction to breathing in humans

Breathing refers to the movements that cause air to be moved into and out of the lungs.

It is important not to confuse **breathing** and **respiration**. Breathing is a **physical process** involving movements, whereas respiration is a **chemical process** involving chemical reactions.

Breathing is **essential** to humans for **two** reasons.

- It ensures that air containing **oxygen** is continually drawn into the body. This ensures that humans have a **continual supply** of oxygen to meet the demands of aerobic respiration.
- It ensures that the **carbon dioxide** produced in aerobic respiration is **continually removed** from the body so that it does not build up and poison cells.

The structure of the human respiratory system

The **respiratory system** is responsible for **breathing** in humans. The system begins with the **nasal cavities** and **mouth** which join together in the **pharynx** or **throat**. The pharynx leads into the **larynx** or **voice-box**, which is situated at the top of a tube known as the **trachea**. The trachea leads downwards and branches into two tubes, known as **bronchi** (singular: **bronchus**). Each bronchus leads into a **lung**.

On entering a lung, a bronchus divides repeatedly into smaller and smaller tubes called **bronchioles**, which branch throughout the lung. Each bronchiole ends in a cluster of pocket-shaped air sacs called **alveoli** (singular: **alveolus**). The outside of each alveolus is surrounded by a **network** of **blood capillaries**. Each lung is composed of millions of bronchioles and alveoli.

The lungs are situated inside the **chest cavity** or **thorax** and are surrounded by the **ribs**, which form the **rib cage**. The ribs have two sets of muscles running between them, the **internal intercostal muscles** and the **external intercostal muscles**. The ribs and intercostal muscles form the walls of the thorax, and a dome-shaped sheet of muscle, called the **diaphragm**, stretches across the floor of the thorax.

Each lung is surrounded by two thin layers of tissue called **pleural membranes** which have **pleural fluid** between them. The inner pleural membrane surrounds the outside of the lung tissue, and the outer membrane lines the rib cage and diaphragm.

The structure of the respiratory system is illustrated in Figures 9.17 to 9.19.

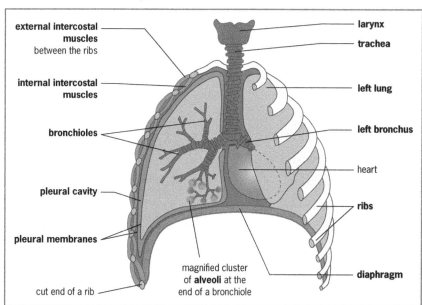

Figure 9.17 *Structure of the human thorax*

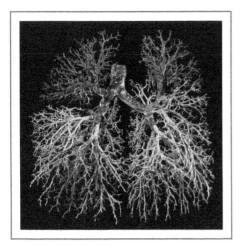

Figure 9.18 *A resin cast of the bronchial tree*

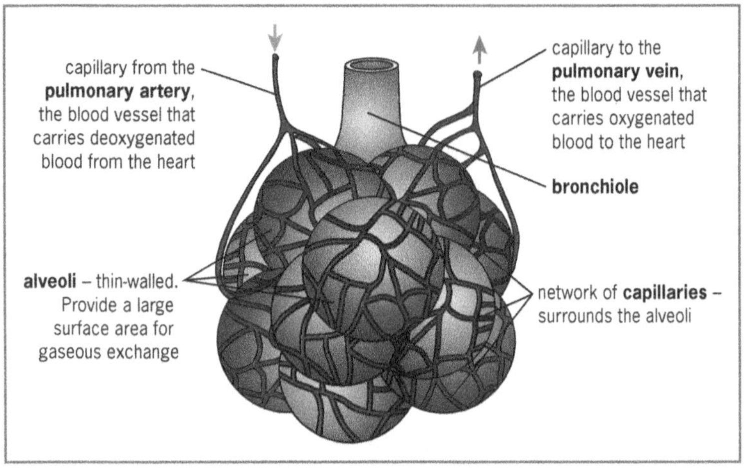

capillary from the **pulmonary artery**, the blood vessel that carries deoxygenated blood from the heart

capillary to the **pulmonary vein**, the blood vessel that carries oxygenated blood to the heart

bronchiole

alveoli – thin-walled. Provide a large surface area for gaseous exchange

network of **capillaries** – surrounds the alveoli

Figure 9.19 *Surface view of a cluster of alveoli showing the blood supply*

The mechanism of breathing

Breathing is brought about by **two** sets of muscles: the **intercostal muscles** between the ribs and the **diaphragm muscles**. These muscles contract and relax and this brings about **movements** of the rib cage and diaphragm, which cause the **volume** of the chest cavity to change. The pleural membranes and pleural fluid form an **airtight cavity** between the lungs and the rib cage and diaphragm, which adheres (sticks) the lungs to the rib cage and diaphragm. Therefore, any changes in the volume of the chest cavity cause the volume inside the lungs to change and this, in turn, causes the **pressure** inside the lungs to change and air to move into or out of the lungs, as explained in Table 9.15.

Table 9.15 *The mechanism of breathing summarised*

	Features	Inhalation (inspiration)	Exhalation (expiration)
1	External intercostal muscles	Contract	Relax
	Internal intercostal muscles	Relax	Contract
	Ribs and sternum	Move upwards and outwards	Move downwards and inwards
2	Diaphragm muscles	Contract	Relax
	Diaphragm	Moves downwards or flattens	Domes upwards
3	Volume inside thorax and lungs	Increases	Decreases
	Pressure inside thorax and lungs	Decreases	Increases
4	Movement of air	Air moves into the lungs due to the decrease in pressure	Air moves out of the lungs due to the increase in pressure

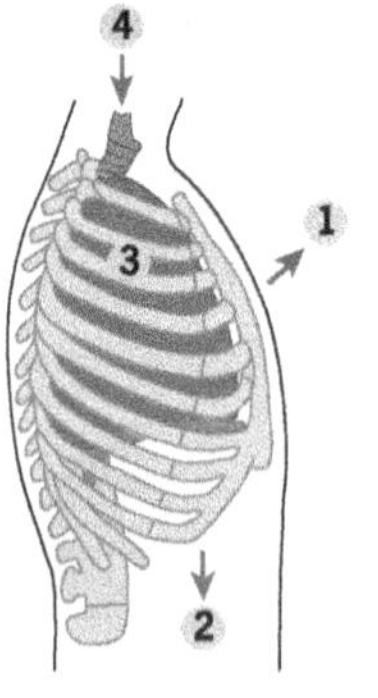

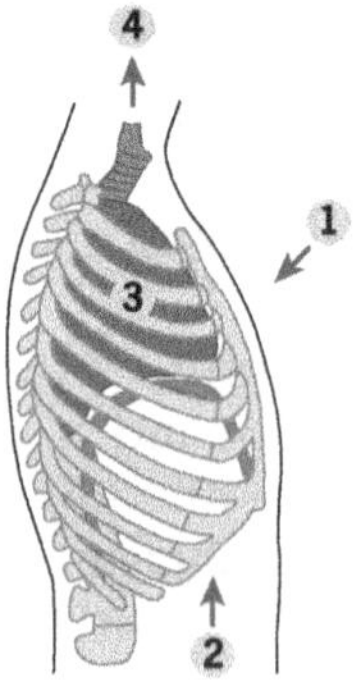

As air enters the lungs during **inhalation**, it passes through the bronchi and bronchioles and into the alveoli, where **gaseous exchange** occurs between the air and the blood passing through the capillaries surrounding the alveoli. Some of the **oxygen** in the inhaled air diffuses into the blood whilst **carbon dioxide** diffuses out of the blood into the air in the alveoli, and is **exhaled** (see page 194).

The role of kinetic energy in breathing

Air moves into and out of the lungs mainly due to the **kinetic energy** of its molecules. The molecules in any gas, including air, possess large amounts of kinetic energy (see Table 18.4 on page 406), they move around freely and rapidly, and they always move from areas of **high pressure** to areas of **low pressure**. During **inhalation**, the pressure inside the lungs **decreases**, which causes the air molecules to move from a region of higher pressure outside the body, into the lungs. During **exhalation**, the pressure inside the lungs **increases**, which causes the air molecules to move out of the lungs into a region of lower pressure outside the body.

The composition of inhaled and exhaled air

The **composition** of **inhaled air** is the same as the atmosphere. **Exhaled air** contains less oxygen than inhaled air and more carbon dioxide and water vapour, as summarised in Table 9.16.

Table 9.16 *The composition of inhaled and exhaled air compared*

Component	Inhaled air	Exhaled air	Reason for the differences
Oxygen (O_2)	21%	16%	Oxygen diffuses into the blood from the inhaled air and is used by body cells in respiration.
Carbon dioxide (CO_2)	0.04%	4%	Carbon dioxide is produced by body cells during respiration and excreted by the lungs.
Nitrogen (N_2)	78%	78%	Nitrogen gas is not used by body cells.
Water vapour (H_2O)	Variable	Saturated	Moisture from the respiratory system evaporates into the air being exhaled.

Cardiopulmonary resuscitation (CPR)

CPR is an emergency procedure performed on a person whose heart has stopped beating (cardiac arrest) and/or who has stopped breathing (respiratory arrest). During CPR, the rescuer performs **chest compressions** to maintain circulation so that oxygen can be delivered to vital organs. **Rescue breathing** or **mouth-to-mouth resuscitation** can also be performed to deliver oxygen to the victim's lungs by persons who are **trained** to carry out CPR. When doing this, the rescuer forces exhaled air containing about 16% oxygen into the victim's lungs. The **steps** used when performing CPR are described on page 250.

Gaseous exchange and its importance

Gaseous exchange is the process by which oxygen diffuses into an organism and carbon dioxide diffuses out of an organism through a respiratory (gaseous exchange) surface.

Gaseous exchange is **important** to all living organisms that respire aerobically for **two** reasons.

* It is the means by which living organisms obtain the **oxygen** they need to sustain aerobic respiration from their environment. This ensures that their cells are provided with the **energy** they need to carry out life processes.
* It is the means by which living organisms get rid of the **carbon dioxide** produced by their cells during aerobic respiration. This ensures that the carbon dioxide does not build up and poison their cells.

Breathing movements speed up the supply of oxygen to **respiratory surfaces** and the removal of carbon dioxide from these surfaces in organisms that breathe; for example, humans and fish.

Respiratory surfaces

Respiratory surfaces or **gaseous exchange surfaces** are surfaces within living organisms through which gases are exchanged, and they have several **adaptations** which make the exchange of gases through them as **efficient** as possible.

- They have a **large surface area** so that large quantities of gases can be exchanged.
- They are very **thin** so that gases can diffuse through them rapidly.
- They have a **rich blood supply** (if the organism has blood) to quickly transport gases between the surface and the body cells.
- They are **moist** so that gases can dissolve before they diffuse through the surface.

The respiratory surface and gaseous exchange in humans

In humans, **gaseous exchange** occurs in the **lungs** between the air in the **alveoli** and the blood passing through the capillaries surrounding the alveoli. The **walls** of the **alveoli** form the **respiratory surface**.

- **Oxygen** in the inhaled air **dissolves** in the moisture lining the alveoli, **diffuses** into the **red blood cells** in the blood passing through the capillaries surrounding the alveoli and binds to the haemoglobin to form **oxyhaemoglobin.** The red blood cells then carry the oxygen in the form of oxyhaemoglobin to all the body cells, where the oxygen is released, diffuses into the cells and is used in **aerobic respiration.**
- **Carbon dioxide**, produced in respiration, **diffuses** from the body cells into the blood. Most of it dissolves in the **plasma**, whilst some enters red blood cells. The plasma and red blood cells carry the carbon dioxide to the lungs, where it diffuses from the blood in the capillaries surrounding the alveoli into the air in the alveoli, and is exhaled.

The process of gaseous exchange is illustrated in Figure 9.20.

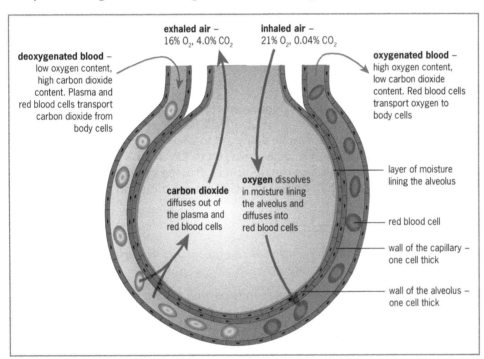

Figure 9.20 *Gaseous exchange in an alveolus*

The respiratory surface and gaseous exchange in a fish

Gaseous exchange occurs in the **gills** of fish. A bony fish (a fish whose skeleton is composed of bone) usually has four gills at each side of its pharynx. The gills are protected at each side by a **gill cover** or **operculum**. Each gill has two rows of long, thin, finger-like projections called **gill filaments** attached to an arch of bone known as a **gill arch** or **gill bar**, as shown in Figure 9.21. Each **filament** has a wall that is **one cell thick** and a **network of capillaries** inside. The **walls** of the **filaments** form the **respiratory surface**.

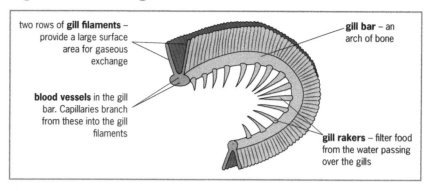

two rows of **gill filaments** – provide a large surface area for gaseous exchange

blood vessels in the gill bar. Capillaries branch from these into the gill filaments

gill bar – an arch of bone

gill rakers – filter food from the water passing over the gills

Figure 9.21 *The gill of a fish showing the gill filaments*

To enable **gaseous exchange**, the fish takes water into its mouth. This water then passes over the gills and moves between the gill filaments. **Oxygen**, which is dissolved in the water, diffuses from the water, through the walls of the filaments and into the blood passing through them. At the same time, **carbon dioxide** diffuses from the blood into the water being passed out of the gills.

The respiratory surface and gaseous exchange in a flowering plant

Gaseous exchange occurs in the **leaves**, **stems** and **roots** of plants by **direct diffusion** between the **air spaces** around all the cells in these organs and the **cells** themselves. Gases diffuse between the **atmosphere** and the air spaces in leaves through the **stomata** (singular: **stoma**), as shown in Figure 9.22 on page 196, and between the atmosphere and the air spaces inside bark-covered stems and roots through the **lenticels** (see Figure 5.9 on page 83). The **walls** and **membranes** of all the **cells** inside the leaves, stems and roots form the **respiratory surface**.

Leaves carry out **two** processes: **respiration** and **photosynthesis**.

- **Respiration** uses oxygen and produces carbon dioxide, and occurs throughout the day and night.
- **Photosynthesis** uses carbon dioxide and produces oxygen, and occurs during the day only.

Movement of gases into and out of **leaves** depends on the time of day.

- During the **night**, only **respiration** occurs. **Oxygen** diffuses **into** the leaves and **carbon dioxide** diffuses **out**.
- During the **day**, the rate of **photosynthesis** is greater than the rate of respiration. **Carbon dioxide** diffuses **into** the leaves and **oxygen** diffuses **out**.

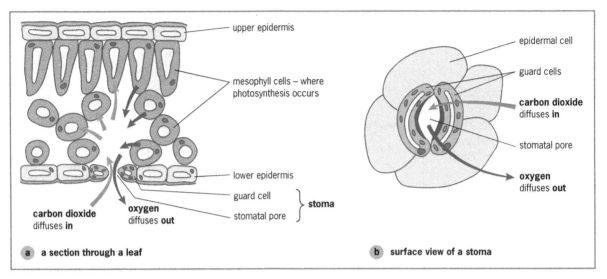

Figure 9.22 *Gaseous exchange in a leaf during the day*

Respiratory surfaces summarised

Table 9.17 summarises the features common to the respiratory surfaces of a human, a fish and a flowering plant to ensure the efficiency of gaseous exchange occurring through them.

Table 9.17 *A summary of the features of the respiratory surfaces of different organisms*

Adaptation of the respiratory surface	Organism		
	Human	Fish	Flowering plant
Large surface area	Each alveolus has a pocket shape and a human has two lungs, each with over 350 million alveoli creating a very large surface area of about 90 m².	Most fish have eight gills, each with a large number of long, thin filaments arranged in two rows, creating a very large surface area.	Leaves are broad, thin and numerous, stems and roots have a branching structure, and leaves, stems and roots are made up of a very large number of cells, creating a very large surface area.
Thin	The walls of the alveoli are only one cell thick.	The walls of the filaments are only one cell thick.	Cell walls and membranes are extremely thin.
Rich blood supply	A network of capillaries surrounds each alveolus.	A network of capillaries is present inside each filament.	No blood supply; direct diffusion occurs between the air and the cells.
Moist	The walls of the alveoli are lined with a thin layer of moisture.	A fish lives in water containing dissolved oxygen.	All the cells are covered with a thin layer of moisture.

The effects of smoking on gaseous exchange

The term **smoking** usually refers to the act of **inhaling smoke** produced by burning plant material in **cigarettes**, **cigars**, **pipes** and **hookahs**. It also refers to inhaling the **vapour** produced by **electronic cigarettes** or **e-cigarettes**, known as **vaping**. The most commonly smoked plant materials are **tobacco** and **marijuana**. The smoke from **tobacco** contains over 7000 different chemicals, the main components being **nicotine**, **carbon monoxide** and **tar** (see Figure 9.23 on page 197).

Inhaling the **smoke** produced when smoking tobacco or marijuana, or the **vapour** produced when vaping, affects the **gaseous exchange** process in a variety of ways.

- It reduces the amount of **oxygen** carried by the blood. This is because the **carbon monoxide** present in the inhaled smoke binds more readily to haemoglobin than oxygen does. This reduces **respiration** in body cells and the smoker's ability to exercise.

- It causes increased **mucus** production in the airways and it paralyses the **cilia** (microscopic hair-like structures) lining the airways which help move the mucus out of the airways, therefore the mucus is not removed. This excess mucus then makes it harder for **oxygen** in inhaled air to reach the alveoli and **carbon dioxide** to be removed. It also causes the smoker to develop a **persistent cough**.

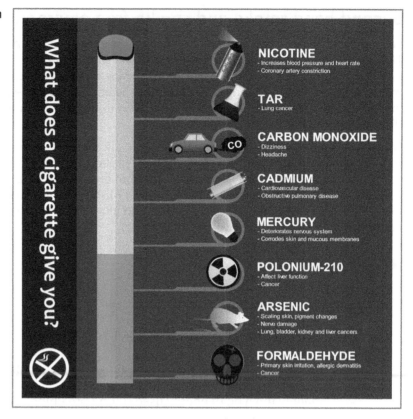

Figure 9.23 *Some components of cigarette smoke*

- It irritates and inflames the walls of the **bronchi** and **bronchioles**. This makes it harder for **oxygen** in inhaled air to reach the alveoli and **carbon dioxide** to be removed, and can lead to the smoker developing **chronic bronchitis**.

- It causes the walls of the **alveoli** to become less elastic and the walls between the alveoli to break down, which decreases their surface area. This reduces **gaseous exchange**, makes exhaling difficult and causes air to remain trapped in the lungs, a condition known as **emphysema**.

- It can lead to the development of **lung cancer**. This happens when abnormal cells grow uncontrollably and form tumours within the lungs. These tumours replace normal, healthy lung tissue and this reduces **gaseous exchange**.

Note: Chronic bronchitis and emphysema are two types of **chronic obstructive pulmonary disease** or **COPD**, as illustrated in Figure 9.24.

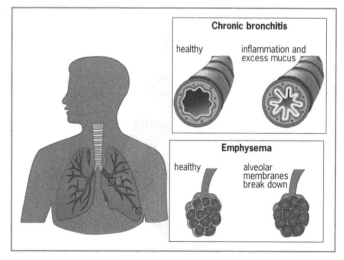

Figure 9.24 *Chronic obstructive pulmonary disease (COPD)*

Second-hand smoke and smoke-free environments

Second-hand smoke consists of smoke exhaled by smokers and smoke from the lit ends of cigarettes. This smoke contains the same chemicals that the smoker inhales in mainstream smoke, however, it has a higher concentration of some **cancer-causing chemicals** or **carcinogens** and smaller particles than mainstream smoke, and it poses considerable **health risks** to non-smokers who are exposed to it. For example, it increases a non-smoker's risk of developing asthma and other respiratory disorders, heart disease, stroke and cancer.

Smoke-free environments, where smoking is not allowed, are extremely **important** because they protect individuals against exposure to second-hand smoke. They help reduce air pollution and contribute to improved air quality. This reduces the harmful effects that air pollutants have on the health of individuals and on the environment (see pages 415 to 416), creates healthier environments and lowers healthcare costs associated with smoke-related illnesses. They also aim to reduce smoking in general and to help people to stop smoking all together.

Recalling facts

1. Define breathing.

2. Describe the structure of a human lung.

3. Explain how air is moved into the lungs during inhalation.

4. Identify the type of energy used during breathing and explain the role it plays in the breathing process.

5. a What is CPR?
   b Outline the principles involved in performing CPR.

6. a What is gaseous exchange?
   b Explain the importance of gaseous exchange to living organisms.

7. Identify the respiratory surface in EACH of the following organisms:
   a a flowering plant.   b a human.

8. Identify the respiratory surface in a bony fish and explain FOUR ways in which the surface is adapted to maximise gaseous exchange.

9. a Name TWO plant materials that are commonly smoked.
   b Explain THREE ways smoking affects the gaseous exchange process.

Applying facts

10. Pneumothorax is a condition that occurs when air enters the pleural cavity. Explain why a person suffering from this condition experiences difficulty breathing.

11. Ashton did not do any science subjects when he was at school, and he is convinced that the air he exhales contains only carbon dioxide. Write an explanation that you could give to Ashton to try and convince him that he is incorrect.

12. For oxygen to diffuse from the air in the alveoli into the blood, a steep concentration gradient must be maintained between the air and the blood. Suggest how this gradient is maintained.

13 Explain why gaseous exchange in leaves depends on the time of the day.

 14 Kofi, who smokes 20 cigarettes a day, noticed that 'No Smoking' signs had recently appeared in the park near his home. Explain why the authorities decided to prohibit smoking in the park.

Analysing data

15 Lung volumes can be tracked using a digital spirometer linked to a computer. To determine the effect of exercise on the volume of air taken in by a student per minute, a student was asked to breathe into the spirometer whilst standing still. He was then told to jog on the spot for a given period of time, after which he was told to stop. The spirometer trace is shown in Figure 9.25.

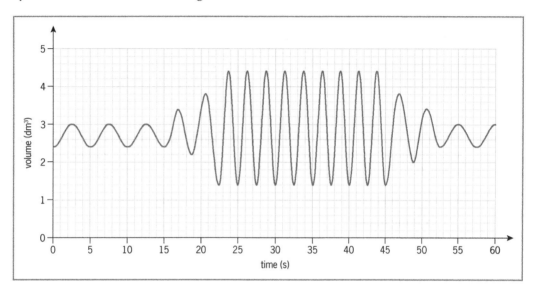

Figure 9.25 *Spirometer trace showing a student's tidal volume before, during and after jogging*

a How long was the student standing still for before being told to jog on the spot?

b How long did the student jog for? Explain how you deduced your answer.

c What volume of air did the student inhale and exhale per breath whilst:

   i standing still?   **ii** jogging?

   Show how you arrived at each answer.

d Determine the student's breathing rate in breaths per minute whilst:

   i standing still.   **ii** jogging.

   Show how you arrived at each answer.

e Calculate the volume of air that the student inhaled and exhaled per minute whilst:

   i standing still.   **ii** jogging.

   Show your working for each answer.

f Explain fully why jogging caused the volume of air inhaled and exhaled by the student per minute to change.

16 The graph in Figure 9.26 shows the average number of cigarettes smoked per person per year and the age-adjusted death rates from lung cancer in males and in females per 100 000 population in the United States (US) between 1930 and 2010.

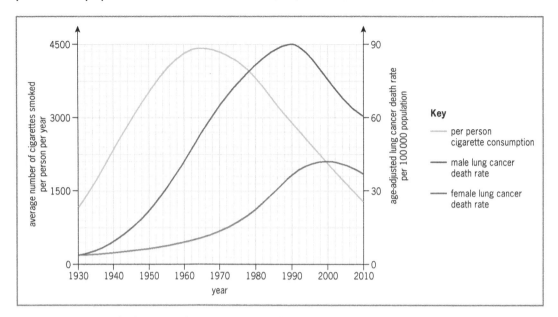

Figure 9.26 *Graph showing the average number of cigarettes smoked per person per year and the age-adjusted death rates from lung cancer in males and in females in the United States (US) between 1930 and 2010*

a In what year was the number of deaths from lung cancer in the US at its highest:

   i among males?   **ii** among females?

b Compare the pattern of deaths due to lung cancer in males and in females.

c i In 1964, the Surgeon General of the US released a report on the negative health effects of tobacco smoking. What conclusion can be drawn about the effect of this report on the smoking habits of US inhabitants?

   ii Explain how you arrived at your conclusion in **c i**.

d Describe and explain what the graph suggests about the link between cigarette smoking and deaths due to lung cancer in US males.

e Suggest the MOST likely reason why the number of deaths from lung cancer was lower each year in females than in males.

10 Fossil fuels and alternative sources of energy

We receive our energy on Earth **from the Sun** in the form of solar radiation. **Plants absorb this energy** during **photosynthesis** and convert it to **chemical energy**, which is then **passed on to animals** as they eat the plants. Energy stored in **plants** and **animals** therefore acts as **fuel**, allowing living organisms to move around and to **do work**. Also, after hundreds of millions of years, energy stored in the **fossils of plants and animals** can become fuels in the form of crude oil, natural gas and coal.

Although a great deal of energy used by humans today is derived from fossil fuels, use of these fuels **produces several pollutants** that have negative effects on our health and on the environment. This, together with other factors mentioned in this chapter, has led to the realisation that there is an **urgent need** to seek and utilise **alternative** and **renewable** sources of energy.

Learning objectives

- Describe **types of fossil fuels** and their **formation**.
- Describe the **mining** and **refining** of fossil fuels.
- Explain the **interconversion of energy** using fossil fuels.
- Discuss the **advantages** and **disadvantages** of using fossil fuels.
- Describe **non-renewable, renewable** and **alternative sources of energy**.
- Appraise the use of **alternative** sources of energy in the **Caribbean**.

Types of fossil fuels and their formation

*Fossil fuels are buried combustible **deposits of decayed** plant and **animal** matter that have been converted to **crude oil, natural gas** and **coal** by subjection to **heat** and **pressure** in the Earth's crust for millions of years.*

Fossil fuels store **chemical potential energy** that is released when the fuel is burnt.

Table 10.1 *Types of fossil fuels*

Fossil fuel	Description	Formation
Crude oil	A yellow-to-black mixture comprised mainly of **solid** and **gaseous hydrocarbons** dissolved in **liquid hydrocarbons**. Hydrocarbons are compounds consisting entirely of hydrogen and carbon.	Produced as the remains of microscopic **marine animals** and **plants** fell to the **ocean floor** where they were covered by mud and subjected to intense **heat** and **pressure**. After millions of years these fossilised organisms converted to crude oil (petroleum). Crude oil is generally found **within layers of sandstone**.
Natural gas	A mixture mainly of **hydrocarbon gases**, the dominant constituent being **methane**.	Formed together with coal and crude oil. It is generally found **trapped** under **impermeable rock**.
Coal	A black or dark brown rock consisting mainly of **carbon**.	Produced as the remains of plants of **swampy, forested areas** were covered by dirt and rock and subjected to intense **heat** and **pressure**.

Charcoal is not a fossil fuel since it is formed by heating materials such as wood in a low-oxygen environment. It is therefore a renewable form of energy (see page 210).

Mining crude oil and natural gas

Oil rigs drill to depths of **several thousand metres**. Oil is **pumped** from these depths but can also rise through pipes with the help of **pressure** from nearby deposits of **trapped natural gas**. Figure 10.1 illustrates typical placement of these rigs.

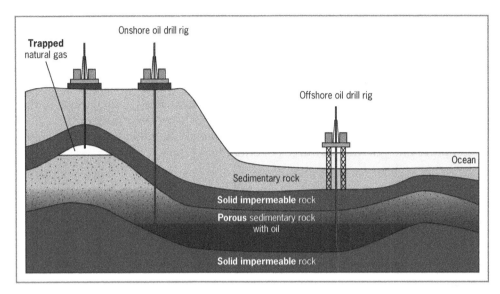

Figure 10.1 *Mining crude oil*

Refining crude oil by fractional distillation

Crude oil is a mixture of hydrocarbons of **differently sized molecules**. The **larger the molecule**, the **higher its boiling point** (or condensing point). The crude oil is **heated** to over **400 °C** in a **furnace** where **most of it vaporises** and is then passed to a **fractionating tower.**

The **larger** hydrocarbon **molecules condense first** and **sink** to the bottom where they are drained into trays. The **remaining** hydrocarbon molecules **rise** within the tower as **vapours**, **condensing** into trays at the **levels** having the temperatures of their **boiling points.** The condensed oils are individually drained from the trays and collected.

Hydrocarbon gases that are not cooled enough to condense, exit from the top of the tower.

The process is illustrated in Figure 10.2 on page 203.

Liquified petroleum gas (LPG) is a mixture of hydrocarbon gases which is used as a source of energy.

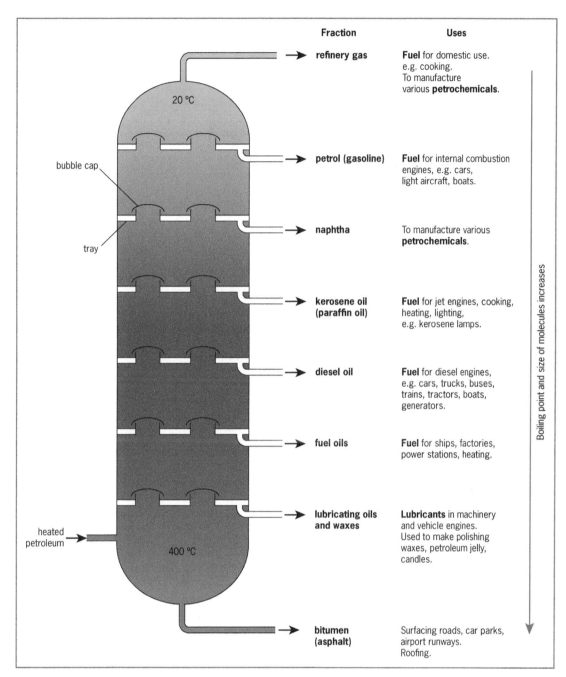

Fraction	Uses
refinery gas	**Fuel** for domestic use. e.g. cooking. To manufacture various **petrochemicals**.
petrol (gasoline)	**Fuel** for internal combustion engines, e.g. cars, light aircraft, boats.
naphtha	To manufacture various **petrochemicals**.
kerosene oil (paraffin oil)	**Fuel** for jet engines, cooking, heating, lighting, e.g. kerosene lamps.
diesel oil	**Fuel** for diesel engines, e.g. cars, trucks, buses, trains, tractors, boats, generators.
fuel oils	**Fuel** for ships, factories, power stations, heating.
lubricating oils and waxes	**Lubricants** in machinery and vehicle engines. Used to make polishing waxes, petroleum jelly, candles.
bitumen (asphalt)	Surfacing roads, car parks, airport runways. Roofing.

bubble cap

tray

heated petroleum

20 °C

400 °C

Boiling point and size of molecules increases

Figure 10.2 *Refining crude oil by fractional distillation*

Interconversion of energy using fossil fuels

The following diagrams show interconversion of energy in different situations.

Gasoline-fuelled car accelerating on level road

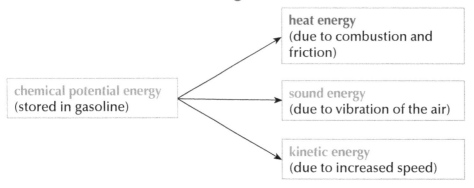

Aircraft taking off

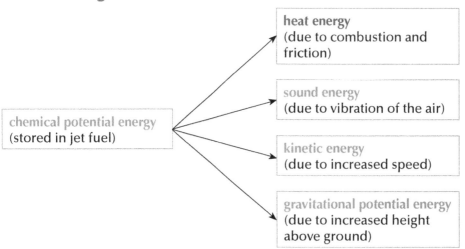

Electrical generation using fossil fuels

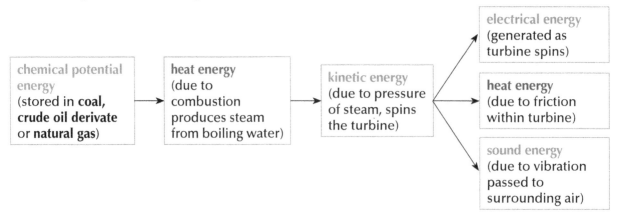

Interconversion of energy using fossil fuels in power plants

Fuel oil and diesel are typically used in the Caribbean for generating electricity in power plants. Figure 10.3 on page 205 illustrates the process.

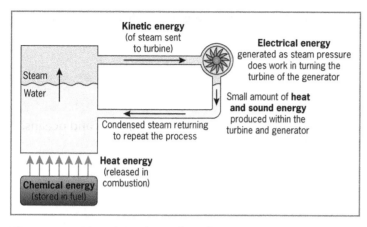

Figure 10.3 *Electricity from diesel*

Advantages and disadvantages of using fossil fuels

Advantages

- **Relatively cheap.**
- **Polymorphic**, meaning they can be used as solid coal, liquid petroleum derivatives or as natural gas.
- **Has a high energy density**, so that a small amount of fuel can produce a large amount of energy.
- **Great economic benefit** as they contribute heavily to national economies.
- **Have shaped our infrastructure** and are the basis of transportation as well as of many products used in our daily lives such as plastics, synthetic fibres, pharmaceuticals, detergents and cosmetics.
- **Predictable**, unlike solar and wind energy which depend on inconsistent and varying weather.
- **Can be stored easily** to be used when required.
- **Relatively easy to use** in liquid or gaseous form since they can be extracted efficiently by rigs, transported through pipelines and converted readily into other forms of energy using a well-established infrastructure.
- **Large reserves** even though they are not renewable. Estimates suggest our oil reserves will last another **50 years** or more, depending on improvements in extraction technologies.

Disadvantages

- **Non-renewable** in the **short term** as they take millions of years to produce and are therefore **exhaustible**; even though there are large reserves now, these reserves are limited.
- **Negative environmental effects: acid rain, global warming** and **climate change**.

Acid rain

The burning of fossil fuels produces oxides of **sulfur** and **nitrogen** (see Table 10.3 on page 209) which dissolve in rainwater to form acids.

*Acid rain, also known as 'acid deposition', is the precipitation of **highly acidic** droplets primarily produced by **oxides of sulfur and nitrogen**. It includes rain, snow, fog, hail and even acidic dust.*

This acidic deposition flows to streams, rivers, lakes and oceans, harming the environment in key ways (see Figure 10.4), such as the following.

- **Increases the bleaching** of coral reefs.
- **Damages soils** and **forests**.
- **Corrodes** metallic objects, buildings and landscapes.
- **Dissolves metals** such as aluminium, forming solutions which then flow to rivers, lakes and oceans, contaminating and poisoning fish and plant life.

Figure 10.4 *Acid rain*

Global warming and the greenhouse effect

Energetic radiation from the Sun is mainly of a **high frequency** which **penetrates** our atmosphere and warms the Earth. This high frequency radiation consists mainly of **visible light** and **ultraviolet (UV)** radiation. The Earth's surface then emits **lower frequency infrared (IR)** radiation which is **absorbed by certain gases** in the atmosphere known as **greenhouse gases** – mainly **carbon dioxide (CO_2)**, **methane (CH_4)**, **nitrous oxide (N_2O)**, **ozone (O_3)**, **water vapour (H_2O)** and **chlorofluorocarbons** (gases composed of chlorine, fluorine and carbon that are known as **CFCs**). As the gases absorb IR radiation, they become warm and emit their own radiation, much of it returning to Earth and preventing our lakes and oceans from freezing. This process is illustrated in Figure 10.5 on page 207.

However, with the **increased burning** of trees as forests are cleared and the **extensive use** of **fossil fuels**, the levels of greenhouse gases have risen to the extent that the planet is experiencing **global warming**. At the time of writing of this text, **2023 was the hottest year on record!**

Table 10.2 *Greenhouse gases*

Greenhouse gas	Generation of greenhouse gas
Carbon dioxide (CO_2)	• Burning fossil fuels • Deforestation (released as trees are burned or cut down) • Respiration
Methane (CH_4)	• Livestock manures • Leaked from sites containing gaseous fossil fuels
Nitrous oxide (N_2O)	• Fertilisers • Some industrial processes
Ozone (O_3)	• UV radiation can break O_2 into individual atoms which then combine to produce O_3 • Electrical discharges from lightning or the spark plugs of engines
Water vapour (H_2O)	• Evaporation from oceans, lakes and rivers • Respiration • Burning of fossil fuels • Burning or decomposition of other carbon-containing compounds
Chlorofluorocarbons (known as CFCs)	• Refrigerants • Aerosol propellants • Industrial processes

The **glass** of a **greenhouse** traps heat in a similar way to **greenhouse gases**. The glass allows high frequency radiation to enter but prevents much of the lower frequency infrared (IR) radiation from leaving (see Figure 10.6).

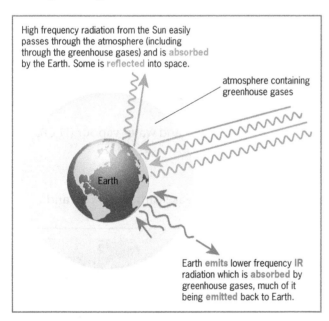

High frequency radiation from the Sun easily passes through the atmosphere (including through the greenhouse gases) and is absorbed by the Earth. Some is reflected into space.

atmosphere containing greenhouse gases

Earth

Earth emits lower frequency IR radiation which is absorbed by greenhouse gases, much of it being emitted back to Earth.

Figure 10.5 *The greenhouse effect*

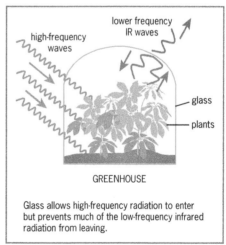

lower frequency IR waves

high-frequency waves

glass

plants

GREENHOUSE

Glass allows high-frequency radiation to enter but prevents much of the low-frequency infrared radiation from leaving.

Figure 10.6 *The greenhouse*

Effects of climate change due to global warming

Global warming has resulted in significant **changes in climate**, more **severe weather**, the **melting** of **polar ice caps** and a **deterioration** of the **ecology** of the planet.

Figure 10.7 *Loss of habitat*

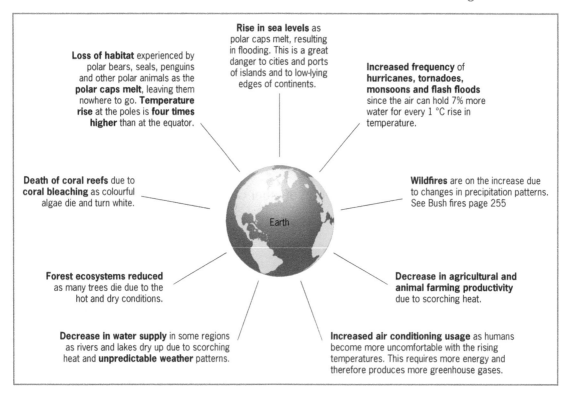

Loss of habitat experienced by polar bears, seals, penguins and other polar animals as the **polar caps melt**, leaving them nowhere to go. **Temperature rise** at the poles is **four times higher** than at the equator.

Rise in sea levels as polar caps melt, resulting in flooding. This is a great danger to cities and ports of islands and to low-lying edges of continents.

Increased frequency of **hurricanes, tornadoes, monsoons and flash floods** since the air can hold 7% more water for every 1 °C rise in temperature.

Death of coral reefs due to **coral bleaching** as colourful algae die and turn white.

Wildfires are on the increase due to changes in precipitation patterns. See Bush fires page 255

Forest ecosystems reduced as many trees die due to the hot and dry conditions.

Decrease in agricultural and animal farming productivity due to scorching heat.

Decrease in water supply in some regions as rivers and lakes dry up due to scorching heat and **unpredictable weather** patterns.

Increased air conditioning usage as humans become more uncomfortable with the rising temperatures. This requires more energy and therefore produces more greenhouse gases.

Earth

Figure 10.8 *Effects of global warming*

Air pollution from burning fossil fuels

Complete combustion of pure hydrocarbons yields carbon dioxide (CO_2) and water vapour (H_2O).

$$\text{hydrocarbon} \rightarrow CO_2 + H_2O$$

However, fossil fuels contain contaminants, and so when burnt, they release carbon dioxide and water vapour as well as carbon monoxide (CO), other harmful gases and particulate matter.

$$\text{fossil fuel} \rightarrow CO_2 + H_2O + CO + \text{harmful gases} + \text{particulate matter}$$

Burning fossil fuels results in air pollution. The **main contributors** to this contamination are:

- **electricity** and **heat production**
- **transport** by road, sea and air
- processes of the **manufacturing industry** (see Figure 10.9).

Figure 10.9 *Air pollution from fossil fuels*

Table 10.3 *Harmful emissions released on burning fossil fuels*

Harmful emission	Negative effect
Carbon monoxide	Produced by **incomplete** combustion. • Combines with the **haemoglobin** in the blood, making it **incapable of transporting oxygen.** • Causes **headache**, **nausea** and **dizziness** and can result in **unconsciousness** and **death.** • Causes **eye irritation.**
Nitric oxide (NO) Nitrogen dioxide (NO$_2$) Sulfur dioxide (SO$_2$)	• Produce **acid rain** (see page 205) by dissolving in rainwater. This produces negative **effects** on animals and plants. • Can produce **respiratory disorders** when combined with other pollutants to form **smog.**
Nitrous oxide (N$_2$O)	• A potent **greenhouse gas** and therefore produces **global warming** and **climate change.**
Volatile organic compounds (VOCs)	Can produce **photochemical smog** when combined with oxides of nitrogen, which can cause the following: • **weakened immune** system • **heart** problems • **respiratory** problems • **eye irritation.**
Particulate matter (very small particles)	Very small particles produced by incomplete combustion. • May cause **irregular heartbeat** and **non-fatal heart attack.** • May cause **respiratory** problems and **lung cancer.** • Causes **eye irritation.** • Results in **reduced photosynthesis** as leaves can be covered.
Heavy metal ions	Mercury, lead, cadmium and other heavy metals. • **Harmful** to animals and plants.

Other problems associated with using fossil fuels

Table 10.4 *Other problems associated with using fossil fuels*

Problem	Negative effect
Pollution from unburnt fuel	**Oil spills** damage our environment, including its plants and animals. **Natural gas** consisting mainly of **methane** (a greenhouse gas) can leak to the air as it is extracted, processed and transported.
Rising health care costs	**Government funding** of healthcare facilities to deal with illnesses associated with pollutants from fossil fuels is a **burden** to economies.
Competition from renewable technologies	**Technologies in renewables** such as solar and wind energy, are improving yearly and so **prices are dropping** for these types of energy. However, **fossil fuels are not a technology**, and so will always maintain a certain cost which is **not likely to be lowered.**

Notes:

Tetraethyl lead is a **poisonous** substance previously added to gasoline to improve its efficiency. Dangerous **lead compounds** expelled by vehicular exhausts have caused this additive to be **banned.**

Carbon dioxide is a **greenhouse** gas emitted by **internal combustion engines (ICEs)**. It is generally **not considered a contaminant**, but plays a major role in **global warming** and **climate change.**

Non-renewable, renewable and alternative sources of energy

Non-renewable energy sources are those which are not readily replenished, so that available quantities become less with use.

Examples are **fossil fuels** and **radioactive materials**.

Renewable energy sources are those which **are readily replenished** (sustainable) by natural processes.

Examples are **solar**, **hydro-electric**, **geothermal**, **tidal** and **wind** energy. Organic matter such as **wood** and **biomass** are considered renewable if the vegetation from which they were obtained is **replanted**.

Due to the problems associated with fossil fuels, it is necessary to use alternative sources of energy.

Alternative energy sources are those which are **not** fossil fuels.

Most alternative sources of energy:

* are **renewable**,
* produce zero or **minimum net environmental pollution**,
* require **minimum operational costs**, although initial plant costs may be high.

Table 10.5 *Uses of various alternative sources of energy*

Energy source	Uses
Solar	**Solar water heaters** These heat water directly with solar radiation (see also Figure 12.14 on page 271). In regions of the northern hemisphere they should be placed on a **south-facing** roof to receive the rays most effectively. *Solar water heater* **Advantages** • **Low maintenance** and **operating costs**. • **Clean** source of energy. • **Limitless supply** of free sunshine. **Disadvantages** • Poor performance on **cloudy days** and so may need to be supplemented by an electric heater. • Initial **set up costs** can be **high** for lower income people. **Photovoltaic (PV) panels** These convert **light** energy into **electrical** energy. As with solar water heaters, in the northern hemisphere they should be placed on a **south-facing** roof. The **tilt** of the solar panel should always allow **rays** to reach it almost **perpendicularly**. More expensive PV systems have **motors** which automatically **adjust** the panels to face the Sun, but these require more maintenance. The conversion to electrical energy is **more efficient** if the panels are **kept cool**. *PV panels*

Energy source	Uses
	Advantages • **Low maintenance** and **operating costs.** • **Clean** source of energy. • The energy can be **returned to the electrical grid** where it would reduce the cost of the total energy consumed by the owner. It can also be **stored in batteries** to be used **at night** or in **remote areas** which otherwise have no access to electricity. • **Limitless supply** of free sunshine is available. **Disadvantages** • **High set up costs** due to **expensive** panels and associated **equipment, extensive installation** and **technical electrical expertise** required. • Poor performance on **cloudy days.** • Large production **requires much space.** • **Low efficiency** of conversion to electrical energy. **Solar cookers and furnaces** These use mirrors to reflect solar energy to a furnace or pot which should be painted matt black (see also Figure 8.8 on page 148). Some solar cookers use **plane mirrors**, but others use **parabolic mirrors** to more effectively focus the solar radiation. **Advantage** • Reduces carbon footprint, meaning it reduces pollution due to fossil fuels. **Disadvantages** • Is **unreliable** since some days there may be very little sunshine. • **Takes longer** to cook, even on sunny days. • Cannot be used at **night.** 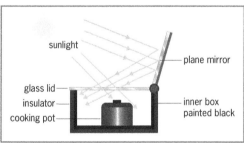 *Solar cooker (plane reflector)* *Solar cooker (parabolic reflector)* **Solar dryers** **Direct solar dryers** are racks on which items are laid to receive sunshine directly in the open air. **Indirect solar dryers** dry items in partially enclosed containers. • Solar radiation enters through a glass cover, warming the air beneath it.

Energy source	Uses

- The **glass cover traps heat** as it does in a **greenhouse** (see also Figure 10.6 on page 207).
- The **black metal grill** is a **good absorber** of the radiation (see also Table 12.2 on page 270).
- Air below the cover is heated and rises through the chamber by **convection**, sucking in cool unsaturated air from outside.
- The warm air leaving the top is humid since it contains moisture from the fish, meats, fruits, and crops that are being dried. Items placed in the dryer become **dehydrated** as the high temperature causes their moisture to **evaporate**.

Advantages

- **Cheap** and easy to build.
- **Indirect solar dryers** are **hygienic** compared to open air solar drying. The transparent cover of a solar dryer protects against rain, dew, dust and airborne insects.
- **Environmentally friendly** producing no pollution.
- **Economical** since the energy it uses is free.
- **Durable** since most last over 15 years with minimum maintenance.

Disadvantages

- **Unreliable,** since on some days there may be very little sunshine.
- **Untimely,** since adequate sunshine may not coincide with the drying season for certain crops.
- **Large surface area** required (for direct dryers).

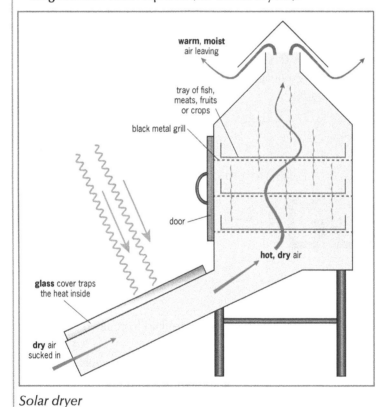

warm, moist air leaving

tray of fish, meats, fruits or crops

black metal grill

door

hot, dry air

glass cover traps the heat inside

dry air sucked in

Solar dryer

Energy source	Uses
Biofuels or biomass	These provide energy from **plant and animal matter**. Although they produce carbon dioxide when burnt, the plants from which they are formed removed carbon dioxide from the air when they were alive, **cancelling the effect on environmental pollution**. Various biofuels are outlined below. **Wood** Wood can be burnt directly to be used as a fuel for cooking or for keeping us warm. **Advantages** • **Cheap.** • Requires **no maintenance**. • Ash can be used as a **fertiliser**. **Disadvantages** • **Pollutes** the air with smoke and soot which is unsafe for us to breathe. • **Increases global warming** as it produces carbon dioxide. • **Large storage** area required. • **Deforestation** can cause problems of **soil erosion** and the **ability to remove carbon dioxide** from the air. The cut trees also generate more CO_2 as they decay. **Biogas** Biogas is obtained from the **decay** of **plant** and **animal wastes** such as **dung** or **sewage** in the **absence of oxygen**. It is mainly composed of **methane** and is used for **cooking, heating boilers** or **driving electrical generators** on farms. The gas can be used directly to supply a stove, or it may be burnt to provide energy to turn the dynamo of an electrical generator. 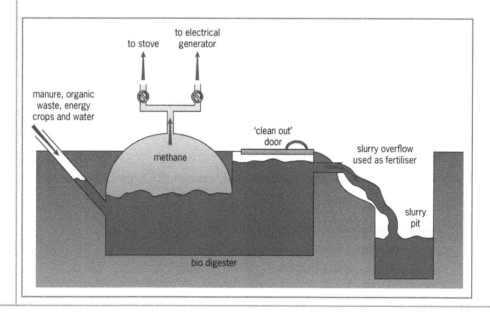

Energy source	Uses

Advantages

- **Cheaper** than natural gas as it does not require much equipment and expertise.
- **Producing** it **does not harm** the **environment**.
- Is a **renewable** resource. Unlike natural gas which is non-renewable, animal and plant waste will always be available.
- **Requires no energy input** to the process of production.
- **Utilises organic waste** such as **animal manure** from open fields which produces methane (a greenhouse gas). It also removes other biodegradable wastes such as those from **slaughterhouses** and the **sludge** from **wastewater** treatment plants. These wastes would otherwise **contaminate landfills** and **pollute water supplies**.
- **Organic fertiliser** is produced as a by-product in the generation of biogas. This is **safer than chemical fertilisers** which have long term **toxic effects**. Organic fertilisers also make plants **resilient to disease**.
- A **healthier alternative** to burning wood in rural areas since it does not contaminate the environment with pollutants that are harmful to our respiratory system.

Disadvantages

- **Impurities** in biogas make it a poor choice for operating equipment since they **corrode machinery**, resulting in high maintenance costs. It is better used for cooking, heating or lighting.
- **Inefficient conversion** to energy since it takes a great deal of organic waste. This discourages governments to set up large-scale biogas plants.
- The **foul odour** of biogas makes it difficult to set up in **residential** or **commercial** areas.
- **Low temperatures** reduce the efficiency since the bacteria that causes the conversion to biogas becomes less active.

Biodiesel

Biodiesel is produced from **vegetable oils**, **animal oils/fats** or **waste cooking oils** by a **chemical process** known as **transesterification**.

Advantages

- **Less polluting** than petroleum diesel.
- We can **dispose of used cooking oil** by recycling it to biodiesel, reducing the dependence on fossil fuel.
- **Lower viscosity** than petroleum diesel and so can replace it in diesel engines.

Disadvantages

- **More expensive** than petroleum diesel.
- **Destroys rubber hoses** and **clogs fuel filters**.
- **Increases** use of **fertilisers**.

Energy source	Uses
	Gasohol Gasohol is made of **gasoline mixed with ethanol** produced from the fermentation of crops such as sugar cane. **Advantages** • **Cheaper** than regular gasoline. • **Less polluting than gasoline** as it emits **less harmful gases** when burnt. • The ethanol component is **renewable** and the amount of fossil fuel is reduced. • Produces **better engine performance** than gasoline. **Disadvantages** • Agricultural land used to produce ethanol instead of food results in **less food** and **increased costs** as the price of land rises. • **Reduced mileage** obtained since gasohol has less energy content per litre. • **Some gasoline engines cannot run on gasohol** unless they are modified.
Wind	**Kinetic energy** from the wind can be used to turn the turbines of electrical generators. **Offshore** wind farms obtain **stronger, more consistent winds** than onshore wind farms. They also have **less visual impact** but are **more expensive to construct and maintain**.   *Onshore wind farm* *Offshore wind farm* **Advantages** • On average, **strong** and **steady** winds blow in the Caribbean. • Many **job opportunities** requiring **several skills** are created by the wind energy industry. • **Clean** since there are no harmful emissions after the plant is constructed. • **Renewable** with free energy input. • **Relatively low maintenance costs.** • **Reduces the reliance on fossil fuels** and their associated problems. • **No air pollution** or **global warming**. • The location used for onshore wind farms can be used at the same time for purposes such as agriculture since the **turbines do not alter the land**. • **Onshore** utility-scale plants produce electricity at very **competitive rates**. • Advancements in **technology** make wind energy even **cheaper**. • Electricity produced from wind turbines can be **stored in batteries** for later use.

Energy source	Uses

Disadvantages

- **High cost** in **constructing** the plant. The sheer size of these wind turbines is revealed in the illustrations above!
- Any **fluctuation in wind speed** means that production may be low even when demand may be high.
- **Noise pollution** and **unpleasant scenery**.
- A **hazard to birds** which may crash into a turbine's rotating blades.
- **Vulnerable** to stormy weather.

Hydro

Water collected behind a dam can be released to turn the turbines of electrical generators. The image here shows the intense power of the water as it drops through the opened gates of the dam through the turbines to the lower level.

Gravitational potential energy is transformed to **kinetic energy** as the water falls, and this is then transformed to **electrical energy** by the generator connected to the turbines.

Hydro-electric plant

Advantages

- **Reduces the reliance on fossil fuels** and their associated problems.
- **Clean** since there are no harmful emissions after the plant is constructed.
- **Renewable** with free energy input.
- The water can be channelled to provide **irrigation** and **water parks** and can be **purified for drinking**.
- **Low maintenance** and **operating costs**.
- **Can produce electricity at any time**, day or night, by opening the gates to release the energy. This contrasts with solar energy conversion where generation can only occur during the day.
- The **timing** of the electrical generation can be **controlled** to release more energy whenever the demand for it is high. It therefore works well in combination with solar and wind energy systems when sunshine and wind speed are low.

Disadvantages

- **High set up cost** of constructing the plant. These are massive power plants.
- **Displaces communities** previously residing around the waterway.
- **Disturbs the ecology** of the water bodies. **Riverbeds downstream** could receive **less sediment** which may damage the fishing industry there. **Water supply** may be **diverted** by the dam upstream, leaving locations downstream with less water.
- **Difficulty** of finding a location that:
  - has an **adequate** and **consistent** water supply throughout the year
  - is **close to power lines**
  - would **not significantly harm** the surrounding ecology.

Energy source	Uses
Tidal	**Tidal barrage generators**

Using strategically placed dams, water from the ocean can be **collected at high tide** and then **released at low tide**. Raising the **sluice gates** allows the water to cause powerful pressures that turn the turbines of electrical generators.

Tidal stream generator

Turbines placed in streams of **high velocity water** moving through **constrictions** (narrow waterways) generate the electricity. The disturbed water in the figure below indicates the power being harnessed by a tidal stream generator.

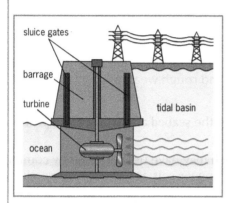 

Tidal barrage generator   *Tidal stream generator*

Advantages

- **Renewable** with free energy input.
- **Clean** since there are no harmful emissions after the plant is constructed.
- **Reliable** output (unlike solar and wind plants) as tides are usually **very predictable**.
- **Strong power output.**
- **Tidal power plants last much longer** than power plants of wind or solar.
- **Coastal areas are protected by the barrages** from stormy weather and high tides.

Disadvantages

- **Scarcity of locations** which have sufficient **difference in levels** between tides.
- Can only be used in **coastal regions**.
- A **hazard to marine life** which may swim into the turbine's rotating blades.
- The **timing of electrical generation** depends on when the tides fall, and this may not coincide with morning or evening which is when demand is highest. A **storage system** of batteries for this **untimeliness** would be necessary. |

Energy source	Uses
Wave	Buoys can be set to rise and fall with the waves, producing kinetic energy to drive electrical generators. **Advantages** • **Renewable**, **infinite** supply of **free energy**. • **Clean** since there are no harmful emissions after the plant is constructed. • **Very reliable** output (unlike solar and wind plants) allowing a **continuous generation of electricity** since the waves are almost always in motion. • Provides a **very high power output**. • **Offshore plants reduce** the **negative environmental effects.** **Disadvantages** • **Very high set up** (**construction**) **costs** for plant and equipment which must be able to resist the environmental elements and rough weather. • Can only be used by **coastal regions**. • Plant equipment can **negatively alter** the **seabed** and **habitat**, and produces sound that can disturb coastal sea animals. • **Uses previously occupied space** which may have been utilised by commercial ships, cruise ships, fishing boats and sporting vessels as well as by recreational areas for beach clubs and restaurants. • **Destroys** the natural **seascape**. • **Stormy weather** significantly **reduces efficiency**.
Geothermal	*Geothermal energy is thermal energy generated in the Earth's **crust** and **mantle** by **radioactivity** and by **friction** between the edges of tectonic plates.* This energy can come to the surface in the form of **lava flows** from erupting volcanoes, **fumaroles** (steam and volcanic gases) and **geysers** (spurts of steam and hot water) from vents in the Earth (see chapter 14, page 315). It can also come to the surface with the help of **human technology**. • **Direct use:** It is common in **volcanic regions** for hot water and steam from hot springs to be used **directly** as the **energy supply for industrial processes** and for **warming buildings**. • **Electrical generation:** Energy plants drill **several kilometres** into the ground and install pipes so that **pressurised water** can be injected into **geothermal reservoirs**. The water absorbs heat from the reservoirs and is forced upward, together with steam, along other installed pipes. The **steam** is used to turn the turbines of **electrical generators**, and the water is then cooled and returned to the **geothermal reservoir** to repeat the process.

Energy source	Uses
	A geothermal energy plant **Advantages** • **Renewable**, as the Earth will continue to emit heat outward for billions of years. • **Relatively clean** as the main emission from most systems is **water vapour**. • **Extremely durable.** Power plants can last for possibly centuries if well managed. • **Very reliable** as they do not depend on weather (unlike solar or wind power plants). • **Minimal space required** by the plant as compared to other power plants. 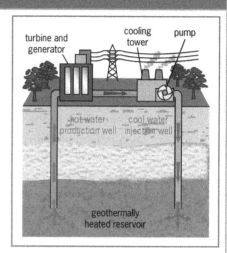 **Disadvantages** • **Small earthquakes** can be produced by injection of high pressure to the system. • **Small amounts of greenhouse gases** are emitted (only a very slight disadvantage). • **Small amounts of toxic elements** can be gathered by the water flow and so the system needs to be carefully managed to ensure adequate insulation from the environment.
Nuclear	This is an **alternative source** of energy that is also **non-renewable**. Energy released by the nuclear **fission** of **uranium** and **plutonium** is used to **produce steam** to turn the turbines of electrical generators.  **Advantages** • Uranium is **available in large quantities.** • The process is **highly efficient** since a small amount of nuclear fuel produces an enormous amount of electricity. • **Inexpensive** since only **small quantities** of nuclear fuel are required. **Delivery and storage** are relatively **cheap** when compared to conventional power plants. • **Reliable** since it does not depend on weather or climatic conditions. • **No greenhouse gases** are produced in the process of nuclear fission. However, if the energy used to mine and refine the ore uses fossil fuels, there will be a small amount of greenhouse gases produced per unit of electricity generated. • Provides a **suitable backup** to **alternative energy sources** (green energy sources) when weather conditions are unsuitable.

Energy source	Uses
	Disadvantages
	• **High set up (construction) costs.**
	• Nuclear fuel is **extremely dangerous** and spent nuclear fuel is **difficult to dispose of.**
	• **Danger** in **mining** and **transporting** radioactive material.
	• **Danger of staff being irradiated** by the radioactive material or being **contaminated** by ingesting or inhaling radioactive material.
	• **A critical malfunction** at the plant can cause huge explosions and result in **radioactive fallout** (the spreading of radioactive material over large regions carried by air masses).
	• **Costly plant closures** are necessary as the plant becomes contaminated with radioactive material after several years of use.

Hydrogen is an energy carrier

Since hydrogen does not exist as an element naturally on Earth, we need to extract it from compounds before using it. For this reason, it is known as an **energy carrier** and not as a renewable energy source.

• **Hydrogen internal combustion engine vehicles** (HICEVs) burn hydrogen to produce energy that provides the thrust necessary to propel vehicles in much the same way as gasoline engines do.
• **Fuel cells** use hydrogen in an **electrolyte** to supply electricity to run the electric motors of electric vehicles.

'Grey' and 'green' hydrogen

*Grey hydrogen is hydrogen produced by a process of **burning fossil fuels** and results in **greenhouse gas** emissions.*

*Green hydrogen (also known as **renewable hydrogen**) is produced by **electrolysis of water** into hydrogen and oxygen using electricity. It does not produce greenhouse gases since the electricity used is **generated from renewable sources**.*

Electrolysis of water: A chemical reaction splits water into hydrogen and oxygen.

$$\text{water} + \text{electricity} \rightarrow \text{hydrogen} + \text{oxygen}$$

Advantages of energy from hydrogen

• **Abundant** and readily **attainable.**
• **Clean** and **renewable.**
• **No harmful emissions** when combusted.
• Has a **high energy density** making it efficient and relatively cheap.
• **Reduces** the reliance on **fossil fuels** since it can supply energy for a wide range of uses.

Disadvantages of energy from hydrogen

- **Expensive to transport** since it must be compressed in strong tanks.
- Can **easily leak** from containers since the gas is comprised of small molecules.
- Is **explosive**.
- Production of **grey hydrogen contaminates** the environment with greenhouse gases and toxic gases.
- **Green hydrogen** does not produce greenhouse gases but is **expensive**.

Zero-energy buildings

Zero-energy buildings (ZEB) or *net zero-energy (NZE)* buildings are those whose annual energy production from renewable sources is equal to their annual energy consumption.

Variables affecting collection of solar and wind energy

Table 10.6 *Variables affecting collection of solar energy*

Variable	Effect
Latitude	The intensity of **received solar energy per unit area (insolation)** decreases at high latitudes due to the increased region of the atmosphere and planet to be warmed by incoming solar beams of given cross-sectional area.
Altitude	High elevations receive more insolation because there is less air above to absorb it.
Season	The daily radiation received depends on the season (see Figure 13.7 on page 294).
Time of day	The intensity of radiation received is greatest when the Sun is directly overhead.
Shadows	Tall buildings, mountains and hills can block the direct rays from the Sun.
Cloud cover	Clouds reduce the received solar radiation by absorbing and scattering it.
Particulate matter	General atmospheric pollution from factories, or dust and sand from quarries or sandstorms, reduce the intensity of solar radiation reaching the planet.

Table 10.7 *Variables affecting collection of wind energy*

Variable	Effect
Wind speed	Strong winds have more kinetic energy to turn the turbines of generators.
Wind consistency	This is necessary for the efficient and continuous production of electricity.
Surface	Speed and consistency are generally higher over the sea than over the land.
Altitude	Wind speed over land is greater at high altitudes as there is then less obstruction from obstacles.
Seasonal weather	Hurricane-prone regions deter the erection of wind turbines due to fear of destruction.

Appraisal of the extent to which alternative sources of energy can be used in the Caribbean

Economic, environmental and social benefits

Several **economic** and **environmental benefits** of renewable energy are listed below.

Economic benefits – more money in pocket

- **New jobs** have become available in research, engineering, manufacturing, installation, marketing and sales of renewable energy products.
- **Cheaper energy** is now available since the natural resources are free.
- **Solar radiation** is **intense** and relatively **consistent** in the region and so costs should reduce as production scales increase.
- **Relatively strong** and **consistent winds** are available, particularly during the winter months, so costs should reduce as production scales increase.
- **Geothermal energy** is available since the region is near to **tectonic plate boundaries**. Tapping on this free energy source would benefit all who use it.
- **Hydropower** has potential in mountainous landscapes. Jamaica, St. Vincent and the Grenadines, Dominica and Suriname have hydro-electric plants.
- **Otherwise-unproductive lands** can now be **productive** as they can be used for wind farms or for growing crops to produce biofuels such as corn ethanol.
- **Increased property value** results if solar water heaters or PV systems are installed.
- **Greater energy independence** is obtained since there is less reliance on **imported fuel** and **fluctuating prices**. Also, if **the national grid** is down, homes can have their own renewable energy stored in batteries.
- **Stable energy costs** are obtained. After installation, operational costs are usually minimal, and renewable energy such as solar, wind, hydro-electric, wave or geothermal energy are continuously supplied and never depleted as are coal, oil and natural gas.

Environmental benefits – safer and cleaner surroundings

- **Improved air quality** is obtained since harmful polluting emissions of burnt fossil fuels are reduced. The health of individuals is therefore improved.
- The **threat of possible oil spills** is reduced if renewables replace fossil fuels.
- **Reduction in global warming** will result since greenhouse gases will be significantly reduced. People may therefore be relieved of the devastating destruction of climate change.

Social benefits – happier, healthier and less stressed

The economic and environmental benefits described all have a **positive social** impact as they improve the general wellbeing of the members of communities. Individuals and families can feel more secure and capable in running their homes and are often **happier**, **healthier** and **less stressed**.

General problems of implementing the switch to alternative sources of energy

- **Lack of adequate education** in technologies.
- **Local banks** are hesitant to offer loans since they lack understanding of the technologies.
- **Foreign banks** are hesitant to offer loans to governments due to lack of transparency and accountability, and to local installers who have no firm or long-term credit history in the field.
- **Large scale generation** of power is **difficult** when compared to generation from fossil fuels.
- **Intermittent energy** is obtained from solar and wind if the sunshine and breezes are inconsistent.

- The **ecology of locations** can be **damaged** by some types of renewable energy plants as they can disturb wildlife and the migration patterns of animals.
- The **construction costs** of renewable energy plants are **generally high**.
- **Visual and noise pollution** is often a consequence of renewable energy plants.

Despite the benefits of utilising renewable energy, the general problems associated with it prevent us from relying completely on it. A **mixture of various types of renewable energy** would be better, with careful consideration of the pros and cons associated with the mix **at the location**. A reserve of energy from fossil fuels can be used as a **back-up** should any of the renewable types fall short in production. With improved technologies and increasing awareness of climate change, the Caribbean is destined to be a significant producer of alternative energy.

Recalling facts

1
  a Define the term 'fossil fuels'.

  b List the three types of fossil fuels.

  c Which type of fossil fuel is generally found:

    i trapped in chambers under impermeable rock?

    ii in areas which were once swampy and forested?

    iii within layers of sandstone?

2
  a What is the temperature at the base of a crude oil fractionating tower?

  b Why is the crude oil heated?

  c In terms of the sizes of long-chain hydrocarbon molecules, which ones condense first in the tower?

  d How are the different oil components collected?

  e What exits the top of the tower?

  f What is drained from the bottom of the tower?

3
  a Why is charcoal not considered a fossil fuel?

  b How are the molecules of hydrocarbon gases different than those of hydrocarbon liquids?

  c What is LPG?

4
  a Write a simple **generalised equation** to show what occurs during the burning of fossil fuels.

  b List FIVE harmful emissions released by burning fossil fuels.

  c State TWO negative effects of unburnt fossil fuels.

5
List TWO ways that EACH of the following greenhouse gases may be generated: carbon dioxide; methane; water vapour; chlorofluorocarbons; ozone; nitrous oxide.

6
  a Define 'acid rain'.

  b What are the acidic oxide gases that mainly produce acid rain?

  c List FOUR harmful effects of acid rain.

7 Draw a well labelled diagram to show how radiant energy transfer results in global warming.

8 **a** Define:
   i renewable energy   **ii** non-renewable energy   **iii** alternative energy.
   b List FIVE types of renewable energy.
   c State with reason, ONE alternative source of energy that is non-renewable.
   d List ONE other type of non-renewable energy.

9 Draw a diagram of a fractionating column used in an oil refinery, showing how the liquid fractions and the hydrocarbon gases are obtained from the system.

Applying facts

10 Draw an **arrow diagram** to describe the energy changes occurring as an aircraft rises from a runway.

11 Describe in **words** the energy changes occurring in a diesel-powered electrical generation plant.

12 Discuss FIVE advantages and TWO disadvantages of using fossil fuels.

13 Discuss FOUR ways in which global warming is detrimental to our planet.

14 Akil's dad warned him that due to harmful exhaust emissions, it is dangerous to be in an enclosed garage for more than a few minutes when the motor of a car with an internal combustion engine is running.
   a Explain how inhaling carbon monoxide can cause death.
   b Describe TWO negative effects that may result from inhaling volatile organic compounds (VOCs) and particulate matter from the exhaust emissions.

15 Ahren has just qualified as an electrical engineer and is advising his dad on the installation of a photovoltaic (PV) system. They live in a remote location in the Blue Mountains of Jamaica where there is no electricity from the grid. The weather in the region is often rainy and windy.
   a What is the function of a PV system?
   b Why is it preferable in Jamaica to place the PV collecting panel on a south-facing roof?
   c Considering temperature effects, why are the panels installed with a space underneath?
   d Discuss THREE advantages and TWO disadvantages of installing the PV system.
   e Recommend a suitable backup system which can also be installed.
   f Ahren tells his dad he wants to soon make their home a '**net-zero-energy building**'. What does he mean?

16 Renata lives in an industrial area which is burdened with particulate matter and acidic gases.
   a What mainly produces these atmospheric pollutants?
   b How do these particles and acidic gases affect the population?
   c How can the **particulate matter** be removed before reaching the air?
   d State with a reason the type of neutralising agent she should use to remove the **acidic gases**.

e How can this burden be made worse during the rainy season?

f Explain how government regulation to prevent atmospheric pollution can boost the economy in the industrial area.

17 Tre is to design a solar dryer.

a Draw a diagram of a possible design he may use.

b Describe how it works.

c State THREE advantages and TWO disadvantages of the solar dryer.

18 Biogas, biodiesel and gasohol are three biofuels. For EACH of these, answer the following.

a Briefly describe how it is produced.

b State TWO advantages and TWO disadvantages of its use.

19 **a** List THREE advantages and TWO disadvantages of a hydro-electric plant.

b Why are solar and wind power plants not as reliable as hydro-electric power plants?

c Explain how the timing of electrical generation can be controlled in a hydro-electric plant to suit demand.

20 **a** Why is hydrogen not considered a renewable energy source?

b What is meant by:

i grey hydrogen?   **ii** green hydrogen?

c State TWO advantages and TWO disadvantages of obtaining energy from hydrogen.

21 Discuss THREE economic benefits and TWO environmental benefits of using renewable energy in the Caribbean.

Analysing data

22 Figure 10.10 shows the power output during a 24 hour period from Kamala's 5 kW PV solar panel.

a What time was:

i sunrise?   **ii** sunset?

b When was the received solar power maximum?

c What was the maximum power output?

d For how many hours was daylight incident on the panel?

e When was the power output 3 kW?

f Explain how it is possible for Kamala to still obtain energy from her system at night even though the panels are not receiving energy.

g Sketch how the graph may look on a cloudy day. The axes of your graph should indicate the same ranges as in Figure 10.10.

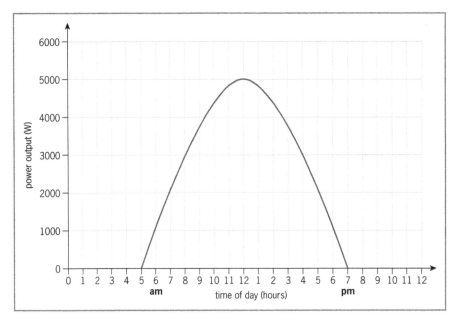

Figure 10.10 *Question 22*

11 Electricity and lighting

Electricity plays a significant role in our everyday lives. It is essential in running our homes and workplaces, providing us with lighting, heating, television, cell phones and other necessary requirements.

It is a **clean form of energy** which can be **transported over long distances** through electrical wires, and it **can be stored** in batteries and devices known as capacitors.

We need to be cautious when handling electrical devices to avoid **electrical shock** which can be dangerous and may even cause **electrocution** (see later in this chapter).

Current electricity and its applications

Learning objectives

- Describe **conductors**, **semiconductors** and **insulators**, giving examples and their uses.
- Investigate the **conductivity** of various materials.
- Learn to draw **circuit diagrams** using **circuit symbols**.
- Understand **series** and **parallel electrical circuits**.
- Use the equations, $V = IR$ (Ohm's law) and $P = IV$
- Calculate **energy consumption** using $E = Pt$
- Assess the costs contributing to **electricity bills**.
- Discuss the **safety features** used with domestic electrical devices, including the use of **fuses**, **circuit breakers**, **colour-coded wiring**, **earth wiring** and different **wire gauges**.
- Explain the advantages of connecting **domestic devices in parallel**.
- Discuss **energy conservation** measures.
- Compare **artificial sources of light**.

Conductors, semiconductors and insulators

Conductors of electricity are materials containing electrical charges which can flow freely.

Good conductors of electricity include the following examples.

- **Metals** – These contain free electrons (negative charges) that have broken away from the orbits around the nucleus of their atom. The electrons flow in **one direction** when connected across the terminals of a battery.
- **Graphite** (a form of carbon) – Although this is a non-metal, it also contains free electrons (negative charges) and is therefore a good conductor. The electrons flow in **one direction** when connected across the terminals of a battery.
- **Solutions of ionic substances** (electrolytes) such as table salt – These have freely moving, **positive** and **negative** charges (ions) that travel in **opposite directions** when connected across the terminals of a battery.
- **Molten ionic substances** – These also contain freely moving **positive** and **negative** ions that travel in **opposite directions** when connected across the terminals of a battery.

Semiconductors are materials with conductivity between that of good conductors and insulators.

Insulators (or poor conductors) are materials through which electrical charges cannot flow freely.

Poor conductors of electricity are **non-metallic materials** (excluding graphite). These substances do not contain charges that can move freely when connected across the terminals of a battery.

Table 11.1 *Examples of conductors, semiconductors and insulators*

Good conductors	Semiconductors	Insulators
silver, gold, copper, aluminium, graphite, blood and other electrolytes in our body, salt water, molten table salt	silicon, germanium	glass, wood, plastic, rubber, cork, paper

Table 11.2 *Uses of conductors, semiconductors and insulators*

Material	Uses
Conductors	**Electrical wires**
	• **Copper** is commonly used since it is an excellent electrical conductor.
	• **Aluminium** is also a very good conductor. It is preferred to copper for transmitting electricity through power lines over long distances. Being **less dense** than copper, the **power lines are not as heavy**. Aluminium is also **cheaper** per gram than copper.
	• **Silver** conducts electricity better than copper but is expensive and so is only used for special circuits.
	Electrical contacts
	Graphite is used for electrical contacts which must repeatedly connect and disconnect (*make and break*). Unlike metals, which can make poor connections due to the non-uniformity of their surfaces, graphite wears to a smooth surface for greater area of contact.
	Electrolytes in batteries
	• **Lead-acid batteries** used in vehicles utilise **dilute sulfuric acid** as an **electrolyte**.
	• **Alkaline cells** utilise **potassium hydroxide** as the **electrolyte**.
Semi-conductors	**Electronic components**
	Semiconductors are used in the manufacture of light and temperature **sensors**, light-emitting diodes (**LEDs**), **transistors** and several other components found in computers and modern electronic devices.
	Photovoltaic cells
	Solar panels that convert light energy into electrical energy are made of semiconducting materials, the most popular being silicon.
Insulators	**Covers for electrical wires and enclosures for certain electrical appliances**
	Rubber and plastics are used in electrical appliances to provide insulation and so prevent electrical shock.

Experiment to determine if various materials are conductors or insulators

• Set up the circuit as shown in Figure 11.1a on page 229.

• Temporarily join the contact terminals, X and Y, with a short length of connecting wire, and close the switch to connect the lamp directly to the cell. The lamp should glow brightly.

• Open the switch and replace the space between X and Y with small pieces of various materials, one at a time. Suitable solid materials to use are copper, iron graphite, plastic, wood, cloth, rubber, glass and paper. Liquids such as water, cooking oil, solutions of vinegar (a weak acid) and salt water can also be connected between X and Y using electrodes (conducting strips) as shown in Figure 11.1b on page 229.

- In each case, turn on the switch and observe the brightness of the bulb, recording your observations and conclusions in a table like the one shown.

Material	Observation of brightness of lamp	Conclusion: Conductor or insulator?

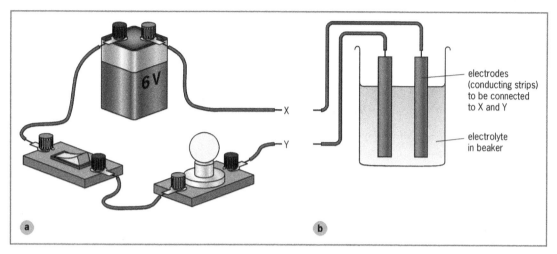

electrodes
(conducting strips)
to be connected
to X and Y

electrolyte
in beaker

a

b

Figure 11.1 *Experiment to determine if various materials are conductors or insulators*

Flow of electricity in circuits

*An **electric circuit** is a complete conducting path or loop through which electrical charges can flow.*

Electrical charges (for example, electrons in metal wires) will not flow if this path is broken.

Circuit diagrams are drawn using various **circuit symbols** representing the electrical components.

Some important circuit components

- **Cell** – A device that provides a **voltage** to a circuit as it converts chemical energy into electrical energy.
- **Battery** – A **group** of **one or more cells.**
- **Resistor** – A component that **opposes** the **flow of current.**
- **Voltmeter** – A device that **measures the voltage** (**potential difference**) between two points in an electrical circuit.
- **Ammeter** – A device that **measures the current** flowing through a point in an electrical circuit.
- **Rheostat (variable resistor)** – A resistor whose **resistance** can be **altered**, usually by a slider control.
- **Fuse** – A metallic resistance wire placed in series with a device, which **protects** a circuit from **excessive current** by becoming hot, melting, and breaking it.
- **Transformer** – A device that **increases** (steps up) or **decreases** (steps down) an **alternating voltage.**
- **Switch** – An electrical component that can **connect** or **disconnect** the conducting path in an electrical circuit.

Table 11.3 *Electrical circuit symbols*

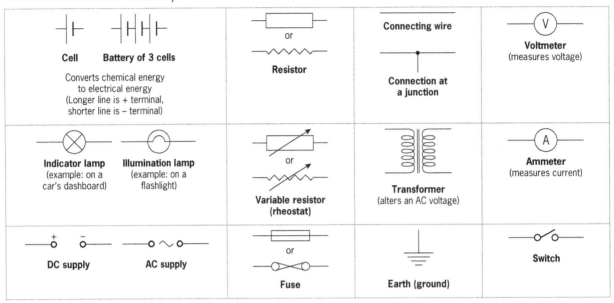

Voltage, current, resistance and power in electrical circuits

Important electrical quantities and their SI base units are defined in Table 11.4.

Table 11.4 *Important electrical quantities and their SI base units*

Quantity	Definition	SI unit
Voltage (V)	Electrical **energy per unit charge** used in **pushing** the electrons through the resistance of the circuit.	volt (V)
Current (I)	**Rate of flow** of **electrical charge** through a circuit.	ampere (A)
Resistance (R)	The **opposition** to the **flow of electrical current** through a material.	ohm (Ω)
Power (P)	The **rate** of **using energy** (the rate of doing work).	watt (W)

*Potential difference (pd) is the **voltage** (energy per unit charge) to **push the electric charges** through a section of the **resistance** of the circuit.*

*Electromotive force (emf) of a cell or battery is the **total voltage (pd)** (total energy per unit charge) that a battery can provide across all the other components in the circuit.*

Cells and batteries behave as **pumps to push electrons**. For this reason, we speak of the **electromotive force** of a cell. When connected to components in a circuit, they provide a **voltage** or **potential difference** across those components to **force** current through them.

A battery of emf 3 V will provide a voltage (**potential difference** or **potential drop**) of 3 V across the resistors in the circuit as illustrated in Figure 11.2.

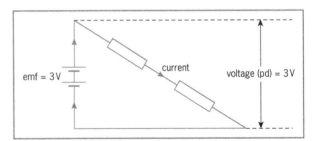

Figure 11.2 *The emf of a battery providing a voltage across the resistors of a circuit*

- **Direction of current** – Current in a circuit flows from the **positive** terminal of a cell or battery through the other components in the circuit and returns to the **negative** terminal of the cell or battery.
- **Electrical current is analogous to water flowing** – We can think of a battery as a water pump raising water to the top of a hill and then releasing it to flow down the hill through the resistance of pebbles or bushes. The stronger the pump (battery), the higher it can raise the water (the greater the voltage or pd it provides) and therefore the faster the water can flow (greater current) **down** the steeper slope.

Some useful equations

voltage = current × resistance

$$V = IR$$

From this equation, we can show that:

$$R = \frac{V}{I}$$

Ohm's law *states that the current through a metallic conductor is proportional to the voltage across it providing the temperature is constant.*

From a **graph of V against I**, of several different values of voltage and corresponding current, the resistance can be found from its gradient (slope). (See question 27, page 249.)

The **power** used by a device depends on the product of the **voltage across** it and the **current through** it.

power = voltage × current

$$P = VI$$

The **power** used by a device can also be found as the **rate of energy** used by it.

$$\text{power} = \frac{\text{energy}}{\text{time}}$$

$$P = \frac{E}{t}$$

From this equation, we can show that:

$$E = Pt$$

Power rating of appliances

Appliances are generally labelled with their **power rating**. This indicates the rate at which they can **do work** or **use energy**. If an appliance is labelled 1500 W, 110 V, this indicates that it should be operated with a voltage of 110 V placed across it. It will then consume a power of 1500 W.

Example 1

A device is rated as 440 W, 220 V. Calculate the following.

a The current flowing in the device when a voltage of 220 V is across it.

b The resistance of the device.

c The energy consumed in 10 minutes.

Solution

a $P = VI$ Lay out the equation as you have learnt it.

  $\dfrac{P}{V} = I$ Make the subject of the equation the quantity you are solving for.

  $\dfrac{440\ W}{220\ V} = I$ Substitute values with respect to SI base units into the equation.

   $2\ A = I$ Represent final answer with correct SI unit.

b $V = IR$

  $\dfrac{V}{I} = R$

  $\dfrac{220\ V}{2\ A} = R$

   $R = 110\ \Omega$

c $P = \dfrac{E}{t}$

  $E = P \times t$

  $E = 440\ W \times (10 \times 60)\ s$ ...remember to convert time to seconds.

  $E = 264\ 000\ J$

Note: We use standard SI base units (see page x) to do our calculations.

Connection of ammeters and voltmeters

Ammeters are used to measure the **current through a point** in a circuit and are connected in **series** with the components through which the current flows. They have **negligible resistance** so as **not to alter the current that was flowing before the measurement**. The ammeter shown in Figure 11.3 is measuring the current through the lamp and the rheostat (variable resistor). Compare the circuit diagram to the photo.

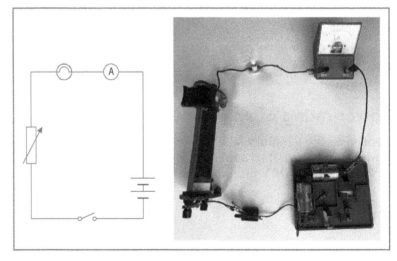

Figure 11.3 *Ammeters are connected in series with components*

Voltmeters are used to measure the **voltage** (potential difference or potential drop) **across a component** and are therefore connected **between two points**, one on either side of the component (resistor or bulb). They have very high resistance so as not to deviate any significant current **and therefore not to alter the current that was flowing before the measurement**. The voltmeter shown in Figure 11.4 is measuring the voltage **across** the lamp. Compare the circuit diagram to the photo.

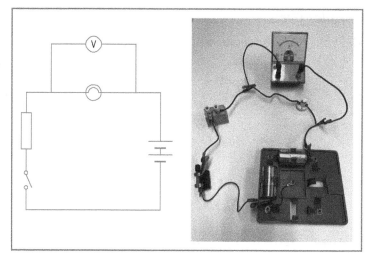

Figure 11.4 *Voltmeters are connected across (in parallel with) components*

Current in series and parallel circuits

Series circuits

In a **series circuit**, components are connected **one in front of the next**, as shown in Figure 11.5. Current leaves the positive terminal of the battery and has only one path around the circuit to the negative terminal.

The motion of the electrical charges must be the same at all points in a series circuit. It can be compared to a line of people, each person walking with their arms resting on the shoulders of the person in front of them. Each person must move at the same speed. **Current at each point in a series circuit must therefore be the same.**

If the circuit wire is cut at any point, the charge at the point must stop, and therefore all the other charges must immediately stop and the current drops to zero.

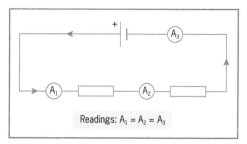

Figure 11.5 *Current in a series circuit is everywhere the same*

Parallel circuits

In a **parallel circuit**, components are connected **in different branches** as shown in Figure 11.6. Current leaves the positive terminal of the battery, splits into branches at point X, recombines at point Y, and then flows to the negative terminal of the battery.

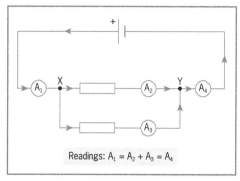

Figure 11.6 *The sum of currents in parallel branches is equal to the current outside the branches.*

Voltage in series and parallel circuits

Series circuits

When components are connected in series, the voltage supplied by the cell or battery is split amongst the components **in proportion to their resistances**. The **sum** of the voltages across all the resistors is equal to the emf of the cell or battery.

In Figure 11.7 on page 234, since R_1 has **twice the resistance** as R_2, V_1 obtains **twice the share of the voltage** from the battery as V_2.

Parallel circuits

The voltage across **components in a parallel** circuit is **always the same** no matter what the resistances are!

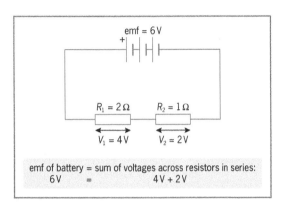

emf of battery = sum of voltages across resistors in series:
  6 V   =   4 V + 2 V

Figure 11.7 *The **sum** of voltages across components in a series circuit is equal to the emf*

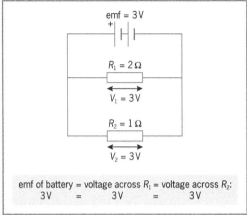

emf of battery = voltage across R_1 = voltage across R_2:
  3 V   =   3 V   =   3 V

Figure 11.8 *The voltage across components in a parallel circuit is the same*

Example 2

Figure 11.9 shows a battery of emf 12 V connected to a resistor of resistance 6 Ω. Calculate the following.

a The current flowing in the circuit.

b The power used by the resistor.

c The energy used by the resistor in:

  i 20 seconds.

  ii 2 minutes.

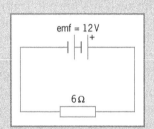

Figure 11.9 *Example 2*

Solution

a

$V = IR$	Lay out the equation as you have learnt it.
$\dfrac{V}{R} = I$	Make the subject of the equation the quanity you are solving for.
$\dfrac{12\ V}{6\ \Omega} = I$	Substitute values with respect to SI base units into the equation.
$2\ A = I$	Represent final answer with correct SI unit.

b
$$P = VI$$
$$P = 12\ V \times 2\ A$$
$$P = 24\ W$$

c i
$$P = \frac{E}{t}$$
$$P \times t = E$$
$$24\ W \times 20\ s = E$$
$$480\ J = E$$

c ii
$$P = \frac{E}{t}$$
$$P \times t = E$$
$$24\ W \times (2 \times 60)\ s = E \qquad \textit{... we must convert time to seconds}$$
$$2880\ J = E$$

Example 3

Figure 11.10 shows a circuit containing a battery of emf 3 V which delivers a current of 0.5 A. The variable resistor (rheostat) is adjusted to a value of 4 Ω and the resistance of the lamp is 2 Ω. Calculate the following.

a The total resistance in the circuit.

b The pd (voltage) across:

  i the lamp.   **ii** the variable resistor.

c The power used by:

  i the lamp.   **ii** the variable resistor.

d The power provided by the battery.

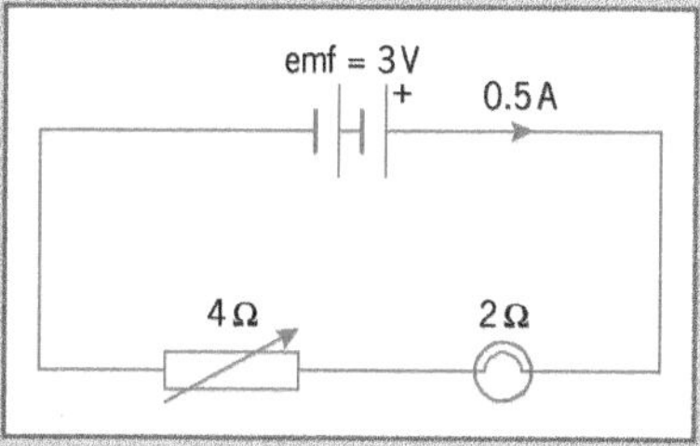

Figure 11.10 *Example 3*

Notes:

- For **cells in series**, the total emf of the battery is the sum of the emfs of the individual cells. So, if the cells are similar, they each provide 1.5 V.

- **Lamps have resistance.**

- For **resistors in series**, the **total resistance** is the **sum of** the individual **resistances**: $R = R_1 + R_2$

- The battery places its emf of 3 V across both resistors: some across the rheostat and the remainder across the lamp.

- **Current is the same at all points in a series circuit** and so the same 0.5 A flows through each resistor.

- The power **delivered by the battery** is the same as the total power **consumed by the resistors** (the variable resistor and the lamp).

Solution

a   Total resistance, $R = R_1 + R_2$ $R = 4\,\Omega + 2\,\Omega = 6\,\Omega$

b i $V = IR$

                  $V = 0.5\,A \times 2\,\Omega$ Using: current through lamp × resistance of lamp.

                  $V = 1\,V$

  ii $V = IR$

                  $V = 0.5\,A \times 4\,\Omega$ Using: current through rheostat × resistance of rheostat.

                  $V = 2\,V$

c i $P = VI$

                  $P = 1\,V \times 0.5\,A$ Using: voltage across lamp × current through lamp.

                  $P = 0.5\,W$

  ii $P = VI$

                  $P = 2\,V \times 0.5\,A$ Using: voltage across rheostat × current through rheostat.

                  $P = 1\,W$

d   At the battery: $P = VI$

                  $P = 3\,V \times 0.5\,A$ Using: voltage (emf) of battery × current from battery.

                  $P = 1.5\,W$

Alternatively, the power provided by the battery is the same as the power consumed by the two resistors, and this is: 0.5 W + 1 W = 1.5 W

Consumption of electricity in the home

The electric power grid provides us with voltages we can use to run our electrical devices including our refrigerators, lights, ovens, TVs and many others.

Alternating current (AC) repeatedly reverses direction.

The **AC frequency** in most Caribbean territories and the US is **50 Hz**.

The **electric company delivers AC** to the **power outlet sockets** in our homes (see Figure 11.11). The **voltage** supplied to the outlet sockets varies from island to island in the Caribbean. In Barbados and Trinidad, it is 115 V and in Jamaica it is 110 V. Guyana offers 120 V and 240 V supplies.

Figure 11.11
Power outlet socket

Direct current (DC) flows in one direction only.

Batteries produce DC. The cylindrical cells that we typically use for our torchlights and remote controls in our homes deliver a DC voltage of 1.5 V. When we place them in series (one behind the other with the bump on the top of one meeting the flat surface on the base of the other), we are making a battery. If we place TWO such cells in series, our battery will have a voltage of 2 × 1.5 = 3 V. In this way we can make batteries of several different voltages.

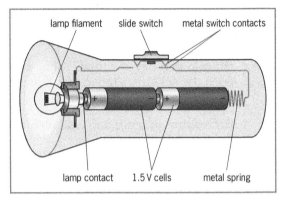

Figure 11.12 *Torchlight with 3 V battery*

Advantages of parallel connection of appliances in domestic wiring

- **Appliances may be manufactured to operate on standard voltages.** When appliances are connected in parallel, they each get the voltage of the supply. Appliances connected in parallel in Guyana can each receive 120 V. However, if connected in series, each appliance would only receive a share of this voltage with the total of all the shared voltages adding to 120 V.
- Appliances can be controlled by **individual switches**.
- Appliances can **draw different currents** from the same voltage and therefore **operate at different powers** (P = VI).

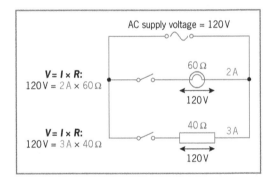

Figure 11.13 *Advantages of parallel connection*

Measuring electrical energy consumption using the kilowatt-hour

The **joule** is a very small quantity of energy compared to the mean daily electrical energy consumption in any home. Instead, we use the more appropriate unit, the **kilowatt-hour** (kW h).

$$E = P \times t$$
$$1\,J = 1\,W \times 1\,s$$
$$1\,kW\,h = 1\,kW \times 1\,h = 1000\,W \times (60 \times 60\,s) = 3\,600\,000\,J$$

Calculate the total weekly energy used in a home in kW h, given the following information about appliance use.

- Five 40 W lamps used for 6 hours each night.
- One 1600 W electric kettle used for 15 minutes ($\frac{1}{4}$ h) every morning.
- One 200 W refrigerator always in use (24 hours, 7 days per week).
- One 1000 W electric oven used for 2 hours on Mondays, Wednesdays and Fridays (3 times per week).

Solution

Appliance	Power (kW)	Time (h)	Energy (kW h)
Five 40 W lamps	5 × 0.040	6 × 7	8.4
One 1600 W kettle	1 × 1.6	$\frac{1}{4}$ × 7	2.8
One 200 W refrigerator	1 × 0.200	24 × 7	33.6
One 1000 W electric oven	1 × 1	2 × 3	6.0
TOTAL (kW h)			**50.8**

Notes:

- In these calculations, power must be expressed as kW (not W) and time must be expressed in h (not s) since energy must be expressed as kW h.
- The value of each appliance in column 4 is obtained by multiplying the values of columns 2 and 3.

Electricity meters

Electricity meters are usually read monthly, and the energy used within the period is found by subtracting the previous reading from the current reading.

Digital meters

- These are easier to read than analogue meters (see Figure 11.14).

Analogue meters

- The dials are read from left to right.
- The hands on successive dials rotate alternately clockwise and anti-clockwise.
- The digits selected are those to which the hands point or have just passed.
- The reading shown in Figure 11.15 is 05358 kW h.

Figure 11.14 *Digital electric meter*

Figure 11.15 *Analogue electric meter*

Charges on our electricity bills

- **Energy charge** – This may be on either a fixed or a variable rate.
  - **Fixed (flat) rate** – For example, $0.25 per kW h charged for all electricity used.
  - **Variable (block) rate** – For example, the first 100 kW h charged at $0.80 per kW h, and further charges charged at $0.50 per kW h.
- **Fixed charge** – A fixed charge may be applied to cover administrative costs and/or meter rentals.
- **Fuel adjustment charge** – A charge per kW h to cover fluctuating fuel costs.

On 30th June, a customer's meter reading was 22 538 kW h and on 31st July it was 22 689 kW h. Calculate the electricity bill for the period given the following added information.

- Energy is charged on a block rate. The first 100 kW h is charged at $0.50 per kW h and any additional usage is charged at $0.40 per kW h.
- There is also a fuel adjustment charge of $0.010 per kW h and a rental fee of $10.00.

Solution

First calculate the energy used: 22 689 kW h – 22 538 kW h = 151 kW h

Then calculate the cost:

- Energy (variable rate)
  - first 100 kW h: $\quad 100 \text{ kW h} \times 0.50 \dfrac{\$}{(\text{kW h})} = \$50.00$
  - remaining 51 kW h: $\quad 51 \text{ kW h} \times 0.40 \dfrac{\$}{(\text{kW h})} = \$20.40$
- Fuel adjustment: $\quad 151 \text{ kW h} \times 0.010 \dfrac{\$}{(\text{kW h})} = \$1.51$
- Rental: $\quad = \$10.00$

TOTAL CHARGE	$81.91

Average power consumed by some commonly used appliances

Table 11.5 shows the average power consumed by several commonly used appliances. Note that appliances which produce a **heating effect** generally use more power than others.

Table 11.5 *Average power consumed by some commonly used appliances*

Appliance (heating type)	Power (W)	Appliance	Power (W)
Microwave	1000	Wi-Fi router	5
Electric kettle	1200	Tablet	10
Hair dryer	1200	Laptop	60
Toaster oven	1200	43-inch LED TV	80
Clothes iron	1200	65-inch LED TV	100
Air fryer	1500	Running treadmill	300
Electric oven	2000	Refrigerator	400
Electric clothes dryer	5400	CRT TV	500

Safety features of electrical devices

Fuses and circuit breakers

A **fuse** is a short wire that melts and breaks a circuit when the **current exceeds a certain value**.

A **circuit breaker** is an electromagnetic switch that breaks the circuit when the **current exceeds a certain value**.

Fuses and circuit breakers have similar roles in protecting an electrical circuit. Figures 11.16 and 11.17 respectively show a typical **fuse** and a set of FIVE **circuit breakers** in the distribution box of a home.

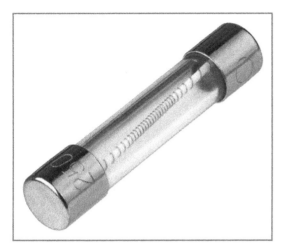

Figure 11.16 *A typical fuse*

Figure 11.17 *Circuit breakers in a distribution box*

Placement of fuses and circuit breakers

Fuses and circuit breakers should be placed **in series with devices** to protect them from excessive currents that could **overheat** and **destroy the components** of the circuit and could **cause an electrical fire**.

A fuse can be fitted in a **distribution box** or **within a plug**, or it can be built into **an appliance** (for example in a microwave oven).

Choosing a suitable current rating for a fuse

The **current rating** of a fuse or circuit breaker is the **current which is slightly greater** than that which should flow in the circuit **during normal operation**.

Example 6

A toaster rated at 1300 W is to be used on a 110 V electrical mains supply.

a Calculate the amperage (current in A) that it takes.

b State, with reasons, which of the following fuses would be suitable to protect the device:
   3 A, 5 A, 13 A, 20 A

c Calculate the energy consumed by the toaster when used for 3 minutes.

Solution

a $P = VI$
Lay out the equation as you have learnt it.

$\therefore I = \dfrac{P}{V}$
Make the subject of the equation the quantity you are solving for.

$I = \dfrac{1300\ \text{W}}{110\ \text{V}}$
Substitute values using SI base units into the equation.

$I = 11.8\ \text{A}$
Represent final answer with correct SI unit.

b The 13 A fuse is most suitable since its current rating is just above the normal operational current the toaster was designed to take.

- The 3 A and 5 A fuses will 'blow' as soon as the device is switched on.

- The 20 A fuse will allow a much larger current to flow than is necessary, which can result in overheating or damage to the components and may even cause an electrical fire.

c $P = \dfrac{E}{t}$

$\therefore E = P \times t$

$E = 1300\ \text{W} \times (3 \times 60\ \text{s})$

$E = 234\ 000\ \text{J}$

Three-core flex used in domestic wiring

Appliances are generally connected to the electrical mains supply by means of a flexible cable known as a **three-core flex.** This is comprised of three individually insulated wires known as the **live** wire, the **neutral** wire and the **earth** (or **ground**) wire that are connected to the electrical mains supply by a **three-pin plug.**

Many appliances in the Caribbean are sourced from the UK, Europe, the USA or Canada. Table 11.6 and Figures 11.18 and 11.19 show the colour codes used to distinguish the live, neutral and earth wires in those regions.

Table 11.6 *Domestic wiring colour codes*

	LIVE	NEUTRAL	EARTH
UK and Europe	Brown	Blue	Green and yellow striped
USA and Canada	Black	White	Green or bare copper (USA)/green or green and yellow striped (Canada)

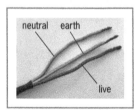

Figure 11.18 *Colour code used in the UK and Europe*

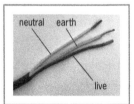

Figure 11.19 *Colour code used in the USA and Canada*

Live and neutral wires

The **live** and **neutral wires** are connected to the terminals of the appliance and carry the current under normal operation. **No current flows in the earth wire during normal operation.** See Figure 11.20 on page 241.

Earth wire and short circuits

Figure 11.21 shows how the **case of a device** can become electrified if it is a conductor and is accidentally connected to the circuit by means of a conducting material. If **no earth wire** is connected and someone touches the case, they may receive an **electric shock** as a current will then flow through them between the ground and the case. This change in path of the current is known as a **short circuit**. It results in a **larger than usual current** since **some of the resistance is bypassed**.

As a safety precaution, many appliances are fitted with an **earth wire** connected between the case of the appliance and ground, and with a **fuse** connected in the **live wire** as shown in Figure 11.21.

As soon as the short circuit occurs, the high current flows in the **live and earth wires** instead of in the **live and neutral** wires.

Two advantages of this system are as follows.

1. **The device is protected** from the high current since the fuse will blow and therefore immediately break the circuit.

2. **Personal electric shock is prevented** since, with the fuse blown, the case is no longer electrified and is therefore no longer a danger.

If the case of the device is not a conductor, the earth wire is not usually required. This is shown in the lighting circuit of Figure 11.22.

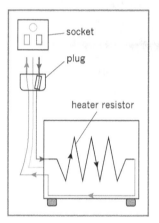

Figure 11.20 *Current flow under normal operation*

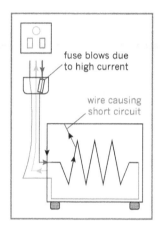

Figure 11.21 *Current flow during short circuit*

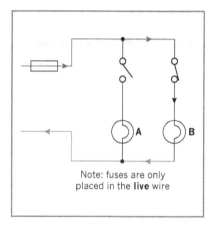

Figure 11.22 *Lighting circuits usually have no earth wire*

Wiring a three-pin plug

1. Cut off about **4 cm** of the **plastic** flex casing.

2. Strip **1 cm** of the insulation from each of the three cables using a wire stripper.

3. Tightly twist the strands of each cable.

4. The brass terminals of the plug should be marked L, N, E. One by one, twirl each cable in a **clockwise** direction around its terminal, ensuring that there are **no exposed strands** and then tighten the screw to hold it firmly. Brass connections are used since brass is a good conductor and does not corrode easily.

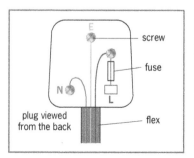

Figure 11.23a *Wiring of a three-pin plug with a fuse*

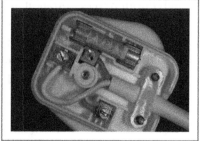

Figure 11.23b *Three-pin plug with fuse in live wire*

Thick wires are required for circuits with high currents

High powered circuits draw large currents. They must be fitted with thick wires through which current can flow easily. They will then have less chance of overheating, **melting insulation**, **destroying electrical components** and producing **electrical fires.** The following circuits require thick wires.

- **Heavy-duty appliances** – These include water heaters, refrigerators, electric stoves, electric ovens, washing machines, electric clothes dryers and power tools such as electric saws, grinders and demolition hammers (see Figures 11.24a and 11.24b).
- **Circuits in the home connected to several power outlets** – The current flowing in these circuits is the sum of the currents taken by the appliances being used at the same time. If we connect a washing machine, blender, toaster, microwave oven, hair dryer, clothes dryer and electric iron to the same power outlet, we will more than likely cause an electric fire (see Figure 11.37 on page 253).
- **Overhead cables** – Are used for **long-distance transmission** of electricity (See Figure 11.24c).

a Dryer and washing machine   **b** Demolition hammer   **c** Electric grid

Figure 11.24 *High powered circuits requiring thick wires*

Danger of electrical shock

We can receive an electrical shock if we touch a live wire when some other point of our body is grounded (earthed). Current will then flow between the **live wire** and the **ground.**

- Since our skin is not such a good conductor, small voltages will give us only a slight shock.

If we are **wet**, however, we become **better conductors** and the electrical shock is more **severe.** Large voltages can produce large currents and therefore result in **electrocution.**

Electrocution is execution by electricity.

- Our **body fluids** (blood and water) are **good conductors.** Even when our skin is dry, a voltage can be high enough to penetrate it and to drive a current through our body fluids which may be strong enough to even **stop our heart.**
- Our **muscles may suddenly contract** causing us to be **jolted** from our position, or we may **uncontrollably clutch the live wire**, preventing others from freeing us.
- **Severe burns** may be produced as the high current through our body can **destroy our cell tissue.**

Energy conservation measures

Energy conservation is the effort to reduce wasteful energy consumption by using fewer energy services and/or more efficient energy services.

Electrical appliances, particularly high-powered heating devices such as hair dryers, electrical ovens and electric clothes dryers, can be **costly to operate** (see Table 11.5). We need to **conserve energy**.

Conserving energy is beneficial to us for the following reasons:

* **To reduce expense** – Most Caribbean islands import large quantities of oil as the energy source to run their electrical generators. This expense is relayed on to the end user.
* **To reduce pollution of the environment** – By consuming less energy, we reduce our reliance on fossil fuels which are destroying the environment.

Energy wastage due to faulty electrical appliances

* **Corrosion of parts** of circuits can sometimes result in current leakages.
* **Poor lubrication** of moving parts can lead to energy loss as heat due to friction.
* **Faulty thermostats** cause overheating of heaters, and excessive cooling in fridges and air conditioners.

Ways to reduce energy consumption in the home

* **Install high efficiency**, **certified** appliances.
* **Install occupancy sensors**. These electronically sense the number of persons in a room and automatically adjust systems such as lights, temperature and air conditioning.
* **Use energy efficient lighting** such as LED (Light-Emitting Diode) or fluorescent bulbs.
* **Use LED-LCD** (light-emitting diode-liquid crystal display) or **plasma TV screens** since they are more energy efficient than the old **CRT** (cathode ray tube) screens (Figure 11.38 on page 253). LED-LCD is the most efficient.
* **Switch off lights** and **unplug appliances** which are not in use.
* **Install photovoltaic (PV) systems** to produce electricity from sunlight (Table 10.5 on page 210).
* **Install solar water heaters** (Table 10.5 on page 210).
* **Cover saucepans** when cooking to prevent wastage of energy to the air.
* **Use pressure cookers** to cook food faster.
* **Adjust the heat source to the minimum** required to maintain boiling since it will cook the food at the same temperature anyhow.
* **Wash only full loads** in the washing machine.
* **Use clothes lines or racks** instead of electric dryers.
* **Avoid frequent opening of the fridge** door and ensure that its rubber gasket is not worn.
* **Ensure that your home is efficiently designed** to have less dependence on air conditioning. The following measures can help.
  + **Double glazing** of windows.
  + **Proper insulation** of **roofs** and **ceilings**.
  + Walls built with **hollow blocks** (air is a poor conductor).
  + **Curtains** and **awnings** or **hoods** at windows to block solar radiation.
  + **Walls painted white** to reflect solar radiation.
  + **Planting nearby trees** to block direct solar radiation.

Figure 11.25 *Reflecting solar radiation with white exterior walls. Blocking solar radiation with nearby trees*

Comparing artificial sources of light

Fluorescent tubes

These are sealed tubes containing an **inert gas argon** and **mercury vapour** at low pressure. Tungsten electrodes are at the ends of the tube.

- When a **voltage is applied** across the ends of the tube, the tungsten cathode emits electrons.
- The **electrons** are pulled by a voltage through the vapour and **strike the mercury atoms** causing them to **release ultraviolet** radiation.
- The **white phosphor coating** on the inner wall of the tube is a **fluorescent** coating which **absorbs the UV** and immediately emits a **bluish-white light**.

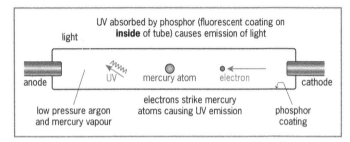

Figure 11.26 *Function of a fluorescent tube*

Figure 11.27 *A fluorescent tube*

Compact fluorescent lamps (CFLs)

These operate on the same principle as the fluorescent tubes and are replacing the less efficient filament lamps since they are designed to fit into the same fixtures.

Light-emitting diodes (LEDs)

These emit light when a current passes through them. They **convert electrical energy very efficiently** to light energy and can produce **soft white** or **'daylight-type'** lighting.

Incandescent (filament) lamps

These consist of a **high resistance coil** made of the metal tungsten kept in a sealed glass enclosure containing an **inert gas** or **vacuum**. An electrical current through the filament heats it to about **2500 °C**, causing it to emit heat and **visible yellowish light**, sometimes referred to as **'warm light'**.

The three bulbs shown in Figure 11.28 were designed to each emit 1100 lumens of light. However, the **incandescent lamp** uses almost seven times the power that the LED uses. The output of an incandescent lamp is about **90% heat and 10% light**, making it much more **costly to operate**.

Table 11.7 shows an extensive comparison of the characteristics of fluorescent, LED and incandescent lamps.

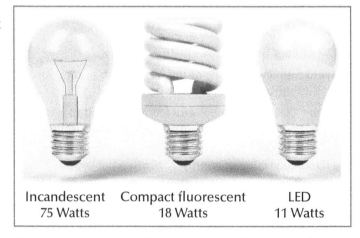

Incandescent	Compact fluorescent	LED
75 Watts	18 Watts	11 Watts

Figure 11.28 *Filament lamp, compact fluorescent lamp, light-emitting diode*

Table 11.7 *Comparison of lamps used for lighting*

Characteristic	Fluorescent	LED	Incandescent
Approximate relative lifetime/hours	10 000	Can be more than 50 000	1000
Efficiency	High	Very high	Poor
Similarity to daylight	Yes. Produce light similar to daylight.	Yes. Some produce light like daylight.	No. Produce a warm white light.
Shadow characteristic	Diffused	Sharp	Diffused
Brightness control	Not as easily controlled	Not as easily controlled Only some are dimmable	Easily controlled by varying the voltage
Consistency of brightness	Dims/flickers with age	Consistent	Consistent
Relative operational cost	Lower	Least	Highest
Relative cost of device	Reasonable	Becoming reasonable	Reasonable
Durability	Easily broken	Withstands bounces	Easily broken
Wastes energy as heat	30% wasted	Very little wasted	90% wasted
Contains toxic mercury	Yes (harms environment)	No	No

Note: Several countries have **banned** the manufacture, sale, distribution and retail of **incandescent lamps** so as to be more energy efficient and therefore less reliant on fossil fuels.

Recalling facts

1. **a** Define each of the following:

   i conductors   **ii** insulators.

   b Prepare a table categorising the following into conductors, semiconductors and insulators: iron, wood, plastic, cork, mercury, germanium, graphite, salt water, aluminium, molten salt, paper, silicon.

2. **a** Which conductor is suitable for electrical contacts that must repeatedly connect and disconnect?

   b Give TWO reasons why aluminium is preferred to copper as a material used to transmit electricity in power lines over long distances.

   c Give TWO uses of semiconductor materials.

   d What role do insulators play in electrical circuits?

3. **a** Define EACH of the following:

   i voltage   **ii** current   **iii** resistance   **iv** power.

   b Write worded equations for relations between each of the following variables:

   i voltage, current and resistance.

   ii power, voltage and current.

   iii power, energy and time.

4 **a** State whether ammeters should be connected in series or in parallel with the component through which they are measuring the current.

   b State, with a reason, why ammeters have very low (almost zero) resistance.

5 **a** State whether voltmeters should be connected in series or in parallel with the component across which they are measuring the voltage (pd).

   b State, with a reason, why voltmeters have very high resistance.

6 Rewrite and complete the following by filling in the missing words.

   a When resistors are connected one in front of the other, we say that they are connected in ....
   The current is the .... everywhere in a series connection.

   b When a circuit divides into two or more branches, we say that the resistors in the branches are connected in ....
   The .... of the currents in the individual branches is .... to the current before and the current after the branched section.

   c When a battery is connected to two or more resistors in series, the ....
   of the voltages across the resistors is .... to the voltage of the battery.

7 Complete Table 11.8.

Table 11.8 *Question 7*

	Series or parallel connection?	Very high or negligible resistance?
Ammeter		
Voltmeter		

8 **a** Define:

   i alternating current (AC).

   ii direct current (DC).

   b The electric company delivers AC to our homes. What is the frequency of this AC in most Caribbean islands?

9 Define:

   i a fuse.   **ii** a circuit breaker.   **iii** the current rating of a fuse.

10 **a** What is the colour code used in the UK and Europe for the live, neutral and earth electrical wires?

   b Through which TWO of the THREE wires does current flow during normal operation?

   c In which of the THREE wires should the fuse be placed?

11 Power tools and heating circuits require high currents. Name THREE such devices.

12 State TWO reasons why appliances should be connected in parallel.

13 **a** Define *electrocution*.

   b If we are dry, small voltages will give us only a slight shock. However, if we are wet, the electrical shock can be severe. What does this tell us about our bodies' resistance under both conditions?

   c Even when dry, if our skin is broken or bruised, electricity can easily enter our bodies. Explain how this can result in electrocution.

14 **a** Define *energy conservation*.

b Give TWO MAIN reasons for conserving energy.

c For EACH of the following, list THREE ways we can reduce our energy consumption.

   i In the kitchen and laundry room without replacing anything.

   ii By installing special devices or systems.

   iii By designing the building to reduce entry of solar radiation and so limit dependence on air conditioners.

15 Draw a well labelled diagram of a fluorescent tube and explain its function.

16 **a** What is the metal used for the filament of an incandescent lamp?

b What is the approximate temperature of the filament when emitting light?

c What colour is the emitted light?

d What is between the filament and the glass bulb?

e What makes this type of lamp very inefficient?

f Does the lamp contain mercury?

17 Complete Table 11.9.

Table 11.9 *Question 17*

Characteristic	Fluorescent	LED	Incandescent
Relative lifetime			Shortest
Relative efficiency	High		
Durability		Withstands bounces	Easily broken
Wastes energy as heat	30% wasted	Very little wasted	
Contains toxic mercury			
Relative operational cost	Low		Highest
Consistency of brightness	Flickers with age	Consistent	

Applying facts

18 **a** Draw a circuit diagram to show a battery of TWO **cells** in series being used to power TWO **lamps** in series. Your circuit must include a **switch**, an **ammeter** to measure the current in the lamps and a **voltmeter** to measure the voltage across ONE of the lamps.

b If the lamps have equal resistance and the emf of the battery is 3 V, what is the voltage across EACH lamp?

19 **a** Draw a circuit diagram to show a battery of TWO **cells** in series being used to power TWO **lamps** in parallel. Your circuit must include a **switch**, an **ammeter** to measure the current in ONE of the lamps, an ammeter to measure the current **leaving the battery** and a **voltmeter** to measure the voltage across **the parallel section**.

b If the emf of the battery is 3 V, what voltage is across each lamp?

20 A 12 V battery is connected across a 20 Ω resistor. Determine:

a the current it takes.

b the power consumed.

c the energy it uses in 3.0 minutes.

21 a Anita's mum has an electric kettle rated at 1100 W and an electric oven rated at 2100 W. Determine the current they EACH use if they are each supplied with a voltage of 120 V.

b FOUR fuses are available for her use with current ratings 5 A, 10 A, 13 A, 20 A. State which fuse should she select for the kettle and which for the oven, giving reasons for your answers.

c Explain in detail what occurs within a fuse when it blows.

d Anita wants to purchase an electric treadmill, but her mum says that it will use more energy than the electric oven. State why Anita's mum is more than likely, incorrect.

22 Determine the following for the circuit shown in Figure 11.29.

a The voltage of each cell.

b The total resistance of the circuit.

c The current delivered.

d The voltage across R_1.

e The voltage across R_2.

f The power used by R_1.

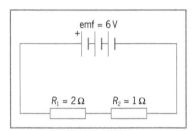

Figure 11.29 *Question 22*

23 Jacob's energy usage for the month is 180 kW h. What is this in joules (J)?

24 Calculate the total weekly energy used in a home in **kW h**, given the following information about appliance use.

• EIGHT 60 W lamps used for 8 hours each night.

• ONE 1500 W electric kettle used for 15 minutes ($\frac{1}{4}$ h) every morning.

• ONE 200 W refrigerator always in use (24 hours, 7 days per week).

• ONE 2000 W electric oven used for 2 hours on Tuesdays, Thursdays and Saturdays (3 times per week).

25 On 30ᵗʰ September, a customer's meter reading was 32 396 kW h and on 31ˢᵗ October it was 32 547 kW h. Calculate the electricity bill for the period given the following added information.

• Energy is charged on a block rate. The first 100 kW h is charged at $0.50 per kW h and any additional usage is charged at $0.40 per kW h.

• There is also a fuel adjustment charge of $0.010 per kW h and a rental fee of $10.00.

26 Determine the reading shown on Jodi's analogue electric meter shown in Figure 11.30.

Figure 11.30 *Question 26*

11 Electricity and lighting

27 Table 11.10 shows readings obtained in an investigation to determine the relation between the voltage across a component to the current flowing through it.

Table 11.10 *Question 27*

Voltage (V/V)	0.4	1.0	1.6	2.2	2.8	3.4
Current (I/A)	0.2	0.5	0.8	1.1	1.4	1.7

a Plot a graph of the voltage V across the component against the current I through it.

b Determine the gradient (slope of the graph).

c State Ohm's law.

d Do these readings demonstrate Ohm's law?

e What does the gradient of this graph represent?

Reducing the impact of electrical and fire hazards

Learning objectives

- Discuss first aid methods for **treating electrical accidents**.
- Discuss the **hazards** associated with electricity.
- Discuss the '**fire triangle**' and the various **types of fires**.
- Discuss the various types of **fire extinguishers** and the various methods of extinguishing fires.
- Evaluate the various types of conventional **protective gear**/wear.

We need to be extremely cautious when using electricity as accidents may occur that can result in injuries ranging from minor to extremely severe. The following describes how we can provide first aid treatment for some accidents.

Treating a victim of an accident resulting in electrical shock

- **Switch off the electrical supply** if the victim is still connected to it. If that is not possible, then separate the victim from the supply using an insulating material such as a dry wooden stick. **Never** touch the victim directly.
- **Assess the victim's condition** and then call for emergency medical help. Place the phone on speaker mode near to the patient allowing the emergency aid to communicate with you.
- If the victim's **heart has stopped beating** (cardiac arrest), and/or if he or she has **stopped breathing** (respiratory arrest), **cardiopulmonary resuscitation** (CPR) should be performed.

Cardiopulmonary resuscitation

This consists of two procedures, **chest compressions** and **mouth-to-mouth resuscitation** (rescue breathing). These are illustrated in Figure 11.31.

If the victim is unresponsive or gasping for air, this may suggest cardiac arrest. **Chest compressions should be performed** to stimulate blood circulation and so provide oxygen to vital organs:

* **Loosen clothing** around victim's neck and chest and lay him or her **on their back.**
* **Kneel** next to the victim's shoulders, place the heel of one hand over the centre of the victim's chest and place the other hand over the first, interlocking the fingers.
* With straight elbows, **push firmly down on the victim's chest** so that it is compressed by approximately **5 cm** and then release the compression so that it returns to its original formation.
* **Perform 30 chest compressions** at a rate of **100 to 120 per minute.**

If the victim is not breathing, and a person trained in CPR is available, **mouth-to-mouth resuscitation should be performed:**

* Gently **tilt the head backwards** to open the airways by lifting the chin.
* **Open the victim's mouth** and remove any debris that may cause the airways to be blocked.
* **Pinch the victim's nostrils** to close them.
* **Inhale, seal your lips** over the victim's mouth and **breathe out** into his or her mouth for **1 second.**
* If the chest rises and there is no response from the victim, give a second rescue breath.
* Continue to alternate, **30 chest compressions** at a **rate of 100 to 120 per minute** with **two rescue breaths** until the victim is breathing again or medical help arrives. If the victim's breathing resumes, he or she should be placed in the **recovery position** shown in Figure 11.32.

Figure 11.31 *Chest compressions and rescue breathing*

Figure 11.32 *Recovery position*

Electrical burns

* **Touching an electrified object** – The current causing the burn can flow only if it has a path **into and out of** the victim's body and therefore there must be at least **TWO points of contact.** One point must be connected to one terminal of the electrical source; the other point may be connected, either to ground or to the other terminal of the source.

  This can occur if a person touches an electrical supply with their hand and is standing on the ground with their **bare feet** (no shoes and so no insulation). Electricity will then flow **between the source and the ground** through the victim.

* **Being in the path of an 'arc blast' (arc flash)** – Extremely bright sparks with temperatures of thousands of degrees Celsius can occur between broken wires of powerful electrical circuits. If a person's body intercepts such an arc, they will receive a burn which may be severe.

Treating a victim of an accident resulting in burns

Minor burns

These are burns affecting only the **outer layer of skin**, and which are **less than 5 cm in diameter**. They may be treated as follows.

- **Wash hands** with antibacterial soap before tending to the patient.
- **Remove clothing** that is not stuck to the burn.
- **Soak** the affected area with cool running water for several minutes. Do not use ice since this may damage the tissue even more.
- **Clean** the affected area with mild soap and soothe with aloe vera.
- **Cover** with a sterile, non-adhesive gauze.
- **Take a pain reliever** such as ibuprofen, aspirin or acetaminophen.

More severe burns

These are burns that have **damaged underlying layers of skin**, especially burns on the face or large areas of the skin. They should be seen **immediately** by a **doctor**.

Burns are rated as between **1st degree** and **4th degree** .

1st degree burns are minor and only affect the outer layer of skin, the **epidermis.**

2nd degree burns damage the **epidermis** and the underlying layer, the **dermis**. They generally produce **blisters**.

3rd degree burns damage **all layers of the skin**. Since the nerve endings are damaged, there is **no pain**.

4th degree burns are the most severe and are **life threatening**. They damage **all layers** of the skin as well as the underlying **bones**, **muscles and tendons**.

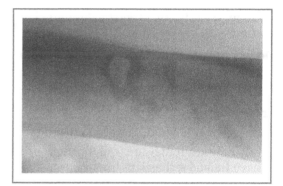

Figure 11.33 *Blister of a 2nd degree burn*

Hazards associated with electricity and methods of preventing them

We should act responsibly with respect to electrical use. Appliances and equipment should always be **handled with care** and **maintained** in good working condition to avoid harm to humans and other organisms, and to protect other aspects of the natural and built environment. Several electrical hazards and ways of preventing them are outlined in the following examples.

Illegal connection to power grid

To save money, some people may try to cheat the system by **connecting illegally** to the electrical grid.

Other consumers of electricity must then pay more per unit of energy.

If the installer of the illegal connection is not a **certified technician**, the system may be vulnerable to overload and may result in electrocution or an electrical fire.

Prevention:

- **Laws** are set in place to deter illegal connection to the grid.
- Each installation is to be **inspected by a certified inspector.**

Flying kites near power lines

Retrieving kites entangled in power lines can be very dangerous. If the kite is made of metal parts or metal wires, or if it is wet, it becomes even more conductive and can lead to electrocution.

Prevention:

- **Release your kite** if it drifts close to power lines.
- **Never** construct your kite with **metal components**.
- **Never** fly a kite in the **rain**.
- **Report kites entangled in power lines** to the appropriate authorities so that they may send trained technicians to remove them.

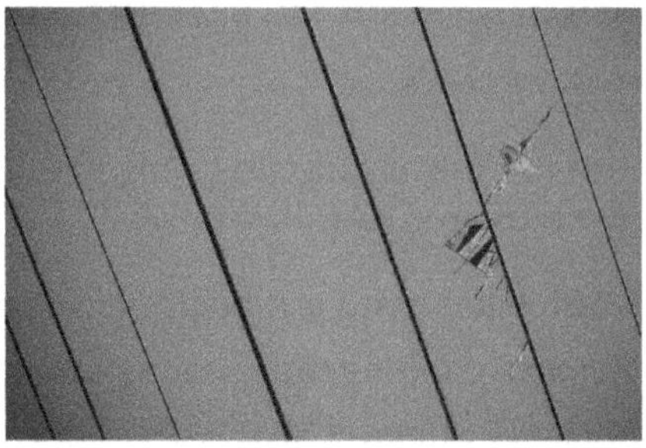

Figure 11.34 *Kite entangled on power line*

Picking fruit or trimming trees near power lines

Trees in contact with power lines can cause **electrocution** of those who touch them. If the tree is wet, its conductivity is greater and there is a higher chance of electrocution.

It is **dangerous** to use **picking poles** to pick fruit near to, or in contact with, **power lines**.

Do not attempt to retrieve a person in contact with a power line or trapped in a tree which is in contact with a power line. Only trained experts should attempt this.

Prevention:

- Check to see that trees are not in contact with, or close to, power lines. If they are, call the **appropriate authorities** to have **trained technicians** trim the trees.

Figure 11.35 *Trees entangled in power lines*

- **Do not use fruit picking poles or ladders** (especially those made of metal) near to power lines.
- If the weather is **rainy** the risk of electrocution increases due to increased conductivity, so be extra careful around trees or bushes entangled with electrical wires.
- Immediately call the **emergency hotline** of the electric company to retrieve anyone from a tree or bush who has been electrically shocked.

Working with electrical equipment in wet conditions

Wet environments provide an easy conducting path for high currents that can lead to **electrocution**.

Prevention:

- Wear **dry insulated boots** and **gloves** when working on electrical equipment in damp conditions.
- **DO NOT work on electrical equipment in the rain.**

Faulty electrical equipment

Loose electrical contacts or **damaged power cords** having exposed conducting wire can produce short circuits resulting in **overheating, electrical fires** and **electrocution**.

Figure 11.36 *Damaged power cord*

Prevention:

- Always **maintain electrical equipment** using **certified technicians**.

Overloading electrical circuits

By connecting too many appliances at the same time to the same circuit, we stand the chance of **overloading** the circuit. The chance is greater if the appliances are **high powered devices**, such as heaters or power tools. **Each appliance draws its own current** and so the total current may be more than the allowed value for the electrical wires. The wires and electrical components of the circuit may overheat and be destroyed, and an electrical fire may ensue.

Prevention:

- **Reduce** the **number of appliances** connected to the circuit.
- **Thicker wires** should be used to take larger currents.

Figure 11.37 *Electrical fire caused by overloading a circuit*

CRT (cathode ray tube) TVs and screens

- CRT TVs contain **capacitors** that can store voltages of over **25 000 V** and **can cause electrocution.**
- The TV tube contains a **vacuum tube that can implode** if its case is broken. After the implosion, there is an **explosion of glass** and other fragments.
- The glass screens **contain lead**, a **poisonous** metal. This poses a major **problem for disposal.**

Prevention:

- These TVs should be **repaired by qualified technicians.**
- They should be **handled with care.**
- They should be **recycled by a regulated body** so that the glass can be utilised.

Figure 11.38 *CRT TV*

Computers, laptops, cell phones and tablets

These devices **do not** emit **high frequency, ionising** radiation and so **do not** affect our **DNA. Scientific opinion** on whether they can cause cancer is therefore **unclear.**

They emit a lesser energetic radiation which is a **non-ionising, low frequency** radiation (known as 'electromagnetic field' radiation or **EMF radiation**).

- EMF radiation is believed to cause **headaches** and **fatigue.**
- In large doses it can have a slight **heating** effect.

Prevention:

- **Reduce the time** spent **in front of the device and screen.**
- Use **modern devices** which utilise **LCD** or **LED** instead of the old CRT computer screens which emit more dangerous EMF radiation.
- Avoid placing cell phones close to the **head.** Use them on **speakerphone mode** or use **hands-free** devices such as **Bluetooth** or **earphones.**
- Avoid putting laptops near the **abdomen** since **heating** can have **negative effects** on the **reproductive system.**

Microwave ovens

Microwaves are **not ionising radiation**; they are **less energetic, non-ionising, low frequency**, EMF radiation.

Microwaves **do not decrease the nutrients** in food any more than other cooking techniques.

They have been in use for over 70 years and still there is **no credible evidence** that these ovens can cause cancer or be harmful to humans if used correctly.

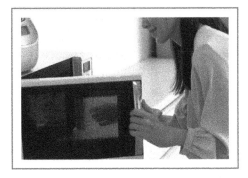

Figure 11.39 Protective mesh on glass door prevents microwaves from exiting

- They contain a **transformer** which steps the **voltage up to about 5000 V** and then **stores** it in a **capacitor.** Even with the switch off, the capacitor can store the charge at this **dangerously high voltage.**
- They have a **heating effect.**

Prevention:

- Circuits in these devices should only be **repaired by qualified technicians.**
- The **metal casing** of the oven, as well as the **metal mesh** on the glass door, **prevent** the EMF waves from **exiting.** The oven is designed for the emission of the waves to **cease** as the **door is opened.** However, as a precaution, one should be at least an arm's length from a microwave oven in operation.

Other hazards and methods of preventing them

Table 11.11 *Other hazards commonly encountered and methods of preventing them*

Hazard	Reason for danger	Prevention
Radiation from • **X-ray machines and** • **radioactive materials**	This is **ionising** radiation. It can **damage** and **destroy body cells** and can result in the **development of cancer.**	Stay away from these ionising radiations as much as possible. • **Lead-lined covers** should be used to block **X-rays** from parts of the body which are not being imaged. • **Radioactive materials** should always be **stored in lead** containers **labelled** as being dangerous and should only be accessible by **authorised personnel.**
Faulty gas supplies	Combustible gases are **harmful if inhaled** and can **cause fires** if they contact very hot surfaces or flames.	**Always maintain** gas hoses and associated equipment. Immediately disconnect the supply if a fire ignites.
Careless handling of hot kitchen appliances and equipment	Contact with **hot surfaces** or pans can result in severe **burns**; contact with **hot liquids** or steam can produce **scalds.**	**Carefully manoeuvre** hot kitchenware by the handles, using **insulated mittens.**
Overheating of cooking oils	Excessive heating can **ignite the oil**, which can **explosively splatter** and produce **violent** flames.	**Always monitor** heated cooking oil; **never** leave it unattended.

Fires and various methods of extinguishing them

Elements required for fires to exist

Figure 11.40 *The fire triangle*

- The elements **FUEL**, **OXYGEN**, and **HEAT** are required **together** to **start** and **sustain** a fire. They constitute the '**fire triangle**' (see Figure 11.40).
- Removing any one or more of these will stop the fire.

Table 11.12 *Removing elements of the 'fire triangle'*

Element(s) removed	Method of removal
Oxygen	**Covering** with an inert material such as a fire blanket (non-combustible blanket), sand, carbon dioxide or inert chemical agent to **separate oxygen** from the burning material (fuel).
Heat	Adding a material which has a **high capacity for absorbing heat** from the fire. For some fires, water is a suitable extinguishing agent (see Table 11.13 on page 256). If the material is cold, it is more effective.
Fuel	**Clear the area** of material which can act as a fuel (material which can be burnt). In the case of a flammable gas fire, we can **turn off the gas supply**.

Types of fires

Electrical fires – If an appliance has a **short circuit** resulting in a fire, it should immediately be **unplugged** from its socket. The most common extinguishing agent for this type of fire is **carbon dioxide**, and if immediately employed, will rapidly stop the fire. These fires are generally **small** and often **indoors**, and so can be adequately smothered by the carbon dioxide to **displace (remove) oxygen** from the burning material without winds pushing it away. However, if the fire is in a **small, confined space**, it is advisable not to use carbon dioxide as it will **reduce the ability to breathe freely**.

Chemical fires – Fires in laboratories and in some factories usually involve chemicals producing **toxic gases** which can harm and even kill surrounding animals, including humans. Such fires are best extinguished by **qualified fire fighters** wearing '**atmosphere respirators**' to protect them from the **poisonous gases**. These respirators are connected to tanks containing clean air for the firefighters to breathe (see Figure 11.41 on page 256).

Bush fires (wildfires) – These fires are generally very **widespread** for the following **reasons**.

- **In dry periods**, the leaves of plants can burn very quickly.
- **A substantial amount of fuel** for combustion is provided by dense bush and large trees.
- **The convection wind produced** by the hot gases, rising and sucking in more air, amplifies the combustion. Together with the **natural winds** of the region, these fires tend to be extremely **fast growing** and **difficult to control**.

Wildfires can quickly scorch thousands of acres of land and can be extremely dangerous if they **encroach on villages or towns**, especially if the winds are strong.

The scorched region will be more **exposed to the Sun**, and with most of the **plants** and **animals** of the habitat **killed**, the ecosystem becomes stressed. This can cause the **topsoil** to **erode rapidly** due to **winds in the dry season** and **water in the wet season**.

Such fires are **best extinguished by qualified fire fighters**.

- It is necessary to quickly **de-bush** and **clear debris** from the area **upwind** of the fire. In so doing, **the fuel** is removed and the danger is reduced.

- For fires that are **very widespread** across **thickly forested** or **mountainous** terrain, it is often necessary for aircraft to drop hundreds of thousands of gallons of **water** and **chemicals** onto the burning material **to remove heat**. These **'water bombs'** are usually comprised of water and a fire retardant (see Figure 11.42).
- Smaller bush fires can be extinguished by **water hoses** connected to a **large water reservoir**.

Figure 11.41 *Extinguishing a chemical fire using an atmosphere respirator*

Figure 11.42 *Extinguishing a bush fire using water bombs*

Types of fire extinguishers

*A **fire extinguisher** is a small and portable **hand-held vessel** containing a wet or dry **chemical agent under pressure** which can be discharged to extinguish small fires.*

Figure 11.43 shows that each type of extinguisher has a **colour-coded band** to easily distinguish the various types available.

Classes of fires

Fires can be classified into several groups or **classes**. The type of extinguishing agent which should be used to stop a fire depends on the class of the fire, as shown in Table 11.13. The element of the fire triangle which is removed in each case is printed in red to promote easy recognition.

Figure 11.43 *Different types of fire extinguishers*

Table 11.13 *Extinguishing agents used with various classes of fire*

Class of fire	Example of material being burnt (fuel)	Extinguishing agent	Additional information
A **Common combustible solids**	Bush, wood, paper, cloth, rubber, trash, plastic	Drench with **water** or cover with **foam**, **dry powder** (a dry chemical agent) or sand to remove OXYGEN and absorb HEAT. Clearing unburnt material from around the fire can remove the FUEL.	Carbon dioxide (CO_2) does **not remove sufficient heat** to be very effective for this type of solid fuel since gases only absorb small quantities of heat. If the gaseous cover is insufficient, the material will quickly **reignite**.

Class of fire	Example of material being burnt (fuel)	Extinguishing agent	Additional information
B (i) **Flammable liquids**	Gasoline, oil, grease, paint, solvents	**Carbon dioxide, foam, sand, dry powder.** Removes OXYGEN and absorbs HEAT.	**Water cannot be used** since it will quickly **boil** and **splatter**, spreading the fire.
B (ii) **Flammable gases**	Propane, butane, methane	**Turn off gas** supply to remove FUEL. **Dry powders** can also be used to remove OXYGEN and absorb HEAT.	Stopping the gas supply is the best way to stop the fire. Alternatively, special powders known as ABC powders may be used (see note after end of table).
C **Electrical equipment**	Faulty electrical appliances which have short circuited	Cover with CO_2 or **dry powder** to remove OXYGEN and absorb HEAT.	These fires are usually small and indoors and so there is **no wind** to blow away the CO_2. **Water cannot be used** since it **conducts electricity** and will cause **electrocution**.
D **Combustible metals**	Lithium, sodium, potassium, magnesium	**Dry powder agents** are used which must be **specific to the type of metal**. These remove OXYGEN and absorb HEAT.	**Water and CO_2 cannot be used** since they may **react** with these metals; water may even **decompose** due to the extreme temperature, producing **explosive hydrogen**!
K **Organic fats and oils**	Cooking oil, animal fats	A **wet chemical agent** is the only extinguishing agent which can effectively remove OXYGEN and absorb HEAT by smothering the burning material.	A fire blanket may also be useful but is not as effective.

Notes:

- **ABC powders** are powdered agents that can be used for **classes A, B and C**.
- **Classes D and K** can only be extinguished by a single type of extinguisher particular to its class.

Table 11.14 *Summary of extinguishers needed for different classes of fire*

Class of fire		Water	Foam	Carbon dioxide	ABC powders	Specific powders	Wet chemical
A	Combustible solids; for example, wood, paper, textiles, plastics	✓	✓		✓		✓
B	Flammable liquids; for example, gasoline, oil		✓	✓	✓		
	Flammable gases; for example, methane, propane				✓		
C	Electrical equipment			✓	✓		
D	Flammable metals; for example, lithium, sodium, potassium, magnesium					✓	
K	Cooking oil and animal fats found in kitchen						✓

Methods of extinguishing a fire

To extinguish a fire, we need to remove **at least one** of the three elements (heat, oxygen, or fuel) of the fire triangle.

Removing heat – by applying a cold agent to the fire, or one which can absorb a large quantity of heat. Good examples of such agents are **water**, **foam** and a **wet chemical agent**, but all extinguishing agents will absorb some heat. As mentioned earlier, aircraft drop thousands of gallons of water and chemical agents onto forest fires.

Removing oxygen – Burning can only occur if the fuel is in contact with oxygen. Extinguishing agents all **starve** burning substances of oxygen.

- **Foams** are useful for **displacing oxygen** from around the burning materials of class **A and B** fires.
- **Carbon dioxide** is a **dense gas** that does not react with most burning fuels and will descend on the fire, pushing away the less dense air. It is used for extinguishing class **B and C** fires.
- **ABC powders** are very useful for **displacing oxygen** from classes **A, B and C** fires. These are usually bicarbonates which **release CO_2** when they are heated by the fire.
- **Special dry powders** (**powdered graphite, granular sodium chloride** or **copper based powder**) must be used on class **D** (metal) fires.
- **Fire blankets** are **flexible**, **heat resistant** and made of **inert** (unreactive) material. Their main component is woven fibreglass and they are used to extinguish small class **A and B** fires. They are often useful in the kitchen to put out class **K** fires, although these fires are best controlled by a wet chemical agent.
- Besides removing heat, **wet chemical agents** form a soap-like barrier over the very hot cooking oils and fats of class **K** fires.

Removing fuel – by switching off the supply or by otherwise removing the fuel source.

- Turning off flammable gas supplies.
- Removing combustible material such as bush or trash that is close to the fire.

Conventional protective gear/wear

Protective gear is necessary for several reasons.

- **Prevents injury** from physical **accidents.**
- **Prevents harm** from dangerous **chemical exposure.**
- **Shields from harmful electromagnetic radiation**, such as bright light, UV radiation or X-rays.
- **Shields** from **hot materials.**
- **Increases efficiency** and **productivity** since we can work faster and therefore produce more.
- **Prevents** the spread of **infection.**

Table 11.15 *Applications of protective gear/wear in work and in sport*

Gear/wear	Protection	Examples of users
Gloves	• Thick, padded, heavy duty, leather gloves protect the hands from being **cut** and **bruised.**	• Construction workers
	• Gloves made of sterile latex, nitrile rubber, PVC or neoprene protect from **germs** and **viruses.**	• Doctors, nurses, chemists
	• Anti-corrosive gloves protect the hands from **corrosive chemicals.**	• Farmers, gardeners
	• Heat insulating gloves protect the hands from **hot objects.**	• Cooks

Gear/wear	Protection	Examples of users
Boots	• Heavy duty leather boots, usually with a steel cover over the front, protect the feet from being **cut** and **bruised**. • Waterproof and anticorrosive rubber boots protect against some **pathogens** and **dangerously reactive chemicals**. • Light duty sports boots protect the feet from being bruised.	• Construction workers, farmers, gardeners • Fire fighters, gardeners • Cricketers, footballers, hikers
Goggles	• Protect the eyes from **airborne particles**, **splashing chemicals** or **water**. • Dark goggles or visors protect the eyes from **sparks** and **ultraviolet radiation**.	• Swimmers, chemists, gardeners • Welders
Earmuffs	• Protect the ears from **loud noises** and **low temperatures**.	• Construction workers, skiers, airport workers
Helmets	• Protect the head from **cuts, bruises** and skull and **brain damage** by absorbing shock and preventing penetration. • Some have visors and cages to protect the face from **airborne objects**.	• Construction workers, cyclists, climbers • Cricketers, hockey players
Coats/aprons	• Protect against **caustic chemicals**, **hot materials**, and **ionising radiation** (for example, **X-rays**) in **laboratories**, **hospitals**, **industrial sites** and **kitchens**.	• Doctors, nurses, chemists, factory workers, cooks, surgeons
Respirators	• **Filter particles** such as **dust and smoke** from the air. • Some have **canisters** attached to **filter harmful gases** and **toxic sprays**. • Some **provide clean air** for environments with limited air.	• Construction workers, fire fighters • Painters, fumigators • Astronauts, fire fighters
Chest guards	• Protect against obtaining **broken bones** and **damaged organs**.	• Racing drivers
Back brace	• Support and **protect the spine** when **lifting heavy objects**.	• Construction workers, dock workers, weightlifters
Groin boxes	• Protect the groin from **fast-moving cricket balls**.	• Cricketers
Sports pads	• Protect the **elbows**, **knees** and **shins** from the impact of **collisions**.	• Cricketers, skateboarders

Figure 11.44 *Spraying herbicide*

Figure 11.45 *Welding*

Figure 11.46 *Spray painting*

Recalling facts

1 Electrical burns can range from minor to extremely severe.

  a How should a minor burn (1st degree burn) be treated?

  b Which layer/s of the skin is/are affected by a minor burn?

  c Burns that are extremely severe are 4th degree burns. Describe the damage caused by a 4th degree burn.

2 How do governments help to reduce illegal connection to the electric grid?

3 **a** What is the first thing that must be done to terminate a flammable gas fire?

  b What else can be done to help in the process of extinguishing such a fire?

4 **a** Name TWO sources of ionising radiation.

  b How can ionising radiation harm our bodies?

  c State TWO ways of reducing the amount of ionising radiation entering our bodies.

5 Power-strips can be used to give power to several appliances. State, with a reason, what is likely to happen if we plug several high-powered devices into a power strip.

6 **a** Do microwave ovens emit ionising radiation?

  b Why is there a metal mesh (grill) on the glass door of a microwave oven?

  c Explain why it is advisable that only qualified technicians should repair microwave ovens.

7 Give THREE reasons why Josh should not dispose of an old CRT TV by breaking it into pieces in his backyard.

8 **a** What are the THREE elements required for a fire to exist?

  b Draw a diagram of the fire triangle.

  c In terms of these elements, what must be done to extinguish a fire?

9 Complete Table 11.16 by inserting a ✓ to indicate suitable extinguishing agents for each class of fire. Some classes can be extinguished by more than one type of extinguisher.

Table 11.16 *Question 9*

Class of fire		Water	Foam	Carbon dioxide	ABC powders	Specific powders	Wet chemical
A	Combustible solids; for example, wood, paper, textiles, plastics						
B	Flammable liquids; for example, gasoline, oil						
	Flammable gases; for example, methane, propane						
C	Electrical equipment						

Applying facts

10   **a** State THREE properties that the material of a fire blanket should have.

       b Ryanna is setting up her kitchen in a new restaurant. She purchases a fire blanket and hangs it in a readily accessible location. However, she was told that there is only one type of extinguishing agent that can efficiently extinguish class K fires. Name this agent.

11   **a** Ezra works in a machine shop where he has to weld many types of metals. Only ONE type of extinguishing agent is required for these class D fires. Describe this extinguishing agent.

       b Why is water unsuitable for stopping these fires?

12   **a** Give THREE reasons why bush fires (wildfires) are generally widespread.

       b Describe how these fires can stress the ecosystem.

       c Who should take charge of extinguishing these fires?

       d Describe how bush fires are generally tackled.

13 Vashti works in a large laboratory which stores and uses chemicals, many of which are highly toxic.

       a Who should take charge of extinguishing fires that may occur on site?

       b How are fire fighters able to breathe good air when in the vicinity of the toxic fumes?

14   **a** Jono's dad lectured him on precautions he should take when he sets out to fly his kite. What should be his advice and reasons for it, if:

          i the kite drifts near to power lines?

          ii rain begins to fall?

          iii the kite becomes entangled in nearby power lines?

       b Jono wanted to make the ribs of his kite out of aluminium since it is a metal of low density. Explain why this would not be a good idea.

15 Alicia was walking around her neighbourhood after a thunderstorm when she saw a boy stuck between the branches of a large mango tree through which power lines were threaded. The boy was clinging to a nearby aluminium ladder propped onto the tree.

       a Explain why Alicia should not try to pull him from the branches.

       b What should be Alicia's first response to help the boy?

       c State, with reasons, TWO mistakes the boy made in trying to pick the mangos.

16 Complete Table 11.17.

Table 11.17 *Question 16*

Gear/wear	User	Protection provided
Gloves	Construction worker	
Gloves	Doctor or nurse	
Boots	Fire fighter	
Helmets	Cyclist	
Respirators	Construction worker	
Coats/aprons	Chemist	
Earmuffs	Airport worker	
Dark goggles	Welder	

12 Temperature control and ventilation

Heat energy transfers from places of higher temperature to places of lower temperature by three methods: **conduction**, **convection** and **radiation**. The transfer of heat energy to or from a body can result in a **change in temperature** or a **change in state**, but never both at the same time. Understanding the methods of heat transfer is fundamental in understanding how devices such as cookware, stoves, ovens, vacuum (Thermos) flasks, solar water heaters, refrigerators, air conditioners and other devices, work.

Temperature control is also important, and so we will learn of **thermometers**, devices which **measure temperature**; and of **thermostats**, devices which **regulate temperature** in refrigerators and ovens. In the Caribbean, **hot, humid climates** can pose **health problems** and therefore we should take measures to overcome these problems by providing adequate **ventilation** in our homes and workplace.

Learning objectives

- Describe and demonstrate the methods of **heat transfer: conduction**, **convection** and **radiation**.
- Describe **applications** of heat transfer including the occurrence of **land** and **sea breezes**, and devices such as **vacuum (Thermos) flasks** and **solar water heaters**.
- Explain the principle by which **thermostatically controlled** household appliances operate.
- Describe various types of **thermometers** in relation to the principles by which they work.
- Discuss the **advantages** and **disadvantages** of different **types of thermometers**.
- Describe **temperature regulation** in **humans**.
- Explain the need for **proper ventilation** including the use of **air conditioners**, **humidifiers** and **dehumidifiers**.

Processes of heat transfer

Walking bare footed on a hot tar road can become unbearable due to thermal **conduction** from the road. Looking down from a roof into an active chimney is extremely uncomfortable due to heat transferred upward by **convection** currents rising within the chimney. Standing near a beach bonfire warms us due to outward **radiation** of electromagnetic waves from the burning twigs. These examples demonstrate the **three processes** by which **heat** can be **transferred** from one point to the next.

*Conduction is the process of heat transfer through a medium by the **relaying** of energy between particles colliding with each other.*

*Convection is the process of heat transfer in a medium by the **movement** of its particles between regions of **different density**.*

*Radiation is the process of heat transfer by means of **electromagnetic waves**.*

Table 12.1 *Heat transfer through solids, liquids, gases and a vacuum*

Conduction	Occurs mainly in solids – to a greater extent in metals than in non-metals – less through liquids, and very poorly through gases. Cannot occur through a vacuum.
Convection	Occurs mainly in liquids and gases. Cannot occur through a vacuum.
Radiation	Occurs mainly through gases and through a vacuum.

Conduction

Conduction explained by kinetic theory

Non-metals

Figure 12.1a shows what happens when one end of a non-metallic bar is warmed. The vibrating particles there (**atoms or molecules**) absorb **heat energy** causing their **kinetic energy** to increase. The particles therefore **vibrate faster** and with **greater amplitude.** They collide more vigorously with the neighbouring particles, **relaying** energy from particle to particle along the bar. The temperature of a substance is proportional to the speed of its particles, and so the temperature at the cooler end of the bar increases.

Metals

A similar process occurs in metals as shown in Figure 12.1b. Metals contain vibrating **cations** (positively charged ions). When a metal bar is heated, the heat energy supplied is converted to kinetic energy of the cations, causing them to vibrate faster and with greater amplitude. They collide more vigorously with the neighbouring cations, **relaying** energy from cation to cation along the bar.

Unlike non-metals, metals contain **freely moving (translating) electrons** which also absorb **heat energy** when heated. These electrons then translate faster and transfer their increased **kinetic energy** to the vibrating cations on collision.

Since **metals have two modes** of transferring heat by conduction whereas non-metals only have one, **metals are better conductors**.

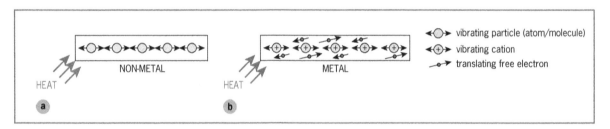

Figure 12.1 *Conduction in non-metals and in metals*

Experiment to compare thermal conduction through solids

Figure 12.2a on page 265 shows three rods of equal length being heated by the same flame. A bit of wax is placed at the end of each rod. The wax melts first from the copper, then from the iron, and finally from the wood, demonstrating that copper is the best conductor of the three materials and wood is the worst.

Figure 12.2b on page 265 shows a wooden rod joined to a copper rod. Paper is tightly wrapped around the region where the rods are joined. When the combined rod is lowered over a flame, the paper chars over the wood but not over the copper. Heat conducted through the paper to the copper quickly spreads through the copper, since copper is a good thermal conductor. However, since wood is a poor thermal conductor, heat conducted to it through the paper collects at the interface with the paper, causing it to char.

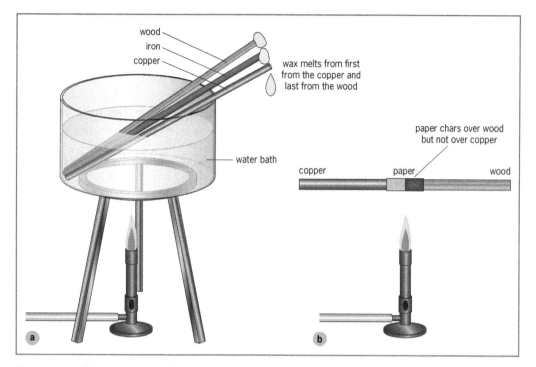

Figure 12.2 *Demonstrating conduction in solids*

Experiment to demonstrate that water is a poor thermal conductor

Figure 12.3 shows a piece of ice wrapped in copper mesh and submerged in a test tube of water. The weight of the mesh keeps the ice at the bottom of the tube. The water, **heated at the top to avoid convection**, rapidly comes to a boil, although the ice remains solid for quite some time. Since the only process by which heat can transfer from water at the top of the tube to ice at the bottom is by conduction, water must be a poor thermal conductor.

Note: The experiment was not performed with the ice floating at the surface as the tube is heated from the bottom; there would then be TWO possible methods of heat transfer, conduction and convection, that could melt it.

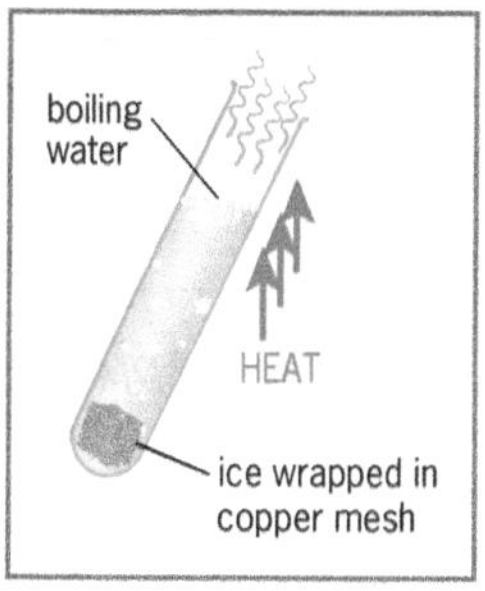

Figure 12.3
Demonstrating that water is a poor conductor

Good and poor thermal conductors

Metals are **good thermal conductors** and are useful in the manufacture of important devices.

- The **bases and sides** of **kettles, pots** and **pans** are usually made of **copper, aluminium or stainless steel** so that heat can readily pass through them to the food by conduction.
- **Boilers** that are heated externally are generally made of alloys such as **steel**. They need to be strong and able to transfer the heat by conduction from the burning fuel to the liquids they contain.
- **Heat exchangers** such as **radiators** are generally made of **aluminium**. A radiator transfers heat by conduction from the fluid it contains to its outer surface, which then **conducts** the heat to the air that is blown through it and **radiates** heat to the environment.

Non-metals are **poor thermal conductors** and are used daily for many purposes.

- The **handles** of **cooking utensils** and **garden tools** are made of poor conductors such as **plastic** or **wood** to reduce the conduction of heat to those who hold them when they are hot. **Leather gloves** are also used when handling hot pots and pans since leather is a poor thermal conductor.

- **Water heater storage tanks** are lagged with **polyurethane** to reduce outward thermal conduction (see the solar water heater shown in Figure 12.14, page 271).
- **Bricks, clay** and materials such as **grasses** are used to build places of shelter that reduce conduction of heat into and out of them, allowing homes to stay cooler during hot periods and warmer during cold periods.
- **Igloos** reduce outward conduction of heat since ice is a poor thermal conductor (Figure 12.4a).

Air is a **very poor thermal conductor.**

- **Woollen jackets** keep us warm since they have **air pockets** trapped between fibres and so reduce heat from conducting outward from our bodies.
- **Expanded polystyrene** (EPS) contains much air and is used as a thermal insulator, reducing the conduction of heat through the walls of **buildings, refrigerators, ovens** and **water heater storage tanks.**
- **Roofs** made of **leaves**, such as those from palm trees, trap air and therefore insulate shelters.
- **Feathers, hair,** and **fur** insulate animals from the cold. Air trapped by these covers offers further protection. Birds **fluff their feathers** to trap more air when necessary (Figure 12.4b).
- **Concrete blocks** and **clay blocks** containing **air pockets** act as thermal insulators, reducing conduction of heat into and out of buildings (Figure 12.4c).

Figure 12.4 *Applications of poor thermal conductivity*

Why a stone floor seems cooler than a rug

Figure 12.5 shows a person with **body temperature 37 °C** standing with one foot on a rug and the other on a stone floor. The stone and the rug are initially at the same temperature of **25 °C**. To the person it seems that stone floors are cooler than rugs. This misconception occurs because the stone is a much better thermal conductor than the rug. Heat flowing from the person to the stone can **quickly spread out within the stone**, but most of the heat flowing from the person to the rug **remains in the region just under the foot**. The temperature of the rug just under the foot therefore soon becomes **37 °C**, giving the impression that the rug was always warmer.

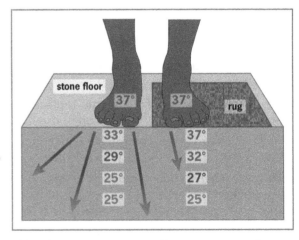

Figure 12.5 *Why a stone floor seems cooler than a rug*

Convection

Convection explained by kinetic theory

Figure 12.6 illustrates the process of convection. On warming a liquid or gas **from below**, the increased thermal energy in its lower region gives the particles there more kinetic energy, causing them to **translate** more vigorously and **take up more space**. The region therefore becomes **less dense**, resulting in its particles **rising** and **cooler, more densely packed** particles falling in to take their place.

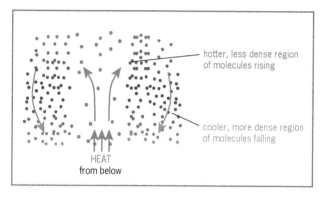

Figure 12.6 *Convection in liquids and gases*

Experiment to demonstrate convection in liquids

A crystal of **potassium permanganate** (purple in colour) is added to a beaker of water and is then heated from below, as shown in Figure 12.7a. As the crystal dissolves it forms a purple solution which rises from the heated region and displays the path of the **convection current**.

Notes:

Copper sulfate crystals (blue) can be used instead of potassium permanganate.

Instead of using crystals, **tiny flakes of aluminium** can be placed in the heated region of the water. The flakes will be seen glittering as they rise and fall in the convection current.

Experiment to demonstrate convection in gases

A small hand-held fan is placed in the air just over a flame, as shown in Figure 12.7b. The upward air draught of the convection current will create a force on the fan, causing it to spin.

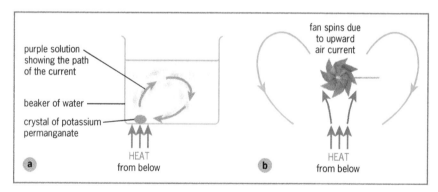

Figure 12.7 *Demonstrating convection in liquids and gases*

Phenomena involving convection

Land and sea breezes

During the day, the Sun's **radiation** warms the land more than it warms the sea. As the air **in contact** with the land is heated by **conduction**, it becomes **less dense** and **rises by convection**, allowing denser air from over the sea to take its place in the form of a **cool onshore breeze**. These convection currents cause coastal regions not to experience the extremely high temperatures during the day that can occur further inland.

The air in contact with the land further inland also becomes hot during the day but cannot rise since there is **no nearby cooler**, denser surrounding air **to take its place** (Figure 12.8a).

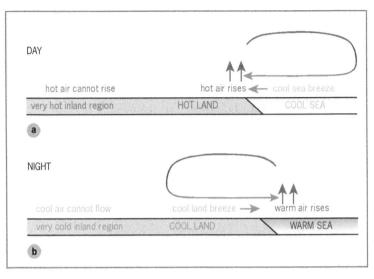

Figure 12.8 *Land and sea breezes*

During the night, the land **radiates** heat at a **higher rate** than the sea and therefore the surface of the land becomes cooler than that of the sea. Air in contact with the sea is warmed by **conduction**. The warm air is then less dense and rises by **convection**, pulling denser air from over the land to take its place in the form of a cool offshore breeze (Figure 12.8b).

The air in contact with the ground further inland also becomes cool at night but **cannot flow** from the region since there is **no nearby rising warmer air** for it **to take the place of**.

Convectional rainfall

During the day, the Sun's **radiation** warms the rivers, lakes and oceans, producing an increased amount of **evaporation**. Air in **contact** with the water is warmed by **conduction** and then becomes **less dense** and rises by **convection**. As the convection current rises, the water **vapour** it contains **cools**, **condenses** to form **clouds** and brings **rain** (see Figure 12.9). This type of rainfall is particularly dominant in equatorial regions such as **Guyana**.

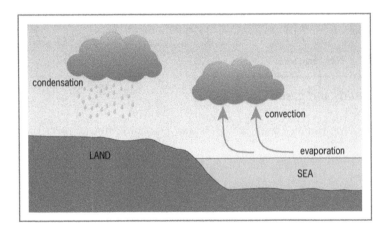

Figure 12.9 *Convectional rainfall*

Using convection currents to obtain fresh air

The air around miners in underground tunnels can become very poor due both to the **surrounding materials**, and to the **depletion of oxygen** and **increase** of **carbon dioxide** as the workers **respire**. By boring vertical shafts as shown in Figure 12.10, and by creating a small fire at the base of one of the shafts, a convection current can be set up to bring fresh air into the tunnel.

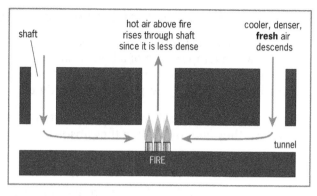

Figure 12.10 *Fresh air from convection currents*

Other applications of convection currents

- **Air conditioners** are placed at high levels in rooms. The air they cool becomes denser and falls, allowing warmer, less dense air to rise and be cooled.
- **Heaters** are placed near to the floor. The air they heat becomes less dense and rises, allowing cooler, denser air to fall and be heated.
- **Ice** floats to the top of a glass of water since it is less dense than water. It cools the liquid in **contact** with it by **conduction** causing it to become **denser** and to fall, thereby setting up a **convection current**. Warmer water rises to take its place and becomes chilled by **conduction** due to **contact** with the ice. In this way the entire glass of water eventually becomes chilled.

Radiation

All matter emits a type of electromagnetic radiation known as **infrared radiation**. As our nerve endings absorb this radiation, we detect a sensation of **warmth**.

- **Hotter** bodies emit **more radiation** and **higher frequency** radiation than cooler bodies.
- Electromagnetic radiation is the **only means** by which thermal energy can be **transported through a vacuum**. This is how we receive our **warmth from** the **Sun** through the **vacuum of space**.

Experiment to show that thermal radiation can pass through a vacuum

The jar in Figure 12.11 is first evacuated by means of a pump and the heater is then switched on. By touching the glass enclosure with the hand, it will be observed that it soon becomes warmer, demonstrating that radiation can be **transferred** from the heater to the glass by being **transported** through the vacuum.

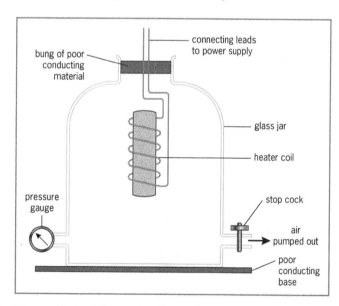

Figure 12.11 *Thermal radiation propagating through a vacuum*

Emitters and absorbers of thermal radiation

All bodies **emit** and **absorb** thermal radiation. Figure 12.12 shows how the temperature of a body relative to its surroundings determines whether it is a net emitter or net absorber of radiant energy at any given time.

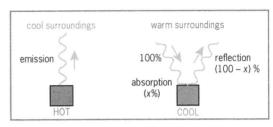

Figure 12.12 *Emitters and absorbers of radiation*

- Bodies that are hotter than their surroundings are net emitters; they emit more than they absorb.
- Bodies that are cooler than their surroundings are net absorbers; they absorb more than they emit.
- The surface of a body will usually reflect some radiation. Clearly, a good absorber is a poor reflector, and a poor absorber is a good reflector.

Effect of colour and texture on emission and absorption of radiation

Table 12.2 *The colour and texture of a surface affects the absorption and emission of thermal radiation*

matt / dull / rough / black	shiny / smooth / polished / silver (or white)
Good absorbers (poor reflectors)	Poor absorbers (good reflectors)
Good emitters	Poor emitters

To determine whether an object is a good emitter or absorber of radiation:

- First, **determine if the object is a net absorber or net emitter.** This depends on its temperature relative to the surroundings – not on its texture or colour!
- Then, **examine its surface texture and colour** to determine how good an absorber or emitter it is.

Examples:

- A refrigerator is an **absorber** since it is cooler than its surroundings.
  Painting it **shiny white** makes it a poor absorber (good reflector) preventing heat from entering.
- An oven is an **emitter** since it is hotter than its surroundings.
  Painting it **shiny white** makes it a poor emitter, preventing heat from leaving.

Example 1

a To be most efficient, which of gloss black, matt black, gloss white or matt white is best to paint the outside of a refrigerator?

Solution

1. **Temperature relative to surroundings:** The contents of a refrigerator are cooler than the surroundings. It is therefore a **net absorber** of radiation.
2. **Physical properties of surface:** An efficient refrigerator should prevent heat from entering. It should therefore be painted gloss white to be a **poor absorber.**

b To be most efficient, which of gloss black, matt black, gloss white or matt white is best to paint the outside of an oven?

Solution

1. **Temperature relative to surroundings:** When cooking, the contents of an oven are very hot relative to the surroundings. It is therefore a **net emitter** of radiation.
2. **Physical properties of surface:** An efficient oven will prevent heat from leaving. It should therefore be painted gloss white to be a **poor emitter.**

c Akil works in the freezer room of an ice company. State, with reasons, whether he should wear a black or a white suit and whether it should have a rough or glossy texture.

The vacuum flask

The vacuum flask, shown in Figure 12.13, has several features that can reduce thermal energy transfer, and so maintain its contents at an almost constant temperature.

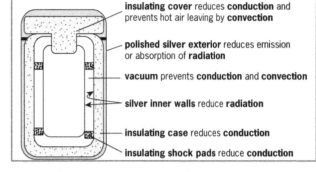

insulating cover reduces **conduction** and prevents hot air leaving by **convection**

polished silver exterior reduces emission or absorption of **radiation**

vacuum prevents **conduction** and **convection**

silver inner walls reduce **radiation**

insulating case reduces **conduction**

insulating shock pads reduce **conduction**

Figure 12.13 *The vacuum flask*

- The **vacuum** within the double walls **prevents** energy transfer by **conduction** and **convection**.
- The **double walls** are made of **glass**, a poor conductor, to **reduce conduction** to or from the contents of the flask.
- The **inner-facing walls** of the vacuum region are **silver-coated**. If the contents of the flask are hot, thermal energy will be conducted from it through the first wall of the vacuum and then radiated though the vacuum to the facing wall. Since silver is a **poor emitter**, the energy radiated is minimised, and since it is also a **poor absorber**, very little is absorbed by the facing wall (a large amount is reflected). If the contents of the flask are cold, heat trying to enter from the outside will be similarly minimised.
- The **cover**, **case** and **shock pads** are made of **insulating** material to **reduce conduction**.
- The **cover** also **prevents convection** as it stops hot air from rising and leaving the flask.
- The **outer wall of the case** is **polished silver**. If the contents are hot, radiation emitted is minimised since **shiny silver surfaces are poor emitters** of radiation. If the contents are cold, radiation absorbed is also minimised since **shiny surfaces are also poor absorbers** (good reflectors) of radiation.

The solar water heater

The features of the solar water heater are illustrated in Figure 12.14.

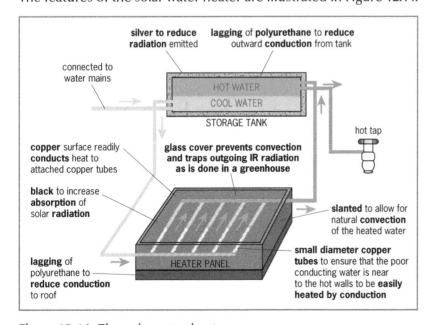

silver to reduce radiation emitted

lagging of polyurethane to reduce outward **conduction** from tank

connected to water mains

HOT WATER
COOL WATER

STORAGE TANK

hot tap

copper surface readily **conducts** heat to attached copper tubes

glass cover prevents convection and traps outgoing IR radiation as is done in a greenhouse

black to increase **absorption** of solar **radiation**

slanted to allow for natural **convection** of the heated water

lagging of polyurethane to **reduce conduction** to roof

HEATER PANEL

small diameter copper tubes to ensure that the poor conducting water is near to the hot walls to be **easily heated by conduction**

Figure 12.14 *The solar water heater*

- **Flow between the tank and the heater panel.** During the day, as the water is warmed in the heater panel, it becomes less dense and rises by **natural convection** to the **storage tank**. At the same time, cooler, denser water falls to the **heater panel** where it is in turn heated.
- **Flow between the water mains supply, through the tank, to the user's hot water tap.** When the hot tap is opened, cool water from the mains supply can enter the bottom of the storage tank and force hot water from the top outward to the hot tap.
- All **hot water** entries and exits are at the **top**, and all **cool water** entries and exits are at the **bottom**, of the panel and tank.
- **Water** is a **poor thermal conductor** and therefore the less dense hot water in the tank remains hot although it rests on the denser, cooler water below it.
- If the tank is too heavy for the roof, it may be placed on the ground. However, an electric **pump** will then be required to **force** the **hot, less dense** water **downward** to the storage tank, and the **cooler, denser** water, **upward** to the heater panel on the roof. This is clearly more costly.

Other applications of absorption and emission of thermal radiation

- **Painting houses white** keeps them cooler in hot climates since white is a **poor absorber (good reflector)** of thermal radiation (see Figure 11.25 on page 243).
- **Cricketers** wear **white** clothing so that they are **poor absorbers (good reflectors)** of solar radiation.
- **Space suits** should be **shiny silver**.
  - When solar radiation is incident on the astronaut, the suit will act as a **poor absorber (good reflector)** and so **prevent him or her from overheating**.
  - When the astronaut is in the shade from radiation, space can become very cold, and he or she then becomes an emitter. A shiny silver suit is a **poor emitter** and so he or she **stays warm**.
- **Fire fighters** should wear **shiny silver** if they are entering burning buildings so that they are **poor absorbers (good reflectors)** of the heat radiation.

Comparing the emissive and absorptive properties of matt black and shiny silver surfaces

Figure 12.15a indicates that although the matt black surface and the shiny white or silver surface are both at the temperature of the hot water, the matt black surface is emitting more radiation.

Figure 12.15b indicates that although the matt black surface and the shiny white or silver surface are both receiving the same radiation from the flame, the matt black surface is absorbing more (reflecting less) radiation.

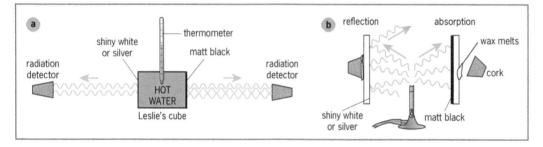

Figure 12.15 *Comparing the emissive and absorptive properties of matt black and shiny silver surfaces*

Thermostats in household appliances

*A **thermostat** is a device that automatically regulates temperature, or that activates a device at a certain critical temperature.*

- For **electric ovens**, an electric thermostat will switch the heating circuit **off** when the **temperature** rises **above** a **certain** value.
- For **air conditioners** and **refrigerators**, an electric thermostat will switch the motor **off** when the **temperature** falls **below** a **certain** value.
- For **gas ovens**, the thermostat will **reduce** the flow of gas to be burnt as the **temperature rises**.

The bimetallic strip

*A **bimetallic strip** consists of two strips of different metals joined along their length.*

If one metal expands more than the other as the temperature changes, the strip will bend. Two suitable metals for use in a bimetallic strip are **brass** and **invar**. Brass expands much more than invar when heated and so the strip bends significantly with an increase of temperature. If initially straight, **heating** causes the strip to bend such that **brass** is on the **outside of the curve**. Brass also contracts more on cooling, so if the temperature returns to the initial temperature, the strip will straighten. Further **cooling** will then cause **brass** to be on the **inside of the curve**.

Bimetallic strips can be used to regulate temperature by switching electrical circuits on and off, as explained in two of the following thermostat applications.

An alternative pair of metals for a bimetallic strip is **brass** and **iron** (see Figure 12.16).

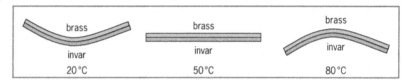

Figure 12.16 *Effect of temperature on bimetallic strip*

Thermostat used in an electric oven

An electric thermostat connected to the heater of an oven is shown in Figure 12.17. With the switch on, the **heater warms the oven**. The bimetallic **strip then bends**, causing the graphite **sliding contacts** to **separate** and the **circuit to break**. With the **heater disconnected**, the oven **cools**, the bimetallic strip **straightens**, the contacts **reconnect**, and the process repeats. The temperature is therefore prevented from rising above a set value.

The temperature **control knob** is an adjusting screw that can be advanced so that it forces the sliding contacts further over each other. The bimetallic strip must then bend more to break the circuit.

By connecting the thermostat to the electrical pump of a refrigerator with the **positions of the brass and invar switched**, the thermostat can be

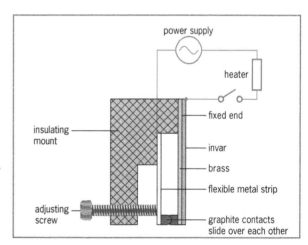

Figure 12.17 *Thermostat used in an electric oven*

used to **prevent a refrigerator from becoming too cold**. As the **temperature** in the refrigerator **reduces**, the bimetallic **strip will bend outwards**. At a certain **set temperature**, the **contacts separate**, breaking the circuit and **switching off** the refrigerator.

Thermostat used in an electric iron

An electric iron is shown in Figure 12.18. As the **heater warms,** the bimetallic **strip bends downward**, separating the sliding contacts and **breaking the circuit**. The **heater then cools**, the bimetallic **strip straightens**, and the **contacts reconnect**, restarting the heating process.

By advancing the adjusting screw, the bimetallic strip is under greater tension and therefore a higher temperature is required before the strip bends sufficiently for the contacts to separate and break the circuit.

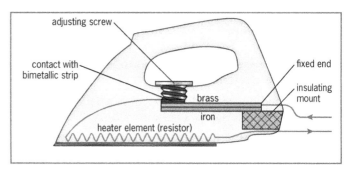

Figure 12.18 *'Thermostat used in an electric iron'*

Thermostat used in a gas oven

Figure 12.19 shows a thermostat used in a gas oven. As the **temperature** of the oven **rises**, the **brass tube expands more** than the invar rod attached to it. The **valve head** therefore **moves to the left**, narrowing the channel and so **reducing the flow of gas** to the burners. As the **oven cools**, the brass tube **contracts**, pushing the rod **to the right** and **increasing the flow of gas** to the burners.

By turning the **adjustable knob**, the **valve head can screw further onto the attached invar rod** and therefore **reduce the gas flow** to a set rate with **less rise in temperature**.

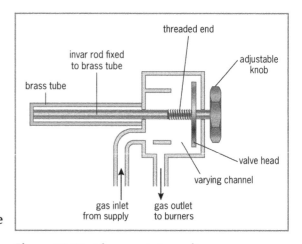

Figure 12.19 *Thermostat used in a gas oven*

Temperature, humidity and the importance of proper ventilation

Temperature is the degree of hotness of a body measured on a chosen scale.

The **temperature of a body** depends on the **kinetic energy** of its **particles**; the **faster** the particles, the **higher** is the **temperature** of the body.

Note: Heat is not temperature.

Heat is thermal energy in the process of transfer from a region of higher temperature to a region of lower temperature, due to the temperature difference between them.

A **thermometer** is an instrument used to measure temperature and so must have an attached temperature scale. Two important temperature scales are the **Celsius** temperature scale and the **Kelvin** temperature scale (also known as the **absolute** or **thermodynamic** temperature scale).

The **SI unit of temperature** is the **kelvin (K)**, but it is also common in science to express temperatures in **degrees Celsius (°C)**.

Celsius temperature scale

Water is a very common substance, and the temperatures of its freezing and boiling points can be determined with minimal effort. Numbers have been assigned to represent the temperatures at these fixed points, known as the **upper fixed point** and the **lower fixed point**.

On this scale, two simple values, 0 °C and 100 °C, are used as the fixed points. Since there are 100 intervals between the fixed points, we refer to the Celsius scale as a **centigrade scale**.

The **lower fixed point (0 °C)** is the temperature of **pure melting ice** at **standard atmospheric pressure**.

The **upper fixed point (100 °C)** is the temperature of **steam from pure boiling water** at **standard atmospheric pressure**.

Liquid-in-glass thermometers and how they work

Some thermometers contain a liquid in an enclosed glass tube with a bulb at one end. Almost all the liquid is contained in the bulb. On heating the bulb, the liquid expands along the narrow capillary bore of the tube which has a scale marked on it.

- **Mercury** or **alcohol** is commonly used as the liquid in such a thermometer.
- Glass is a poor thermal conductor and so the bulb is made with a **thin wall** to facilitate the easy **transfer of heat** through it.
- The **bore** of the tube is very **narrow** so that any change in volume of the liquid will result in a noticeable change in length of the liquid thread.
- The **bulb** is relatively **large** so that the corresponding expansion or contraction of the liquid in it is noticeable along the length of the capillary bore for small changes in temperature. The **larger** the bulb, the **longer** can be the stem and the greater can be the separation of the intervals on the scale, making the instrument more **precise**.
- The **scale** is usually marked on the stem to **reduce parallax error** when taking readings.

Laboratory mercury thermometer

Figure 12.20 shows a liquid-in-glass mercury thermometer which is generally designed to read temperatures between **−10 °C and 110 °C**. It is useful for use in the school laboratory since experiments generally performed there are within this range.

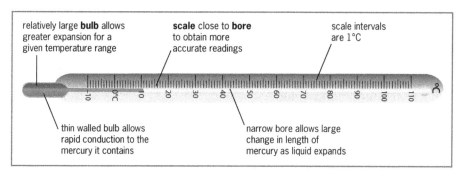

Figure 12.20 *Liquid-in-glass laboratory mercury thermometer*

Alcohol thermometer

Alcohol boils at a **lower temperature** and **freezes** at a **much lower temperature** than mercury. Alcohol thermometers are therefore used for measuring a **different range** of temperature than mercury thermometers. Figure 12.21 shows a typical alcohol thermometer.

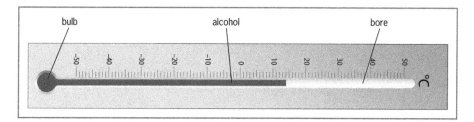

Figure 12.21 *A typical alcohol thermometer*

Advantages of using mercury instead of alcohol in a thermometer

- Mercury is a metal and so has a **higher conductivity** than alcohol. This allows heat transfers to and from the mercury to occur at a higher rate, causing the thermometer to **respond more rapidly**.
- Being a metal, not much heat is needed to enter or leave mercury for its temperature to adjust to that of the body being measured. The thermometer therefore **responds more rapidly**, and the **temperature** of the **body being measured** is **not significantly altered**.
- The boiling point of mercury is **357 °C**, whereas that of ethyl alcohol is only **78 °C**. Mercury thermometers are therefore more suitable for most laboratory experiments done at school. If alcohol was used as the liquid in the thermometer, it would **evaporate** and **distill** on the upper part of the bore, giving inaccurate readings for most temperatures measured in the school laboratory.
- Mercury is **bright silver** and can be **seen easily**, whereas alcohol is **colourless** and must be **tinted** to make it visible.

Disadvantages of using mercury instead of alcohol in a thermometer

- Mercury is much more **expensive** than alcohol.
- Mercury vapour is **toxic** whereas alcohol vapour in moderate amounts is **not toxic**.
- Mercury freezes at **−39 °C** whereas ethyl alcohol freezes at **−114 °C**. Mercury thermometers are therefore **less suitable** for measuring **very cold temperatures**.
- Alcohol **expands** about **six times** as much as mercury for the same temperature change. The stem of an alcohol thermometer is therefore **six times longer** than that of a mercury thermometer of the same size bulb and of the same width of bore. This causes the **intervals** on the mercury thermometer to be **closer together**, preventing it from being read with as great a **precision**.

Example 2

On the stem of the mercury thermometer shown in Figure 12.22, the distance between the fixed points, 0 °C and 100 °C, is 20 cm. The bulb of the thermometer is submerged in warm water and the mercury thread rises to a point which is 12 cm from the 0 °C marking on the scale. Given that the expansion of mercury is directly proportional to its increase in temperature, calculate the temperature of the water.

Solution

A distance of 20 cm represents a temperature change of 100 °C

∴ a distance of 1 cm represents a temperature change of $\dfrac{100}{20}$ °C   i.e. 5 °C

∴ a distance of 12 cm represents a change of 12 × 5 °C = 60 °C

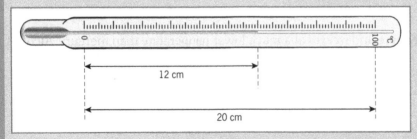

12 cm

20 cm

Figure 12.22 *Example 2*

Clinical thermometers

Clinical thermometers are important for monitoring a person's health. Table 12.3 indicates how a person's condition can vary with temperature.

Table 12.3 *Relation between patient's temperature and patient's condition*

Temperature, θ/°C	Condition
$\theta < 35$	Hypothermia (intense shivering, numbness, confusion, hallucinations, coma that can lead to death)
$36.5 < \theta < 37.5$	Normal body temperature
$\theta < 38$	Either fever or hyperthermia (an uncontrollable rise in body temperature that can lead to death)
$\theta < 42$	Usually, death

Clinical liquid-in-glass mercury thermometer

A clinical thermometer (Figure 12.23) can be the liquid-in-glass type and therefore has many of the features of the mercury-in-glass laboratory thermometer. However, the following should be noted.

- Its range is from **35 °C to 43 °C**, since this is the range of temperature for living humans.
- The interval between markings on the scale is **0.1 °C** (not 1 °C, as in the laboratory thermometer) so that a very **precise reading** can be obtained. This is important since a **slight change in temperature** can indicate a **serious change in health**.
- There is a narrow constriction in the bore. When the thermometer is removed from the patient, the **sudden change in temperature** causes a **rapid contraction** of the mercury. As the mercury rushes toward the bulb, the **thread breaks** at the **constriction**, leaving the remainder above the break to be read by the doctor or nurse.
- **Alcohol cannot be used** in these thermometers since, unlike mercury, **it will not break at the constriction**.
- Since mercury is **toxic**, this type of clinical thermometer is being replaced by electronic, digital thermometers.

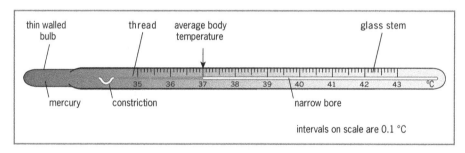

Figure 12.23 *Clinical liquid-in-glass mercury thermometer*

Digital thermometers

These thermometers have sensors that **produce voltages** dependent on the **temperature of their environment**. The sensors are connected to a digital display, which indicates the temperature. There are different types of digital thermometers with temperature-sensing abilities that depend on different physical principles.

- **Infrared digital thermometers** produce voltages dependent on the frequencies of thermal radiation.
- **Thermocouple digital thermometers** produce voltages dependent on the temperature difference between two junctions in a circuit.
- **Thermistor digital thermometers** produce voltages dependent on their variation of resistance with temperature.

Figure 12.24 shows a clinical thermometer. It has a **thermistor**, made of a **ceramic semiconductor** material, as a **temperature sensor**. The **resistance** of the thermistor **changes** as the **temperature changes** and this produces a corresponding **voltage**, which is then converted to a **temperature reading** in a display window.

- The **tip is placed on the body** being measured and a **rapid** reading is obtained.
- Some digital thermometers have an **auto shut-off** feature used to save on battery life.
- Some can **store past readings**.
- They produce **accurate** readings within the range of temperature of living humans.

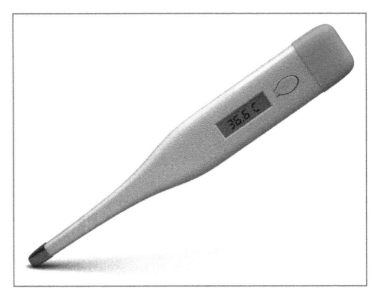

Figure 12.24 *Digital thermometer*

Maximum and minimum thermometer

A maximum and minimum thermometer is used to measure the maximum and minimum temperatures reached in a particular place over a period of time (see Figure 12.25).

- As the **temperature increases**, alcohol in the left tube expands **through** the left steel index and presses on the mercury, causing it to force the right steel index upwards.
- The indexes have a light spring that holds them against the tube.
- As the **temperature decreases**, alcohol in the left tube contracts, pulling the mercury with it. If the mercury reaches the left index, it forces it upwards. Alcohol in the right tube flows **through** the index.

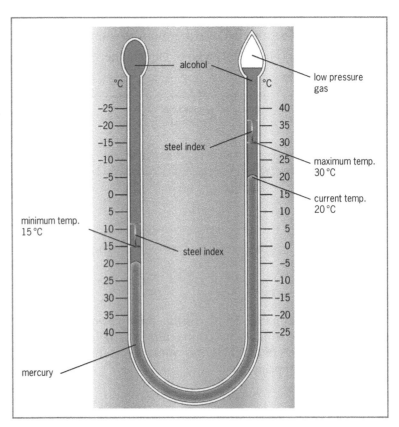

Figure 12.25 *Maximum and minimum thermometer*

- The **highest and lowest temperatures** of the period can be read from the **bottom of the indexes**. The diagram indicates that the highest temperature of the period was 30 °C and the lowest temperature was 15 °C.
- The current temperature can be read from the mercury level in either scale. The diagram indicates that the current temperature is 20 °C.
- After reading the scales, a **magnet** is used to **return the indexes**, so they once more touch the mercury.

Temperature regulation in humans

Humans must maintain a **constant** internal body temperature of about **37 °C** for **enzymes** to function properly, as discussed on page 81. **Sweating** plays a crucial role in reducing a person's body temperature if the temperature **rises** above normal (see Figure 5.6, page 81). As the **water** in sweat **evaporates**, it takes heat energy from the body, thereby **cooling** the body. This is because the process of converting a liquid to vapour requires **energy** to overcome the attractive forces between the liquid molecules, known as the **latent heat of vaporisation**.

Latent heat of vaporisation is the amount of heat energy that is needed to convert a unit mass of a liquid into a vapour without changing its temperature.

Water has a **high** latent heat of vaporisation because the attractive forces between its molecules are **strong**. Therefore, when water in sweat evaporates from the surface of the skin it removes large amounts of heat energy from the skin. This makes sweating a very effective method of cooling the body.

Effect of changes in body temperature on metabolic rate

Chemical reactions occur constantly in all living cells in order to sustain life. These reactions are referred to as the body's **metabolism** and the rate at which they occur is known as the **metabolic rate**. Metabolic rate is a measure of the amount of **energy** per unit time that a person needs to keep the body functioning. Metabolic rate varies among individuals and **changes** in a person's **body temperature** can affect this rate. This is because the rate of chemical reactions and the rate of enzyme activity are both affected by temperature (see page 180).

- If the body temperature **rises** above normal; for example, during exercise, illness or when the environmental temperature is high, a person's metabolic rate **increases**. This is because as temperature increases, the rate of enzyme activity increases.
- If the body temperature **drops** below normal; for example, when the environmental temperature is low, a person's metabolic rate **decreases**. This is because as temperature decreases, the rate of enzyme activity decreases.

Importance of proper ventilation

Ventilation is the process by which clean air is provided to a space and stale air is removed from it.

To remain healthy and comfortable, the air around us should have the following properties.

- An adequate **oxygen** level.
- An adequate **humidity** level.
- An adequate **temperature**.
- Be **free of dust, pollen** and **toxic contaminants**.
- Be **free of mould** and **bacteria**.

Problems of inadequate ventilation of enclosed spaces

- As we breathe, **oxygen levels fall** and **carbon dioxide** and **water vapour levels rise, reducing** the **ease of respiration.**
- Exhaled **water vapour** causes **increased humidity, reducing** the **cooling effect** of evaporation.
- **Microorganisms** (such as mould) rapidly multiply in warm, humid environments, creating an **unhealthy, musty odour.**
- **Toxins** and **dust** can **interact negatively** with our bodies.

Natural ventilation

Natural ventilation is ventilation produced by natural breezes or natural convection currents.

- On a **windy day,** windows/vents on **different sides of a room** allow clean air to enter and stale air to be pushed out (see Figure 12.26a).
- When there is **no natural breeze** an open window/vent **on a higher level** allows stale, less dense, warm air to exit by convection, and cooler, denser, fresh air to be sucked in through an open window/vent **on a lower level** (see Figure 12.26b).

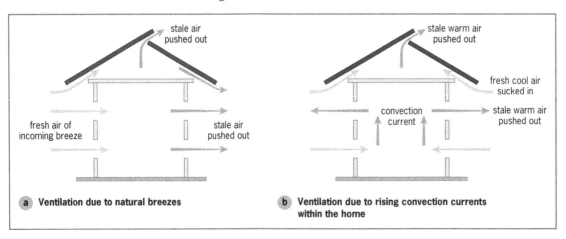

Figure 12.26 *Some design features promoting improved natural ventilation*

Mechanical ventilation

Mechanical ventilation is ventilation produced by devices such as fans, air conditioners, air purifiers, humidifiers and dehumidifiers.

- **Bathroom exhaust vents** powered by motorised fans can remove air with undesirable odours.
- **Kitchen exhaust vents above stoves** (some motorised) can remove hot air and contaminants.
- **Fans cool us by increasing the rate of evaporation** of our perspiration and by **replacing warm, moist air** from around our bodies with **cool, less humid air.** Electric fans are common in the Caribbean.
- **Air conditioners (ac units) extract warm, moist air** from a room and replace it with **cooler, less humid air.** The air is cooled as it touches the cold coils of the ac unit. The water vapour in it condenses and is allowed to drain outside the building. Air conditioners therefore also act as **dehumidifiers** since **air holds less water** vapour at **lower temperatures.**
- **Dehumidifiers** should be used in highly humid rooms such as cellars to prevent build-up of mould. Figure 12.27a on page 281 shows a dehumidifier.
- **Air purifiers** remove contaminants from the air. They are fitted with **several filters** specifically designed to remove airborne allergens, such as pollen and mould spores, as well as bacteria, viruses, and smoke. Figure 12.27b on page 281 shows an air purifier.
- **Humidifiers** should be used in rooms where the air is very dry. Figure 12.27c on page 281 shows a humidifier.

a Dehumidifier showing tank of **water removed** from moist air. **b** Air purifier removing **allergens and odours** from dog and carpet. **c** Humidifier showing **moisture being sprayed** into dry air.

Figure 12.27 *Dehumidifier, air purifier and humidifier*

Temperature and humidity

*Relative humidity is the amount of water vapour present in the air expressed as a percentage of the total amount it can hold **at that temperature**.*

A relative humidity of **between 30% and 50%** is **recommended** for comfortable and healthy living.

The air in the Caribbean generally has a relative humidity level between 60% and 90%! Being close to the equator, the **higher temperature causes increased evaporation** from the sea which surrounds our islands.

Negative effects of high humidity

- Leads to **early decay** of **building materials**, especially damp wooden structures.
- Promotes the development of **fungi**, including **mould** (see Figure 12.28), which can lead to **allergic reactions** in humans.
- Produces **distasteful odours**.
- Promotes the development of **bacteria** and **viruses**.
- Encourages the growth of **dust-mites**.
- On a hot and humid day our body temperature can rise significantly, causing the production of excessive sweat that is unable to evaporate. This can lead to **dehydration** – especially if we are engaged in very active physical work or exercise – since our **higher metabolic rate** will further increase our body temperature. If our body temperature rises above 40 °C, **heatstroke** may result, bringing with it a range of symptoms including nausea and vomiting, headaches and dizziness, gasping for breath, seizures, kidney failure, and even a state of coma.

Figure 12.28 *Mould and mildew due to high humidity*

Coma is a state of prolonged unconsciousness where the victim cannot respond to external stimuli.

Negative effects of low humidity

- It can **dehydrate mucous membranes** such as the lining in the nose and throat and can result in **respiratory distress**.
- Materials may shrink or **become brittle** and **crack**.
- Surfaces of some materials tend to become **electrically charged** resulting in the **destruction of semiconducting devices** and **attraction of dust**.

Recalling facts

1. **a** Define the following forms of heat transfer:
    i conduction   **ii** convection   **iii** radiation.
    b i State the relative conductivities of solids, liquids and gases.
       ii Is conduction greater in metals or is it greater in non-metals?
       iii What is the only form of heat transfer that can occur through a vacuum?

2. Name a suitable material from which each of the following should be made:
    a the handle of a saucepan.
    b the base and sides of a saucepan.

3. Define the following:
    a a bimetallic strip.   **b** a thermostat.   **c** temperature.

4. **a** What is the normal body temperature of a human, in °C?
    b What is a person's most likely medical condition if their body temperature:
       i falls to 34 °C?   **ii** rises to 40 °C?

5. **a** What is meant by the term 'metabolic rate'?
    b Explain the effects that any changes to a person's body temperature have on the person's metabolic rate.

6. **a** Define 'ventilation'.
    b Differentiate between natural ventilation and mechanical ventilation.
    c What are the FIVE main characteristics of a room with suitable ventilation?
    d List FIVE devices which can be installed in a home to improve ventilation.

7. **a** Define relative humidity.
    b What range of relative humidity is recommended for healthy living?
    c What is the range of relative humidity generally experienced in the Caribbean?
    d Why does the Caribbean region have such a high humidity level?
    e List FOUR negative effects of high humidity.
    f List TWO negative effects of low humidity.

Applying facts

8 For EACH of the following, describe an experiment with the aid of a diagram to show that:

  a copper is a better conductor than wood.

  b water is a poor thermal conductor.

  c convection can occur in liquids.

9 **a** Explain how Isha's quilted blanket can keep her warm on a cold night.

  b Explain why Isha's house, which is made of hollow concrete blocks, will keep her cooler during a hot summer's day than Ishmael's house, which is made of solid concrete blocks.

  c State, with a reason, which house will be warmer during a cold winter's night.

10 Explain each of the following.

  a A convection current is produced when a block of ice is placed into a bowl of water.

  b Coastal regions obtain sea breezes during the day.

11 Answer the following questions of these FOUR surfaces:
smooth, shiny silver / rough, matt silver / smooth, shiny black / rough, matt black.
Which is the best:

  a absorber of thermal radiation?

  b emitter of thermal radiation?

  c reflector of thermal radiation?

12 Since the Moon has no atmosphere, there is no insulation from the Sun's rays. During a lunar day the temperature is 120 °C, but this falls to –130 °C during a lunar night! Rico has volunteered to be an astronaut and has been given special suits to wear to protect himself from the blistering temperature and the intense cold. State, with reasons, the texture and colour suit he should wear:

  a during the day. **b** during the night.

13 Figure 12.29 shows the features of Accalia's solar water heater.

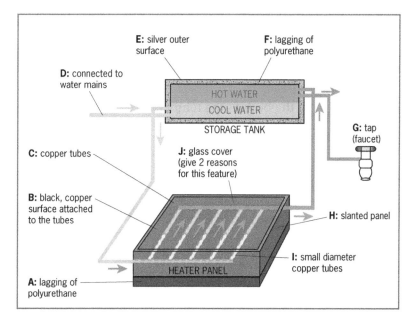

Figure 12.29 *Question 13*

a State the reason for EACH feature of her water heater system.

b Why does the hot water in the tank not transfer any significant amount of heat to the cold water below it?

c Kody's home has the storage tank in the garage instead of on the roof above the panel. Water heated in the panel will therefore not be able to reach the tank by natural convection. What added component must he have to ensure that hot water reaches the tank?

14 Figure 12.30 shows a thermostat used in an electric oven.

a Explain the following.

  i The lower end of the bimetallic strip moves to the right when the temperature rises.

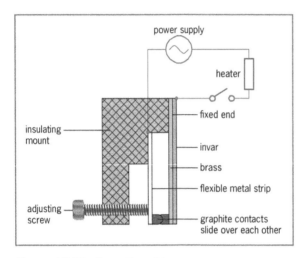

Figure 12.30 *Question 14*

  ii The current through the heater is cut off when the temperature rises to a certain value.

  iii Shortly after, the current flows again and the process repeats, thereby approximately maintaining the temperature.

b How can the thermostat be set to maintain a higher temperature?

15 Figure 12.31 shows a laboratory liquid in glass mercury thermometer. Explain the following.

a The mercury moves along the bore as the temperature rises.

b The bulb of the thermometer has thin walls.

c The bore along which the mercury moves is very narrow.

d The scale is marked on the stem.

Figure 12.31 *Question 15*

16 State TWO advantages and TWO disadvantages of using mercury instead of alcohol in a liquid-in-glass thermometer.

17 Figure 12.32 shows a clinical liquid-in-glass thermometer.

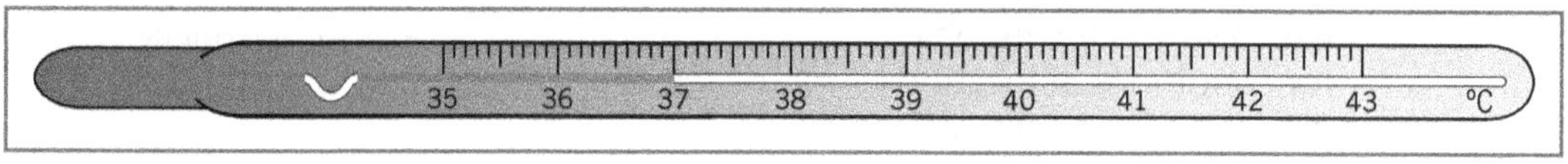

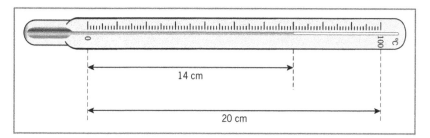

Figure 12.32 *Question 17*

a What is the temperature reading on the thermometer?

b Why is there a narrow constriction in the bore?

c Why is the range of the scale only from 35 °C to 43 °C?

d Give a reason for the interval spacing representing 0.1 °C whereas in the laboratory type thermometer it is 1 °C.

18 Explain the importance of water's high latent heat of vaporisation to the human body.

19 Name the device that would be most suitable to improve ventilation in the following cases.

a A very dry room.

b A room which contains lots of allergens from dogs and cats.

c A damp cellar smelling strongly of mould.

d An enclosed office with adequate humidity and which is free of allergens and mould, but which is uncomfortably hot.

e A hot room which needs to have opened windows.

20 Calculate the temperature shown by the thermometer in Figure 12.33.

Figure 12.33 *Question 20*

Analysing data

21 Answer the following by examining Figure 12.34, which shows the graphs for conditions at locations P and Q over a range of temperature.

a At 25 °C, what mass (in grams) of water per kilogram of air is present:

  i at P?

  ii at Q?

b At 40 °C, what mass (in grams) of water per kilogram of air is present

  i at P?

  ii at Q?

c State, with a reason, which of the locations is more likely to experience heavy rainfall.

d At which location would a given temperature seem lower than at the other?

e Which location has adequate relative humidity?

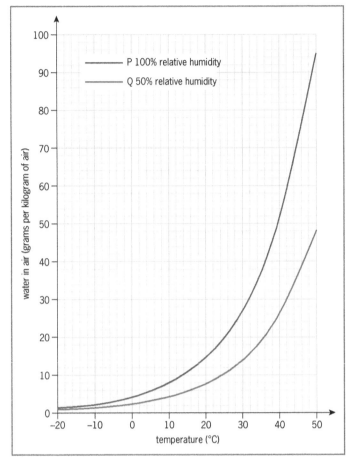

Figure 12.34 *Question 21*

Section C
Our Planet

The topics covered in this section are:

- The universe and our solar system
- The terrestrial environment
- Water and its uses
- Water pollution, water purification and flotation
- Navigational and water safety devices, and scuba diving
- The statics and dynamics of forces and their applications
- The human skeleton
- Metals and non-metals
- Chemicals used in the home
- Matter, mixtures and their separation
- Pollutants and the environment

13 The universe and our solar system

The universe is extremely vast. It takes light just 8 minutes to travel 152 000 000 km from the Sun – our nearest star – to Earth, but more than 4 years to reach us from the next nearest star! Scientists believe that there are more stars in the universe than there are grains of sand on the entire Earth!

Learning objectives

- Identify the **components** of the **universe**.
- Explain how **satellites** can remain in **orbit**.
- Describe the various **types of satellites** and their **uses**.
- Describe the **solar system**.
- Discuss how **Earth is affected by other bodies**.
- Discuss **exploration** of the **universe**.

The universe is comprised of several types of celestial bodies. Table 13.1 summarises these components.

Table 13.1 *Important components of the universe*

Celestial body	Description
Earth	The celestial body in our solar system that is **home to humans**. Over **70%** of its surface is **water** and its atmosphere contains **21%** oxygen, which is essential to **sustain life**.
Star	A **luminous sphere** composed of plasma and held together by gravitational forces.
Sun	An **average star** and the closest to Earth.
Planets	Celestial bodies that have all three of the following properties. • **Rotate on an axis** as they **revolve around a star** in an **elliptical orbit**. • Are **large** enough to have **gravitational forces** which cause them to be **spherical**. • Have **cleared their orbital paths** of most bodies.
Planetoids	Planetoids of our solar system: **Ceres**, **Pluto**, **Haumea**, **Makemake** and **Eris**. They have the following properties. • **Orbit a star** (the Sun in our solar system). • Are **not spherical** due to their small size and therefore weaker gravitational field. • Have **orbits that are intercepted** by other bodies; for example, asteroids.
Solar system	The **solar system** has the **Sun as its focus** and is orbited by several bodies (see Figure 13.6).
Asteroids	• **Rocky masses** that orbit the Sun. • Has **no atmosphere** as it is too small to have a gravitational field sufficiently strong to contain one. • Are **not spherical** due to their weak gravitational field.

Celestial body	Description
Asteroid belt	The **asteroid belt** is an orbital path around the Sun between Mars and Jupiter containing **millions of asteroids** and **one dwarf planet**, **Ceres**.
Meteoroids	Meteoroids are smaller than asteroids and also orbit the Sun. They are usually the **remnants of comets** or broken pieces of asteroids.
Meteors	These are **bright trails of light** (known as shooting stars) produced when meteoroids or other objects experience **friction** on passing through the atmosphere.
Meteorites	The **remains of meteoroids** or other debris that have **fallen to the Earth's** surface.
Comets	Masses of **frozen water** and **super-cold carbon dioxide**, **methane** and **ammonia** 'ices' mixed with lesser quantities of **rock** and **dust** which orbit the Sun in highly **eccentric** paths. They have extreme trajectories which carry them very close to the Sun and then very far from the Sun. When they are close to the Sun the **ice vaporises**, producing a **'tail' of gas and dust** which is always directed away from the Sun. If a planet's orbit passes through this material, the material falls onto the planet as **meteor showers**.
Kuiper belt	A donut shaped region **beyond Neptune** where **icy bodies** and **dwarf planets** (except for Ceres) revolve around the Sun in elliptical orbits.
Galaxy	A group of billions of stars.
Milky Way	The galaxy containing our solar system.
Universe	The **entire cosmic system** composed of **all matter and energy** of billions of galaxies.

Location of Earth in the universe

Earth

Our solar system

Small part of the observable universe

Milky Way

Figure 13.1 *The location of Earth in the universe*

The Milky Way galaxy

- The Milky Way is a typical spiral galaxy made of **hot gases**, **dust** and over **200 billion stars.**
- It has a diameter of about **100 000 light-years** (light takes approximately 100 000 years to cross it).
- It is bulged at the centre and has **four spiral arms** where the stars are most concentrated.
- Our solar system is located midway between the centre and the outer edge of the galaxy.
- As the spiral arms rotate around the centre of the galaxy, **hot gases** and **dust** are forced through them causing the **birth of more stars.**
- At its centre is a huge **black hole** with a **mass** that is **billions of times greater** than that of the **Sun.**

Characteristics of outer space

- Outer space is the expanse that lies between celestial bodies such as the stars and planets.
- Outer space is mostly empty of matter (it is mainly a **vacuum**), but there are clouds of both **cosmic dust** and a **plasma** of **hydrogen** and **helium.**
- In areas of outer space where there are no large celestial bodies nearby, **gravitational forces** are **extremely small.**
- There is **no air to breathe**, and **sound cannot be transmitted.**
- As a body travels away from the Sun or any star, its **temperature continuously falls.**
- **Radiation levels** in space are **extremely dangerous.**
- **Dark matter** is matter that we know is there, but so far have not been able to detect directly.

How do bodies stay in orbit?

*A **satellite** is a body that orbits another body of **larger** mass.*

Natural and artificial satellites

Satellites may be **natural** or **artificial** (made by humans). The Earth is a **natural satellite** of the Sun and the Moon is a natural satellite of the Earth. Examples of artificial satellites are **weather satellites** and **communication satellites** that orbit Earth as they transmit radio and television programmes.

Gravitational forces keep satellites in orbit

The force necessary to keep a satellite in orbit depends on its **mass**, **speed** and **orbital radius.** This force is provided by gravity.

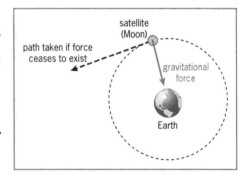

- The **force of gravity** on a satellite has a **particular value** which is just sufficient to **prevent** it from **shooting out of its orbit** as shown in Figure 13.2.
- The force is always **directed to the centre of the orbit.**
- The **greater** the **mass** and/or **speed** of the satellite, the **greater** the required **force.**
- The **greater** the **radius of the orbit**, the **smaller** the required **force.**

Figure 13.2 *Gravitational forces keep satellites in orbit*

Types of artificial satellites

Geostationary satellites

These orbit with a **period of 24 hours** in the same direction as the Earth revolves and are **always directly above** the **same point** on the **equator** (see Figure 13.3).

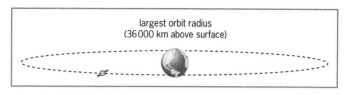

largest orbit radius
(36 000 km above surface)

Figure 13.3 *Geostationary satellite*

Uses

- **Communication** – Some geostationary satellites relay radio, television and telephone signals. Since they are **always above the same point on the Earth**, their **signals can be located easily**.

- **Storm monitoring** – Since geostationary weather satellites are **always above the same hemisphere**, they can provide continuous data from observing a region within that hemisphere. This makes them useful for monitoring **large scale weather systems** such as hurricanes.

Polar satellites

These have orbits that are almost parallel to the longitudinal lines of Earth, so they can obtain data from around the planet in an **east-west** direction as the Earth spins beneath them on its axis, as well as in a **north-south** direction as they proceed along their orbits (see Figure 13.4).

smallest orbit radius
(approx. 1000 km above surface)

Figure 13.4 *Polar satellite*

Uses

- **Monitoring weather patterns**.
- **Mapping** and **surveying**.
- **Military applications** – such as locating an enemy or assessing land features for strategic warfare.

Polar satellites have some **advantages** over geostationary satellites.

- They can monitor conditions **anywhere** around the **entire planet**. A number of polar satellites may be used together with geostationary satellites to monitor weather conditions anywhere at any time.

- They produce **images of good resolution** since they orbit **close to the Earth's surface**.

- One complete polar orbit takes about **90 minutes**, so each polar satellite orbits the Earth several times in 24 hours, enabling it to observe the **entire surface of Earth** in that time.

Satellite navigational systems

Several satellite navigational systems are currently in use. One such system is the **Global Positioning System** (**GPS**) of satellites developed and operated by the USA (see Figure 13.5). It consists of approximately **30 satellites** orbiting in **6** circular paths with orbital periods of about **12 hours**. The minimum number of satellites needed to provide full coverage at any location on Earth is **24**.

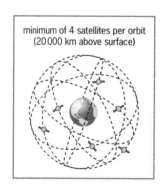

minimum of 4 satellites per orbit
(20 000 km above surface)

Figure 13.5 *GPS satellites*

Use

They produce information of **location and time** at various points on or above the Earth's surface (see chapter 15, page 344, Navigational devices used at sea).

Other artificial satellites

The International Space Station, the Hubble Space Telescope and the James Webb Space Telescope are discussed later in this chapter on page 298 and 299.

A closer look at our solar system

Our **solar system** has the Sun at its centre, and planets, planetoids (dwarf planets), moons, asteroids, meteoroids, comets and meteors which orbit it in **elliptical paths** (see Figure 13.6).

Figure 13.6 *Our solar system*

The planets can be divided into the following two groups.

Terrestrial planets – Mercury, Venus, Earth and Mars. They have **hard rocky** surfaces and are **smaller** and **warmer** than the other planets.

Gas giants – Jupiter, Saturn, Uranus and Neptune. They have **no solid surfaces** and are composed of **gaseous hydrogen** and **helium**, and **liquid ammonia**. They are **larger** and **colder** than the terrestrial planets and each has a **ring system** of dust and/or ice around it.

The **asteroid belt** and **Kuiper belt** are described in Table 13.1 on page 289 and illustrated in Figure 13.6.

Table 13.2 *Characteristic features of the planets of our solar system*

Planet	Characteristic features
Mercury	• The **smallest** planet. • Rotates slowly, taking 59 Earth days to make 1 rotation, but orbits the Sun in just 88 Earth days. Approximately 3 Mercury days occur during 2 Mercury years! • The only planet with virtually **no atmosphere** to prevent heat from entering or leaving it. • The side facing the Sun is **very hot** and the opposite side is **very cold**.
Venus	• A dense atmosphere of **carbon dioxide** traps heat by the **greenhouse effect** (see page 207) making it the **hottest** planet, although it is not the closest to the Sun. • Rotates very slowly about its axis, taking 243 Earth days to make 1 rotation. This is even longer than a year on Venus, which is 225 Earth days! • Spins about its axis in the **opposite direction** to the other planets. • Covered by an opaque cloud of **sulfuric acid**. • **Brightest** planet since sunlight is reflected from the thick cloud which surrounds it. • More than a thousand **large volcanoes** are scattered over its landscape.
Earth	• **Largest** of the **terrestrial** planets. • Completes 1 rotation in 24 hours and 1 revolution in 365¼ days. • **Supports life** since its temperature allows water to exist in the liquid state. • Has a **strong magnetic field** that protects it from the **solar wind** (high speed electrical charges streaming out from the Sun).
Mars	• Known as the **red planet** due to the rusted **iron** in its surface of rock, ice and dust. • Has **2 moons**, Phobos and Deimos. • Has the **largest dust storms**. • Has the **tallest mountain** and **largest volcano** in our solar system. • There is evidence of the **presence of water** on Mars, which could enable life to exist. However, evidence of life has not yet been detected on Mars. • The **second smallest planet**; it is **half the size of Earth** but has the same land area. • UV and cosmic radiation penetrate the thin atmosphere, consisting mainly of carbon dioxide. This radiation **sterilises** the surface. • The thin atmosphere causes ice to change directly to vapour, **leaving the planet dry**.
Jupiter	• Has the **shortest day** of all the planets; rotates once every 9 h 55 min. • Has a **Great Red Spot**, which is a huge raging storm. • Has the **largest mass** and **volume**. • Has 95 moons; the largest, **Ganymede**, is larger than Mercury! • Has a ring system of **dust** particles.
Saturn	• Known for its profound **ring system** which is made mainly of ice and dust particles. • Has 146 **moons**, all of which are have a surface temperature well below 0 °C. The largest, Titan, is larger than Mercury.
Uranus	• Known as an 'ice giant' and has a ring system of ice and dust. • Its axis of rotation is tilted at an angle of 98°, giving the illusion that it is **on its side**.
Neptune	• Known as an 'ice giant' and has a **ring system** of ice and dust.

Table 13.3 *Comparing and contrasting the planets with Earth*

Planet	Distance from Sun (km)	Diameter (km)	No. of known moons	Mean temp. (°C)
Mercury	60 million	5 000	0	167
Venus	110 million	12 000	0	464
Earth	150 million	13 000	1	15
Mars	230 million	7 000	2	−65
Jupiter	780 million	143 000	95	−110
Saturn	1430 million	121 000	146	−140
Uranus	2870 million	51 000	28	−195
Neptune	4500 million	50 000	16	−200

How Earth is affected by other bodies

Day and night are the result of the rectilinear propagation of light

As the Earth spins on its axis, the surface that **faces the Sun** experiences **daylight** and the surface on the **side away from the Sun** experiences **night**. The Earth rotates about its axis once every 24 hours and so most places on the planet will undergo a period of daylight and a period of darkness in this time.

Seasons are a consequence of the tilted axis of the Earth's rotation

The axis of rotation of the Earth is tilted at **23.5°**. This results in the northern hemisphere receiving more hours of daylight than the southern hemisphere for six months (summer), and then more hours of darkness than the southern hemisphere for the next six months (winter), as shown in Figure 13.7.

The 'midnight sun' and 'polar nights'

From **March to September**, the **North Pole** receives **6 months of daylight**, and the **South Pole** receives **6 months of darkness**. From **September to March**, the **North Pole** receives **6 months of darkness** and the **South Pole, 6 months of daylight**. These **6-month periods** of **day** and **night** are respectively known as the 'midnight sun' and 'polar nights'.

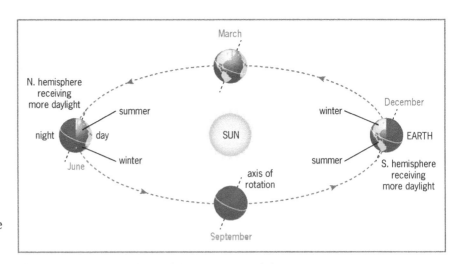

Figure 13.7 *Day, night and the seasons of the year*

We see the Moon by reflection

The Moon is **non-luminous** and is therefore seen from the Earth by **reflection** of light from the Sun. The orbit of the Moon usually passes outside the Earth's umbra (cone of complete shadow). Light always reflects such that its angle of incidence (i) is equal to its angle of reflection (r). If the reflected ray is directed to Earth, the Moon will be visible. Therefore, sometimes we can see the Moon **during the day** and at other times, **during the night** (see Figure 13.8).

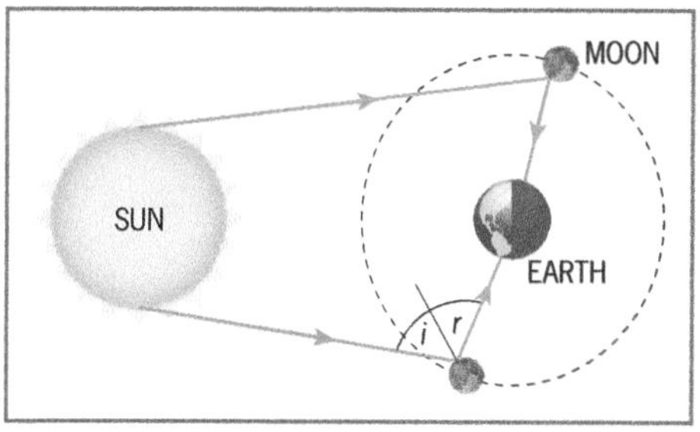

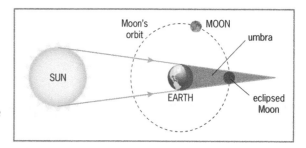

Figure 13.8 *We see the Moon during the day and during the night*

Eclipse of the Moon (lunar eclipse)

*A **lunar eclipse** occurs when the Earth passes between the Sun and the Moon and casts a shadow over the Moon.*

Occasionally, the Moon enters the shadow of the Earth and becomes only dimly visible (see Figure 13.9). Light from the Sun can no longer reach it to be reflected to Earth, and a lunar eclipse occurs. It can take as much as **1½ hours** before it emerges from the other edge of the shadow. An eclipse of the Moon only occurs when there is a '**full moon**', that is, when the Sun and the Moon are on opposite sides of the Earth as in Figure 13.12 on page 296. On such an occasion, the full moon becomes obscured as it passes through the Earth's umbra.

Figure 13.9 *Eclipse of the Moon*

Eclipse of the Sun (solar eclipse)

Occasionally, the orbit of the Moon can pass through the rays directed from the Sun to the Earth (see Figure 13.10). It is then possible for the Moon's umbra to reach the surface of the Earth, covering a relatively small area of surface from which a **total solar eclipse** is observed. Persons engulfed in the partial shadow of the penumbra observe a **partial solar eclipse**.

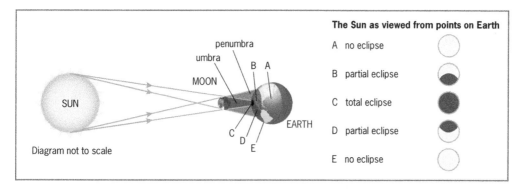

Figure 13.10 *Total eclipse of the Sun*

Annular eclipse of the Sun

During some solar eclipses, the **umbra does not reach the surface of Earth**, and a **bright ring** is seen surrounding the shadow produced by the Moon. For example, see Figure 13.11; an annular eclipse is observed from point A.

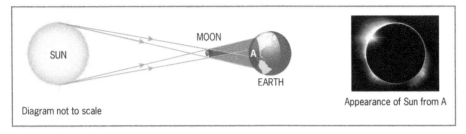

Diagram not to scale

Appearance of Sun from A

Figure 13.11 *Annular eclipse of the Sun*

The Moon over a period of 30 days

The moon takes **29½ days** (approximately 30 days) to orbit the Earth and to return to the same position relative to the Sun as seen by an observer on Earth. The **inner ring** of Figure 13.12 shows how the **side facing the Sun is always lit** and the opposite side is always in darkness. The **outer ring** shows the Moon as **viewed from Earth**.

When the Moon is between the Earth and Sun, we view the side that is in darkness: a *new moon*.

For the next few days an increasing amount of light from the Sun reflects from the Moon's surface producing a *waxing crescent*, until half of the disc appears lit, and we observe the *first quarter moon*.

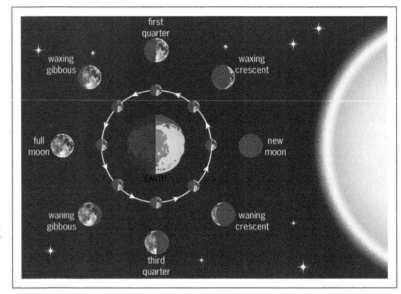

Figure 13.12 *Observing the Moon over a period of 30 days*

As the moon continues in its orbit, an increasing amount of its surface reflects light producing a *waxing gibbous*, until a *full moon* is observed after approximately 15 days. The reflected light then becomes less, displaying a *waning gibbous* and then a *third quarter moon*, and finally a **waning crescent** and a **new moon** as the cycle completes.

- **Gibbous** and **crescent** refer to the Moon's **shape**.
- **Waxing** and **waning** refer to the Moon's reflection of **more light** and **less light**, respectively.

The **position of the Moon** in its orbit also affects the **tides** (see chapter 14 page 313).

Human exploration of the universe

Humans have been interested in space exploration for a very long time. Astronomers have used telescopes to study celestial bodies but until the latter half of the 20th century, did not have the technology to undertake physical exploration. Today however, powerful spacecraft have been developed to probe the universe for useful information.

Reasons for exploration of the universe

Exploration of deep space is extremely challenging due to **cost** as well as to the **high quality instruments** required to execute successful missions. Nevertheless, humans need to persist in their efforts so that they can succeed in obtaining the many benefits that space exploration has to offer.

Table 13.4 *Reasons for space exploration*

Reason	Details
Satisfy our curiosity	Find answers to questions of the evolution of the universe and our place in it.
Scientific research	Some scientific research is best done in space to eliminate variables such as gravity.
Asteroid collisions	Approximately every 10 000 years an asteroid collides with Earth. On September 26, 2022, the **asteroid, Dimorphos**, was successfully **deflected** by the **kinetic impact** of NASA's Double Asteroid Redirection Test (DART) spacecraft. Dimorphos was not a threat to Earth, but now we know it may be possible to avoid future collisions.
Mining	Many useful substances can be mined in space from planets, moons and asteroids to provide fuel, construction materials, fertilisers and life support for space explorers. • **Iron, nickel, platinum** and **rare earth metals** for **construction** and **technology**. • **Carbon dioxide, methane** and **ammonia** can be collected for **life support** and **fuel**. • **Water-ice** from the Moon and Mars can be used for **drinking** and for making hydrogen and oxygen. **Hydrogen** can be used as a **fuel**. • **Helium** can be used for **cooling rocket fuel** and for producing **superconductors**.
Technology	**Expand technologies** and give birth to new industries.
Unity	Foster **peaceful cooperation** with other nations to reap the benefits of unity.
Migration	• **Population increase** may reach levels that the Earth cannot sustain. • **Climate change** may force us to search for a less harmful environment.

Characteristics of outer space which make its exploration challenging

Table 13.5 *Problems of space exploration and how we can deal with them*

Challenge	Action required
Lack of atmosphere	• **Oxygen**, stored as a liquid, must be **added** constantly to the air of a spacecraft. • **Carbon dioxide** must be **removed** constantly from the air. • **Temperature** and **pressure** levels must be carefully **maintained**. • Sound cannot propagate through a vacuum so communication outside the space vehicle is done with the use of **radio waves**.
Weightlessness	• Astronauts need to adjust to their immediate environment as being one in which **nothing has weight**. • Food must be in **liquid or semi-liquid** form so that it may be **sucked** from its container and then forced down the oesophagus using the muscles. • **Urine and body waste** must be passed to **sealed containers**. • It is recommended that astronauts exercise **2½ hours per day, 6 days per week** to avoid **muscle atrophy** (shrinking of the muscles) and **reduced bone mass**.

Challenge	Action required
Food and water supply	• Foods are **dehydrated** or **freeze-dried** to reduce their mass and to avoid spoilage. They can be rehydrated before consumption. • Water is **recycled** from **sweat**, **breathing** and **urine**.
Cosmic radiation	• **Special clothing** must be worn to protect against the **high radiation** levels in space. • Space vehicles must be designed to provide **protection from radiation**.
Psychological stress	• **Being confined** and isolated so far from home strongly affects mental health and **mental motivational therapy** is necessary.
Highest standard of technology	• The **technologies** are very **complex** and **costly** since failures can be disastrous.
Communication delays	• Communication **delays due to distances** are managed by many technologies including **predictive** and **autonomous** systems that carry out actions without waiting on instructions from Earth.

The International Space Station (ISS)

Table 13.6 *The International Space Station*

Brief description	• This is the **largest artificial satellite** put into space by humans. It has laboratories, living quarters, docking ports for space vehicles, solar panels to provide power and a crew of about six, whose responsibilities include maintaining the space station.
	 International Space Station (ISS)
Orbit	• A **low orbit** with an average height of **400 km** and orbital period of **90 minutes**.
Functions	• Used as an **intermediate port** for space exploration. • Performs **scientific research** under the conditions of a **space environment**.
Ownership	• It was built in orbit at a cost of 100 billion dollars by space agencies from four countries (**USA**, **Russia**, **Canada**, and **Japan**) and one collection of countries (**Europe**). Each of these space agencies has a control centre on Earth.

The Hubble Space Telescope

The Hubble Space Telescope (HST), shown in Figure 13.13, has **revolutionised our understanding of the universe** through its **imagery**.

It observes **nearby current events** and **events far into our distant past**, billions of light-years away. It has helped to:

- determine the **rate of expansion** of the universe
- observe **collisions** of comets with Jupiter
- produce **high resolution images** of celestial bodies
- reveal the **birth and death of stars**
- witness the **merging of galaxies**
- increase our understanding of **black holes.**

Figure 13.13 *The Hubble Space Telescope*

The James Webb Space Telescope

The James Webb Space Telescope (JWST) is the **largest** and **most powerful** telescope ever constructed (see Figure 13.14).

Its mission includes the following objectives.

- Learning of the **beginnings** of the **universe, galaxy formation** and **evolution** of the cosmos.
- Studying the **formation** of **stars** and **planetary systems.**
- Analysing the **atmospheres of exoplanets** (planets outside our solar system) so that humans can investigate the possibility of **life in other systems.**

Figure 13.14 *James Webb Space Telescope*

Comparison of the HST and the JWST

Table 13.7 *A brief comparison of the Hubble Space Telescope and the James Webb Space Telescope*

Aspect	James Webb Space Telescope	Hubble Space Telescope
Launched	25th December 2021	25th April 1990
Wavelength range	Uses **infrared** detectors that can: • **avoid** the **interference of ultraviolet radiation** and **visible light** • **peer through dust** and **cosmic clouds** that block visible light • view **older**, more **distant galaxies.**	Uses detectors of **ultraviolet radiation, visible light** and **small wavelength infrared.**
Mirror size	**Larger** receiving mirror.	**Smaller** receiving mirror.
Location	**1 500 000 km** from Earth. It is not orbiting Earth.	**Low Earth orbit**, just **540 km** above Earth's surface.
Maintenance	**Cannot be maintained by astronauts** since it is at a distance beyond current human space flight capability.	**Can be maintained by astronauts** in space since it is in low orbit.

Exploring Mars

Other than Venus, Mars is the **nearest** planet to Earth. Venus has a high average surface **temperature of 467 °C** together with **sulfuric acid rain**; Mars is therefore rather easier to explore.
Although space exploration is expensive, scientists are eager to explore Mars for several reasons.

- To search for **biosignatures** which can indicate **if there was or is life on Mars.**
- To mine for **important materials.**
- To develop **new technologies** and **scientific theories.**
- To learn how we may **adjust to** drastic changes in **climatic conditions.**
- To investigate the possibility of **future colonisation.**

Atmosphere on Mars

To deal with the difficulties of Mars exploration, we need to understand its weather and climate.

Table 13.8 *Atmosphere on Mars*

Feature	Details
Composition	CO_2 (95%) N_2 (nearly 3%) Ar (2%) O_2 (< 0.2%)
	H_2O vapour, CO, noble gases (very small quantities)
Density	Very **thin atmosphere** (only 2% of atmospheric density on Earth)
Pressure	1000 pascals (only 1% of atmospheric pressure on Earth)
Temperature	**Lower temperature** (average of –60 °C) than that of Earth since it is **further from the Sun.**
	Colder upper atmosphere than that on Earth since, although there is much CO_2, the very thin atmosphere results in **less greenhouse warming.**
Dust storms	Dust storms are common occurrences on Mars.

Spacecraft used to obtain information of Mars

Flybys – Space probes which get close enough to gather information, and then shoot off into space.

Orbiters – Satellites placed around planets to:

- **gather information** from the surroundings
- **collect data** from landers and rovers
- **relay data** and information to Earth.

Landers – Space probes which land and remain on a planet to:

- **gather information** and relay it to Earth via orbiters
- **deliver rovers** to the planet.

Rovers – These are remotely controlled, robotic, motorised vehicles (including a recent small helicopter named *Ingenuity*). Mars rovers are important for the following purposes.

- To **discover** and relay information of the **geology of the surface.**
- To **study** the **climate** and **radiation levels** so that engineers can better protect astronauts.
- To **search** for **ancient microbial life** using information of the history of the planet.
- To **gather knowledge** necessary for future efficient exploration.
- To **collect surface samples** for future return to Earth where they will be further analysed.
- To **demonstrate technological development.**

Important Mars rovers

- **Sojourner** (NASA – **landed in 1997**)
  A small vehicle, just 2 feet long. It stayed within 12 metres of the **lander**, as it gathered and relayed information to Earth. The outcomes of this mission included:

  - the collection of many rock samples and the analysis of their chemistry
  - more than 550 images of the Mars surface
  - information on weather factors on Mars
  - information that Mars was once warm, wet and potentially habitable.

  It lasted almost 4 months, which was 12 times its design lifetime. This pioneering rover **revolutionised the approach to exploration for future missions.**

- **Spirit** and **Opportunity** (NASA – **landed in 2004**)
  This pair of rovers (known as twins) were placed on opposite sides of Mars to investigate the **geology of the surface**. They confirmed that **water existed** on the planet in the **ancient past**. *Spirit* ceased operation in 2010 after it got stuck in the sand. *Opportunity* stopped communicating in 2018 during a dust storm after it was no longer able to recharge its batteries. *Opportunity* holds the record of being the longest lasting rover ever placed on another planet.

- **Curiosity** (NASA – **landed in 2012**)
  This rover is the size of an SUV and is still in operation. It investigates:

  - the **geology** and **climate** of Mars
  - the **possibility** that the planet once supported **life**; in 2018 it **discovered organic molecules** that indicate **life could have existed there.**

Figure 13.15 *Sojourner, Opportunity and Curiosity*

- **Perseverance** (NASA – **landed in 2021**)
  Perseverance is mainly being used to study **astrobiology**, including the search for **ancient and current life** on Mars and to determine if humans can live there. It will do so by investigating the **Jazero Crater**, which is believed to have once contained a **lake** with conditions **suitable for microbial life.**

  It has a **7-foot mechanical arm**, and **23 cameras** uniquely designed for **navigation, landscape viewing** and **scientific investigation.** The mechanical arm has **drilling capability** and **sensitive cameras and detectors** to collect and analyse **rocks** and **regolith** (loose soil covering rocks). Three of its cameras used for **microbial analysis** are:

  - **PIXL** – uses **X-rays** to **identify chemicals** and take **close-up photos.**
  - **SHERLOC** – uses **ultraviolet light** (**UV**) to search for **microbial life.**
  - **WATSON** – uses **light** to help SHERLOC with **texture** and **wide-angle imaging.**

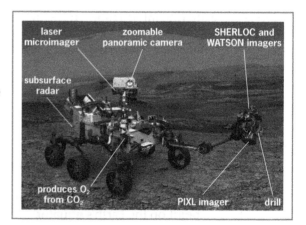

Figure 13.16 *Perseverance, the most technologically advanced rover*

- *Ingenuity* (NASA – landed in 2021 with *Perseverance*)
  A helicopter used as an **engineering test** for **future helicopters**. It performed 72 flights before it was damaged and went out of service. Scientists and engineers, however, obtained valuable information from the test flights and are planning to send TWO helicopters to be used as backup to *Perseverance* in retrieving the samples it collects.
- *Zhurong* (Chinese National Space Administration (CNSA) – **landed in 2021**)
  Equipped with scientific instruments to analyse the Martian surface, study its geology and search for evidence of past or current life.

Returning the samples collected by Perseverance to Earth

The samples collected by *Perseverance* will be **drilled extractions** from the **Jezero Crater**. They will be small and cylindrical (like pieces of school chalk), and each will have a mass of about ½ ounce. They will be placed in a cached deposit in the rover and then await collection on the surface of the planet in **triple-sealed tubes**.

- **Dispatching**
  A **Sample Retrieval Lander** (SRL) should be launched by 2026 and should reach Mars by 2027. It will bring **two mini helicopters** (designed as a result of what was learned from *Ingenuity*), a rocket called the **Mars Ascent Vehicle** (MAV), and a **loading arm**.
  Perseverance, and the helicopters (which will be used as backup), will bring the sample tubes to the SRL, and the loading arm will place the tubes in the MAV.
- **Dropping into Mars orbit**
  The samples will **ascend** from the Martian surface in the MAV to **await capture** by the **Earth Return Orbiter** (ERO).
- **Transporting to Earth**
  The ERO will arrive in orbit around Mars by 2030. It will **rendezvouz with and capture** the samples by 2031, and then bring them to Earth where they will be **dropped** in the **Utah desert** in 2033 for further investigation. This will be the first interplanetary spacecraft to capture hardware in orbit from another planet and return it to the Earth's surface, making a full round trip to Mars and back!

Exploring Jupiter

Jupiter is the **largest planet** in our solar system and is known as the '**king of planets**'. Landers and rovers are not used on Jupiter since its **surface is not solid.** Initially, several **flybys** were sent to gather information of conditions around Jupiter but now **orbiters** are doing the investigating.

Orbiters are gathering information on the planet and its **many moons**, **dust rings**, **magnetic field** and **auroras**. They are also investigating the amounts of **water** and **ammonia** in its atmosphere and the possibility that **humans** could **survive** on its **icy moons**.

Recalling facts

1. a Distinguish among meteoroids, meteors and meteorites.
   b Distinguish between planets and planetoids.

2. a State the period of a geostationary satellite and describe its path relative to a fixed point on the Earth's equator.
   b State TWO uses of geostationary satellites.
   c How does the orbit radius of a geostationary satellite compare with that of other satellites?

3 a Describe the orbital path of a polar satellite.

b State TWO uses of polar satellites.

4 a How many orbital paths does the GPS system of satellites have?

b What is the minimum number of satellites in the GPS system that must be functioning to provide full coverage at any point on Earth?

5 a Name the planets belonging to the following groups in order of increasing orbital radius.

  i The terrestrial planets.

  ii The gas giants.

b For each of the following items, identify the planet of our solar system that is:

  i the smallest

  ii orbited by 95 moons

  iii known for its profound ring system

  iv the largest

  v spinning on its side with its axis of rotation tilted at 98°

  vi known as the 'red planet'

  vii the hottest

  viii known for having many volcanoes

  ix orbited by a moon larger than Mercury

  x the brightest when viewed from Earth

  xi virtually without an atmosphere

  xii known for its 'great red spot'

  xiii covered by dense carbon dioxide and a cloud of sulfuric acid

  xiv known for its dust storms.

6 a State TWO functions of the International Space Station (ISS).

b Rewrite and complete the following sentences about the ISS.

  i It orbits at a height of about ………… km and has a period of ……. minutes.

  ii The number of crew members is generally about ……… .

7 The following questions are about the Hubble Space Telescope and the James Webb Space Telescope.

a Which can view older and more distant galaxies?

b Which is in a low Earth orbit?

c Which uses infrared detectors to peer through dust and cosmic clouds?

d State, with a reason, which cannot be maintained by astronauts.

e Which is the newest?

8 Outline the use of each of the following spacecraft: flybys, orbiters, landers, rovers.

9   **a** Explain why polar satellites:

   i   produce images of better resolution than geostationary satellites

   ii can obtain information from around the planet, but geostationary satellites can only obtain information from ONE of its hemispheres.

   b What is the approximate orbital period of a polar satellite and how is this advantageous to its use?

10 Draw a ray diagram showing the formation of a lunar eclipse.

11 Draw a single diagram to illustrate the positions of the Sun, Earth and Moon during a *new moon*, a *full moon*, a *first quarter moon* and a *third quarter moon*.

12 Kewell wants to be an astronaut so that he can explore space.

   a State THREE reasons why space exploration can be important to humans.

   b How can Kewell deal with the challenges of:

   i   consuming food?

   ii obtaining water?

   iii muscle atrophy (shrinking of the muscles)?

   iv maintaining correct levels of oxygen and carbon dioxide in his spacecraft?

14 The terrestrial environment

Our terrestrial environment is very dynamic and is influenced by several variables. The interaction of different types of air masses can bring fresh or polluted air to regions and can affect our weather. Variations in temperature and pressure can lead to storms and hurricanes. The relative position of the Moon can affect our tides, and this can lead to coastal erosion. Volcanoes and earthquakes can also produce drastic transformation in our landscapes and seascapes.

Learning objectives

- Describe the **types of air masses** and the **effects of pollutants** spread by air masses.
- Explain how various **types of fronts** can affect the **weather**.
- Examine the **weather patterns** in the Caribbean including the **seasons**, **tropical depressions**, **tropical storms** and **hurricanes**.
- Explain the **regular nature of tides** and the sudden and unpredictable nature of **tsunamis**.
- Explain the causes of the various types of **volcanic eruptions** and describe the **ecological consequences** they bring.
- Examine the relationship between **earthquakes** and **volcanoes**.
- Be familiar with the use of the **seismograph** and the **Richter scale**.

Air masses

Air masses are extensive bodies of air with approximately uniform characteristics of temperature and humidity at any given altitude.

The longer an air mass remains over a particular region, the more it will acquire the properties resulting from its contact with the Earth's surface in that region. These air masses affect the **weather** and can transport **pollutants** over **thousands of kilometres** to other parts of the Earth. Air masses affecting North America and the Caribbean are shown in Figure 14.1.

Table 14.1 *The main types of air masses*

Type	Region of formation on surface of Earth	Characteristics
Maritime tropical (mT)	Tropical and sub-tropical **seas** and **oceans**, such as the Caribbean Sea	hot/moist
Continental tropical (cT)	Large **arid land** areas, such as the deserts in the southwest of the USA (in California, Nevada, Arizona and New Mexico)	hot/dry
Maritime polar (mP)	Polar **oceans**, such as the Atlantic, east of Newfoundland	cool/moist
Continental polar (cP)	Large **land** areas near to poles, such as Canada	cool/dry

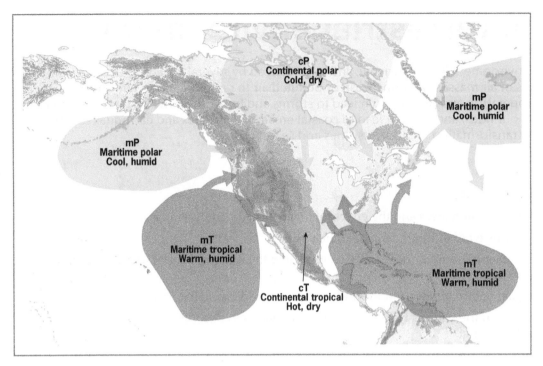

Figure 14.1 *Air masses affecting North America and the Caribbean*

Table 14.2 *Pollutants transported by air masses*

Pollutant	Associated problems
Harmful gases from industrial processes	Carbon monoxide (CO), nitrogen oxides (NO, NO_2) and sulfur dioxide (SO_2) emitted from industrial processes can produce **acid rain**. NO_2 and SO_2 cause **respiratory problems** (see Table 10.3, page 209).
Landfill fumes	Landfill fumes create risks to animals, plants and the environment in general. • **Hydrogen sulfide** and **methane** can cause **stress**, **fatigue**, **headaches** and even **respiratory problems**. • **Awful odours** from decayed organic materials can reduce the quality of life. • **Soil and water contamination** can result as the gases penetrate the earth and dissolve in water supplies. This problem is extremely difficult to correct. • **Methane can explode** at landfills and plays a significant role in **global warming**. • **Harmful bacteria** can be transported by landfill fumes.
Particulate matter	Produced by **industrial processes**, **dust storms** and **volcanic eruptions.** • **Reduction in photosynthesis** can occur as smoke and dust can cover the leaves of plants. • **Respiratory problems** occur when the particles enter our airways. • **Harmful bacteria** can be transported as particulate matter.
Radioactive fallout	Material from **nuclear explosions** can be shot high into the air and transported for hundreds of miles before returning to the surface to contaminate crops and grasses. Animals, including humans, who consume them will also be contaminated. • **Ionising radiation** from the radioisotopes can lead to severe illness and cancer. • **Psychological stress** may occur due to uncertainty of becoming critically ill. • **Environmental contamination** negatively affects ecosystems including wildlife and water supplies. • **Agricultural economy declines** due to inability to use the soil for crops.

Saharan dust storms

These are formed when **very warm air** over a **hot desert** produces a low-pressure region causing a strong **updraft** of fine particles of sand as high as **5 km**. The **larger** of the particles fall into the **Atlantic Ocean** but the **smaller** ones are carried by air masses as far as the **Caribbean islands** and the **Americas**.

Problems

- Can transport **pathogenic bacteria** which can lead to **deadly diseases** such as **cholera**.
- Causes **respiratory irritation** and **allergic reactions**.

Benefits

- Provides important **nutrients** such as **iron to marine bacteria**, and much needed **phosphorus and other nutrients to the soils** of the Amazon, the southern United States and the Caribbean.
- **Weakens tropical cyclones.**

Note: Saharan dust plays a complicated role in global warming.

- **Cooling effect** – Dust particles can prevent sunlight from reaching Earth by **reflecting it back into space.**
- **Warming effect** – Radiation **reflected** from and **emitted** by the **Earth's surface** can be **absorbed** by dust particles suspended in the air. These particles **then emit** radiation in all directions, much of it returning to Earth.
- **Increased precipitation** – Dust in the air can act as **condensation nuclei**, facilitating the formation of clouds and increasing the possibility of **precipitation**.

The net effect is to produce varying weather patterns dependent on geographical location and timing of the dust storms.

Volcanic ash and gases

These shoot tens of kilometres into the air and can travel **thousands of kilometres** from the volcano.

Problems

- Produce **respiratory illness.**
- Block sunlight **reducing photosynthesis** and plant growth.

Benefits

- **Ash** can bring essential **nutrients** for **plant growth**, and **minerals** that can **balance soil pH** and **improve soil structure**.
- Finely crushed **basalt** added to arable soils improves crop yields due to the increased content of **calcium**, **potassium** and **other essential nutrients**.

Local fronts and their effect on weather

*A **front** is a boundary or transition zone formed where air masses of different temperatures meet.*

At a front, warm, less dense air rises above cooler air. If the rising air is humid, its water vapour may condense as it cools to produce rain.

Table 14.3 *Fronts and their weather map symbols*

Type of front	Cold front	Warm front	Stationary front	Occluded front
Map symbol	▲▲▲▲	⌒⌒⌒⌒	▲⌒▲⌒	▲▲⌒▲ or ▲▲▲▲

Cold fronts and warm fronts

The weather conditions produced by cold and warm fronts are illustrated in Figure 14.2.

*A **cold front** is the boundary where a **cold air mass advances** into a warm air mass.*

During winter in the northern hemisphere, cold polar air masses from the USA **plough under** warm, moist, maritime tropical air masses of the Caribbean, forcing them upwards with a **steep gradient**.

*A **warm front** is the boundary where a **warm air mass advances** towards a cold air mass.*

During the winter in the northern hemisphere, warm, moist maritime tropical air masses from the Gulf of Mexico move northward and **glide over** cool dry continental polar air masses from Canada, forced upward with a **gentle gradient**.

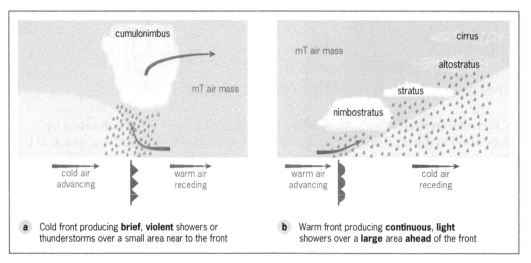

a   Cold front producing **brief, violent** showers or thunderstorms over a small area near to the front

b   Warm front producing **continuous, light** showers over a **large** area **ahead** of the front

Figure 14.2 *Weather at a cold front and at a warm front*

Table 14.4 *Comparing the weather produced by cold fronts and by warm fronts*

	Cold front	Warm front
Action	Cold polar air mass **ploughs under** warm tropical air mass.	Warm tropical air mass **glides over** cold polar air mass.
Gradient at boundary	**Steep**	**Gentle**
Temperature	Becomes **cooler**	Becomes **warmer**
Clouds	**Vertical cumulonimbus** clouds form rapidly due to rapidly rising air.	**Horizontal stratus-type** clouds form slowly due to gently rising air.
Showers	**Brief, intense** showers with possible thunderstorms at the front.	**Continuous, light to moderate** showers ahead of the front – can last for a few days.
Region affected	Relatively **small** due to the steep gradient between the air masses.	Relatively **large** due to the slight gradient between the air masses.
Frontal speed	**Fast**, compared to warm fronts.	**Slow**, compared to cold fronts.

Stationary front

*A **stationary front** occurs at the boundary between two air masses of different temperature when neither air mass is capable of displacing the other.*

Weather at the stationary front is normally clear to partly cloudy, but if there is moisture, there can be light or heavy rain which may fall for long periods until the front moves again (see Figure 14.3a).

Winds blowing parallel to the front as shown in Figure 14.3b helps to keep the front stationary. If the wind direction changes, the front can begin to move again, becoming a cold front or a warm front depending on which air mass advances against the other.

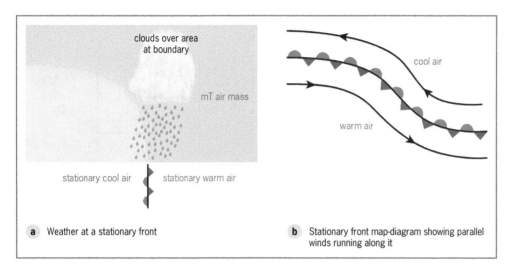

a   Weather at a stationary front

b   Stationary front map-diagram showing parallel winds running along it

Figure 14.3 *Weather at a stationary front*

Occluded front

*An **occluded front** occurs when a cold front catches up with a warm front, raising the warm air between them upward and away from the ground.*

Cold fronts advance faster than warm fronts. Figure 14.4a shows a cross-section just before the formation of an occluded front.

- The cold air mass ploughs into the warm air, squashing it onto the cool air ahead of the warm front.
- The warm air rises **steeply** at the **cold front**, producing **cumulonimbus** clouds.
- The warm air rises **more gently** at the **warm front**, producing **stratus** clouds.
- The cold front catches up with the warm front, squeezing the hot air mass **off the ground** and producing **major precipitation** as shown in Figure 14.4b. This is the last stage of the storm since the hot air has now all been lifted.

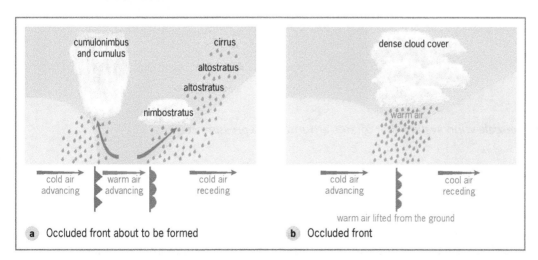

a   Occluded front about to be formed

b   Occluded front

Figure 14.4 *Weather at an occluded front*

Figure 14.5 shows a sequence of map diagrams during the formation of an occluded front. When the **cold front catches up with the warm front**, an occluded front is formed and they '**zip together**'. Note that **winds** in the **northern hemisphere** blow **anti-clockwise** around a **low-pressure** centre.

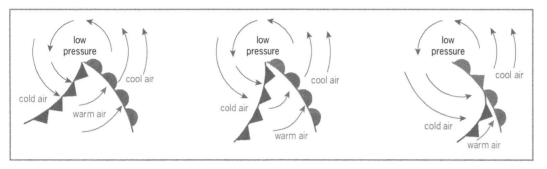

Figure 14.5 *Map diagram showing the formation of an occluded front*

Weather patterns in the Caribbean

The seasons

- **Dry season: November to April** (**6 months**); temperature, humidity and amount of rainfall are **lowest**.
- **Wet season: May to October** (**6 months**); temperature, humidity and amount of rainfall are **highest**.
- **Atlantic hurricane season: June to November** (**6 months**); coincides with much of the wet season.

Temperature and rainfall

Temperature

- **Day** – between 30 °C and 34 °C.
- **Night** – between 20 °C and 26 °C.

Rainfall

The ITCZ (Intertropical Convergence Zone) is a **low-pressure belt** that encircles the Earth near the equator where the northeast (NE) trade winds and the southeast (SE) trade winds meet (see Figure 14.6). The belt drifts a bit above the equator in summer and a bit below the equator in winter. As the **warm**, **humid winds** converge, they are forced upward, cool, and produce **clouds**, **heavy rainfall** and **thunderstorms**.

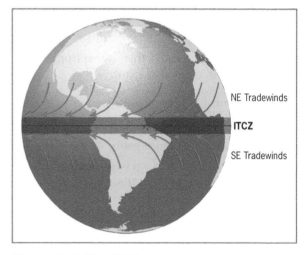

Figure 14.6 *The ITCZ*

Cyclones

A cyclone is a large-scale wind system that rotates around a low-pressure centre.

Tropical cyclones

- Temperatures in excess of **27 °C** can cause large areas of hot, moist air to expand and rise, producing regions of **low pressure**.
- Winds pulled by the low-pressure region are deflected by the Earth's rotation in an **anti-clockwise** rotation in the **northern hemisphere** and in a **clockwise** rotation in the **southern hemisphere**.

- As water vapour condenses, the **latent heat of condensation** released further **heats** the air, **sucking water vapour** from over the ocean at an **increased rate** and producing **cumulonimbus** clouds and **torrential rains**.
- The **eye** of the storm (its centre) is a **calm low-pressure** region with **few clouds** and **little or no rain**.
- The eye is surrounded by the **eyewall**. This is the most destructive region of the hurricane, as it is where the **strongest winds** and **heaviest rainfall** occur.

Figures 14.7 and 14.8 illustrate the appearance and features of a hurricane.

Figure 14.7 *Satellite view of a hurricane showing the eye, dense cloud and spiralling rain bands*

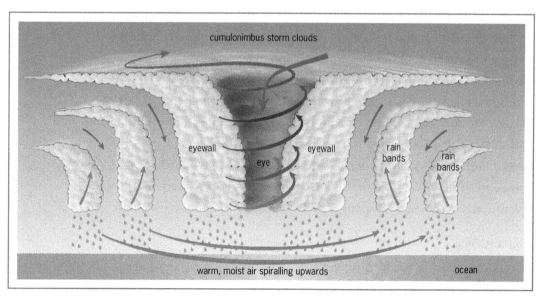

Figure 14.8 *Cross-section through a hurricane*

Table 14.5 *Classification of tropical cyclones*

Classification	Tropical depression	Tropical storm	Hurricane
Wind speed (km/h)	less than 63	63 to 117	greater than 117
Wind speed (mph)	less than 39	39 to 73	greater than 73

Saffir-Simpson Hurricane Wind Scale: Hurricanes are further classified using numbered categories 1 to 5, with category 5 being the most dangerous, having wind speeds **above 252 km/h (157 mph)**!

Weather during the passing of a hurricane

- Hurricanes in the Atlantic progress **westward** across the ocean, strengthening until reaching land.
- The approaching storm is signalled by a **drop in atmospheric pressure.** Wind gusts become strong and dark **nimbus clouds** (**rain clouds**) appear in bands bringing **heavy rain.**
- As the eye approaches, the high winds and heavy rainfall become severe, destroying buildings, uprooting trees and causing landslides.
- On **arrival of the eye** the pressure drops significantly and **calm sets in.**
- As the **eye passes,** the **rain returns** and the **wind speed increases** once more, this time in the **opposite direction.** The very **low-pressure** region of the storm **pulls water upward** producing **high sea levels** which, together with strong onshore winds, can produce a **storm surge** and result in coastal flooding.
- This bad weather persists for some time, gradually weakening as the storm leaves the region.
- Wind speed **decreases over the land:**
  - ◆ due to **friction** with the landscape
  - ◆ since the storm is **no longer supplied with energy** by evaporation from the ocean.

Hurricane preparedness

- Ensure that all animals are sheltered and have food to sustain them for 2 weeks.
- Have charged battery packs or generators available in case the electricity is cut off.
- Stay tuned to the news media via a battery-operated radio.
- Ensure your flashlights and lamps are functioning and that you have spare batteries.
- Ensure that your medical kit is adequately stocked.
- Secure doors and windows with straps or shutters.
- Store all important documents and personal possessions in a waterproof container.
- Store loose indoor objects in cupboards.
- Store all loose outdoor objects in a secure shed or garage.
- Trim or remove any damaged trees and remove any trees that may fall onto buildings.
- Have a 2-to-3-week stock of canned and dried foods, which do not require refrigeration.
- Have a 2-to-3-week store of clean water.
- Have a full tank of fuel in your car. If your car is electric, ensure that it is fully charged.
- Have a gas stove and a full bottle of gas to fuel it; do not depend on piped natural gas.
- Know the whereabouts of the nearest secure shelter in case you need to evacuate.

After the hurricane

- Listen to news updates to learn of any problems outside. For example, there may be flooded areas, fallen trees and roads blocked by dislodged objects.
- Boil or use sterilising tablets to purify drinking water which may now be contaminated.

Tides and their effects

Tides are the **changes in sea levels** on Earth caused by the **gravitational attractions** of the Sun and the Moon on the Earth and by the **rotation of the Earth**.

High tides and low tides

High tides occur on the sides of the Earth **closest to the Moon** and **furthest from the Moon** as shown in Figure 14.9. Since the Earth takes 24 hours to rotate once on its axis, there are **two high tides** and **two low tides** which occur simultaneously around the Earth on a **daily** basis.

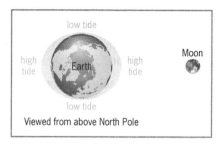

Figure 14.9 *High tides and low tides*

Spring tides and neap tides

The Moon takes **29½ days** (approximately one month) to orbit the Earth and to return to the same position relative to the Sun as seen by an observer on Earth (Chapter 13, Figure 13.12 on page 296).

Spring tides occur **twice each month**, at **new moon** and **full moon** phases (see Figure 14.10). This is when the gravitational attraction of the Earth by the Sun is along the same line as the gravitational attraction of the Earth by the Moon, producing a maximum combined attraction of the Earth. These tides are therefore the **highest high tides** and **lowest low tides.**

Neap tides occur **twice each month**, at the **first quarter** and **third quarter** phases of the Moon (see Figure 14.11). This is when the gravitational attraction of the Earth by the Sun and the gravitational attraction of the Earth by the Moon produce a minimum combined attraction of the Earth. These tides are therefore the **lowest high tides** and the **highest low tides.**

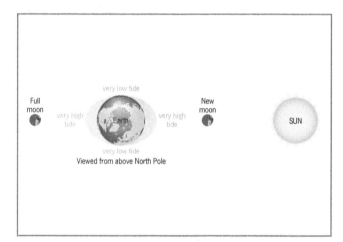

Figure 14.10 *Spring tides*

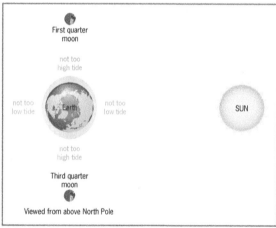

Figure 14.11 *Neap tides*

Tidal waves and tsunamis

*A **tidal wave** is a **regularly reoccurring, shallow-water wave** caused by the **gravitational interactions** of the Sun, Earth and Moon.*

Tidal waves can **intensify** due to **frictional drag** from winds.

Tidal waves are not tsunamis although in the past they referred to the same thing.

*A **tsunami** is a **large deep-water wave** produced by a **sudden** disturbance of a **large volume** of water by an event such as a coastal **landslide**, an underwater **volcano** or **earthquake**, or a huge **meteorite** crashing into the ocean.*

Table 14.6 *Comparing tidal waves and tsunamis*

	Tidal wave	Tsunami
Cause	**Changing tides** and the gravitational interactions among the Earth, Moon and Sun.	**Seismic events** such as underwater earthquakes, volcanic eruptions, landslides or **cosmic events** such as huge asteroids crashing into Earth.
Nature	**Predictable** and **regularly** occurring since they depend on the changing of the tides.	Generally, **unpredictable** and sudden.
Impact	The energy is carried by the body of water **near the surface**. This can be significant but is generally less destructive than tsunamis.	Extremely destructive since the energy may be carried by the **entire volume** of water down to the ocean floor.

Tsunamis, from creation to aftermath

Creation – A **sudden** and significant disturbance **far below the surface** displaces **a large volume** of water sending a wave **in all directions**. Large celestial bodies crashing into the Earth can also produce tsunamis.

Propagation – The wave progresses at speeds of up to **800 km/h** but with **small amplitude** of about 1 m in deep water. As it approaches land, **friction** slows it down significantly, causing the amplitude to suddenly increase – at times to over **30 m** (100 feet).

Impact – Just before reaching the coast, water is sucked outward and upward into the swell (see Figure 14.12). With the **energy compressed**, the **impact force increases** dramatically, **flattening buildings** as far as **1.5 km inland**. Towering waves slam into the shoreline, continuing for **several hours**. The '**run-up**' of water generally reaches more than **15 km inland**, destroying infrastructure (see Figure 14.13) and taking lives. **As the water retreats** back into the ocean, it **drags debris** with it, causing even more destruction!

Aftermath – Operations are usually immediately put in place to **rescue** and **relieve** those in need. Communities then need to **survey** the damage, **rebuild** the infrastructure and make a dedicated effort to **restore normalcy**.

Figure 14.12 *Tsunami just before impact*

Figure 14.13 *Devastation caused by a tsunami*

In 2004, a tsunami in the Indian Ocean took the lives of over **200 000** people throughout southern Asia. Locations vulnerable to tsunamis should always have well-planned **evacuation routes** (see Figure 14.14).

Protection against the perils of tsunamis

- **Sea walls** and **channels** should be constructed to help block the onslaught of the wave energy.
- **Pressures** and **seismic activity** should be **carefully monitored.**
- A **good network** to **relay evacuation alarms** on a timely basis should be employed.

Figure 14.14 *Evacuation route*

Storm surges and tidal bores

A **storm surge** occurs when the **eye of a hurricane** sucks ocean water into a swell and pulls it onto a coastal region. If this occurs during a **spring tide**, the **sea level can rise significantly**.

Tidal bores occur at the **mouths of rivers** when the flow of water downstream meets a **rising high tide** and raises the water level even higher.

Volcanic eruptions

*A **volcano** is an opening in a planet's crust from which molten lava, rock fragments, ashes, dust and gases are ejected from far below the surface.*

*__Fumaroles__ are small vents which emit only **steam** and **volcanic gases**.*

__Geysers__ are small vents that emit steam and hot water due to geothermal activity.

__Calderas__ are bowl-shaped depressions formed when a volcano collapses into an old empty vent.

Formation of volcanoes

The Earth's core consists of very hot **molten rock** known as **magma** which is constantly trying to expand outward. Large sections of **solid rock**, known as **tectonic plates**, slowly **drift** on the magma. When these plates **move away** (diverge) from each other or **collide** (converge) against each other, magma can make its way upward to the surface through cracks and fissures.

Cooling near the surface usually causes the magma to **solidify** and **blocks the flow** through the vent. This results in an increase of pressure in the vent, causing it to blow its cap off in an **explosive** manner. **Pyroclastic** materials (rocks, cinder, ashes and gases) as well as **molten lava** (magma that has reached the surface) are thrown high into the air and produce thick clouds of pungent smoke. Smaller vents known as **fumaroles** emit only steam and gases such as carbon dioxide (CO_2), sulfur dioxide (SO_2), hydrogen sulfide (H_2S), hydrogen fluoride (HF) and hydrogen chloride (HCl). As the materials pour from the vent or as they fall to the ground, they can form steep or gentle slopes dependent on the **viscosity** of the lava (see Table 14.7).

Table 14.7 *Factors that result in different types of volcanic eruptions and their formations*

Cause	Effect
Viscosity of magma	• **Viscous** lava is thick and contains **a lot of silica**. It **moves slowly** and **solidifies quickly** to produce **steep slopes**. It tends to block the vent, leading to **explosive** eruptions as the pressure increases and eventually blows the top off.
	• **Non-viscous** lava is sometimes referred to as **basaltic** lava. It contains a lot of **basalt**, but very little silica. It **quickly spreads**, forming **gentle slopes**. This type of lava does not block the vents to cause explosions.
Tectonic plate setting	• **Convergent boundaries** – If an oceanic plate collides with a continental plate, it forces itself **under** the continental plate. This **subduction** produces deep ocean trenches and powerful earthquakes and volcanoes, leading to the formation of mountain ranges.
	• **Divergent boundaries** – If tectonic plates move away from each other, magma rises from the mantle to fill the space. **Shield volcanoes**, **mid-ocean ridges** and **volcanic islands** are normally formed in this way.
Water	• **High water content** results in intense steam pressure that can produce **violent explosions** and scatter solid rock fragments, ash and cinder.
	• **Low water content** results in steady lava flows that are **not explosive**.
Gases	• Volcanoes also emit carbon dioxide (CO_2), sulfur dioxide (SO_2) and hydrogen sulfide (H_2S). High concentrations of gases have the same effect on the explosive nature of volcanoes as does high water content.

Main types of volcanoes

Cinder cone volcano (Figure 14.15)

- **Small** and simple, with a **single vent**.
- **Wide crater**.
- **Erupts only once** (monogenetic).
- The lava is slightly **basaltic** but not as easy flowing as that of a shield volcano.
- Solidifies to **block** the single **vent**.
- Has a lot of **steam** and **gases** that cause the vent to **explode violently**.
- **Molten lava** and **pyroclastic** material are shot **high into the air** and **quickly cool**.
- Rock, ash and cinder fall as **volcanic bombs** producing a steep, **conical** mound of **loose material**.
- **Spattering** occurs if the lava is more basaltic. It is welded together on spattering from the vent.

If the lava is more basaltic, the less violent eruption produces a **spatter cone volcano**.

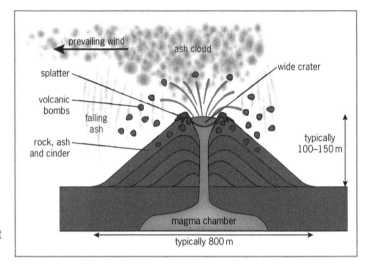

Figure 14.15 *Cinder cone volcano*

Shield volcano (Figure 14.16)

- **Massive**, usually with **multiple vents**.
- **Non-viscous** basaltic lava of low silica content produces **gentle eruptions** which can flow steadily for **hundreds of kilometres**.
- Has an appearance of a **gently sloped** warrior's shield.
- **No explosions** since there is very little gas.
- Most characteristic of **ocean island volcanism** at hotspots (where the lava is hotter than average) and **continental rift volcanism** where the crust is being stretched by plate movements.

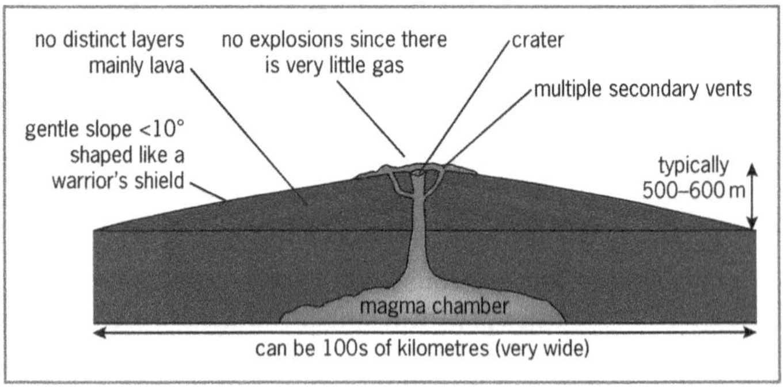

Figure 14.16 *Shield volcano*

Composite or stratovolcano
(Figure 14.17 on page 317)

- **Massive** due to the quantity of volcanic material ejected, with parasitic **cones** developed at **secondary** vents, forming huge mountainous landscapes.
- **Viscous magma** containing lots of **silica** moves **slowly** when ejected, **quickly solidifying** to produce a conical shape with **steep slopes** near the vent but **gentler slopes** near the base.
- **Explosions** are produced due to **steam** in the vent shooting rock, ash and pumice into the air.

- The **unblocked vent** then allows the **outflow of lava** but quickly solidifies and reseals until the buildup of gases quickly blows its top once more.

- These alternating **explosive** and then **gentle** eruptions produce a **layered stratum**.

  ◆ **Explosive stage** – Rock, ash, solid lava and some of the molten lava are shot upward; the molten lava solidifies in the air before striking the ground.

  ◆ **Gentle stage** – Molten lava escapes the unblocked vent and runs down the slope where it solidifies.

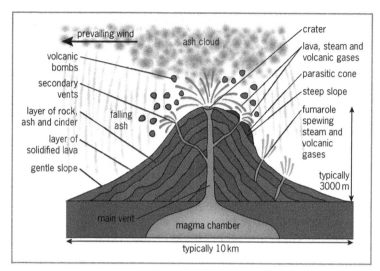

Figure 14.17 *Composite or stratovolcano*

Table 14.8 *Comparative summary of the main types of volcanoes*

	Cinder cone	Shield	Composite or stratovolcano
Size	Small	Wide	Tall
Viscosity of magma	Low to middle	Low (contains much basalt)	High (contains much silica)
Gentle or explosive eruptions	Explosive due to gas/steam pressures.	Gentle due to: • very little gas/steam pressures • non-viscous magma not blocking vent.	Explosive due to: • gas/steam pressures • viscous magma easily solidifying to block vent.
Example	• San Juan Valley, Dominican Republic (inactive) • Paricutin, Mexico (inactive)	• Kilauea, Hawaii (active)	• Soufrière Hills, Montserrat (active) • Mount St. Helens, USA (active)

Figure 14.18 *Paricutin, Mexico [left], Kilauea, Hawaii [centre], Soufrière Hills, Montserrat [right]*

Kick'em Jenny – a submarine volcano

- Kick'em Jenny is an **active submarine volcano** located 8 km (5 miles) north of Grenada (see Figure 14.19).

- It is part of the **Lesser Antilles Volcanic Arc** which is formed due to the subduction of the dense **oceanic South American tectonic plate** beneath the less dense **Caribbean tectonic plate** (see Figure 14.20).

- It is **1300 m above the sea floor** and **180 m below the sea surface.**

- It erupted in 1939 sending a cloud of steam and debris almost **300 m** into the air and causing a small tsunami. Since then, it has erupted at least **12 times.**

- It produces both **explosive** (violent) and **effusive** (gentle) eruptions.

- There is a **maritime exclusion zone** of radius **1.5 km** around the volcano.

- The volcanic islands of the Lesser Antilles were initially all submarine volcanoes as evidenced by analysis of the solidified lavas found there.

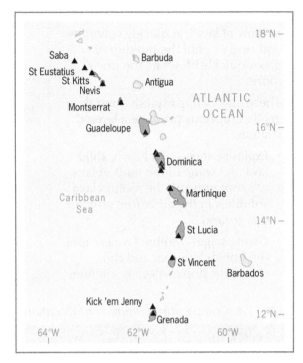

Figure 14.19 *Volcanic arc of the Caribbean*

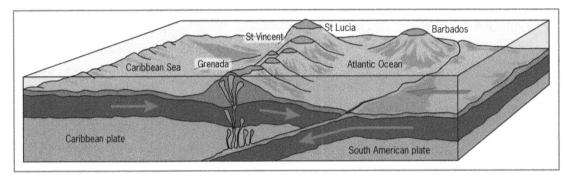

Figure 14.20 *Lesser Antilles Volcanic Arc created as the South American plate subducts beneath the less dense Caribbean plate*

Ecological consequences of volcanoes

Table 14.9 *Ecological consequences of volcanoes*

Negative	Positive
• Rapidly **flowing** volcanic **materials** instantly **destroy** plants, animals and anything else in their path.	• Volcanic material can contain **important minerals** such as copper and gold.
• **Ash** can **block sunlight, reducing photosynthesis** and **plant growth.**	• **Weathered lava** becomes **fertile soil** after a period of time.
• Ash and volcanic gases can **cause respiratory illness.**	• **Hot springs** provide **geothermal energy.**
• **Landslides** produced can cause massive **destruction.**	• Hot springs can be used for **therapy.**
• **Decaying animals**, killed by the volcano, can **pollute** the environment, including its water supplies.	• **Tourism** can be boosted by **extraordinary** volcanic **landscapes** such as calderas.
• **Active volcanoes** are unsafe and **reduce tourism.**	
• Beautiful landscapes are destroyed.	

Earthquakes

Earthquakes are produced when the forces between tectonic plates result in sudden bursts of energy in the form of shock waves known as *seismic waves*.

- The **hypocentre** or **focus** is the point **below** the surface where the earthquake originates.

- The **epicentre** is the point on the surface directly **above** the focus where vibrations are usually strongest.

- A **seismograph** is a device that measures movement of the ground by producing a graph (seismogram) which indicates the **amplitudes** of the vibrations **over time** (see Figure 14.21).

- The **Richter scale** is a scale of 1 to 10 used to **compare** earthquakes.

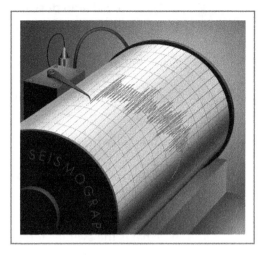

Figure 14.21 *Seismograph*

Table 14.10 *Interpreting the Richter scale*

Scale value	Effect
< 5	Generally, no damage, but indoor objects can vibrate and rattle.
5–6	Damages poorly constructed buildings.
6–8	Damages well-built structures; major damage occurs even 250 km from the epicentre.
8–9	Damages even 'earthquake-resistant' buildings.
> 9	Near-total destruction, producing permanent changes even to the natural landscape.

Table 14.11 *Relationship between volcanoes and earthquakes*

Volcanoes	Earthquakes
Occur along the **edges of tectonic plates**.	Occur along the **edges of tectonic plates**.
Result from **magma being forced upwards** as plates interact with each other.	Result from **vibrations produced** as plates interact with each other.
Volcanoes can cause earthquakes as pressure from the magma can crack rocks and so produce vibrations.	**Earthquakes can cause volcanoes** by creating cracks for magma to rise through or by weakening the top of a magma chamber, allowing the release of pressure.

Recalling facts

a Define the term 'air mass'.

b Create a table of the FOUR main types of air masses using the following column headers.

Type of air mass	Characteristics	General region in which found	Example of state, country, ocean or sea in which found

Air masses can transport pollutants, two of which are landfill fumes and particulate matter. State THREE problems associated with EACH of these pollutants.

3
   a How are Saharan dust storms formed?

   b List TWO problems and TWO benefits of Saharan dust.

4
   List TWO problems and ONE benefit of volcanic ash and gases.

5
   Define each of the following weather terms:

   a front   **b** cold front   **c** warm front

   d stationary front   **e** occluded front.

6
   a State the range of months representative of each of the following seasons in the Caribbean:

      i dry season   **ii** wet season   **iii** hurricane season.

   b What is the average temperature range experienced during the day in the Caribbean?

   c What effect does the ITCZ have on the weather?

7
   a Define a 'cyclone'.

   b What critical ocean temperature, if exceeded, is likely to result in a tropical depression?

   c In which direction do winds deflect when pulled by a low pressure region in the northern hemisphere?

   d As water vapour condenses in the clouds, latent heat of condensation is released and the air becomes warmer. What effect does this have on a storm?

   e Describe the weather in the eye of a storm system.

   f Describe the weather in the eyewall of a storm system.

8
   a The wind speed in a particular tropical cyclone is 90 km/h (56 mph). Is this a tropical depression, a tropical storm or a hurricane?

   b What wind speed must a category 5 hurricane exceed?

   c Give TWO reasons why the wind speed of a hurricane decreases as it passes over land.

   d Explain why the sea level rises and produces a storm surge on impact of a hurricane.

   e How can the tides make a storm surge more profound?

9
   a State FIVE ways you can prepare for a hurricane.

   b State TWO precautions you should take after the passing of a hurricane.

10
   a What are tides?

   b Draw a diagram showing how the position of the Moon relative to the Earth affects the tides.

   c Draw another diagram with the addition of the Sun to show the occurrence of spring tides.

11
   a Define the following:

      i tidal wave   **ii** tsunami.

   b Contrast tidal waves and tsunamis with reference to:

      i how they are produced.

      ii the magnitude of their impact.

12

a Define the following:

    i volcano   ii fumarole   iii caldera.

b How is the viscosity of magma affected by:

    i the amount of silica it contains?

    ii the amount of basalt it contains?

c Name TWO acidic gases emitted from the vents of volcanoes.

13 Define the following:

    i earthquake   ii seismograph   iii the Richter scale.

Applying facts

14 Justin lives in St. Vincent and witnessed the La Soufrière volcano, which is a composite or stratovolcano.

a What is the effect of the build-up of steam and gases in the vent of such a volcano?

b The magma contained from it contained much silica. How does this affect its viscosity?

c What can you say about the speed at which this magma would have flowed?

d Comment on the steepness of the slopes of such a volcano:

    i around the vent.   ii near its base.

15 a Hawaii is a country known for 'shield' volcanism. Comment on this type of volcanism in terms of **size**, **viscosity** of magma, **steepness** of slopes and **intensity** of eruptions.

b Describe the movement of plates that generally produces shield volcanoes.

16 Shinaya lives in the Lesser Antilles just 8 km (5 miles) from an active submarine volcano.

a On which Caribbean island does Shinaya live?

b What is the name of the volcano?

c The Lesser Antilles Volcanic Arc was formed by the subduction of one tectonic plate below the next. Name these tectonic plates, and state which plate forced itself below the other.

d How are people such as tourists and fisherfolk prevented from going too close to the volcano?

17 Discuss the costs and benefits of the ecological consequences of volcanoes.

Analysing data

18 For each whole number increase on the Richter scale, the amplitude of the vibration of an earthquake increases by a factor of 10 and the energy released by the earthquake increases by a factor of about 30.

If an earthquake, rated as 5 on the Richter scale, has an amplitude X and releases energy Y, write expressions in terms of X and Y for the amplitude and energy released if its Richter scale value was:

a 6   b 7.

15 Water and the aquatic environment

Water is essential for life on Earth. The bodies of living organisms contain between 60% and 70% water and water covers about 71% of the Earth's surface. Water provides a **habitat** for aquatic organisms and humans **use** water in very many different ways. Water can also become **polluted** by human activities.

Water and its uses

Learning objectives

- Discuss the **properties** of **water.**
- Distinguish between **hard water** and **soft water.**
- Explain the **uses** of **water.**
- Describe various **methods** used **locally** for **fishing.**

Properties of water

At the temperatures found on Earth, **water** is the only natural substance that exists in **all three** physical states: solid, liquid and gas. Based on its **chemical composition**, water can be classified into **pure water**, **fresh water** and **seawater.**

- **Pure water** contains only water (H_2O) molecules. It does not contain any other substances.
- **Fresh water** contains a very low concentration of dissolved salts. Fresh water is found in lakes, ponds, rivers and streams.
- **Seawater** contains a higher concentration of dissolved salts than fresh water. Seawater is found in oceans and seas.

Pure water has several unique **chemical** and **physical properties** which are affected by the presence of **dissolved salts.**

Chemical properties of pure water, fresh water and seawater

The **chemical properties** of pure water, fresh water and seawater are compared in Table 15.1.

Table 15.1 *The chemical properties of pure water, fresh water and seawater compared*

Property	Pure water	Fresh water	Seawater
Chemical composition	Contains water molecules only.	Contains a very low concentration of dissolved ions, including sodium, chloride, magnesium, sulfate, calcium, potassium and hydrogencarbonate ions.	Contains a higher concentration of dissolved ions than fresh water, including sodium, chloride, magnesium, sulfate, calcium, potassium and hydrogencarbonate ions.
Salinity (concentration of dissolved salts)	Zero.	Less than 0.5 parts per thousand (ppt) or 0.05%.	Approximately 35 parts per thousand (ppt) or 3.5%.

Property	Pure water	Fresh water	Seawater
pH	7.0, i.e. neutral.	Typically 6.5 to 7.5, i.e. very slightly acidic to neutral to very slightly alkaline in certain locations.	Typically 7.5 to 8.5, i.e. slightly alkaline.

Note: The composition of dissolved salts and the pH of fresh water depend on a variety of factors, such as the composition of the surrounding rocks and soil, use of the surrounding land and human activity.

Physical properties of pure water, fresh water and seawater

The presence of **dissolved salts** in water **decreases** the melting point of pure water and **increases** its boiling point, density and electrical conductivity. The **physical properties** of pure water, fresh water and seawater are compared in Table 15.2.

Table 15.2 *The physical properties of pure water, fresh water and seawater compared*

Property	Pure water	Fresh water	Seawater
Melting point at standard pressure	0 °C	Approximately 0 °C	Typically −1.9 °C
Boiling point at standard pressure	100 °C	Approximately 100 °C	Typically 100.7 °C
Density at standard temperature and pressure	1 g cm^{-3}	Approximately 1 g cm^{-3}	Typically 1.025 g cm^{-3}
Electrical conductivity	Very low	Slightly higher than pure water	High
Taste	Tasteless	Almost tasteless	Salty

Effects of fresh water and seawater on aquatic organisms

Aquatic organisms are faced with challenges created by the differences in concentration between the fluids inside their bodies and the surrounding water.

- **Fresh water** is **more dilute** than the body fluids of organisms living in freshwater environments, therefore they are at constant risk of water **entering** their bodies and body cells by **osmosis**. To prevent this from happening, they have developed certain adaptations. For example, a single-celled **amoeba** has a **contractile vacuole** that slowly fills up with water entering the cytoplasm and, when full, expels the water from the cell. Some of the water passing over the **gills** of **freshwater fish** to enable gaseous exchange (see page 195) enters their bodies by osmosis. At the same time, the gill filaments **actively absorb salts** from the water passing over them into the blood, and the kidneys produce **large volumes** of very **dilute urine** to remove excess water from their bodies.

- **Seawater** is **more concentrated** than the body fluids of many organisms living in seawater environments, therefore they are at risk of water **leaving** their bodies and body cells by **osmosis**. Like organisms living in fresh water, they have developed certain adaptations to prevent this from happening. **Marine (seawater) fish** lose water from their **gills** by osmosis as seawater passes over them, therefore they constantly **drink** seawater. At the same time, the gill filaments **actively excrete salts** from their bodies into the water passing over the filaments and the kidneys produce very **small volumes** of **concentrated urine** to help retain water in their bodies. **Marine invertebrates**, however, have developed body fluids that are the **same** concentration as the seawater to prevent water moving out of their bodies. These include starfish, jellyfish and lobsters.

The effects that fresh water and seawater have on fish are summarised in Figure 15.1 on page 324.

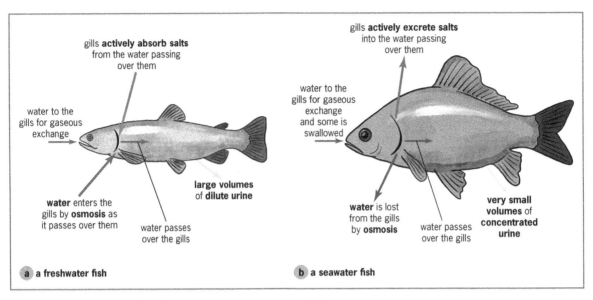

Figure 15.1 *Effects of fresh water and seawater on fish*

Characteristics of hard and soft water

Water used by humans for domestic, industrial and agricultural purposes can be classified as **hard** or **soft** based on its **mineral content**, especially the concentration of **calcium** and **magnesium salts** such as calcium and magnesium hydrogencarbonate, or calcium and magnesium sulfate. These minerals can affect the quality of the water and its suitability for different purposes in a variety of ways.

Hard water

Hard water contains **high** levels of dissolved calcium (Ca^{2+}) and magnesium (Mg^{2+}) ions. Because of this, it does not lather easily with **soap**, which is a compound called **sodium octadecanoate**. When soap is added to hard water, insoluble compounds called calcium and magnesium octadecanoate form, which are also known as **soap scum** or just **scum**. This reduces the lathering ability of soap because it only lathers when all the calcium and magnesium ions have been converted to scum (see page 402).

When hard water is **heated**, the dissolved minerals that it contains can precipitate out, in other words, they can form solid particles. These particles, which are mainly calcium and magnesium carbonate, can then form solid deposits, known as **limescale** or **kettle fur**, on surfaces such as inside pipes and kettles (see Figure 15.2). Hard water is typically found in areas where the rocks contain mainly calcium carbonate (limestone) or other calcium compounds; for example, calcium sulfate.

Figure 15.2 *Limescale (calcium carbonate) deposited on the heating element of a kettle*

Soft water

Soft water contains very **low** concentrations of dissolved calcium and magnesium ions. Soft water lathers easily with soap, it does not form scum and it does not form limescale when heated. Soft water is typically found in granite-, slate- or sandstone-rich areas and where water is treated by water treatment processes (see page 334). Rainwater is also soft.

Advantages and disadvantages of hard and soft water

Hard and **soft water** both have certain advantages and certain disadvantages, as summarised in Table 15.3.

Table 15.3 *Advantages and disadvantages of hard and soft water*

Type of water	Advantages	Disadvantages
Hard water	• When drunk, it is good for building strong bones and teeth due to the presence of calcium ions, and good overall health due to the presence of magnesium ions. • It does not dissolve lead from pipes, so does not contribute to lead poisoning in homes that still have lead water pipes. • It tastes better than soft water.	• The **scum** that forms with soap discolours clothes and forms an unpleasant grey, greasy layer around sinks, baths and showers. • It **wastes** soap because all the calcium and magnesium ions have to be removed as scum before the soap lathers. • It causes **limescale** to be deposited in boilers, hot water pipes, kettles and other household appliances. This can block pipes, waste electricity and reduce the lifespan of household appliances.
Soft water	• It has better cleaning power than hard water because it does not form unpleasant scum or discolour clothes. • It does not waste soap because it lathers immediately. • Limescale does not build up in boilers, hot water pipes, kettles and other household appliances. This maintains the efficiency of plumbing systems, extends the lifespan of household appliances and saves energy. • It is gentler on the skin and hair than hard water.	• It does not help build strong bones and teeth because it lacks calcium ions and is not as good for overall health as hard water because it lacks magnesium ions. • It dissolves lead from lead water pipes, so it can cause lead poisoning. • If softened using an ion exchange process, it has a higher content of sodium ions than normal, which may lead to hypertension when drunk.

Softening hard water

There are two **types** of water hardness: **temporary hardness** and **permanent hardness**.

* **Temporary hardness** is caused by dissolved **calcium** and **magnesium hydrogencarbonate**. It is found in limestone-rich areas and **can** be removed by **boiling** the water.
* **Permanent hardness** is caused by dissolved **calcium** and **magnesium sulfate**. Permanent hardness **cannot** be removed by **boiling**.

Hard water can be converted into **soft water**, in other words, **softened**, by removing the dissolved calcium and magnesium ions. This can be done in a variety of ways, including **boiling** the water, adding **washing soda** and **distillation**.

- **Boiling** the water removes **temporary hardness** only. It causes dissolved calcium and magnesium hydrogencarbonate to decompose and form **insoluble** calcium and magnesium carbonate. These insoluble carbonates settle within the water or are deposited on surfaces as **limescale**, and this removes the dissolved calcium and magnesium ions from the water.
- **Adding washing soda,** which is **sodium carbonate**, to the water causes dissolved calcium and magnesium ions to form **insoluble** calcium and magnesium carbonate which settle, thereby removing the dissolved ions from the water.
- **Distillation** involves boiling the water and condensing the steam. The condensed steam forms **pure distilled water** and any dissolved salts are left behind (see pages 411 to 412).

To compare the of hardness of water before and after softening

The hardness of water samples can be compared by determining how much **soap** must be added to form a **permanent lather**, as described in Steps **1** and **2** in Figure 15.3. To determine the effect of boiling on water hardness, the method can be repeated, as described in Step **3**. Question 14 on page 331 gives possible results of the investigation to analyse.

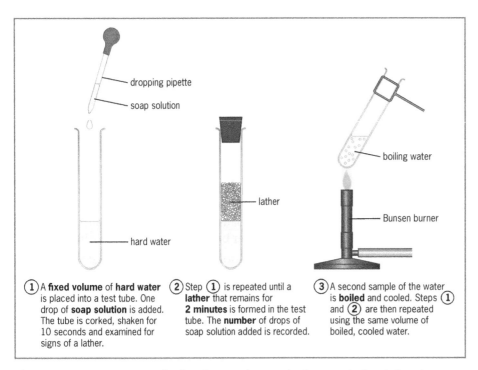

(1) A **fixed volume** of **hard water** is placed into a test tube. One drop of **soap solution** is added. The tube is corked, shaken for 10 seconds and examined for signs of a lather.

(2) Step **(1)** is repeated until a **lather** that remains for **2 minutes** is formed in the test tube. The **number** of drops of soap solution added is recorded.

(3) A second sample of the water is **boiled** and cooled. Steps **(1)** and **(2)** are then repeated using the same volume of boiled, cooled water.

Figure 15.3 *To compare the hardness of water before and after it has been softened by boiling*

The experiment can be repeated using water to which **washing soda** has been added, and again using water that has been **distilled**, in order to assess the effectiveness of the different methods that can be used to soften water.

Uses of water

Uses of water in life processes

Water is essential for a variety of different processes occurring in living organisms due to its **unique properties**, one of the most important being that it **dissolves** a very large number of substances. For this reason, it is known as the 'universal solvent'.

- Water **dissolves** chemicals so that **metabolic (chemical) reactions** can occur in cells; for example, it dissolves the reactants need for respiration. Enzymes which catalyse (speed up) these reactions also need to be dissolved in order to function.

- Water **dissolves** substances so that they can be **transported** around the bodies of living organisms. For example, blood plasma dissolves and transports the products of digestion and waste products around the human body, and a solution of sucrose and amino acids is transported through the phloem of plants (see page 70).

- Water **dissolves** waste substances so that they can be **excreted** from the bodies of living organisms. For example, urine contains urea dissolved in water.

- Water present in digestive juices **dissolves** the digestive enzymes which are essential for **digestion**. It **dissolves** the products of digestion so that they can be absorbed into the body from the intestines.

- Water acts as a **reactant** in certain chemical reactions occurring in living organisms. For example, it is essential to break down large, complex molecules such as polysaccharides, proteins and lipids during **digestion**, and it reacts with carbon dioxide to produce glucose during **photosynthesis** in green plants.

Uses of water in the home

Water has a variety of very important uses in the **home**.

- Water is used directly for **drinking** and it can also be used to make a variety of beverages such as tea, coffee and lemonade.

- Water is used in various ways for **cooking**. It is used to wash and prepare fresh produce such as fruits and vegetables, and to boil, steam or poach foods such as rice, pasta, eggs, vegetables and seafood. It is also used as an ingredient in many food items such as soups, stews, sauces, gravies, baked goods and jellies.

- Water is used for **washing** and **cleaning** purposes, both inside and outside the home. It is used for bathing or showering and brushing teeth, for washing hands, dishes and clothes, for cleaning floors, surfaces and windows, for flushing toilets and for washing patios, driveways and cars.

Only about 1% of the world's fresh water is accessible for humans to use. This is because most of it is frozen in glaciers and polar ice caps, or stored in groundwater. Therefore it is crucial that **water wastage** and **water conservation** are constantly monitored and addressed for **environmental sustainability**. Overusing and wasting water can lead to the depletion of water sources which, in turn, can lead to a decrease in worldwide water availability and water security, food scarcity and starvation, and the loss of habitats for freshwater organisms. A variety of measures can be implemented to **conserve** water in the home.

- **Meter** all domestic water supplies.

- Regularly check all water pipes and places where water is used for **leaks**, and immediately **repair** any leaks that are found.

- Install **water-saving devices** and **appliances** such as **low-flow** shower heads and taps, **low-flush** or **dual-flush** toilets, **aerators** on taps, and **water-efficient** washing machines and dishwashers.

- **Do not** leave taps running when brushing teeth, shaving, washing dishes and defrosting food.

- Use **grey water** to flush toilets, wash cars and water gardens. Grey water is water that has been used for washing dishes, clothes or fresh produce.

- Collect **rainwater** and use it to wash cars and water gardens.

A household's **water consumption** or **usage** over a 30-day period can be determined by taking a **water meter reading**, and noting the date and time when the reading is taken. A second reading is then taken 30 days after the first, at exactly the same time of day. The initial reading is subtracted from the second reading to determine how much water has been used over the 30-day period. If this is done every 30 days, households can **monitor** their water usage and identify **trends**, and it can help them find ways to **conserve water.**

Uses of water in agriculture

Water plays a crucial role in many aspects of **agriculture**.

- Water is used to **irrigate** crops. This helps to ensure that the crop plants receive the water they need for photosynthesis, which maximises yields, especially in areas with insufficient rainfall.

- Water is essential for **hydroponics**, which involves growing crop plants in a solution that is rich in nutrients (see page 26).

- Water is essential for **aquaculture** and **mariculture**. **Aquaculture** involves breeding, rearing and harvesting aquatic organisms in aquatic environments; these are environments with fresh water, brackish water such as that found in estuaries, and seawater. **Mariculture** is a specialised type of aquaculture that involves farming marine organisms in seawater environments only. Organisms commonly farmed in aquatic environments include freshwater fish such as tilapia, trout and salmon, marine fish such as sea bass, tuna and salmon, shellfish such as oysters, mussels, clams, shrimp, prawns and lobsters, and aquatic plants such as seaweed. These organisms can be farmed in ponds, lagoons, artificial freshwater and seawater tanks, and cages and pens located in lakes and in the open sea (see Figure 15.4).

Figure 15.4 *Cages used to farm fish*

- Water is essential for rearing **livestock**, mainly as drinking water for the animals and for maintaining cleanliness.

- Water is used to dissolve **pesticides** so that they can be sprayed on crops.

Other uses of water

Water has a large number of **other** important uses.

- Water is used for a variety of **recreational activities** including swimming, boating, surfing, water skiing, paddle boarding, scuba diving, cruising, water parks, fishing and ice skating (when it is frozen).

- Water is used for **fighting fires** due to its ability to cool the burning material (see page 258). The steam produced when the water is heated also displaces air containing oxygen from around the fire.

- Water is used to **generate electricity**. **Thermoelectric** power plants use a source of fuel, such as oil, to boil water. The steam produced is used to turn turbines, which drive a generator. The generator then converts the mechanical energy from the turbines into electrical energy. **Hydroelectric** power plants use the kinetic energy of flowing water to turn the turbines to generate electricity (see Figure 15.5). **Tidal power**, created by the rise and fall of the tides, and **wave power**, created by ocean waves, can also be used to generate electricity.

Figure 15.5 *Flowing water can be used to generate electricity*

Fishing methods used in the Caribbean

Fishing is a vital part of the economy of Caribbean countries because it provides both **employment** and **food**. Whilst some fish are caught in fresh water, most commercial fishing is carried out at sea using a variety of methods. These are summarised in Table 15.4 and three are shown in Figure 15.6.

Table 15.4 *Fishing methods used in the Caribbean*

Method	Description
By hand	Shellfish, including crabs, oysters and sea eggs (sea urchins), are **handpicked** from intertidal zones or from the seabed by free divers and scuba divers.
Spearfishing and harpoon fishing	**Spears** and **harpoons** are held by hand or are shot from special guns. Free divers or scuba divers use spears to catch smaller fish, such as snappers. Harpoons are used from boats to catch larger fish, such as tuna.
Netting	Fish are caught within the mesh of **nets**. The mesh size determines the size of the fish caught; the smaller the mesh size, the smaller the fish caught. Methods of net-fishing include: • **Cast netting** – A **circular net** with weights around its edge is thrown in shallow water close to shore. As the net sinks, it covers any fish below and traps them as the net edges are drawn together. • **Purse seining** – A **wall of netting**, with weights at the bottom and supported by floats at the top, is launched from a boat in a **circle** around a shoal of fish. A drawstring is pulled to close the bottom of the net and the fish are hauled aboard the boat. • **Trawling** – One or two boats tow a large **trawl net** through the water. Mid-water trawling catches fish in the open ocean. Bottom trawling catches fish close to or on the seabed and can damage the seabed.
Lining	Fish are caught using **lines**. Methods of lining include: • **Hand line** or **rod and line** – A baited hook on a line is thrown into the water. As a fish bites the bait, the hook catches in its mouth and the fish is pulled or reeled in. • **Long-lining** – A long **main line** is held floating horizontally near the surface. Shorter, vertical, **branch lines** with baited hooks are attached to it at intervals to catch fish swimming below the main line. Long-lining can kill seabirds and turtles.
Fish pots and traps	**Baited cages** made of chicken wire attached to a wooden frame are placed on the seabed with a surface buoy attached. Fish and shellfish enter through a cone-shaped funnel or trap door and cannot get back out. Lost traps can turn into 'death traps' for fish.
Fish farming	Freshwater and seawater fish, and shellfish are raised commercially in **tanks**, **enclosures** such as ponds or **cages** submerged in natural bodies of water (see page 328). Species farmed include tilapia, carp, oysters and shrimp.

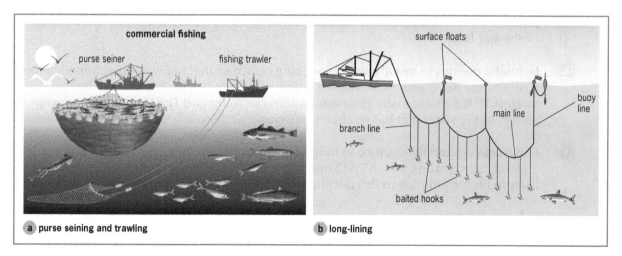

a purse seining and trawling **b** long-lining

Figure 15.6 *Purse seining, trawling and long-lining*

Recalling facts

1 Distinguish between fresh water and seawater in terms of:
   a their chemical composition.   **b** their density.   **c** their pH.
   d their boiling points.   **e** where they can be found.

2 Explain the challenges faced by freshwater fish and how their bodies are adapted to overcome these challenges.

3 Give THREE differences between hard water and soft water.

4 The formation of scum and limescale can both pose problems to households with hard tap water. Explain how scum and limescale are formed and give ONE disadvantage to the formation of EACH.

5 Distinguish between temporary water hardness and permanent water hardness.

6 Identify THREE ways water can be softened.

7 Outline the role played by water in the life of a monkey.

8 Give THREE ways water is used:
   a in the home.   **b** in agriculture.   **c** to generate electricity.

9 Describe how fisherfolk of the Caribbean use EACH of the following methods to catch fish:
   a trawling   **b** long-lining   **c** fish pots.

Applying facts

10 Suggest why salt is often spread on the roads in many countries during the winter months when it snows.

11 Explain fully why a marine fish such as a barracuda dies rapidly if it is transferred to a freshwater lake.

12 Henrietta decides to install a water softening device so that her water is softened before it comes into her home. However, her neighbour, Solly, prefers his water to be hard. Suggest THREE reasons why Henrietta softens her water and THREE reasons why Solly prefers to use water that has not been softened.

13 Fish stocks around the Caribbean have been gradually declining over recent years. Suggest, with reasons, which TWO methods used by Caribbean fisherfolk are MOST likely to be contributing to this decline.

Analysing data

 14 To compare the hardness of four samples of tap water A, B, C and D, taken from four different locations, and the effect that boiling has on each sample, Kevon followed the method described in Figure 15.3 on page 326. His results are given in Table 15.5.

Table 15.5 *Number of drops of soap solution needed to form a permanent lather in four samples of tap water before and after boiling*

Water sample	Number of drops of soap solution to form a long-lasting lather	
	before boiling	after boiling
A	11	5
B	2	2
C	17	2
D	6	6

a i Give ONE limitation of the method used by Kevon.

  ii Identify TWO precautions that Kevon should take to ensure the accuracy of his results.

b i Explain the results obtained by Kevon for sample A.

  ii Describe how you could confirm your explanation in **b i**.

c i Which water sample is MOST likely to have been taken from a limestone-rich region?

  ii Explain your answer to **c i**.

d State, with a reason in EACH case, which TWO samples are MOST likely to have been taken from areas without rocks containing limestone.

e i Which water would be the BEST for building strong bones and teeth?

  ii Give a reason for your choice in **e i**.

 15 The Granville family of four decide to monitor their daily water consumption. To do this, they read their water meter at 9:00 am on every fourth Saturday for 24 weeks, starting on 1st March. Their readings are given in Table 15.6.

Table 15.6 *A household's water usage over a 36-week period*

Date of meter reading	Meter reading (m³)	Water usage (m³)
1st March	2216	–
29th March	2241	
26th April	2267	
24th May	2291	
21st June	2314	
19th July	2344	
16th August	2376	

a Complete Table 15.6 to give the family's water usage per 30-day period.

b Determine the average daily water usage per person over the 24-week period. Show how you arrived at your answer.

c Describe the trends shown in the family's water usage over the 24-week period.

d Suggest ONE reason for the sudden change in water usage in July.

e Identify FOUR measures that the Granville family could implement to reduce their water usage.

Water pollution, water purification and flotation

Learning objectives

- Evaluate the **effects** of **water pollution** on **aquatic life**.
- Investigate the **methods** used to **purify water**.
- Understand and apply the **principle of Archimedes** and the **law of flotation**.

Water pollution

Pollution is the contamination of the natural environment by the release of unpleasant and harmful substances or forms of energy into the environment.

A ***pollutant*** is any unpleasant and harmful substance or form of energy that causes contamination of the natural environment when released.

Water can become **polluted** by waste or harmful substances being **released directly** into **bodies** of **water** such as lakes, streams, rivers, estuaries and oceans from industrial, agricultural and domestic sources, or by being **washed off** the land into the water. These pollutants make the water unsuitable for aquatic organisms to live in and for humans to use. Table 15.7 gives examples of some of the main water pollutants, their sources and their effects on aquatic organisms.

Table 15.7 *Sources of water pollutants and their effects on aquatic life*

Pollutant	Source	Harmful effects
Nitrates and phosphates (plant nutrients)	• Fertilisers used in agriculture. • Synthetic detergents. • Improperly treated sewage.	• Cause **eutrophication**, in which these added plant nutrients enrich the aquatic environment and cause the rapid growth of green plants and algae. This growth causes the water in lakes, ponds and rivers to turn green (see Figure 15.7 on page 333) and this reduces the amount of **light** reaching aquatic plants below. When the plants and algae die, they are decomposed by **aerobic bacteria**, which multiply and use up the **dissolved oxygen** in the water. This causes other aquatic organisms, such as fish, to die.
Pesticides, including insecticides, fungicides and herbicides	• Used in agriculture to control pests, pathogens and weeds. • Used to control vectors of disease, e.g. mosquitoes.	• Can be directly **toxic** to aquatic organisms, including fish. • Can accumulate in the tissues of aquatic organisms and become **higher in concentration** up food chains where they can harm the health of the top consumers; for example, large fish such as tuna, sharks and marlin, fish-eating mammals such as dolphins, whales and manatees, and fish-eating birds such as pelicans and eagles.
Oil	• Oil spills originating from oil tankers, offshore oil rigs and pipeline leaks. • Industrial activities such as oil refining. • Runoff from roads and car parks.	• Chemical constituents of oil can be directly **toxic** to aquatic organisms, including fish. • Forms **slicks** on the surface of water, which prevent **oxygen** from dissolving for aquatic organisms to use in respiration and block out **light** for aquatic plants to use in photosynthesis. • **Coats** sea birds and mammals with oil causing birds to be unable to fly and both to be unable to keep warm. • **Smothers** and **kills** plants and animals living on the shore (see Figure 15.8 on page 333).

Pollutant	Source	Harmful effects
Heavy metals ions such as mercury and lead	• Industrial waste.	• Can be directly **toxic** to aquatic organisms or become **higher in concentration** up food chains, harming the health of top consumers.
Suspended solid particles	• Soil erosion, which leads to silt and soil being washed into bodies of water when it rains. • Industrial waste.	• Reduce **light penetration**, which reduces photosynthesis in aquatic plants and coral polyps, leading to reduced growth. • **Clog** the gills of fish, which reduces or prevents gaseous exchange and can result in death. • **Smother** bottom-dwelling organisms such as corals.
Organic matter	• Untreated or improperly treated sewage and industrial waste. • Manure and other farmyard waste.	• Reduces the amount of **oxygen** dissolved in the water because aerobic bacteria multiply and use up dissolved oxygen as they decompose the organic matter. Aquatic organisms then die due to a shortage of oxygen, and their decomposition depletes dissolved oxygen levels even further.

Figure 15.7 *Eutrophication*

Figure 15.8 *A shore crab covered in oil*

The effects of water pollution on aquatic ecosystems

Water pollution can have a serious and detrimental impact on **coral reefs**, **mangrove swamps** and other **wetland ecosystems**, including freshwater swamps, marshes and bogs. These are some of the most **biologically diverse** ecosystems on Earth. Loss of organisms within these ecosystems as a result of pollution disrupts food chains and webs (see pages 161 to 163), leads to an overall loss of biodiversity and can ultimately destroy the ecosystems.

Coral reefs (see Figure 15.9a) are particularly affected by reduced light penetration and smothering caused by **solid particles** in the water, which causes the death of the coral polyps, and to the toxic effects of **chemical pollutants** such as pesticides, heavy metals and oil from oil spills, which kills the polyps and reef organisms, including sponges, sea stars, lobsters, octopuses and reef fish. They are also affected by **reduced oxygen** levels caused by eutrophication, oil and organic matter from improperly treated sewage, which causes the death of polyps and other reef organisms.

Mangrove swamps (see Figure 15.9b) are similarly affected by **oil** from oil spills smothering the roots of the mangrove trees, which prevents gaseous exchange. They are also affected by the toxic effects of **chemical pollutants** and by **reduced oxygen** levels caused by eutrophication, oil and organic matter, which lead to the death of mangrove trees and mangrove organisms, including oysters, crabs, shrimp and fish, especially juvenile reef fish.

Other **wetland ecosystems** are affected by **sediment** building up and reducing the depth of the water and altering the habitat for organisms living in the wetlands such as frogs, toads, snails, crayfish, snapping turtles, catfish and other fish. The toxic effects of **chemical pollutants** and **reduced oxygen** levels caused by eutrophication, oil and organic matter also lead to the death of wetland plants and animals.

a a coral reef

b roots of mangrove trees

Figure 15.9 *Aquatic ecosystems can be affected by water pollution*

Methods of purifying water for domestic use

Sources of water for domestic use

Water for use in homes comes from a variety of **sources** including surface water sources such as **springs**, **rivers**, **lakes** and **reservoirs**, and groundwater sources such as **aquifers**. To make the water **potable**, in other words safe to drink and use in food preparation, it must be **treated** to remove harmful contaminants such as bacteria, viruses, dissolved chemicals and suspended solid particles. This usually occurs in **large-scale** water treatment plants. After treatment, the water should be clear and not discoloured, and it should have an acceptable taste and odour, and be safe for human consumption.

Seawater and **brackish water**, that is water which is slightly salty, can also serve as **sources** of potable water, especially in coastal areas. To make the water potable, it must be **desalinated**, in other words, have the salts removed. Most desalination methods use large amounts of **energy**, therefore seawater and brackish water are typically used as sources of water in locations where other sources are insufficient.

After treatment or desalination, the water is then piped to homes where it can be further purified to ensure that it is absolutely safe for human consumption (see page 335).

Desalination of seawater for domestic use

Desalination removes salts and other impurities from seawater and brackish water. This is usually carried out in a **desalination plant** and can be done by a variety of methods, two of the main ones being **distillation** and **reverse osmosis**.

- During **distillation**, the water is boiled and the steam is condensed to produce **distilled water** (see page 411). The dissolved salts and other impurities are left behind. To reduce the energy costs in areas with a lot of sunshine, solar energy can be used to heat the water in a **solar still**, however this is only practical on a small scale.

- During **reverse osmosis**, water is forced through a **semi-permeable membrane** under pressure. Only the water molecules are forced through the membrane and all the dissolved salts and other impurities are left behind on the pressurised side. This method uses less energy than distillation.

Water purification methods in the home

A variety of methods can be used to **purify** water in the home. These are particularly useful if the **quality** of tap water is questionable or there are concerns about certain **contaminants** in the water; for example, microorganisms such as viruses, bacteria and protozoans, and chemical contaminants such as heavy metals and pesticides. These methods include **boiling, filtration, chlorination, distillation** and **additives**.

- **Boiling** – The water is brought to a **rolling boil** for at least 1 to 3 minutes to kill harmful microorganisms. After boiling, the water is covered and allowed to cool.

- **Filtration** – The water is passed through a **filter** to remove unwanted particles. **Domestic filters,** such as filter jugs, and inline water filters that filter the water before it comes through the tap, usually contain a **filter cartridge** (see Figure 15.10). These cartridges can contain a variety of **different materials** depending on the contaminants to be removed.

  - **Fibre mesh filters** contain a mesh made of fibres such as polyester, polypropylene, cellulose and, sometimes, glass fibres. Fibre mesh filters vary in pore size and typically remove particulate matter from the water; the size of the particles removed depends on the pore size of the mesh.

  - **Ceramic filters** contain a porous ceramic material of variable pore size. They typically remove suspended particulate matter, and those with the smallest pores are capable of filtering out bacteria and protozoans from the water.

  - **Activated carbon filters** use activated carbon, which is often made from charcoal, to remove many dissolved chemical contaminants, dissolved organic compounds, odours and unpleasant tastes from the water.

  Activated carbon particles or granules are often incorporated into fibre or ceramic filters to improve their effectiveness.

Figure 15.10 *New cartridges for a domestic water filter on the left and used cartridges on the right*

- **Chlorination** – **Chlorine tablets** are added to the water. These contain chemicals that release **chlorine** into the water when dissolved, and the chlorine is very effective in killing viruses, bacteria and protozoans. Alternatively, 2 drops of **chlorine bleach** can be added to each litre of water if chlorine tablets are unavailable. The bleach releases chlorine which kills harmful microorganisms.

- **Distillation** – The water is boiled to produce steam which is condensed to form **pure distilled water.** This leaves any impurities and contaminants, including microorganisms, behind.

- **Additives** – Certain substances are **added** to the water to purify it. For example, **powdered alum (potassium aluminium sulfate)** is added to cause fine suspended particles to clump together and settle, leaving clear water above.

Density, upthrust and flotation

*The **density** of a body is its mass per unit volume.*

Mass is the quantity of matter making up a body.

Weight is the gravitational force of a planet or other large object on a body.

$$\text{density} = \frac{\text{mass}}{\text{volume}} \qquad \text{i.e. } \rho = \frac{m}{V} \qquad \text{Density can be expressed in } \frac{g}{cm^3} \text{ or } \frac{kg}{m^3}$$

Note: From the above equation we can derive an equation to express mass:

mass = density × volume $m = \rho V$

The weight of a body depends on the **gravitational field strength at the location** (see Chapter 16). On Earth, the generally accepted value for the **gravitational field strength**, g, is **10 N/kg**.

A body falling in this field has an **acceleration due to gravity**, g, of **10 m/s^2**.

- **Gravitational field strength** and **acceleration due to gravity** are given the same symbol, g, and their units are equivalent. They can be used interchangeably.
- When using the value **g = 10 m/s^2**, **always express mass in kg** within the equation to **calculate weight**.

    weight (W) = mass (m) × gravitational field strength (g)
        weight = mass × acceleration due to gravity

An object of mass **1 kg** has a weight of **10 N** since:

$$W = mg = 1 \text{ kg} \times 10 \frac{\text{N}}{\text{kg}} = 10 \text{ N}$$

$$W = mg = 1 \text{ kg} \times 10 \frac{\text{m}}{\text{s}^2} = 10 \text{ N}$$

Example 1

Figure 15.11a shows an irregularly shaped stone of mass 40 g gently lowered into a displacement can filled with water to the level of the spout. The overflow is collected in a measuring cylinder and measured as 20 cm^3. Determine the density of the stone.

Solution:

$$\rho = \frac{m}{V} = \frac{(40 \text{ g})}{(20 \text{ cm}^3)} = 2 \text{ g/cm}^3$$

Note 1: If the stone fits into the measuring cylinder, as in Figure 15.11b, the volume of a given amount of water in the cylinder can be measured before and after immersing the stone in it. The difference in volumes then represents the volume of the stone.

Note 2: To find the volume of a substance which is soluble in water (e.g. table salt), we place it in a solvent in which it is insoluble (e.g. kerosene).

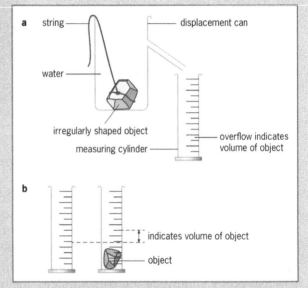

Figure 15.11 *Example 1*

Experiment: To determine the density of a piece of cork

Method

- Measure the mass of the cork using a sensitive electronic balance.
- Tie the stone firmly to the cork with a piece of string and lower into a displacement can filled to the spout with water as shown in Figure 15.12 on page 337.
- Measure the volume of water that overflows into the measuring cylinder.

- Repeat the process, this time with the stone alone being tied to the string.
- Find the volume of the cork by subtracting the second volume reading from the first.
- Calculate the density of the cork using the equation $\rho = \dfrac{m}{V}$.

Precautions

- Take eye-level readings of the volume in the measuring cylinder to avoid parallax error.
- Take readings from the bottom of the water meniscus.
- Lower the stone gently into the water to avoid excessive water splashing over.

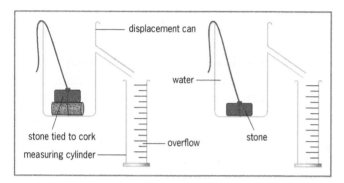

Figure 15.12 *To determine the density of a piece of cork*

The principle of Archimedes

The *principle of Archimedes* states that when a body is wholly or partially immersed in a fluid it experiences an *upthrust* equal to the weight of the fluid displaced (pushed away).

Figure 15.13 shows an experiment verifying the principle using numerical data.

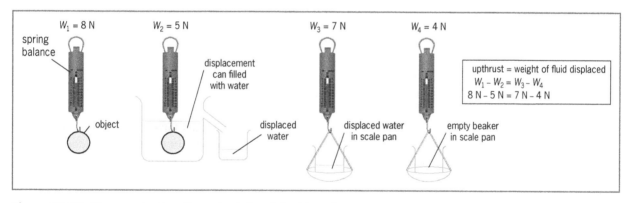

Figure 15.13 *Demonstrating the principle of Archimedes*

Principle of flotation

The *principle of flotation* states that the *weight* of a floating body is equal to the *upthrust* on it.

Note:

Principle of Archimedes:	weight of fluid displaced = upthrust
Principle of flotation:	weight of fluid displaced = upthrust = weight of body

There are three situations that may apply (see also Figure 15.14).

- **Sinking** – An object will sink in a fluid if its density is greater than that of the fluid. The weight of the object is then greater than the upthrust (weight of fluid displaced).
- **Floating** – A heavy ship made of steel will float. This is so since its rooms contain air and therefore the overall density of the ship and its contents is much less than that of steel alone. The entire ship does not displace water since some of it is still above the surface. It displaces just enough water to provide an upthrust equal to its weight.

    A ship travelling from the sea into the mouth of a river sinks deeper into the fresh water than it does in the seawater, thereby displacing more of the less dense fresh water, and so maintaining the upthrust at a value equal to its weight. A similar occurrence results when a ship travels from high latitude, cool waters to less dense, warmer tropical water.
- **Rising** – Hot air is less dense than cool air. A hot air balloon rises since the weight of its rubber casing plus the hot air inside of it is less than the upthrust on it (the weight of cool air it pushes away).

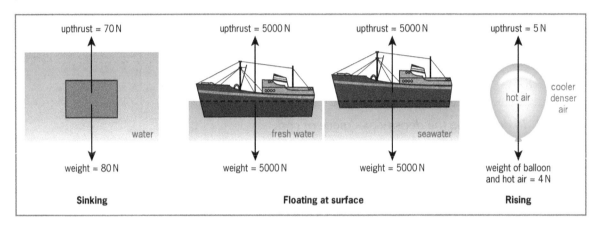

Figure 15.14 *Sinking, floating and rising*

Upthrust and submarines

Figure 15.15 shows a toy submarine having a ballast tank which can hold water.

- If water is taken into the tank until the submarine's **total weight** exceeds the weight of water displaced (upthrust), the submarine will accelerate downwards. The resultant force on it is downward and it will descend without the use of its engines.
- To accelerate upwards, air under pressure expels water from the ballast tank, decreasing the total weight of the submarine. When decreased to a value less than the weight of water displaced (upthrust), the submarine can accelerate upwards without the use of its engines.
- Floating occurs if the weight of the submarine is equal to the weight of water displaced (upthrust).

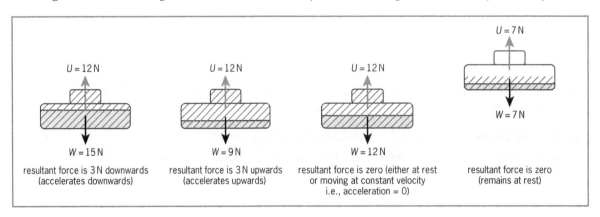

Figure 15.15 *Upthrust and submarines*

Upthrust and balloons

Figure 15.16a shows a balloon containing air. If the air in the balloon is heated, it will become less dense and will expand. The weight of the balloon is unchanged, but the upthrust on it will increase since it now displaces more of the cooler surrounding air. It will accelerate upwards if its weight plus the weight of the air it contains is less than the weight of the cooler air it pushes away (upthrust).

If the balloon contains a gas of low density such as helium, as in Figure 15.16b, its weight plus the weight of gas in it will be less than the weight of air it displaces (upthrust). It therefore accelerates upwards.

Immersing an object in a denser fluid will provide greater upthrust since the weight of fluid displaced is proportional to its density.

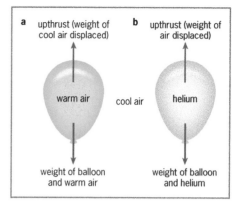

Figure 15.16 *Upthrust and balloons*

Table 15.8 *Floating and sinking in relation to density*

For a totally immersed body:		
Weight of body > upthrust	Immersed body sinks through fluid	Density of body > density of fluid
Weight of body < upthrust	Immersed body rises through fluid	Density of body < density of fluid
Weight of body = upthrust	Body floats fully immersed	Density of body = density of fluid
For a body (e.g. a football) floating partially immersed at the surface:		
Weight of ball = upthrust	Ball floats at surface, partially immersed	Mean density of ball including air it contains < density of fluid

Example 2

A sphere of volume 200 cm³ and density 6 g/cm³ is suspended by string below the surface of water.

a Calculate:

 i its mass   ii its weight.

b Determine the volume of water displaced.

c Given that the density of the water is 1 g/cm³, calculate:

 i the mass of water displaced   ii the weight of water displaced   iii the upthrust.

Solution:

a i For a sphere, density $= \dfrac{\text{mass}}{\text{volume}}$

$\therefore$ mass = density × volume

$$\text{mass} = 6\,\frac{g}{cm^3} \times 200\ cm^3$$

$$\text{mass} = 1200\ g$$

 ii First express mass in kg:

$$\text{mass} = 1200\ g = \frac{1200}{1000}\ kg = 1.2\ kg$$

$\therefore$ weight = mass × acceleration due to gravity

$$\text{weight} = 1.2\ kg \times 10\,\frac{N}{kg}$$

$$\text{weight} = 12\ N$$

The unit for acceleration due to gravity was expressed as N/kg instead of m/s² so that the final answer in N is more obvious.

b Volume of water displaced = volume of sphere = 200 cm³.

c i For water displaced: density $= \dfrac{mass}{volume}$ $\therefore$ mass $=$ density $\times$ volume

$$mass = 1\,\frac{g}{cm^3} \times 200\ cm^3$$

$$mass = 200\ g$$

ii First express mass in kg:

$$mass = 200\ g = \frac{200}{1000}\ kg = 0.2\ kg$$

$\therefore$ weight $=$ mass $\times$ acceleration due to gravity

$$weight = 0.2\ kg \times 10\,\frac{N}{kg}$$

$$weight = 2\ N \quad \dots \text{weight of water displaced}$$

iii Upthrust $=$ weight of water displaced $= 2\ N$

Plimsoll line

*A **plimsoll line** is a line marked on a ship that indicates the maximum depth to which it should sink in the water in which it is loaded.*

Several 'load lines' (shown in Figure 15.17 with a key) are used corresponding to the density of the water **where the ship is loaded**. This makes it safe to travel between waters of different densities.

The 'LR' line indicates the classification society, in this case it is Lloyd's Register, a leading provider of services for marine industries.

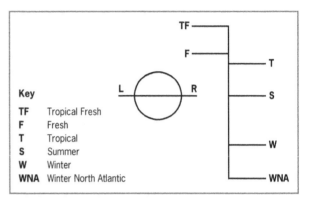

Key
TF   Tropical Fresh
F   Fresh
T   Tropical
S   Summer
W   Winter
WNA Winter North Atlantic

Figure 15.17 *Plimsoll line*

Recalling facts

1 What is meant by the term 'pollution'?

2 Identify the sources of the following water pollutants:
  a oil   **b** pesticides
  c nitrates and phosphates.

3 Outline the harmful effects of oil on aquatic life.

4 Give an account of how EACH of the following is being impacted by water pollution in the Caribbean:
  a mangrove swamps   **b** coral reefs.

5 Identify the main sources of water used in homes.

6 **a** What is meant by the term 'desalination'?
  b Explain TWO ways that seawater can be desalinated for domestic use.

7 **a** Define density.
  b Write a general equation which can be used to calculate density.

8 State:
  a the principle of Archimedes   **b** the principle of flotation.

9 **a** What is a Plimsoll line?

    b Explain why shipping companies should follow the regulations set out by the Plimsoll line marked on their ships.

Applying facts

Note: acceleration due to gravity can be taken as 10 m/s^2 or 10 N/kg.

10 In August 1999, hundreds of dead fish started to appear floating in the sea and washed up on the beaches along certain shorelines of many of the Caribbean's Windward Islands. Identify FOUR different water pollutants that could have been the cause of these deaths and explain how EACH pollutant named could have led to the fish kills.

11 Farmer Fred begins to realise that the water in several of the ponds on his farm is starting to turn green.

    a What is the MOST likely cause of this?

    b Explain the long-term effects that this will have on the organisms in Farmer Fred's ponds.

12 Shauna regularly uses insecticides to control insect pests on the crops that she grows on her farm, which is close to the coast. Provide an explanation to convince her that these insecticides can harm large fish living in the sea many miles away.

13 What features make water potable?

14 After Hurricane Maria hit the Caribbean in 2017, the public water supplies of several countries became contaminated. Explain the measures that households in these countries could have taken to make their water safe to drink.

15 A block of density of 2 g/cm^3 has a volume of 4 cm^3.

    a Calculate its mass:

        i in grams.   **ii** in kilograms.

    b Calculate its weight in newtons.

16 **a** Calculate the density of the following.

        i A stone of mass 400 g and volume 200 cm^3.

        ii A large boulder of mass of mass 4000 kg and volume 2.0 m^3.

        iii A block of mass 40 g and volume 80 cm^3.

    b State, with a reason, whether the block in part **a iii** will sink or float in water of density 1 g/cm^3.

    c Calculate the weight in newtons of the block in part **a iii**.

17 Describe a simple experiment to determine the density of a small glass marble, stating two precautions you should take.

18 A sealed balloon filled with a low-density gas such as hydrogen, accelerates upward through the atmosphere. Explain this phenomenon in terms of Archimedes' principle.

19 Explain why the water line on the side of a ship rises as it travels from a cool temperate region to warmer Caribbean waters.

Navigational and water safety devices, and scuba diving

Learning objectives

- Understand the **function** and **importance** of various **navigational devices** used at **sea**.
- Identify **water safety devices**.
- Discuss the **effects** of **scuba diving** and **free diving** on the **human body**.

Importance of navigational devices used at sea

Efficient and effective maritime navigation can only be achieved with the help of a set of devices, each providing a necessary and unique piece of information.

Compasses

*A **magnetic compass** consists of a magnetised needle mounted on a pivot such that it can spin freely and point along the Earth's magnetic field to the **Earth's 'magnetic north'**.*

As shown in Figure 15.18, the instrument is generally mounted on a fixed base on which is marked the **cardinal points**: north (N), south (S), east (E) and west (W), and a **scale** showing rotation through 360°.

*A **gyrocompass** consists of a **fast-spinning disc** which together with the **rotation of the Earth** determines the geographical direction **pointing to the Earth's 'true north'**.*

The instrument has a **lubber line** which aligns with the scale to indicate the direction, as shown in Figure 15.19. Readings of 0°, 90°, 180° and 270° respectively indicate the directions due north, due east, due south and due west.

Figure 15.18 *Magnetic compass*

lubber line

Figure 15.19 *Gyrocompass*

Advantages of gyrocompass over the magnetic compass for navigation

- Points to **true north** determined by the axis of rotation of the Earth, unlike the magnetic compass which points to **magnetic north** (see Figure 15.20).

- Gyrocompasses are **more accurate**. Magnetic compasses are affected by the large **steel hulls of ships** which **alter magnetic field directions**.

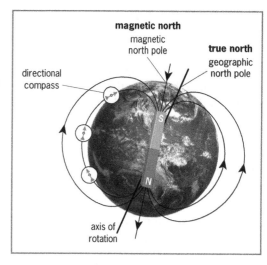

Figure 15.20 *'Magnetic north' and 'true north'*

Sound navigation and ranging (sonar)

Ultrasonic waves can be used to detect the depth of water. Owing to ultrasound's high frequencies relative to those of audible sound, it undergoes relatively **slight diffraction** and produces a more **focused beam**. An ultrasonic pulse is emitted by a **transmitter, T**, as shown in Figure 15.21, and a **timer is started** simultaneously. A **receiver, R**, detects the reflected pulse and records the time taken for the round trip. A computer then calculates the **depth, x**, of the water using:

$$\text{speed} = \frac{\text{distance down and up}}{\text{time}} \qquad \text{speed} = \frac{2x}{\text{time}}$$

The speed of sound in water is approximately 1500 m/s.

Sonar plays a **critical role** in **maritime navigation**, as follows.

- **Safer navigation** is achieved as sonar helps ships to avoid obstacles such as reefs, shipwrecks and submerged rocks **in real-time**.

- **Detailed mapping** of the seabed can be produced.

- **Search and rescue operations** for distressed submerged vessels are more efficient using sonar.

- **Fisheries** use sonar to **locate schools** of fish.

- **Scientists** use sonar to **study marine ecosystems**.

- **Submarines** can better **prevent collisions** with other vessels and with the natural environment.

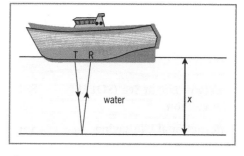

Figure 15.21 *Depth sounding using echoes*

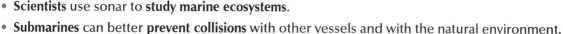

Example 3

A ship emits an ultrasonic wave to the seabed and receives the **echo** 0.2 s later. Given that the speed of sound in the water is 1500 m/s, determine the depth, x, of the seabed below the ship.

Solution:

Since the sound wave travels down and then up, the total distance travelled in the 0.2 s is 2x.

$$\text{speed} = \frac{\text{distance}}{\text{time}}$$

$\therefore$ distance = speed × time $2x = 1500 \text{ m/s} \times 0.2 \text{ s}$ $2x = 300 \text{ m}$ $x = \frac{300 \text{ m}}{2}$ $x = 150 \text{ m}$

Radio detection and ranging (radar)

Radar can be used to prevent collisions at sea by providing **bearings** of other vessels and objects, their **speeds** and **distances** away. It is particularly useful when visibility is poor, e.g. during bad weather or at night. A **rotating transmitter** on the vessel sweeps a narrow beam of **radio wave pulses** across the water surface between the vessel and the horizon. If the pulses meet an object, part of its energy is **reflected back to a receiver** on the vessel. The object is **displayed on a screen** as a series of 'blips'.

Global Positioning System (GPS)

This is a system of satellites (see page 291) that is used to determine the exact **position** of a sea vessel. The system consists of about **30 satellites** orbiting the Earth at an altitude of **20 000 km**.

Radio wave pulses emitted by the satellites are **received by the GPS** receiver. Knowing the speed of radio waves and the time taken to the receiver, the distances are calculated (distance = speed × time). Using **distances** from **three** satellites to a particular location, the **GPS calculates the position** of the ship (latitude and longitude) by a method known as **trilateration**. These systems can also **measure speed** since that is simply how **position changes with time.**

Maritime safety standards

The following are some of the codes and conventions enforced by the International Maritime Organisation (IMO) and other organisations worldwide.

Table 15.9 *Some international codes and conventions for maritime safety standards.*

Standard	Details
International System Management (ISM) Code	Regulates safety management objectives for shipping companies focusing on operational safety, pollution prevention and crew welfare.
Safety of Life at Sea (SOLAS) Convention	Sets minimum standards for ship construction, equipment and operation.
International Life-saving Appliance (LSA) Code	Sets requirements for lifeboats, life rafts and protective gear.
Procedure for Port State Control (PSC)	Sets procedure for inspections to see that foreign vessels comply with safety and environmental regulations on entering a port.
Fire Test Procedures (FTP) Code	Assesses fire resistance of materials used on ships.
Cargo Stowage and Securing (CSS) Code	Lays guidelines for handling and securing of cargo to prevent damage.

Water safety devices

Water safety devices include **life jackets**, **life rafts** and **inflatable tubes** (see Figure 15.22 on page 345). They are designed to ensure the safety of people taking part in water-related sporting or recreational activities. They can be **worn** by people to help keep them **afloat** during activities such as swimming and snorkelling, and in the event of an accident occurring during activities such as sailing, canoeing, kayaking and paddleboarding. They are also **carried** on board various larger watercraft and sea-going vessels, such as powerboats, ferries and cruise ships, for use in an emergency.

- **Life jackets** or **personal flotation devices (PFDs)** keep a person afloat even when unconscious. They are designed to keep a person's head above water and are worn by persons taking part in water-related activities. Life jackets are always carried on larger watercraft and sea-going vessels as part of their safety equipment. They contain either **foam**, which is waterproof and naturally buoyant, or are **inflated** when needed by a cartridge of carbon dioxide. The person is kept afloat because the weight of the water displaced by the jacket is more than the weight of the jacket.

- **Life rafts** are inflatable boats of various sizes. They are usually made of reinforced rubber or neoprene, and are carried by larger watercraft and sea-going vessels as part of their safety equipment. They can be **inflated manually** by pulling a cord to activate a **carbon dioxide cylinder** or they can **inflate automatically** when the raft comes into contact with the water. People in need of rescue can then climb on board.
- **Inflatable tubes** or **rings** are buoyant flotation devices that are worn around a person's waist and can be used to keep non-swimmers and those learning to swim afloat.

a   life jacket   b   inflatable life raft   c   inflatable tube

Figure 15.22 *Water safety devices*

Effects of diving on the human body

Free diving and **scuba diving** are two ways humans can venture into the underwater world. When **free diving**, divers rely on holding their breath while underwater (see Figure 15.23a). Before diving, they usually take one or two deep breaths to increase the amount of oxygen in their bodies and reduce the amount of carbon dioxide, which reduces the urge to breathe. Free divers also use a variety of **techniques** to conserve oxygen and maximise their time underwater; for example, staying relaxed, streamlining their bodies and limiting unnecessary movement. They can also undergo training to develop their breath-holding and free diving skills.

When **scuba diving**, divers use self-contained underwater breathing apparatus (scuba) in order to breathe underwater. This usually consists of a **scuba tank** (see Figure 15.23b) filled with either **compressed air** or a **compressed breathing gas mixture** such as nitrox, which contains a higher percentage of oxygen and lower percentage of nitrogen than air.

a   free divers   b   a scuba diver

Figure 15.23 *Divers exploring the undersea world*

All divers experience **increasing pressure** from the water surrounding them as they descend, and this affects the body and can lead to a number of potential **hazards**. Most of these can affect scuba divers, not free divers, and include **decompression sickness**, **nitrogen narcosis**, **barotrauma** and **air embolism**. Figure 15.24 shows how the concept of pressure increasing as depth increases can be demonstrated.

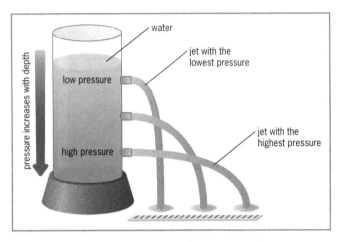

Figure 15.24 *Demonstrating that pressure increases with depth*

Decompression sickness

Decompression sickness is also known as '**the bends**'. The solubility of gases in liquids increases as pressure increases; therefore, as a diver **descends** and inhales air from the tank, the increased pressure causes the gases in the air, particularly **nitrogen**, to dissolve into his or her blood and tissue fluids. The **deeper** the diver goes and the **longer** the diver's time at depth, the **greater** the amount of nitrogen that dissolves.

As the diver then **ascends** to the surface, the pressure **decreases** and this causes the dissolved nitrogen to come out of solution. If the ascent is made **slowly** enough and the diver makes any necessary **decompression stops**, the nitrogen is eliminated from the blood and tissue fluids gradually and safely. However, if the diver ascends **too quickly** and does not make the required decompression stops, the nitrogen comes out of solution too quickly and forms **nitrogen bubbles** in the blood and tissue fluids during or soon after the ascent. These bubbles cause **symptoms** of decompression sickness to develop, which vary and include joint pain, pressure bruising of the skin, tingling or numbness in the hands, feet, arms and legs, dizziness, shortness of breath and paralysis, and it can be fatal.

Decompression sickness is **treated** by the diver being **recompressed** in a **decompression chamber**, also known as a **recompression chamber**, as soon as possible (see Figure 15.25). This reduces the size of the nitrogen bubbles and helps the nitrogen to dissolve back into the blood and tissue fluids, and it relieves the symptoms experienced by the diver. The diver is also given **pure oxygen** to breathe, which promotes the **diffusion** of oxygen into the blood and tissue fluids, and of the nitrogen back out. The diver remains under pressure in the chamber long enough for his or her symptoms to be fully alleviated and all the nitrogen to be removed safely from the body. The pressure within the chamber is then slowly decreased to atmospheric pressure.

Figure 15.25 *A diver being treated for decompression sickness in a decompression chamber*

Nitrogen narcosis

At depths greater than **30 m**, the nitrogen dissolved into a diver's blood and tissue fluids has a **narcotic effect** on the diver similar to that of drinking alcohol. This narcotic effect, known as **nitrogen narcosis**, impairs the diver's judgment, sense of perception and decision making, reduces his or her coordination and creates a sense of detachment from the environment. This effect increases as the diver goes deeper, leading to confusion and disorientation, which increase the risk of accidents happening. The effects of nitrogen narcosis can be reversed by ascending to a **shallower depth**. Additionally, using a breathing gas mixture such as nitrox can help reduce the severity of the effects.

Barotrauma

Barotrauma refers to an injury that occurs when there is a **pressure difference** between air-filled cavities inside the body and the surrounding environment. There are several types of barotraumas depending on the part of the body affected, including **ear barotrauma** and **lung barotrauma**.

- **Ear barotrauma** can occur when there is a difference in pressure between the air inside the middle ear and the surrounding environment and can affect free divers as well as scuba divers. As a diver **descends**, his or her **ear drums** are pushed **inwards** by the increasing pressure, causing discomfort and pain. If the diver continues to descend, the ear drums can become damaged and can eventually **rupture (burst)**, causing the diver to develop vertigo. To prevent this from happening, the diver must **equalise** the pressure on each side of the ear drums whilst descending by pinching the nose and forcing air from the throat up each Eustachian tube into the middle ear (see Figure 6.8 on page 94).

- **Lung barotrauma** can occur when there is a pressure difference between the air inside the lungs and the surrounding environment. It happens if a scuba diver inhales and then holds his or her breath, or fails to exhale sufficiently, during the ascent. The air that the diver inhales from the tank is at the same pressure as the surrounding water and as the diver then **ascends**, the surrounding pressure **decreases** and the air inside the lungs **expands**. If this air cannot escape, it stretches the lung tissue and this can cause the walls of the alveoli to **rupture**. This can cause symptoms such as chest pain, difficulty breathing and coughing up blood. In severe cases, air may enter the pleural cavity (see Figure 9.17 on page 191) and cause a **collapsed lung** or it may enter the bloodstream, which can lead to an **arterial gas embolism**. To prevent this from happening, a diver must ascend slowly and exhale during the ascent.

Embolism

An **embolism** is a medical condition caused by the **obstruction** of a blood vessel. In the case of a scuba diver, the obstruction can be caused by **air bubbles** that form in the bloodstream as a result of damage to the walls of the alveoli during ascent or by **nitrogen bubbles** that form in the bloodstream during a rapid ascent without the required decompression stops. If an air or nitrogen bubble blocks an artery, known as an **arterial gas embolism**, it cuts off the blood supply to the region of the body supplied by the artery and can lead to a stroke, heart attack and even death. Immediate recompression in a decompression chamber is essential to reduce the size of any bubbles in the diver's blood.

Recalling facts

1
  a Briefly describe the structure and function of each of the following:
     i a magnetic compass   ii a gyrocompass.
  b State TWO advantages of the gyrocompass over the magnetic compass for navigation.

2
  a Briefly explain how sonar is used to detect the depth of water below a maritime vessel.
  b State THREE ways that sonar can be used in the efficient functioning of maritime vessels.
  c List TWO devices used in maritime navigation other than compasses and sonar.

3
  a What are water safety devices designed to do?
  b Distinguish between a life jacket and a life raft.

4 What is the difference between free diving and scuba diving?

5
  a Identify FOUR hazards faced by a scuba diver.
  b Outline why scuba diving becomes more dangerous as a diver goes deeper.

Applying facts

6 A SONAR transmitter below a ship sends an ultrasonic wave to the seabed and receives the reflected echo 0.50 seconds later. Given that the speed of sound in water is 1500 m/s, determine the depth, x, of the seabed below the ship.

7 Marley invites his friend, Ravi, to go sailing with him and insists that Ravi wears a life jacket, but Ravi cannot understand why because he is a very good swimmer. Write an explanation that Marley could use to convince Ravi of the need to wear the life jacket.

8 Provide an explanation for each of the following.
  a Both free divers and scuba divers can suffer from ear barotrauma.
  b A lung barotrauma can affect a scuba diver but not a free diver.

9 Bertie set off to dive down the side of a barrier reef from its top at about 25 m to the sandy seabed at about 35 m, but as he approached the sand he started to feel detached from his surroundings and began to lose his ability to coordinate his actions. Petra, on the other hand, decided to remain at the top of the reef, but overstayed her time there and then ascended to the surface without making the required stops. After her ascent, she began to develop joint pain and numbness in her arms.
  a Explain the causes of the symptoms experienced by Bertie and by Petra.
  b What must Bertie do to relieve his symptoms?
  c Suggest TWO other symptoms that Petra might develop if she does not seek immediate treatment.
  d Outline the treatment that Petra must undergo to ensure that her symptoms do not worsen and that she makes a full recovery, and explain fully the principles behind the treatment.

16 Forces

Forces play a key role in understanding how bodies interact with each other. In this chapter we will learn how forces are responsible for maintaining the equilibrium of systems at rest and how they can be used in machines to make our work easier. Forces can also cause bodies to accelerate along a straight line, as a car does on a highway, or to accelerate in circular motion, as the Earth does in revolving around the Sun.

The statics and dynamics of forces and their applications

Learning objectives

- Define **force** and identify various forms of force.
- Explain **lift forces, frictional forces** and **centripetal forces** together with their applications.
- Define **centre of gravity** and relate it to the types of **equilibrium** of a body.
- Understand the **conditions for equilibrium** under a system of coplanar parallel forces.
- Define **momentum** and state and apply the **law of conservation of linear momentum**.
- State and apply **Newton's laws of motion**.
- Explain the **functions** and describe the **terms** and **applications** associated with **simple machines**.

Force

*A **force** is a push or pull which changes, or tends to change, the **size**, **shape** or **motion** of a body.*

Principles of forces

Force is a **vector** quantity and so its **magnitude** (size) and **direction** are significant. If several forces act on a body along a straight line, we sum them by taking one direction as positive and the other as negative.

The **newton, N**, is the SI unit of force.

Determining the resultant vector for vectors acting along the same line

Figure 16.1 shows how we can calculate the resultant force of several forces. For the cases shown, we have assigned forces acting to the right as positive and forces acting to the left as negative.

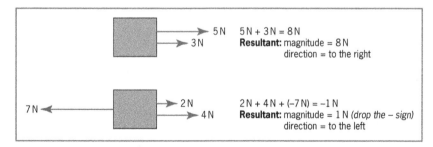

Figure 16.1 *Finding the resultant force of several forces*

Contact and non-contact forces

A force (push or pull) can be exerted on body A due to **contact** with body B, or it can be exerted on body A **from a distance** if it is in a **field** of body B.

Contact forces (mechanical forces)

- **Thrust** is the force exerted by a person or system (e.g. a motor) in pushing an object.
- **Tension** and **compression** are forces produced within a spring or elastic material being stretched or compressed. These forces act in directions which oppose the deformation of the material by pulling or pushing respectively on objects connected at their ends.
- **Normal reaction** is the contact force acting perpendicularly **from a surface** as a reaction to a force acting **onto the surface** from another body.
- **Buoyancy** force is an upward force from a fluid onto a body **submerged** in the fluid (see page 337).
- **Lift** is an **aerodynamic** force caused by the motion of an object through the air (see page 354).
- **Friction** is the **opposing** force which **acts along the surface** of contact of a body, moving or tending to move relative to another body (see later in this chapter for more on friction).
- **Drag** is the **opposing** force which **acts along the surface** of a body as it moves through a **fluid**.

Non-contact forces (field forces)

- **Gravitational force** is the force between **masses** due to their position within a gravitational **field**.
- **Nuclear force** is the force binding **subatomic particles** due to their position within a nuclear **field**.
- **Electric force** is the force between **charges** due to their position within an electric **field**.
- **Magnetic force** is the force between **magnetic poles** due to their positions within a magnetic **field**.

Free-body force diagrams

A free-body force diagram is important in analysing a body's behaviour under the action of several forces (see Figure 16.2). It shows the **forces** acting **ON** the **body**. For this CSEC course, these are the following.

1. **Field** force: The **weight** acting at the **centre of gravity** (see page 355).
2. **Contact** forces: Forces from the **environment** acting at **contact** points.

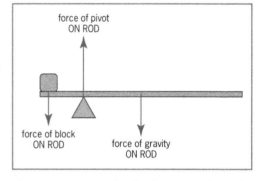

Figure 16.2 *Free-body diagram of a rod in equilibrium*

Newton's laws of motion

Table 16.1 *Newton's laws of motion*

1st law	If there is **no resultant force** on a body, it continues in its state of **rest** or at **constant velocity** *(no acceleration)* in a straight line.
	resultant force = 0 $\qquad$ ∴ acceleration = 0
2nd law	If there is a **resultant force** (net force) on a body it produces a proportional acceleration.
	resultant force = mass × acceleration $\qquad F_R = ma$
	If the resultant force is doubled on a given mass, its acceleration will also double.
3rd law	If body A exerts a force on body B, then body B exerts an **equal** but **oppositely directed** force on body A. *(Every **action** has an **equal**, but **oppositely** directed **reaction**.)*

Note: A body can never have **both** forces of a **Newton's 3rd law pair** acting on it. For example, if we are investigating the **behaviour of the ROD** shown in Figure 16.2, we are only concerned with the forces **ON THE ROD**. We are NOT concerned with the downward force of the rod **ON THE PIVOT** or the upward force of the rod **ON THE BLOCK**.

Figure 16.3a shows a person of weight 400 N standing in an elevator that accelerates upward. The floor of the elevator provides an upward force of 500 N on the person. These two forces do **NOT** form **Newton's 3rd law pair** since **both** act on the person (the **same body**).

Figure 16.3b illustrates that there are **TWO Newton's 3rd law pairs** of forces in action. Note how the phrases in bold print for the pairs of forces are reversed. Knowing this should make it easy to identify **Newton's 3rd law pairs** of forces.

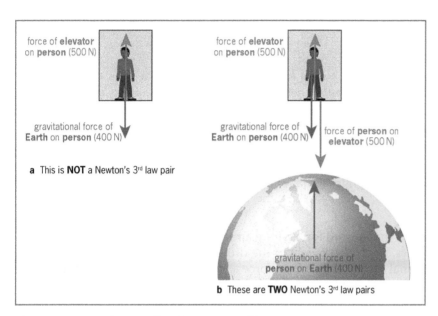

force of **elevator** on **person** (500 N)

gravitational force of **Earth** on **person** (400 N)

a This is **NOT** a Newton's 3rd law pair

force of **elevator** on **person** (500 N)

gravitational force of **Earth** on **person** (400 N)

force of **person** on **elevator** (500 N)

gravitational force of **person** on **Earth** (400 N)

b These are **TWO** Newton's 3rd law pairs

Figure 16.3 *Understanding Newton's 3rd law*

Applications of Newton's laws

- As our **foot presses backward on the ground**, an equal force from the **ground presses forward on our foot**, enabling us to walk or run.
  (**3rd law: action = reaction**)

- A rocket, with its engines off, moves through outer space at constant velocity in a straight line. The resultant force on the rocket is zero; there is no forward force since the engines are off and there is no opposing force since there is no atmosphere to create friction with its surface, and this is in outer space where gravitational forces are negligible.
  (**1st law: uniform velocity** (no acceleration) if $F_R = 0$)

  If an astronaut steps out of the rocket as it moves at 200 m/s and then gently releases the door handle, he or she will continue to move at 200 m/s alongside the vehicle. The velocity of the astronaut is 200 ms^{-1} and remains at 200 ms^{-1} until some resultant force acts to change this.
  (**1st law: uniform velocity** (no acceleration) if $F_R = 0$)

- As a car crashes into a wall, a force acts against its motion for a brief interval of time. It quickly decelerates to rest (experiences an acceleration with a direction in opposition to its motion).
  (**2nd law: $F_R = ma$**)

  If the occupants are not wearing seatbelts, they will continue their motion until they collide with the windscreen, dashboard, or some other object.
  (**1st law: $F_R = 0$ if $a = 0$**)

  An opposing force on collision decelerates them to rest.
  (**2nd law: $F_R = ma$**)

- As an aircraft accelerates along a runway, the backrest of the seat presses forward on its occupant. This produces a resultant force causing the passenger to accelerate.
  (2nd law: $F_R = ma$)

  The forward force of the **seat** onto the passenger's **back** gives rise to a backward force from passenger's **back** onto the **seat**.
  (3rd law: action = reaction)

- If the aircraft moves at **constant velocity**, the resultant force on the occupant along the line of motion must be zero. The passenger will no longer feel the seat pushing on his/her back or friction at the arms.
  (1st law: $F_R = 0$ if $a = 0$)

  As the aircraft **decelerates to rest** due to the **opposing force** of the **brakes** on its **wheels**, the occupant also **decelerates to rest** due to the **opposing resultant force** from the **seatbelt, handrests** and **seat**.
  (2nd law: $F_R = ma$)

  The forward force of the passenger's **body** on the **seatbelt** is equal in magnitude to the backward force of the **seatbelt** on the passenger's **body**.
  (3rd law: action = reaction)

- As a raindrop falls through the air, it **accelerates** initially since the only force on it is the force of gravity (its **weight**).
  (2nd law: $F_R = ma$)

  As the **velocity** of the drop **increases**, the **upward force** of the **air friction** on it **increases** and hence the **resultant force** on the drop **decreases**. Soon, the **weight** of the drop is **equal in magnitude** but **opposite in direction** to the opposing frictional force; the **resultant force** and **acceleration** are then **zero** and the velocity no longer increases. This maximum velocity reached is known as the **terminal velocity**.
  (1st law: $F_R = 0$ if $a = 0$)

- As a child springs upward from a trampoline, an upward force from the trampoline acts on his/her feet resulting in an acceleration.
  (2nd law: $F_R = ma$)

  The force exerted by the **child** on the **trampoline** is equal but opposite in direction to the force exerted by the **trampoline** on the **child**.
  (3rd law: action = reaction)

- As water spouts from a rotating garden sprinkler, the force of the **sprinkler on** the **water** results in an equal but oppositely directed force of the **water** on the **sprinkler**. This causes the sprinkler arm to rotate.
  (3rd law: action = reaction)

- A stone being **whirled in a circle** at the end of a string is constantly **changing direction** and therefore **changing velocity** (recall that velocity is a vector). It is therefore accelerating (even though its speed, which is not a vector, may be constant). It accelerates under the influence of the tension in the string (see centripetal force on page 356).
  (2nd law $F_R = ma$).

Example 1

Cimron pushes a block of weight 40 N across the floor using a force of 26 N (see Figure 16.4). The frictional force opposing the motion is 14 N. Determine the acceleration.

Solution:

When forces are in perpendicular directions, we can analyse in those directions separately.

- **Vertically** – acceleration is zero, and therefore the resultant vertical force must also be zero. (Newton's 1st law: $F_R = 0$ if $a = 0$)
  The weight must be equal, but opposite in direction to the normal reaction so that they cancel.
- **Horizontally** – there is a resultant force, and therefore an acceleration.

$$\text{weight} = \text{mass} \times \text{acceleration due to gravity}$$

Therefore $\text{mass} = \dfrac{\text{weight}}{\text{acceleration due to gravity}}$

So mass $m = \dfrac{40\ \text{N}}{10\ \text{m/s}^2}$

$$m = 4.0\ \text{kg}$$

resultant force $F_R = ma$

$$26\ \text{N} - 14\ \text{N} = 4.0\ \text{kg} \times a$$

$$\dfrac{12\ \text{N}}{4.0\ \text{kg}} = a$$

$$3.0\ \text{m/s}^2 = a$$

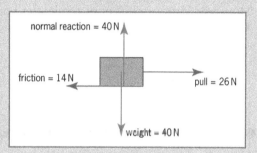

Figure 16.4 *Example 1*

More on friction

Advantages

- Friction provided by the brakes of vehicles **reduces speed.**
- Friction between tyres and road surfaces allows cars to **go round corners** and to **accelerate.**
- Friction enables us to **walk** and **run** as explained in the application of Newton's 3rd law above.
- Friction helps us to **grip objects**, preventing them from slipping away.

Disadvantages

- Friction **makes us do more work** when we try to slide objects across surfaces.
- Tyres with **worn treads** can **cause accidents** since they do not provide sufficient friction.
- Friction **produces heat**, which can affect the proper functioning of machinery.
- Friction **erodes** and can **destroy surfaces.**
- Friction **shortens the lives of electric motors** by increasing the loads they must overcome.

Reducing friction

- **Lubricating oil** or **grease** can provide a layer between surfaces to reduce friction.
- **Sanding** or **polishing** surfaces reduces friction by making the surfaces smooth.
- **Streamlined shapes** reduce frictional drag forces on bodies moving through fluids.
- **Rollers** placed under objects reduce friction by preventing their surfaces from **sliding** over other surfaces. Vehicles have wheels for a similar reason.

Aerodynamic lift force on the wings of planes and birds

As the wing of a plane moves forward, air moves smoothly along its gently sloped, **streamlined** surface. Air over the wing moves faster than air under the wing because it travels a longer path. Since air above the wing is then more spread out, it exerts less pressure and the excess pressure from below produces an upward force known as the lift force (see Figure 16.5). Birds can glide through the air for a similar reason.

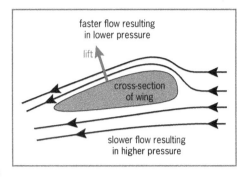

Figure 16.5 *Aerodynamic lift*

- Figure 16.6 shows an aircraft moving with constant horizontal velocity. Since the acceleration is zero, the resultant force must also be zero. The engine thrust and the drag force must therefore cancel each other. (1st law: $F_R = 0$ if $a = 0$)

- However, if the aircraft now **accelerates horizontally**, the **resultant force will no longer be zero** and so the forward thrust of the engine would be greater than the frictional drag. (2nd law: $F_R = ma$)

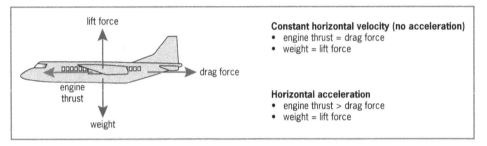

Figure 16.6 *Forces on aircraft in horizontal flight*

Effect of winds on motion of aircraft

A **tailwind** blows in the direction of travel of the aircraft and tends to **increase** its speed.

A **headwind** blows in the opposite direction to the aircraft and tends to **reduce** its speed.

A **crosswind** tends to cause the aircraft to **shift off course**. Figure 16.7 shows how the pilot must steer the plane through a crosswind blowing due north in order to continue its motion due east.

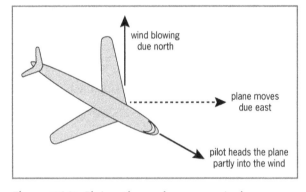

Figure 16.7 *Flying through a crosswind*

Gravitational force

*Gravitational force is the **attractive** force between bodies due to their **masses**.*

- Planets of **larger mass** exert **greater gravitational forces**. The weight of a body on Earth is about 6 times its weight on the Moon, since the mass of the Earth is about 6 times that of the Moon.

- The **further apart** objects are, the **smaller are the gravitational forces** on them. As a rocket rises above the Earth, the gravitational force on it decreases until it becomes zero in outer space. However, it still has the same mass since it is still made of the same quantity of matter.

See Chapter 15, page 335.

Example 2

The acceleration due to gravity on Earth is 10 m/s², on Mars it is 3.7 m/s² and in outer space it is 0 m/s². Determine the weight of a body of mass 5.0 kg:

a on Earth   **b** on Mars   **c** in outer space.

Solution:

a weight = 5.0 kg × 10 m/s² = 50 N

b weight = 5.0 kg × 3.7 m/s² = 18.5 N

c weight = 5.0 kg × 0 m/s² = 0 N

Centre of gravity

*The **centre of gravity** of a body is the point through which the **resultant** gravitational force on the body may be **considered** to act.*

Each atom or molecule has its own weight. The centre of gravity (C of G) is that point where the resultant of all these forces **appears to act** (see Figure 16.8).

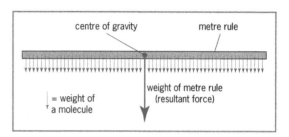

Figure 16.8 *Centre of gravity*

Location of the centre of gravity of regular shapes and solids

The centre of gravity of a **regular shape**, such as a circle or square, and a **regular solid**, such as a sphere or cube, is at its **geometric centre** if made of a material of **uniform density** throughout. Its location for various shapes is described below.

Shapes

- **Rectangle:** intersection of the diagonals.
- **Triangle:** intersection of its medians (lines drawn from the vertices to **bisect** the opposite sides).
- **Circle:** midpoint of its diameter.

Solids

- **Uniform thin rod:** on the midpoint of its length along its axis.
- **Non-uniform thin rod:** the point where a fine edge placed under the rod keeps it in balance.
- **Uniform cuboid:** the point of intersection of its diagonals from opposite vertices.
- **Uniform sphere:** the midpoint of its diameter.

Experiment to find the centre of gravity of an irregularly shaped lamina

- Hang a lamina so that it can swing freely from a pin placed through a small hole near its edge.
- Hang a plumbline (a small weight attached at one end of a string) from the pin and mark its position with small crosses on the lamina.
- Repeat the procedure by suspending the lamina from another hole near its edge.
- The centre of gravity is at the point of intersection of the drawn lines.
- Repeat the procedure once more from a third point near the edge of the lamina to check that the third line drawn across the lamina intersects at the same point as the first two (see Figure 16.9).

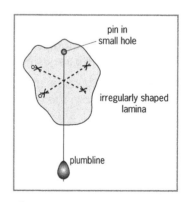

Figure 16.9 *Finding the centre of gravity of an irregular lamina*

Centripetal force and circular motion

*A **centripetal force** is the force on an object that is necessary to keep it moving in **circular motion**.*

A centripetal force always acts towards the **centre** of curvature of the path. It **increases** under any of the following conditions.

1. The **mass** of the object **increases**.
2. The **speed** of the object **increases**.
3. The **radius** of the curved path **decreases**.

Figure 16.10 shows different situations involving centripetal force.

For example, consider a ball at the end of a string being **whirled in a horizontal circle**. The string pulls outwards **on the hand**, but also exerts an inwards **centripetal force on the ball** towards the **centre of the circular path**. Releasing the string reduces the force in it to zero. The ball shoots off at a tangent to the circle and then takes a curved path to the ground due to the Earth's gravitational force.

Similarly, a car **moving around a curve** requires a **centripetal force** to do so. This force is caused by **friction** between the tyres and the road surface. If oil is spilled on the road, the reduced friction would not be sufficient to maintain circular motion and the vehicle will slide off at a tangent to the curve.

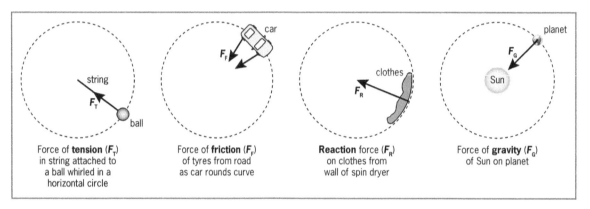

Figure 16.10 *Various types of forces acting as centripetal forces*

Satellites depend on **the force of gravity** to provide the **centripetal force** to keep them in orbit.

• To **remain in orbit**, the gravitational force must be **equal** to the required centripetal force.
• If the gravitational force is **larger**, the satellite will **spiral inwards** until it crashes to the planet.
• If it is **smaller**, the satellite will **move outwards into space**.

Moments, equilibrium and stability

When we open a door, sit on a seesaw, use a spanner, raise the handles of a wheelbarrow or use a bottle opener, we are using forces that have a **turning effect** or **moment** about some point (a **pivot**).

*The **moment** of a force about a point is the **product** of the **force** and the **perpendicular distance** of its line of action from the point.*

$$\text{moment} = \text{force} \times \text{perpendicular distance from force to pivot} \qquad M = Fd_\perp$$

The **SI unit** of moment is the **newton metre (N m)**. Other units may be used, such as **N cm**.

Note: Work (see Chapter 10) is the product of a force and the **distance moved in the direction** of the force. Its unit is also the newton metre. To indicate the difference between moment and work, the unit joule (J) is assigned to work.

Example 3

The trapdoor shown in Figure 16.11 is uniform and of mass 1600 g. Calculate the following.

a The weight of the trapdoor.

b The **anti-clockwise moment** about the hinge exerted by the force of 8 N.

c The **clockwise moment** about the hinge created by the weight of the trapdoor.

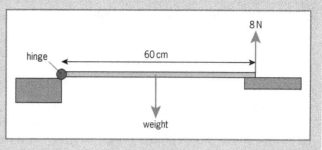

Figure 16.11 *Example 3*

Solution:

a First express the mass in kg: 1600 g = 1.6 kg

Then weight = mass × acceleration due to gravity = $1.6 \text{ kg} \times 10 \dfrac{m}{s^2} = 16 \text{ N}$

b Anticlockwise moment about hinge = 8 N × 60 cm = 480 N cm

c Since the door is **uniform**, the centre of gravity is in the middle, i.e. 30 cm from the hinge.

∴ clockwise moment about hinge = 16 N × 30 cm = 480 N cm

Note: Since moments are taken about the hinge, we measure each distance from the force to the hinge.

Conditions for equilibrium under the action of coplanar parallel forces

Coplanar forces are those which act in the **same plane**.

1. The sum of the **forces in any direction** is equal to the sum of the **forces in the opposite direction**.
2. The sum of the **clockwise moments** about any point is equal to the sum of the **anti-clockwise moments** about that same point.

For a system of coplanar **parallel forces in equilibrium**, this second rule is known as the **principle of moments**.

Example 4

To verify the principle of moments

A uniform metre rule of weight 4 N is suspended from its midpoint by a small piece of string attached to a spring balance.

Objects of weight 8 N and 6 N are now hung from the rule using two additional pieces of string and their positions are adjusted until the rule is once more horizontal (see Figure 16.12).

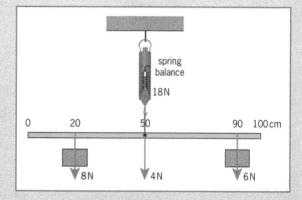

Figure 16.12 *Example 4*

The following observations are noted:

1. sum of **upward forces** = sum of **downward forces**

reading on spring balance = 8 N + 4 N + 6 N

18 N = 18 N

The free-body diagram: First, insert the non-contact force (weight or gravitational force ON THE RULE) and then the THREE contact forces where the attached strings are pulling ON THE RULE.

2. sum of **anti-clockwise moments** = sum of **clockwise moments** ... (about centre of rule)

$$8 \text{ N} \times (50 - 20) \text{ cm} = 6 \text{ N} \times (90 - 50) \text{ cm}$$

$$8 \text{ N} \times 30 \text{ cm} = 6 \text{ N} \times 40 \text{ cm}$$

$$240 \text{ N cm} = 240 \text{ N cm}$$

Note: We have taken moments about the centre of the metre rule. The weight of the rule (4 N) and the tension (18 N) in the string attached to the spring balance have no moment since these forces pass through the pivot and therefore have no distance from the pivot. Moments about the centre are only due to the 8 N and 6 N forces.

Example 5

Figure 16.13 shows blocks A and B resting on a uniform metre rule of weight 2 N.

a Redraw the diagram and insert FOUR arrows to indicate:

i the weight (force of gravity) **of the rule**

ii the forces of A and B **on the rule**

iii the force (*R*) of the triangular pivot pressing **on the rule**.

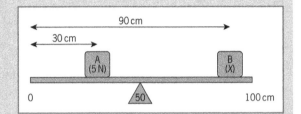

Figure 16.13 *Example 5*

b Calculate *X* by taking **moments** about the 50 cm mark.

c Calculate *R* by equating the **upward** and **downward forces.**

Solution:

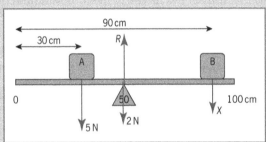

a Figure 16.14 *Example 5 solution*

Note where each of the arrows **originates** in this free-body diagram.

b sum of **anti-clockwise moments** = sum of **clockwise moments** ... (about centre of rule)

$$5 \text{ N} \times (50 - 30) \text{ cm} = X \times (90 - 50) \text{ cm}$$

$$5 \text{ N} \times 20 \text{ cm} = X \times 40 \text{ cm}$$

$$100 \text{ N cm} = 40X \text{ cm}$$

$$\frac{100 \text{ N cm}}{40 \text{ cm}} = X$$

$$2.5 \text{ N} = X$$

sum of **upward forces** = sum of **downward forces**

$$R = 5 \text{ N} + 2 \text{ N} + 2.5 \text{ N}$$

$$R = 9.5 \text{ N}$$

Stable, unstable and neutral equilibrium

A body is in **stable equilibrium** if, when slightly displaced, its **centre of gravity rises** and a **restoring moment** is created which returns it to its original equilibrium position (its base).

A body is in **unstable equilibrium** if, when slightly displaced, its **centre of gravity falls** and a **toppling moment** is created which removes it from its original equilibrium position.

A body is in **neutral equilibrium** if, when slightly displaced, its **centre of gravity remains** at the same level and **no moment** is created, leaving the body in the displaced position.

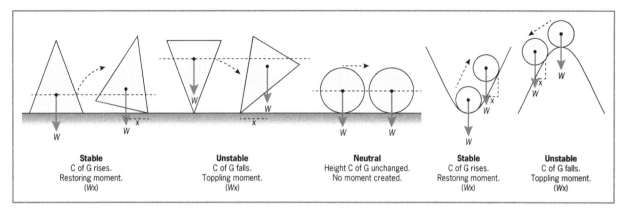

Figure 16.15 *Stable, unstable and neutral equilibrium*

Factors affecting the stability of an object

Figure 16.16 shows how the following factors affect stability.

1. Height of centre of gravity.

2. Width of base.

3. Weight.

- Go-karts have wide wheelbases and low centres of gravity in order to be more stable. When tilted, restoring moments are created which return them to their bases.

- Large cargo buses have their baggage compartments below the floor in order to lower their centres of gravity so as to enhance stability.

- A larger weight increases the restoring moment of a stable body thereby increasing its stability. It also increases the toppling moment of an unstable body, thereby decreasing its stability.

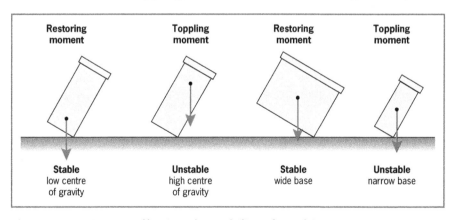

Figure 16.16 *Factors affecting the stability of an object*

Maximum loading capacity and tare weight

Loading the top of a vehicle such as a van or bus raises its centre of gravity, making it less stable. Commercial vehicles therefore cannot exceed a maximum loading capacity. Their **tare weight** (unloaded weight) and their **maximum loaded weight** must be clearly marked on their sides for inspection by users.

Other applications of equilibrium

Homeostasis and biological equilibrium

Homeostasis is the self-regulating process by which biological systems maintain stability by monitoring and maintaining the various **physiological** and **behavioural** processes necessary for them **to function optimally**.

Key applications are outlined in Table 16.2.

Table 16.2 *Applications of equilibrium in the body*

Osmoregulation	Our kidneys are important in maintaining the **balance of water and electrolytes** in the body. They ensure that cells neither swell nor shrink excessively and so can function normally.
pH regulation	Maintaining a suitable **balance between acids and bases** is accomplished by buffering systems, respiratory control of carbon dioxide and regulation of hydrogen and bicarbonate ions by the **kidney**.
Hormonal regulation	**Hormones** such as insulin and glucagon **regulate glucose levels** when blood sugar levels rise. Other hormones regulate other equilibria.
Blood pressure regulation	Signals sent from the **hypothalamus** to the heart, blood vessels and kidneys help **maintain blood pressure** within a range that prevents **hypertension** (high blood pressure) and **hypotension** (low blood pressure).
Thermoregulation	In order to maintain body temperature between 36.5 °C and 37.5 °C, our **central nervous system** sends information from temperature receptors in our body to the hypothalamus in the brain. The information is processed and appropriate responses to increase or decrease the temperature are sent to trigger necessary actions. If **too cold**, increased metabolic rate (shivering) or the constricting of blood vessels can be performed. If **too hot**, the body can sweat and dilate blood vessels to increase heat loss. A **behavioural response** may also be triggered, causing the person to seek shade or to drink water.
Pharmaconetics	The **equilibrium between drug concentration** in the bloodstream and its **target site** requires knowledge of the kinetics and dynamics of drug distribution, absorption, metabolism and excretion.
Respiratory regulation	**Equilibrium between carbon dioxide and oxygen** is crucial for efficient gas exchange. Carbon dioxide diffuses from blood to alveolar gas and oxygen diffuses into the blood to oxygenate our tissues.

Reversible reactions and chemical equilibrium

Reversible reactions are those in which the conversion of reactants to products and the conversion of products to reactants occur simultaneously. For example:

ammonium chloride $\rightleftharpoons$ ammonia + hydrogen chloride

When the reaction begins, the forward reaction occurs faster since there are no products yet. However, as the reaction proceeds, the rate of the backward reaction increases and the rate of the forward reaction decreases, until the rates of reaction are in **chemical equilibrium**. This condition can only be achieved if the reaction takes place in a **closed container**, so that the **concentrations of the products and the reactants** remain constant.

Linear momentum

*The **linear momentum** of a body is the product of its mass and velocity.*

$$\text{momentum} = \text{mass} \times \text{velocity} \qquad p = m \times v$$

SI unit of momentum: Since momentum = mass × velocity, the unit of momentum is **kg m/s**.

Example 6

If Usain Bolt has a mass of 90 kg, calculate his momentum when running at a speed of 12.4 m/s.

Solution:

$p = m \times v$

$p = 90 \text{ kg} \times 12.4 \dfrac{m}{s}$

$p = 1116 \text{ kg m/s}$

Example 7

Car A of mass 2000 kg moves east at 20 m/s and car B of mass 2400 kg moves west at the same speed (see Figure 16.17). What is their total momentum?

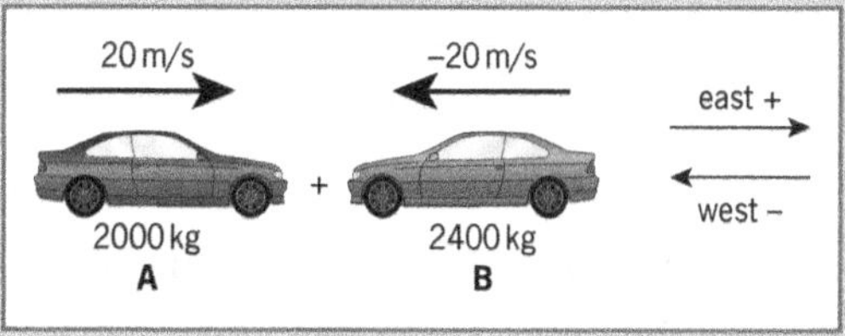

Solution:

Since the cars move in opposite directions, we can designate **east as positive** and **west as negative**.

Figure 16.17 *Example 7*

$p = (m_A \times v_A) + (m_B \times v_B)$

$p = (2000 \text{ kg} \times 20 \text{ m/s}) + (2400 \text{ kg} \times -20 \text{ m/s})$

$p = 40\,000 \text{ kg m/s} - 48\,000 \text{ kg m/s}$

$p = -8000 \text{ kg m/s}$

Total momentum: **magnitude:** 8000 kg m/s   **direction:** to the west

Note: we drop the negative sign since it simply means 'west'.

Conservation of momentum

*The **law of conservation of linear momentum** states that for a system of colliding objects, their **total momentum before** the collision is equal to their **total momentum after** the collision.*

Example 8

A toy car of mass 2 kg and speed 8 m/s to the right, collides head-on with another of the same mass which is initially stationary. Determine the following.

a The total momentum before the collision.

b The total momentum after the collision.

c The magnitude (size) of their common velocity after the collision if they stick together.

d The magnitude (size) of the velocity of B after the collision if A becomes stationary.

Solution:

a Total momentum before the collision (taking to the right as positive) is given by:

$p = (m_A \times v_A) + (m_B \times v_B)$

$p = (2 \text{ kg} \times 8 \text{ m/s}) + (2 \text{ kg} \times 0 \text{ m/s})$

$p = 16 \text{ kg m/s} + 0 \text{ kg m/s}$

$p = 16 \text{ kg m/s}$ **direction:** to the right

b From the principle of conservation of linear momentum, the **total momentum after the collision** must also be 16 kg m/s to the right.

c After the collision, the masses are **stuck together** and therefore have a **common velocity, v** (see Figure 16.18).

$p = (m_A + m_B)v$

$16 \text{ kg m/s} = (2 \text{ kg} + 2 \text{ kg})v$

$16 \text{ kg m/s} = (4 \text{ kg})v$

$v = \dfrac{16 \text{ kg m/s}}{4 \text{ kg}}$

$v = 4 \text{ m/s}$ to the right

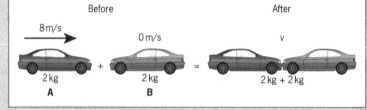

Figure 16.18 *Example 8c solution*

d After the collision, **A becomes stationary** (see Figure 16.19):

$p = (m_A \times v_A) + (m_B \times v_B)$

$16 \text{ kg m/s} = (2 \text{ kg} \times 0 \text{ m/s}) + (2 \text{ kg} \times v)$

$16 \text{ kg m/s} = 0 + (2 \text{ kg} \times v)$

$16 \text{ kg m/s} = (2 \text{ kg} \times v)$

$\dfrac{16 \text{ kg m/s}}{2 \text{ kg}} = v$

magnitude: 8 m/s

direction: to the right

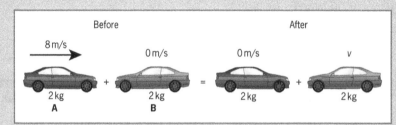

Figure 16.19 *Example 8d solution*

Machines

*A **machine** is a device that makes doing work (transferring energy) **easier**.*

A machine **does not make work less**; it simply **alters the force and distance components** of work.

Recall Chapter 8 page 140: **work** (or **energy**) = **force** × **distance** (in direction of force)

Say an object of weight 20 N is to be raised through a distance of 4 m.

Actual job without a machine is calculated as: work or energy output = 20 N × 4 m = 80 J

With a machine A, this may be calculated as: work or energy input = 10 N × 8 m = 80 J

With a machine B, this may be calculated as: work or energy input = 40 N × 2 m = 80 J

- **Load** is the force to be overcome without the use of the machine (usually the weight of the object). In the above example, the load is 20 N.
- **Effort** is the force required when using the machine. In the above example, the effort using machine A is 10 N and using machine B is 40 N.

For simplicity of the calculations, it was assumed that there is no energy lost due to friction or any resistance when using machines, A and B.

Force and distance multipliers

*A **force multiplier** is a machine that alters the forces so that the effort is **smaller** than the load.*

Machine A is a **force multiplier**. It is particularly useful if the user is not strong enough to apply 20 N and would like to **reduce the force**. However, by using **half the force**, the object must now be moved through **twice the distance**.

*A **distance multiplier** is a machine in which the distance moved by the effort is **smaller** than the distance moved by the load.*

Machine B is a **distance multiplier.** It is useful if the user has no problem with the force but would like to **reduce the distance** through which the force must be moved. The actual job requires a distance of 4 m, but using this machine the user only needs to push the object through 2 m.

Work or energy conversion

*Useful work or energy output is the work or energy converted in moving the **load without the machine**.*

useful energy output = load × distance moved by load

*Work or energy input is the work or energy converted by the **effort** in **using the machine**.*

energy input = effort × distance moved by effort

*The **law of conservation of energy** states that energy cannot be created or destroyed but can be transformed from one type to another.*

The total energy input must be equal to the total energy output. However, only part of the output is **useful** since some is always **wasted** due to friction or resistive forces other than the load.

Efficiency of a machine expressed as a percentage

$$\text{efficiency} = \frac{\text{useful work (energy) output}}{\text{work (energy) input}} \times 100\%$$

$$\text{efficiency} = \frac{\text{load} \times \text{distance moved by load}}{\text{effort} \times \text{distance moved by effort}} \times 100\%$$

At times, calculations may be simplified by assuming that the machine is 'ideal' (100% efficient) and there is no loss of energy output.

Inefficiencies of machines and ways to overcome them

Table 16.3 *Inefficiencies and ways to overcome them*

Factors causing inefficiency	Overcoming the inefficiency
Friction wastes energy in bearings, joints, gear wheels, axles of pulleys, pistons and cylinders.	• **Lubricating oil** will reduce friction. • A **fine powder** reduces friction on inclined planes.
Corrosion leads to instability and increased friction.	• **Rustproofing** of iron or steel parts using special paints and greases prevents corrosion.
The weight of the lower rising block (the moving harness holding the lower pulley/s) of a pulley system adds to the load. See Figure 16.25 on page 367 (block and tackle).	• These pulleys and their harnesses should be made of **light materials** such as aluminium.

Mechanical advantage

Mechanical advantage is the force amplification benefit to the user of a machine.

• Mechanical advantage (MA): $\mathbf{MA = \dfrac{load}{effort}}$

• If the MA of a machine **decreases**, it indicates that the machine is becoming **less efficient**.

Three simple machines

Table 16.4 *Three simple machines*

Levers	Levers each consist of a rigid beam or rod that can rotate on a fixed pivot. An effort applied at one point along the beam or rod can move a load from some other point along it. Figures 16.20 to 16.24 on pages 365 and 366 show the various classes into which levers may be divided, with reference to practical levers commonly encountered and levers of the mammalian skeleton.	
Inclined planes	Inclined planes each have a flat, sloping surface along which an object can be pushed or pulled to a higher level; for example, from the road into the back of a truck. The longer the slope, the more gradual it is, and the easier it becomes to force the object up the incline.	
Pulleys	Pulleys each consist of a wheel on an axle that carries a rope (string or belt) wrapped around its circumference. An effort applied to one end of the rope (string belt) creates a tension that is transmitted throughout its length and moves an attached load. Pulleys are particularly useful in raising loads through large distances. Systems of several pulleys can be arranged to lift very heavy loads, as shown in Figures 16.25 and 16.26 on pages 367 and 368.	

Types of levers

Levers may be divided into three classes depending on the relative positions of the pivot and the points of application of the effort and load.

Table 16.5 *Distinguishing the classes of lever*

Class 1	Load and effort are on different sides of pivot.	Effort can be lesser or greater than load.
Class 2	Load is between effort and pivot.	Effort is always less than load.
Class 3	Effort is between load and pivot.	Effort is always more than load.

In each case shown in Figures 16.20 to 16.24, an effort (*E*) is balancing a load (*L*) and the lever is pivoted at P.

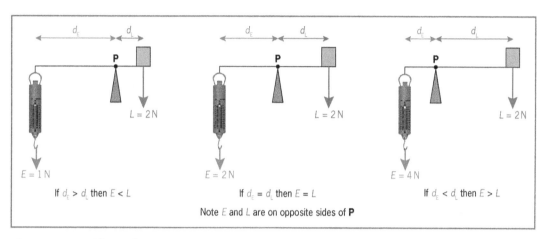

Figure 16.20 *Class 1 lever*

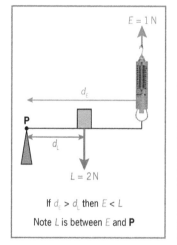 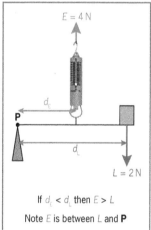

Figure 16.21 *Class 2 lever*   Figure 16.22 *Class 3 lever*

Notes:

- **Class 1 levers** can be **force** or **distance multipliers**.
- **Class 2 levers** are always **force multipliers**.
- **Class 3 levers** are always **distance multipliers**.

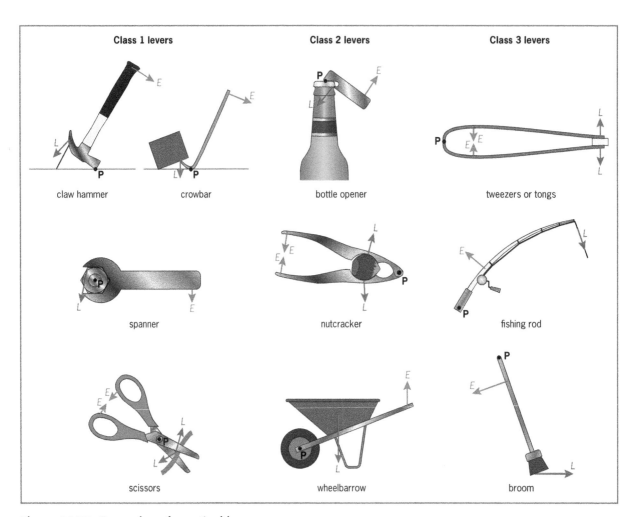

Figure 16.23 *Examples of practical levers*

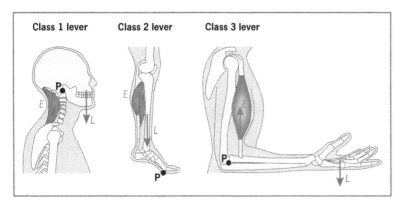

Figure 16.24 *Levers in the mammalian skeleton*

A closer look at pulleys

- For simplicity, the following pulley systems are assumed to be 'ideal' (completely efficient) and therefore the work or **energy input** is **equal** to the work or **energy output**.

- An **effort** applied to the string sets up an **equal tension** within it. It is the tensions, (**T**), which **raise the load, (L)**.

In each pulley system of Figure 16.25, the **sum** of the **tensions**, (**T**), **raising the load** is equal to the **load, (L)**, and therefore the greater the number of strings raising the load, the smaller is the required effort.

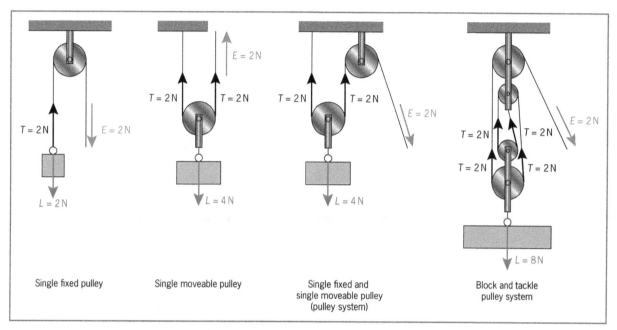

Figure 16.25 *Different types of pulley arrangements*

Single fixed pulley

- The **load is equal to the effort** and $MA = \dfrac{L}{E} = \dfrac{2\,N}{2\,N} = 1$

There are two reasons why we would use this pulley although the effort is not less than the load.

1. The user may use his/her body weight to provide part of the effort since he/she is pulling downward.

2. Loads may be raised to great heights without the user having to move through those heights.

Single moving pulley

- The **load is twice the effort** and $MA = \dfrac{L}{E} = \dfrac{4\,N}{2\,N} = 2$

Single moving and single fixed pulley

This is like the single moving pulley except that the user can stand on the ground and pull downward using his/her weight to provide the effort.

- The **load is twice the effort** and $MA = \dfrac{L}{E} = \dfrac{4\,N}{2\,N} = 2$

Fixed and moving pulleys – block and tackle

- In the block and tackle of Figure 16.25, the **load is four times the effort** and MA $= \dfrac{L}{E} = \dfrac{8\,N}{2\,N} = 4$

Draglines use pulley systems

Figure 16.26 shows a mechanised dragline excavator that is used in large-scale works. It has a scoop attached only by cables and is controlled by a system of pulleys, chains and ropes that lift the scoop.

Figure 16.26 *Mechanised dragline excavator*

Gears

Figure 16.27 shows connected cogged wheels having identically spaced teeth. The wheel with the lesser number of teeth will spin faster than the other.

A **bicycle** regulates its gears in this way. The pedals produce a rotation in the larger cogged wheel, which causes rotation of the back wheel connected to it via the chain.

From the diagram, for every one revolution of the pedals, the back wheel makes 1.5 rotations.

$$\text{gear ratio} = \frac{\text{no. of teeth of driving wheel}}{\text{no. of teeth of driven wheel}} = \frac{24}{16} = 1.5$$

By switching between several cogged wheels, different gear ratios can be produced.

Gears in the transmission of a car work with the same basic principle. As the pistons of the engine move up and down, they transfer their motion via a crank shaft to the **driving cogged wheel** which then relays motion to the **driven cogged wheel**.

driving cogged wheel connected to pedals

driven cogged wheel connected to back wheel of bicycle

chain

16 teeth

24 teeth

Figure 16.27 *Cogged wheels of a bicycle*

Example 9

Mohammed uses a bar as a lever to lift a stone of weight 400 N through a distance of 15 cm. He exerts an effort of 100 N through a distance of 75 cm. Determine the following.

a The useful energy converted in lifting the **load.**

b The energy converted by the **effort** using the machine.

c The efficiency.

d The mechanical advantage.

Solution:

a Useful energy converted in lifting the load = load × distance moved by load

$$= 400 \text{ N} \times 0.15 \text{ m} = 60 \text{ J}$$

b Energy converted by the effort using the machine = effort × distance moved by effort

$$= 100 \text{ N} \times 0.75 \text{ m} = 75 \text{ J}$$

c Efficiency = $\dfrac{\text{useful work (energy) output}}{\text{work (energy) input}}$ × 100% = $\dfrac{60 \text{ J}}{75 \text{ J}}$ × 100% = 80%

d Mechanical advantage = $\dfrac{\text{load}}{\text{effort}} = \dfrac{400 \text{ N}}{100 \text{ N}} = 4$

Example 10

Figure 16.28 shows a block of mass 6 kg being raised to a height of 2 m using an **inclined plane**. The block is pushed by an effort of 15 N up the incline through a distance of 10 m.

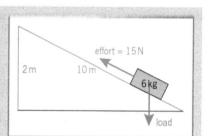

a Calculate the following.

  i The weight of the load.

  ii The energy converted if the block was lifted vertically.

  iii The energy converted by the effort in using the machine.

  iv The efficiency.

Figure 16.28 *Example 10*

b Which is less, the useful work output or the work input?

c Account for the difference between the work output and work input.

d How does the user benefit by using such a ramp?

e Is this machine a force multiplier or distance multiplier?

f Calculate the mechanical advantage.

Solution:

a i weight = mg ∴ weight = 6 kg × 10 $\dfrac{\text{m}}{\text{s}^2}$ = 60 N

  ii useful energy output = load × distance moved by load

$$= 60 \text{ N} \times 2 \text{ m} = 120 \text{ J} \quad \dots \text{(use the force and distance that are } \textbf{parallel})$$

  iii energy input = effort × distance moved by effort

$$= 15 \text{ N} \times 10 \text{ m} = 150 \text{ J} \quad \dots \text{(use the force and distance that are } \textbf{parallel})$$

  iv Efficiency = $\dfrac{\text{useful energy output}}{\text{energy input}}$ × 100%

$$= \dfrac{120 \text{ J}}{150 \text{ J}} \times 100\% = 80\%$$

b The useful work output is less. You can never get out more than you put in!

c The energy input of 150 J was partly converted to useful energy output of 120 J. The remaining 30 J was wasted as heat and sound due to friction between the block and the incline.

energy input (150 J) → **useful** energy output (120 J) + **wasted** energy output (30 J)

d The user benefits by using the ramp since, although the work input is greater than the work output (150 J > 120 J), the required **effort of 15 N** is much less than the **load of 60 N.**

e It is a force multiplier since the effort of 15 N seemingly amplifies to raise the larger load of 60 N.

f Mechanical advantage $= \dfrac{\text{load}}{\text{effort}} = \dfrac{60\ \text{N}}{15\ \text{N}} = 4$

Recalling facts

1 **a** Define force.

b Give TWO examples of contact forces and TWO examples of non-contact forces.

c Why is force considered a vector quantity?

2 State Newton's THREE laws of motion.

3 **a** Define friction.

b State TWO of EACH of the following:

  i benefits of friction.   **ii** problems of friction.

c State THREE ways by which friction can be reduced.

4 **a** Identify the forces A, B, C and D in the free body diagram of Figure 16.29 to show the engine thrust, weight, lift force and drag force.

b Figure 16.30 shows the cross-section of an aircraft wing.

  i Redraw the diagram to show the air flow above and below the wing as the wing moves to the right.

  ii Where is the air flow fastest?

  iii Where is the air pressure lowest?

  iv Indicate on the diagram the direction of the force caused by the difference in pressures.

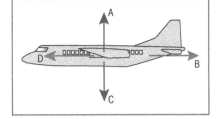

Figure 16.29 *Question 4a*

Figure 16.30 *Question 4b*

5 **a** Define the centre of gravity of a body.

b Briefly describe how you can find the centre of gravity of a non-uniform rod.

6 **a** What is a centripetal force?

b Jaden ties a stone to the end of a string and whirls it in a horizontal circle above his head. How would **increasing** EACH of the following affect the force (tension) in the string?

    i The speed of the stone.

    ii The length of the string.

    iii The mass of the stone.

c What provides the centripetal force for each of the following motions?

    i The Moon in orbit around the Earth.

    ii A car going around a bend on a level road.

7 **a** Define the moment of a force about a point.

b State an appropriate SI unit for a *moment*.

c State the TWO conditions necessary for equilibrium under the action of coplanar parallel forces.

8 **a** Define EACH of the following types of equilibrium:

    i stable equilibrium   **ii** unstable equilibrium   **iii** neutral equilibrium.

b How do the following affect the stability of a body?

    i The height of its centre of gravity.

    ii The width of its base.

9 Draw a diagram to show that a moment is created when a body in stable equilibrium and initially resting on its base, is slightly displaced. Indicate any change in height of its centre of gravity.

10 **a** Define linear momentum.

b State an appropriate SI unit for momentum.

c Is momentum a scalar or a vector quantity?

d State the law of conservation of linear momentum.

11 Define the following:

a a machine (in terms of work)

b a force multiplier

c mechanical advantage.

12 **a** Distinguish between class 2 and class 3 levers.

b Which class of lever is always:

    i a force multiplier?

    ii a distance multiplier?

c Which of the following are class 2 levers? wheelbarrow, spanner, tweezers, scissors, nutcracker, hammer, bottle opener

d What class of lever is associated with each of the diagrams of the mammalian skeleton shown in Figure 16.31?

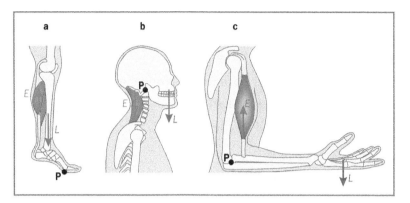

Figure 16.31 *Question 12*

Applying facts

13 A breadfruit has a mass of 2 kg on Earth and is taken to planet X where the gravitational pull is 10 times greater. On Earth, the acceleration due to gravity is 10 m/s².

a What is the weight of the breadfruit on Earth?

b On planet X, what is:

    i the mass of the breadfruit?   **ii** the weight of the breadfruit?

14 Jason drags a block of weight 25 N horizontally across a floor at constant velocity, using a horizontal string tied to one end of the block. The tension in the string is 12 N and there is a frictional force of 7 N.

a Besides the forces already mentioned, name the fourth force acting on the block and give its value.

b Draw a free body diagram of the block, showing the values of the FOUR forces acting.

15 What is the resultant **horizontal** force on each block shown in Figure 16.32?

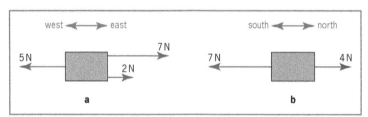

Figure 16.32 *Question 15*

16 State which of Newton's laws is applicable to EACH of the following situations.

   a As Xavier presses the throttle of his racing car, the backrest of his seat presses forward on him causing him to accelerate.

   b When the car reaches its top speed, there is no more acceleration and the resultant horizontal force on it becomes zero.

   c Xavier suddenly presses the brake, bringing the car to rest in a very short time. His body lunges forward, exerting a strong force on the seatbelt which simultaneously produces an intense force that presses back on him, bruising his chest.

17 **a** Tamesha, of mass 40 kg, accelerates down the slide at 6.0 m/s². Determine the resultant force causing her acceleration.

   b Anita's toy boat moves at constant speed of 2 m/s in a straight line (no acceleration).

   i What is the resultant force on the boat?

   ii If the forward force of the engine is 80 N, state, with a reason, the value of the drag force.

18 Figure 16.33 shows a uniform metre rule of weight 4 N with a load *L*, resting on it at the 80 cm mark. The system is in equilibrium.

   a At what position on the rule does its weight act?

   b Redraw the diagram and add an arrow to represent the third force necessary to sustain equilibrium.

   c Calculate the value of *L*.

   d What is the value of the third force mentioned in part **b**?

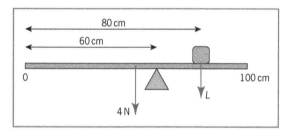

Figure 16.33 *Question 18*

19 Damani, a roller skater of mass 60 kg, is moving due east at 5.0 m/s when he crashes into Joan, of mass 40 kg, who was standing stationary. Joan immediately grabbed onto him and the two moved on together with a common velocity.

Determine the following.

   a The momentum of EACH immediately **before** the collision.

   b The **total** momentum immediately **before** the collision.

   c The **total** momentum immediately **after** the collision.

   d Their common velocity after the collision.

20 A block of mass 20 kg is to be raised through a height of 2 m. Natasha found it difficult to lift the block vertically and so she used the ramp shown in Figure 16.34.

a Determine the following.

  i The weight of the load.

  ii The energy used by the effort in pushing the block along the ramp (work input).

  iii The energy Natasha would have used if she had lifted the block vertically (work output).

  iv The mechanical advantage of the inclined plane.

  v The efficiency of the machine.

b By using the inclined plane, Natasha did more work than if she had lifted the block vertically. Explain why she still preferred to use the machine.

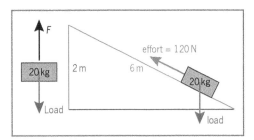

Figure 16.34 *Question 20*

Analysing data

21 Figure 16.35 shows a graph of load against effort when a machine was used to raise various objects.

a Determine the gradient (slope) of the graph.

b What does the gradient represent?

c What is the value of the load when the effort needed is 5 N?

d What load would correspond to an effort of 10 N?

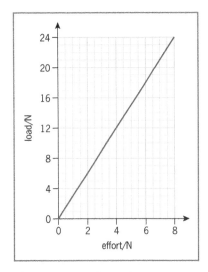

Figure 16.35 *Question 21*

The human skeleton

Learning objectives

- Relate the **structure** of the **skeleton** to its **functions**.
- Identify the different **types** of **joints** found in the **human skeleton**.
- Explain **how** the **skeletal muscles function** in the **movement** of a **limb**.

Structure of the human skeleton

The **human skeleton** serves as a **framework** for the body and is surrounded by skeletal muscles. The skeleton of an adult human is composed of 206 bones of different shapes and sizes, which are held together at **joints** by tough, elastic **ligaments**. **Movement** in humans is brought about by **skeletal muscles** working across these **joints**. The major bones of the skeleton are shown in Figure 16.36.

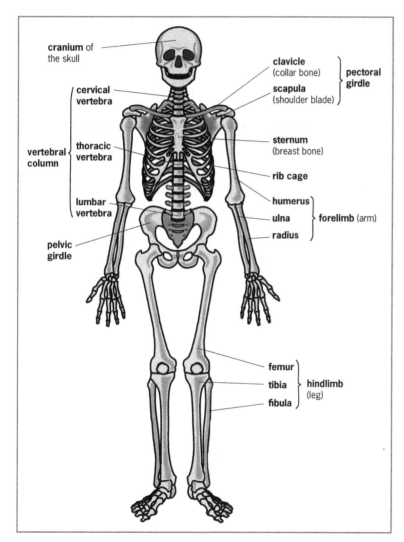

Figure 16.36 *The human skeleton*

The skeleton is made mainly from **two** types of tissues: **bone** and **cartilage**, and it can be divided into the **axial skeleton** and the **appendicular skeleton**.

The axial skeleton

The **axial skeleton** forms the central axis of the body and consists of the **skull**, the **vertebral column**, the **ribs** and the **sternum**. The **skull** is made up of the **cranium** and **upper jaw**, which are fused, and the **lower jaw**, which articulates with the upper jaw. The **cranium** consists of eight fused bones, and it encloses and protects the brain and sense organs of the head. Movement of the **lower jaw** enables a person to chew and talk.

The **vertebral column** or **spine** is composed of 33 bones known as **vertebrae**. The vertebrae of the neck are known as **cervical vertebrae**, those in the chest region are known as **thoracic vertebrae** and those of the lower back region are known as **lumbar vertebrae**. Each vertebra has a hole in the centre through which the **spinal cord** runs, and **intervertebral discs** of cartilage lie between adjacent vertebrae. These discs allow for some movement of the vertebral column and act as a cushion to **absorb shock**. The column supports the head and the body, protects the spinal cord which runs through it and allows some movement.

Twelve pairs of **ribs** are attached to the vertebral column, and together with the **sternum** or **breast bone**, they form the **rib cage**. The rib cage encloses and protects the heart, lungs and major blood vessels, and movements of the ribs and sternum are essential for **breathing**.

The appendicular skeleton

The **appendicular skeleton** consists of the **pectoral** and **pelvic girdles**, the **arms** (forelimbs) and the **legs** (hindlimbs). The **girdles** connect the limbs to the axial skeleton. The **pectoral girdle** is made up of two flat, triangular shaped **scapulae** or **shoulder blades** and two long, thin **clavicles** or **collar bones**. Each scapula has a socket for the ball of the humerus to fit into and articulate with. The **pelvic girdle** is a basin-shaped structure composed of two broad, flat **hip bones**. Each hip bone has a socket for the ball of the femur to fit into and articulate with. The hip bones are fused to the bottom of the vertebral column to provide **support** for the lower body and to transmit the **thrust** from the legs to the vertebral column, which moves the body forwards.

The **limbs** are composed of long bones which have **joints** between them to allow for easy **movement**. Each forelimb is made up of the **humerus**, **radius** and **ulna** and the bones of the wrist, hand and fingers. Each hindlimb is made up of the **femur**, **tibia** and **fibula** and the bones of the ankle, foot and toes. The main function of the **arms** is to grasp and manipulate objects, and the long bones allow the arms to have a long **reach**. The main functions of the **legs** are for support and movement, and the long bones permit long **strides** to be taken.

Functions of the skeleton

The human skeleton has **five** main functions.

Movement

The skeleton is jointed and muscles work across these joints to bring about **movement**. Most movement is brought about by the **legs** and **arms**, whilst the **vertebral column** allows some movement.

Protection

The skeleton provides **protection** for the internal organs of the body. The **skull** protects the brain and sense organs of the head, namely the eyes, ears, nasal cavities and tongue. The **vertebral column** protects the spinal cord. The **rib cage** and **sternum** protect the lungs, heart and major blood vessels. The **pelvic girdle** protects the internal reproductive organs, bladder and lower part of the digestive system.

Support

The skeleton **supports** the body's soft parts and internal organs, and it provides the framework that gives **shape** to the body. The **vertebral column**, **pelvic girdle** and **legs** are mainly responsible for providing support.

Production of blood cells

Red blood cells, most white blood cells and platelets are produced in the **red bone marrow**, which is found in the spongy bone inside **flat bones**, mainly the pelvis, scapula, ribs, sternum, cranium and vertebrae, and in the **ends** of the **long bones** of the limbs, mainly the humerus and femur.

Breathing

Alternate contractions of the internal and external intercostal muscles between the ribs bring about movements of the **rib cage**, which cause air to be drawn into the lungs during inhalation and expelled from the lungs during exhalation (see Table 9.15 on page 192).

Joints

*A **joint** is formed where two bones meet.*

Most joints allow the rigid skeleton to **move**. Based on their structure, joints can be classified into three types: fixed joints, partially movable joints and movable joints.

Fixed joints or fibrous joints

In **fixed joints**, the bones are joined firmly together by **fibrous connective tissue** that allows **no** movement. For example, the cranium of the skull is made of eight bones joined by fixed joints, as shown in Figure 16.37, and each hip bone of the pelvic girdle is made of three bones joined by fixed joints.

fixed joints between the bones of the cranium

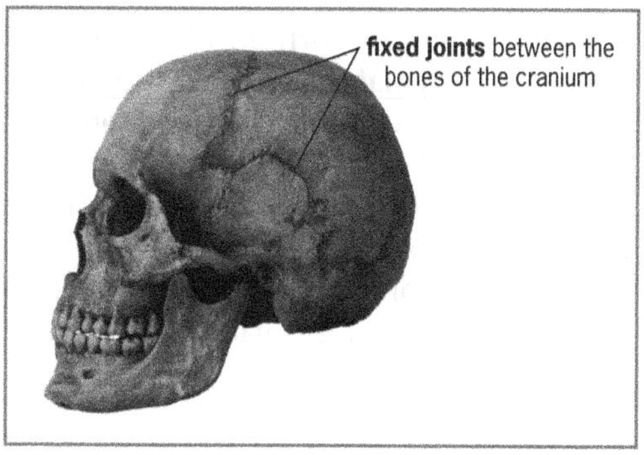

Figure 16.37 *Fixed joints between the bones of the cranium*

Partially movable joints or cartilaginous joints

In **partially movable** joints, the bones are separated by **cartilage pads** which allow **slight** movement. For example, the vertebrae that make up the vertebral column are separated by intervertebral discs of cartilage which allow limited movement.

Movable joints or synovial joints

Synovial joints are adapted to allow **friction-free** movement. In these joints, the articulating surfaces of the bones are covered with a layer of slippery cartilage known as **articular cartilage** and the bones are held together by tough, slightly elastic **ligaments** that form the **capsule** around the joint. The capsule is lined with the **synovial membrane** and the **synovial cavity** between the bones is filled with **synovial fluid**.

There are several different types of synovial joints including **hinge joints**, **ball and socket joints** and **gliding joints**. The structure of a hinge joint and a ball and socket joint, and the functions of the different parts are shown in Figure 16.38 on page 378.

* **Hinge joints** are formed where the **ends** of bones meet. They allow movement in **one plane** (direction) only. This limited movement provides **strength** and the joints are capable of bearing heavy loads. The elbow and knee joints, and the joints in the fingers and toes are all hinge joints.

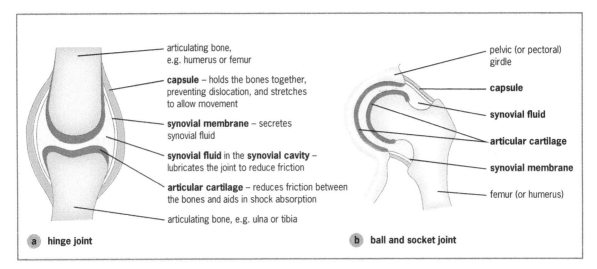

Figure 16.38 *Structure of a hinge joint and a ball and socket joint, and functions of the different parts*

- **Ball and socket joints** are formed where a **ball** at the end of one bone fits into a **socket** in the other bone. They allow **rotational** movement in **all planes**. This free range of movement provides less support and makes the joints more susceptible to dislocation than a hinge joint. The shoulder and hip joints are ball and socket joints.

- **Gliding joints** are formed where the articulating surfaces of bones are **flat** or **nearly flat**. They allow the bones to **glide** or **slide** past each other in various directions along the **same plane** as the articulating surfaces. The amount of movement in the joints is small compared with other types of synovial joints. Gliding joints are found between the bones that make up the wrists, the bones of the wrists and the hands (see Figure 16.39), the bones that make up the ankles and the bones of the ankles and feet. In all these places, the joints provide **flexibility** and **stability**.

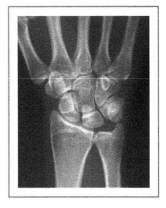

Figure 16.39 *Gliding joints are found between the bones of the wrist*

Movement of a limb

When a muscle contracts it **shortens** and exerts a **pull**, but it cannot exert a push when it relaxes, therefore it can pull a bone in one direction, but cannot push it back to its original position. Because of this, **two** muscles are always needed to produce movement at a movable joint. These muscles are known as an **antagonistic pair** because they work against each other. One member of the pair is known as the **flexor muscle** and the other is known as the **extensor muscle** (see Figure 16.40 on page 379).

- The **flexor muscle** is the muscle that brings about the **bending** of a hinge joint when it contracts, and when moving a ball and socket joint, it moves the arm or leg **forwards** at the shoulder or hip.

- The **extensor muscle** is the muscle that brings about the **straightening** of a hinge joint when it contracts, and when moving a ball and socket joint, it moves the arm or leg **backwards** at the shoulder or hip.

Both the flexor and the extensor muscles are attached, by **tendons**, to the bone that does not move at one of their ends and to the bone that does move at the other end. These points of attachment are known as the **origin** and **insertion** of the muscle. The **origin** is the point of attachment to the bone that does not move and it is usually as **far** away from the joint as possible. The **insertion** is the point of attachment to the bone that moves and it is usually very **close** to the joint. This arrangement maximises the **efficiency** and **effectiveness** of muscles to bring about movement.

Movement of the elbow joint

The **antagonistic pair** of muscles that bend and straighten the **elbow joint** are known as the **biceps muscle** and **triceps muscle**.

- The **biceps** is the **flexor** muscle.
- The **triceps** is the **extensor** muscle.

To **bend** the elbow joint, the **biceps contracts** and the triceps relaxes. To **straighten** the elbow joint, the **triceps contracts** and the biceps relaxes. This is illustrated in Figure 16.40.

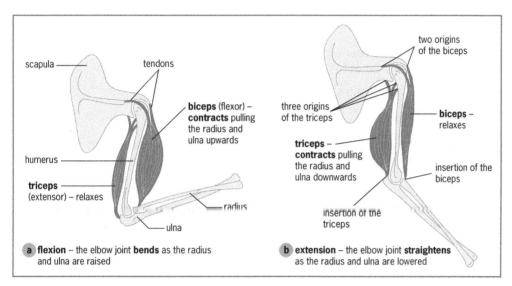

scapula

tendons

biceps (flexor) – **contracts** pulling the radius and ulna upwards

humerus

triceps (extensor) – relaxes

radius

ulna

a **flexion** – the elbow joint **bends** as the radius and ulna are raised

two origins of the biceps

three origins of the triceps

biceps – relaxes

triceps – **contracts** pulling the radius and ulna downwards

insertion of the biceps

insertion of the triceps

b **extension** – the elbow joint **straightens** as the radius and ulna are lowered

Figure 16.40 *Movement of the elbow joint*

Recalling facts

1 Construct a table that lists all the bones of the axial skeleton in the left column and all the bones of the appendicular skeleton in the right column.

2 **a** List FIVE functions of the human skeleton.
b Discuss how the different parts of the skeleton perform any THREE of the functions listed in **a**.

3 What is a joint?

4 Name the type of joint found:
a between the bones of the wrist. **b** between the bones of the cranium.
c at the hip. **d** at the knee.

5 Give the function of EACH of the following parts of a synovial joint:
a capsule **b** synovial membrane **c** articular cartilage.

6 What are antagonistic muscles and why are they needed to bring about movement of a joint?

7 **a** Distinguish between a flexor muscle and an extensor muscle.
b Identify the flexor muscle and the extensor muscle responsible for moving the elbow joint.

8   Explain clearly why blood needs bones.

9   A group of scientists found the skeleton of an ancient human.

   a Suggest TWO features they should look for in order to identify the bones of the girdles.

   b Suggest TWO features they should look for in order to identify the limb bones.

   c How do the features you referred to in **b** make the limb bones suitable for their functions?

10   As Clifton runs around the athletics track at school, several joints in his legs allow his legs to move, especially those at his knees and his hips.

   Explain how the joints at his knees and hips differ:

   a in terms of their structure.   b in terms of their function.

11   People sometimes find that they need to replace one or both of their hip joints to retain their ability to walk as they grow older. Suggest TWO reasons why this might be necessary.

12   As part of his daily exercise routine, Gareth performs 40 biceps curls. To do this, he holds a dumbbell in each hand and then bends and straightens his elbow joints 40 times. With the aid of a simple labelled diagram, explain fully how the muscles in Gareth's arms function as he carries out his biceps curls.

17 Metals and non-metals

Chemical elements can be classified as **metals** or **non-metals**, and **materials** used in everyday life can be classified as **metallic** or **non-metallic materials** based on their properties. Each class of materials has its own unique properties which make the materials suitable for different **uses**. **Metals** differ in their reactivity and the more reactive ones are affected by chemicals in the environment, which cause them to **corrode**.

Learning objectives

- Relate the **properties** of **metals** and **non-metals** to their **uses**.
- Compare the **reactivity** of **metals**.
- Discuss the **advantages** and **disadvantages** of using **cooking utensils** and **cans** made of **aluminium**.
- Discuss the **benefits** of using **alloys** to make **household items**.
- Examine **conditions** which cause **rusting**.
- Discuss **methods** used to **prevent tarnishing** of **metals**.

Properties and uses of metals

Most **metals** have the following **common physical properties**.

- They have **high melting points**. As a result of this, all metals are found in the **solid** state at room temperature, with the exception of mercury, which is a liquid. The high melting points make metals suitable for use when high temperatures are required such as in furnaces, engines and many industrial processes.
- They are **good electrical conductors**, meaning that **electricity** passes through them easily. Because of this, metals are used to make electrical wires, circuits and electronic components.
- They are **good thermal conductors**. This means that **heat** passes through them easily. This makes metals suitable for use in many industrial processes where heat transfer is essential, and to make heat exchangers and cooking utensils.
- They are **malleable**, meaning that they can be hammered, rolled or pressed into different shapes (see Figure 17.1), and they are **ductile**, meaning that they can be drawn out into wires. These properties make metals useful for making metal tools and sculptures, decorative metalwork, jewellery, metal sheets, foil, electrical wires and cables.
- They have **high tensile strengths**. This means that they are **strong** and can withstand tension, heavy loads and stress without becoming deformed or breaking. This makes them valuable for use in the construction industry and to manufacture components used in the automotive and aerospace industries, machinery used in many industries and military equipment.
- They have **high densities**, meaning that they have a relatively high mass per unit volume. This makes metals heavy and, therefore, useful for applications where weight is required, such as ballast in ships, counterweights in elevators and diving weights. Their high density also makes them useful to make radiation shields.
- They are **shiny** in appearance or can be **polished** to make them shiny. Because of this, metals are said to have a **high lustre** and they are used to make jewellery and for other decorative purposes.
- They are **sonorous**, meaning that they make a sound when hit. This makes metals useful in making musical instruments.

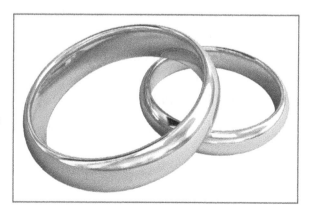

Figure 17.1 *Metals are malleable and shiny*

The **common properties** outlined above **vary** from metal to metal, and this makes certain metals **more suitable** than others for specific jobs. The specific properties and uses of some important metals are outlined in Table 17.1.

Table 17.1 *Properties and uses of some important metals*

Metals	Specific properties making the metal suitable for its uses	Uses
Aluminium	• Good conductor of electricity and heat. • Relatively low density. • Very malleable and ductile. • Very shiny and reflective. • Resistant to corrosion.	To make overhead electrical cables, cooking utensils, cans to store drinks (see page 387), foil for cooking and window frames. **Alloys** made mainly of aluminium are used to construct aircraft.
Copper	• Good conductor of electricity and heat. • Very malleable and ductile. • Very resistant to corrosion.	To make electrical wires, bases of saucepans and water pipes.
Iron	• High tensile strength. • Very malleable and ductile. • Easily welded.	To make ornamental iron work. **Steel**, an **alloy** made mainly of iron, is used to construct buildings, bridges, oil rigs, ships, trains and motor vehicles, and to make wire, nails, cutting tools, drill bits and many household items (see page 388).
Zinc and **tin**	• Resistant to corrosion.	To coat iron and steel items to prevent rusting; for example, zinc is used to coat nails and roofing sheets, and tin is used to coat 'tin cans' (see page 391).
Silver and **gold**	• Very shiny. • Very malleable and ductile. • Very resistant to corrosion.	To make jewellery and medals. Silver is also used to make cutlery and ornaments. Gold is also used in dentistry to make crowns and fillings.

Properties and uses of non-metallic materials

Non-metallic materials include **natural** materials; for example, wood, rubber and textiles made from natural fibres, and **manufactured** materials such as plastics, glass, ceramics, carbon fibre and textiles made from synthetic (man-made) fibres. These materials have very **variable physical properties**, as follows.

• They are all **poor electrical** and **thermal conductors**; in other words, they are **insulators**.
• Some are **flexible**, whilst others are **brittle**.
• Some are **strong**, whilst others have **low tensile strengths**.
• Most are **dull** in appearance.
• Some have **high densities**, whilst others have **low densities**.

Non-metallic materials have a great many **uses** because of their variable properties.

Wood

Wood is a hard, fibrous material obtained from the trunks and branches of trees. It is fairly easy to work with, shape, carve and join, it is a good insulator and it is fairly flexible, which allows it to bend without breaking. Wood can be divided into two kinds: **hardwoods**; for example, mahogany and purple heart, and **softwoods**; for example, pine and cedar. Most hardwoods are hard, strong and durable, whereas most softwoods are softer, easier to work with and not as durable.

Wood is **used** to build houses (see Figure 17.2) and boats, and to make furniture, flooring, cupboards, window frames, doors, decorative items, musical instruments, toys, tool handles and handles for saucepans.

Figure 17.2 *Wood is used to build houses*

Plastics

Most **plastics** are made using chemicals obtained from petroleum (crude oil) and they are composed of very large organic molecules known as **polymers**. They include polyethylene, polystyrene, polyvinyl chloride (PVC), polyesters and nylon. Plastics are durable, strong, light in weight, easy to mould, join, spin into fibres and colour, they are good insulators and they can be rigid or flexible. Plastics have a large number of uses because many of these properties make them **superior** to many other materials. However, plastics can have serious **harmful** effects on the environment (see pages 422 to 423).

Plastics are **used** to make bottles for drinks and cleaning products, food containers, shopping and garbage bags, toys, handles on saucepans, packaging materials, insulation for electrical wires, water pipes, guttering, window frames, clothing, boat sails, carpets, ropes, fishing lines and furniture.

Ceramics

Ceramics are made from soft, non-metallic materials which become **hard** and **brittle** when heated. **Clay** is the main raw material for most ceramics. Other materials, including **feldspar**, **silica**, **alumina** (aluminium oxide) and **calcium carbonate**, can be added to the clay in varying amounts to **modify** and **improve** the properties of the final products so they are well suited for their specific uses.

The raw materials are mixed with water to form a malleable paste, which is then **shaped** into the desired form (see Figure 17.3), dried to remove excess moisture and heated in a **kiln** to temperatures of 1300 °C or higher; a process known as **firing**. During firing, chemical changes occur within the ceramic materials which make them **harder** and **stronger**. After firing, the ceramic items are cooled slowly and they can then be **glazed** to give them a protective, non-porous coating and attractive appearance.

Figure 17.3 *Shaping a ceramic item before firing*

Ceramics include stoneware, earthenware, porcelain and bone china, and they possess a **wide range** of **properties**. Most are hard, strong, durable and resistant to heat, chemicals and scratching. They can be made into almost any shape and they are good thermal and electrical insulators. Because of their **unique** combination of properties, ceramics have a very wide range of uses; however, they are **brittle**, which means they shatter when hit, and this limits their uses under certain circumstances.

Ceramics are **used** to make bricks for building purposes, floor tiles, wash basins, toilets, cookware, tableware, a variety of decorative items and components for electrical devices and for car, aircraft and spacecraft engines. They are also used in the medical field to make artificial hips and knees, and dental implants.

Textiles

Textiles are materials composed of **natural fibres** such as cotton, wool, silk, linen and jute, or **synthetic fibres** such as nylon, polyester and acrylic, or a mixture of both. The fibres are **woven**, **knitted**, **crocheted** or otherwise **intertwined** to create textiles for a variety of purposes (see Figure 17.4). After production, the textiles can then undergo various finishing processes to improve their appearance, texture and performance. For example, they can be dyed to add colour or printed to add patterns. They can also be treated to improve their softness, strength or water resistance.

Textiles exhibit a wide range of **properties** that determine their suitability for different uses. Most are strong, flexible, durable and good thermal insulators. Most are also hard to rip or tear and can be dyed easily, and some are elastic, meaning that they can be stretched and return to their original shape.

Figure 17.4 *Textiles can be produced by weaving fibres*

Textiles are **used** to make clothing and accessories of all kinds, bed sheets, towels, curtains, covers for furniture and car seats, carpeting, camping gear, boat sails, bandages, surgical gowns and many other items.

Materials used in sporting equipment

Materials used in making **sporting equipment** have evolved from the readily available and mainly natural materials, such as wood, leather, gut, rubber and steel, to a variety of **high-technology materials**, which are aimed at enhancing **performance**, increasing the **durability** of the equipment and improving **safety** and **comfort**. These materials include **carbon fibre** and **graphite composites**, which are made by embedding fibres made from carbon atoms in a resin, usually made of epoxy; **glass fibre composites** made by embedding glass fibres in a resin, usually epoxy; **Kevlar** made from long, rigid, parallel, synthetic fibres; **aluminium** and **aluminium alloys**; and **titanium** and **titanium alloys**.

The different properties of these materials make some of them **more appropriate** than others when making specific items of sporting equipment, as outlined in Table 17.2 on page 385.

Table 17.2 *Properties of materials used to make sporting equipment*

Material	Properties	Sporting equipment made
Carbon fibre and **graphite composites**	Strong, lightweight, stiff, durable, good impact and fatigue resistance, allow freedom of design.	Tennis and badminton rackets (see Figure 17.5), bicycle frames, golf club shafts, hockey sticks, fishing rods, sailboat masts, skis, racing car parts.
Glass fibre composites	Strong, relatively lightweight, durable, can be made rigid or flexible, good impact resistance, easy to make and to mould into complex shapes.	Surfboards, skis, snowboards, boat hulls, kayaks, pole vaulting poles, fishing rods.
Kevlar	Extremely strong, tough, lightweight, durable, resistant to stretching, cutting and abrasion.	Racing boat sails (see Figure 17.6), protective clothing used in cycling, motor sports, fencing, speed skating, rock climbing.
Aluminium and **aluminium alloys**	Strong, lightweight, durable, can be formed into complex shapes.	Baseball bats, tennis and badminton rackets, hockey sticks, bicycle frames, javelins.
Titanium and **titanium alloys**	Strong, lightweight, durable, extremely resistant to corrosion, fatigue and stress.	Bicycle frames and components, tennis rackets, golf clubs, archery equipment, racing car components.
Wood	Strong, flexible, good shock absorber, easy to shape and customise to the individual, has a classic look and good feel.	Cricket and baseball bats, hockey sticks.
Rubber	Elastic, good shock absorber, durable, resistant to wear and tear, non-slip.	Baseballs, tennis balls, soccer balls, rugby balls, grips on tennis rackets and golf clubs.
Leather	Durable, flexible, provides a good grip.	Baseball, cricket and boxing gloves.

Figure 17.5 *A graphite composite badminton racket*

Figure 17.6 *A racing boat with Kevlar sails*

The reactivity of metals

Some metals react **vigorously**, even violently, with other chemical substances such as **acids**, **oxygen** and **water**, whilst others are relatively **unreactive**. Potassium, sodium, calcium and magnesium are the most reactive whilst aluminium, zinc, iron and tin are less reactive, and copper, silver and gold are relatively unreactive.

Reactions of metals with dilute acids

When a metal reacts with dilute hydrochloric or sulfuric acid, it forms a **salt** and **hydrogen**. Salts formed when a metal reacts with **hydrochloric acid** are known as **chlorides** and salts formed when metals react with **sulfuric acid** are known as **sulfates**. The reaction can be summarised by the following general word equation:

$$\boxed{\text{metal} \; + \; \text{acid} \longrightarrow \text{salt} \; + \; \text{hydrogen}}$$

For example:

aluminium + hydrochloric acid $\longrightarrow$ aluminium chloride + hydrogen

iron + sulfuric acid $\longrightarrow$ iron sulfate + hydrogen

To **determine** which of the following metals, aluminium, copper, iron, tin, silver and zinc, react with dilute hydrochloric acid, 4 cm³ of the acid is poured into each of six test tubes. A small, clean piece of one of the metals is added to each of the tubes, as shown in Figure 17.7. Each tube is shaken and observed for signs of **effervescence** or **bubbling**, which indicates the metal is reacting with the acid and producing hydrogen gas. The **relative strength** of effervescence is also noted to determine the **order of reactivity** of the metals.

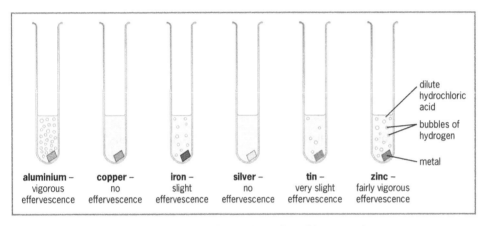

Figure 17.7 *Observing reactions of metals with a dilute acid*

Based on the relative strength of effervescence, the **order of reactivity** of the metals from the most reactive to the least reactive is: aluminium, zinc, iron and tin, with copper and silver not reacting.

Reactions of metals with oxygen

When a metal reacts with oxygen, it forms a **metal oxide**:

$$\boxed{\text{metal} \; + \; \text{oxygen} \longrightarrow \text{metal oxide}}$$

For example:

zinc + oxygen $\longrightarrow$ zinc oxide

Reactions of metals with water as steam

When a metal reacts with **water** in the form of **steam**, it forms a **metal oxide** and **hydrogen**:

$$\boxed{\text{metal} \; + \; \text{steam} \longrightarrow \text{metal oxide} \; + \; \text{hydrogen}}$$

For example:

tin + steam $\longrightarrow$ tin oxide + hydrogen

Table 17.3 *Summary of the reactions of some specific metals with dilute acids, oxygen in air and water*

Metal	Description of the reaction with dilute acids	Description of the reaction when the metal is heated in air	Description of the reaction with water
Aluminium (Al)	Reacts vigorously.	Burn when heated strongly, especially if powdered.	Do not react with cold or hot water. React with steam.
Zinc (Zn)	Reacts fairly vigorously.		
Iron (Fe)	Reacts slowly.	Burn when powdered and heated strongly.	
Tin (Sn)	Reacts very slowly.		
Copper (Cu)	Do not react with dilute acids.	Does not burn when heated, but forms an oxide coating if heated very strongly.	Do not react with water or steam.
Silver (Ag)		Does not react, even when heated very strongly.	

Aluminium cooking and canning utensils

Aluminium is a very **useful** metal, despite the fact that it is a fairly reactive metal. This is because the surface of any aluminium item is coated in a thin layer of **aluminium oxide**, which is relatively **unreactive**. This layer sticks to the metal surface and protects it against **corrosion** (see page 389).

Two major **uses** of aluminium are to make **cooking utensils** such as pots, pans, pressure cookers and baking trays (see Figure 17.8), and to make **cans** which are used to store a variety of beverages and some foods.

Using cooking and canning utensils made of aluminium has some **advantages** and some **disadvantages**, which are summarised in Table 17.4. Some of these disadvantages can be overcome or reduced by increasing the **thickness** of the

Figure 17.8 *Aluminium cooking utensils*

aluminium oxide layer on cooking utensils by a process called **anodising**. This has an added advantage because the thickened layer readily absorbs dyes, so the utensils can be attractively coloured.

Table 17.4 *Advantages and disadvantages of using cooking and canning utensils made of aluminium*

Advantages	Disadvantages
• The utensils are **resistant to corrosion** due to their aluminium oxide coating. This makes them durable and gives them a long life. • The utensils are **unreactive** due to the aluminium oxide coating, therefore they are usually not affected by acidic or alkaline foods. • The utensils are very **good conductors** of heat. This allows for efficient cooking. • The utensils are **light in weight** because aluminium has a low density. This makes them easy to transport and handle. • The utensils can be polished to have a **shiny**, attractive appearance.	• The utensils can be **scratched** or **dented** easily, and they **warp** easily because aluminium is a soft metal. • The utensils can be **stained** easily, especially if cooking very acidic foods such as tomatoes and citrus fruits. • If the utensils are used to cook or store very **acidic foods**, the acid may **react** with the aluminium oxide coating. This reduces its effectiveness and causes aluminium ions to enter the food and alter the taste. Aluminium has also been implicated in increasing a person's risk of developing **Alzheimer's disease**. • If the utensils are **scratched** or **damaged**, aluminium ions may **leach** into food during cooking or storage, possibly altering its taste and increasing the risk of Alzheimer's disease.

Alloys in the home and workplace

Metals are not used very often in their pure form. Instead, two or more metals are **mixed** to produce an **alloy**. Sometimes a non-metal may also be added to the mixture. To make an alloy, the metals are heated until they melt, mixed thoroughly and then cooled. Alloys are produced to **improve** or **modify** the properties of metals. Alloys are usually **harder, stronger**, more **malleable** and more **resistant to corrosion** than the pure metals. Alloys commonly used in the home and workplace include **steel**, **stainless steel**, **brass** and **soft solder**. The composition, properties and uses of these alloys are given in Table 17.5.

Table 17.5 *Alloys commonly found in the home and workplace*

Alloy	Composition	Properties	Uses
Steel	**Iron** alloyed with up to 1.5% **carbon.**	Harder and stronger than iron, and more malleable and ductile.	In the construction of buildings, bridges, ships and motor vehicles. To make 'tin cans' to store food, tools, nails, door hinges, gates, fences and cookware.
Stainless steel	Usually about 70% **iron** alloyed with 20% **chromium** and 10% **nickel.**	Harder, stronger and much more resistant to corrosion than iron or steel, malleable and ductile. Has a very shiny, attractive appearance.	To make cutlery, cooking utensils, kitchen equipment and appliances, sinks and surgical equipment.
Brass	**Copper** alloyed with up to about 45% **zinc.**	Harder, stronger and denser than copper, malleable, ductile and resistant to corrosion. Has an attractive golden-yellow colour.	To make door and window fittings, taps, lamp fittings, nuts and bolts, ornaments and musical instruments.
Soft solder	About 60% **tin** alloyed with 40% **lead.**	Has a relatively low melting point, so melts easily when being used. More malleable and ductile than tin and lead.	To join metal items together at relatively low temperatures, e.g. electrical wires and water pipes.

Electroplating

Electroplating is another technique that can be used to **modify** the properties of metal objects. The process uses an **electric current** to **coat** the object with a thin layer of an unreactive or less reactive metal. It is used to **protect** the original metal object from corrosion and wear, to make it look more **attractive** or to make an inexpensive object appear more **valuable. Silver, nickel, chromium** and **tin** are often used to electroplate objects made of **steel**. This is because steel corrodes (rusts) easily, but is relatively inexpensive, whereas silver, nickel, chromium and tin are resistant to corrosion and have a shiny, metallic appearance, but they are relatively expensive. Therefore, the durability and appearance of inexpensive steel objects can be improved by electroplating.

Figure 17.9 *Chrome-plated rims*

Many automotive parts, household fixtures and parts of household appliances are made of steel which has been electroplated with **chromium**; for example, kitchen and bathroom taps, and bumpers and rims of cars (see Figure 17.9). 'Tin cans', which are used to store food and beverages, are made of steel that has been electroplated with a thin layer of **tin**. Silver cutlery, and items of silver and gold jewellery are often made from copper or brass that has been electroplated with **silver** or **gold**.

Tarnishing and rusting

Tarnishing and **rusting** are two forms of **corrosion**. Corrosion occurs when the **surface** of a metal **reacts** with chemicals in the environment, mainly oxygen and moisture, and it is speeded up by the presence of certain pollutants.

Tarnishing

A metal **tarnishes** when its freshly polished surface reacts with **oxygen**, or sometimes **sulfur dioxide**, in the air. This forms a thin layer of the **metal oxide** or **metal sulfide** on the surface of the metal, which is also known as **tarnish**. This layer causes the metal to become **dull** and sometimes **discoloured**, and it generally adheres (sticks) to the surface and **protects** the rest of the metal from reacting. Metals that are particularly prone to tarnishing in this way include **aluminium**, **copper** and **nickel**, and the alloys **brass** and **bronze** (an alloy of copper and tin). **Silver** also tarnishes, however, this occurs by its surface reacting with hydrogen sulfide or sulfur dioxide in the air to form black **silver sulfide** (see Figure 17.10). Only the **top layers** of a metal are affected by tarnishing, and the tarnish can usually be removed by polishing the metal or using chemical metal cleaners.

Figure 17.10 *Tarnished (left) and polished (right) silver salt and pepper shakers*

Rusting

Rusting occurs when **iron** and **steel** objects are exposed to both **oxygen** and **water** (**moisture**) in the air. The iron, oxygen and water react and form **hydrated iron oxide**, which is also known as **rust**. The following word equation shows the formation of rust.

$$\text{iron + oxygen + water} \longrightarrow \text{hydrated iron oxide (rust)}$$

Rust does not stick to the metal as tarnish does, instead it **flakes off**. This exposes fresh iron to the environment, which rusts and the rust flakes off. This process continues, causing the iron to gradually wear away. Rusting can be both damaging and costly (see Figure 17.11).

Figure 17.11 *Rust damages objects made of iron and steel*

Investigating the conditions needed for rusting

The **conditions** needed for **rusting** can be investigated by setting up three test tubes, as illustrated in Figure 17.12 on page 390. The test tubes are then left for a week at room temperature and observed for any changes in the appearance of the nails.

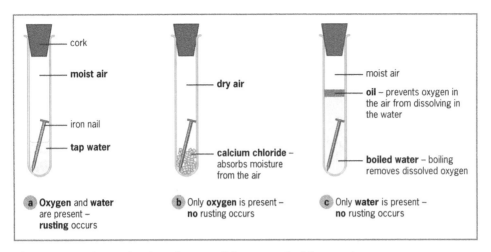

Figure 17.12 *Investigating the conditions needed for rusting*

Factors affecting the rate of rusting

The **rate** at which iron and steel rust is affected by a variety of **environmental** factors.

- **Temperature** – The higher the atmospheric temperature, the faster rusting occurs.
- **Humidity** – The more water vapour in the air, the faster rusting occurs.
- **Salts** – Any salts, especially sodium chloride, dissolved in the moisture in the air speed up the rusting process. Iron and steel fixtures in homes located near the **sea** rust at a faster rate than normal because they are constantly exposed to **sea spray.**
- **Pollutants** – Certain pollutants in the atmosphere speed up rusting; for example, sulfur dioxide, nitrogen oxides and carbon dioxide speed up the process due to their acidic nature. Iron and steel fixtures in homes near to **industrial plants**, especially those that burn fossil fuels, rust faster than normal because of the **emissions** produced by these plants (see page 416).

The **climate** of the **Caribbean**, characterised by high temperatures and high humidity, significantly increases the rate of rusting of iron and steel objects and structures compared to cooler and dryer climates. Additionally, the high salt content of the air, especially in coastal regions, speeds up rusting.

Methods to reduce or prevent tarnishing and rusting

Objects and structures made from metals and alloys that are prone to **tarnishing**, and iron and steel that will **rust**, especially when outdoors, can be **protected** against tarnishing and rusting in a variety of ways. Most of these prevent chemicals in the air from coming into **contact** with the metal from which the object or structure is made. It is important to prevent tarnishing and rusting to maintain the appearance, value, durability and lifespan of metal items.

Proper storage and using a drying agent

Metal objects can be stored in **dry, moisture-free** environments in order to reduce or prevent tarnishing and rusting. The best way to achieve this is by sealing the objects in airtight containers or bags. **Desiccants** that absorb moisture, such as packets of silica gel, can also be added to the storage containers or bags to absorb any moisture present (see Figure 17.13). This is particularly useful to preserve the original **shiny appearance** of objects prone to tarnishing; for example, items of silver jewellery.

Figure 17.13 *Silica gel used to absorb moisture*

Non-metallic protective coatings

Metal objects and structures can be **coated** with **paint**, **grease**, **oil** or **plastic**. The coatings create physical **barriers** between the objects and the surrounding environment which prevent oxygen, moisture and other pollutants from being able to react with the metal. For example, steel structures such as railings, gates and bridges, and the bodies of motor vehicles can be painted to prevent them from rusting and enhance their appearance, whilst machinery and engine parts can be protected from rusting by using grease or oil, and plastic coatings can be used to protect wire mesh fencing from rusting. **Clear lacquer** or **varnish** can also be used to protect metal objects against tarnishing, whilst still preserving the original shiny appearance of the object.

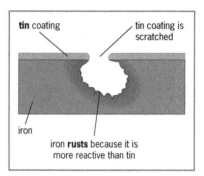

Figure 17.14 *Iron rusts if the metal it is plated with is scratched*

Electroplating

Elecroplating, explained on page 388, is mainly used to prevent iron and steel objects from **rusting**. However, if the metal coating is scratched or damaged in any way, the iron or steel will then rust because iron is more reactive than any of the metals that are used for the plating. This is shown in Figure 17.14, where the iron object has been electroplated with tin.

Galvanising

Galvanising is used to prevent iron and steel objects from **rusting**. It involves **coating** the object with a thin layer of **zinc**. To do this, the object is cleaned thoroughly and then immersed in a bath of molten zinc at about 450 °C. After a fixed time, the object is removed, cooled and a layer of zinc solidifies and forms a coating over its surface. On exposure to the air, the surface of the zinc oxidises and an adherent layer of unreactive **zinc oxide** forms, which protects the surface. If the zinc coating is scratched or damaged, the zinc is oxidised instead of the iron or steel because zinc is more reactive. This, therefore, protects the iron or steel against rusting, as shown in Figure 17.15. The zinc is said to provide **sacrificial protection**. Steel roofing sheets, nails and wire used in fencing are often galvanised (see Figure 17.16).

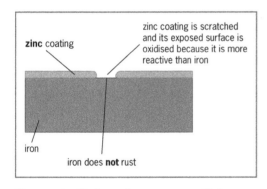

Figure 17.15 *Iron does not rust if the zinc coating is scratched*

Figure 17.16 *Galvanised roofing sheets*

Alloying

Alloying involves mixing two or more metals (see page 388). This can be done to prevent iron from **rusting** by alloying the iron with **chromium** and certain other metals, such as nickel and manganese, to form **stainless steel**. On contact with the air, the chromium at the surface of the stainless steel is oxidised to form an extremely thin layer of unreactive **chromium oxide**, which protects the steel and prevents the iron in it from being oxidised to rust (see Figure 17.17 on page 392).

a steel rusts   b stainless steel does not rust

Figure 17.17 *Alloying iron to form stainless steel protects against rusting*

Recalling facts

1 Construct a table to compare the following physical properties of metallic and non-metallic materials: appearance, electrical and thermal conductivity, tensile strength and density.

2 Suggest TWO reasons for EACH of the following.
  a Iron is used to make decorative gates.
  b Silver is used to make jewellery.
  c Aluminium is used to make overhead electrical cables.

3 Distinguish between the following non-metallic materials:
  a plastics and wood   **b** ceramics and textiles.

4 Suggest, with reasons in each case, what material would be the MOST appropriate for making:
  a a soccer ball   **b** a frame for a bicycle
  c a tennis racket   **d** a racing boat sail.

5 Which of the following metals react with oxygen, steam and dilute acids: aluminium, copper, iron, silver, tin and zinc?

6 Identify the products of a reaction between:
  a a metal and steam   **b** a metal and an acid   **c** a metal and oxygen.

7 **a** Explain why aluminium can be used to make cooking utensils even though it is a fairly reactive metal.
  b State THREE advantages of using cooking utensils made from aluminium.

8
  a What is an alloy?

  b State the composition of stainless steel and give THREE reasons why it is used in place of steel to make cutlery.

9 Provide a suitable definition for electroplating and explain why the process is used.

10 Distinguish between tarnishing and rusting and write a word equation to summarise rusting.

11 Identify FOUR different ways of protecting metallic objects against tarnishing and rusting.

Applying facts

12 Why it is easy to predict the physical properties of metallic materials, but those of non-metallic materials cannot be predicted easily?

13 Explain why wood is suitable for making chairs and other furniture, but ceramics are generally unsuitable.

14 Cricket bats are usually made from a type of wood known as willow. Suggest and explain what properties willow might have that make it the most suitable wood for making cricket bats.

15 Write a word equation for EACH of the following reactions.

  a Copper reacting with oxygen.

  b The reaction between zinc and sulfuric acid.

  c The reaction between iron and steam.

  d Tin reacting with hydrochloric acid.

16 Kiana often uses aluminium pots when cooking, however, she recently noticed that her favourite pot had some scratches on its inside. What advice would you give her and why?

17 Explain why certain metals become more useful when they are mixed with another metal.

18 Why can the process of anodising, which increases the thickness of the oxide layer on a metal, be used to protect aluminium objects from corrosion, but not iron objects?

19 Explain how the experiment described in Figure 17.12 on page 390 could be adapted to:

  a determine the effects of seawater on the rate of rusting.

  b compare the effectiveness of using paint and oil to prevent rusting.

20 It has been found that corrosion of a metal is speeded up if the metal is in contact with a less reactive metal and rainwater. Under these circumstances, the less reactive metal does not corrode. Explain the consequences of using uncoated iron nails to secure roofing sheets made of the following:

  a iron coated with zinc   **b** iron coated with tin.

21 Suggest the reason why iron railings tend to rust more at the bottom of the railings than at the top.

18 Household chemicals

Household chemicals are non-food chemicals that are commonly found and used in and around the home. They play essential roles in everyday life, from maintaining cleanliness and hygiene, to enhancing comfort and improving the household environment. Understanding their uses, what they are composed of and how to handle them properly is key to using them effectively, safely and responsibly.

Chemicals used in the home

Learning objectives

- Discuss the **use** of **common household chemicals**.
- Discuss the **safe** and **economic use** of **household chemicals**.
- Examine the **properties** of **acids**, **bases** and **salts**.
- Classify **household chemical** into **acids**, **bases** and **salts**.
- Explain the **effects** of **cleaning agents** on **household appliances**.
- Distinguish between **soapy** and **soapless detergents**.

The use of common household chemicals

Household chemicals include **water**, **cleaning** products, **hygiene** products, **healthcare** products and **pest control** products.

Water

Water is the **most common** chemical used in the home because of its **solvent properties**. Water is known as the **'universal solvent'** because it is capable of **dissolving** more substances than any other liquid. It is used to do laundry, wash dishes, clean floors, and for bathing, flushing toilets, watering gardens, cooking and drinking. Because water dissolves so many substances, most household chemicals in the liquid state contain water as a **solvent**; for example, window cleaners and liquid bleaches. Water is also relatively inexpensive, readily available in most households and it is non-toxic, making it safe for its many uses.

Hard surface cleaners

Hard surface cleaners are designed to clean and sanitise non-porous surfaces such as countertops, floors, appliances and bathroom fixtures. They include **disinfectants**, which are chemicals used to destroy or inhibit the growth of microorganisms in or on non-living objects; for example, **pure alcohols** such as ethanol and propanol, **chlorine-releasing** compounds such as sodium hypochlorite found in household bleaches, and **quaternary ammonium salts** found in disinfectants such as Lysol (see Figure 18.1).

Figure 18.1 *Common disinfectants*

Household **ammonia**, which is a dilute solution of ammonium hydroxide, is used to remove oils, fats, grease and grime (greasy dirt) on hard surfaces. It does this by breaking these substances down due to its **alkalinity**. It is particularly useful for cleaning windows and mirrors because it evaporates quickly, which helps to avoid streaking. Other **degreasers**, used to remove grease and grime, contain **solvents** such as ethanol or propanol, which dissolve greasy substances, or **alkaline substances** such as sodium hydroxide, which break down the grease. In addition to being used as disinfectants, **household bleaches**, especially chlorine bleaches, can be used to remove stains, mould and mildew from hard surfaces. They do this by oxidising the stains to their colourless form and killing the mould and mildew.

Personal hygiene products

Personal hygiene products are extremely important to maintain personal cleanliness, good health and wellbeing (see Figure 18.2). Products such as **hand** and **bath soap** or **body wash** should be used daily to clean the hands and body to remove dirt, oils, sweat and bacteria. **Shampoo** should be used once or twice a week to clean the hair and scalp, and **conditioner** should be used on the hair after shampooing to detangle, moisturise, nourish and hydrate the hair, giving it a soft, silky feel and healthy shine, and to help protect it against damage. **Deodorants** and **antiperspirants** are used to help control body odour by inhibiting the growth of odour-forming bacteria, masking unpleasant odours and reducing sweat production. **Toothpaste** and **mouthwash** are essential for maintaining oral hygiene by helping to prevent cavities, gum disease and bad breath, and **moisturisers** are used to keep the skin moist, soft and flexible, and they help protect the skin against environmental damage.

Figure 18.2 *Personal hygiene products*

Laundry products

Laundry products are essential for cleaning clothing and other textiles, such as towels and bedding (see Figure 18.3). **Soaps**, also known as **soapy detergents**, have been used historically for this purpose. However, they have been largely replaced by **soapless** or **synthetic detergents**, also known simply as **detergents**, because of the detergents' improved cleaning power, especially when used in hard water (see page 402). Both soapy and soapless detergents remove greasy dirt from fabrics by lifting the dirt from the surface of the fabric and keeping it suspended in the water so it can be washed away (see Figure 18.9 on page 401). The cleaning power of detergents can be improved by adding **enzymes** to break down biological stains and **optical brighteners** to make white fabrics appear whiter and brighter. **Fragrances** are also often added to give a pleasant odour to the laundered items.

Figure 18.3 *Laundry products*

Fabric softeners can be added to laundry when it is being rinsed. These contain **quaternary ammonium salts** that soften fibres in fabrics by untangling and lubricating them. This reduces cling caused by static and reduces wrinkling, which makes ironing easier. They also add a pleasant fragrance.

Kitchen cleaners

Kitchen cleaners are used to maintain cleanliness in the kitchen. These include **dishwashing liquid**, which is a detergent used to remove grease, food residue and bacteria from dishes, utensils and cookware. **Oven cleaners** are designed to remove baked-on food and grease that accumulate inside ovens (see Figure 18.4). Most contain a strong alkali, such as **sodium hydroxide**, which breaks down the baked-on food and grease. **Salt** (**sodium chloride**) can be used as an abrasive cleaner when mixed with a small amount of lemon juice to create a paste, which can then

Figure 18.4 *Oven cleaners*

be used to scrub away stains in tea and coffee cups, on countertops and chopping boards, and in sinks. Salt can also be used to absorb spills of oil or grease so that they can wiped away more easily.

Vinegar is a dilute solution of **ethanoic (acetic) acid** that can be added to water and used to clean countertops, sinks, floors and other kitchen surfaces. It leaves glass surfaces streak-free and is particularly useful for removing limescale (calcium carbonate) deposits from appliances. **Baking soda (sodium hydrogencarbonate)** is mildly abrasive and can be used to scrub surfaces such as sinks, stovetops and countertops without scratching them. It is also very good at absorbing odours; for example, from inside refrigerators and garbage cans. **Baking powder (sodium hydrogencarbonate** mixed with an **acidic** component) can be used in a similar way to baking soda, but it is less abrasive and not as effective at absorbing odours.

Healthcare products

Various chemical products play an essential role in maintaining and improving **health** within households. **Antacids** contain **basic** chemicals that are used to **neutralise** excess hydrochloric acid in the stomach (see page 399). **Antiseptics** are chemicals that are used to destroy, or inhibit the growth of, microorganisms on living tissue; for example, in a cut or wound, and include **hydrogen peroxide**, **rubbing alcohol** (which is about 70% propanol) and **iodine solution** (see Figure 18.5).

Hand sanitisers are used to reduce or eliminate microorganisms on hands and reduce the spread of infections when soap and water are not available. **Alcohols** can be used as **disinfectants** or **antiseptics** to reduce the spread of infections within the home, and they are also used in alcohol-based hand sanitisers. **Painkillers** are used to relieve pain. Some can only be obtained with a prescription, including opioids such as codeine, methadone and morphine, whilst others such as paracetamol or acetaminophen, aspirin and ibuprofen can be bought over the counter.

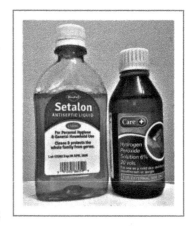

Figure 18.5 *Common antiseptics*

Eco-friendly household chemicals

Eco-friendly household chemicals, especially cleaning products, should be used whenever possible to help create healthier living spaces and minimise damage to the environment that can be caused by many household chemicals. They are usually made from **plant-based ingredients** that are effective cleaning agents without having the harmful effects of harsh, synthetic chemicals, and they often contain **natural additives**. Ingredients include lemon juice, orange oil, vinegar, baking soda, coconut oil and essential oils, such as lavender oil. Being made of natural ingredients, these products are **biodegradable** and **non-toxic**.

The safe use of household chemicals

Using household chemicals **safely** is essential to prevent accidents, protect the user and those close by from any harmful effects of the chemicals, and minimise harm to the environment. The following guidelines should be followed to ensure the safe use of household chemicals.

- **Read** all labels very carefully, always follow the instructions given and use only as directed.
- Use only the **amount** of the chemical needed to do the job.
- Use chemicals in **well-ventilated** areas and avoid inhaling the fumes.
- **Never mix** household chemicals, especially chlorine bleach and products containing ammonia, because mixing them can produce toxic gases or possibly cause other dangerous reactions.
- Wear the appropriate **protective clothing**, such as gloves and goggles, when using harmful chemicals and do not use chemicals near food.

- **Wash hands** immediately after using any household chemicals.
- **Store** all chemicals in their original containers, and ensure the containers are tightly sealed and out of reach of children.

The economic use of household chemicals

Using household chemicals **economically** involves trying to maximise their efficiency and minimise waste. This can be achieved in the following ways.

- Use the **recommended quantity** of household chemical for each job. Avoid using more than necessary to do a job, always measure the recommended amount, do not guess, and dilute chemicals following the instructions given.
- Buy household chemicals that are used frequently in **bulk** and store them properly to prevent them from degrading. However, only buy sufficient to ensure that it will all be used before its expiration date.
- Buy household chemicals that have **long shelf lives**. This helps to ensure that all the chemical is used before it expires.

Safety symbols on chemicals

A number of chemicals, including household chemicals, are potentially harmful and they carry **safety symbols** to warn users about the **potential hazards** associated with their use. These symbols are crucial for ensuring that chemicals are handled, stored, used and disposed of safely. Figure 18.6 gives some of the more common safety symbols. The same symbols may also appear on a white background inside a red diamond as shown in Figure 18.7.

Figure 18.6 *Some important safety symbols*

Figure 18.7 *Safety symbols on a can of insecticide*

Properties of acids, bases and salts

The **properties** of **acids** and **bases** are **opposite** to each other, and they have the ability to **neutralise** each other. When an acid reacts with a base, the reaction always forms a **salt** and **water**.

Acids

Acids are substances that form positive **hydrogen ions** (H^+ **ions**) when they dissolve in water. Solutions of acids are described as being **acidic**, and they have the following properties.

- They have a **sour** taste.
- They are **corrosive**.

- They change blue litmus to **red.**
- They have a pH value of **less than** 7.

Hydrochloric acid, **sulfuric acid** and **nitric acid** are the common acids found in the laboratory, whilst **citric acid** and **ascorbic acid** (**vitamin C**) are found in fruits.

Bases

Bases are chemically opposite to acids. Bases include **metal oxides**; for example, calcium oxide, and **metal hydroxides**; for example, magnesium hydroxide and **ammonia.**

Some bases are **soluble** in water and these are known as **alkalis.** Alkalis include **sodium hydroxide, potassium hydroxide, calcium hydroxide** and **ammonium hydroxide,** formed when ammonia dissolves in water. Alkalis form negative **hydroxide ions** (**OH$^-$ ions**) when they dissolve in water. Solutions of alkalis are described as being **alkaline,** and they have the following properties.

- They have a **bitter** taste.
- They are **corrosive.**
- They feel **soapy.**
- They change red litmus to **blue.**
- They have a pH value **greater than 7.**

The concept of pH

Solutions of **acids** and **alkalis** can be classified as **strong** or **weak** and their **strength** can be measured on the **pH scale.** The pH scale is a numbered scale ranging from **0** to **14.** A solution with a pH of **7** is **neutral.** Solutions with a pH **less** than 7 are **acidic,** and the **lower** the pH, the **stronger** the acid. Solutions with a pH **greater** than 7 are **alkaline,** and the **higher** the pH, the **stronger** the alkali.

The pH of a **solution** can be **measured** in the laboratory by using **universal indicator.** This is a chemical substance whose **colour** changes depending on the pH of the solution. It can be in paper form or solution form. When using **universal indicator paper,** a small piece of the paper is dipped into the solution and its colour is compared with a pH colour chart. Figure 18.8 shows the pH scale and the colour of universal indicator paper at different pH values.

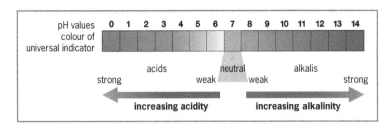

Figure 18.8 *The pH scale*

Salts

Salts are compounds formed when bases react with acids. Salts formed by hydrochloric acid are called **chlorides**, salts formed by sulfuric acid are called **sulfates** and salts formed by nitric acid are called **nitrates.** Other salts include **carbonates, hydrogencarbonates** and **phosphates.**

base + acid ⟶ salt + water

Classification of household chemicals as acids, bases and salts

Household chemicals can be classified into **acids**, **bases** and **salts**, as shown in Table 18.1. Most salts are **neutral**, however, some can be acidic and some can be basic. Their **pH values** can be determined using **universal indicator**, as explained on page 398. If universal indicator paper is used to determine the pH of a solid, the solid must first be dissolved in distilled water to create a **solution** that can then be tested.

Table 18.1 *Classification of some common household chemicals as acids, bases or salts*

Classification	Household chemical	Main chemical component
Acid	• Limescale remover	• Phosphoric, sulfamic or citric acid
	• Toilet bowl cleaner	• Hydrochloric or citric acid
	• Rust remover	• Phosphoric or oxalic acid
	• Battery acid	• Sulfuric acid
	• Vinegar	• Ethanoic (acetic) acid
	• Aspirin	• Acetylsalicylic acid
Base	• Drain cleaner	• Sodium or potassium hydroxide
	• Oven cleaner	• Sodium or potassium hydroxide
	• Chlorine bleach	• Sodium hypochlorite
	• Household ammonia	• Ammonia
	• Antacid	• Magnesium hydroxide or aluminium hydroxide
Salt	• Washing soda (also basic)	• Sodium carbonate
	• Toothpaste (also basic)	• Sodium fluoride or sodium monofluorophosphate, and sodium hydrogencarbonate
	• Epsom salt	• Magnesium sulfate
	• Baking soda (also basic)	• Sodium hydrogencarbonate
	• Table salt	• Sodium chloride
	• Washing soda (also basic)	• Sodium carbonate
	• Antacid (also basic)	• Sodium hydrogencarbonate or calcium carbonate

Neutralisation reactions

A **neutralisation reaction** is a reaction between a base and an acid to form a salt and water. Neutralisation reactions play an important part in various aspects of daily life, including **agriculture**, **health**, **nutrition**, **cooking** and **sanitation**, as outlined in the following examples.

* Neutralisation is important in managing the **pH of soil**. Most soils tend to be acidic, especially after fertilisers have been added to them, and most plants grow best in soils that are neutral. Therefore, **calcium hydroxide** (**lime**) or finely ground **calcium carbonate** (**limestone**), both of which are basic, can be added to these soils to neutralise them.

* **Antacids** are used to treat conditions such as **indigestion** and **acid reflux**. One or more of their active ingredients are basic, as shown in Table 18.1, and these neutralise excess hydrochloric acid in the stomach, which helps relieve symptoms of these conditions.

* **Toothpaste** contains certain basic ingredients which neutralise any acids produced by bacteria in the mouth, and this helps to prevent **tooth decay**.

* **Baking soda**, being basic, can be used to treat **bee stings**, which contain methanoic (formic) acid; and **vinegar**, being acidic, can be used to treat wasp stings, which are basic. In each situation, the venom in the sting is neutralised and this helps to reduce itching, pain and swelling.

- Neutralisation reactions occur in the **digestive system** to maintain the optimum pH levels for enzyme activity. This mainly occurs in the small intestine, where any hydrochloric acid entering from the stomach is neutralised by **sodium hydrogencarbonate** present in the pancreatic juice (see Table 9.10 on page 182).

- **Baking soda** is used in baking as a **leavening agent**, which causes baked goods to rise. When added to acidic ingredients such as buttermilk, yoghurt, lemon juice or cocoa powder in cake mixtures, doughs or batters, the basic baking soda reacts with the acidic ingredients producing **carbon dioxide** gas. The gas causes the mixture to rise, and become light and fluffy.

- Many **household cleaning products** are designed to clean as a result of neutralisation reactions; for example, rust removers and limescale removers (see page 401).

- Neutralisation plays a crucial role in **wastewater** and **sewage treatment plants**, where it is used to adjust the **pH** of the **treated wastewater** to a neutral level before the water is discharged into the environment. This prevents any environmental damage that could be caused by the water being acidic or alkaline. It is also used in **water treatment plants** to adjust the pH of the **treated water** to a neutral level.

Studying neutralisation

Neutralisation can be studied by placing an acid into a small conical flask and adding a few drops of **universal indicator solution**, which turn the solution in the flask **red**. An alkali is then added dropwise from a dropping pipette and colour changes are observed. As the alkali is added, the **acidity** of the solution **decreases** until it becomes **neutral**, which is indicated by the gradual colour change of the solution from **red** to **green**. As more alkali is then added, the solution gradually becomes **more alkaline** and the colour gradually changes to **dark blue** (see Figure 18.8 on page 398).

The effects of cleaning agents on household appliances

A variety of **cleaning agents** are used to clean **household appliances**. These work in different ways.

- They can clean appliances by acting as **abrasives** to **physically** remove dirt and stains when they are rubbed onto hard surfaces. **Scouring powders** clean in this way.

- They can clean appliances by acting as **surfactants**, as seen in the action of **detergents**.

- They can clean appliances by their **chemical action**, as seen in the action of **rust removers**, **limescale removers** and **oxidising agents**.

Scouring powders

Scouring powders contain **fine particles** of an insoluble mineral, such as limestone, quartz or silica, mixed with other powders and chemical cleaners to help them clean, such as a detergent or a bleaching agent. Before use, they are mixed with water to form a thick paste, and the mineral particles act as an **abrasive** when rubbed on hard surfaces, which removes any solid dirt. Scouring powders should be used with care because they can damage hard surfaces.

Detergents

Both **soapy** and **soapless detergents** can be used to remove grease and dirt from appliances. **Detergent molecules** are long molecules composed of **two** parts: a **hydrophilic head**, which is water-loving and oil-hating, and a **hydrophobic tail**, which is water-hating and oil-loving. Detergents work in the following way.

- They **lower** the surface tension of the water, allowing it to **spread out** and **wet** surfaces more efficiently; in other words, they act as **surfactants** or **surface-active agents**.

- They **break up** and **disperse** grease and dirt.

The action of detergents is explained in Figure 18.9 on page 401.

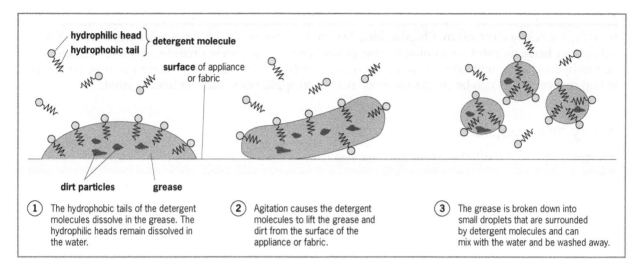

 is at the top of the page. The figure's internal labels and step text:

hydrophilic head
hydrophobic tail } detergent molecule

surface of appliance or fabric

dirt particles   grease

(1) The hydrophobic tails of the detergent molecules dissolve in the grease. The hydrophilic heads remain dissolved in the water.

(2) Agitation causes the detergent molecules to lift the grease and dirt from the surface of the appliance or fabric.

(3) The grease is broken down into small droplets that are surrounded by detergent molecules and can mix with the water and be washed away.

Figure 18.9 *How detergents remove grease and dirt*

Rust removers

Rust removers usually contain an acid such as **phosphoric** or **oxalic acid**. The acid reacts with the **rust** or **iron oxide**, which is basic, and this forms a soluble salt that can be washed away leaving the bare iron or steel. Care must be taken when using rust removers because they can be harmful to the skin.

Limescale removers

Limescale removers contain an acid such as **phosphoric**, **sulfamic** or **citric acid**. The acid reacts with the basic **limescale** or **calcium carbonate** deposits that build up inside kettles and shower heads, and around taps. The reaction forms a soluble salt that can be washed away. Care must be taken when using limescale removers because they can be harmful to the skin.

Oxidising agents

Several household chemicals act as **oxidising agents**, such as **chlorine bleach**, **hydrogen peroxide** and other **oxygen bleaches**. These chemicals remove coloured stains by oxidising them to their colourless form.

Cleaning metal appliances

Household appliances can be made out of a variety of **metals**, such as aluminium, copper, iron, tin, zinc and silver, and their alloys. These need to be cleaned regularly to remove any grease, dirt, tarnishing, corrosion, stains and discolouration, and to keep them shiny. When doing this, it is important to use the correct cleaning agents to avoid scratching the appliances, causing them to corrode or discolour, or damaging their surfaces in any other way.

Most metals appliances can be cleaned using a **mild detergent**, such as dishwashing liquid mixed with warm water, to remove grease and dirt. Diluted **vinegar** can also be used to remove mineral deposits such as limescale, and a paste made of **baking soda** and water can be applied using a soft cloth to remove stains. After cleaning, the surfaces should be **rinsed** with water and **dried** thoroughly using a clean, dry, microfibre cloth to prevent any corrosion. **Cleaners** and **polishes** designed specifically for each metal can also be used.

Abrasive cleaners, such as scouring powders, should be avoided because they can scratch metal surfaces, especially aluminium. Chlorine bleaches should also be avoided because they can discolour metals. Any harsh cleaners containing strong alkalis, such as sodium hydroxide, and strong acids, such as hydrochloric acid, should not be used because they can cause corrosion or pitting. However, certain rust removers can be used to remove rust from appliances made of iron or steel.

Soapy and soapless detergents

Detergents can be classified as soapy and soapless.

- Soapy detergents are often known simply as soaps. They are made by boiling animal fats or vegetable oils with concentrated potassium or sodium hydroxide solution, both of which are strong alkalis. One example of a soapy detergent is sodium octadecanoate, also known as sodium stearate.
- Soapless detergents are also called synthetic detergents and are often known simply as detergents. They are made from chemicals obtained from petroleum. One example of a soapless detergent is sodium dodecyl sulfate.

Scum formation

Soapy detergents do not lather easily when used in hard water (see page 324). Hard water contains dissolved calcium and magnesium ions, and these ions react with sodium octadecanoate (soap) and form insoluble calcium or magnesium octadecanoate, also known as scum (see Figure 18.10).

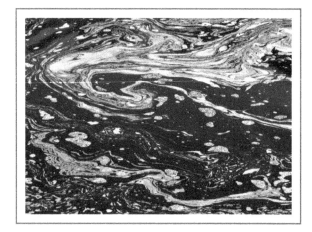

Figure 18.10 *Soap scum floating on water*

hard water + soap ⟶ scum

When scum forms, it removes the soap from the water, which prevents the soap from doing its job of removing greasy dirt. It is only when all the calcium and magnesium ions have been removed from the water as scum that any remaining soap molecules will form a lather and do their job of removing the dirt. Scum is an unpleasant, greasy substance that can build up in clothes and discolour them. It also forms an unpleasant grey, greasy layer on hard surfaces such as around sinks, baths and showers.

Soapless detergents do not form scum when added to hard water, therefore they begin to do their job of removing dirt as soon as they are added to the water.

Advantages and disadvantages of soapy and soapless detergents

Both soapy and soapless detergents have advantages and disadvantages associated with their production and use. These are summarised in Table 18.2 on page 403.

Table 18.2 *Advantages and disadvantages of soapy and soapless detergents*

	Soapy detergents	Soapless detergents
Advantages	• They are manufactured from fats and oils which are **renewable** and will not run out. • They are **biodegradable**, meaning that they are broken down by microorganisms in the environment, therefore they do not cause foam to form on waterways such as lakes and rivers. • They do not contain phosphates, therefore they **do not** cause **pollution** of aquatic environments by causing eutrophication. • They contain **fewer irritants** than soapless detergents because they are made form natural fats and oils and have fewer synthetic additives.	• They **lather** very easily in hard water, therefore smaller amounts are needed than soapy detergents to achieve the same result, making them **more cost-effective**. • They **do not** cause scum to form, therefore they are **more efficient cleaning agents** than soapy detergents. • They tend to be **less expensive** to produce than soapy detergents.
Disadvantages	• They **do not** lather easily in hard water, therefore larger amounts are needed than soapless detergents, making them **less cost-effective**. • They form unpleasant **scum** in hard water, which makes them **less efficient cleaning agents** than soapless detergents. • They tend to be **more expensive** to produce than soapless detergents.	• They are manufactured from petroleum, a **non-renewable** resource that will eventually run out. • Some are **non-biodegradable**. These can cause **foam** to build up on waterways, which prevents oxygen dissolving for aquatic organisms, resulting in their death (see Figure 18.11). Most modern soapless detergents are biodegradable. • Some contain **phosphates** that are added to improve their cleaning ability. These **pollute** aquatic environments by causing **eutrophication** (see Table 15.7 on page 332). • They contain **more irritants**, especially skin irritants, than soapy detergents because they contain more synthetic additives to enhance their cleaning power.

Figure 18.11 *Foam build-up on a river caused by using soapless detergents*

Recalling facts

1. Identify the MAIN reason why water is the most commonly used chemical in the home.

2. Give the use of EACH of the following household chemicals and give THREE examples of EACH.
   a Personal hygiene products.   b Kitchen cleaners.
   c Healthcare products.   d Hard surface cleaners.

3. Distinguish between disinfectants and antiseptics, and give TWO examples of EACH.

4. List FOUR pieces of advice that you could give to Jerome on how to safely use the drain cleaner that he just purchased.

5. Give the meaning of the following safety symbols that may be found on chemical products.

a   b   c   d

6. Excluding their pH values, give THREE differences between an acid and an alkali.

7. Describe the pH scale and explain what it is used to measure. Your answer must include the range of the scale and the pH values of acids, alkalis and neutral substances.

8. a What is a salt?
   b Name THREE different household chemicals that are acidic, THREE that are basic and THREE that are salts.

9. a What is neutralisation?
   b Explain how neutralisation reactions function in EACH of the following: agriculture, nutrition and sanitation.

10. Most agents used to clean household appliances work either chemically or as abrasives. Give ONE example of an agent that cleans by its abrasive action and ONE that cleans by its chemical action. In EACH case, explain how the cleaning agent functions.

11. Outline the BEST way to clean a stainless steel refrigerator.

12. Distinguish between a soapy detergent and a soapless detergent.

13. a Explain how scum is formed and write a word equation to summarise the process.
    b Explain why the formation of scum is undesirable.

Applying facts

14 To remove the greasy stains on her countertops, Willa decides to make a mixture of household ammonia and chlorine bleach.

    a Suggest why Willa chose EACH of the household chemicals.

    b What advice would you give Willa and why?

15 Audley likes to keep his home spotlessly clean, but finds he is spending over his budget on cleaning products. Outline FOUR ways he could reduce this expenditure.

16 Explain how you would compare the pH values of vinegar, household ammonia and Epsom salt.

17 How does toothpaste help to reduce tooth decay?

18 Explain why it is always advisable to try to clean a small, inconspicuous area of any metal appliance with a newly purchased cleaner before using it to clean the entire appliance.

19 Write an argument that you could put forward to support the use of soapy detergents in preference to soapless detergents.

Analysing data

20 Three brands of limescale remover: 'Lime Gone', 'Lime Vanish' and 'Lime Go', all sell for the same price. Science student, Shanik, was asked to determine which would be most cost effective to remove the limescale from shower heads. To do this, she measured 10 cm³ of dilute sodium hydroxide solution, poured it into a small conical flask and added 10 drops of universal indicator solution. She then added 'Lime Gone' from a dropping pipette, whilst swirling the flask, and counted the number of drops needed to turn the solution green. She repeated the test with 'Lime Vanish' and 'Lime Go'. Her results are given in Table 18.3.

Table 18.3 *Number of drops of limescale remover added*

Limescale remover	Number of drops added
Lime Gone	25
Lime Vanish	32
Lime Go	19

    a i What was the colour of each solution in the conical flask immediately after adding the 10 drops of universal indicator solution?

      ii Give a reason for your answer to **a i**.

    b Explain why each solution turned green after a certain number of drops of the limescale remover had been added.

    c i What colour would each solution turn if Shanika continued to add drops of the limescale remover?

      ii Explain your answer to **c i**.

    d i Which of the three brands of limescale remover would be most cost effective?

      ii Explain your answer to **d i**.

Matter, mixtures and their separation

Learning objectives

- Differentiate among the **properties** of the **states** of **matter**.
- Discuss **changes** of **state**.
- Examine the **properties** of **mixtures**.
- Determine **appropriate separation techniques** for the **components** of **mixtures**.

The states of matter

Matter is anything that occupies space and has mass.

All **matter** is made of **particles** and it can exist in various forms or **states**. The **three** states of matter that are most common on Earth are the **solid**, **liquid** and **gaseous** states. **Three** different **types** of particles make up these three common states: **atoms**, **molecules** and **ions**, and the differences between the states lie in the **energy** and **arrangement** of their particles.

Particles in the **solid** state have the least amount of energy; they simply vibrate about their mean position and they are packed closely together. Particles in the **liquid** state have medium amounts of energy; they move slowly past each other and they have very small spaces between. Particles in the **gaseous** state have the greatest amount of energy; they move about rapidly and they have large spaces between. The **properties** of solids, liquids and gases are summarised in Table 18.4.

Table 18.4 *The properties of the three common states of matter compared*

Property	Solid	Liquid	Gas
Shape	Fixed.	Takes the shape of the part of the container it is in. The surface is always horizontal.	Takes the shape of the entire container it is in.
Volume	Fixed.	Fixed.	Variable – it expands to fill the container it is in.
Arrangement of particles	Packed closely together, usually in a regular way:	Have very small spaces between and are arranged randomly:	Have large spaces between and are randomly arranged:
Forces of attraction between the particles	Strong.	Weaker than those between the particles in a solid.	Very weak.
Energy possessed by the particles	Possess very small amounts of kinetic energy.	Possess more kinetic energy than the particles in a solid.	Possess large amounts of kinetic energy.
Movement of the particles	Vibrate about their mean position.	Move slowly past each other.	Move around freely and rapidly.

Changes of state

Matter can exist in any of the three states, depending on its **temperature**. It can be **changed** from one state to another by **adding** or **removing heat** because adding or removing heat causes a change in the **energy** and **arrangement** of the particles. The different changes of state are summarised in Figure 18.12 and explained below.

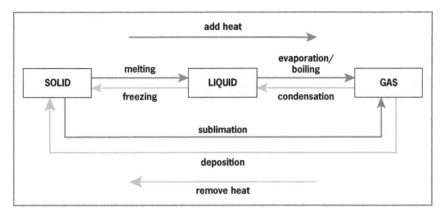

Figure 18.12 *Summary of the changes of state*

Melting

When a **solid** is **heated**, its particles **gain** kinetic energy and begin to vibrate more vigorously. Eventually the particles are able to overcome the strong forces of attraction between them and are able to move freely past each other, forming a **liquid**. The solid is said to **melt**. The temperature remains constant whilst the solid is melting because all the heat energy being supplied is used to overcome the forces of attraction between the solid particles. This temperature is known as the **melting point**.

Melting point is the constant temperature at which a solid changes into a liquid.

Evaporation

When a **liquid** is **heated**, its particles **gain** kinetic energy and move faster. Some of the particles near the surface of the liquid have enough kinetic energy to overcome the forces of attraction between them and are able to leave the liquid and become a **vapour**. These particles are said to **evaporate**.

Boiling

When the temperature of the **liquid** being **heated** reaches a certain point, it will start to **boil**. At this point, the liquid particles have gained enough kinetic energy and started to move fast enough to change into a **gas,** both within the liquid and at its surface. The temperature remains constant whilst the liquid is boiling because the heat energy being supplied is used to overcome the forces of attraction between the liquid particles. This temperature is known as the **boiling point**.

Boiling point is the constant temperature at which a liquid changes into a gas.

Boiling differs from evaporation in two ways.

* Boiling occurs at a **specific temperature**, whereas evaporation can take place at any temperature.
* Boiling takes place **throughout** the liquid, whereas evaporation takes place only at the surface of the liquid.

Condensation

When a **gas** is **cooled**, its particles **lose** kinetic energy and begin to move more slowly. The forces of attraction between the particles become stronger, causing the particles to move closer together, forming a **liquid**. The gas is said to **condense**.

Freezing

When a **liquid** is **cooled**, its particles **lose** kinetic energy and begin to move more slowly. The forces of attraction between the particles become stronger, causing the particles to move even closer together, forming a **solid**. The liquid is said to **freeze** and the temperature at which this occurs is known as the **freezing point**.

Freezing point is the constant temperature at which a liquid changes into a solid.

The freezing point of a **pure** substance has the same value as the melting point; for example, water has a freezing point and a melting point of 0 °C.

Sublimation and deposition

When the forces of attraction between the particles in a **solid** are **weak**, the addition of a small amount of heat can cause the **solid** to change directly into a **gas** without passing through the liquid state. The solid is said to **sublimate** or **sublime**, and the change in state is known as **sublimation**. If the **gas** is then cooled it will change directly back to the solid. The gas is said to **deposit**, and the change of state is known as **deposition**.

Figure 18.13 *Snowflakes form by deposition*

Examples of substances which undergo sublimation and deposition are iodine, carbon dioxide (dry ice), ammonium chloride and naphthalene, used to make moth balls. If the atmosphere is cold enough, **snow** forms by deposition. This happens when **water vapour** in the air deposits onto particles in the air such as dust and forms ice crystals, which gradually increase in size to form **snowflakes** (see Figure 18.13).

Plasma

*A **plasma** is an electrically charged gas.*

Plasma is known as the fourth state of matter. It is rare on Earth, but the Sun and other stars are composed mainly of plasma. Plasma is thought to be the most common state in the universe. Plasmas are an **ionised gases** consisting of negatively charged **electrons** and positively charged **ions**, which possess very large amounts of kinetic energy. A plasma is usually formed when a gas is heated strongly enough that the atoms in it lose one or more electrons; in other words, they **ionise**. Plasmas can emit **light** of various colours, depending on the specific gas involved in their formation.

Figure 18.14 *An aurora in Iceland*

Like gases, plasmas do not have fixed shapes or volumes. **Unlike gases**, plasmas conduct an electric current and are attracted to magnetic fields. On Earth, plasmas are found in neon signs, fluorescent light bulbs, lightning and auroras, also known as the northern or southern lights (see Figure 18.14).

Mixtures

Mixtures are composed of two or more substances that are **physically combined**. Each component in the mixture retains its own individual properties and has not undergone any chemical reaction with any other component. The proportions of the components of mixtures can vary and they can be **separated** from each other by physical means (see pages 411 to 413). **Solutions**, **suspensions** and **colloids** are all mixtures.

Solutions

*A **solution** is a homogeneous (uniform) mixture of two or more substances; one substance is usually a liquid.*

A **solution** is made by **dissolving** one substance in another. The substance that does the **dissolving** is called the **solvent** and the substance that **dissolves** is called the **solute**.

*A **solvent** is a chemical substance that dissolves another chemical substance to form a solution.*

*A **solute** is a chemical substance that can be dissolved by another chemical substance to form a solution.*

The **solvent** is the substance that is present in the higher or highest concentration, and a solution may contain one or more solutes dissolved in the solvent. Solvents are usually liquids and solutes can be solids, liquids or gases. A **solution** usually appears **transparent**, and the components do not separate if left undisturbed.

Based on the **nature** of the **solvent**, solutions can be classified into **two** types: **aqueous solutions** and **non-aqueous solutions**.

Figure 18.15 *Carbonated drinks are solutions of carbon dioxide gas, sugar and various other solutes dissolved in water*

- **Aqueous solutions** have **water** as the solvent. Water is known as the 'universal solvent' because it can dissolve a large number of substances. Examples of aqueous solutions include sea water, acids, iced tea, carbonated drinks and rum (see Figure 18.15).

- **Non-aqueous solutions** have substances other than water as the solvent. Common **non-aqueous solvents** include ethanol, kerosene, gasoline, turpentine, acetone and methylated spirits, which is a mixture of ethanol and a small amount of methanol. These solvents are capable of dissolving substances that are usually insoluble in water.

Solvents play an important role in removing **stains** and certain other substances, such as oil and grease, in the home and places of work. They do this by **dissolving** the stains, oil or grease.

- If the stain is soluble in **water**, it can be removed by soaking in water.

- If the stain is insoluble in water, but soluble in a **non-aqueous solvent**, it can be removed by soaking in the appropriate non-aqueous solvent; for example, **acetone** can be used to dissolve nail polish, **turpentine** to dissolve oil-based paints, **methylated spirits** to dissolve greasy dirt on surfaces such as glass, and **tetrachloroethane** is used in dry cleaning to dissolve greasy dirt and stains from clothes.

Suspensions

*A **suspension** is a heterogeneous (non-uniform) mixture in which minute, visible particles of one substance are dispersed in another substance, which is usually a liquid.*

A **suspension** appears **opaque** and the dispersed particles will eventually **separate out** if the suspension is left undisturbed (see Figure 18.16). Examples of suspensions include muddy water, and chalk dust or flour stirred in water, all of which contain solid particles suspended in a liquid, and the particles will settle if left undisturbed. Oil shaken vigorously in water is an example of liquid particles suspended in a liquid; the oil breaks up into fine droplets, which join back together and form a layer of oil when left undisturbed.

Figure 18.16 *Particles in a suspension settle out*

Colloids

*A **colloid** is a heterogeneous mixture in which minute particles of one substance are dispersed in another substance, which is usually a liquid. The dispersed particles are larger than those of a solution, but smaller than those of a suspension.*

A colloid can appear **translucent** or **opaque** and the dispersed particles **do not** separate out if left undisturbed. Examples of colloids include: smoke, which is a colloid of a solid in a gas; fog, a colloid of a liquid in a gas; gelatin, a colloid of a solid in a liquid; and whipped cream, a colloid of a gas in a liquid. Mayonnaise, milk and emulsion paint are colloids known as **emulsions**. They contain minute liquid droplets, such as droplets of oil, dispersed in a water-based mixture.

Comparing solutions, colloids and suspensions

Figure 18.17 compares the particle sizes in a solution, a colloid and a suspension, and Table 18.5 compares the properties of the three types of mixtures.

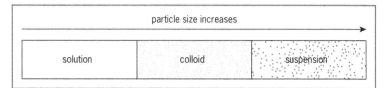

Figure 18.17 *Comparing the particle sizes in a solution, a colloid and a suspension*

Table 18.5 *Comparing the properties of solutions, colloids and suspensions*

Property	Solutions	Colloids	Suspensions
Size and visibility of dispersed particles	Extremely small. Not visible, even with a microscope.	Between those in a solution and those in a suspension. Not visible, even with a microscope.	Larger than those in a colloid. Visible to the naked eye.
Separation of components on standing	Dispersed particles do not separate out if left undisturbed.	Dispersed particles do not separate out if left undisturbed.	Dispersed particles separate out if left undisturbed.
Passage of light and appearance	Light usually passes through, making them appear **transparent**.	Most will scatter light, making them appear **translucent**. Some are **opaque**.	Light does not pass through, so they appear **opaque**.
Separation of components by filtration	Dispersed particles cannot be separated by filtration.	Dispersed particles cannot be separated by filtration.	Dispersed particles can be separated by filtration.

Classification of household chemicals

Nearly all **household chemicals** are **mixtures** and can be classified as **solutions**, **colloids** or **suspensions**. Table 18.6 classifies some of the common household chemicals.

Table 18.6 *Classification of some common household chemicals as solutions, colloids or suspensions*

Solutions	Colloids	Suspensions
• Chlorine bleach	• Aerosol sprays, e.g. insecticides	• Liquid scouring (abrasive) cleaners
• Limescale remover	• Liquid detergents	• Metal polish
• Window cleaner	• Shaving cream	• Calamine lotion
• Household ammonia	• Hand cream	
• Vinegar	• Conditioner	
• Hydrogen peroxide		
• Rubbing alcohol		
• Iodine solution		

Separation techniques

Mixtures form a part of our everyday lives and the **separation** of these mixtures into their component parts can be important. Various **techniques** are available to achieve this, and these are dependent on the **physical properties** of the components to be separated. These techniques include **distillation**, **filtration**, **chromatography**, **crystallisation** and **evaporation**.

Distillation

Distillation separates the components of a solution based on differences in their **boiling points**. It involves heating the solution in a **distillation flask**, which causes the component with the **lowest** boiling point to vaporise first. The vapour is allowed to pass through a **condenser** where it cools and condenses back to a liquid known as **distillate**, which is then collected.

There are several types of distillation, including **simple distillation**, which is used to separate the components of solutions when their boiling points are significantly different; for example, to separate a sodium chloride (salt) solution into solid sodium chloride and water. The principles of simple distillation are explained in Figure 18.18. During the process, the concentration of the solution in the distillation flask increases and the solute can then be obtained by evaporating the remaining water from it.

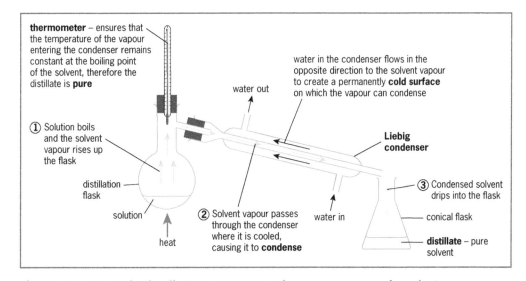

Figure 18.18 *Simple distillation to separate the components of a solution*

Distillation can be **used** to produce **distilled water** from tap water and to **desalinate** seawater or brackish water to produce **fresh water** in a **desalination plant** (see page 334). It is also used to produce a variety of **spirits** and **fortified wines** in the **wine-making industry**. To produce spirits such as **brandy**, grapes are fermented to make a **base wine**. The base wine is then distilled to concentrate the alcohol and flavours, which collect as the distillate, and the distillate is then aged in wooden barrels to form brandy. Fortified wines such as **port** and **sherry** are produced by adding the brandy to wine.

Filtration

Filtration separates the components of a mixture made of **solid** particles suspended in a **liquid** or **gas**. The components are separated due to their different **particle sizes**, using the appropriate **porous** material that allows the smaller liquid or gas particles to pass through and retains the larger solid particles. The principles of filtration are explained in Figure 18.19.

Filtration is **used** in **cooking** to separate solid food items such as potatoes or pasta from the water they have been cooked in, or to remove coffee grounds or tea leaves from the liquid when making coffee or tea. It is also used in **water filtration systems** to remove impurities from tap water (see page 335), **air purifiers** to remove dust and other airborne particles from indoor air, and **fuel filters** to remove particles of impurities from the fuel entering car engines.

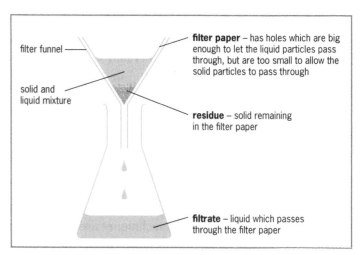

Figure 18.19 *Separating the components of a suspension by filtration*

Chromatography

Chromatography separates several **solutes** present in a solution. The solutes are usually coloured, such as the dyes in black ink or pigments in chlorophyll, and they are able to move through some kind of stationary material when dissolved in a solvent. There are several **types** of chromatography, including **paper chromatography**, which uses absorbent paper such as filter paper as the stationary material. The solutes are separated based on **two** factors.

- How **soluble** each solute is in the solvent used, which is usually water or ethanol.
- How strongly each solute is **attracted** to the stationary material used.

The principles of paper chromatography are explained in Figure 18.20.

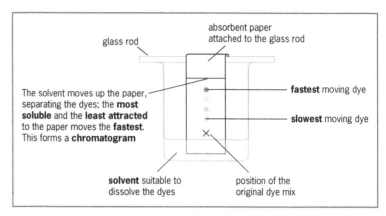

Figure 18.20 *Separating the coloured dyes in a mixture by paper chromatography*

The **principles** of chromatography can be used to explain the **bleeding** of **colours** from one garment to another during washing. Coloured dyes are often soluble in water and when garments are washed together, any water-soluble dyes from new garments in particular, can dissolve in the washing water and move to a neighbouring garment, causing the neighbouring garment to become coloured. This happens if the garments are made of **different types** of fabrics, and the fabric of the neighbouring garment **attracts** one or more of the dyes more readily than the fabric of the original garment.

Crystallisation

Crystallisation separates and retains the solid solute from a solution. The solution is placed in a container and the solvent is allowed to **evaporate** slowly, usually at room temperature, leaving the solid behind in the form of **crystals.**

Crystallisation is one of the processes involved in the production of **sugar** from **sugar cane.** Cane juice containing the dissolved sugar is obtained by crushing sugar cane stalks and it is concentrated to form a thick syrup by heating it to evaporate most of the water. Once the syrup is concentrated enough, the sugar in it begins to **crystallise**, forming **sugar crystals**, which are then separated from the remaining thick, viscous syrup, known as molasses, by a process called **centrifugation.** Crystallisation can also occur in **honey**, which is a very concentrated solution of sugars, mainly glucose and fructose. Over time, the **glucose** can crystallise in the honey because it is less soluble in water than fructose. This gives the honey a gritty texture.

Evaporation

Evaporation separates and retains the solid solute from a solution by **heating** the solution to evaporate the solvent. Evaporation is **used** to produce **table salt** from seawater or brine (concentrated salt solution). In hot climates, the seawater or brine is left in shallow ponds or pans, and the **heat** from the Sun causes the water to evaporate, leaving salt crystals behind, which are then cleaned to remove any impurities (see Figure 18.21). Alternatively, brine can be heated to a temperature which is just below the boiling point of water, usually about 80 to 90 °C, in large containers to evaporate the water and leave salt crystals.

Figure 18.21 *Salt evaporation ponds and salt mounds*

Recalling facts

1. Water can exist as solid ice, liquid water and gaseous steam. Explain the differences among these three states of matter in terms of their volume, the arrangement of their particles, the movement of their particles and the forces of attraction between their particles.

2. By reference to particles, explain what happens when the following occur and, in EACH case, name the change of state.

   a A gas is cooled until it becomes a liquid.

   b A solid is heated until it becomes a liquid.

3. What happens when a gas undergoes deposition?

4. What is a plasma and how is it formed?

5 How would you describe a mixture?

6 Distinguish among a solution, a suspension and a colloid in terms of:

   a particle size

   b appearance

   c separation of the components on standing.

7 Explain the relationship among a solution, a solvent and a solute.

8 Distinguish between an aqueous solution and a non-aqueous solution.

9 Name TWO household chemicals that are solutions, TWO that are suspensions and TWO that are colloids.

10 Explain the principles involved in obtaining:

   a pure water from seawater

   b sugar crystals from sugar cane juice

   c table salt from seawater.

Applying facts

11 Explain clearly the reason for EACH of the following by referring to particles.

   a Oxygen gas readily takes the shape of the container it is in.

   b Liquid bromine can be compressed very slightly by applying pressure.

   c The volume of ethanol slowly decreases when it is left on a laboratory bench.

12 Account for the fact that a solid lump of carbon dioxide (dry ice) that is left on a table at room temperature gradually decreases in size until it eventually disappears.

13 Wendell fell during a football game and got grass stains on his new white shirt. His friend Darius suggested using methylated spirits to remove the stains, whereas Aisha suggested using soap and water and Zara suggested using acetone. Plan and design an investigation to determine which of his friends' suggestion would be the best to remove the grass stains. The design must include a hypothesis to be tested, the aim of the investigation, the method and the expected results.

14 Explain EACH of the following.

   a Smoke is classified as a colloid.

   b Seawater is transparent.

   c The dispersed particles in muddy water can be separated by filtration.

15 Nadine, a forensic scientist, has a sample of black ink from a crime scene and wants to find out if the ink came from Lyle's or Blake's pen. Outline the method Nadine could use to determine whose pen the ink came from.

16 You are provided with a jar containing a mixture of salt (sodium chloride) and sand. Plan and design an experiment to separate the mixture into salt crystals and sand.

19 Pollutants and the environment

Human activities produce waste and harmful substances which, if released into the environment, can **pollute** the air, the land and water, and cause harm in many other ways. In order to reduce the harmful effects of any waste to a minimum or to prevent them totally, and to maintain a clean and healthy environment, all waste must be properly treated and properly disposed of.

Learning objectives

- Discuss the **effects** of **air pollution**.
- Justify the **importance** of **community hygiene** to the **environment**.
- Identify the different **types** of **waste**.
- Discuss the **impact** of **improper waste disposal**.
- Discuss the **recommended practices** for **proper waste management**.
- Discuss the **advantages** of using **plastics**.
- Discuss the **negative effects** of **plastics** on the **environment**.
- Discuss the **benefits** of **recycling plastics**.

Air pollution and its effects

Air pollution is caused by the release of unpleasant and harmful substances into the **atmosphere** (see Figure 19.1). A large number of **human activities** release air pollutants, including the combustion of fossil fuels in industry, power plants, motor vehicles, ships and aircraft, mining and quarrying, various manufacturing processes, smoking cigarettes and agricultural activities such as livestock farming and rice agriculture. In addition, certain **natural activities** contribute to this pollution, including wildfires, volcanic eruptions, lightning strikes and dust storms.

Figure 19.1 *Combustion of fossil fuels in industry contributes to air pollution*

The major air pollutants include **sulfur dioxide, carbon monoxide, carbon dioxide, nitrogen oxides, methane, volatile organic compounds, carbon particles** or **soot** in smoke and other fine **particulate matter**. These pollutants can have a detrimental effect on both **human health** and the **environment**.

Effects of air pollution on human health

Air pollution is one of the leading causes of **disease** globally. Exposure to polluted air, especially in urban areas and industrial regions, is linked to a variety of health issues, including **allergies**, **asthma**, **lung cancer**, other **respiratory disorders** and **cardiovascular disease**. Young children, older adults, people who work or are active outdoors and those with heart or lung diseases are particularly vulnerable.

Figure 19.2 *A child using an inhaler to control asthma*

- Certain air pollutants can trigger or worsen **allergies** in susceptible individuals, especially asthma and hay fever (see pages 115 to 116). **Carbon particles** and other **particulate matter** in smoke can irritate the eyes, nasal passages and airways. They can also make individuals more susceptible to other allergens and can carry these other allergens into the respiratory system during inhalation. **Nitrogen oxides** can weaken the body's defenses against allergens.

- Some air pollutants, especially some of the **volatile organic compounds**, are known to be **carcinogenic.** This means that they have the potential to cause cancer. When inhaled, these pollutants increase a person's risk of developing **lung cancer** in particular.

- **Sulfur dioxide**, **nitrogen oxides**, **carbon particles** and other **particulate matter** can irritate and inflame the airways and cause, or worsen, the symptoms of a variety of **respiratory disorders**, including chronic bronchitis, asthma and emphysema (see page 197). They can also make a person more susceptible to **respiratory infections**, such as acute bronchitis and pneumonia.

Effects of air pollution on the environment

Air pollution poses a significant threat to the **environment** due to the adverse effects it has on ecosystems and natural processes worldwide.

- **Sulfur dioxide** and **nitrogen oxides** react with water vapour and oxygen in the air to form sulfuric acid and nitric acid, respectively. These acidic solutions then fall to Earth as **acid rain** which has a pH of about 4.5 or lower. Acid rain damages **crops, trees** and other **plants**, mainly by harming their leaves, which reduces photosynthesis and makes plants more vulnerable to disease. This reduces crop yields and has caused the decline or destruction of forests in several regions of the world (see Figure 19.3). It turns **soils acidic**, which makes certain mineral nutrients unavailable to plant roots, and it causes **bodies** of **water** such as ponds, lakes, streams and rivers to become **acidic**, which harms aquatic organisms. It also **corrodes** structures such as buildings and statues.

Figure 19.3 *Trees damaged by acid rain*

- **Particulate matter** and **carbon particles** can settle on the leaves of plants. This **reduces** the amount of **light** that reaches the leaves, which reduces photosynthesis. The particles can also **block** the **stomata** of leaves, which prevents carbon dioxide from diffusing into the leaves to be used in photosynthesis, and this also reduces photosynthesis.

- **Carbon dioxide**, **nitrogen oxides** and **methane** are known as **greenhouse gases** because they are **enhancing** the **greenhouse effect**. This enhancement is causing a gradual increase in the Earth's temperature, known as **global warming**, which is leading to **global climate change** (see pages 206 to 208).

Community hygiene

Community hygiene refers to the practices that promote and maintain health and cleanliness within communities. It involves individuals, households, local authorities and community organisations working together to ensure that public spaces and shared environments are **clean** and **safe**, and that they promote **good health**. Community hygiene involves the following.

- Ensuring the proper disposal of **all waste** produced within communities.
- Providing everyone with clean and safe **drinking water**.
- Promoting good **personal hygiene**, such as regular washing of hands, body and hair and taking care of teeth.
- Managing **pests** and **vectors** of disease, such as rodents and mosquitoes.
- Maintaining the cleanliness and tidiness of **public spaces**, such as parks, streets, markets and communal areas.
- **Educating** members of communities about the importance of promoting good community hygiene.

Types of waste

Waste produced by humans can be divided into **five** categories: **domestic waste**, **industrial waste**, **biological waste**, **chemical waste** and **electronic waste**.

- **Domestic waste** is produced by households. It includes **sewage** and **refuse**. **Sewage** is wastewater that comes from toilets, showers, baths, washing machines, dishwashers and sinks. Its contents include human faeces and urine, detergents and food particles. **Refuse** consists of **solid waste**, including plastics, paper, cardboard, glass, metal, food and garden waste, and other materials discarded from everyday activities.

- **Industrial waste** is generated by **industrial activity**, including manufacturing, mining, food and construction industries. It includes **solid waste** such as scrap metal, plastics and construction debris, **sewage** or **liquid waste** which is often contaminated with chemicals, heavy metals, oils and greases, and **gaseous waste** which contains gases such as sulfur dioxide, nitrogen oxides, volatile organic compounds and carbon dioxide. The components depend on the specific industries involved.

- **Biological waste** contains, or has been contaminated by, potentially **hazardous biological materials** such as bacteria, viruses and human cells. It is also known as **biohazardous waste** and it usually comes from hospitals and other healthcare facilities, laboratories and research institutions (see Figure 19.4). It can contain human blood, blood products, tissues and organs, surgical dressings and gloves, syringes, needles, blood vials, culture dishes and scalpels.

Figure 19.4 *Biohazardous waste*

- **Chemical waste** contains potentially **harmful chemicals** produced mainly by industrial processes, laboratories and agricultural activities. It can contain mineral oils, cyanides, acids and alkalis, solvents, heavy metals such as mercury and lead, radioactive waste, expired drugs and pesticides.

- **Electronic waste** or **e-waste** consists of discarded **electrical** or **electronic devices**, such as computers, tablets, mobile phones and televisions, whose components contain potentially harmful chemicals, including lead, cadmium and mercury. They can also contain plastics, glass and certain valuable metals, such as gold, silver and palladium, which can be recovered and recycled.

Biodegradable and non-biodegradable waste

Waste can also be categorised as **biodegradable** and **non-biodegradable** based on whether or not it can be broken down or decomposed naturally by **biological processes**.

- **Biodegradable waste** can be broken down by the action of living organisms, mainly bacteria and fungi, into harmless materials that can be recycled into the environment. It includes food waste from homes, schools, restaurants and the food industry, most paper, farmyard and garden waste, bagasse from the sugar industry, natural fabrics such as cotton and wool, and some plastics.

- **Non-biodegradable waste** cannot be broken down by living organisms, therefore it remains in the environment. It includes metal, glass, rubber, construction waste, synthetic fabrics such as nylon and polyester, and most plastics.

The impact of improper waste disposal

Improper disposal of waste poses a significant **threat** to the environment, public health and the overall wellbeing of communities. Improper disposal practices include waste being incorrectly stored and not collected regularly, being dumped into bodies of water, open dumps and other open areas, being burnt, not being recycled, wherever possible, and untreated (raw) or partially treated sewage being released onto the land and into bodies of water (see Figure 19.5). Waste which is not disposed of correctly creates an **eyesore** and **unpleasant odours**, causes **pollution** and an increase in the size of **pest populations**, and it leads to the spread of **pathogens** and **parasites**.

| a | improperly stored and uncollected refuse | b | raw sewage being discharged into the sea |

Figure 19.5 *Improper waste disposal poses a threat to human health and the environment*

Pollution

Improper waste disposal leads to the **pollution** of **land**, the **air** and **water**, including surface water, groundwater, sources of potable (drinkable) water and bodies of water such as lakes, rivers and oceans.

- **Toxic chemicals** in the waste can seep out and contaminate the soil and water.
- **Plastics** in the waste can persist in the environment for hundreds of years, polluting the land and gradually breaking down into smaller pieces known as **microplastics**, which contaminate the soil, affect plant growth and harm animals that ingest them. Plastics can also enter bodies of water where they are directly harmful to aquatic organisms (see page 422).
- **Greenhouse gases**, such as methane and carbon dioxide, can be released into the atmosphere from the breakdown of any organic material in the waste. These gases contribute to the **greenhouse effect** (see pages 206 to 207).
- **Hydrogen sulfide gas** can be released into the air from any organic matter in the waste being broken down anaerobically (without oxygen). This creates foul odours and is extremely **toxic**; even low concentrations irritate the eyes and respiratory system.
- **Plant nutrients** such as nitrates and phosphates in improperly treated or untreated sewage can pollute water, leading to **eutrophication** (see Table 15.7 on page 332).

Increased pest populations

Waste that has not been disposed of properly provides a **breeding ground** for **pests** and **vectors** of disease (see pages 128 to 129). This causes their population numbers to increase, which increases the **damage** caused by the pests and the spread of **infectious diseases** transmitted by vectors.

Spread of pathogens and parasites

Pathogenic microorganisms, mainly bacteria, some viruses and some fungi, and **intestinal parasites** or their **eggs**, which are present in human faeces, raw or partially treated sewage and solid waste, can enter water supplies and contaminate potable water. This leads to the spread of **infectious diseases** such as cholera, typhoid fever and dysentery, and **parasites** such as the protozoan, *Giardia*, which causes a diarrhoeal illness known as giardiasis, the roundworm known as *Ascaris*, and several different hookworms and flukes.

Recommended practices for waste management

A variety of **waste management practices** can be used to minimise the impact posed by improper waste disposal on the environment, public health and the wellbeing of communities.

Refuse, reduce, reuse, repair, refill, repurpose and recycle

The amount of **solid waste** that has to be disposed of can be decreased considerably by practising the **7Rs** of waste management.

- **Refuse** means to actively **avoid** or **decline** buying or using products that create unnecessary waste. For example, rejecting items that are over-packaged or cannot be recycled.
- **Reduce** means to **cut down** on what is produced, what is purchased and what is used. For example, the manufacture and use of disposable or single-use plates, cutlery and bags should be reduced to a minimum.
- **Reuse** means to **use** the same item **again**, preferably many times, for its original purpose or function without any significant alterations. For example, glass bottles and cloth shopping bags can be used many times for the same purpose.
- **Repair** means to **mend** items that are broken or damaged, if possible, instead of discarding them. For example, a table leg that has broken or a refrigerator that has stopped working.
- **Refill** means to **replenish** a container with its original contents or an alternative product. For example, water bottles can be refilled with water and ink cartridges can be refilled with ink.
- **Repurpose** means to find a **new** use for an item that is **different** to its original use. For example, old tyres can be repurposed to make tyre gardens.
- **Recycle** means to **separate**, **recover** and **reprocess** materials into new raw materials that can then be used to make new products. For example, plastics can be shredded, melted and turned into new plastic items such as plastic wood or fibres for clothing.

Composting

Waste **organic matter** can be converted into a nutrient-rich material known as **compost** by a natural process called **composting**. Organic waste that can be composted includes food waste such as fruit and vegetable peelings, coffee grounds, tea leaves and crushed eggshells, and garden waste such as grass cuttings, leaves and weeds. Composting can be carried out in compost heaps or specialised composters at home (see Figure 19.6), or in a commercial composting facility, where agricultural waste such as crop residues and manure can be used. Bacteria and fungi in the waste break it down **aerobically** to produce **compost**, which can then be used as a **soil conditioner** or **mulch**.

Figure 19.6 *Producing compost in a home composter*

Biogas production

Organic waste such as manure, crop residues, food waste and sludge from sewage treatment plants can be used to produce a renewable energy source called **biogas**. The waste is placed into an **anaerobic digester** (see Figure 19.7) and certain **bacteria** that are present naturally in the waste break it down **anaerobically**. This produces **biogas**, which is a mixture of about **60% methane**, **40% carbon dioxide** and traces of other gases. Biogas can be used as a **fuel** for cooking, heating and to generate electricity. The **residue** remaining is rich in mineral nutrients and can be used as a **fertiliser**.

Figure 19.7 *Producing biogas on a farm*

Proper sewage disposal practices

Sewage should be disposed of in a way that humans and animals cannot come into contact with it, and in a way that it does not contaminate water supplies and the environment. To achieve this, it can be disposed of in an **on-site sewage system,** such as a **septic tank**, **cesspool** or **suckwell**, each of which treats the sewage close to a building and releases the treated water into the same area. A **soakaway** can also be used to collect and disperse surface runoff.

Alternatively, sewage can be treated in a **sewage disposal system**, which consists of a network of underground pipes of varying sizes, known as **sewers**, which collect and transport the sewage to a **sewage treatment plant**, where it is treated (see Figure 19.8). Treatment removes contaminants from sewage to produce treated wastewater, known as **effluent**, which is safe to release into the environment. The process also produces semi-solid **sludge**, which undergoes further treatment so that it can be used as a **fertiliser**. Households, schools, offices, hospitals and factories must also have adequate **toilet facilities** that are linked to sewage systems to properly dispose of faeces and urine.

Figure 19.8 *Sewage flowing through a sewer*

Proper collection and disposal of refuse

Refuse should be **separated** into different types before collection and disposal. **Organic waste** should be separated out and **composted**, and **recyclable materials**, such as glass, paper, metal and plastic, should be separated out, collected separately and transported to a **recycling facility**. The remaining refuse should be **stored** in durable bins with tight-fitting lids and **collected** at least once per week by an enclosed truck that compacts the refuse and transports it to a **disposal facility**. In communities where appropriate sites are available, **landfills** usually provide the most economical means for disposal of refuse. Another method that can be used is **incineration**.

Benefits of community hygiene

Good **community hygiene** has many **benefits**.

- It helps prevent the spread of **infectious diseases**.
- It helps promote good overall **public health**.

- It helps protect the **environment.**
- It helps improve the **aesthetic value** of communities and the overall **quality of life.**
- It helps strengthen **community spirit.**

Plastics

Plastics are synthetic (manufactured) materials made from **polymers.** Polymers are very large molecules known as macromolecules, which are made from small, repeating molecules known as **monomers** that are linked together, usually in chains. The **properties** of plastics make them **superior** to many other materials, as a result they are used extensively in today's world (see page 383). However, their extensive use poses serious **threats** to living organisms and the environment.

Advantages of using plastics

Two of the main **advantages** of using plastics are their **ease of production** and their **durability.**

Ease of production

Plastics are relatively **easy to produce** compared with other materials for a variety of reasons, and this contributes significantly to their widespread use.

- Most plastics are made from petrochemicals obtained from **petroleum** (**crude oil**) which is **widely available.**
- Plastics are **cost-effective** to produce, being cheaper than alternatives such as metals, glass and ceramics.
- Plastics offer manufacturers a high degree of **design flexibility.** This is because they can be manufactured using a **wide variety** of **production processes**, which can be adapted easily to produce a wide range of different **shapes** and **sizes** that are difficult to achieve with alternative materials.
- Plastics can be **customised** by manufacturers for **specific uses.** This is because a variety of **additives** and **modifiers** can be added to them during the manufacturing process to achieve different desired properties such as flexibility, strength and a wide range of colours.

Durability

Plastics are extremely **durable**, which contributes to their **long life** and makes them ideal for a wide range of uses. It also means that they require **minimal maintenance** compared with alternative materials such as wood and metal, and this saves time and resources.

- Plastics are resistant to **wear** and **physical damage.** This makes them suitable for making items such as furniture, automotive parts, construction materials, protective equipment and packaging.
- Plastics are resistant to **corrosion** and attack by other **chemicals** such as acids, alkalis and solvents. This makes them ideal for outdoor use; for example, to make outdoor furniture, water pipes, window frames, playground equipment and fencing. It also makes them valuable for storing chemical products and for use in the chemical processing industry, where exposure to harsh chemicals is common.
- Most plastics are resistant to **biological decay**, which makes them well-suited for outdoor use and also for making medical equipment and food packaging.

Use of plastics in the medical and construction industries

In addition to being relatively **easy to produce** and **durable**, plastics have certain other unique properties that make them well-suited for use in the **medical** and **construction industries.**

- Certain types of plastics are **biocompatible**, meaning that they are well-tolerated by the body, therefore they can be used to make a variety of medical devices and implants.

- Plastics can withstand a variety of **sterilisation methods**, such as autoclaving and irradiation, and this ensures medical equipment is sterile and safe for use.
- Plastics can be **moulded** into complex shapes with great precision, allowing intricate medical devices to be made and customised to specific needs. It also allows a wide range of products to be made for use in the construction industry, and for architects and designers to create innovative and attractive structures.
- Most plastics are **lightweight**, which makes them suitable for making medical devices that need to be worn by patients or carried (see Figure 19.9). It also makes building materials easier to transport, handle and install than other materials such as metals and concrete.
- Plastics are **waterproof**, therefore they can provide a barrier against moisture. This makes them ideal for producing medical devices, packaging for pharmaceuticals and construction materials.
- Plastics are very good **electrical** and **thermal insulators**, which makes them ideal for insulating electrical wires and also very useful to improve the energy efficiency of buildings, which reduces heating and cooling costs.

Figure 19.9 *An artificial hand made from plastic*

Negative effects of plastics on the environment

Plastics can have significant **harmful effects** on ecosystems and the environment.

- Various **toxic chemicals** are released into the environment during the manufacture of plastics. Some continue to be released from plastic items during their use and when disposed of, and many of these chemicals are persistent, meaning that they remain in the environment causing harm for many years.
- Most plastics are **non-biodegradable**, meaning that they cannot be broken down or decomposed by living organisms, mainly bacteria and fungi. When disposed of, they build up and remain in the environment for hundreds of years, causing land and water pollution.

Figure 19.10 *A turtle mistakes a plastic bag for food*

- Plastics are directly harmful to **aquatic organisms** such as sea turtles, whales, dolphins, fish and aquatic birds, often leading to injury or death by the plastics entangling the organisms, being ingested by them (see Figure 19.10), or by causing their suffocation. Organisms that ingest pieces of plastic often die of starvation because their stomachs become filled with these pieces and they stop eating.
- Many plastics gradually break down over time into fragments known as **microplastics**, which are less than 5 mm in size (see Figure 19.11). These microplastics are widespread in the environment, being present in oceans, seas, bodies of fresh water, the soil and the air. The tiniest of these can enter the bodies of organisms, where they are found to have harmful effects on tissues and organs.

Figure 19.11 *Microplastics*

- Many plastics are **flammable**, therefore they pose fire hazards.
- Plastics produce **dense smoke** and **poisonous gases** when burnt, including dioxins, furans and volatile organic compounds. These lead to air pollution and serious health problems such as asthma and other respiratory illnesses, immune system damage, cancer and damage to the nervous and reproductive systems.
- Plastics are made from petroleum, which is a **non-renewable resource**. Their manufacture is contributing to the depletion of petroleum worldwide. Based on known reserves and annual production levels in 2019, it was estimated that petroleum will only last until 2052.

Benefits of recycling plastics

Disposing of plastics poses a huge problem in today's world. When disposed of in landfills, most will remain for hundreds of years because they do not degrade, and they cannot be burnt safely because they produce dense smoke and toxic gases. Therefore, the best solution is to **recycle** them (see page 419).

Plastics are classified into different **types** based on their **chemical composition**, and their ability to be **recycled** depends on their type. The different types of plastics that can be recycled are recognised by **Resin Identification Codes (RICs)** or **recycling codes**. Each code consists of a number from 1 to 7 inside a triangle of arrows, as shown in Figure 19.12. The **number** identifies the **type** of plastic.

Recycling plastics has many environmental and economic **benefits**.

Figure 19.12 *A Resin Identification Code on a plastic item*

- It **conserves natural resources**, mainly petroleum, by reducing the quantity of new raw materials that are needed to manufacture plastics.
- It **reduces energy consumption**, mainly because processes used to obtain the raw materials, such as extraction and refining, are not involved, and fewer steps and lower temperatures are usually needed for processing recycled plastic.
- It **reduces** the **volume** of solid waste that must be disposed of in landfills. This reduces the amount of land taken up by landfills and the pollution of the air, soil and groundwater that can occur if landfills are not operated properly.
- It **lowers greenhouse gas emissions** and the emissions of other air pollutants. This is because it requires less energy than producing plastics from new raw materials, and this energy is usually produced by burning fossil fuels, which releases these pollutants.
- It **reduces** the **loss** of potentially useful materials and it keeps materials in use for as long as possible, which creates a more sustainable economy.
- It **reduces pollution** of land and water that can result from the disposal of plastics.
- It **creates jobs** because people are needed to collect, sort, process and manufacture recycled materials, and this helps improve the economy of countries.

Recalling facts

1
  a Explain how fine particulate matter in smoke can worsen a person's allergies.
  b Identify FOUR other health conditions that can result from air pollution.

2
  Explain how acid rain is formed and outline the effects it has on plant life.

3
  a What is meant by 'community hygiene'?
  b Identify the different ways that hygiene can be maintained within a community and suggest FOUR benefits of good community hygiene.

4
  Distinguish among the FIVE different categories of waste produced by humans.

5
  a Provide FOUR examples of improper waste disposal practices.
  b Identify FOUR reasons why it is necessary to dispose of all human waste properly.

6
  What is the principal aim of practising the 7Rs of waste management?

7
  Explain the following terms as they relate to the 7Rs of waste management and support each explanation with TWO examples:
  a repurpose   **b** reduce   **c** reuse   **d** recycle.

8
  Farmer Fabio generates large quantities of organic waste on his farm.
  a Identify FOUR possible sources of this waste.
  b Explain TWO methods Farmer Fabio can employ to dispose of the waste that can benefit the operations on his farm.

9
  a What is sewage?
  b Outline how a sewage disposal system functions.
  c Rural areas of many countries of the world lack sewage disposal systems. Identify THREE ways households in these areas can safely dispose of the sewage they produce.

10
  a What are plastics?
  b 'Two reasons why plastics are used so extensively in today's world are because they are relatively easy to produce and they are very durable.' Provide evidence to support this statement.

11
  Discuss THREE properties of plastics that make them suitable for use in the medical industry and THREE different properties that make them suitable for use in the construction industry.

Applying facts

12
  Construct a table to identify the effect that EACH of the following air pollutants has on human health and on the environment: sulfur dioxide, carbon dioxide, nitrogen oxides, methane, volatile organic compounds and fine particulate matter. Write the words 'no effect' where appropriate.

13
  Explain why many plastics are classified as being non-biodegradable, but wood is classified as biodegradable, even though both are composed of organic compounds.

14 According to a World Bank report, the proper disposal of waste is a universal issue that matters to every single person in the world. Explain FIVE reasons that you could put forward in support of this statement.

15 Householders in many countries place all their refuse in one bin for collection. What recommendations would you give to these households to improve their waste disposal practices?

16 As a cost-cutting measure, the Ministry of Health of your country proposes that domestic refuse should be collected once every 2 weeks instead of the normal weekly collection. What would your reaction be to the proposal and why?

17 A poll commissioned by the World Wildlife Fund and the Plastic Tree Foundation in 2024 found that 85% of the 24 000 people from 32 different countries that took part in the poll were in favour of a worldwide ban being placed on single-use plastics. Suggest and explain FIVE possible reasons why so many people support such a ban.

18 As Javon throws a plastic detergent bottle into his refuse bin, he notices a triangle of arrows on the bottom with the number 5 inside and asks you what it means.

   a Provide a suitable explanation that you could give to Javon to answer his question.

   b What advice would you give to Javon about how to dispose of his detergent bottle? Give FIVE reasons to support your advice.

Analysing data

19 Figure 19.13 shows data taken from a study by the World Bank into the waste management practices of households without waste collection services in three islands of the Caribbean. Uncollected plastics accounted for 14.1% of the uncollected waste in Grenada, 10.9% in Jamaica and 18.0% in St. Lucia. Use this information, and that given in the bar graph, to answer the questions that follow.

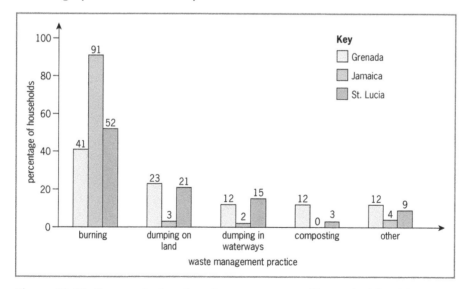

Figure 19.13 *Bar graph showing the percentage of households without waste collection services using different waste management practices in three islands of the Caribbean*

a i Which method of disposal of uncollected waste was used MOST frequently by households in the three countries?

ii Which method of disposal of uncollected waste was used LEAST frequently by households in the three countries?

iii Suggest ONE 'other' way households in the three countries could dispose of their uncollected waste.

b i In which country are people MOST likely to suffer from respiratory disorders due to the waste management practices of households without collection services? Explain your answer.

ii Name TWO respiratory disorders that the people identified in **b i** might experience.

c i Uncollected waste from which TWO countries is likely to cause the greatest harm to the marine environment? Give TWO reasons to support your answer.

ii Outline THREE possible harmful effects of the uncollected waste from the countries identified in **c i** on the marine environment.

d Which disposal practice is most likely to contribute to the occurrence of dengue fever within the three countries? Explain your answer.

Index

Figure and tables are indicated by an f and t following the page number

Acknowledgements

Photo credits:

p16: Vinod Kumar Pillai / Alamy Stock Photo, p107: Alfred Pasieka / Science Photo Library, p175: Phanie – Sipa Press / Alamy Stock Photo, p192: Pako Mera / Alamy Stock Photo, p217: PA Images / Alamy Stock Photo, p251: rfranca / Alamy Stock Photo, p252: Guy Corbishley / Alamy Stock Photo, p275: Marharyta Stoika / Alamy Stock Vector, p301: Science History Images / Alamy Stock Photo, p314: AFP / Stringer, p345: G.I. Dobner / Alamy Stock Photo, p378: Radu Bercan / Alamy Stock Photo, p385: Thornton Cohen / Alamy Stock Photo, p389: Science History Images / Alamy Stock Photo, p392: camac / Alamy Stock Photo, p392: Oleksandr Chub / Alamy Stock Photo, p395: all photos – Anne Tindale, p396: Anne Tindale, p397: right photo – Anne Tindale, p423: Allexxandar / Alamy Stock Photo

All other photos © Shutterstock.com